HANDBOOK OF MOTIVATION AND COGNITION ACROSS CULTURES

HANDBOOK OF MOTIVATION AND COGNITION ACROSS CULTURES

RICHARD M. SORRENTINO AND SUSUMU YAMAGUCHI

AMSTERDAM • BOSTON • HEIDELBERG • LONDON • NEW YORK • OXFORD
PARIS • SAN DIEGO • SAN FRANCISCO • SINGAPORE • SYDNEY • TOKYO
Academic Press is an imprint of Elsevier

ELSEVIER

Academic Press is an imprint of Elsevier
525 B Street, Suite 1900, San Diego, CA 92101-4495, USA
30 Corporate Drive, Suite 400, Burlington, MA 01803, USA
32 Jamestown Road, London NW1 7BY, UK
Radarweg 29, PO Box 211, 1000 AE Amsterdam, The Netherlands

First edition 2008

British Library Cataloguing in Publication Data
A catalogue record for this book is available from the British Library

Library of Congress Cataloging-in-Publication Data
A catalog record for this book is available from the Library of Congress

ISBN: 978-0-12-373694-9

For information on all **Academic Press** publications
visit our web site at books.elsevier.com

Typeset by Charon Tec Ltd., A Macmillan Company.
(www.macmillansolutions.com)

Printed and bound in USA

08 09 10   10 9 8 7 6 5 4 3 2 1

CONTENTS

3

UNCERTAINTY REGULATION: THE MASTER MOTIVE?   49

RICHARD M. SORRENTINO, ANDREW SZETO, JOHN B. NEZLEK,
SATORU YASUNAGA, SADAFUSA KOUHARA, AND YASUNAO OHTSUBO

4

IMPLICIT THEISM   71

ERIC LUIS UHLMANN, T. ANDREW POEHLMAN, AND JOHN A. BARGH

5

DO IMPLICIT MOTIVES ADD TO OUR UNDERSTANDING OF PSYCHOLOGICAL AND BEHAVIORAL OUTCOMES WITHIN AND ACROSS CULTURES?   95

JAN HOFER AND MICHAEL HARRIS BOND

6

A CROSS-CULTURAL ANALYSIS OF
SELF-VERIFICATION MOTIVES   119

TAMMY ENGLISH, SERENA CHEN, AND WILLIAM B. SWANN JR.

7

AN ATTRIBUTION THEORIST ADDRESSES THE
CO-EXISTENCE OF THEORETICAL GENERALITY AND
CULTURAL SPECIFICITY   143

BERNARD WEINER

8

RE-THINKING CULTURE AND PERSONALITY: HOW SELF-REGULATORY UNIVERSALS CREATE CROSS-CULTURAL DIFFERENCES   161

E. TORY HIGGINS, ANTONIO PIERRO, AND ARIE W. KRUGLANSKI

9

GOAL PURSUIT IN THE CONTEXT OF CULTURE   191

GABRIELE OETTINGEN, A. TIMUR SEVINCER, AND PETER M. GOLLWITZER

10

UNVEILING AGENCY: A MOTIVATIONAL PERSPECTIVE ON ACCULTURATION AND ADAPTATION   213

MICHELLE GEZENTSVEY AND COLLEEN WARD

11

A SITUATED COGNITION PERSPECTIVE ON CULTURE: EFFECTS OF PRIMING CULTURAL SYNDROMES ON COGNITION AND MOTIVATION   237

DAPHNA OYSERMAN AND SPIKE W. S. LEE

12

THE FUNDAMENTAL TOOLS, AND POSSIBLY UNIVERSALS, OF HUMAN SOCIAL COGNITION   267

BERTRAM F. MALLE

13

CROSS-CULTURAL DIFFERENCES VERSUS UNIVERSALITY IN COGNITIVE DISSONANCE: A CONCEPTUAL REANALYSIS   297

BERTRAM GAWRONSKI, KURT R. PETERS, AND FRITZ STRACK

PART II

MOTIVATION AND COGNITION FROM A CULTURAL PERSPECTIVE   315

14

THE ROLE OF LANGUAGE IN THE PERCEPTION OF PERSONS AND GROUPS   317

MINORU KARASAWA AND ANNE MAASS

15

CULTURE AND INTERGROUP RELATIONS: THE ROLE OF SOCIAL REPRESENTATIONS OF HISTORY   343

DENIS J. HILTON AND JAMES H. LIU

16

MOTIVATED EXPRESSION OF SELF-ESTEEM ACROSS CULTURES   369

SUSUMU YAMAGUCHI, CHUNCHI LIN, HIROAKI MORIO, AND
TAICHI OKUMURA

17

CULTURE, NARRATIVE, AND HUMAN AGENCY   393

YOSHIHISA KASHIMA, KIM PETERS, AND JENNIFER WHELAN

18

CULTURE, COGNITIONS, AND LEGAL DECISION-MAKING   423

JUSTIN D. LEVINSON

19

THE PSYCHOLOGICAL PROCESS OF COPING WITH THREAT AND ITS CULTURAL MAINTENANCE FUNCTION   443

Emiko S. Kashima

20

VALUES AND SOCIAL AXIOMS   471

Kwok Leung and Fan Zhou

21

COGNITIVE, RELATIONAL, AND SOCIAL BASIS OF ACADEMIC ACHIEVEMENT IN CONFUCIAN CULTURES: PSYCHOLOGICAL, INDIGENOUS, AND CULTURAL PERSPECTIVES   491

UICHOL KIM AND YOUNG-SHIN PARK

22

DIALECTICAL EMOTIONS: HOW CULTURAL EPISTEMOLOGIES INFLUENCE THE EXPERIENCE AND REGULATION OF EMOTIONAL COMPLEXITY   517

JENNIFER L. GOETZ, JULIE SPENCER-RODGERS, AND KAIPING PENG

23

CULTURE, EMOTION, AND MOTIVATION   541

DAVID MATSUMOTO AND JESSIE WILSON

PART III

MEASUREMENT   565

24

MEASURING COGNITION AND MOTIVATION ACROSS CULTURAL GROUPS   567

RON FISCHER AND VIVIAN MIU-CHI LUN

PREFACE

This handbook is the result of the two co-editors joining forces in order to call others to do likewise and bridge the field between experts in motivation and cognition, and experts in cross-cultural research. Being well evidenced by a recent surge of research interest in the area of culture and psychology, the cultural perspectives are now recognized as indispensable for research in cognition, motivation, and their interplay. It is now widely recognized that both cognition and motivation are culturally embedded, as this handbook is devoted to this issue.

Although interests in cross-cultural research in psychological functioning have long been prevalent especially among psychological anthropologists (such as the culture-and-personality school), the mainstream social psychologists have not paid much attention to cultural research until 1990s, when they faced challenges from cultural psychology and indigenous psychology. Advocates of both cultural psychology and indigenous psychology have been criticizing mainstream psychology as being, among other things, bounded by its ungrounded commitment to natural science orientations. On one hand, cultural psychologists questioned the validity of assumed solutions applicable to all people in all cultures. They also criticized the assumed "psychic unity" that people are fundamentally the same. Indigenous psychologists, on the other hand, argued that human mentality needs to be understood in a particular cultural context. For both parties, the assumption of universality of human mental functioning was too simplistic.

The assumed universality of empirical law becomes questionable once psychic unity of human being is challenged. Stimulated by such challenges, empirical work has flourished in the past 10 years. A growing number of social psychologists in North America launched cross-cultural projects. Also, Asian social psychologists started to raise their voices from a cultural perspective. The establishment of the Asian Association of Social Psychology in 1995 was symbolic of growing Asian voices.

As the mainstream psychology met with challenges from cultural psychology and indigenous psychology, the editors of this volume met at a Society for Experimental Social Psychology conference (which is undoubtedly a meeting of mainstream social psychologists) in New Orleans in this period of the rise of cross-cultural research. Rather than confronting with each other, we learned from each other and agreed to launch this project. We invited authors from both social psychology and cross-cultural psychology, expecting that they would elucidate the interplay among motivation, cognition, and culture for the readers. Hopefully, this volume will prove useful for a rapidly growing number of scholars interested in the interplay among motivation, cognition, and cultures.

In publishing this book, we wish to express sincere appreciation to many people. Most important, we want to thank the contributors to this volume, whose enthusiasm and commitment to the project is reflected in their respective chapters. We joyfully learned tremendously from each chapter. In addition, we are also grateful to Barbara Makinster, Senior Developmental Editor, for her efficiency in guiding the book throughout the entire production process. One of us (RMS) would also like to thank his fourth year honors psychology class for their helpful comments on many of the first drafts of chapters in this book. We had many enjoyable discussions, much of which was passed back to the contributors. Finally, but not the least important, we would like to thank our wives and children, grand children, and mothers for their affection and support during this project: Judy, Eric, Emily, Michael, Giuliana, Rose, Rumiko, Aya, Megumi, and Kazuko.

LIST OF CONTRIBUTORS

John A. Bargh Department of Psychology, PO Box 208205, Yale University, New Haven, CT 06520-8205, USA

Michael Harris Bond Department of Psychology, Sino Building, Chung Chi College, The Chinese University of Hong Kong, Shatin, New Territories, Hong Kong, SAR, China

Serena Chen Department of Psychology, 3413 Tolman Hall, #1650, University of California, Berkeley, CA 94720-1650, USA

Tammy English Department of Psychology, 3210 Tolman Hall, #1650, University of California, Berkeley, CA 94720-1650, USA

Ronald Fischer Centre for Applied Cross-Cultural Research, Victoria University of Wellington, School of Psychology, PO Box 600, Wellington, New Zealand

Bertram Gawronski Department of Psychology, The University of Western Ontario, Social Science Centre, London, Ont., Canada N6A 5C2

Michelle Gezentsvey School of Psychology, Victoria University of Wellington, Wellington, New Zealand

Jennifer L. Goetz Department of Psychology, University of California, 3210 Tolman Hall #1650, Berkeley, CA 94720-1650, USA

Peter M. Gollwitzer 6 Washington Place, Room 781, New York, NY 10003, USA

E. Tory Higgins Psychology Department, 401-D Schermerhorn Hall, Columbia University, New York, NY 10027, USA

Denis J. Hilton Laboratoire Dynamiques Sociocognitives et Vie Politique, Maison de la Recherche, Bureau B430, Universite de Toulouse II-le Mirail, 5, allees Antonio Machado, 31058 Toulouse Cedex 9, France

Jan Hofer Department of Human Sciences, Development and Culture, University of Osnabrück, Seminarstrasse 20, D-49069 Osnabrück, Germany

Minoru Karasawa Department of Psychology, Graduate School of Environmental Studies, Nagoya University, B4-1 (780) Furo-cho, Chikusa-ku, Nagoya 464-8601, Japan

Emiko S. Kashima School of Psychological Science, La Trobe University, Bundoora, Victoria 3086, Australia

Yoshihisa Kashima Department of Psychology, The University of Melbourne, Parkville 3010, Victoria, Australia

Heidi Keller Fachbereich Humanwissenschaften, Differentielle Psychologie und Persönlichkeitsforschung Seminarstrasse, 20 49074, Universität Osnabrück, D-49069 Osnabrück, Germany

Uichol Kim College of Business Administration, Inha University, 253 Yonghyun-dong Nam-gu, Inchon, 402-751, Korea

Sadafusa Kouhara Faculty of Human Science, Yamaguchi Prefectural University, Sakurabatake 3-2-1, Yamaguchi 7538502, Japan.

Arie W. Kruglanski Department of Psychology, University of Maryland, College Park, College Park, MA 20742, USA

Julius Kuhl Fachbereich Humanwissenschaften, Differentielle Psychologie und Persönlichkeitsforschung, Seminarstrasse 20 49074 Universität Osnabrück, Osnabrück, Germany

Spike W. S. Lee Department of psychology, University of Michigan, Ann Arbor, MI 48109, USA

Kwok Leung Department of Management, City University of Hong Kong, Tat Chee Avenue, Kowloon, Hong Kong

Justin D. Levinson University of Hawaii, William S. Richardson School of Law, 2515 Dole Street, Honolulu, HI 96844, USA

Chunchi Lin Department of Psychology, 3424 Tolman Hall, #1650, University of California, Berkeley, CA 94720-1650, USA

James H. Liu Centre for Applied Cross-Cultural Research, Victoria University of Wellington, School of Psychology, PO Box 600, Wellington, New Zealand

Vivian Miu-Chi Lun Centre for Applied Cross-Cultural Research, Victoria University of Wellington, School of Psychology, PO Box 600, Wellington, New Zealand

Anne Maass DPSS, Università di Padova, Via Venezia, 8, 35139 Padova, Italy

Bertram F. Malle Department of Psychology, Institute of Cognitive and Decision Sciences, 1227, University of Oregon, Eugene, OR 97403-1227, USA

David Matsumoto Department of Psychology, San Francisco State University, 1600 Holloway Avenue, San Francisco, CA 94132, USA

Hiroaki Morio Faculty of Business Administration, Sapporo University, 7-3-1 Nishioka 3Jo, Toyohira-ku, Sapporo 062-8520, Japan

John B. Nezlek Department of Psychology, College of William & Mary, PO Box 8795, Williamsburg, VA 23187-8795, USA

Gabriele Oettingen 6 Washington Place, Room 455, New York, NY 10003, USA

Yasunao Ohtsubo Department of Psychology, Fukuoka University of Education, Akama-Bunkyo-machi 1-1, Munakata-shi, Fukuoka 811-4192, Japan.

Taichi Okumura Department of Educational Psychology, Graduate School of Education/Faculty of Education, The University of Tokyo, Hongo 7-3-1, Bunkyo-ku, Tokyo 113-0033, Japan

Daphna Oyserman Department of Psychology, Institute for Social Research, University of Michigan, 426 Thompson Avenue, Room 5240, Ann Arbor, MI 48109-1248, USA

Young-Shin Park Department of Education, Inha University, 253 Yonghyun-dong Nam-gu, Inchon, 402-751, Korea

Kaiping Peng Department of Psychology, University of California, 3210 Tolman Hall, Berkeley, CA 94720-1650, USA

Kim Peters School of Psychology, The University of Exeter, Perry Road, Exeter, EX4 4QG, England

Kurt R. Peters Department of Psychology, The University of Western Ontario, Social Science Centre, London, Ont., Canada N6A 5C2

Antanio Pierro Development of Psychology of the Process of Development and Socialization, University of Rome, La Sapienza, Rome, Italy

T. Andrew Poehlman Southern Methodist University, Edwin L. Cox School of Business, PO Box 750333, Dallas, TX 75275-0333, USA

A. Timur Sevincer Department of Psychology, Universität Hamburg, Germany

Richard M. Sorrentino Psychology Department, University of Western Ontario, London, Ont., Canada n6g3v4

Julie Spencer-Rodgers Department of Psychology, University of Victoria, Victoria, BC, Canada V8W 3P5

Fritz Strack Universität Würzburg, Lehrstuhl für Psychologie II, Röntgenring 10, 97070 Würzburg, Germany

William B. Swann Jr. Department of Psychology, The University of Texas at Austin, Austin, TX 78712, USA

Andrew Szeto Psychology Department, University of Western Ontario, London, Ont., Canada n6g3v4

Eric Luis Uhlmann Ford Motor Company Center for Global Citizenship, Kellogg School of Management, Northwestern University, Donald P. Jacobs Center, 2001 Sheridan Road, Evanston, IL 60208-2001, USA

Colleen Ward School of Psychology, Victoria University of Wellington, Wellington, New Zealand

Bernard Weiner Psychology Department, University of California at Los Angeles, USA

Jennifer Whelan Department of Psychology, The University of Melbourne, Parkville 3010, Victoria, Australia

Jessie Wilson 328 Lenox Avenue #2, Oakland, CA 94610, USA

Susumu Yamaguchi Department of Social Psychology, Graduate School of Humanities and Sociology/Faculty of Letters, The University of Tokyo, Hongo 7-3-1, Bunkyo-ku, Tokyo 113-0033, Japan

Satoru Yasunaga Department of Psychology, Faculty of Literature, Kurume University, 1635 Mii, Kurume, Fukuoka 839-8502, Japan

Fan Zhou RM 805-10, School of Management, Zhejiang University, Hangzhou, Zhejiang Province, China

1

MOTIVATION AND COGNITION ACROSS CULTURES

RICHARD M. SORRENTINO[*] AND SUSUMU YAMAGUCHI[†]

Psychology Department, University of Western Ontario, London, Ontario, Canada
†Department of Social Psychology, University of Tokyo, Tokyo, Japan

This handbook has its historical roots in the late 1970, early 1980 period. During that time social cognition was in its heyday and social motivation was flat on its back. The reason for this, according to Sorrentino and Higgins (1986, Chapter 1) can perhaps be traced back to the rise of behaviorism in North American psychology. Until that point, various views relating motivation and/or cognition to behavior were flourishing. Darwin (1872) carried considerable weight, as did Freud (1917/1955) and McDougall (1908), in putting forth instinct as the underlying motivational force accounting for behavior. On the other hand, others were putting forth a primarily cognitive and/or rational viewpoint as the basis for behavior. James (1890), for example, stressed the importance of will and the self in determining what he called voluntary behavior. The structuralists and functionalists as well as the phrenologists (e.g., Galton, 1883; Titchener, 1899), argued that the mind and various streams of consciousness were all that were worthy of study. There was, however, a third and ultimately, overwhelming, viewpoint that won the day – behaviorism. This school of thought rejected all other approaches – or any approach that focussed on the internal machinations of the individual. Watson (1930, p. 5) the "father of behaviorism" said:

> The Behaviorist began his own formulation of the problem of psychology by sweeping aside all medieval conceptions. He dropped from his scientific vocabulary all subjective terms such as sensation, perception, image, desire, purpose, and even thinking, and emotion as they were subjectively defined.

This statement, which reflected the predominant feeling among North American psychologists at the time, obviously did little to promote the fields of motivation, cognition, and social psychology. It is interesting that cognition was the last of the three areas to fully recover from the attack of the behaviorists.

> The behaviorist program and the issues it spawned all but eliminated any serious research in cognitive psychology for 40 years. The rat supplanted the human as the principal laboratory subject, and psychology turned to finding out what could be learned by studying animal learning and motivation.
>
> Anderson (1980, p. 9)

Motivation, however, could not be swept aside as a by-product of learning principles, as Hull (1943) had hoped to do. Tolman's (1932, 1959) empirical demonstrations of purposive behavior in animals met the rat behaviorists head on, until they were forced to embrace the concept of motivation as something other than a learning phenomenon. Social psychology was also soon to re-emerge, largely through the influence of Lewin (1935, 1951), whose field theory had concepts that were strikingly similar to those of Tolman (see Atkinson, 1964).

It is important to note that these theories were not motivational or cognitive, but both. The expectancy-value theories of Tolman and Lewin took account of both motivational and cognitive factors when attempting to predict behavior. Tolman, in predicting maze behavior, spoke of the expectancy of the goal and the demand for the goal. Lewin, in research on level of aspiration and decision making, spoke in terms of potency and valence. When a rat moves through a maze or a human moves through his or her life space, it is done purposively, and both motivation and cognition are important elements in accounting for this behavior.

Although Tolman's points were well taken, prompting Hull and the neo-Hullians (e.g., Miller, 1948; Spence, 1956) to modify their viewpoint, the influence of B. F. Skinner (e.g., Skinner, 1953), a staunch theoretical behaviorist, continued to dominate in that area. Within social psychology, however, models involving the interactive effects of motivation and cognition flourished well into the early 1970s. This was a direct consequence of Lewin's charismatic appeal, which enabled him to pass many of his theoretical ideas to his students and associates and to their students (e.g., Festinger, Cartwright, Zander, Back, Atkinson, Deutsch, Kelley, Schachter, Zajonc). Indeed, much of social psychology up to that point could be traced to Lewin and others (e.g., Bruner, Heider, Newcomb) who saw the importance of both motivation and cognition in their theories.

In the 1970s, a major shift in emphasis began occurring in social psychology; cognition emerged as the dominant force, and motivation declined to a secondary element. This reversal may be directly attributable to the rejection of motivational concepts in the study of cognition and perceptual processes in general psychology. As Anderson (1980) pointed out, cognitive psychology did not begin to emerge from the attack of the behaviorists until this time. He cited three areas that account for the information-processing approach that emerged in the late 1960s and early 1970s: human factors research in World War II (see Broadbent, 1958; Atkinson & Schiffrin, 1968), interest in artificial intelligence (e.g., Newell & Simon, 1972), and psycholinguistics (e.g., Chomsky, 1957). Anderson cited Neisser's (1967)-*Cognitive Psychology* as the book that gave "a new legitimacy to the field." Motivation had little place in these three areas. These nonmotivational information-processing concepts began to influence research and theory in social psychology in the late 1970s, with the premise that cognition can account for many behaviors that others claimed to be motivated.

In an earlier period, the premise had been quite the opposite. The "New Look" argued that motivation could account for many responses that others claimed to be strictly perceptual. Bruner (1957, p. 123), for example, wrote:

> About ten years ago I was party to the publication of an innocent enough paper entitled, 'Value and Need as Organizing Factors in Perception.' It was concerned with what at that time was the rather obscure problem of how extra-stimulus factors influenced perception, a subject then of interest to only a small band of us – Gardner Murphy, Nevitt Sanford, Muzafer Sherif, and a few others. Obviously, Professor Boring is quite right about the mischievousness of the Zeitgeist, for the appearance of this paper seemed to coincide with all sorts of spirit-like rumbling within the world of psychology that were soon to erupt in a most unspirit-like torrent of research on this very topic – perhaps three hundred research reports and theoretical explications in the ten years since then.

Bruner then went on to present, in this classic article, his views on perceptual readiness, in which the New Look plays an important role. His notion regarding category accessibility, for example, was that it was determined by learning and by "the requirements of search dictated by need states and the need to carry out habitual enterprises such as walking, reading, or whatever it is that makes up the round of daily, habitual life" (Bruner, 1957, pp. 148–149). He concluded his article with the following statement:

> In conclusion, it seems appropriate to say that the ten years of the so-called New Look in perception research seem to be coming to a close with much empirical work accomplished – a great deal of it demonstrational, to be sure, but with a promise of a second ten years in which hypotheses will be more rigorously formulated and, conceivably, neural mechanisms postulated, if not discovered. The prospects are anything but discouraging.

The New Look is gone. Bruner was correct in that the New Look carried on for 10 years and, indeed, might have had its heyday in the 1960s. The notion of motivational influences on perception and cognition was highly discussed, though always controversial in perception (e.g., Dember, 1960) and cognition (e.g., Harper et al., 1964). In the Harper et al. (1964) book, there is a section of particular relevance to the present volume. It is entitled, *Cognition, Motivation and Personality*, and it includes articles that deal with effects of motivational processes on cognition (Henle, 1964) and cognitive aspects of motivation (Prentice, 1964) as well as some very interesting contributions by investigators of social behavior. Here we have Schachter and Singer's (1962) classic article on cognitive, social, and physiological determinants of emotional state; Festinger's articles on the motivating effects of cognitive dissonance (Festinger, 1958) and the psychological effects of insufficient rewards (Festinger, 1961); and many others (e.g., Pettigrew, 1958; Berkowitz, 1960; Secord & Backman, 1960).

Hence, as a consequence of the New Look, there was a very rich sense of the interplay among motivation, cognition, and social behavior.

In the early 1980s, all of this camaraderie between motivational and cognitive theorists faded. In books on sensation and perception (e.g., Levine & Shefner, 1981; Coren et al., 1984), the New Look and motivation are mentioned rarely if at all. Similarly, no mention of the New Look or motivation is made in Anderson's (1980) cognitive psychology book, *Cognitive Psychology and Its Implications*. When it comes to social psychology, the situation was similar. For example, in a highly influential book by Nisbett and Ross (1980), the New Look is discussed, as is motivation, but both are treated as peripheral to central human inference processes. In much of psychology, then, the New Look and its impact were no longer felt. Indeed, in some areas of social cognition, there was evidence of hostility toward anyone who would dare use the term "motivation" in anything other than a pejorative manner. One of our undergraduate students, for example, on arriving at a graduate center well known for social cognition, proudly presented the results of his honors thesis (subsequently published in the *Journal of Personality and Social Psychology*) at a conference. The student was cautioned by his new advisor not to mention the study "around here" – the reason being that since the study involved a motivational construct, the student might jeopardize his standing with the faculty.

What appears to account for the demise of the New Look is the fact that motivation was seen as an alternative explanation for a cognitive process. Rather than studying the interaction of motivational and cognitive processes, a battle developed regarding which of the two, motivation or cognition, was a better explanation for the phenomenon. Dember (1960), for example, pointed out that in the classic experiment by Bruner and Goodman (1947), in which children overestimated the size of coins compared to neutral discs, the results might not be due to motivation, as was originally proposed, "but more simply by a culturally acquired association between value and size" (Dember, 1960, p. 340). Research on perceptual defense (e.g., Postman et al., 1948; Blum, 1954) also fell under heavy criticism, mostly because of methodological shortcomings.

In the 1970s and early 1980s, social psychologists were quick to jump on the bandwagon. Social-cognitive theorists also attempted to put motivational theories to rest with alternative explanations. Thus, for Nisbett and Ross (1980, p. 247), biases and problems in inference or behavior are often due to information-processing errors and cognitive limitations – the notion of "people as faulty computers." Self-serving biases in attribution and prejudice, for example, may not be at all motivational:

> In both cases nonmotivational factors seem sufficient to account for most of the phenomena. In the case of so-called ego-defensive biases in attribution, it is clear that actors usually hold preconceptions and possess evidence that on purely intellectual grounds would seem to justify, if not demand, asymmetric responses to success and failure. In the case of prejudice, it seems clear that stereotypes of ethnic or racial groups are similar to the schemas or theories that encapsulate socially based knowledge of many other categories of people, objects, or events.

A similar "faulty computer" perspective on judgmental errors and biases may be found in the works of Cantor and Mischel (1977), Dawes (1976), Markus (1977), Hamilton (1979), and Miller and Ross (1975).

Contrary to the history of research and theory in social psychology, and in spite of the teachings of many current practitioners' advisers whose lineage could be traced back to Heider and Lewin, the "cold" approach became the predominant theme in the study of social behavior. Indeed, even motivational theories of achievement behavior were under attack from cognitive theorists. Trope (1975) argued that differences in behavior as a function of achievement-related motives are primarily due to differences in cognitive information seeking, not affective arousal. He and Weiner (1972) argued that preferences for tasks of intermediate difficulty on the part of success-oriented persons (see Atkinson, 1964; Atkinson & Raynor, 1974) are due to the fact that such tasks are most diagnostic of the person's ability, rather than being due to the interaction of motivational and situational components that the affective theory specifies. In the area of social behavior, then, cognitive theories became the Weltanschaung.

It was during this time that one on the most cognitive of cognitive social psychologist, Tory Higgins, arrived at my (RMS) university and remained there for a few years before moving on. Whereas Tory was a strict cognitive theorist at the time, I was trying to defend motivational theorists. Before long, we began trying to convince the other that our field was more important than the other's. It did not take long for us to realize that both motivation and cognition were not only important, but also must be considered together. In so doing, we developed the notion of the Warm Look. We argued that just as "hot" cognitions are insufficient explanations for information processing and perceptual processes, so, too, is the "cold" approach an inadequate explanation for social phenomena. The Warm Look reflects the blending of "cold" cognitive and "hot" motivational processes; motivation and cognition are, in fact, inseparable. Sorrentino and Higgins (1986, Chapter 1, p. 8) wrote,

> Behavior is not a product of hot cognitions, as suggested by the New Look perspective, nor of cold cognitions, as suggested by the 'faulty computer' perspective. In addition, it is not simply that cognition leads to motivation and motivation leads to cognition. Rather, each is a property or facet of the other. They are synergistic in that they operate together to produce combined effects. What we are saying, then, is that whatever determines behavior is neither hot nor cold – it is warm.

Following our synthesis of ideas, it became apparent that we should try to do what we can to help bring the two fields back together. In order to accomplish this, we decided that we would come up with the first handbook of motivation and cognition. We contacted the best people we could think of who were experts in either motivation or cognition and asked them if they would be willing to write a chapter emphasizing the synergism of motivation and cognition. The original *Handbook of Motivation and Cognition* (Sorrentino & Higgins, 1986) was highly cited and became so successful that two more volumes were produced (Higgins & Sorrentino, 1990, Vol. 2; Sorrentino & Higgins, 1996, Vol. 3).

The present handbook is a natural extension of this series. Recognizing the importance of motivation and cognition to the study of cross-cultural research, Susumu and I contacted some of the people that contributed to the original series and asked them to write a chapter stating how their current research and theory was affected by differences across cultures. As a result, we got some very interesting chapters in the current volume. These chapters are included in the first part of the book, where we have loosely clustered together those chapters which attempt to show the importance of motivation and cognition for the study of cultural differences and similarities. In the original volume, Julius Kuhl (1986, p. 407) nicely defined affect, motivation, and cognition:

> It is assumed that cognitive, emotional, and motivational subsystems relate to the world in three different ways. The term cognition is reserved for those processes that mediate the acquisition and representation of knowledge about the world, i.e., processes that have a representative relation to the world of objects and facts. Emotional (affective) processes evaluate the personal significance of those objects and facts. Motivational processes relate to the world in an actional way, e.g., they relate to goal states of the organism in its attempt to produce desired changes in its environment.

Kuhl went on to discuss some interesting interactions among the three subsystems in terms of three motivational phenomena: choice, persistence, and effort. His discussion is a tour de force that shows why each of these subsystems must be taken into account in any theory of human behavior. In Chapter 2 of this volume, he and Heidi Keller aim to improve our understanding of the role of emotion across cultures by taking a closer look at the cognitive, emotional, and developmental differences that have been observed in cross-cultural research on independent and interdependent orientations; providing a theoretical explanation for the observed pattern of cognitive, emotional, and developmental differences between cultures that lean more toward individualistic or interrelated orientations; elaborating the role affect regulation plays in modulating the interaction between diverging cognitive processing styles; and deriving from this theoretical analysis an elaborated model extending the framework of independence and interdependence to overcome some conceptual difficulties involved in this contrast.

In the original volume, Judy Short and I (Sorrentino & Short, 1986) presented our initial theory of uncertainty orientation. We tried to show that previous research and theory on achievement behavior may have confused information value with affective value. We introduced our views on uncertainty orientation with the notion that uncertainty orientation is primarily an informational variable, whereas achievement-related motives are primarily affective variables. Thus, all those aspects of achievement situations that are informational in nature (e.g., information about the self or the environment) are related to individual differences in uncertainty orientation. All those aspects that are related to affective arousal (feeling good or bad about the self or the environment) are due to achievement-related motives (as well as to any other source of motivation aroused by the situation). In Chapter 2 of the present volume, I, along with Andrew Szeto, John Nezlek, Satoru Yasunaga, Sadafusa Kouhara, and Yasunao Ohtsubo extend this theory to cross-cultural studies. We present research suggesting that although controversy currently rages regarding whether individualism and collectivism truly distinguish Eastern and Western societies, or whether it may be more meaningful to speak of an independent versus interdependent self, or whether people have or do not have self-esteem, a plausible major distinction may be that most East–West differences might be a function of how these societies cope with uncertainty, and how this shapes the behavior of its constituent members. We also show that so-called differences in emotional responding and self-esteem may be a function of underlying individual differences in achievement-related motives and whether the individual's means of handling uncertainty are consistent with his or her culture's method of resolving uncertainty.

Perhaps one of the most provocative chapters in the original series was that by Bargh (1990). There he presented one of his most complete statements regarding nonconscious motivation and cognition. Bargh raised the issue of how much control a person exercises over his or her own thought and behavior in social situations. What other agents of control exist and what is the extent of their influence? Bargh argues that while responses may be strongly influenced by the environment and preconscious processes, an intervening intention is required to make the response itself. Intentional, goal-directed responding can overcome automatic tendencies in information processing and action. Bargh suggests that the key question then becomes, "Where do goals come from?" He proposes that instead of being under "executive" control, much goal-setting activity may be initiated by patterns of environmental features. It may be the environment itself that activates the goal or intent. More specifically, chronic representations of goals (or intents) and those environmental features with which they are frequently and consistently associated (e.g., because these are the situations in which the goals are typically pursued) may become interconnected in memory. Thus, goals or intentions would be automatically activated whenever relevant situational features were present in the environment. And these goals and intentions can guide thought and behavior outside of awareness in the service of the individual and not simply to satisfy the desires or demands of the social environment.

John, along with Eric Uhlmann, and Andrew Poelhman, continues to be provocative in Chapter 4 of this handbook. These co-authors tackle the fascinating topic of the universality of religion, but from an implicit motivation and cognitive framework. Rather than attempt a comprehensive theory of the ultimate origins of religious faith, they discuss evidence for two classes of empirically supported psychological contributors: *cognitive defaults* and *existential needs*. Both of these sets of variables exert a profound yet largely implicit (i.e., intuitive, unconscious) influence on the development, content, transmission, and maintenance of religious faith. Theistic cognition is so deeply ingrained that even atheists, agnostics, and less religious people display implicit responses consistent with religious beliefs.

William Swann was also a contributor to the original series (Swann, 1990). Swann considers the interplay of self-enhancement and self-verification. He asks, "What do people want to believe about themselves?" He argues that both self-enhancement and self-verification processes are sufficiently robust that neither can be ruled out. It is true both that people like to be liked and that people are motivated to maintain an idea about themselves. And these motivations can work together (e.g., high self-esteem persons) or be in conflict (e.g., low self-esteem persons). With respect to social feedback in particular, people are motivated both to receive positive feedback about themselves (because of their need for praise and love) and to receive feedback that is consistent with their self-beliefs (because of their need to believe that the social world is predictable and controllable). Swann proposed that the process of self-enhancement requires only that the feedback be identified as favorable or unfavorable. In contrast, the process of self-verification requires identification of the self-attribute contained in the feedback, accessing stored beliefs about one's self-attributes, and comparing these self-attributes. Swann suggests that this difference means that self-verification has more complex conditional rules for approaching and avoiding feedback than does self-evaluation, which, in turn, means that self-verification requires additional mental work. He then described a variety of motivational implications of this difference in mental effort, such as the effects of depriving people of cognitive resources or manipulating the accessibility or certainty of people's self-beliefs.

In this handbook, the goal of Chapter 6 by Tammy English, Serena Chen, and William Swann is to assess the likelihood that self-verification is a culture general phenomenon. To this end, they first provide an overview of self-verification theory and research, and then discuss whether the roots of self-verification extend to cultures outside of North America and, if so, what form self-verification strivings would take in these cultures. Ultimately, they propose that self-verification strivings are universal, although cross-cultural differences in conceptions of the self may result in cultural variation in the ways they are pursued.

Weiner (1986) developed his ideas concerning the importance of attributional theory to the study of motivation and emotion. In Chapter 7 of this handbook, he contends that attribution theory as a theory, that is, as a set of interrelated constructs, is not in need of alteration. However, one must be very careful in the assumptions being made when contrasting ethnic groups, cultures, genders, and so forth. Success for one may be failure for another; causal information for one may be perceived as useless for another; causes salient to one group may be in the far background for the other; and so on. That is, content must be distinguished from process inasmuch as content may be culturally specific whereas process is culturally general. This means that the theorist must be alert for differences between cultures. However, one must be equally alert to convert phenotypic disparities into genotypic similarities. What appears to be a qualitative difference between cultures may be subject to a similar conceptual analysis. That is, the unique is nonetheless included within more general laws.

Tory Higgins along with his students (Higgins et al., 1986) presented the initial formulation of self-discrepancy theory. This evolved into regulatory-focus theory (see Chapter 8) and Tory, along with, Antonio Pierro and Arie Kruglanski (another contributor to the series, see Kruglanski 1990, 1996), in Chapter 8, expand this theory across cultures. They consider how the regulatory focus distinction between promotion concerns with accomplishment and aspirations and prevention concerns with safety and responsibilities, and the regulatory mode distinction between loco-motion concerns with movement from state to state and assessment concerns with making comparisons, could provide a new perspective on cultural differences in trait strength. From this *self-regulatory perspective*, traits like extraversion or con-scientiousness are conceptualized as *strategic conduits* or *channels* in the service of promotion, prevention, locomotion, or assessment orientations. That is, rather than themselves reflecting something basic about individuals' motivational predis-positions, such traits are considered as providing support for more fundamental and general self-regulatory concerns. This conceptualization includes a new perspective on why Japan and USA, for example, vary in self-esteem levels.

Gollwitzer (1990), then working with Heinz Heckhausen prior to Heckhausen's passing, asked the question, "How do people choose, plan, enact, and evaluate actions?" Four distinct phases in the course of action were described; delibera-tion, implementation, goal achievement, and evaluating outcomes of the action. Peter Gollwitzer suggests that the concept of "mind-set" can be used to spec-ify the distinct tasks or demands to be solved at each of the four phases. In this handbook, Peter Gollwitzer, along with Gabrielle Oettingen and Timur Sevincer (Chapter 9) state that the role of culture in goal pursuit may be discussed at vari-ous levels of analysis, and that cultural norms and values might affect the deter-minants of goal setting and goal striving, desirability, and feasibility. They then address the following questions. Does culture affect what future outcomes and behaviors are perceived as desirable and thus qualify as potential aspired – to goal states? And does culture affect how people perceive the feasibility of realiz-ing these desired futures? They also examine whether and how culture influences the processes that lead people to commit to goals, and whether it influences the translation of set goals into action (i.e., goal striving).

Along with contributors to the original series, we sought out others who had something to say about the influence of motivation and cognition across cultures. In Chapter 5, Jan Hofer and Michael Bond make a case for using implicit meas-ures in cross-cultural psychology. They argue that implicit measures may be even more useful in such investigations because they rely less heavily on the sophis-ticated cognitive processes that compromise the validity of explicit measures when used cross-culturally. Implicit measures alert psychologists to the power of situations in evoking the constructs being implicitly tapped. Their cross-cul-tural consideration of implicit measures leads into a discussion of culture's role in infusing situations with shared meaning, "the very stuff of social psychology." This shared meaning interacts with the personalities of cultured carriers of that meaning to yield predictable behavior.

Michelle Gezensvey and Colleen Ward, Chapter 10, attempt to synthesize the-ory, concepts and models from two domains of psychological research: motivation and acculturation. From the cross-cultural vantage point, a motivational analy-sis offers a new perspective on the acculturation process. From the motivational vantage point, the chapter demonstrates that key theoretical constructs and processes can be extended to a new area of investigation – culture contact and change.

In Chapter 11, Daphna Oyserman and Spike Lee point out that, although the correlational evidence supports the claims made by individualism and collectivism models of culture, without experimental evidence, the process by which culture matters remains hidden. In this chapter, their goal is to illuminate at least part of this hidden process, focussing on *how* individualism and collectivism as cultural syndromes likely influence cognitive content, procedures, and motivations. By articulating what turns on culturally characteristic motivations and studying the extent that these motivations map on to individualism and collectivism or other cultural syndrome models, research on the interface between culture and motivational processes provides a new frontier on cultural psychology.

Bertram Malle (Chapter 12) argues that, in response to the variety of tasks and demands in social life, humans have evolved a suite of interrelated subsystems that together form what may be called the social-cognitive toolbox. This toolbox contains abstract concepts (e.g., agency and intentionality); processes of gaze following, automatic empathy, mimicry, and joint attention; and increasingly complex functions of imaginative simulation and mental state inference. These tools belong together not because they form a module or are implemented in the same brain areas; what unites them is their responsiveness to the social environment with its challenges of ambulant intentional agents-minded, intelligent, and unique individuals. In this chapter, Malle discusses extant knowledge on each social-cognitive tool and asks whether there are compelling data for or against universality of that tool.

Rounding out this section of the book, Bertram Gawronski, Kurt Peters, and Fritz Strack, Chapter 13, tackle cognitive dissonance theory. They provide a conceptual reanalysis of inconsistency processes that aims at specifying different sources of cross-cultural differences in dissonance-related phenomena. The central claim of their reanalysis is that the general processes associated with cognitive inconsistency are universal, even though cross-cultural differences pertaining to the contents of belief systems may function as important moderators of the outcomes of these processes.

Part II of the book consists of leading cross-cultural researchers for whom we asked the question, "How does culture affect the way people think and act?" Minoru Karasawa and Anne Maass (Chapter 14) kick off this part by discussing three functions of language in social cognition. First, they analyze the way in which language drives attention, arguing that subtle differences in language use determine what the listeners will focus on, what will attract their attention, and also what they may overlook or ignore. Second, they review research showing that linguistic choices of the speaker affect inferences that the listener is likely to draw about the speaker as well as the object of the conversation. Finally, taking an embodiment perspective, they argue that our perception and imagery of social reality is, in a subtle manner, influenced by the way in which language is written.

Chapter 15 by Denis Hilton and James Liu explicates their use of the concept of social representations of history, and show how it can function with respect to group identity construction and agenda setting. They speculate that these representations include "charters" that serve a normative function of warranting group attitudes and actions by explaining them in terms of key events in the group's history. They also discuss other ways in which charters can be changed or contested, and conclude by reviewing studies that show the relevance of representations of history for group identities and collective emotions, such as collective guilt.

In Chapter 16, Susumu Yamaguchi, Hiroaki Morio, and Chunchi Lin challenge the self-criticism view of self-esteem among Japanese citizens. They point out that cross-cultural differences in self-evaluations and self-esteem, especially between Japan and North America, fit very well with the self-criticism hypothesis at the country level. However, if one takes a closer look at the individual level data and analyze them as such, the attractiveness of the self-criticism hypothesis fades away. At the individual level, available evidence indicates that high self-esteem is associated with higher academic achievement, higher expectation of performance, and more persistent both in Japan and North America. High self-esteem people among Japanese also show more confidence in their social skills and initiate contacts more easily than their low self-esteem counterparts, like high self-esteem people in North America. Furthermore, high self-esteem is strongly associated with higher expressed psychological well-being again like in North America.

Chapter 17 by Yoshihisa Kashima, Kim Peters, and Jennifer Whelan points out that culture is part of human nature. *Homo sapiens* have evolved to construct culture. Human ontogeny presupposes cultural input; children become fully human to the extent that they are enculturated into the meaningful world of the human social reality. Whereas culture may influence genetic evolution in the long run, cultural evolution proceeds much more quickly than biological evolution. Much of human adaptation (or otherwise) to our natural and social environment has to be driven by cultural evolution. In this sense, human agency, either individual or collective, is fundamentally cultural. A question they address in this chapter, however, is how such enculturated agency is possible.

Chapter 18 by Justin Levinson states that the collaboration between psychological and legal scholarship is only just beginning. Recent interdisciplinary projects have demonstrated that an important accomplishment – the building of an accurate and culturally competent legal behavioral model – is within reach. Building such a model has major societal ramifications, from protecting victims of racial and cultural discrimination to ensuring a behaviorally and economically efficient system of rules. This chapter brings up to date legal scholarship incorporating cognitive, social and cultural psychology, highlights new interdisciplinary research directions, and challenges psychologists and legal scholars to increase collaborations.

In Chapter 19, Emiko Kashima argues that, given the overwhelming advantage of culture for individual and group survival, a psychological mechanism that ensured the individual's adherence to, and within-group maintenance of, the shared knowledge would have been critical. While some animal species including humans physically threaten others to dominate and gain own advantages, humans are unique in their ability to threaten self as well as others by using culturally shared meanings. Likewise, humans are capable of symbolically alleviating the psychological injuries experienced by self and other. In other words, culture is both an antecedent and a consequence of threat for an individual, with an important group-level implication of knowledge preservation. The more the given meaning is activated, used, and encoded in the memory of the people who participated in the event, the more likely it becomes that this meaning is used in the future of people.

Chapter 20, by Kwok Leung and Fan Zhou, provides a critical analysis of the relationships between two classes of generalized motivational and cognitive constructs: values and social axioms. Different from previous works on motivational and cognitive processes, research on these two constructs has taken into account the influence of culture, and their cultural generality has been demonstrated by large-scale cross-cultural research. The chapter also explores the interplay between values and social axioms in influencing behavior, and presents a number of directions for future research.

Uichol Kim and Young-Shin Park, in Chapter 21, discuss differences between Korean and other East Asian cultures with the United States and other Western cultures. They see basic differences in attitudes and goals with regard to academic achievement as strongly rooted in Confucianism and Buddhist beliefs in the former and more individualist attitudes in the latter groups. Findings from quantitative and qualitative analyses lead them to question the validity of Western theories that focus narrowly on individualistic values.

Chapter 22 by Jennifer Goetz, Julie Spencer-Rodgers, and Kaiping Peng, discusses how culture influences the experience and regulation of emotional complexity, or the co-occurrence of positive and negative emotions. Research in this chapter suggests that beliefs about the nature of contradiction, interconnections, and change in the world relate to the subjective experience of complex emotions. Individuals from dialectical cultures that tolerate contradiction report feeling emotional complexity more frequently, are more comfortable with emotional complexity, and may be less likely to regulate it. These findings raise questions about emotional co-occurrence, as well as the role of culture in emotional experience.

In Chapter 23, David Matsumoto and Jessie Wilson describe a theory of how emotions serve as one important source of motivation by priming individuals to behave in certain ways. They also argue that the functions of culture – as a meaning and information system – are to prevent social chaos, maintain social order, and ensure group efficiency, given the ecological environment and the resources available in it to survive. They believe that when emotions are elicited, culture calibrates the primed individual to the behavioral repertoires available and necessary in that culture as identified by the social roles, norms, and expectations in order to serve as motivators for desired behaviors. They also believe that culture calibrates the behaviors of the perceivers of emotion, thereby ensuring the regulation of social interaction.

Finally, in Part III (Chapter 24), Ron Fischer and Vivian Miu-Chi Lun state that we need to address to what extent existing psychological tests are adequate and can be used with culturally diverse populations. The aim of their chapter is therefore to (a) outline criteria and principles for assessing equivalence and bias (or cultural fairness) of psychological tests, (b) provide a brief review of methods that could be used for examining the applicability of tests, (c) provide a selected review of specific tests and domains and their cross-cultural applicability, and (d) present some avenues for further research.

REFERENCES

Anderson, J. R. (1980). *Cognitive psychology and its implications*. San Francisco: Freeman.

Atkinson, J. W. (1964). *An introduction to motivation*. Princeton, NJ: Van Nostrand.

Atkinson, J. W., & Raynor, J. O. (1974). *Motivation and achievement*. Washington, DC: Winston.

Atkinson, R. C., & Shiffrin, R. M. (1968). Human memory: A proposed system and its control processes. In K. Spence & J. Spence (Eds.), *The psychology of learning and motivation* (Vol. 2, pp. 90–195). New York: Academic Press.

Bargh, J. A. (1990). Auto-motives: Preconscious determinants of social interaction. In T. Higgins & R. M. Sorrentino (Eds.), *The handbook of motivation and cognition: Foundations of social behavior* (Vol. 2, pp. 93–130). New York: The Guilford Press.

Berkowitz, L. (1960). The judgmental processes in personality functioning. *Psychological Review*, *67*, 130–142.

Blum, G. S. (1954). An experimental reunion of psychoanalytic theory with perceptual vigilance and defense. *Journal of Abnormal and Social Psychology*, *49*, 94–98.

Broadbent, A. E. (1958). *Perception and communication*. New York: Pergamon Press.

Bruner, J. S. (1957). On perceptual readiness. *Psychological Review*, *64*, 123–152.

Bruner, J. S., & Goodman, C. C. (1947). Value and need as organizing factors in perception. *Journal of Abnormal and Social Psychology*, *42*, 33–44.

Cantor, N., & Mischel, W. (1977). Traits as prototypes: Effects on recognition memory. *Journal of Personality and Social Psychology*, *31*, 38–49.

Chomsky, N. (1957). *Syntactic structures*. The Hague: Morton.

Coren, S., Porac, C., & Ward, L. M. (1984). *Sensation and perception* (2nd ed.). Orlando, FL: Academic Press.

Darwin, C. (1872). *The expression of emotions in man and animals*. New York: Appleton.

Dawes, R. M. (1976). Shallow psychology. In J. S. Carroll & J. W. Payne (Eds.), *Cognition and social behaviour* (pp. 3–11). Hillsdale, NJ: Erlbaum.

Dember, W. N. (1960). *The psychology of perception*. New York: Holt, Rinehart and Winston.

Festinger, L. (1958). The motivating effect of cognitive dissonance. In G. Lindzey (Ed.), *Assessment of human motives* (pp. 65–86). New York: Holt, Rinehart and Winston.

Festinger, L. (1961). The psychological effects of insufficient reward. *American Psychologist*, *16*, 1–11.

Freud, S. (1955). A childhood recollection from Dichtung and Wahrheit. In J. Strachey & A. Freud (Eds.), *The standard edition of the complete psychological works of Sigmund Freud* (Vol. 17). London: Hogarth Press. (Original work published in 1917)

Galton, F. (1883). *Inquiries into human faculty and its development*. London: Macmillan.

Gollwitzer, P. M. (1990). Action phases and mind sets. In E. T. Higgins & R. M. Sorrentino (Eds.), *The handbook of motivation and cognition: Foundations of social behavior* (Vol. 2, pp. 53–92). New York: The Guilford Press.

Hamilton, D. L. (1979). A cognitive attributional analysis of stereotyping. In L. Berkowitz (Ed.), *Advances in experimental social psychology* (Vol. 12, pp. 53–84). New York: Academic Press.

Harper, R. J. C., Anderson C. C., Christensen, C. M., & Hunka, S. M. (Eds.) (1964). *The Cognitive process: Readings*. Englewood Cliffs, NJ: Prentice-Hall.

Henle, M. (1964). Some motivational processes on cognition. In R. J. C. Harper, C. C. Anderson, C. M. Christensen, & S. M. Hunka (Eds.), *The cognitive processes: Readings* (pp. 389–399). Englewood Cliffs, NJ: Prentice-Hall.

Higgins, E. T., & Sorrentino, R. M. (1990). *The Handbook of Motivation and Cognition: Foundation of Social Behavior, Vol. 2* . New York: The Guilford Press.

Higgins, E. T., Strauman, T., & Klein, R. (1986). Standards and the process of self-evaluation: Multiple affects from multiple stages. In R. M. Sorrentino & E. T. Higgins (Eds.), *The handbook of motivation and cognition: Foundations of social behavior* (pp. 23–63). New York: The Guilford Press.

Hull, C. L. (1943). *Principles of behaviour*. New York: Appleton-Century.

James, W. (1890). *The Principles of psychology (Vols. 1 & 2)* . New York: Holt.

Kruglanski, A. W. (1990). Motivations for judging and knowing: Implications for causal attribution. In E. T. Higgins & R. M. Sorrentino (Eds.), *The handbook of motivation and cognition: Foundations of social behavior* (Vol. 2, pp. 333–368). New York: The Guilford Press.

Kruglanski, A. W. (1996). A motivated gatekeeper of our minds: Need for closure effects on interpersonal and group processes. In R. M. Sorrentino & E. T. Higgins (Eds.), *The handbook of motivation and cognition: The interpersonal context* (Vol. 3, pp. 465–496). New York: The Guilford Press.

Kuhl, J. (1986) Motivation and information processing: A new look at decision making, dynamic change and action control. In R. M. Sorrentino and E. T. Higgins (Eds.), *The Handbook of Motivation and Cognition: Foundations of Social Behavior* (pp. 404–434). New York: The Guilford Press.

Levine, M. V., & Shefner, J. M. (1981). *Fundamentals of sensation and perception*. Reading, MA: Addison-Wesley.

Lewin, K. (1935). *A dynamic theory of personality*. New York: McGraw-Hill.

Lewin, K. (1951). *Field theory in social science*. New York: Harper & Brothers.

Markus, H. (1977). Self-schema and processing information about the self. *Journal of Personality and Social Psychology, 35*, 63–78.

McDougall, W. (1908). *Introduction to social psychology*. London: Methuen.

Miller, N. E. (1948). Studies of fear as an acquirable drive: I. Fear as motivation and fear-education as reinforcement in the learning of new responses. *Journal of Experimental Psychology, 38*, 89–101.

Miller, A. T., & Ross, M. (1975). Self-serving biases in the attribution of causality: Fact or fiction?. *Psychological Bulletin, 82*, 213–225.

Neisser, U. (1967). *Cognitive psychology*. New York: Appleton-Century-Crofts.

Newell, A., & Simon, H. A. (1972). *Human problem solving*. Englewood Cliffs, NJ: Prentice-Hall.

Nisbett, R., & Ross, L. (1980). *Human inferences: Strategies and shortcomings of social judgment*. Englewood Cliffs, NJ: Prentice-Hall.

Pettigrew, T. F. (1958). The measurement and correlates of category width as a cognitive variable. *Journal of Personality, 26*, 532–544.

Postman, L., Bruner, J. S., & McGinnis, E. (1948). Personal values as selective factors in perception. *Journal of Abnormal and Social Psychology, 43*, 142–154.

Prentice, W. C. H. (1964). Some cognitive aspects of motivation. In R. J. C. Harper, C. C. Anderson, C. M. Christensen, & S. M. Hunka (Eds.), *The cognitive processes: Readings* (pp. 400–411). Englewood Cliffs, NJ: Prentice-Hall.

Schachter, S., & Singer, J. E. (1962). Cognitive, social, and physiological determinants of emotional state. *Psychological Review, 69*, 379–399.

Secord, P. F., & Backman, C. W. (1960). Personality theory and the problem of stability and change in individual behaviour: An interpersonal approach. *Psychological Review, 68*, 21–32.

Skinner, B. F. (1953). *Science and human behavior*. New York: Free Press.

Sorrentino, R. M., & Higgins, E. T. (1986). Motivation and cognition: Warming to synergism. In R. M. Sorrentino & E. T. Higgins (Eds.), *The handbook of motivation and cognition: Foundations of social behavior* (pp. 3–19). New York: The Guilford Press.

Sorrentino, R. M., & Higgins, E. T. (1996). *The handbook of motivation and cognition: The Interpersonal Context. Vol 3*. New York: The Guilford Press.

Sorrentino, R. M., & Short, J. C. (1986). Uncertainty orientation, motivation, and cognition. In R. M. Sorrentino & E. T. Higgins (Eds.), *The handbook of motivation and cognition: Foundations of social behavior* (pp. 379–403). New York: The Guilford Press.

Spence, K. W. (1956). *Behavior theory and conditioning*. New Haven: Yale University Press.

Swann, W. B. (1990). To be adored or to be known?: The interplay of self-enhancement and self-verification. In E. T. Higgins & R. M. Sorrentino (Eds.), *The handbook of motivation and cognition: Foundations of social behavior* (Vol. 2, pp. 408–450). New York: The Guilford Press.

Titchener, E. B. (1899). Structural and functional psychology. *Philosophical Review, 8*, 290–299.

Tolman, E. C. (1932). *Purposive behavior in animals and men*. New York: Century.

Tolman, E. C. (1959). Principles of purposive behaviour. In S. Koch (Ed.), *Psychology: A study of a science* (Vol. 2, pp. 92–157). New York: McGraw-Hill.

Trope, Y. (1975). Seeking information about one's own ability as a determinant of choice among tasks. *Journal of Personality and Social Psychology, 52*, 1004–1013.

Watson, J. B. (1930). *Behaviourism*. New York: Norton.

Weiner, B. (1972). *Theories of motivation: From mechanism to cognition*. Chicago: Markham.

Weiner, B. (1986). Attribution, emotion, and action. In R. M. Sorrentino & E. T. Higgins (Eds.), *The handbook of motivation and cognition: Foundations of social behavior* (pp. 379–403). New York: The Guilford Press.

PART

I

CULTURE FROM A MOTIVATION AND COGNITION PERSPECTIVE

2

AFFECT-REGULATION, SELF-DEVELOPMENT AND PARENTING: A FUNCTIONAL-DESIGN APPROACH TO CROSS-CULTURAL DIFFERENCES

JULIUS KUHL AND HEIDI KELLER

University of Osnabrück, Osnabrück, Germany

One of the most obvious ways in which people differ relates to social distance: Within any culture of the world people differ in the preferred degree of closeness and relatedness to others. For many centuries, even before psychology became a science, individual differences in relatedness have been described in terms of personality constructs such as warm-aloof, social-reserved, and the like. These constructs are mirrored in personality dimensions, e.g., introversion versus extraversion (Eysenck, 1967; McCrae & Costa, 1987), or personality disorders (Costa & Widiger, 1994), such as schizoid versus histrionic personality disorders, which are characterized by extreme degrees of emotional separateness ("independence") versus affective sharing ("interrelatedness"), respectively (Millon, 1981; Kuhl, 2001). In recent years, a similar distinction has been made to describe cross-cultural differences. Western cultures (e.g., the USA) seem to place more emphasis on individualism and independence whereas eastern cultures (e.g., Japan) seem to be more oriented toward interrelatedness and interdependence (Triandis, 1995; Markus & Kitayama, 2004).

Emotion is perhaps the most striking feature in which the constructs of independence and interdependence differ. According to a common stereotype, joy and warmth are feelings that seem to describe a socially oriented, interdependent person rather than an independent individual who is less involved in social contact or keeps a distance to others. In a similar vein, extraverts have been postulated and found to be more sensitive than introverts to reward, positive affect and social contact (Gupta & Nagpal, 1978; Gray, 1987). However, differences among independent and interdependent cultures seem to be more complex than simple models of similar personality constructs may suggest. For example, even heightened rather than reduced sensitivity for positive affect has been observed in individuals from an independent culture when an emotion (i.e., pride) was assessed that is better consistent with a cultural context that emphasizes individual rather than collective achievement (Kitayama et al., 2003b).

It is the aim of this chapter to take a few steps toward improving our understanding of the role of emotion across cultures by (1) taking a closer look at the cognitive, emotional, and developmental differences that have been observed in cross-cultural research on independent and interdependent orientations; (2) providing a theoretical explanation for the observed pattern of cognitive, emotional, and developmental differences between cultures that lean more toward individualistic or interdependent orientations; (3) elaborating the role affect regulation plays in modulating the interaction between diverging cognitive processing styles; and (4) derive from this theoretical analysis an elaborated model extending the framework of independence and interdependence to overcome some conceptual difficulties involved in this contrast.

INDEPENDENT AND INTERDEPENDENT ORIENTATIONS: FINDINGS FROM CROSS-CULTURAL RESEARCH

From a developmental point of view, the two cultural syndromes of independence and interdependence can be conceived of as two idealized developmental pathways toward desirable endpoints in specific cultural environments (Keller, 2007). Although any given culture should be regarded as a mixture of those two orientations (Kitayama, 2000; Keller et al., 2002; Keller, 2007), western civilization typically emphasizes independence in terms of individuality, self-expression, personal sufficiency, and an independently oriented conceptual self (see Neisser, 1988) that is separated from others by emphasizing differences rather than communalities between one's own and others' needs and values (Kessen, 1979). In contrast, eastern cultures lean toward interdependence as described by interpersonal harmony, social hierarchy, and humility giving rise to an interdependently oriented self that shares its values and preferences with the immediate social environment (Greenfield et al., 2003).

DIACHRONIC AND SYNCHRONIC
PARENTING STYLES

Cross-cultural research has revealed a variety of differences between independent and interdependent cultural orientations. For example, the independent orientation is associated with an individualistic socialization strategy characterized by mentalistic language (Meins et al., 2002; Wang & Brockmeier, 2002; Demuth et al., 2007) which focuses on individual needs, wants, and ideas. For example, a mother may verbally express her perception of the child's emotional state along with an attempt to help cope with ("Don't be afraid: look, you can pet the dog and it is very kind to you"). In addition, the independent orientation is characterized by a distal parenting style involving face-to-face interaction and object play (Keller, 2003; Keller et al., 2004). For example, during face-to-face interaction (e.g., mother's responding to the child's eye contact or smile), the distance between mother and infant is larger compared to the close body contact that is more frequent in interdependent cultures. By exercising prompt and appropriate responsiveness that is *contingent* upon the infant's signals, caretakers promote the foundation for the development of agency and control (Keller et al., 2005a) and emotion regulation (Keller & Gauda, 1987). For example, when the child expresses distress, a mother from an independent culture may respond very promptly (sometimes within a few hundred milliseconds) by softening her voice, changing the child's body position, or any other measure that might make the child feel more comfortable. However, the very short interaction latencies during the first weeks of life are gradually increased, which helps the child tolerate uncomfortable states of mind for more extended periods of time. We will use the term *diachronic* to refer to this feature of the independent socialization pattern: A diachronic socialization style (i.e., interactive behavior characterized by caretakers' delayed responding) is characterized by increasing latencies of parental responses rather than an emphasis on synchronization of mother–child behaviors. The diachronic style facilitates an increasing separation of own and others' mental states, needs, and expectations: Gradually increasing the time elapsed between the child's expressive behavior and the caretaker's response promotes the development of separate rather than united cognitive-emotional representations of own and other's states.

In contrast, the interdependent orientation has been characterized by a cooperative style, minimization of conflict, and flexible adaptation to situational demands rather than rigid *self-control*, that is control of the environment according to ego-centered goals and intentions (Markus & Kitayama, 1991; Triandis, 1995). During the first weeks of life the interdependent orientation can be observed in frequent synchronization of behaviors performed by the infant and the caretaker. Mother and child may typically be in close body contact and share simultaneous rather than sequential ("diachronic") experiences, e.g., when mother and child are involved in synchronized dancing or rocking movements as well as co-occurring smiling and vocalizing (Keller et al., 2008).

This interdependent orientation seems to be promoted by a socialization strategy characterized by a proximal rather than distal parenting style (e.g., frequent carrying, close body contact, co-sleeping, and immediate or anticipatory attention to infants' negative signals) and an emphasis on implicit hierarchy and authority promoting a teacher–apprentice relationship between the infant and parents, older siblings, or other relatives (Keller, 2003; Greenfield, 2004).

DIFFERENT FORMS OF AFFECT REGULATION

One important outcome of the different socialization strategies associated with independent and interdependent orientations (i.e., diachronic and synchronic styles) is especially relevant for the central topic of this chapter: Diachronic and synchronic parenting styles should result in different modes of affect regulation. Different cultural orientations can be associated with characteristic differences in relational patterns (Takahashi, 1986; Kitayama & Park, in press) that may result in divergent forms of affect regulation. For example, the diachronic style frequently involves caretakers' *contingent* (i.e., conditional) responding to the child's signals: Mother's soothing is made contingent (i.e., dependent) upon the child's signals of distress. In contrast, early in infancy, the synchronic style associated with interdependent orientations is frequently characterized by mothers' *anticipatory* behavior (preventing an aversive state from occurring in the first place): Whereas the diachronic style responds to the child's signals of distress, the synchronic style is characterized by attempts to avoid distress from occurring whenever possible. For example, the latter style is directed at preventing potentially inconsistent or conflict-arousing experiences by immediate or even anticipatory responses of caretakers to a potentially threatening or otherwise difficult to integrate situation (Rothbaum et al., 2000a, b). In sum, contingent (diachronic) responding to the infant's signals (with gradually increasing latencies) amounts to a pattern of emotion regulation that differs from synchronic interaction styles and anticipatory parenting (Shaver & Mikulincer, 2007).

Different emotions are emphasized in socialization strategies across cultures (Miller & Sperry, 1987; Matsumoto & Kupperbusch, 2000). However, little empirical evidence is available on cross-cultural differences in the development of affect regulation. From a theoretical point of view one can expect clear-cut differences between diachronic and synchronic styles. Diachronic parenting expects more tolerance toward negative emotions (e.g., frustration or anxiety) and emphasizes the development of self-regulation of affect: A child that frequently experiences his own emotional state separately from the state of his or her caretaker may develop a stronger need to acquire self-regulatory coping strategies. On the other hand, an infant who frequently experiences unity between his own and others' emotional states can rely much more on social regulation of emotional states. We will return to this issue later in this chapter.

DIFFERENCES IN SELF-REPRESENTATIONS
ACROSS CULTURES

From a personality perspective, research on cognitive, motivational, and self-regulatory differences among cultures defines an enormous challenge to the specification of individual processes and mechanisms mediating culturally transmitted differences in cognition, emotion, and behavior. Despite all the differences in the cultural sources of behavior, the final common pathway of those sources is the individual: Irrespective of whether culture-specific patterns of behavior are derived from interdependent or individualistic concerns, they eventually have to be enacted through individual actors. What are the mental mechanisms promoting the particular types of behaviors that specific cultures expect from individuals? A pattern emerging from many studies suggests independent orientation to be associated with an individualistic self-representation (e.g., an emphasis on one's own as opposed to others' needs), independence (e.g., freedom of choice), ego-control (e.g., controlling the environment including others according to one's own explicit goals), and self-esteem (i.e., associating a sense of worth with oneself as an individual rather than with the group one is belonging to).

Research on cognitive and emotional characteristics underlying the individualistic pattern suggests that this pattern is characterized by the following: First, free ("self-expressive") choice as a prerequisite for individual motivation, i.e., motivation depends on the degree to which the individual has free choice among action alternatives (Iyengar & Lepper, 1999; Kitayama & Uchida, 2005). Second, the independent in contrast to the interdependent orientation is also associated with the well-known effect of dissonance reduction (e.g., exaggerating the personal value of an object or an action when it was freely chosen, especially when one's choice seems underjustified (Harmon-Jones & Mills, 1999; Kitayama et al., 2004). For example, when participants from an independent culture "freely" decide to participate in a boring experiment, they subsequently tend to exaggerate its attractiveness or value, presumably to avoid their individualistic self (which assumes the responsibility for the choice) to feel inconsistent or "irrational" when it chooses a rather unattractive activity.

Third, the independent orientation is also associated with disengaging emotions (e.g., pride or anger) rather than engaging emotions such as shame or feelings of indebtedness: Pride or anger focus on individual concerns (e.g., personal success or frustration, respectively) whereas shame (and a perhaps similar form of socially referenced guilt) has some reference to one's social role (Kitayama et al., 2003b). Fourth, self-esteem is a predictor and mediator of well-being and happiness in independent cultures only: Within independent cultures happiness is primarily derived from the degree to which a sense of worth is associated with the individual (self-esteem) rather than being based on how well the relevant group is doing (Uchida et al., 2003).

Finally, independent orientations are associated with better attention to and memory of own social behavior compared to other persons' behaviors and states (Kitayama et al., 2003) and a more analytic as opposed to a holistic and context-sensitive mode of information-processing (Nisbett et al., 2001; Kitayama, 2002). Holistic processing can be described in terms of simultaneous (parallel) processing of many pieces of information (e.g., the emotional signals from all family members surrounding a child during a common meal). This mode of processing is more conducive to an interdependent orientation whereas analytic processing with its limited-capacity characteristic seems to be better suited for focusing on one's own interests at the expense of social concerns. For example, analytical processing with its emphasis on analyzing the parts of a whole picture is conducive to see one's own individual (ego) needs *in contrast* to the needs of others rather than processing the needs of all members of a group simultaneously ("holistic processing") to come up with a solution that simultaneously satisfies several people. In the studies cited in the preceding paragraphs, participants with an *interdependent* cultural orientation typically did not show the mentioned effects observed in independent cultures or showed a similar effect only when experimental conditions provided for social embeddedness of the behavior in question (e.g., dissonance effects were observed only when choice was made by a family member).

THEORETICAL ANALYSIS: UNDERLYING MECHANISMS

What are the mechanisms underlying culture-specific associations or interactions among cognitive, emotional, and developmental characteristics? For example: Why are independent individuals more likely to perceive their own needs and values in opposition to the needs of others? Why are their selves more conceptual and analytic (focusing on the parts rather than the whole) whereas interdependence seems to be associated with holistic processing? Could there be any simple mechanism explaining these and various other characteristics of independent (as compared to interdependent) individuals such as mentalistic language, distal parenting style, disengaging emotions, and an analytic rather than holistic mode of information-processing? In this section, we will elaborate the process-oriented approach described in the previous section by focusing on a functional-design analysis of the mechanisms underlying cross-cultural differences in affect regulation.

The theory of personality systems interactions (PSI) has been developed to understand patterns of cognitive, emotional, and behavioral characteristics that can be observed among people with or without a shared cultural environment (Kuhl, 2000a, b, 2001). It integrates theoretical and empirical work from the areas of personality, development, cognition, and neurobiology into a coherent architecture of interacting personality systems. The classical distinction between analytic and holistic processing ("thinking versus feeling") is elaborated by specifying the functional characteristics of information-processing systems involved including units that are necessary for the control of action (e.g., a memory system specialized on the maintenance of uncompleted intentions). In addition, these two modes of processing are extended by subdividing either mode into a high-level and a low-level system (Figure 2.1). According to PSI theory, the analytical mode can be subdivided into a high-level system supporting analytical thinking (including a subsystem for maintaining

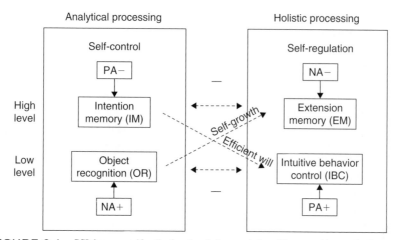

FIGURE 2.1   PSI theory specifies the functional characteristics of four cognitive-motivational systems and their interactions modulated by high (+) versus low (−) positive affect (PA) and negative affect (NA) including two self-regulatory modes: analytical self-control (or "ego-control") and holistic self-regulation. Note that antagonistic (inhibitory) relationships between systems (depicted by dashed arrows) can be overcome by an affective change because each system is modulated by a different type of affect.

difficult intentions in memory until they can be carried out: Figure 2.1) and a low-level *object recognition system* that decontextualizes perceptual objects (or conceptual categories) to facilitate later recognition irrespective of the context in which they are encountered on a later occasion (e.g., enabling organisms to recognize a dangerous object even when it reappears in a new context). Since object recognition separates objects from their contexts, it fits better with the analytical mode (focusing on isolated parts) than with holistic processing. Likewise, systems supporting holistic processing are subdivided into a high-level system (*extension memory*) and a low-level system (*intuitive behavior control*). The holistic low-level system (i.e., *intuitive behavior control*) supports intuitive (context-sensitive) online control of ongoing behavior wherever well-learned, ready-to-go routines for action are available. Extension memory (EM) provides extended networks of meaning, values, and options for action in order to integrate separate (decontextualized) objects into new overarching contexts of related experiences. For example, EM may integrate contradicting propositions ("too humble is half proud": Peng & Nisbett, 1999) or it may integrate many single characteristics of a friend into a coherent picture, including a variety of situations one has interacted with her, what one knows about her childhood, her abilities, future plans, etc.).

ACTION CONTROL: ENACTING DIFFICULT INTENTIONS

Whenever spontaneous enactment of an action is difficult, an intention has to be formed and maintained in intention memory (IM) until it can be enacted (Figure 2.1). Maintaining an intention in memory is important when it cannot be carried out immediately (e.g., because one has to wait for the right moment or find the best way to proceed). As long as enactment of an intention has to be postponed (e.g., when one is trying to think of a good answer to a teacher's question), the connectivity between IM and intuitive behavior control (IBC) has to be inhibited for that intention in order to prevent premature action (e.g., giving a spontaneous, but wrong answer). This "volitional" inhibition (i.e., the inhibition of the enactment of an intention) is indicated in Figure 2.1 by the dashed diagonal indicating the inhibition of "efficient will." Volitional inhibition which prevents premature (impulsive) action is mediated by the reduction of positive affect associated with hesitation, behavioral inhibition, or (in severe cases) by dejected mood (indicated in figure by "PA−," which activates IM, but not its connection with IBC). This inhibitory link between IM and IBC is depicted by the dashed diagonal arrow between IM and IBC in Figure 2.1.

As soon as the right moment for enactment has arrived, the IM–IBC connectivity has to be restored, i.e., an interaction (i.e., communication) between IM and the IBC system has to be established (Figure 2.1: diagonal connection from IM to IBC). According to recent findings, the interaction between IBC and IM (which is more relevant for achievement motivation than for social interaction: Kazén & Kuhl, 2005) is facilitated by a change from low positive affect, PA− (see Figure 2.1), presumably activating IM, to high positive affect, PA+ (Figure 2.1), which instigates the transition from IM to intuitive enactment, a process that has been called *action control* (Kuhl, 1984), *self-control* (Kuhl & Fuhrmann, 1998), or *volitional facilitation* (1st affect–cognition interaction assumption of PSI theory: Kuhl & Kazén, 1999; Kazén & Kuhl, 2005). According to PSI theory, volitional facilitation (action control) can be described in terms of an efficient interaction between IM and IBC. To the extent that the independent orientation can be characterized by a controlling style which imposes one's own interpretations, needs, and intentions on others (Keller et al., 2006), self-control can be regarded as the dominant form of volition in independent cultures which is reflected, e.g., in a long tradition in philosophy (as well as in psychology) of identifying "the will" with conscious and deliberate action control based on one's own (ego-related) needs and goals.

SELF-REGULATION AND SELF-GROWTH: DEVELOPMENT AND MAINTENANCE OF AN INTEGRATED SELF

However, action control (or "self-control") is not the only mode of volition, according to PSI theory (although volition has often been reduced to this mode by authors from cultures with a predominant independent orientation). Another mode of volition is self-regulation. Not unlike a democratic voting procedure, self-regulation takes in many personal and others' needs, values, and experiences before making a decision regarding a course of action (Kuhl & Fuhrmann, 1998; Koole & Kuhl, 2003; Kuhl & Koole, 2004). Within the framework of PSI theory, this integrative function of willful action heavily depends on the parallel-holistic processing capacity of EM which is defined as a memory system that integrates an extended network of (even remote) semantic associations (e.g., Beeman et al., 1994) and inferences from autobiographical episodes and object recognition. The close connection between high negative affect (NA+) and object recognition (see Figure 2.1) can be illustrated by the fact that under stress people focus on relevant details rather than on the whole which facilitates coping with the immediate source of danger, but which also impairs a deeper, context-sensitive form of coping (e.g., by perceiving a failure in the context of the successes one has experienced rather than overgeneralizing it).

According to PSI theory, excessive degrees of negative affect or stress (unless they can be downregulated) impair access to EM and the integrated self (2nd affect–cognition interaction assumption of PSI theory). Examples for this relationship can be found in everyday experience: It is difficult to "see the whole" when one feels afraid or is in pain. In this case, attention focuses on isolated details ("objects") rather than on a coherent picture of the whole. Experimental evidence for impaired access to EM as a function of excessive negative affect has been reported even for the functions of EM that are not directly self-referential (e.g., intuitive coherence judgments: Baumann & Kuhl, 2002; Bolte et al., 2003) as well as its self-referential functions (Kuhl & Kazén, 1994; Baumann & Kuhl, 2003; Kazén et al., 2003).

The interaction between EM and object recognition systems is relevant for the second central task of personality functioning (in addition to action control): *Self-development* as reflected by a growing self system that integrates more and more isolated experiences ("objects") from autobiographical episodes into a coherent network of context-specific options for action. According to PSI theory, the diachronic form of self-growth requires continuous integration of *isolated* (decontextualized) experiences (encoded by the object recognition system) into the integrated self (Figure 2.1). Unexpected or threatening experiences are encoded as isolated mental "objects" unless they can be assimilated into the integrated self. As long as an aversive experience (e.g., loss of a partner) cannot be integrated, it can become the target of uncontrollable rumination (Kuhl & Beckmann, 1994a, b). The integrated self system is the self-referential part of EM, i.e., it provides an extended, holistic perception of oneself rather than focusing on just one detail that happens to be of interest (e.g., a person's nose, his bank account, or a particular habit). Research suggests that the integrated self yields a holistic picture of the whole person, and is closely connected with his or her emotions and needs, and integrates even opposing emotions within the same domain (Showers & Kling, 1996; Schore, 2003).

In more abstract terms, the features describing the functional profile of the integrative self include (1) high-level parallel (holistic) processing according to connectionistic principles (e.g., multiple constraint satisfaction: Rumelhart & McClelland, 1986) and (2) close interaction with somatosensory perception (body contact) and autonomic nervous activities (emotion). (3) Since the holistic (or "integrated") self integrates innumerable personal experiences, its contents cannot become conscious at once (see Kuhl, 2000a, b, 2001, for empirical evidence for these and additional functional characteristics of personality systems). It should be noted that the diachronic integration of isolated experience ("objects") into the self cannot be generalized to interdependent cultures. To the extent that these cultures place more emphasis on synchronic interaction, self-growth primarily draws upon *assimilation* of new experience. In contrast to *integration*, assimilation can be accomplished within the holistic mode, e.g., when an interdependent child gradually extends her schema of caretakers when she is exposed to the people around her. In contrast, within an independent culture, a child that has been exposed to intensive dyadic interactions with her mother and father may not easily assimilate another person into her schema of self-relevant interaction partners. Instead, this learning process may require integration in terms of a discontinuous revision of the existing self-schema (i.e., accommodation). A neuro-cognitive model of these two different modes of learning has been elaborated elsewhere (McClelland et al., 1995). This model is compatible with our aligning cross-modal integration with the discontinuous learning process of accommodation. This process has the advantage that it can even integrate new experience when it is too discrepant from the existing self-schema in order to be incorporated by gradual (continuous) changes of assimilative learning (Piaget, 1952).

EXPLAINING CROSS-CULTURAL DIFFERENCES

How can PSI theory account for the pattern of findings discriminating independent and interdependent orientations described in an earlier section? The observation that participants from independent cultures are characterized by *separation* both with regard to social interaction and in their perceiving their own needs and preferences as separate from those of others can be explained as a direct consequence of the "either-or" characteristic of analytical thinking (Kuhl, 2001). The discounting principle is an example for this mode of thinking: Once one potential cause has been discovered for an observed effect (e.g., heavy drinking as a cause of a headache), additional potential causes are discounted (Kelley, 1972). Presumably, this and other forms of dichotomous ("either-or") thinking are fostered by a distal style of early socialization that emphasizes verbal and analytical thinking ("mentalistic language") and deemphasizes warmth and positive affect (e.g., trust) that would promote a sense of relatedness. This hypothesis can be derived from the first modulation assumption of PSI theory which states that lack of positive affect, PA−, activates dichotomous analytical thinking and IM (see Figure 2.1: arrow from PA− to IM). In sum, the competitive orientation associated with the independent orientation (e.g., "either my or their needs can be satisfied; either proposition A or the opposite proposition B is true") is an example of dichotomous thinking. This relationship between dichotomous, analytical thinking and an independent orientation leads us to expect that the analytical mode of processing is fostered by the socialization style that is typical of independent cultures, e.g., relying on social distance rather than warmth, delayed ("diachronic") affect regulation, analytical reasoning, and explicit mentalistic language rather than relatedness, immediate ("synchronic") affect regulation, and more implicit and body-oriented forms of communication).[1]

THE ROLE OF AFFECT REGULATION

According to PSI theory, a shift from an analytic (e.g., object recognition) to a holistic system (e.g., the integrated self) and vice versa is facilitated through affective change (Figure 2.1). Take, e.g., the case that negative affect (NA+) activates object recognition thereby inhibiting high-level holistic processing (depicted in Figure 2.1 by the dashed line from object recognition to the integrated self). In this case, the integration of isolated objects of experience into a coherent self is impaired until downregulation of negative affect can be accomplished (i.e., a shift from NA+ to NA− in Figure 2.1). This mechanism explains why *emotional autonomy*, i.e. the ability to regulate one's own emotions even without external support, is promoted in cultures that aim at the integrated self as a developmental ideal: Whenever somebody can modify his own emotional state according to situational demands, he or she can switch among analytical and holistic modes (Figure 2.1: OR to EM) thereby facilitating the interaction among those modes (including the development of an integrated self which depends on that interaction). It should be noted that neither analytical nor holistic processing alone is sufficient for the development of what we call an integrated self because this form of self-growth depends on continuous interactions among those two modes of processing (Figure 2.1). Note that this type of cross-modal interaction is not reflected in the dichotomy of independent versus interdependent orientations which are based on either analytical (independent) or holistic (interdependent) processing styles. Although the interdependent self is able to reconcile opposing arguments or emotions (Peng & Nisbett, 1999), we reserve the term *integration* for the diachronic learning process by which the holistic self incorporates isolated experiences that have been processed for some time by analytical object recognition (strictly speaking, something has to be processed in isolation first before it can be integrated). In contrast, the interdependent form of self-growth may more appropriately be described in terms of assimilation, fusion, or blending of opposites rather than accommodative integration.

---

[1]Later in this chapter, we will qualify these assumptions concerning different socialization styles across cultures: Compared to interdependent styles, independent socialization does not necessarily promote less warmth and closeness. Instead, in independent socialization interpersonal warmth is typically based on close personal interaction with an individual caretaker rather than with a social group. However, even when even amounts of warmth are involved in caretaking, the independent style presumably tolerates or even promotes longer periods of emotional distance (and frustration resulting from it) than interdependent socialization.

THE FUNCTIONAL BASIS OF AUTONOMY

Our account of the cross-modal integration process (i.e., from analytical isolation to holistic incorporation) is in accordance with an argument derived from self-determination theory which states that neither independent nor interdependent cultural orientations per se are conducive to loss of autonomy and its risks for well-being and health as long as autonomous agency in the sense of self-determination is maintained (Chirkov et al., 2003). Our argument converges with self-determination theory in postulating that the development of an autonomous and integrated self is neither identical with a holistic and interdependent self nor with an analytical and independent ego per se. Instead, the autonomous self is defined by intrapersonal harmony ("self-congruence"). This state can be achieved in two ways. This first (interdependent) route to personal harmony is based on short-term (or even synchronic) alignment of all psychological systems (including analytical and holistic systems). The second route to self-congruence requires an extended period of "independence" of analytical and holistic processing (delayed integration): It integrates contrasting arguments or painful experiences *later in time* ("diachronically"), i.e., only *after* they have been "independently" processed.

The latter form of self-congruence and autonomy is aiming at achieving an increasing capacity to shift among emotional states and the epistemic systems associated with them. As a result, the ability should increase to tolerate prolonged periods of opposing emotional states and the cognitive modes of processing associated with them because the ability to shift among emotional states and cognitive styles reduces the risk to get stuck in an emotional state or processing mode: For example, when I know that I can motivate myself whenever I want to, it is easier for me to tolerate prolonged periods of frustration (e.g., when facing a difficult task). The central cultural aim of cross-modal integration (rather than holistic blending) of contrasting arguments or experiences can be seen in the optimization of dyadic interaction: In dyadic relationships, cross-modal integration promotes the balance between autonomy support (i.e., respecting each other as unique individuals) and community (i.e., developing an integrated perspective on common values and goals). We will return to this important consequence of affect-regulatory competence in a later section that focuses on the cultural implications of emotional and cognitive *endurance* as we call this particular ability to maintain an emotional state or cognitive mode for prolonged periods of time (even if that state is rather unpleasant).

Experimental evidence confirms the claim that affect-regulatory competence facilitates adaptation of individuals to their cultural environment, at least within independent cultures. For example, participants from cultures emphasizing an independent orientation are better adjusted to many social demands when they are action-oriented in the sense that they maintain their ability to take the initiative and act by downregulating negative affect after failure or upregulating positive affect when confronted with difficult demands (Beckmann & Kuhl, 1984; Kuhl & Beckmann, 1994a, b; Koole & Jostmann, 2004; Koole & van den Berg, 2005).

Specifically, when compared to participants who cannot easily regulate their emotions (so-called state-oriented individuals), action-oriented participants maintain or even increase their level of performance (e.g., short-term memory span) when exposed to threats or demanding tasks (Kuhl & Helle, 1986; Jostmann & Koole, in press), implicitly perceive themselves as more autonomous and self-assured (Koole, 2004), obtain higher scores on well-being scales while reporting less psychological symptoms (Hautzinger, 1994; Baumann et al., 2005; 2007), and are less affected by subliminal affective primes (Jostmann et al., 2005). In addition, action-oriented participants have better self-access as indicated by better discrimination between their own and others' choices (Kuhl & Kazén, 1994; Baumann & Kuhl, 2003), keep less context-irrelevant and more relevant intentions active in memory (Goschke & Kuhl, 1993; Jostmann & Koole, in press), and enact more of their intentions (Kuhl & Helle, 1986; Fuhrmann & Kuhl, 1998).

According to PSI theory, affect regulation (i.e., action orientation) is a prerequisite for cross-modal interactions among analytical and holistic systems that contribute to the transition from independence to integration. Specifically, counterregulation of emotional states facilitates both volitional efficiency (i.e., enacting one's intentions) and maintain one's health and develop one's self through integration of contrasting experiences (depicted by the two diagonal arrows in Figure 2.1): Either aspect of personality functioning is impeded by insufficient positive or excessive negative affect, respectively (whose counterregulation is captured by two subscales of action orientation: Kuhl & Beckmann, 1994a, b). However, it remains to be seen whether these relationships between self-regulation of affect, on the one hand, and performance, self-access, and health, on the other hand, can be generalized to interdependent cultures. It could well be that the interdependent orientation is better compatible with state rather than with action orientation because the former relies on others to help regulate individual emotions (see Koole et al., 2005, for this and other potential benefits of state orientation). Empirical findings are consistent with this hypothesis (Olvermann et al., 2004).

In sum, according to PSI theory, the role of affect regulation is not confined to its functions for maintaining a balanced mood state, well-being and health: Over and above those known functions, self-regulation of affect is the prerequisite for shifting among analytic and holistic cognitive systems and the effects of context-sensitive interaction among systems for personal growth and the maintenance of well-being and health. However, the hypothesis that self-regulation of affect is more crucial for adjustment in independent than in interdependent cultures needs further exploration in future research.

ACQUISITION OF AFFECT REGULATION: SYSTEMS CONDITIONING

Because of the enormous functional significance of affect regulation, the way this self-regulatory capacity is acquired during development is especially relevant. PSI theory offers a functional model of this learning process: The systems condition-ing model (SCM) is a generalization of the well-known model of classical con-ditioning from the reinforcement of links between stimuli to the reinforcement of new connections among psychological systems. Acquisition of affect regulation is regarded as a conditioning process because self-regulation of affect is tantamount to the regulation of affect through a system (i.e., the self) that is not identical with the primary affect-generating system (e.g., relevant parts of the limbic system of the brain). In other words, for the acquisition of *self*-regulation of *affect*, new con-nections have to be established between the two systems involved (i.e., the self and the affect-generating system). According to the classical conditioning model, new connections in the brain are strengthened whenever the two stimuli to be connected (i.e., CS and UCS, as e.g., Pavlov's bell and the meat he showed to his dogs) occur in close temporal succession followed by an appropriate rein-forcement (the UCR as, for instance, saliva secretion). The SCM extends this basic model to the formation of new connections among macro-systems. To the extent that the self is to learn to regulate emotions, the connection between the self and affect-generating systems has to be strengthened. Applying clas-sical conditioning to the level of connectivity among systems, the SCM posits that self-regulation of affect is learned whenever external regulation of affect (through activation or de-activation of primary affect-generating systems) is successfully performed in close temporal proximity to the activation of the self system, e.g., briefly after a child has engaged in self-expressive activity (which presumably requires activation of the self). Interestingly, self-expression of emo-tional distress is associated in infants with activation of the prefrontal part of the right hemisphere (Fox & Davidson, 1987), the same region that is also activated when adults are asked to perform self-referential tasks such as recognizing their own face (Keenan et al., 2001) or deciding whether or not adjectives shown in succession match their personality (Craik et al., 1999). Whenever that part of the brain is active (e.g., when a child expresses distress or when a patient feels "understood") and affect regulation is brought about by an external agent (e.g., mother, teacher, therapist), the connectivity between the self and primary affect-regulatory systems is strengthened, according to the SCM. As a result, the child or patient, respectively, literally learns to *self*-regulate his or her emotions. In sum, the SCM specifies the learning mechanism underlying the old hypothesis (Vygotsky, 1978) that self-regulation develops through internalization of exter-nal regulation (mothers soothing the infant)

MECHANISMS UNDERLYING CROSS-CULTURAL DIFFERENCES IN AFFECT REGULATION

The SCM specifies the learning mechanism underlying what has been called the responsive and sensitive maternal style that is associated with secure mother–child attachment (Ainsworth et al., 1978). It should be noted, however, that this type of affect regulation is not universal: It is typical of the "independent" cultural orientation which emphasizes the development of an independent self (or an integrated self: Kağitçibaşi, 2007). Why should parents from independent cultures be especially keen to promote the development of self-regulation of affect in their children? The capacity to self-regulate changes among contrasting emotional states facilitates interactions between epistemic systems associated with such affective changes, according to affect–cognition interactions postulated in PSI theory (Figure 2.1). Since the interaction between analytic and holistic cognitive systems is considered a necessary condition for self-growth and action control (i.e., efficient will), the development of these two aspects of personality functioning is facilitated through the ability to self-regulate affect (i.e., to switch among contrasting emotional states).

EXTENDING THE DICHOTOMY OF INDEPENDENT AND INTERDEPENDENT ORIENTATIONS

The foregoing application of PSI theory illustrates how this functional account provides a reasonable explanation for the pattern of differences between independent and interdependent orientations. PSI theory can also be applied to extend this dichotomy. In fact, a close examination of the literature on cross-cultural comparisons of cognitive-emotional orientations confirms our earlier conclusion that the independent–interdependent dichotomy does not suffice to account for cultural differences: For example, it does not provide a satisfactory explanation of the development of an integrated self. At first glance, one might expect the interdependent orientation to promote an integrative self. However, as mentioned earlier, interdependent personality may be more similar to interpersonal fusion than to interpersonal integration: In contrast to the process of integrative self-development described in the preceding paragraph, self-development in interdependent cultures does not seem to be based on integration of contradicting emotions or cognitions *after they have been encoded separately in a decontextualizing system (i.e., in the object recognition system).*

At first glance, this statement seems to contradict empirical evidence suggesting that interdependent cultures are characterized by a preference for contradictory arguments or experiences and their prompt integration (Peng & Nisbett, 1999). For example, Chinese participants respond to social conflicts (e.g., when a mother wants her daughter to study for school rather than go out) with attempts to reconcile opposing views. Moreover, Chinese participants prefer "dialectical" proverbs that appear paradoxical from a logical point of view ("Too humble is half proud" which contradicts the meaning of "humble"). In contrast, Americans more frequently take one of two opposing positions in social conflicts and prefer nondialectical proverbs such as "One against all is certain to fall" (Peng & Nisbett, 1999). It should be noted, however, that resolution of conflict and reconciliation of contradictory positions can be accomplished without cross-modal interactions between analytical and holistic modes of processing: In the example cited, Chinese participants' integrative or "dialectic" responses were characterized by *simultaneity* of self-exposure to contradictory arguments or emotions, by promptness of reconciling opposing views, and by the intuitive nature of this process. These three features suggest that the eastern form of "dialectics" does not require diachronic (i.e., temporally extended) interactions between analytical processing of opposing views and later integration on the basis of high-level holistic processing. Instead, it seems more plausible to assume that, in interdependent cultures, integrative solutions are typically found by rapid or even synchronic cooperation between analytical and holistic processing systems or by capitalizing on the integrative capacity of holistic processing alone (cf. the feature of *multiple constraint satisfaction* of connectionist networks: Rumelhart & McClelland, 1986). The term *synlecticism* might be more appropriate than *dialecticism* for describing this form of synchronized (parallel) perception of opposing arguments or perspectives.

SYNCHRONIC SOCIALIZATION AND SOCIAL-COGNITIVE FUSION

This synchronic view on interdependent integration is based on our developmental argument that interdependent parenting is characterized by attempts to *prevent* infants to experience aversive states in the first place. This is to say that, in interdependent in contrast to independent parenting, conflicting emotions or cognitions should not occur frequently as *isolated instances processed at temporally distant occasions* (at least during early stages of development). The lower frequency (or duration) of aversive states results from the immediacy or even anticipation of the infant's needs, interests, or other concerns that need to be "integrated" (Greenfield, 2004; Keller et al., 2005b). In-depth analysis of interdependent socialization behavior reveals early care patterns that mainly focus on the suppression or prevention of signs of negative emotionality (Keller, 2007). Immediacy or anticipation of aversive states may not only prevent aversive states from perseverating, but it may also promote a feeling of "us," some form of union and social fusion rather than a clear-cut perception of a "you" that is separate from "me." Empirical findings suggest that feelings of empathy and relatedness (or "affiliation") are more closely associated with the holistic capacity of the right than with the analytical processing mode of the left hemisphere of the brain (Adolphs et al., 2000; Schore, 2003; Kuhl & Kazén, 2008). It should be noted that the interdependent representation of mother–infant (or others–infant) unity does not exclude the occurrence and representation of negative states or unsatisfied needs. The difference is one of degree: According to our reasoning, interdependent mothers do not systematically prolong negative states to the same extent as independent mothers do (in order to promote emotional and epistemic endurance as a basis for repeated shifts between emotional states and epistemic systems to facilitate self-growth).

During infancy, interdependent mothers try to minimize the expression of negative effect and do not try to prolong the expression of positive affect. This finding can be interpreted as a sign of avoiding rather than promoting emotional and epistemic endurance. In contrast, independent mothers clearly prolong and maintain the expression of positive affect in infants when they engage the infant in smiling and vocalizing turn taking (Keller et al., 2008). They also leave room for the child to experience negative affect. They mainly react to clear expressions of crying instead of responding to more subtle signs already. They want to find out why the infant cries before they respond and develop and test hypotheses like hungry, tired, bored, annoyed. With this attitude they also react to the child's agency in expressing needs and wishes and refer to intentional control. This interactional style provides the infant, with or without her mother's explicit intention, with the experience of emotional and epistemic endurance. Sometimes folk theories support this strategy with claims like "crying strengthens the lungs." According to PSI theory, the endurance-promoting style can facilitate the development of an integrated self unless it overtaxes the affect-regulatory competence of the child. With its early emphasis on prevention of aversive states and interpersonal fusion, interdependent socialization may not primarily aim at promoting the high-level (cross-modal) form of self-growth. However, at a later stage of infancy, the focus on interdependent socialization shifts from parental anticipation of the infant's needs to the infant's anticipation of needs and expectations of others.

DIACHRONIC SOCIALIZATION AND SOCIAL-COGNITIVE INTEGRATION

How can the diachronic interaction among analytic and holistic modes of processing be described in more specific functional terms? Integration, in contrast to fusion or assimilation, requires a prolonged separation between *heteronomous* systems (i.e., analytic versus holistic). Independent socialization can be regarded as a necessary (but not sufficient) condition for this diachronic form of cross-modal interaction. An example for a prolonged separation of those systems would be a parent from an independent culture who tolerates an extended phase of focusing on negative affect and its consequences (letting the child cry for a while): During this phase, the child's object recognition system might be dealing with a family member's unfriendly behavior without any interaction with the integrated self (EM) that would bring that experience in contact with prior positive experiences with that unfriendly person. In contrast, the immediate or anticipatory counterregulation of negative states that is associated with interdependent socialization strategies can accomplish "integration" (i.e., assimilation) *within* the holistic mode of processing (or in virtually synchronic interaction among analytic and holistic systems) because no experience (e.g., the unfriendly family member) has to be singled out for a prolonged period of time and processed in isolation before it can be integrated or assimilated, respectively.

It may be concluded that, from a functional-design point of view, the integrated self cannot be fully accommodated by the concepts of interdependence because of the mismatch between the early parental style associated with interdependence (i.e., prevention of negative affect and interpersonal fusion) and the type of integration required for the diachronic form of self-development. On the other hand, the independent orientation is not capable either to accommodate the development of integrative self: Recall that the independent self operates in the either-or mode of analytical processing. Therefore, we must conclude that it does not have the parallel-holistic capacity required for the integrative task of coherent self-construction. For example, perceiving and accepting that oneself has both loving and aggressive feelings toward the same person is not easily compatible with either-or thinking. Our functional analysis of the mechanisms underlying self-development arrives, then, at the conclusion that the development of an integrative self requires another cultural orientation that is not covered by the independent or interdependent orientations. We propose that this third cultural orientation promoting the development of an integrative self represents the *original* developmental ideal of so-called independent cultures. This is to say that the description of the "independent" orientation in the cross-cultural literature focuses on a reductive (or even degenerated) form of the original developmental ideal of cultures that are described as relying on an independent orientation (see Chirkov et al., 2003, for a similar view). The origins of this reduction from integration to independence can be traced back to Greek philosophy (Artistole's formal logic) and the European tradition of rationalism, idealism, and enlightenment (*Aufklärung*). The cultural origins of diachronic dialecticism can be traced back to the Jewish-Christian tradition of promoting self-development on the basis of self-confrontation with rather than avoidance and repression of pain and anxiety.

It is the integrative potential (presumably associated with holistic agency) that self-determination theorists associate with the term *autonomy*. Using the term autonomy to denote the degree to which people act in accordance with their authentic interests or integrated values and desires without ignoring the needs and values of others (Deci & Ryan, 2000), our functional account explains why autonomy in this sense is associated with greater well-being across cultures (Chirkov et al., 2003): Holistic integration of own and others' needs on the level of agency increases the likelihood that many needs, own and others', even potentially conflicting ones, are taken into account and that behaviors are found that can do justice to many needs rather than handling different needs (e.g., for achievement versus affiliation) in an exclusive or antagonistic manner. Moreover, our functional account, based on PSI theory, explains why beneficial somatic effects are associated with holistic processing: Because the epistemic system supporting this holistic mode of processing (associated with the right hemisphere of the brain) is closely connected with the autonomous nervous system (e.g., Wittling, 1990), regulation of emotional and somatic processes can be better accomplished by holistic compared to analytic processing. It should be noted, however, that the dominance of the analytical mode, as in the independent orientation, can be fully adaptive as well (or "autonomous" in the self-determination sense) if that mode is in balanced interaction with holistic processing to the effect that own and others' needs and expectations are satisfied. According to our model, analytical can be in harmony with holistic processing on the level of the integrated self which combines low-level analytical processing (perceiving discrete objects) with the holistic competence of the integrated self (Table 2.1). On the phenomenological level, this balanced interaction can be recognized by the endorsement of independent decisions and actions (Deci & Ryan, 2000) by the "whole person." A balanced interaction among analytical and holistic systems can be regarded as the functional basis of the phenomenological concept of the "whole person."

RISKS OF AUTONOMY THROUGH DIACHRONIC INTEGRATION

According to PSI theory, integration or autonomy (Chirkov et al., 2003) turns into its reductive form ("independence") when independent socialization strains (or even overstrains) a child's emotional endurance. For example, when a mother often leaves her baby boy in a negative mood for prolonged periods or engages in any form of autonomy neglect, PSI theory predicts inhibited self-access and strong activation of object recognition resulting in his perceiving things independently of their context (see Figure 2.1: NA+ activates object recognition). When he develops a categorical sense of self (around 2 years of age), the tendency of the object recognition system to separate things from their context may also extend to his self-concept. We use Freud's concept of *ego* to denote this analytical self-concept that separates the self from its social context. In sum, according to PSI theory, whether diachronic socialization promotes the development of an integrated or independent self (i.e., holistic self-regulation or analytical ego-control) depends on whether or not this form of socialization overtaxes the child's affect-regulatory capacity.

Based on a model combining agency and relatedness, Kağitçibaşi (1996) introduced a concept which is similar to our notion of the integrated self. She describes her concept of the "autonomous-related" self as a combination of autonomy and relatedness: According to her proposal, individuals having an autonomous-related orientation are characterized by combining both spontaneously rather than externally controlled behavior (autonomous agency) *and* an attentional focus on others (relatedness). The theoretical convergence between Kağitçibaşi's behavioral description of the autonomous-related self and our functional-design account of the integrated self is remarkable: Despite starting from quite different conceptual positions the two approaches lead to similar conceptualizations of a third type of cultural orientation. The two approaches are complementary in that the functional-design approach elaborates the mechanisms underlying the observable cultural differences described by the behavioral approach. Specifying the underlying mechanisms is useful, not only for a better understanding of cultural differences, but also for discovering and overcoming the limitations of seemingly general models of the architecture and dynamics of personality.

A FUNCTIONAL TAXONOMY OF FOUR
CULTURAL ORIENTATIONS

The (neuro-)psychological mechanisms underlying the different cultural orientations can be summarized in terms of an elaborated classification of cultural orientations. The functional basis of our taxonomy is illustrated in Table 2.1: According to this taxonomy which is based on PSI theory, two psychological dimensions form the basis of the three cultural orientations discussed until now and a fourth orientation is added (to be explained later). The two dimensions refer to the mode of processing underlying agency (analytic versus holistic) and the processing mode presumably associated with synchronic versus diachronic parenting. The first dimension relates to mode of agency: Self-initiated, spontaneous action (agency) can be either based on the ego's narrow focus on one intention or goal (supported by analytical processing) or on the extended focus of the integrated self taking many needs and goals (own and others) into account.

The second dimension relates to the synchronic versus diachronic type of development (Table 2.1): Behaviors associated with synchronic interaction (e.g., anticipation of needs and synchronization of body movement) presumably rely even more on intuitive behavior than the diachronic style. On the other hand, the discrete processing quality of object recognition may be more important for diachronic than for synchronic interaction because diachronic interaction separates subjective states into discrete (decontextualized) entities ("objects") rather than forming a continuous flow of mutual interaction. We will explain in this chapter, how the four cultural orientations can be described more precisely. However, it should be noted that the four-fold taxonomy, just like the classical dichotomous classification, cannot be identified with specific countries or continents. Nonetheless, we expect that the cultural differences between countries can be better described by the pattern of relative strengths of each of the four orientations than by a dichotomous scheme.

TABLE 2.1   A Functional Taxonomy of Four Cultural Orientations Toward Self-development

	Mode of early development	
	Synchronic	Diachronic
Mode of agency (high-level processing)	*Intuitive behavior control* (IBC) (low-level holistic processing)	*Object recognition* (OR) (low-level analytical processing)
Analytic (ego) *Intention memory*	Interdependent ego (Selflessness)	Independent ego (Self-control)
Holistic (integrated self) *Extension memory*	Interrelated self (Self-embeddedness)	Integrated self (Self-maintenance)

TWO MODES OF AGENCY

How can the first dimension related to mode of agency be described in more detail? The difference between analytical and holistic modes can be elaborated by looking at some properties that are unique to the analytical mode. Analytic processing operates in a step-by-step fashion through time by combining elements that have been extracted from their context ahead of time. Cognitive activities drawing from this type of processing range from object recognition (e.g., recognizing a table across contextual changes in distance, hue, color, shape etc.), formation of clear-cut rather than fuzzy concepts (e.g., "a bachelor is an unmarried person"), and dichotomous ("either-or") categorical thinking (e.g., dividing the world into the "good" and the "evil") to comparative judgment (e.g., "A is greater than B") and logical reasoning ("If fever is always caused by an infection and Helen has a fever, then Helen has an infection").[2]

As explained earlier in this chapter, the independent orientation can be related to analytical processing: The analytical self (i.e., the *ego*) focuses on one self-attribute at a time rather than taking the full picture into account (as the integrated self). Moreover, in combination with diachronic parenting, the analytical ego is separated from others in an either-or fashion, that is self and others are perceived as separate objects: Either my own or others' needs can be satisfied, I focus either on my own interests or take normative standards into account (which are seen in opposition to my own needs, when the analytical ego is combined with object recognition). According to our model, this conflict-oriented mode of dealing with own and others' needs, derives from the assumption that the *independent* orientation is a combination of analytical thinking and the diachronic style of parenting: Children not only learn to perceive themselves and others as separate entities (analytical agency), but also acquire the ability to tolerate extended phases of ego-focus or other-focus, respectively (diachronic interaction). One empirical hypothesis that can be derived from this assumption predicts that two subforms of independent orientations should be observed within independent cultures: In addition to an ego-centered type, there should be an other-focused ("altruistic") type whereas individuals integrating these two orientations should be less frequent in this culture. In contrast to its interdependent form, independent altruism is characterized by exclusiveness of the altruistic perspective rather than by merging own and others' concerns. Another hypothesis that can be derived from the model predicts that independent cultures as specified in our model (e.g., some European societies), should foster the development of abstract ideals more than pragmatic values because the independent orientation places more emphasis on abstract

---

[2]The fact that the premise is wrong (fever is not always caused by an infection) illustrates the limitations of analytical processing: neurobiological evidence suggests that empirical insights preventing conclusions from empirically false assumptions require termination of logical and initiation of experiential processing which requires access to the right rather than the left ("analytical") hemisphere (Deglin & Kinsbourne, 1996).

processing (i.e., analytical thinking and object recognition) than on behavior control, according to our model (Table 2.1).

When a bias toward analytical processing is combined with a synchronic rather than a diachronic style of parenting, a cultural orientation is expected that emphasizes what we call the "*interdependent* ego" (Table 2.1). This orientation is introduced in addition to the three orientations elaborated in earlier sections of this chapter. It is characterized by a combination of the either-or mode of analytical thinking and synchronic *fusion* rather than diachronic separation of self and others (or opposing emotions and cognitions). For example, own and others' needs are perceived as separate and often opposing states. Within the common independent–interdependent dichotomy, the "interdependent ego" may be a subtype of the "independent" orientation because it shares with this orientation the analytical mode of agency (ego-control). However, the combination of analytical agency and the synchronic interactional style may foster a cultural orientation that deserves the label "interdependent" because self and others are not represented as separate entities despite the analytical mode of agency. An example may be a one-sided "positivism" in child-rearing preventing children from experiencing states of frustration and from learning to alternate between tolerating and counterregulating aversive states. Carried to the extreme, this orientation is characterized by a strong ego that cannot perceive the individuals' own and others' needs separately. The failure to separate own and others' needs on an analytical level can result in putting others into the service of the ego or the other way around (putting the ego into the service of others' needs). Narcissistic personality may be an example of a form of ego-focus associated with social fusion rather than independence: In contrast to the independent form of egoism, a narcissistic person does not reliably discriminate between own and others' needs which may result in non-intentional social exploitation (i.e., taking advantage of others without explicit intentionality or even misperceiving one's exploitative behavior as being altruistic). As discussed for the independent orientation, the combination of analytical processing and interdependence (social fusion) may also result in the opposite, overly altruistic, style: When own and others' needs are not perceived as separate and independent entities, the ego may also operate in the service of others (in extreme cases even in a self-destructive way). However, in contrast to the independent case, the risk of self-destructive altruism should be smaller here because own and others' concerns are combined here (recall that the independent orientation allows for either the self or other perspective only).

MODES OF PARENTING

Let us now turn to the two forms of parenting. First, holistic agency can be exercised either with a diachronic or with a synchronic style of parenting (Table 2.1). The synchronic case should be most compatible with the concept of interdependence in cross-cultural research (discussed throughout this article). For example, a girl having an interrelated self does not typically process her own and others' needs, thoughts, and emotions in a contrasting way, perceiving others as independent from her own self. Instead, she perceives her own states embedded in the context of the needs and feelings of significant others. This holistic fusion of self and others should facilitate behavior that is socially accepted. In contrast, the integrative self which presumably results from a combination of holistic processing and diachronic development (Table 2.1) integrates own and others' needs in a different way. The difference can be described in terms of conflict tolerance: The integrated self can tolerate even prolonged states of interpersonal conflict whereas the interrelated self is oriented toward interpersonal harmony. Conflict tolerance can have the advantage that it enables people to come up with advanced integrative solutions finding better ways of integrating own and others' needs. On the other hand, conflict tolerance entails the risk of escalating conflict when it is taken to the extreme so that it over-strains the integrative competence of the people involved.

CONCLUSIONS AND OUTLOOK

We hope that our functional account of cultural orientations will guide future research into the mechanisms underlying cultural differences in order to elaborate psychological theories to accommodate personality development across cultures. We used a recently developed theory of personality (i.e., PSI theory) to integrate various cultural orientations. It can be concluded from this analysis that PSI theory can accommodate all four cultural orientations described in our taxonomy (Table 2.1). The new distinctions proposed are subtle, but revealing, especially with regard to the distinction between integrative and interdependent (in our terminology, "interrelated") orientations. For example, Peng and Nisbett (1999) note the difficulty, both for interdependent and independent perspectives, to resolve Needham's paradox: In light of the remarkable achievements of Chinese science who understood phenomena such as magnetism, acoustic resonance, and the true reason for the tides more than 1500 years before Western scientists did, it is difficult to understand why the Chinese form of (synchronic) dialectic thinking was not able to develop quantum physics. According to many historians of physics, this unique achievement of Western science is attributable to its one-sided reliance on "billiard ball" physics until, after centuries of elaborations, the limitations of this paradigm could be recognized. Assuming that this paradigm was primarily based on the Western analytical form of logical thinking, we propose that the scientific revolution brought about by quantum physics is a good example of the benefits of a diachronic and cross-modal form of dialectics. In contrast to Eastern forms of synchronic "integration" (naïve dialecticism), the Western form of diachronic integration (cross-modal dialecticism) focuses on one position or paradigm, respectively, for an extended period of time. It carries its potential to its ultimate limits of analytical understanding, which presumably provides the cue that is necessary for a profound integration of contradictory observations. From this perspective, it is not surprising that innovative steps toward quantum physics were made possible by Western physicists like Bohr and Einstein, who introduced a considerable amount of intuitive-holistic thinking to the otherwise extremely analytical orientation of Western science. This example for an extreme extension of the time period between analytical and holistic modes of processing highlights what we consider to be the unique advantage of the diachronic form of dialectics when it works at its optimum level: A more and more advanced abstraction ("compression") of analytical knowledge which eventually provides its temporally distant interaction partner (i.e., holistic processing) with a highly sophisticated analytical input enabling holistic processing to arrive at a considerably higher level of integration than could be accomplished by instant (synchronic) integration of contradictory evidence through holistic processing. However, these benefits of diachronic integration can be outweighed by its risks which occur when analytical thinking is dissociated from holistic appreciation of intra- and interpersonal values, needs, and ecological conditions for living (Horkheimer & Adorno, 1976).

Finally, our functional-design analysis of cultural differences may open new perspectives for one of the most intriguing questions for future research: How can problems in cross-cultural communication be better understood and resolved? Uncovering the functional features of analytic versus holistic modes of processing as well as synchronic and diachronic developmental styles may help understand the risks and limitations of cross-cultural dialog. For example, any attempt of representatives from a diachronic culture, especially when combined with a preponderance of analytic processing (i.e., the independent orientation, according to Table 2.1), to confront individuals from a synchronic background with arguments capitalizing on the separation of rational and emotional views (i.e., creating a distance between opposing emotional states and contrasting cognitive stances) can be emotionally unbearable and cognitively difficult to understand from the synchronic point of view. An example is Pope Benedict's speech at the University of Regensburg where he cited some critical remarks by a medieval emperor about Mohammed: Although it may not be uncommon for an individual from a diachronic background to be exposed to critical remarks that are not necessarily the speaker's own opinion, this dialectic separation of own and opposing views may be difficult to appreciate for an audience socialized within a synchronic developmental context.

The expectations sometimes expressed by individuals having a diachronic developmental background that communication and peace could be improved if only people from some interdependent cultures would go through their historical period of "enlightenment" (which was characterized by the separation of rational thinking from holistic feeling in western cultures) reveals just another culturally biased belief because this expectation implicitly imposes the diachronic model of development with its diachronic dialectics of the relationship between opposing emotions, opinions, and modes of processing on people from cultures that derive their woes and foes from fundamentally different cognitive-emotional dynamics. On the other hand, the inability or unwillingness of individuals coming from a synchronic background to separate and tolerate opposing positions from each other and to distinguish a rational analysis of a conflict from an emotional and holistic appreciation of the needs and values involved may be one of the most difficult impediments to cross-cultural communication for individuals that have been socialized within a diachronic developmental context. To the extent that future research will focus on the functional mechanisms involved in diverging modes of processing and development, we can expect new progress in understanding misunderstanding across cultures.

REFERENCES

Adolphs, R., Damasio, H., Tranel, D., Cooper, G., & Damasio, A. R. (2000). A role for somatosensory cortices in the visual recognition of emotion as revealed by three-dimensional lesion mapping. *The Journal of Neuroscience, 20,* 2683–2690.

Ainsworth, M. D. S., Blehar, M. C., Waters, E., & Wall, S. (1978). *Patterns of attachment: A psychological study of the strange situation.* Hillsdale, NJ: Erlbaum.

Baumann, N., & Kuhl, J. (2002). Intuition, affect, and personality: Unconscious coherence judgments and self-regulation of negative affect. *Journal of Personality and Social Psychology, 83,* 1213–1223.

Baumann, N., & Kuhl, J. (2003). Self-infiltration: Confusing assigned tasks as self-selected in memory. *Personality and Social Psychology Bulletin, 29,* 487–497.

Baumann, N., Kaschel, R., & Kuhl, J. (2005). Striving for unwanted goals: Stress-dependent discrepancies between explicit and implicit achievement motives reduce subjective well-being and increase psychosomatic symptoms. *Journal of Personality and Social Psychology, 89,* 781–799.

Baumann, N., Kaschel, R., & Kuhl, J. (2007). Affect sensitivity and affect regulation in dealing with positive and negative affect. *Journal of Research in Personality, 41*(1), 239–248.

Beckmann, J., & Kuhl, J. (1984). Altering Information to gain action control: Functional aspects of human information-processing in decision-making. *Journal of Research in Personality, 18,* 223–237.

Beeman, M., Friedman, R. B., Grafman, J., Perez, E., Diamond, S., & Lindsay, M. B. (1994). Summation priming and coarse coding in the right hemisphere. *Journal of Cognitive Neuroscience, 6,* 26–45.

Bolte, A., Goschke, T., & Kuhl, J. (2003). Emotion and intuition. *Psychological Science, 14,* 416–422.

Chirkov, V., Ryan, R. M., Kim, Y., & Kaplan, U. (2003). Differentiating autonomy from individualism and independence: A self-determination theory perspective on internalization of cultural orientations and well-being. *Journal of Personality and Social Psychology, 84,* 97–110.

Costa, P. T. & Widiger, T.A. (Eds.) (1994). *Personality disorders and the five-factor model of personality.* Washington, DC: American Psychological Association.

Craik, F. I. M., Moroz, T. M., Moscovitch, M., Stuss, D. T., Winocur, G., Tulving, E., & Kapur, S. (1999). In search of the self: A positron emission tomography study. *Psychological Science, 10,* 26–34.

Deci, E. L., & Ryan, R. M. (2000). The "what" and "why" of goal pursuits: Human needs and the self-determination of behavior. *Psychological Inquiry, 11,* 319–338.

Deglin, V. L., & Kinsbourne, M. (1996). Divergent thinking styles of the hemispheres: How syllogisms are solved during transitory hemisphere suppression. *Brain and Cognition, 31,* 285–307.

Demuth, C., Keller, H., & Yovsi, R. D. (2007). The study of cultural developmental pathways – A multi-perspective approach, University of Osnabrück, Germany. Paper presented for publication.

Eysenck, H. J. (1967). *The biological basis of personality.* Springfield, IL: Charles C. Thomas.

Fox, N., & Davidson, R. A. (1987). Electroencephalogram asymmetry in response to the approach of a stranger and maternal separation in 10-month-old infants. *Developmental Psychology, 23,* 233–240.

Fuhrmann, A., & Kuhl, J. (1998). Maintaining a healthy diet: Effects of personality and self-reward versus self-punishment on commitment to and enactment of self-chosen and assigned goals. *Psychology and Health, 13,* 651–686.

Goschke, T., & Kuhl, J. (1993). The representation of intentions: Persisting activation in memory. *Journal of Experimental Psychology: Learning, Memory, and Cognition, 19,* 1211–1226.

Gray, J. A. (1987). *The psychology of fear and stress* (2nd ed.). Cambridge: Cambridge University Press.

Greenfield, P. M. (2004). *Weaving generations together. Evolving creativity in the Maya of Chiapas.* Santa Fe, NM: Sar Press.

Greenfield, P. M., Keller, H., Fuligni, A., & Maynard, A. (2003). Cultural pathways through universal development. *Annual Review of Psychology, 54,* 461–490.

Gupta, B. S., & Nagpal, M. (1978). Impulsivity/sociability and reinforcement in verbal operant conditioning. *British Journal of Psychology, 69,* 203–206.

Harmon-Jones, E., & Mills, J. (1999). *Cognitive dissonance: Progress on a pivotal theory in social psychology.* Washington, DC: American Psychological Association.

Hautzinger, M. (1994). Action control in the context of psychopathological disorders. In J. Kuhl & J. Beckmann (Eds.), *Volition and personality: Action versus state orientation* (pp. 209–215). Hogrefe: Seattle.

Horkheimer, M., & Adorno, T. W. (1976/2007). *Dialectic of enlightenment.* Stanford, CA: Stanford University Press.

Iyengar, S. S., & Lepper, M. R. (1999). Rethinking the value of choice: A cultural perspective on intrinsic motivation. *Journal of Personality and Social Psychology, 76,* 349–366.

Jostmann, N. B., & Koole, S. L. (2006). On the waxing and waning of working memory: Action orientation moderates the impact of demanding relationship primes on working memory capacity. *Personality and Social Psychology Bulletin, 32,* 1716–1728.

Jostmann, N. B., Koole, S. L., van der Wulp, N. Y., & Fockenberg, D. A. (2005). Subliminal affect regulation: The moderating role of action vs. state orientation. *European Psycholgist, 10,* 209–217.

Kağıtçibaşi, C. (1996). The autonomous-relational self: A new synthesis. *European Psychologist, 1,* 180–186.

Kağıtçibaşi, C. (2007). *Family, self, and human development across countries. Theory and applications* (2nd ed.). Mahwah, NJ: Erlbaum.

Kazén, M., & Kuhl, J. (2005). Intention memory and achievement motivation: Volitional facilitation and inhibition as a function of affective contents of need-related stimuli. *Journal of Personality and Social Psychology, 89,* 426–448.

Kazén, M., Baumann, N., & Kuhl, J. (2003). Self-infiltration and self-compatibility checking in dealing with unattractive tasks and unpleasant items: The moderating influence of state vs. action-orientation. *Motivation and Emotion, 27,* 157–197.

Keenan, J. P., Nelson, A., O'Connor, M., & Pascual-Leone, A. (2001). Self-recognition and the right hemisphere. *Nature, 409,* 305.

Keller, H. (2003). Socialization for competence: Cultural models of infancy. *Human Development, 46,* 288–311.

Keller, H. (2007). *Cultures of infancy.* Mahwah, NJ: Erlbaum.

Keller, H., & Gauda, G. (1987). Eye contact in the first months of life and its developmental consequences. In H. Rauh & H. C. Steinhausen (Eds.), *Psychobiology and early development. Advances in psychology* (46, pp. 129–143). North-Holland: Amsterdam.

Keller, H., Yovsi, R. D., & Voelker, S. (2002). The role of motor stimulation in parental ethnotheories. The case of Cameroonian Nso and German women. *Journal of Cross-Cultural Psychology, 33,* 398–414.

Keller, H., Lohaus, A., Kuensemueller, P., Abels, M., Yovsi, R. D., Voelker, S., Jensen, H., Papaligoura, Z., Rosabal-Coto, M., Kulks, D., & Mohite, P. (2004). The bio-culture of parenting: Evidence from five cultural communities. *Parenting: Science and Practice, 4,* 25–50.

Keller, H., Kärtner, J., Borke, J., Yovsi, R. D., & Kleis, A. (2005a). Parenting styles and the development of the categorial self. A longitudinal study on mirror self recognition in Cameroonian Nso farming and German families. *International Journal of Behavioral Development, 29*(6), 496–504.

Keller, H., Voelker, S., & Yovsi, R. D. (2005b). Conceptions of parenting in different cultural communities. The case of West African Nso and Northern German women. *Social Development, 14,* 158–180.

Keller, H., Lamm, B., Abels, M., Yovsi, R. D., Borke, J., Jensen, H., Papaligoura, Z., Holub, C., Wingshan, L., Tomiyama, A. J., Su, Y., Wang, Y., & Chaudary, N. (2006). Cultural models, socialization goals, and parenting ethnotheories. A multicultural analysis. *Journal of Cross-Cultural Psychology*, *37*, 155–172.

Keller, H., Otto, H., Lamm, B., Yovsi, R. D., & Kärtner, J. (2008). The timing of verbal/vocal communications between mothers and their infants: A longitudinal cross-cultural comparison. *Infant Behavior and Development, 31*, 217–226.

Kelley, H. H. (1972). *Causal schemata and the attribution process.* New York: General Learning Press.

Kessen, W. (1979). The American child and other cultural inventions. *American Psychologist, 34*, 815–820.

Kitayama, S. (2000). Cultural psychology of the self: A renewed look at independence and interdependence. In C. von Hofsten & L. Bäckmann (Eds.), *Psychology of the turn of the Millenium* (pp. 305–322). Hove, East Sussex: Psychology Press.

Kitayama, S. (2002). Culture and basic psychological processes – Toward a system view of culture: Comment on Oyserman et al.. *Psychological Bulletin, 128*, 89–96.

Kitayama, S., & Uchida, Y. (2005). Interdependent agency: An alternative system for action. In R. Sorrentino, D. Cohen, J. M. lson, & M. P. Zanna (Eds.), *Culture and social behavior: The Ontario symposium* (Vol. 10, pp. 165–198). Mahwah, NJ: Erlbaum.

Kitayama, S., & Park, H. (2007). Cultural shaping of self, emotion, and well-being: How does it work? *Personality and Social Psychology Compass, 1*(1), 202–227.

Kitayama, S., Mesquita, B., & Karasawa, M. (2003b). The emotional basis of independent and interdependent selves: Socially disengaging and engaging emotions in the US and Japan. Unpublished manuscript, University of Michigan.

Kitayama, S., Uchida, Y., Mesquita, B., & Saito, K. (2003). Culture and social relationship: Perception and memory of reciprocal exchange. Unpublished manuscript, University of Michigan.

Kitayama, S., Snibbe, A., Markus, H. R., & Suzuki, T. (2004). Is there any free choice? Self and dissonance in two cultures. *Psychological Science, 15*(8), 527–533.

Koole, S. L. (2004). Volitional shielding of the self: Effects of action orientation and external demands on implicit self-evaluation. *Social Cognition, 22*, 100–125.

Koole, S., & Jostmann, N. (2004). Getting a grip on your feelings: Effect of action orientation and social demand on intuitive affect regulation. *Journal of Personality and Social Psychology, 87*, 974–990.

Koole, S. L., & Kuhl, J. (2003). In search of the real self: A functional perspective on optimal self esteem and authenticity. *Psychological Inquiry, 14*, 43–49.

Koole, S. L., & van den Berg, A. (2005). Lost in the wilderness: Terror management, action orientation, and nature evaluation. *Journal of Personality and Social Psychology, 88*, 1014–1028.

Koole, S. L., Kuhl, J., Jostmann, N., & Vohs, K. D. (2005). On the hidden benefits of state orientation: Can people prosper without efficient affect regulation skills?. In A. Tesser, J. Wood, & D. A. Stapel (Eds.), *On building, defending, and regulating the self: A psychological perspective* (pp. 217–243). London (UK): Taylor & Francis.

Kuhl, J. (1984). Volitional aspects of achievement motivation and learned helplessness: Toward a comprehensive theory of action-control. In B. A. Maher (Ed.), *Progress in experimental personality research* (Vol. 13, pp. 99–171). New York: Academic Press.

Kuhl, J. (2000a). A functional-design approach to motivation and self-regulation: The dynamics of personality systems interactions. In M. Boekaerts, P. R. Pintrich, & M. Zeidner (Eds.), *Handbook of self-regulation* (pp. 111–169). San Diego: Academic Press.

Kuhl, J. (2000b). The volitional basis of personality systems interaction theory: Applications in learning and treatment contexts. *International Journal of Educational Research, 33*, 665–703.

Kuhl, J. (2001). *Motivation und Persönlichkeit: Interaktionen psychischer Systeme. [Motivation and personality: Interactions of mental systems].* Göttingen, Germany: Hogrefe.

Kuhl, J., & Beckmann, J. (1994a). *Volition and personality: Action versus state orientation.* Seattle: Hogrefe.

Kuhl, J., & Beckmann, J. (1994b). *Volition and personality: Action versus state orientation*. Seattle/ Göttingen: Hogrefe.

Kuhl, J., & Fuhrmann, A. (1998). Decomposing self-regulation and self-control: The volitional components checklist. In J. Heckhausen & C. Dweck (Eds.), *Life span perspectives on motivation and control* (pp. 15–49). Mahwah, NJ: Erlbaum.

Kuhl, J., & Helle, P. (1986). Motivational and volitional determinants of depression: The degenerated-intention hypothesis. *Journal of Abnormal Psychology, 95*, 247–251.

Kuhl, J., & Kazén, M. (1994). Self-discrimination and memory: State orientation and false self-ascription of assigned activities. *Journal of Personality and Social Psychology, 66*, 1103–1115.

Kuhl, J., & Kazén, M. (1999). Volitional facilitation of difficult intentions: Joint activation of intention memory and positive affect removes Stroop interference. *Journal of Experimental Psychology: General, 128*, 382–399.

Kuhl, J., & Koole, S. L. (2004). Workings of the will: A functional approach. In J. Greenberg, S. L. Koole, & T. Pyszczynski (Eds.), *Handbook of experimental existential psychology* (pp. 411–430). New York: Guilford.

Kuhl, J., & Kazén, M. (2008). Motivation, affect, and hemispheric asymmetry: Power versus affiliation. *Journal of Personality and Social Psychology*, in press.

Markus, H. R., & Kitayama, S. (1991). Culture and the self. Implications for cognition, emotion and motivation. *Psychological Review, 98*, 224–253.

Markus, H. R., & Kitayama, S. (2004). Models of agency: Sociocultural diversity in the construction of action. In V. Murphy-Berman & J. J. Berman (Eds.), *Cross-cultural differences in perspectives on the self: Nebraska symposium on motivation* (Vol. 49, pp. 1–57). Lincoln: University of Nebraska Press.

Matsumoto, D., & Kupperbusch, C. (2000). Idiocentric and allocentric differences in emotional expression and experience. *Asian Journal of Social Psychology, 4*, 113–131.

McCrae, R. R., & Costa, P. T. (1987). Validation of the five-factor model of personality across instruments and observers. *Journal of Personality and Social Psychology, 52*, 81–90.

McClelland, J. L., McNaughton, B. L., & O'Reilly, R. C. (1995). Why there are complementary learning systems in the hippocampus and neorcortex: Insights from the successes and failures of connectionist models of learning and memory. *Psychological Review, 102*, 419–457.

Meins, E., Fernyhough, C., Wainwright, R., Das Gupta, M., Fradley, E., & Tuckey, M. (2002). Maternal mind-mindedness and attachment security as predictors of theory of mind understanding. *Child Development, 73*, 1715–1726.

Miller, P. J., & Sperry, L. L. (1987). The socialization of anger and aggression. *Merrill-Palmer Quarterly, 33*, 1–31.

Millon, T. (1981). *Disorders of Personality: DSM III. Axis II*. New York: Wiley.

Nisbett, R. E., Peng, K., Choi, I., & Norenzayan, A. (2001). Culture and systems of thought: Holistic vs. analytic cognition. *Psychological Review, 108*, 291–310.

Neisser, U. (1988). Five kinds of self-knowledge. *Philosophical Psychology, 1*, 35–59.

Olvermann, R., Metz-Göckel, H., Hannover, B., & Pöhlmann, C. (2004). Motivinhalte und Handlungs- versus Lageorientierung bei Personen mit independenter versus interdependenter Selbstkonstruktion [Motivational contents and action versus state orientation as a function of independent and interdependent self-construal]. *Zeitschrift für Differentielle und Diagnostische Psychologie, 25*, 87–103.

Peng, K., & Nisbett, R. E. (1999). Culture, dialecticism, and reasoning about contradiction. *American Psychologist, 54*, 741–754.

Piaget, J. (1952). *The origins of intelligence in children*. New York: International University Press.

Rothbaum, F., Pott, M., Azuma, H., Miyake, K., & Weisz, J. (2000a). The development of close relationships in Japan and the United States: Paths of symbiotic harmony and generative tension. *Child Development, 71*, 1121–1142.

Rothbaum, F., Weisz, J., Pott, M., Miyke, K., & Morelli, G. (2000b). Attachment and culture: Security in the United States and Japan. *American Psychologist, 55*, 1093–1104.

Rumelhart, D. E., & McClelland, J. L. The PDP Research Group (1986). *Parallel distributed processing: Explorations in the microstructure of cognition*. Cambridge, MA: MIT. Vol:1

Schore, A. N. (2003). *Affect regulation and the repair of self*. New York: Norton.

Shaver, P. R., & Mikulincer, M. (2007). Adult attachment strategies and the regulation of emotion. In J. J. Gross & R. A. Thompson (Eds.), *Handbook of emotion regulation* (pp. 446–465). New York: Guilford Press.

Showers, C. J., & Kling, K. C. (1996). Organization of self-knowledge: Implications for recovery from sad mood. *Journal of Personality and Social Psychology, 70*, 578–590.

Takahashi, K. (1986). The role of the personal frame mark of social relationships in socialization studies. In H. Stevenson, H. Azuma, & K. Hakuta (Eds.), *Child development and education in Japan* (pp. 123–135). New York: Freeman.

Triandis, H. C. (1995). *Individualism and collectivism*. Boulder, CO: Westview.

Uchida, Y., Kitayama, S., Mesquita, B., Reyes, J. A., & Morling, B. (2003). Culturally contingent correlates of wellbeing and happiness: Self-esteem and social support. Unpublished manuscript: University of Michigan.

Vygotsky, L. S. (1978). *Mind in society: The development of higher psychological processes*. Cambridge: Harvard University Press.

Wang, Q., & Brockmeier, J. (2002). Autobiographical remembering as cultural practice: Understanding the interplay between memory, self and culture. *Culture and Psychology, 8*, 45–64.

Wittling, W. (1990). Psychophysiological correlates of human brain asymmetry: Blood pressure changes during lateralized presentation of an emotionally laden film. *Neuropsychologia, 28*, 457–470.

3

UNCERTAINTY REGULATION: THE MASTER MOTIVE?

RICHARD M. SORRENTINO[*], ANDREW SZETO[*], JOHN B. NEZLEK[†], SATORU YASUNAGA[‡], SADAFUSA KOUHARA[¶] AND YASUNAO OHTSUBO[§]

[*]*Psychology Department, University of Western Ontario, London, Ontario, Canada*
[†]*Department of Psychology, College of William & Mary, Williamsburg, USA*
[‡]*Kurume University, Kurume, Japan*
[¶]*Yamaguchi Prefectural University, Yamaguchi, Japan*
[§]*Psychology Department, Fukuoka University of Education, Fukuoka, Japan*

One undeniable fact about uncertainty is that all situations can be characterized in terms of the degree of uncertainty one perceives in the situation. In any situation, no matter how trivial or how important, whether it be planning dinner or deciding on a career, that situation can be labeled in terms of uncertainty. One may be certain, fairly certain, uncertain, or fairly uncertain as to what he or she will eat for dinner, or who he or she will become. There is simply no situation which cannot be characterized in this manner.[1]

The literature is full of books, chapters, and research articles that list uncertainty as a key word. Just now, as we write this draft, there are 62,900,000 results

---

[1]When I (RMS) discussed this during a Keynote address at the 2006 Japanese Psychological Association in Fukuoka, I said some of you are uncertain whether this will be a good talk, others know it will be. – Nobody laughed.

---

on Google web search, where the word uncertainty is typed in. One of our favorite quotes regarding uncertainty comes from Fiddle (1980, p. 3):

> The twentieth century has been coloured by the principle of uncertainty, taken both in its original Heisenberg meaning of 1927, to refer to a fundamental incommensurability, and in its broadest sense, as a general characteristic of the life of modern man since Einstein's miracle year of 1905 and the killing of the archduke in 1914. Along with relativity, uncertainty is a sort of charismatic concept, exciting those who filter conventional concepts and data through its perspectives.

Eric Fromm (1947) also wrote about the wonderful epistemological value of uncertainty: "The quest for certainty blocks the search for meaning. Uncertainty is the very condition to impel man to unfold his powers." However, it is important to point out that uncertainty is not always thought of as a panacea; one needs only to look at colloquialisms such as "curiosity killed the cat," or "if you put your nose too close to the pot, it could get burned" to realize that resolving uncertainty isn't always a good thing.

Given the incommensurability of this construct, it is no surprise that cross-cultural differences in how people cope with uncertainty would come to the fore. Beginning with Hofstede's (1980) seminal research on ecological differences between cultures, it has been argued that Eastern and Western cultures should differ in how they handle uncertainty. In particular, Eastern countries, such as Japan, should be more uncertainty avoidant than Western countries such as Canada and the United States (e.g., Hofstede, 1980; Shane et al., 1995; Arrindell et al., 1997; Ryan et al., 1999). Hofstede (1991, p. 113) defined uncertainty avoidance as the extent to which the members of a culture feel threatened by uncertain or unknown situations. High uncertainty avoidance cultures view uncertainty as negative and emphasize the use of rules and regulations in order to maintain predictability in the social environment. In contrast, cultures that are low in uncertainty avoidance are generally tolerant of ambiguity and uncertainty. Less emphasis is placed on rules and regulations in these societies than in high uncertainty avoidance societies (Hofstede, 1980).

Triandis (1989, 1990) elaborates on cultural differences in the norms of handling uncertainty through his discussion of loose and tight cultures. He explains that loose cultures, such as those in the West, encourage freedom and deviation from norms, whereas tight cultures, such as many in the East, promote norms and deviation from those norms is punished. Therefore, individuals in tight cultures prefer predictability, certainty, and security, and individuals from loose cultures prefer creativity and diversity (1989, p. 50).

This societal theme has also been alluded to by other theorists and is reflected most prominently in Japanese culture's emphasis on authority and hierarchy. Benedict (1946) suggests that hierarchy and deference to authority is first learned in the family, where the father serves as the apex in the family unit and the exemplar for proper behavior. What is learned within this micro-context is also applied and used in larger societal milieus. For example, Herbig (1995) demonstrates that Japanese industry is replete with certainty. Compared to "frontier thinking" North American industry, where the focus is on new discoveries and exploration of novel ideas, Japanese industry excels at taking existing ideas or products and refining or improving on them (see also Bowonder & Miyake, 1992). This approach allows the Japanese to rework those ideas and technologies that are certain to them, rather than risking time and effort on unproven, and thus uncertain, new ideas and technologies. Finally, and more importantly for us, education in Japan is also a reflection of this emphasis on certainty. Researchers have showed that the Japanese education system is highly organized and hierarchically structured (e.g., Ellington, 1992; Guo, 2005), with a standard set of curricula, texts, and moral teachings for the entire country (Stigler et al., 1987). Japanese children, for example, spend significantly more time in structured instruction than their US counterparts (Stigler et al., 1987), such as unison rote chanting of the multiplication tables (Ellington, 1992). Furthermore, Ellington describes pedagogical techniques used in grade school as those centering on the absorption of factual knowledge (e.g., memorization) and the dissemination of information through lecturing, rather than classroom discussions or the examination of opposing viewpoints. This certainty theme continues in post-secondary education as university students continue to defer to the authority of the professor (Ellington, 1992), sometimes remaining silent in class after questions to avoid confrontations with others or getting the incorrect answer (Nakane, 2006). All these rules, regulations, and structures create social interactions that flow with a tacit script. In other words, everyone knows who they are, how to act, and where they exist within the Japanese social system. For Japanese society to function properly, everything has to be defined, scripted, and practiced, creating a society that has surrounded itself in a cloak of certainty and predictability.

Others have pointed out how countries like Japan promote a self-regulatory style consistent with maintaining certainty. For example, Weisz et al. (1984) discussed differences between Japan and the United States with regard to control. They explained that, compared to American organizations, Japanese organizations are more likely to possess a clear and visible hierarchy among the various levels within a company. Weisz et al. further suggest that this distinction of status within Japanese organizations serves to minimize uncertainty, anxiety, and disappointment (p. 963). Compared to American workers, Japanese workers are more likely to gain control by maintaining certainty surrounding their workplace situations. Finally, Vishwanath (2003) performed an online study where interactants in high uncertainty avoidance cultures, such as Japan, seem to exhibit drastic behavioral changes when faced with limited information within an ambiguous decision context as compared to similar participants in Germany and the United States.

Although we agree with many of the above authors that East-Asian cultures may differ in how they cope with uncertainty compared to Western cultures, we do not agree that this difference is necessarily due to negative affective concerns. Hofstede's (1980) ecological measure of uncertainty avoidance is considered by Hofstede (1980, 1991) to be an affective measure of a society's anxiety regarding uncertainty (see also Matsumoto, 1989). Conversely, our construct of uncertainty orientation, as discussed below, is an individual difference variable concerned with the informational properties of uncertainty. Many of the findings cited above can be interpreted easily as a positive means of coping with uncertainty by constructing a predictable, tight environment, rather than an illustration of anxiety over uncertainty. This is important to us, as the distinction between affect (feeling good or bad) and informational value (attaining clarity or maintaining clarity) plays a key role in much of the research testing the theory of uncertainty orientation (cf. Sorrentino & Roney, 2000). It may also play a key role when it comes to examining cross-cultural differences in the way individuals and cultures handle uncertainty.

INDIVIDUAL AND CULTURAL DIFFERENCES IN UNCERTAINTY ORIENTATION

Uncertainty orientation refers to individual differences in how people handle uncertainty. The theory of uncertainty orientation relies on a broad definition of uncertainty, as specified by Kagan (1972). Kagan thought of uncertainty reduction as a primary motive, with uncertainty originating from either the inability to predict the future or from an incompatibility between two cognitions, a cognition and an experience, or a cognition and a behavior. At opposite ends of a continuum are those considered uncertainty-oriented (UOs) and those considered certainty-oriented (COs). UOs are *high* in the desire to *attain* clarity, but *low* in the desire to *maintain* clarity. Their preferred method of handling uncertainty is to seek information and engage in activities that will directly resolve the uncertainty. Such people can be described as having a strong "need to know." They are people who try to understand and discover aspects of the self and the environment about which they are uncertain. In contrast, COs are *low* in the desire to *attain* clarity but are *high* in the desire to *maintain* clarity. When confronted with uncertainty, COs use indirect methods such as relying on others or heuristic devices such as leadership status, group norms, or source expertise to provide a resolution (Sorrentino et al., 1988; Hodson & Sorrentino, 1997).

The normative expectations for uncertainty orientation may vary across cultures. In some societies, a UO style of coping may be the norm, whereas in others, a CO style may be preferred. To illustrate, three studies comparing Japanese university students with Canadian University students (Shuper et al., 2004; Szeto, 2005; Sorrentino et al., 2008) found that Japanese participants were more CO than they were UO, whereas Canadian participants were more UO than they were CO. These results are consistent with our notion that where Canada may be described as a UO-centric society, Japan may be described as CO-centric.

We measure uncertainty orientation using a resultant measure (see Sorrentino et al., 1992c) composed of a projective measure, *n*Uncertainty (Sorrentino et al., 1992a) that is intended to infer one's desire to directly resolve uncertainty, and an acquiescent-free measure of authoritarianism (Cherry & Byrne, 1977) that is intended to infer one's desire to maintain clarity or predictability. A person high in *n*Uncertainty and low in authoritarianism is assumed to be relatively uncertainty-oriented, or a UO. A person low in *n*Uncertainty and high in authoritarianism is assumed to be relatively certainty-oriented, or a CO. Relative differences on the component measures were also significant and in the expected direction in all three studies with Japanese students significantly lower in *n*Uncertainty and higher in authoritarianism than Canadian students.

Table 3.1 presents a summary of several key studies of uncertainty orientation to date. The studies can be described loosely in terms of two overarching characteristics: motivational arousal and information processing. In terms of motivational arousal, the first three studies we conducted (Sorrentino et al., 1984)

TABLE 3.1   Examples of Research on Uncertainty Orientation

Study	Topic	UOs	COs
Sorrentino et al. (1984)	Three studies showing that uncertainty directs achievement motivation	Achievement motives are engaged when the outcome is uncertain	Achievement motives are engaged when the outcome is certain
Sorrentino and Roney (1986)	Motivational arousal and performance	Strongest effects when self-assessment was relevant	Strongest effects when self-assessment was not relevant
Roney and Sorrentino (1995)	Motivational arousal and performance	Strongest effects when self-discrepancies were relevant	Strongest effects when there were no self-discrepancies
Sorrentino et al. (1996)	Motivational arousal and intelligence	Strongest effects when IQ was assessed	Strongest effects when IQ was not relevant
Sorrentino and Hewitt (1984)	Self-assessment of abilities	Want to find out about a new ability regardless of whether the information may be good or bad	Don't want to find out about a new ability regardless of whether the information may be good or bad
Roney and Sorrentino (1997)	Social comparison	Compare their values with others	Don't compare their values with others
Sorrentino et al. (1992)	Risk-taking	Prefer moderate risk in order to evaluate ability	Prefer low or high risk in order not to evaluate ability
Haynes et al. (2007)	Counterfactual thinking and time perspective	Show greater upward thoughts and derogation of past selves following negative events	Show no tendency toward upward thoughts nor derogation of past selves following negative events

(continued)

TABLE 3.1　(Continued)

Study	Topic	UOs	COs
Huber et al. (1992)	Cooperative learning	Prefer and perform better than with lecture style teaching	Prefer and perform better with lecture style teaching
Brouwers and Sorrentino (1993)	Health compliance behavior	Seek information under life-threatening but preventive conditions	Don't seek information when life-threatening and preventive
Brouwers et al. (2004)	Effects of disclosure of traumatic events	Beneficial effects, skin conductance goes down	Non-beneficial, skin conductance shoots way up
Walker and Sorrentino (2000)	Depression, information seeking, and performance	Greater when depressed in order to restore control	Less when depressed in order to restore control
Sorrentino et al. (1988)	Information processing and self-relevance	Use controlled or systematic processing when issue is self-diagnostic	Rely on heuristic or non-systematic processing when issue is self-diagnostic
Hodson and Sorrentino (2003)	Ingroup versus outgroup information processing	Process information more systematically when group opinions are incongruent with expectations	Process information more systematically when group opinions are congruent with expectations
Shuper and Sorrentino (2004)	Majority versus minority influence on information processing	Process information more systematically when group opinions are incongruent with expectations	Process information more systematically when group opinions are congruent with expectations
Driscoll et al. (1991)	Memory for congruent and incongruent traits	Recall incongruent traits more than congruent ones	Recall congruent traits more than incongruent ones
Sorrentino et al. (1995)	Memory for past events in close relationships	Do not distort their memory of past events	Distort their memory based on their current trust for their partner
Hodson and Sorrentino (1997)	Groupthink	Do not succumb to groupthink	Are affected by groupthink
Sorrentino et al. (2007)	Optimal distinctiveness	Do not show a need for optimal distinctiveness	Show a need for assimilation

integrated self-assessment theories of achievement motivation (e.g., Weiner, 1972; Trope, 1975), or those concerned with finding out about one's ability, with affective theories (i.e., the theory of achievement motivation, Atkinson, 1958; Atkinson & Feather, 1966; and the general theory of achievement motivation, Atkinson & Raynor, 1974), or those concerned with pride in accomplishment and shame over failure. We hypothesized that it is not the relationship between probability of success (Ps) and the incentive value of success (Is) that affective theories predict (i.e., Is $= 1 - $ Ps), nor assessment of abilities, that self-assessment theories predict, that determines motivational arousal. Rather, the degree of uncertainty is the crucial factor. When the uncertainty of the situation matches one's uncertainty orientation, that is, where the situation is relatively uncertain for UOs (e.g., Ps $= 0.50$) and where it is relatively certain for COs (e.g., Ps $= 0.20$ or 0.80), success-oriented people (SOs) are more positively motivated, whereas failure-threatened persons (FTs) are more negatively motivated. By positively motivated, we mean that the desire to succeed is strong and performance is enhanced. By negatively motivated, we mean that fear of failure is strong, and performance is dampened or inhibited.

The above hypothesis was confirmed in Study 1 of Sorrentino et al. (1984), which directly manipulated Ps, and in Studies 2 and 3 of Sorrentino et al. (1984), as well as in Sorrentino and Roney (1986), three studies by Roney and Sorrentino (1995), and by Sorrentino et al. (1996), which used other forms of uncertainty such as task diagnosticity, or self-discrepancies. The Sorrentino et al. (1996) study is especially interesting as the uncertainty here was derived from presenting an intelligence test as a test of intelligence or as a pilot project (i.e., diagnostic or not diagnostic of ability, respectively).

The other key study published in 1984 was related to information processing (Sorrentino & Hewitt). This study directly challenged Trope's (1975) self-assessment theory. Trope argued that people want to find out about a new ability regardless of whether the result is likely to be indicative of being good or poor at that ability, this study showed that Trope was correct only for UOs. COs did not want to find out about a new ability, regardless of the likelihood of outcome. This tendency to want to self-assess by UOs and to *NOT* want to self-assess by COs was the impetus for many of the other studies shown in Table 3.1, including research on social comparison (Roney & Sorrentino, 1997), risk-taking (Sorrentino et al., 1992b), counterfactual thinking (Haynes et al., 2007), the jigsaw method of cooperative learning (Huber et al., 1992), and health-related behaviors (Brouwers & Sorrentino, 1993; Walker & Sorrentino, 2000; Brouwers et al., 2004).

A third study of major importance to us, also falling under the information processing category, was that by Sorrentino et al. (1988). Here we showed that dualistic theories of information processing such as that of Petty and Cacioppo's (1986) peripheral versus central route to persuasion, are moderated by one's uncertainty orientation. UOs will systematically process diagnostic information when it is personally relevant, and rely on heuristics when it is not. COs, on the other hand will process diagnostic information when it is not personally relevant, and rely on heuristics when it is personally relevant.

The information processing part of this study not only played a role in some of the other studies mentioned above, but also led to studies on information processing in groups based on in-group versus out-group influence (Hodson & Sorrentino, 2001) and minority versus majority influence (Shuper & Sorrentino, 2004). Consistent with the notion that incongruence is a form of uncertainty, and congruence is a form of certainty, in both of these studies, UOs were more likely to systematically process the information if it was incongruent with their expectations than if it was congruent, regardless of the source (e.g., in-group or majority disagrees, out-group or minority agrees). COs were more likely to systematically process information when the source was congruent with expectations (e.g., in-group or majority agrees, out-group or minority disagrees). This tendency to process congruent versus incongruent information also manifested itself in a memory study by Driscoll et al. (1991).

The heuristic propensity of COs was again seen in a study on close relationships (Sorrentino et al., 1995), where COs were more likely to have high or low trust for their partners (maintaining certainty) than UOs, and relied more on the heuristic of trust when recalling an event they recorded early in a close relationship. It was also carried forward to group research where we showed that, in a groupthink situation (Janis, 1972), COs were more likely to rely on the leader and show greater biased decisions to a closed leader and unbiased decisions to an open leader than UOs. Reasoning that COs were more reliant on groups than UOs, Hodson and Sorrentino (1997) also showed that only COs displayed in-group bias using the nominal groups paradigm (Tajfel & Turner, 2004). Furthermore, Sorrentino et al. (2008) showed that only COs demonstrate a need for assimilation by using the optimal distinctiveness manipulations of Pickett et al. (2002).

A FORMAL MODEL OF UNCERTAINTY ORIENTATION

Much of the above research led to a mathematical reformulation of the theory of uncertainty orientation (Sorrentino et al., 2003). This reformulation of the theory attempted to account not only for when people should be engaged in a particular activity, but when they should become disengaged.[2] Collapsing across relevant motivational variables, such as achievement-related motives, Figure 3.1 illustrates the model in terms of engagement, disengagement, and the affective consequences associated with this behavior. Briefly, UOs (whose desire to resolve uncertainty, U, is greater than their desire to maintain certainty, C) are more likely to be actively engaged in a situation where uncertainty is greater (i.e., where the probability of uncertainty, Pu, is greater than the probability of certainty, Pc; this is also known as a matched situation) and the personal relevance, R, of the outcome of that uncertain situation is greater. Conversely, COs (C > U) are more likely to be actively engaged in a situation where certainty is greater (Pc > Pu, a matched situation) and the R of the outcome in that certain situation is greater. By active engagement, we mean that the person should increase his or her systematic processing of information and decrease heuristic or more non-systematic forms of information processing. In addition, relevant sources of motivation should be accentuated (see below).

---

[2] See Sorrentino et al. (2003) for the complete mathematical reformulation.

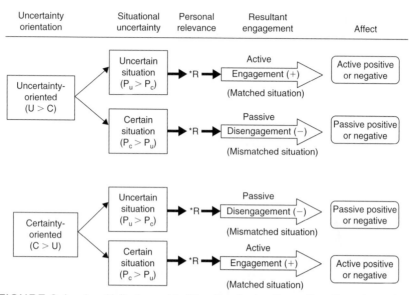

FIGURE 3.1   A multiplicative model of thought and action. *Source*: From Sorrentino et al. (2003, p. 134). Copyright 2003 by Elsevier Science. Adapted with permission.

When the uncertainty of the situation does not match one's uncertainty orientation (i.e., it is an unmatched situation), people become disengaged from the situation. By disengagement, we mean that the person should increase non-systematic forms of information processing and decrease systematic information processing. In addition, relevant sources of motivation should be lessened. It is important to note that engagement can be positive (+) or negative (−) depending on the relevant motives in the situation. For example, if one is success-oriented, then he or she should be positively engaged, particularly when an achievement-oriented situation matches his or her uncertainty orientation, and should perform best under these conditions. If he or she is failure-threatened , then he or she should be negatively engaged, especially when the situation matches his or her uncertainty orientation, and should perform least well under these conditions. This occurs because a matched situation is consistent with the person's uncertainty orientation. It is his or her way of organizing the world such that he or she can cope with uncertainty in the best way possible. In unmatched situations, disengagement will occur and should lead to a relaxing of relevant motives. In turn, this relaxing of relevant motives can lead, for example, to a decrease in performance for SOs, and ironically, an increase in performance for FTs.

This part of the model, as shown in Figure 3.1, is empirically based. In fact, in all of the studies dealing with achievement-related motives described in Table 3.1, the data fit this description. More on this later; for now, it is important to note that, in addition to formalizing the model, Sorrentino et al. (2003) speculated on what should happen when people are engaged or disengaged from an activity in terms of their affective experiences. They put forward the general expectation that people's dispositional affect would be more active than passive (Russell, 1980) when their uncertainty orientation matched the uncertainty inherent in the situation at hand than when they did not match. In mismatched situations, passive emotions should dominate.

Putting informational influences together with motivational and affective experiences, uncertainty orientation can be understood in terms of flow experiences as shown in Figure 3.1. Drawing on Csikszentmihalyi (1975), Sorrentino et al. (2003, p. 145) state that,

> Flow is feeling good about the self while concentrating on the activity at hand. It occurs when the person engages in a situation that has positive information value (attaining or maintaining clarity for uncertainty-oriented vs. certainty-oriented persons, respectively) and the person is positively motivated to undertake the activity; in other words, when positive information value and positive motivation are matched.

It is important to note that uncertainty orientation is neither domain specific nor it is affectively based. Rather, it interacts with the uncertainty of the situation and with affectively based motives such as achievement-related or affiliation-related motives to predict differences in flow behavior. For example, SOs, or those who are motivated by anticipating pride in accomplishment, are more actively engaged in and have more flow experiences in achievement-oriented situations that match their uncertainty orientation than in achievement-oriented situations that do not match their uncertainty orientation (Sorrentino et al., 2003). It is in these former situations that they perform best and enjoy the activity the most. Failure-threatened persons, those who are motivated by anticipating shame over failure, are also actively engaged in achievement situations, although they are likely to have anti-flow experiences in achievement-oriented situations that match their uncertainty orientation than in achievement-oriented situations that do not match their uncertainty orientation (e.g., Sorrentino et al., 1984; Roney & Sorrentino, 1995). Sorrentino et al. (2003, p. 145) define anti-flow as follows: "The person in anti-flow feels badly about the self while acting in or attempting to avoid a situation that he or she fears." He or she exhibits the worst performance and the greatest fear of failure in these situations.[3]

In matched situations, people are in either flow or anti-flow. In contrast, in mismatched situations, people are always in non-flow. Mismatched situations do not activate the self-system, and there is no real importance to the self attached to them. For example, Raynor and McFarlin (1986) distinguish between the self and behavioral systems. We perform some activities because our self-concept is involved, whereas we perform other activities because of extrinsic incentives

---

[3] It should be pointed out that because someone is negatively motivated in one domain does not imply that he or she is negatively motivated in others. For example, a failure-threatened UO might also be affiliation-oriented; consequently he or she might derive more positive affect from uncertain social situations than uncertain achievement-oriented ones.

that are not considered part of the self. Such activities are performed because of necessity. A professor may view the success or failure of his or her research to be a reflection of the self, while he or she views taking out the garbage as having nothing to do with the self. Non-flow activity may be aligned with the behavioral system but not with the self-system.

Sorrentino et al. (2003) cite Russell's (1980) circumplex model as a way of distinguishing between the emotions experienced in flow and non-flow situations. In flow states (either flow or anti-flow), people are more likely to experience active emotions (both positive and negative) such as excited, astonished, alarmed, and angry. In contrast, when they are in non-flow states, people are more likely to experience passive emotions (both positive and negative) such as satisfied, content, bored, and gloomy. Interestingly, the first test of this hypothesis came with an opportunity to study differences in affective experiences between people in Japan and Canada (Sorrentino et al., 2008) as described below.

AFFECTIVE EXPERIENCES AS A FUNCTION OF UNCERTAINTY ORIENTATION AND SOCIETAL UNCERTAINTY

We assume that if UOs and COs from different cultures are put in identical situations, that is, where the amount of perceived uncertainty is the same, then UOs in one culture would act like UOs in another, and COs in one culture would act like COs in another. In fact, in a study involving Japanese participants, Yasunaga and Kouhara (1995) found that UOs preferred to find out new information about the self; that is, they chose items from a test that would resolve uncertainty about a new and important ability. In contrast, COs preferred non-diagnostic items; that is, they chose items that would tell them nothing new about the self. This finding partially replicated the results of a study by Sorrentino and Hewitt (1984) that involved Canadian UOs and COs. In a second study by Yasunaga and Kouhara (2008), Japanese participants were asked how much information they wanted about a new disease. When the disease was life-threatening, UOs wanted to know more information about the disease when it was not certain if there was a cure than when it was certain that there was a cure. In contrast, COs wanted more information when a cure was certain, regardless of threat. This study is a conceptual replication of Brouwers and Sorrentino (1993), which found similar results among Canadians.

Despite this evidence that Japanese and Canadian participants perform in the same manner when one controls for individual and situational uncertainty, the notion of Japan being a CO-centric society and Canada being a UO-centric society suggests that the people in each society have somewhat different everyday life experiences. The literature discussed earlier suggests that in their home, their work or program of study, and in their social activity, people in Japan are more

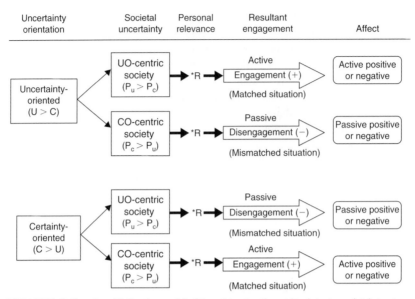

FIGURE 3.2   A multiplicative model of thought and action as it relates to societal structure.

likely to encounter situations structured for COs, whereas people in Canada are more likely to encounter situations structured for UOs.[4] This being the case, one could posit that culture can interact with uncertainty orientation to moderate the outcomes one experiences.

Figure 3.2 illustrates what should happen to affective experiences if one's uncertainty orientation matched or did not match the uncertainty orientation of one's culture. If one's society were UO-centric, for example, then he or she should have more active (flow and anti-flow) experiences than passive or non-flow experiences. The study by Sorrentino et al. (2008) was a direct test of this hypothesis. That is, whereas UOs in Canada will have more active and less passive emotional experiences than COs in Canada, COs in Japan will have more active and less passive emotional experiences than UOs in Japan. Sorrentino et al. tested participants from universities in Japan and Canada, where they described the frequency of experiencing various emotions. As can be seen in Figure 3.3, results are consistent with their hypotheses. Participants whose uncertainty orientation matched that of their country (i.e., UOs in Canada, COs in Japan) experienced more active emotions than mismatched participants (i.e., COs in Canada, UOs in Japan) who experienced more passive emotions.

[4]As a personal anecdote of this difference, two of my (RMS) coauthors (YO and SY) each spent a sabbatical with me in Canada. During their respective visits I invited them to sit in on a fourth year Honours Course in Social Psychology. The course was discussion-oriented and my colleagues were in "shock and awe" to see the students speak freely, often arguing with their professor that their opinion was correct. This would be most unheard of in a fourth year undergraduate course in Japan.

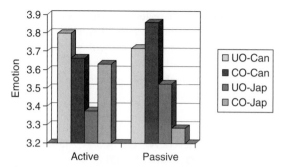

FIGURE 3.3   Mean active versus passive emotion scores as a function of country (Can = Canada, Jap = Japan) and uncertainty orientation (UO = uncertainty-oriented, CO = certainty-oriented).

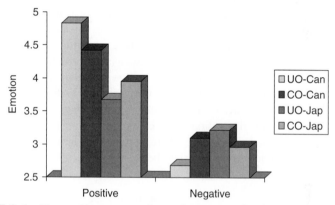

FIGURE 3.4   Mean positive versus negative emotion scores as a function of country (Can = Canada, Jap = Japan) and uncertainty orientation (UO = uncertainty-oriented, CO = certainty-oriented).

These findings follow exactly from what is predicted in Figure 3.2, supporting both the theory and the notion that UOs and COs will differ in each country in their emotional experiences as a function of the impact of their society on their individual level of uncertainty orientation.

Interestingly, as shown in Figure 3.4, Sorrentino et al. (2008) also found that those who matched their country's style of coping with uncertainty not only reported more active than passive experiences than mismatched students, but they also reported experiencing more positive and fewer negative emotions than mismatched students. Given that mismatched students may not have the opportunity to express their motives in order to achieve a flow experience as a function of their relevant motives, this finding is not surprising. In fact, in the Shuper et al. (2004) study described earlier, mismatched people in both countries seem to have higher levels of unrealistic optimism than their counterparts, and exhibited what the investigators interpreted as anxiety and feelings of a lack of freedom in the workplace, as compared to matched participants. These results suggest that living in a culture where the normative way of coping with uncertainty does not match the individual's preferred way of coping with uncertainty may have negative effects on mismatched individuals. This is likely due to the fact that mismatched people will likely engage in everyday activity (e.g., educational and industrial systems) which do not provide them with the opportunity to express positive sources of motivation.

AFFECTIVE EXPERIENCES AS A FUNCTION OF UNCERTAINTY ORIENTATION, ACHIEVEMENT-RELATED MOTIVES, AND CULTURE

Figure 3.5 is an illustration of the full formal model of uncertainty orientation, based on Sorrentino et al. (2003), that takes account of sources of motivation that are relevant in specific situations, such as achievement-related motives in achievement-oriented situations. However, where situational uncertainty was shown in the original model in Figure 3.2, societal uncertainty has been substituted. As can be seen in Figure 3.5, the person who would be in flow (e.g., excited) if the situation was an achievement-oriented one is the success-oriented person (SO, where the motive to succeed, Ms, is greater than the motive to avoid failure, Maf) in a matched situation. The person in anti-flow (e.g., afraid) would be the failure-threatened person (FT, where Maf > Ms) in a matched situation. Those in an mismatched situation would be in non-flow, and either in a state of

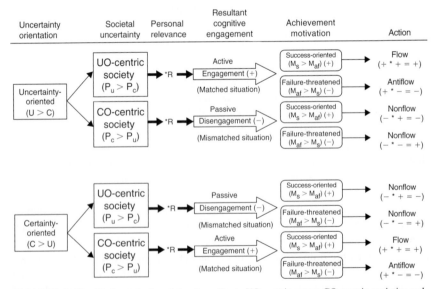

FIGURE 3.5　Mathematical model as it applies to UO-centric versus CO-centric societies and including achievement-related motives.

negative passive affect (e.g., bored) if they were SOs, or positive passive affect (e.g., relieved) if they were FTs.

As predicted from the formal theory, in matched achievement-oriented situations, SOs should perform better than FTs because of flow and anti-flow, but in mismatched situations, FTs may actually perform better than SOs because of the reverse effects of non-flow experiences (e.g., relief versus boredom, respectively). These performance differences due to achievement-related motives in matched and mismatched situations have been observed in all studies shown in Table 3.1 that deal with performance. Extrapolating to the societal level, then, to the extent that one's society shapes achievement-oriented situations in a direction that matches one's uncertainty orientation, we should expect affective experiences in everyday achievement activity to vary accordingly. Thus, in Japan we would expect COs to have the greatest number of flow experiences if they are also success-oriented, and the greatest number of anti-flow experiences if they are failure-threatened. Here SOs should also perform better than FTs. UOs, however, should be in non-flow, with FTs having more positive passive experiences and performing better than SOs, who should have more negative passive experiences. In Canada, we would expect the UOs to be like the COs in Japan, and the COs to be like the UOs in Japan. In other words, there should be a complete reversal of effects as a function of culture, not just a moderation or enhancement of effects by culture.

Although plans for this research are currently underway, the above hypotheses remain to be tested. We do, however, have some auxiliary data from our current research that leads to the intriguing possibility that we are correct in our assumption. These data are part of a larger study by Nezlek et al. (in press) and use the same participants that were used in the study by Sorrentino et al. (2008). In the Nezlek et al. study, participants at four sites (two in the United States, one in Canada, and one in Japan) described their self-esteem and mood, as well as the events that occurred each day for a 2-week period. Multilevel random coefficient modeling analyses found that the self-esteem of Japanese participants changed more in reaction to daily social events (both positive and negative) than it did for North American participants. For negative social events, the Japanese were more reactive in terms of depressed mood than North Americans, whereas they were less reactive in terms of positive affect. In contrast, the Japanese were less reactive to negative achievement events than North Americans in terms of positive affect and anxious mood. These results highlight the greater sensitivity of the self-esteem of the Japanese to social concerns compared to North Americans (see Ho, 1976; Cohen & Hoshino-Browne, 2005; Heine, 2005), and the greater affective sensitivity of North Americans to daily events, particularly in reaction to failure in achievement domains (see Heine et al., 1999). This is an important finding, suggesting domain-specificity, not merely more situational reactivity by the collectivistic Japanese.

Using only the participants from Canada and Japan, where measures of uncertainty orientation and achievement-related motives were also administered,

Sorrentino et al. (2007) addressed the issue of individual differences in affective and self-esteem reactions as a function of culture and success or failure at achievement-oriented activity. More specifically, they examined whether there would be differences in these reactions as a function of uncertainty orientation, achievement-related motives, and country. Multilevel random coefficient modeling analyses revealed significant three factor interactions on all measures of positive and negative mood as well as self-esteem for positive achievement events, but not for negative achievement events.

Figures 3.6 and 3.7 illustrate the significant three factor interactions in differences for mood (where only positive mood is shown) and self-esteem, respectively.

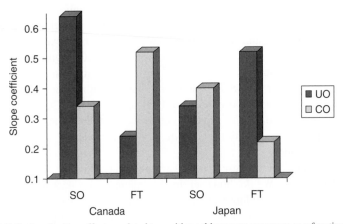

FIGURE 3.6   Positive affect as related to positive achievement outcomes as a function of achievement-related motives (SO or FT), uncertainty orientation (UO or CO), and country.

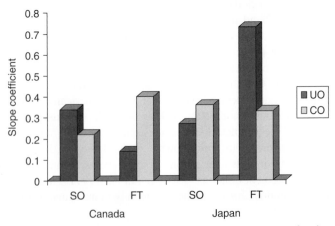

FIGURE 3.7   Self-esteem as related to positive achievement outcomes as a function of achievement-related motives (SO or FT), uncertainty orientation (UO or CO), and country.

The most striking findings related to the theory of uncertainty orientation are the patterns of interaction related to positive mood, positive active mood, and positive passive mood for positive achievement events. In all of these measures, when the situation is matched (i.e., UOs in Canada, COs in Japan), success-oriented persons have higher positive mood than failure-threatened persons (FTs). In mismatched situations (i.e., COs in Canada, UOs in Japan), it is the FTs who show higher positive mood than the SOs. Although the formal model makes no predictions regarding affect *following* successful engagement in achievement activity, this is exactly the interaction predicted by the theory of uncertainty orientation for performance as a function of engaging in achievement-oriented activity, as shown in Figure 3.5. Apparently, for those engaged (i.e., matched), succeeding at achievement-oriented activities is associated more with positive mood in those that strive to attain it (SOs) than by those who prefer to avoid it (FT). Conversely, for those who are disengaged from the activity (i.e., mismatched), those who would normally be fearful if they were engaged are more positive than those who would prefer achievement-oriented activity more engaging to them. The significant pattern of interaction for self-esteem associated with positive achievement events follows the same pattern of interaction. It is also interesting that only the UO/FTs in Japan show higher SE coefficients than the Canadian participants.

The significant three-way interactions for negative active, negative passive, and total negative mood associated with positive achievement events are not illustrated here. However, the one outstanding finding is that mismatched FT participants (i.e., UOs in Japan, COs in Canada) show the least amount of negative mood as compared to the other three combinations within each country. This may be consistent with the theory because of the expectation that it is in mismatched situations that FTs should be least anxious. To also succeed in these situations may be additionally rewarding. This possibility is consistent with the dynamics of success and failure at achievement-oriented activity over time, but is too complex to be presented here.

For negative achievement events, there are no significant three-way interactions on any of the mood measures, nor self-esteem. From what is reported in Nezlek et al. (in press), one might have expected more robust differences in negative mood as a function of achievement-related motives and uncertainty orientation in the Canadian versus Japanese participants, but this was not the case. One wonders to what extent the country level differences found in Nezlek et al. and others are simply a function of uncontrolled variation in relevant underlying motives such as achievement and affiliation motivation. Note, for example, that when we control for achievement-related motives, there are no noticeable country level effects in Figures 3.6 and 3.7. Any differences in affect or self-esteem as a function of country that are associated with positive achievement events are subsumed by the higher order interaction with uncertainty orientation, achievement-related motives, and country. We expect that this will also be true for social events when we include affiliation-related motives in our future research.

That is, so-called country level differences will be subsumed by a higher order uncertainty orientation $\times$ affiliation-related motives $\times$ country interaction. Although much of what we are saying here is conjecture, the data are sufficiently intriguing to carry on this research program and, hopefully, stimulate others to begin examining individual differences within and across countries.

SO, WHAT ABOUT CHINA?

It must be mentioned that we have collected some data comparing Canadian and Chinese children (Szeto et al., 2007). The results were not what we expected, but very intriguing. Here, 507 Chinese and Canadian children in grades 3–6 were tested. After being assessed for their uncertainty orientation, participants were administered measures of self-perceptions for cognitive ability, social competence, behavioral competence, and global self-worth. In addition, the children were rated by their teachers for their language and mathematics ability, and for learning problems. The children were also rated by their peers using the Revised Class Play (Masten et al., 1985). Overall, the results indicated that, in both countries, those who were UO were better adjusted than their CO peers, evincing higher self-ratings, higher teacher-rated academic achievement, and fewer learning problems. Based on our data comparing Japanese university students with Canadian university students as cited above, we would have expected Canadian children to be more UO and Chinese children to be more CO. We would also have expected CO children in China and UO children in Canada to have more positive self, teacher, and peer ratings. This has created considerable uncertainty for us in terms of what Japanese children may be like and what Chinese university students might be like, not to mention how all of this fits into our model. At present, we can only leave you with the same uncertainty.

CONCLUSIONS

Putting the results from the initial stages of our research together, it appears that uncertainty orientation may well be a critical individual difference variable that has important implications for examining differences between and within cultures. Within cultures, the data from Shuper et al. (2004) suggest that people whose predominant style of coping with uncertainty matches that of their society have a better sense of self, perceive more freedom and less anxiety in work situations, and are more realistic about what their future holds than those whose coping style does not match their society's values or beliefs. The results from Sorrentino et al. (2008) suggest that matched individuals also are more actively involved and have greater flow and anti-flow emotional experiences than their mismatched counterparts. Results from Sorrentino et al. (2007) indicate that examining informational and affective measures such as uncertainty orientation and achievement-related motives at the individual level will contribute greatly to our understanding of how culture may influence the motivation, persistence, performance, and affective experiences of its members.

Although this is all extremely encouraging, we have only "scratched the surface" so to speak, and much work needs to be done. We are greatly excited by our current ongoing research that is bringing affiliation-related motives (e.g., affiliation motivation, fear of social rejection) into the fold to examine reactions to social events in interaction with country and uncertainty orientation. Our immediate next step is to examine all of this in other countries such as China and the United States, and to demonstrate that when one controls for the uncertainty of the situation, and relevant motives, people will behave similarly, regardless of country. In the distant future, we also see a full blown test of our model, which includes the dynamical interaction of repeated occasions of success and failure at achievement and social activities (see Sorrentino et al., 2003).

Controversy currently rages regarding whether individualism and collectivism truly distinguish Eastern and Western societies (e.g., Matsumoto, 1999; Oyserman et al., 2002) or whether it may be more meaningful to speak of an independent versus interdependent self, or whether people have or don't have self-esteem (see Ho, 1976; Cohen & Hoshino-Browne, 2005; Heine, 2005 and Chapters 8 and 16 of this volume). A plausible alternative explanation is that East–West differences might be a function of how these societies cope with uncertainty, and how this shapes the behavior of its constituent members.

ACKNOWLEDGMENTS

Research reported in this manuscript was supported by various Social Sciences and Humanities Research Council of Canada grants, and partially supported by a grant for cooperative research in graduate schools from the Japanese government, awarded to the third author. Our thanks to Pei-Shiuan L. Lin, Yang Ye, Susan Sergeant, Michael Bond, and Jan Hofer for their helpful comments regarding this manuscript.

REFERENCES

Arrindell, W. A., Hatzichristou, C., Wensink, J., Rosenberg, E., van Twillert, B., Stedema, J., & Meijer, D. (1997). Dimensions of national culture as predictors of cross-national differences in subjective well-being. *Personality and Individual Differences, 23*, 37–53.

Atkinson, J. W. (Ed.) (1958). *Motives in fantasy, action, and society*. Princeton: Van Nostrand.

Atkinson, J. W., & Feather, N. T. (1966). *A theory of achievement motivation*. New York: Wiley.

Atkinson, J. W., Raynor, J. O. (Eds.) (1974). *Motivation and achievement*. Washington, DC: Winston and Sons.

Benedict, R. (1946). *The chrysanthemum and the sword: Patterns of Japanese culture*. Boston: Houghton Mifflin Company.

Bowonder, B., & Miyake, T. (1992). A model of corporate innovation management: some recent high tech innovations in Japan. *R & D Management, 22*, 319–336.

Brouwers, M. C., & Sorrentino, R. M. (1993). Uncertainty orientation and protection motivation theory: The role of individual differences in health compliance. *Journal of Personality and Social Psychology*, *65*, 102–112.

Brouwers, M. S., Sorrentino, R. M., Roney, C. J. R., & Hanna, S. E. (2004). Predicting the impact of trauma disclosure on physiological responses: How cognitive style challenges our ideas about coping. *Journal of Social and Clinical Psychology*, *23*, 697–715.

Cherry, F., & Byrne, D. (1977). Authoritarianism. In T. Blass (Ed.), *Personality variables in social behavior* (pp. 109–133). HillsDale, NJ: Erlbaum.

Cohen, D., & Hoshino-Browne, E. (2005). Insider and outsider perspectives on the self and social world. In R. M. Sorrentino, D. Cohen, J. M. Olson, & M. P. Zanna (Eds.), *Cultural and Social Behaviour: The Ontario Symposium*, Vol. 10, pp. 49–76.

Csikszentmihalyi, M. (1975). *Beyond boredom and anxiety*. San Francisco: Jossey-Bass.

Driscoll, D. M., Hamilton, D. L., & Sorrentino, R. M. (1991). Uncertainty orientation and recall of descriptive information. *Personality and Social Psychology Bulletin*, *17*, 494–500.

Ellington, L. (1992). *Education in the Japanese life cycle: Implications for the United States*. Lewiston, NY: The Edwin Mellen Press.

Fiddle, S. (Ed.) (1980). *Uncertainty: Behavioral and social dimensions*. New York: Praeger.

Fromm, E. (1947). *Man for himself: An inquiry into the psychology of ethics*. New York: Rinehart.

Guo, Y. (2005). *Asia's educational edge: Current achievements in Japan, Korea, Taiwan, China, and India*. Lanham, MD: Lexington Books.

Haynes, G. A., Olson, J. M., Sorrentino, R. M., Szeto, A. C. H., Wirkki, J. S., & Grigg, M. C. (2007). The effects of temporal framing on counterfactual thinking and self-appraisal: An individual differences perspective. *Social Cognition*, *25*, 339–366.

Haynes, G. A., Sorrentino, R. M., Olson, J. M., Szeto, A. C. H., Wirkki, J. S., & Grigg, M. C. (2007). The role of individual differences and temporal self-appraisal in counterfactual thinking. *Social Cognition*, *25*(3), 339–366.

Heine, S. J. (2005). Constructing good selves in Japan and North America. In R. M. Sorrentino, D. Cohen, J. M. Olson, & M. P. Zanna (Eds.), *Cultural and Social Behaviour: The Ontario Symposium* (Vol. 10, pp. 95–116).

Heine, S. J., Lehman, D. R., Markus, H. R., & Kitayama, S. (1999). Is there a universal need for positive self-regard?. *Psychological Review*, *106*, 766–794.

Herbig, P. (1995). *Innovation Japanese style: A cultural and historical perspective*. Westport, CT: Quorum Books.

Ho, D. Y. F. (1976). On the concept of face. *American Journal of Sociology*, *81*, 867–884.

Hodson, G., & Sorrentino, R. M. (1997). Groupthink and uncertainty orientation: Personality differences in reactivity to the group situation. *Group Dynamics: Theory, Research, and Practice*, *1*, 144–155.

Hodson, G., & Sorrentino, R. M. (2001). Just who favors the ingroup? Personality differences in reactions to uncertainty in the minimal group paradigm. *Group Dynamics: Theory, Research and Practice*, *2*, 92–101.

Hodson, G., & Sorrentino, R. M. (2003). Uncertainty Orientation in the Group Context: Categorization Effects on Persuasive Message Processing. *Journal of Social Psychology*, *143*(3), 212–291.

Hofstede, G. (1980). *Culture's consequences: International differences in work related values*. Beverly Hills, CA: Sage Publications.

Hofstede, G. (1991). *Cultures and organizations: Software of the mind*. London, UK: McGraw Hill.

Huber, G. L., Sorrentino, R. M., Davidson, M., Epplier, R., & Roth, J. (1992). Uncertainty orientation and cooperative learning: Individual differences within and across cultures. *Learning and Individual Differences*, *4*, 1–24.

Janis, I. L. (1972). *Victims of groupthink: A psychological study of foreign-policy decisions and fiascos*. Oxford, England: Houghton Mifflin.

Kagan, J. (1972). Motives and development. *Journal of Personality and Social Psychology*, *22*, 51–66.

Masten, A., Morison, P., & Pelligrini, D. (1985). A revised class play method of peer assessment. *Development Psychology*, *21*, 523–533.

Matsumoto, D. (1989). Cultural influences on the perceptions of emotion. *Journal of Cross-Cultural Psychology, 20,* 92–105.

Matsumoto, D. (1999). Culture and self: An empirical assessment of Markus and Kitayama's theory of independent and interdependent self-construals. *Asian Journal of Social Psychology, 2,* 289–310.

Nakane, I. (2006). Silence and politeness in intercultural communication in university seminars. *Journal of Pragmatics, 38,* 1811–1835.

Nezlek, J. B., Sorrentino, R. M., Yasunaga, S., Otsubo, Y., Allen, M., & Shuper, P. (in press). A cross-cultural study of relationships between daily events and daily well-being. *Journal of Cross Cultural Psychology.*

Oyserman, D., Coon, H. M., & Kemmelmeier, M. (2002). Rethinking individualism and collectivism: Evaluation of theoretical assumptions and meta-analyses. *Psychological Bulletin, 128,* 3–72.

Petty, R. W., & Cacioppo, J. T. (1986). *Communication and persuasion: Central and peripheral routes to attitude change.* New York: Sringer-Verlag.

Pickett, C. L., Silver, M. D., & Brewer, M. B. (2002). The impact of assimilation and differentiation needs on perceived group importance and judgements of ingroup size. *Personality and Social Psychology Bulletin, 28,* 546–558.

Raynor, J. O., & McFarlin, D. B. (1986). Motivation and the self-system. In R. M. Sorrentino & E. T. Higgins (Eds.), *The handbook of motivation and cognition: Foundations of social behavior* (Vol. 1, pp. 315–349). New York: The Guilford Press.

Roney, C. J. R., & Sorrentino, R. M. (1995). Reducing self-discrepancies or maintaining self-congruence? Uncertainty orientation, self-regulation, and performance. *Journal of Personality and Social Psychology, 68,* 485–487.

Roney, C. J. R., & Sorrentino, R. M. (1997). Uncertainty orientation, the self, and others: Individual differences in values and social comparison. *Canadian Journal of Behavioural Sciences, 27,* 157–170.

Russell, J. A. (1980). A circumplex model of affect. *Journal of Personality and Social Psychology, 39,* 1161–1178.

Ryan, A. M., McFarland, L., Baron, H., & Page, R. (1999). An international look at selection practices: Nation and culture as explanations for variability in practice. *Personnel Psychology, 52,* 359–391.

Shane, S., Venkataraman, S., & MacMillan, I. (1995). Cultural differences in innovation championing strategies. *Journal of Management, 21,* 931–952.

Shuper, P. A., & Sorrentino, R. M. (2004). Minority versus majority influence and uncertainty orientation: Processing persuasive messages based on situational expectancies. *Journal of Social Psychology, 144,* 127–147.

Shuper, P. A., Sorrentino, R. M., Otsubo, Y., Hodson, G., & Walker, A. M. (2004). A theory of uncertainty orientation: Implications for the study of individual differences within and across cultures. *Journal of Cross-Cultural Psychology, 35,* 460–481.

Sorrentino, R. M., & Hewitt, E. C. (1984). The uncertainty-reducing properties of achievement tasks revisited. *Journal of Personality and Social Psychology, 47,* 884–899.

Sorrentino, R. M., & Roney, C. J. R. (1986). Uncertainty orientation, achievement-related motives, and task diagnosticity as determinants of task performance. *Social Cognition: A Journal of Social, Personality, and Developmental Psychology, 4,* 420–436.

Sorrentino, R. M., & Roney, C. J. R. (2000). *The uncertain mind: Individual differences in facing the unknown.* Philadelphia, PA: Psychology Press.

Sorrentino, R. M., Short, J. C., & Raynor, J. G. (1984). Uncertainty orientation: Implications for affective and cognitive views of achievement behavior. *Journal of Personality and Social Psychology, 46,* 189–206.

Sorrentino, R. M., Bobocel, C. R., Gitta, M. Z., Olson, J. M., & Hewitt, E. C. (1988). Uncertainty orientation and persuasion: Individual differences in the effects of personal relevance on social judgments. *Journal of Personality and Social Psychology, 55,* 357–371.

Sorrentino, R. M., Hanna, S. E., & Roney, C. J. R. (1992a). A manual for scoring need for uncertainty. In C. P. Smith (Ed.), *Motivation and personality: Handbook of thematic content analysis* (pp. 428–439). Cambridge, UK: Cambridge University Press.

Sorrentino, R. M., Hewitt, E. C., & Raso-Knott, P. A. (1992b). Risk-taking in games of chance and skill: Individual differences in affective and information value. *Journal of Personality and Social Psychology, 62*, 522–533.

Sorrentino, R. M., Roney, C. J. R., & Hanna, S. (1992c). Uncertainty orientation. In C. P. Smith, J. W. Atkinson, & D. C. McClelland (Eds.), *The handbook of thematic analysis* (pp. 419–427). New York: Cambridge University Press.

Sorrentino, R. M., Holmes, J. G., Hanna, S. E., & Sharp, A. (1995). Uncertainty orientation and trust: Individual differences in close relationships. *Journal of Personality and Social Psychology, 68*, 314–327.

Sorrentino, R. M., Brouwers, M. C., Hanna, S. E., & Roney, C. J. R. (1996). The nature of the test taking situation: Informational and affective influences on intelligence test performance. *Learning and Individual Differences, 8*, 105–120.

Sorrentino, R. M., Smithson, M., Hodson, G., Roney, C. J. R., & Walker, A. M. (2003). The theory of uncertainty orientation: A mathematical reformulation. *Journal of Mathematical Psychology, 47*, 132–149.

Sorrentino, R. M., Nezlek, J. B., Yasunaga, S., Kouhara, S., Otsubo, Y., & Shuper, P. (2008). Uncertainty orientation and emotional responses: Individual differences within and across cultures. *Journal of Cross-Cultural Psychology, 39*, 129–146.

Sorrentino, R. M., Seligman, C., & Battista, M. (2007). Optimal distinctiveness, values, and uncertainty orientation: Individual differences on perceptions of self and group identity. *Self and Identity, 6*(4), 322–339.

Stigler, J. W., Lee, S. Y., & Stevenson, H. C. (1987). Mathematics classrooms in Japan, Taiwan, and the United States. *Child Development. Special Issue: Schools and Development, 58*, 1272–1285.

Szeto, A. C. H. (2005). *Compensatory conviction as a function of uncertainty orientation, culture, and explicit and implicit self-esteem*. Unpublished Master of Arts thesis, University of Western Ontario, London, Ontario, Canada.

Szeto, A. C. H., Wang, Z., Chen, X., & Sorrentino, R. M. (2008). Uncertainty regulation and adjustment: An exploration of individual differences in Chinese and Canadian children. Manuscript submitted for review.

Tajfel, H., & Turner, J. C. (2004). The social identity theory of intergroup behavior. In J. T. Jost & J. Sidanius (Eds.), *Political psychology; Key readings in social psychology* (pp. 276–293). New York, NY: Psychology Press.

Triandis, H. C. (1989). The self and social behavior in differing cultural contexts. *Psychological Review, 96*, 506–520.

Triandis, H. C. (1990). Theoretical concepts that are applicable to the analysis of ethnocentrism. In R. W. Brislin (Ed.), *Applied cross-cultural psychology* (pp. 34–55). Newbury Park, CA: Sage Publications.

Trope, Y. (1975). Seeking information about one's own ability as a determinant of choice among tasks. *Journal of Personality and Social Psychology, 32*, 1004–1013.

Vishwanath, A. (2003). Comparing online information effects: A cross-cultural comparison of online information and uncertainty avoidance. *Communication Research, 30*, 579–598.

Walker, A. M., & Sorrentino, R. M. (2000). Information processing or avoidance motivation? Motivation for control in moderate and non-depressives as a function of uncertainty orientation. *Personality and Social Psychology Bulletin, 26*, 436–447.

Weiner, B. (1972). *Theories of motivation: From mechanism to cognition*. Chicago: Markham.

Weisz, J. R., Rothbaum, F. M., & Blackburn, T. C. (1984). Standing out and standing in: The psychology of control in America and Japan. *American Psychologist, 39*, 955–969.

Yasunaga, S., & Kouhara, S. (1995). Uncertainty orientation: Its measurement and validity. *Bulletin of Faculty of Literature* (Vol. 5–6, pp. 35–45). Kurume, Japan, Kurume University: Human Sciences.

Yasunaga, S. & Kouhara, S. (2008). *The role of uncertainty orientation in health protection behavior under conditions of threat and uncertainty*. Manuscript in preparation.

4

IMPLICIT THEISM

ERIC LUIS UHLMANN*, T. ANDREW POEHLMAN[†]
AND JOHN A. BARGH[‡]

*Northwestern University, Evanston, IL, USA
[†]Southern Methodist University, University Park, TX, USA
[‡]Yale University, New Haven, CT, USA

Religion is one of the great human universals and a uniquely difficult phenomenon to explain. Today, as during most (if not all) of human history, just about everyone is a theist who believes in supernatural agents such as gods and souls (Greeley, 1991; Gallup & Linday, 1999; Norris & Inglehart, 2004). Human communities isolated for thousands of years each developed a religious worldview with common elements (Atran, 2002; Tremlin, 2006). Evidence that prehistoric peoples buried flowers and other symbolic items alongside departed group members further testifies to the deep roots of belief in an afterlife (Schwartz, 1998; Hayden, 1993). Yet current accounts of theism, while often compelling, remain largely speculative (for reviews, see Atran, 2002; Wilson, 2002a; Bloom, 2005; Bering, 2006; Dennett, 2006; Tremlin, 2006). This question of ultimate origins (e.g., whether religiosity evolved to address a specific adaptive problem or emerged as a side effect of other evolved human characteristics) is unlikely to be resolved in the foreseeable future.

Rather than to attempt a comprehensive theory of the ultimate origins of religious faith, the present chapter discusses evidence for two classes of empirically supported psychological contributors: *cognitive defaults* and *existential needs*. Cognitive defaults evident in young children predispose children and adults alike to believe in supernatural agents. And religion addresses deep existential issues, for example, the fear of death, that are endemic to the human condition but which materialist philosophies (i.e., belief systems that deny the existence of supernatural forces) have difficulty addressing. Both of these sets of variables exert a profound yet largely implicit (i.e., intuitive, unconscious) influence on the development, content, transmission, and maintenance of religious faith. Theistic cognition is so deeply ingrained that even atheists, agnostics, and less religious people display implicit responses consistent with religious beliefs.

The implicit roots of theistic cognition help account for its universality. Cultures separated by great distances and natural barriers nevertheless developed shared religious beliefs such as the tendency to attribute to human beings souls that survive physical death. As we will argue in greater depth later, because people intuitively distinguish between intentional agents and physical bodies (Bloom, 2004), and have difficulty mentally simulating their own nonexistence (Bering, 2006), religions across the world include the concept of an immortal soul. Belief systems that essentially characterize humans as machines made of meat violate common intuitions and face difficulties gaining adherents (Bloom, 2004). Universal aspects of how the mind works therefore contribute to certain shared aspects of religious faiths across the world.

Indeed, there are fascinating historical examples of parallel religious beliefs in different cultures that are potentially attributable to basic human cognitive and emotional tendencies. Historians and anthropologists have marveled at the similarities between the cultures of the ancient Mayans and Egyptians, who on separate continents evolved similar rituals aimed at dealing with the existential fear of death endemic to the human condition. Indeed, the vast majority of the world's major religions incorporate beliefs addressing such universal existential needs (Becker, 1973; Bering, 2002a; Greenberg et al., in press).

While properties of mind place limiting conditions on what sorts of moral beliefs may characterize a successful religion, the latitude of potential acceptance is obviously large enough to encompass both the Catholic aversion to material gain and the Protestant conviction that the accumulation of wealth through hard work is a spiritual calling (Weber, 1904/1958; Sanchez-Burks, 2002, 2005). In human populations developing based on complex and interacting geographic, ecological, economic, and historical factors, cultural beliefs will ultimately reach different "equilibriums" (Cohen, 2001). In other words, human communities will reach different shared understandings about what to think, how to behave, and expectations about how others will behave and react to one's own actions. Once reached, a cultural equilibrium is perpetuated by the mutually contingent judgments and actions of the individual members of that culture. For example, in historically Protestant cultures characterized by an enhanced commitment to the merit principle, both employers and job applicants know that engaging in nepotistic hiring practices can result in costs to one's social reputation. As a result, decision makers in such cultures are comparatively reluctant to hire incompetent friends and relatives, which helps maintain negative cultural associations with nepotism (Zurcher et al., 1965; Trompenaars & Hampden-Turner, 1993).

This process of cultural persistence is aided and abetted by the readiness with which people act based on simple associations learned from the surrounding cultural context (Greenwald & Banaji, 1995; Banaji, 2001; Rudman, 2004). People tend to act based on common cultural associations whether or not they consciously endorse them. For example, even well-intentioned White Americans accidentally shoot unarmed Black civilians in police simulations in which they are obliged to respond quickly, consistent with the cultural stereotype linking Black Americans and crime (Correll et al., 2002; Greenwald et al., 2003). As we will discuss in more depth later, culturally specific theistic beliefs such as the Protestant link between work and divine salvation can also operate in this way. For example, even less religious and non-Protestant Americans respond to the implicit activation of concepts related to divine salvation by working harder (Uhlmann et al., 2007). Thus, another aspect of implicit cognition – the tendency to act based on shared mental associations – can help explain the persistence of more idiosyncratic theistic beliefs *within* a culture.

The relationship between religious and cultural values is of course both complex and bidirectional. Culture shapes religion, such as when Buddhist beliefs and practices were fused with local values as they spread through Asia. And religion shapes culture, such as with the effects of early Protestant immigration on contemporary American attitudes toward work. And – in our primary thesis – both religion and culture are profoundly shaped by fundamental aspects of human psychology: cognitive defaults and existential needs that propel human beings toward belief in supernatural agents and shape our conceptions of what such agents may be like.

BRIEF NOTE ON TERMINOLOGY

The term *implicit* generally refers to cognitions that are intuitive, spontaneous, effortless, unintentional, uncontrollable, and/or inaccessible to conscious awareness. Each of these characteristics has been identified as a key aspect of implicit mental processes (Nisbett & Wilson, 1977; Bargh, 1994; Greenwald & Banaji, 1995; Wegner & Bargh, 1998; Banaji, 2001; Wilson, 2002b). However, it is relatively rare for any mental process to be purely explicit or purely implicit (Bargh, 1994; Wegner & Bargh, 1998). Therefore, we often use the term implicit in reference to cognitions that are "intuitive, spontaneous, effortless, and which do not *require* a conscious intention on the part of the social perceiver in order to occur" (Uhlmann et al., in press, p. 3). We assume that in many cases, the person in question does have some awareness of the outputs of her implicit cognitions (e.g., perceiving a face in the clouds, viewing the natural world as designed, disgust at heretical arguments), though lacking awareness of their origins.

The terms "theistic" and "theism" are used to refer to belief in supernatural agents, including both gods and souls. While theism is generally used in reference to belief in God or gods, in practice virtually all religions combine belief in gods and souls. (Although some forms of Buddhism lacks official, immortal gods, in practice the Buddha is often treated as a quasi-deity; Slone, 2004). In many traditional religions, disembodied souls are a type of deity (e.g., as in ancestor worship). Due to this reality, and because highly similar psychological processes contribute to belief in nonmaterial yet agentic deities and nonmaterial yet agentic souls, we consider both as examples of implicit theism.

We now turn to the first category of recently identified contributors to the cultural universality of theistic cognition: cognitive defaults evident among young children and infants.

COGNITIVE DEFAULTS

A number of cognitive defaults present early in life implicitly shape theistic cognition. The cognitive science of religion has identified a number of such biases, among them implicit dualism (which separates a person's mind from her body), hypersensitive agency detection (which encourages belief in bodiless deities), simulation constraints (which contribute to belief in an immortal soul), promiscuous teleology (which creates a predisposition toward creationist explanations of how the natural world came to be), and the "curse of knowledge" (which lays the groundwork for belief in an omniscient deity).

Implicit Dualism

As Bloom (2004, p. 191) has observed, "We do not feel as if we *are* bodies; we feel as if we *occupy* them." Even children and infants intuitively distinguish between the physical and psychological. Implicit dualism is the ultimate basis of judgments of intentionality, morality, as well as religious beliefs (Bloom, 2004, 2006; Kuhlmeier et al., 2004).

An established indirect means of assessing infant cognition is the expectancy violation paradigm. This approach uses the length of time that infants look at something to assess whether they find it surprising. The more that an infant looks at something, the more it presumably violates their expectations (Spelke et al., 1992; Wynn, 1992). Woodward (1998) found that infants expected a human hand to pursue an intentional goal. Infants watched either a hand or a rod consistently move toward either a teddy bear or multi-colored ball. When the locations of the two toys were switched, infants were unsurprised that the human hand reached for the same toy as before. But they *were* surprised when the hand went to the same location as before even though the toys had switched places. This pattern of results was not observed for the rod. This suggests that infants expect humans, but not inanimate objects, to act intentionally or purposefully.

Other work suggests that infants are capable of rudimentary judgments of blame. In one study, when an adult began to hand them a toy and then accidentally dropped it, 9-, 12-, and 18-month-old infants reacted less impatiently than when the adult offered it and then intentionally pulled it away (Behne et al., 2005; for a similar finding with chimpanzees, see Call et al., 2004). The ability to attribute intentions to others enables judgments of blame and praise, since individuals are considered most responsible for actions that they intended.

Hypersensitive Agency Detection

In addition to implicitly distinguishing between bodies and souls, humans are predisposed to perceive agency not only in ourselves (Wegner & Wheatley, 1999; Wegner, 2002; Aarts et al., 2004, 2006) but also in the world around us (Guthrie, 1993; Barrett, 2000). Because the costs of failing to perceive a predator are much higher than perceiving a predator when none is there, humans have a hypersensitive agency detection device (Barrett, 2000) that leads us to perceive lurking danger in the woods and faces in the clouds (not to mention the Virgin Mary in a potato chip and Mother Teresa's face in a cinnamon roll; Guthrie, 1993).

Both adults and infants automatically attribute intentions to objects that move as if self-propelled (Heider & Simmel, 1944; Mandler & McDonough, 1993; Gergely et al., 1995; Johnson et al., 1998; Bloom & Veres, 1999; Kuhlmeier et al., 2003). In one classic study of agency detection, adult participants watched a movie in which geometric shapes interacted (Heider & Simmel, 1944). When asked to describe what they saw, virtually all of the participants described the geometric shapes as having intentions and goals. For example, a small triangle and large triangle were described as fighting for the love of a circle, with the small triangle eventually beating out the large triangle. Even though the geometric shapes did not look like any known agent, participants nonetheless perceived them as having intentions. In a remarkable study of infant cognition, 12-month olds watched a yellow circle jump a barrier to get to a red circle. Later, when the barrier was removed, the infants were surprised when the yellow circle did not go directly toward the red circle (Gergely et al., 1995). This suggests that humans are automatically disposed to attribute agency, even in cases in which the purported agent bears no resemblance to existing animal species.

While implicit dualism leads us to anticipate disembodied souls, hypersensitive agency detection disposes us to see agency all around us. Human beings may be implicit animists predisposed to perceive supernatural agents intervening in our lives and environments.

Simulation Constraints

A belief in a soul that outlives the physical body is among the most widely endorsed religious concepts around the world. A full 96% of Americans believe that human beings have souls. Even in the relatively secular nations of Western Europe, most people believe in souls (e.g., 75% of the population of the Netherlands, 73% of Austrians, 60% of Belgians, 70% of Britons, 55% of the French, and 81% of Swedes; Germans are a notable exception with only 37% believing in souls; Norris & Inglehart, 2004). Is this notion mostly culturally learned, or are humans predisposed to believe they and others possess a soul? One means of addressing this issue is to compare young children's beliefs about souls to those of older children and adults. To the extent that the notion of a soul is culturally learned, adults and older children should be more likely than younger children to evidence a belief in souls.

Bering and Bjorklund (2004) presented kindergartners, elementary school children, and adults with a puppet show during which an alligator ate a mouse. Kindergartners believed that the dead mouse no longer needed food or water and that its brain had stopped functioning. But they thought that the mouse still possessed emotions, desires, and epistemic states such as thinking and knowing. Kindergartners were significantly more likely than elementary school children and adults to believe that the mouse still had certain psychological states. For example, kindergartners were twice as likely as elementary school children to believe that the mouse retained epistemic states. Thus, a belief in the afterlife appears a psychological default rather than a culturally acquired notion – if the latter were true, elementary school children and adults should have been more likely than kindergartners to attribute psychological states to a dead being. Kindergartners rarely made any explicit religious references but nonetheless implicitly evidenced afterlife beliefs.

Similarly, Gimenez-Dasi et al. (2005) found that 3-year-old children believed that both God and their best friend would never die, whereas 5-year-olds thought that while their best friend was mortal God was immortal. Again, the cognitive default among young children is that agents are not mortal. As Tremlin (2006) has argued, in some cases "we do not project human-like qualities onto gods but god-like qualities onto humans."

Such responses are partly based on young children's lack of knowledge and experience. However, they also reflect constraints on the ability of children (and to a lesser degree adults) to mentally simulate the experience of not existing (Bering, 2002b, 2006; Bering & Bjorklund, 2004). While virtually everyone has experienced not needing to urinate or eat food, it is impossible to experience not existing. As a result, when people attempt to mentally simulate what it would be like to be dead, they have great difficulty doing so, and often end up attributing states such as thinking and knowing to dead agents. This difficulty in imagining not being alive lays the foundation for explicit afterlife beliefs that develop later in life.

Promiscuous Teleology

Other work suggests an implicit predisposition toward creationism. Young children display promiscuous teleology (Kelemen, 1999, 2004; Kelemen & DiYanni, 2005). That is, they automatically make attributions regarding intentionality when it comes to natural objects. Children believe that natural objects were made by agents for a reason. Kelemen (1999) found that when children and adults were asked what features of fictional prehistoric animals (e.g., a "cryptoclidus") and natural objects (e.g., a pointy rock) were for, only children attributed a function to the natural objects. For example, they believed that the rock was pointy so that people would not sit on it. Only 13% of adults thought that nonliving natural objects (i.e., a pointy rock, still pond, sand dune, and green stone) were made for a purpose, but 78% of first graders did. Evans (2001) asked the children of creationists and noncreationists whether humans, God, or evolution had created animals and the natural world. Children were significantly more likely to make theistic attributions than their parents. Notably, even the children of *noncreationist* parents believed that God had made animals and the natural world. Kelemen (1999) argued that children readily give purpose-based explanations because the human mind is designed for reading intentions (see also Tomasello et al., 2005).

Additional work indicates that even infants are implicitly predisposed to see order as created by intentional agents (Newman et al., 2006). As in the studies on agency detection discussed earlier, the amount of time that infants spent looking at something was used to assess the extent to which it violated their expectations. Either a ball or ball-like agent arranged blocks in either an ordered or disordered configuration. Infants looked longer (i.e., were more surprised) when a ball created order than when it created disorder. This suggests an implicit tendency to perceive ordered patterns as designed by an intentional agent. This helps explain the continuing popularity of William Paley's (1802/2006) argument from design, which contends that the natural world is too complex and ordered to have occurred by chance. Paley's famous example is that when you find a watch on the ground, the complexity of the watch indicates that someone must have made it. While evolutionary theory can account for complex systems arising without intentional intervention (Dawkins, 1986, 2006), natural selection simply lacks the intuitive appeal of theistic explanations. Perceiving the natural world as intentionally made is an additional example of the human tendency to over-attribute intentions (Bloom, 2007).

The Curse of Knowledge

A number of the world's leading religions require the faithful to accept the existence of an all-knowing, all-perceiving deity. While some adults may struggle to accept the existence of this supernatural agent, the concept of an omniscient God capitalizes on cognitive defaults evidenced by young children. An omniscient God is easy for children to comprehend because such a being is consistent with their intuitions about other agents. Children under the age of four are profoundly egocentric and have a difficult time taking the perspective of other agents. As a result, they expect others to know anything that they themselves know (the "curse of knowledge"; Birch, 2005). They further expect Person B to know anything that Person A knows. In other words, their default assumption is that beliefs are universal and infallible.

In one relevant investigation, 4-, 5-, and 6-year-old children watched the experimenter put rocks in a box (Barrett et al., 2001). Children under the age of four thought that their mother would know that the box had rocks in it, and that God would know this too. Five and six-year-olds accurately predicted that their mother would not know what was in the box but still thought that God would know. In an additional experiment, children were shown that there was a wooden block inside a dark box. Three-year-olds believe that both God and a human puppet could see the wooden block, whereas 5-year-olds thought that God but *not* the human puppet could see the block.

The belief that God is all-knowing capitalizes on cognitive defaults evident among young children.[1] Instead of expanding their notion of agents to include an omniscient being, children gradually learn to *reduce* the amount of knowledge they attribute to humans. Rather than requiring an enormous leap of faith, the concept of an omniscient God is something that comes naturally.

Summary

Given these cognitive defaults, it is little wonder that religious beliefs are so widespread. Implicit dualism, hypersensitive agency detection, simulation constraints, promiscuous teleology, and the curse of knowledge are the cognitive foundation on which faith in supernatural agents is built.

EXISTENTIAL NEEDS

In addition to cognitive defaults present in infants and young children, existential needs most clearly present later in life also contribute to religious faith. (The studies reviewed in the upcoming sections used adult participants unless otherwise specified.) Successful religions generally provide an emotionally satisfying framework for understanding the world that is in little danger of disproof. Successful religions mitigate the existential terror of death, serve the implicit motive to justify the existing social order, and fulfill the desire to share a meaningful understanding of the world with other members of one's social group.

The Search for Meaning

While some moral intuitions vary dramatically across cultures, others are quasi-universal (Wilson, 1993; Haidt, 2001; Haidt & Joseph, 2004). People around the world view killing an innocent infant, robbing an elderly grandmother, and other commonly censured acts as absolutely wrong. Belief systems that fail to ascribe moral meaning to human behavior consistent with such intuitions are at a distinct disadvantage to those who do (Bering, 2002a).

One of the major hurdles faced by a materialist worldview is the distinction between what *is* and what *should* be. Materialists are reasonably successful at explaining how things are (e.g., men are nine times as likely to commit violent crimes as women), but have a difficult time justifying what *should* be (e.g., why men should stop committing so many violent acts). In a materialist world there are no deep moral truths, rather social conventions that result from evolved characteristics of mind. Materialism thus leads to relativist moral conclusions that everyday people find intuitively unsatisfying and even grotesque.

Empirical evidence suggests that materialism fails to provide life with the same sense of deep moral significance that successful religions provide (Bering,

---

[1] At the same time, there are aspects of the Jewish, Christian, and Islamic God that are counter-intuitive. For example, both children and adults find it difficult to imagine a supernatural agent who acts outside of time and is present everywhere at once (Barrett, 2004; Barrett & Keil, 1996).

2002a). Religiosity correlates positively with a sense of meaning in life, and negatively with anxiety and depression (Chamberlain & Zika, 1992; Steger & Frazier, 2005; Vilchinsky & Kravetz, 2005; Wulff, 2006). Moreover, the association between religion and well-being is mediated by an enhanced sense of meaning in life (Chamberlain & Zika, 1992; Steger & Frazier, 2005). Religious faith provides psychological benefits that materialist worldviews are unable to replicate.

Another advantage of theistic beliefs over materialist beliefs is that the former are extremely difficult to falsify (Barrett, 2004). Consider the case of Christian prayer, for example. If a believer prays for something that actually comes to pass, she experiences a tremendous validation of her faith. But if the prayer is not immediately answered, it could still be answered later on. And it could also be that either the prayer or the person who made it were not worthy of a divine response. While an answered prayer validates one's faith, an unanswered prayer fails to weaken it to the same degree. While some would-be prophets have made the mistake of giving a precise date for the end of the world and making other falsifiable claims, the theistic claims that tend to last are those invulnerable to disproof. Successful religions provide people with a meaningful framework to understand the world which guarantees their beliefs will never be proven completely false. As such, they provide a degree of existential security that no scientific theory can fully match, because scientific theories must be falsifiable.

Existential Terror of Death

A number of scholars have argued that religion satisfies the powerful (yet often unconscious) need for psychological immortality (Freud, 1946; Becker, 1973). However, empirical evidence that fear of death implicitly contributes to religiosity has only become available relatively recently.

Multiple waves of the World Values Survey indicate that people from underdeveloped countries are considerably more religious than people from industrialized countries (Norris & Inglehart, 2004). The constant existential threat posed by an environment rife with poverty, disease, violence, and political instability leads people to turn to religion for solace (Norris & Inglehart, 2004). As Barrett (2004, p.118) has observed, "if religion is the opiate of the masses, atheism is a luxury of the elite." Only elites have the existential comfort necessary to reject theistic concepts and other aspects of traditional authority; for the poor, the belief in a just world requires an afterlife to balance the equation.

Direct evidence that a fear of death contributes to religiosity is provided by research on Terror Management Theory (TMT; Greenberg et al., in press; Pyszczynski et al., 1997, 1999). Scores of studies demonstrate that asking people to think about their own death leads them to seek symbolic immortality by defending the worldview of their culture (e.g., Rosenblatt et al., 1989; McGregor et al., 1998). Goldenberg et al. (2001) found that asking people to think about their own death led them to deny a connection between human beings and animals – in other words, to cling to the idea that there is something "special" about human beings. Also, priming death increased the extent to which participants believed that God exists and plays an active role in human affairs (Norenzayan & Hansen, 2006). Mortality salience further made people more biased in favor of individuals who shared their religion (Greenberg et al., 1990), and less willing to use a religious symbol in a disrespectful manner (i.e., banging in a nail using a cross; Greenberg et al., 1995). Notably, church attendance and Bible sales rose after the terrorist attacks of September 11, 2001 (Pyszczynski et al., 2003). Consistent with the idea that religious faith addresses existential fears, deeply religious people report less fear of death (Minton & Spilka, 1976; Bolt, 1977; Spilka et al., 1977; Donahue, 1985) and are less likely to respond to mortality salience by defending the cultural worldview (Jonas & Fischer, 2006; see also Dechesne et al., 2003, for evidence that afterlife beliefs mitigate the existential terror of death).

Existential needs are not fully sufficient to explain theism because some religions do not provide much existential comfort (Boyer, 2001). A few even present an existentially terrifying worldview in which malevolent supernatural agents intervene regularly in human affairs. While speculative, it seems possible that religious ideas that do provide existential comfort (e.g., heavenly rewards in the afterlife) are more "contagious" and likely to spread (Sperber, 1985, 1994; Nichols, 2004). This would help explain why certain existentially comforting religions count hundreds of millions of members while existentially terrifying religions are relatively parochial. As discussed in upcoming sections, socially oriented motives also make a major contribution to theistic beliefs.

System Justification

A number of scholars have argued that humans possess an implicit motive to justify the prevailing social order (Jost & Banaji, 1994; Sidanius & Pratto, 1999; Jost et al., 2004). Many people believe the world is a just place, which leads them to blame the victims of tragedies for their misfortune (Lerner & Miller, 1978; Olson et al., 2006). Classic work by Piaget (1932/1965/1978) found that the belief in a just world – as evidenced by a conviction in "immanent justice" – developed early in life. Children were told a story about a child who committed the moral transgression of stealing, and later died when a bridge collapsed. Eighty-six percent of the youngest children thought that it was the moral transgression that caused the bridge to collapse.

Even the victims of social misfortune implicitly justify the social hierarchy (Sidanius & Pratto, 1999; Jost et al., 2004). Low income Americans are significantly *more* likely than high income Americans to believe that economic inequality is legitimate and differences in pay are needed to get people to work hard (Jost et al., 2003). Similarly, Black Americans are more likely than European Americans to explicitly endorse stereotypes of Black people as lazy and irresponsible (Sniderman & Piazza, 1993).

Religious beliefs are among the most effective rationalizations used by both high and low status individuals to rationalize inequality (Sidanius & Pratto,

1999). Obvious cases include the Hindu caste system, the concept of divine right of kings, and the Calvinist principle of earthly rewards. When no natural justification for status differences exists, religion is used to provide supernatural justifications (e.g., moral behavior in a past life, being chosen by God to lead, having the grace of God). Empirical studies confirm that religiosity is positively correlated with authoritarian, anti-egalitarian, and otherwise pro-system beliefs (Altemeyer & Hunsberger, 1992; Altemeyer, 2003). This suggests that the need to justify enormous differences in socioeconomic status is one reason for the pervasiveness and content of theistic beliefs.

Social Intuitionism

The need to belong and affiliate is a fundamental human motive that helps account for why communities generally share the same religious values (Baumeister & Leary, 1995; Tremlin, 2006). Human beings are deeply social creatures who implicitly conform to the values of those around them (Hardin & Higgins, 1996; Haidt, 2001; Sinclair et al., 2005).

Cultural influences on moral beliefs are especially strong at an automatic, implicit level (Schweder, 1991; Banaji, 2001; Haidt, 2001). In ingenious research by Haidt and his colleagues, participants were "morally dumbfounded" when asked to logically justify their opposition to physically harmless yet socially disapproved acts (e.g., using an American flag to clean the toilet; Haidt et al., 1993). Yet such intuitions are easy enough to predict, so long as one is familiar with the person's culture (Schweder, 1991; Haidt, 2001).

Research using implicit measures of attitude (Fazio et al., 1995; Dovidio et al., 1997; Greenwald et al., 1998) indicates that automatic evaluations are highly sensitive to the cultural context (Greenwald & Banaji, 1995; Banaji, 2001; Rudman, 2004), and unconsciously shift to become more like those of other people one likes and respects (Hardin & Higgins, 1996; Sinclair et al., 2005). For example, Sinclair et al. (2005) found that automatic racial attitudes, as assessed by a subliminal priming task, changed to become more like those of a polite research confederate but not a rude research confederate.

Recent work by Epley and his colleagues further underscores the contribution of social affiliation motives to theistic cognition (for a review, see Epley et al., in press). Individuals who self-reported feelings of loneliness were significantly more likely to evidence a belief in God and anthropomorphize inanimate objects (e.g., an alarm clock named "Clocky") and pets (Epley, Akalis, Waytz, & Cacioppo, in press; Epley, Waytz, Akalis, & Cacioppo, in press). And individuals (falsely) told their personality predicted they would be alone later in life became significantly more likely to report a belief in supernatural agents, including God (Epley et al., in press). This converges with earlier studies indicating that single individuals, as well as individuals with insecure personal relationships, are more likely to strongly believe in a personal God (Kirkpatrick & Shaver, 1990; Granquist and Hagekkull, 2000).

Once adopted, such core theistic beliefs are passionately defended (Lord et al., 1979; Kunda, 1990; Tetlock et al., 2000; Pronin et al., 2004). In fact, people find it aversive to even *think* about alternatives to their theistic beliefs. Tetlock et al. (2000) asked participants to read passages containing "heretical counterfactuals." One passage speculated that if Joseph had left Mary in response to her pregnancy, Jesus would have grown up in a single-parent household and his personality would have been different. Fundamentalist Christians reported feeling angered, disgusted, and even violated by such ideas. They also engaged in "moral cleansing," reporting intentions to get more involved in church activities as a way to purify themselves of such thoughts (see also Zhong & Liljenquist, 2006). No such effect was observed for nonreligious counterfactuals. The toxicity of heretical ideas is testament to the emotional commitment created by the shared reality of religion.

Summary

Religious faith capitalizes not only on cognitive defaults evident in children, but also on existential needs most clearly identifiable in adults. These include the desire for meaning, existential terror of death, the implicit need to rationalize the social order, and the desire to share an understanding of the world with other members of one's social group. Empirical evidence further indicates that system justification and social intuitionism address existential terror: people are more likely to defend the current social system and ideologies they share with ingroups when they have recently thought of their own death (Pyszczynski et al., 1997, 1999).

While work with infants and young children indicates that certain aspects of theistic cognition are present early in life, research with adults suggests how universal properties of mind combine with existential and social experiences to produce and maintain religious beliefs. We now turn to the tension that atheist, agnostic, and less religious people experience between their explicit beliefs and implicit theism.

Explicit Versus Implicit Theism

While international surveys indicate that the overwhelming majority of people around the world are theists (Norris & Inglehart, 2004), there are individuals who consistently claim that they do not believe in supernatural agents or immortal souls. Is it as simple as that, or do atheists, agnostics, and less religious people nonetheless experience theistic intuitions? That theistic cognition is based in basic properties of mind shared by all humans (e.g., agency detection, simulation constraints, social intuitionism) predicts that even nonbelievers should at an implicit level experience some theistic cognitions (Bloom, 2007). Just such a dissociation is observed with regards to racial prejudice – even explicitly egalitarian individuals exhibit implicit responses consistent with cultural prejudices (e.g., shooting unarmed black civilians in a police simulation; Correll et al., 2002; Greenwald et al., 2003). Dual process models stipulate that while explicit attitudes determine deliberative, abstract judgments (e.g., judgments of guilt in a criminal case), implicit attitudes influence relatively more spontaneous, spur of-the-moment reactions (e.g., nonverbal behaviors such as how close one chooses to sit to a Black student; Fazio, 1990; Fazio et al., 1995; Dovidio et al., 1997; Wilson et al., 2000; Gawronski & Bodenhausen, 2006). Without drawing any moral comparison between religion and racism, this leads us to expect an uneasy coexistence of explicitly atheist and implicitly theist cognitions in individuals who claim to be nonbelievers.

A number of empirical findings are consistent with just such an implicit–explicit tension. In a structured interview about afterlife beliefs, Bering (2002b) explicitly asked participants whether they thought that "what we think of as the 'soul,' or conscious personality of a person, ceases permanently when the body dies." He classified participants as "extinctivists" if they explicitly rejected the notion that the soul survives physical death. Participants were next presented with vignettes about fictional characters who met abrupt, accidental deaths. For instance, one vignette described a history teacher who, while trying to get to his class on time, crashed his car into a utility pole and died. Participants were asked what faculties the man still possessed. Remarkably, many extinctivists agreed that the dead man "knew that he was dead." One extinctivist responded "Yeah, he'd know, because I don't believe in the afterlife. It is nonexistent; he sees that now." Providing further evidence that belief in souls is strongest at an implicit level, extinctivists took twice as much time to indicate that epistemic states cease upon death as it took them to indicate that biological processes cease upon death. Taken together, these results suggest that many extinctivists nonetheless implicitly believe in a soul that survives physical death.

In another relevant investigation, participants were offered a contract selling their soul to the experimenter for the sum of 2 dollars (Haidt et al., 2000). The contract prominently stated that the offer was a joke and the contract was not valid. Despite this, four out of five participants refused to sign. Notably, even nonreligious participants overwhelmingly declined the offer, in some cases laughingly admitting that they had no rational reason for doing so. It appears that religious and less religious people share the implicit belief that they have a soul to be sold.

Data reported by Nosek (2002, 2005) provides the most direct evidence for an implicit–explicit tension regarding religion. Participants completed both a questionnaire measure of their attitudes toward evolutionary theory versus creationism and an Implicit Association Test (IAT; Greenwald et al., 1998) of their automatic attitudes toward evolutionary theory and creationism. Strikingly, while a majority of participants explicitly preferred evolutionary theory over creationism, automatic attitudes toward creationism were more positive than those toward evolutionary theory. This dissociation suggests that even when explicit attitudes tend toward materialist explanations of how the world came to exist, implicit cognitions remain consistent with the culture's dominant religion.

It is interesting to speculate about potential role of cognitive development in the tension observed between implicit and explicit theism. Some of the theistic biases observed in young children appear to dissipate substantially over time, for example, the tendency to view natural objects like rocks as made for a purpose (Kelemen, 1999, 2004; Kelemen & DiYanni, 2005). Yet it is difficult to deny the intuitive, implicit appeal of Paley's (1802/2006) related argument from design, and the more logically imposed, deliberative nature of a belief in natural selection (Dawkins, 1986). While speculative, it seems possible that theistic cognitions most strongly evident in children may temporarily re-emerge among adults under conditions that promote implicit processing, such as when the individual's capacity to reason carefully is reduced by a concurrent cognitively demanding task (e.g., trying to remember an eight-digit number; Gilbert et al., 1988; Gilbert & Osborne, 1989). We leave empirical tests of this hypothesis to future research.

In sum, theistic cognition is intuitive, spontaneous, and implicitly shapes relevant judgments and behaviors. Indeed, universal properties of mind make it practically inevitable that theistic ideas will manifest themselves in the implicit cognitions of both explicit believers and explicit nonbelievers. Theistic cognition is near-universal at an explicit level and quite likely universal at an implicit level. We now turn to a culturally specific expression of implicit theism: the association between work and divine salvation in United States of America.

Implicit Puritanism in America

> Christ by a wonderful Providence hath dispossessed Satan, who reigned securely in these Ends of the Earth, for Ages the Lord knoweth how many, and here the Lord has caused as it were New Jerusalem to come down from Heaven.
> –Puritan minister Increase Mather

The United States is exceptional among developed nations in its extremely high level of explicit religiosity. International surveys indicate that wealth almost universally leads to secularization, such that in Western Europe and economically prosperous East Asian states, religion is gradually fading from public life (Inglehart, 1997; Norris & Inglehart, 2004; Inglehart & Welzel, 2005). Yet in America, the world's economic superpower, a full 94% of the population believes in God, and 65% are sure that Satan exists (Harris, 2004). The majority of Americans are creationists who believe that the universe was created 6,000 years ago (Dawkins, 2006; Harris, 2006). 44% of Americans believe that Jesus will return during the next 50 years, and three times as many Americans endorse intelligent design as endorse evolutionary theory (Greeley, 1991; Gallup & Linday, 1999; Harris, 2006). Based on economic development, 5% of Americans should regard religion as extremely important in their lives, yet the actual figure is 10 times that amount (Wald, 1987).

Indeed, America appears to be on a different developmental course than are other developed nations, in that Americans are virtually as religious today as they were over half a century ago. Contemporary Americans are just as likely as Americans from the 1940s and 1950s to attend church, believe in God and life after death, and rank God as extremely important in their lives as (Lipset, 1996; Norris & Inglehart, 2004; Baker, 2005). Between 1947 and 2001, the percentage of Americans who believe in life after death actually *increased* by 8% (Harris,

2006; Sheler, 2006). And spiritual and religious elements in American television shows have grown 400% since 1993 (Gazzaniga, 2005).

American theism has its roots in the nation's Puritan–Protestant heritage (Sanchez-Burks, 2002, 2005; Uhlmann et al., in press). In contrast to the over-whelmingly male Spanish immigrants to the New World, who sought to make their fortunes, these English colonists came as families and in some cases entire reli-gious congregations (Bellow, 2003). Considered religious fanatics in Europe and subjected to persecution, these Puritan–Protestants sought to create a religious utopia in the New World. They sought to save the world by founding a "city upon a hill" that would, by example, lead other nations to embrace the true faith (Merk, 1963; Gilbert, 1970). This self-selection process resulted in extremely religious communities that exerted a profound influence on the culture of the English colonies (Fisher, 1989). While eventually dwarfed in numbers by waves of immigrants seeking economic opportunities, the Puritan–Protestant settlers, by virtue of having arrived earlier, succeeded at imprinting their values on what eventually became the United States of America (Cohen, 2001). It is this unique cultural history that has allowed the United States to retain high levels of religi-osity in the face of enormous economic prosperity.

Protestant countries were the first to industrialize, due at least in part to Protestant values conducive to capitalism (Weber, 1904/1958; Landes, 1998; Norris & Inglehart, 2004). One ironic result is that Protestantism has become a victim of its own (economic) success. The Reformation ushered in explosive economic growth that has deeply eroded support for the Protestant religion in its birthplace of Western Europe. This leaves the United States as the only major Protestant nation that has yet to secularize. As a result, contemporary Americans may display unique implicit responses that reflect Puritan–Protestant values.

The values of contemporary Americans should differ not only from those of individuals from cultures that are not historically Protestant (e.g., Italy) but also historically Protestant cultures that have since secularized. As noted earlier, humans readily – and implicitly – pick up the associations predominant in their culture (Greenwald & Banaji, 1995; Haidt, 2001). For example, even consciously egalitarian White Americans implicitly associate Black Americans with crime (Correll et al., 2002; Greenwald et al., 2003). A less religious or non-Protestant American should therefore exhibit implicit cognitions consistent with cultur-ally predominant Protestant values. In contrast, contemporary Germans live in a society in which religion has largely faded from public life (Norris & Inglehart, 2004). As a result, they may have not been conditioned with implicit associations reflective of Protestant values.

Perhaps the most exceptional aspect of Puritan–Protestant theology is the link made between work and divine salvation. In contrast to other religious tradi-tions that frown on excessive worldliness and the accumulation of wealth, the early Protestants viewed wealth as a sign that one was among God's chosen. Harvesting the fruits of one's hard work became a moral imperative rather than a practical necessity. While many East Asian cultures likewise emphasize hard work, their ethos is typically a secular one. For example, the Japanese government actively promoted work as a way of fulfilling one's national and family responsibilities (Fukuyama, 1995; Landes, 1998). In contrast, Protestantism made work a religious imperative. As US President Calvin Coolidge once claimed, "The man who builds a factory builds a temple. And the man who works their worships there." (as cited in Davis, 1993, p. 322).

In a number of recent studies, we have examined whether contemporary Americans display implicit Puritanism, for example, by implicitly linking work and divine salvation (Poehlman et al., 2007; Uhlmann et al., 2007). In one investigation, participants unscrambled sentences (Srull & Wyer, 1979) including either concepts related to divine salvation (e.g., *saved, God, angelic*) or nonreligious concepts matched in valence (Uhlmann et al., 2007). Subsequently, all participants completed an anagram task. As expected, American participants in the salvation prime condition solved more anagrams, suggesting that they worked harder on their assigned task. Control groups of Canadian, Italian, and German participants did not evidence this implicit link between work and salvation. No participant believed that the salvation prime had influenced their anagram performance.

Notably, non-Protestant and less religious Americans were just as likely as devout Protestants to respond to the salvation prime by working harder. This suggests that it is exposure to American culture, rather than conviction in any particular faith, which engenders an implicit link between work and divine salvation. The implicit theistic cognition of Americans is therefore traceable to cultural history, different from that of members of other cultures, and rooted in basic properties of how the mind works. Thus, we identify a way in which the *content* of theistic cognition differs between cultures, even as it is rooted in psychological *processes* that are universal. And we again implicate implicit cognition in the maintenance and expression of theistic beliefs.

Of particular interest for future research are the intuitions of individuals from East Asia, known for a strong work ethic lacking in religious overtones (Fukuyama, 1995; Landes, 1998). How might their moral cognitions related to work converge and diverge from those of Americans? As noted, the famed Japanese work ethic is traditionally linked to secular concerns such as duty to country and family. This suggests that for Japanese individuals, implicitly priming stimuli associated with such concerns, such as the national flag or a family portrait, may cause them to work harder at an assigned task. However, Japanese individuals should not respond to implicit primes associated with religion by working harder.

Making a respectable empirical case that a belief is universal or unique to a specific culture is challenging. In some rare cases, one can argue scholars have yet to encounter a culture conspicuously lacking in some common belief, for example, that a human being is more than a machine made of meat. Some cross-national surveys of explicit values have included scores of countries (e.g., Hofstede, 1980), perhaps enough to justify strong claims. Norenzayan and Heine

(2005 p. 767) have proposed some less logistically daunting criteria for cultural universality, for example, replicating a psychological phenomenon in two cultures that are known to be extremely different from one another on relevant dimensions including "social practices, philosophical traditions, language, geography, socioeconomic status, literacy, and level of education". For example, children from both North America and the Baka people of Cameroon both develop an understanding that other people can believe in things that are incorrect (Avis & Harris, 1991). That both North Americans and illiterate pygmy hunter-gatherers share this critical belief suggests that it is a pan-cultural psychological phenomenon (Norenzayan & Heine, 2005).

Our research on the distinctive American link between work and divine salvation employs the approach championed by Seymour Martin Lipset (1996), among the foremost scholars on American values. Lipset has argued that claims of American exceptionalism are best tested by comparing the values of Americans and members of highly similar cultures, such as Canada. That Americans, but not Canadians, responded to a salvation prime by working harder suggests that American attitudes toward work are special and distinctive. Of course, however, much more research is necessary before drawing strong conclusions about American moral exceptionalism.

CONCLUSION

Religion is a human universal that capitalizes on (1) cognitive defaults observable in children and (2) existential needs endemic to the human condition. Human beings are implicit dualists who distinguish between bodies and minds, are biased toward detecting agency in the world around us, have difficulty imagining a future in which physical death brings psychological death, view the natural world as created for a purpose, and find it easy to imagine an omniscient deity. Successful religions provide frameworks for understanding the world which both imbue it with meaning and are immune to falsification. Successful religions further address the existential terror of death, the implicit need to justify the prevailing social order, and the desire to affiliate with members of one's social groups. These variables may not be sufficient to account for the pervasiveness of belief in the supernatural, but they do go a long way toward explaining why religion developed independently in geographically isolated cultures throughout the world. At the same time, they provide a more empirically grounded account of certain aspects of the human collective unconscious (Jung, 1921/1976).

Theistic cognition is so inherent to human psychology that even individuals who claim to be atheists or agnostics evidence implicit responses consistent with a belief in the supernatural. Of course, much of the specific content of religious beliefs varies widely from one culture to another (Cohen, 2001), as with, for example, the implicit Puritanism displayed by contemporary Americans (Poehlman et al., 2007; Uhlmann et al., 2007).

Psychological research, informed by an understanding of implicit cognition, can make a unique contribution to the science of religion. The development, spread, and maintenance of theistic beliefs are by necessity closely tied to basic psychological processes. As Tremlin (2006, p. 74) has argued, "we cannot understand *what* we think until we first understand *how* we think." The nearly universal belief in God and the afterlife appears an inevitable consequence of the natural grooves of human cognition and motivation.

REFERENCES

Aarts, H., Custers, R., & Wegner, D. M. (2004). On the inference of personal authorship: Enhancing experienced agency by priming effect information. *Consciousness and Cognition, 14*, 439–458.

Aarts, H., Wegner, D. M., & Dijksterhuis, A. (2006). On the feeling of doing things: Dysphoria and the implicit modulation of authorship ascription. *Behaviour Research & Therapy, 44*, 1621–1627.

Altemeyer, B. (2003). Why do religious fundamentalists tend to be prejudiced?. *International Journal for the Psychology of Religion, 13*, 17–28.

Altemeyer, B., & Hunsberger, B. E. (1992). Authoritarianism, religious fundamentalism, quest, and prejudice. *International Journal for the Psychology of Religion, 2*, 113–133.

Atran, S. (2002). *In gods we trust: The evolutionary landscape of religion.* New York, NY: Oxford University press.

Avis, J., & Harris, P. L. (1991). Belief-desire reasoning among Baka children: Evidence for a universal conception of mind. *Child Development, 62*, 460–467.

Baker, W. (2005). *America's crisis of values.* Princeton, NJ: Princeton University press.

Banaji, M. R. (2001). Implicit attitudes can be measured. In H. L. Roedeger, III, J. S. Nairne, I. Neath, & A. Surprenant (Eds.), *The nature of remembering: Essays in honor of Robert G. Crowder* (pp. 117–150). Washington, DC: American Psychological Association.

Bargh, J. A. (1994). The four horsemen of automaticity: Awareness, efficiency, intention, and control in social cognition. In R. S. Wyer, Jr. & T. K. Srull (Eds.), *Handbook of social cognition* (2nd ed, pp. 1–40). Hillsdale, NJ: Erlbaum.

Barrett, J. L. (2000). Exploring the natural foundations of religion. *Trends in Cognitive Sciences, 4*, 29–34.

Barrett, J. L. (2004). *Why would anyone believe in God?.* Walnut Creek, CA: AltaMira press.

Barrett, J. L., & Keil, F. C. (1996). Conceptualizing a non-natural entity: Anthropomorphism in God concepts. *Cognitive Psychology, 31*, 219–247.

Barrett, J. L., Richert, R. A., & Driesenga, A. (2001). God's beliefs versus mother's: The development of nonhuman agent concepts. *Child Development, 72*, 50–65.

Baumeister, R. F., & Leary, M. R. (1995). The need to belong: Desire for interpersonal attachments as a fundamental human motivation. *Psychological Bulletin, 117*, 497–529.

Becker, E. (1973). *The denial of death.* New York: Free Press.

Behne, T., Carpenter, M., Call, J., & Tomasello, M. (2005). Unwilling versus unable: Infants' understanding of intentional action. *Developmental Psychology, 41*, 328–337.

Bellow, A. (2003). *In praise of nepotism.* New York, NY: Doubleday.

Bering, J. M. (2002a). The existential theory of mind. *Review of General Psychology, 6*, 3–24.

Bering, (2002b). Intuitive conceptions of dead agents' minds: the natural foundations of afterlife beliefs as phenomenological boundary. *Journal of Cognition and Culture, 2*, 263–398.

Bering, J. (2006). The folkpsychology of souls. *Behavioral and Brain Sciences, 29*, 466–468.

Bering, J. M., & Bjorklund, D. F. (2004). The natural emergence of reasoning about the afterlife as a developmental regularity. *Developmental Psychology, 40*, 217–233.

Birch, S. A. J. (2005). When knowledge is a curse: Biases in mental state attribution. *Current Directions in Psychological Science, 14*, 25–29.

Bloom, P. (2004). *Descartes's baby: How the science of human development explains what makes us human.* Cambridge, MA: Basic Books.

Bloom, P. (2005). Is God an accident?. *The Atlantic, 296*, 105–112.

Bloom, P. (2006). My brain made me do it. *Journal of Culture and Cognition, 6*, 209–214.

Bloom, P. (2007). Religion is natural. *Developmental Science, 10*, 147–151.

Bloom, P., & Veres, C. (1999). The perceived intentionality of groups. *Cognition, 71*, B1–B9.

Bolt, M. (1977). Religious orientation and death fears. *Review of Religious Research, 19*, 73–76.

Boyer, P. (2001). *Religion explained.* New York, NY: Basic Books.

Call, J., Hare, B., Carpenter, M., & Tomasello, M. (2004). 'Unwilling' versus 'unable': chimpanzees' understanding of human intentional action. *Developmental Science, 7*, 488–498.

Chamberlain, K., & Zika, S. (1992). Religiosity, meaning in life, and psychological well-being. In J. F. Schumaker (Ed.), *Religion and mental health* (pp. 138–148). New York, NY: Oxford University Press.

Cohen, D. (2001). Cultural variation: Considerations and implications. *Psychological Bulletin, 147*, 451–471.

Correll, J., Park, B., Judd, C. M., & Wittenbrink, B. (2002). The police officer's dilemma: Using ethnicity to disambiguate potentially threatening individuals. *Journal of Personality and Social Psychology, 83*, 1314–1329.

Davis, K. C. (1993). *Don't know much about history: Everything you need to know about American history but never learned.* New York, NY: HarperCollins.

Dawkins, R. (1986). *The blind watchmaker: Why the evidence of evolution reveals the universe without design.* New York, NY: WW Norton & Co.

Dawkins, R. (2006). *The God delusion.* Boston, Massachusetts: Houghton Mifflin Co.

Dechesne, M., Pyszczynski, T., Arndt, J., Ransom, S., Sheldon, K. M., van Knippenberg, A., & Janssen, J. (2003). Literal and symbolic immortality: The effect of evidence of literal immortality on self-esteem striving in response to mortality salience. *Journal of Personality and Social Psychology, 84*, 722–737.

Dennett, D. C. (2006). *Breaking the spell: Religion as a natural phenomenon.* New York, NY: Viking.

Donahue, M. (1985). Intrinsic and extrinsic religiousness: Review and meta-analysis. *Journal of Personality and Social Psychology, 48*, 400–419.

Dovidio, J. F., Kawakami, K., Johnson, C., Johnson, B., & Howard, A. (1997). On the nature of prejudice: Automatic and controlled processes. *Journal of Experimental Social Psychology, 33*, 510–540.

Epley, N., Akalis, S., Waytz, A., Cacioppo, J. T. (2008). Creating social connection through inferential reproduction: Loneliness and perceived agency in gadgets, gods, and greyhounds. *Psychological Science, 19*, 114–120.

Epley, N., Waytz, A., Akalis, S., & Cacioppo, J. T. (in press). When I need a human: Motivational determinants of anthropomorphism. *Social Cognition.*

Epley, N., Waytz, A., & Cacioppo, J. T. (2007). On seeing human: A three-factor theory of anthropomorphism. *Psychological Review, 114*, 864–886.

Evans, E. M. (2001). Cognitive and contextual factors in the emergence of diverse belief systems: Creation versus evolution. *Cognitive Psychology, 42*, 217–266.

Fazio, R. H. (1990). Multiple processes by which attitudes guide behavior: The MODE model as an integrative framework. In M. P. Zanna (Ed.), *Advances in Experimental Social Psychology* (Vol. 23, pp. 75–109). San Diego, CA: Academic Press.

Fazio, R., Jackson, J., Dunton, B., & Williams, C. (1995). Variability in automatic activation as an unobtrusive measure of racial attitudes: A bona fide pipeline?. *Journal of Personality and Social Psychology, 69*, 1013–1027.

Fisher, D. H. (1989). *Albion's seed: Four British folkways in America.* New York, NY: Oxford University Press.

Freud, S. (1946). *Totem and taboo*. New York, NY: Vintage Books.

Fukuyama, F. (1995). *Trust: The social virtues and the creation of prosperity*. New York, NY: Simon & Schuster.

Gallup, G., & Linday, D. M. (1999). *Surveying the religious landscape: Trends in U.S. beliefs*. Harrisburg, PA: Morehouse publishing.

Gawronski, B., & Bodenhausen, G. V. (2006). Associative and propositional processes in evaluation: An integrative review of implicit and explicit attitude change. *Psychological Bulletin, 132*, 692–731.

Gazzaniga, M. S. (2005). *The ethical brain*. Washington, DC: Dana Press.

Gergely, G., Nádasdy, Z., Csibra, G., & Bíró, S. (1995). Taking the intentional stance at 12 months of age. *Cognition, 56*, 165–193.

Gilbert, F. (1970). *To the farewell address: ideas of early American foreign policy*. Princeton, New Jersey: Princeton University press.

Gilbert, D. T., & Osborne, R. E. (1989). Thinking backward: Some curable and incurable consequences of cognitive busyness. *Journal of Personality and Social Psychology, 57*, 940–949.

Gilbert, D. T., Pelham, B. W., & Krull, D. S. (1988). On cognitive busyness: When person perceivers meet persons perceived. *Journal of Personality and Social Psychology, 54*, 733–740.

Gimenez-Dasi, M., Guerrero, S., & Harris, P. L. (2005). Intimations of immortality and omniscience in early childhood. *European Journal of Developmental Psychology, 2*, 285–297.

Goldenberg, J. L., Pyszczynski, T., Greenberg, J., Solomon, S., Kluck, B., & Cornwell, R. (2001). I am not an animal: Mortality salience, disgust, and the denial of human creatureliness. *Journal of Experimental Psychology: General, 130*, 427–435.

Granquist, P., & Hagekkull, B. (2000). Religiosity, adult attachment, and why "singles" are more religious. *International Journal for the Psychology of Religion, 10*, 111–123.

Greeley, A. M. (1991). American exceptionalism: The religious phenomenon. In B. E. Scafer (Ed.), *Is America different? A new look at American exceptionalism* (pp. 94–115). New York, NY: Oxford University press.

Greenberg, J., Pyszczynski, T., & Solomon, S. (1995). Evidence of a terror management function of cultural icons: The effects of mortality salience on the inappropriate use of cherished cultural symbols. *Personality and Social Psychology Bulletin, 21*, 1221–1228.

Greenberg, J., Landau, M. J., Solomon, S., & Pyszczynski, T. (in press). What is the primary psychological function of religion? In D. Wurff, (Ed.), *Handbook of the psychology of religion*. New York, NY: Oxford University press.

Greenberg, J., Pyszczynski, T., Solomon, S., Rosenblatt, A., Veeder, M., Kirkland, S., & Lyon, D. (1990). Evidence for terror management theory II: The effects of mortality salience on reactions to those who threaten or bolster the cultural worldview. *Journal of Personality and Social Psychology, 58*, 308–318.

Greenwald, A. G., & Banaji, M. R. (1995). Implicit social cognition: Attitudes, self-esteem, and stereotypes. *Psychological Review, 102*, 4–27.

Greenwald, A. G., McGhee, D. E., & Schwartz, J. L. K. (1998). Measuring individual differences in implicit cognition: The implicit association test. *Journal of Personality and Social Psychology, 74*, 1464–1480.

Greenwald, A. G., Oakes, M. A., & Hoffman, H. (2003). Targets of discrimination: Effects of race on responses to weapons holders. *Journal of Experimental Social Psychology, 39*, 399–405.

Guthrie, S. E. (1993). *Faces in the clouds: A new theory of religion*. New York NY: Oxford University Press.

Haidt, J. (2001). The emotional dog and its rational tail: A social intuitionist approach to moral judgment. *Psychological Review, 108*, 814–834.

Haidt, J., & Joseph, C. (2004). Intuitive ethics: How innately prepared intuitions generate culturally variable virtues. *Daedalus, 133*, 55–56. Special issue on human nature.

Haidt, J., Koller, S., & Dias, M. (1993). Affect, culture, and morality, or is it wrong to eat your dog?. *Journal of Personality and Social Psychology, 65*, 613–628.

Haidt, J., Bjorklund, F., & Murphy, S. (2000). *Moral dumbfounding: When intuition finds no reason*. Unpublished manuscript.

Hardin, C. D., & Higgins, E. T. (1996). Shared reality: How social verification makes the subjective objective. In R. M. Sorrentino & E. T. Higgins (Eds.), *Handbook of motivation and cognition. Vol. 3. The interpersonal context* (pp. 28–84). New York: Guilford.

Harris, S. (2004). *The end of faith: Religion, terror, and the future of reason.* New York, NY: WW Norton & Co.

Harris, S. (2006). *Letter to a Christian nation.* New York, NY: Alfred A. Knopf.

Hayden, B. (1993). The cultural capacities of Neanderthals. *Journal of Human Evolution, 24,* 113–146.

Heider, F., & Simmel, M. (1944). An experimental study of apparent behavior. *American Journal of Psychology, 57,* 243–249.

Hofstede, G. (1980). *Culture's consequences: International differences in work-related values.* Beverly Hills, CA: Sage Publications.

Inglehart, R. (1997). *Modernization and postmodernization: Cultural, economic, and political change in 43 societies.* Princeton, NJ: Princeton University press.

Inglehart, R., & Welzel, C. (2005). *Modernization, cultural change, and democracy: The human development sequence.* Cambridge, MA: Cambridge University press.

Johnson, S., Slaughter, V., & Carey, S. (1998). Whose gaze will infants follow? Features that elicit gaze following in 12-month-olds. *Developmental Science, 1,* 233–238.

Jonas, E., & Fischer, P. (2006). Terror management and religion: Evidence that intrinsic religiousness mitigates worldview defense following mortality salience. *Journal of Personality and Social Psychology, 91,* 553–567.

Jost, J. T., & Banaji, M. R. (1994). The role of stereotyping in system-justification and the production of false consciousness. *British Journal of Social Psychology, 33,* 1–27.

Jost, J. T., Banaji, M. R., & Nosek, B. A. (2004). A decade of system justification theory: accumulated evidence of conscious and unconscious bolstering of the status quo. *Political Psychology, 25,* 881–919.

Jost, J. T., Pelham, B. W., Sheldon, O., & Sullivan, B. N. (2003). Social inequality and the reduction of ideological dissonance on behalf of the system: Evidence of enhanced system justification among the disadvantaged. *European Journal of Social Psychology, 33,* 13–36.

Jung, C. G. (1921/1976). *Psychological types.* Princeton, NJ: Princeton University press. (The collected works of C.G. Jung, Vol.6).

Kelemen, D. (1999). Why are rocks pointy? Children's preference for teleological explanations of the natural world. *Developmental Psychology, 35,* 1440–1452.

Kelemen, D. (2004). Are children "intuitive theists"? Reasoning about purpose and design in nature. *Psychological Science, 15,* 295–301.

Kelemen, D., & DiYanni, C. (2005). Intuitions about origins: purpose and intelligence in children's reasoning about nature. *Journal of Cognition and Development, 6,* 3–31.

Kirkpatrick, L. A., & Shaver, P. R. (1990). Attachment theory and religion, childhood attachment, religious beliefs, and conversion. *Journal for the Scientific Study Religion, 29,* 315–334.

Kuhlmeier, V., Wynn, K., & Bloom, P. (2003). Attribution of dispositional states by 12-month-olds. *Psychological Science, 14,* 402–408.

Kuhlmeier, V. A., Bloom, P., & Wynn, K. (2004). Do 5 month old infants see humans as material objects?. *Cognition, 94,* 95–103.

Kunda, Z. (1990). The case for motivated reasoning. *Psychological Review, 108,* 480–498.

Landes, D. S. (1998). *The wealth and poverty of nations: Why some are so rich and some so poor.* New York, NY: W.W. Norton & Co.

Lerner, M. J., & Miller, D. T. (1978). Just world research and the attribution process: Looking back and ahead. *Psychological Bulletin, 85,* 1030–1051.

Lipset, S. M. (1996). *American exceptionalism: A double edged sword.* New York, NY: W.W. Norton & Co.

Lord, C. G., Ross, L., & Lepper, M. R. (1979). Biased assimilation and attitude polarization: The effects of prior theories on subsequently considered evidence. *Journal of Personality and Social Psychology, 37,* 2098–2109.

Mandler, J. M., & McDonough, L. (1993). Concept formation in infancy. *Cognitive Development, 8,* 291–318.

McGregor, H., Lieberman, J. D., Greenberg, J., Solomon, S., Arndt, J., Simon, L., & Pyszczynski, T. (1988). Terror management and aggression: evidence that mortality salience motivates aggression against worldview-threatening others. *Journal of Personality & Social Psychology, 74*, 590–605.

Merk, F. (1963). *Manifest destiny and mission in American history: A reinterpretation*. New York, NY: Knopf.

Minton, B., & Spilka, B. (1976). Perspectives on death in relation to powerlessness and form of personal religion. *Journal of Death and Dying, 7*, 261–268.

Newman, G. E., Keil, F. C., Kuhlmeier, V., & Wynn, K. (2006). *Infants understand that only intentional agents can create order.* Unpublished manuscript.

Nichols, S. (2004). Is religion what we want? Motivation and the cultural transmission of religious representations. *Journal of Cognition and Culture, 4*, 347–371.

Nisbett, R. E., & Wilson, T. D. (1977). Telling more than we can know: Verbal reports on mental processes. *Psychological Review, 84*, 231–259.

Norenzayan, A., & Heine, S. J. (2005). Psychological universals: What are they and how can we know? *Psychological Bulletin, 131*, 763–784.

Norenzayan, A., & Hansen, I. G. (2006). Belief in supernatural agents in the face of death. *Personality and Social Psychology Bulletin, 32*, 174–187.

Norris, P., & Inglehart, R. (2004). *Sacred and secular: Religion and politics worldwide*. New York, NY: Cambridge University Press.

Nosek, B. A. (2002). *Moderators of the relationship between implicit and explicit attitudes*. Doctoral dissertation, Yale University.

Nosek, B. A. (2005). Moderators of the relationship between implicit and explicit evaluation. *Journal of Experimental Psychology: General, 134*, 565–584.

Olson, K. R., Banaji, M. R., Dweck, C. S., & Spelke, E. S. (2006). Children's biased evaluations of lucky versus unlucky people and their social groups. *Psychological Science, 17*, 845–846.

Paley, W. (1802/2006). *Natural theology; or, evidence of the existence and attributes of the deity*. New York, NY: Oxford University Press.

Piaget, J. (1932/1965/1978). *The moral judgment of the child*. Free Press.

Poehlman, T. A., Uhlmann, E. L., & Bargh, J. A. (2007). *Inherited ideology: An implicit link between work and sex morality in American cognition*. Unpublished manuscript.

Pronin, E., Gilovich, T., & Ross, L. (2004). Objectivity in the eye of the beholder: Perceptions of bias in self versus others. *Psychological Review, 111*, 781–799.

Pyszczynski, T., Greenberg, J., & Solomon, S. (1997). Why do we need what we need? A terror management perspective on the roots of human social motivation. *Psychological Inquiry, 8*, 1–20.

Pyszczynski, T., Greenberg, J., & Solomon, S. (1999). A dual-process model of defense against conscious and unconscious death-related thoughts: An extension of terror management theory. *Psychological Review, 106*, 835–845.

Pyszczynski, T., Solomon, S., & Greenberg, J. (2003). *In the wake of 9/11: The psychology of terror*. Washington, DC: American Psychological Association.

Rosenblatt, A., Greenberg, J., Solomon, S., Pyszczynski, T., & Lyon, D. (1989). Evidence for terror management theory: I. The effects of mortality salience on reactions to those who violate or uphold cultural values. *Journal of Personality and Social Psychology, 57*, 681–690.

Rudman, L. A. (2004). Sources of implicit attitudes. *Current Directions in Psychological Science, 13*, 80–83.

Sanchez-Burks, J. (2002). Protestant relational ideology and (in)attention to relational queues in work settings. *Journal of Personality and Social Psychology, 83*, 919–929.

Sanchez-Burks, J. (2005). Protestant relational ideology: The cognitive underpinnings and organizational implications of an American anomaly. *Research in Organizational Behavior, 26*, 267–308.

Schwartz, J. H. (1998). *What the bones tell us*. New York, NY: Henry Holt.

Schweder, R. A. (1991). *Thinking through cultures: Expeditions in cultural psychology*. Cambridge, MA: Harvard University Press.

Sheler, J. S. (2006). The lure of the prophetic world. In P. W. Bernstein & A. Swan (Eds.), *U.S. News & World Report special edition: Mysteries of faith: The prophets* (pp. 4–5). Washington, DC: U.S. News & World Report.

Sidanius, J., & Pratto, F. (1999). *Social dominance: An intergroup theory of social hierarchy and oppression*. New York, NY: Cambridge University Press.

Sinclair, S., Lowery, B. S., Hardin, C. D., & Colangelo, A. (2005). Social tuning of automatic racial attitudes: The role of affiliative motivation. *Journal of Personality and Social Psychology, 89*, 583–592.

Slone, J. D. (2004). *Theological incorrectness: Why religious people believe what they shouldn't*. New York, NY: Oxford University press.

Sniderman, P., & Piazza, T. (1993). *The scar of race*. Cambridge, MA: Harvard University Press.

Spelke, E. S., Breinlinger, K., Macomber, J., & Jacobson, K. (1992). Origins of knowledge. *Psychological Review, 99*, 605–632.

Sperber, D. (1985). Anthropology and psychology: Towards an epidemiology of representations. *Man, 20*, 73–89.

Sperber, Dan (1994). The modularity of thought and the epidemiology of representations. In L. A. Hirschfeld & S. A. Gelman (Eds.), *Mapping the Mind: Domain specificity in cognition and culture* (pp. 39–67). New York, NY: Cambridge University Press.

Spilka, B., Stout, L., Minton, B., & Sizemore, D. (1977). Death and personal faith: A psychometric investigation. *Journal for the Scientific Study of Religion, 16*, 169–178.

Srull, T. K., & Wyer, R. S. (1979). The role of category accessibility in the interpretation of information about persons: some determinants and implications. *Journal of Personality and Social Psychology, 37*, 1660–1672.

Steger, M. F., & Frazier, P. (2005). Meaning in life: One link in the chain from religiousness to well-being. *Journal of Counseling Psychology, 52*, 574–582.

Tetlock, P. E., Kristel, O., Elson, B., Green, M., & Lerner, J. (2000). The psychology of the unthinkable: Taboo trade-offs, forbidden base rates, and heretical counterfactuals. *Journal of Personality and Social Psychology, 78*, 853–870.

Tomasello, M., Carpenter, M., Call, J., Behne, H., & Moll, H. (2005). Understanding and sharing intentions: The origins of cultural cognition. *Behavioral and Brain Sciences, 28*, 675–735.

Tremlin, T. (2006). *Minds and gods: The cognitive foundations of religion*. New York, NY: Oxford University press.

Trompenaars, F., & Hampden-Turner, C. (1993). *Riding the waves of culture: Understanding diversity in global business*. New York, NY: McGraw-Hill.

Uhlmann, E. L., Poehlman, T. A., & Bargh, J. A. (in press). American moral exceptionalism. Chapter to appear in J. T. Jost, A. C. Kay, & H. Thorisdottir (Eds.), *Social and psychological bases of ideology and system justification*. New York, NY: Oxford University Press.

Uhlmann, E. L., Poehlman, T. A., & Bargh, J. A. (2007). *Implicit puritanism in American moral cognition*. Unpublished manuscript.

Vilchinsky, N., & Kravetz, S. (2005). How are religious belief and behavior good for you? An investigation of mediators relating religion to mental health in a sample of Israeli Jewish students. *Journal for the Scientific Study of Religion, 44*, 459–471.

Wald, K. D. (1987). *Religion and politics in the United States*. New York, NY: St. Martin's press.

Weber, M. (1904/1958). *The Protestant ethic and the spirit of capitalism*. New York, NY: Charles Scribner's Sons.

Wegner, D. M. (2002). *The illusion of conscious will*. Cambridge, MA: MIT press.

Wegner, D. M., & Bargh, J. A. (1998). Control and automaticity and social life. In D. T. Gilbert, S. T. Fiske, & G. Lindzey (Eds.), *Handbook of social psychology* (4th ed. (Vol. 1, pp. 446–496). New York, NY: McGraw-Hill.

Wegner, D. M., & Wheatley, T. P. (1999). Apparent mental causation: Sources of the experience of will. *American Psychologist, 54*, 480–492.

Wilson, D. S. (2002). *Darwin's cathedral: Evolution, religion, and the nature of society*. Chicago, IL: University of Chicago press.

Wilson, J. Q. (1993). *The moral sense*. New York: Free Press.

Wilson, T. D. (2002). *Strangers to ourselves: Discovering the adaptive unconscious*. Cambridge, MA: Belknap Press/Harvard University Press.

Wilson, T. D., Lindsey, S., & Schooler, T. Y. (2000). A model of dual attitudes. *Psychological Review, 107*, 101–126.

Woodward, A. L. (1998). Infants selectively encode the goal object of an actor's reach. *Cognition, 69*, 19–32.

Wulff, D. M. (2006). On the benefits, and costs, of being religious. *PsycCRITIQUES*.

Wynn, K. (1992). Addition and subtraction by human infants. *Nature, 349*, 748–750.

Zhong, C., & Liljenquist, K. (2006). Washing away your sins: Threatened morality and physical cleansing. *Science, 313*, 1451–1452.

Zurcher, L. A., Meadow, A., & Zurcher, S. L. (1965). Value orientation, role conflict, and alienation from work: A cross-cultural study. *American Sociological Review, 30*, 539–548.

5

Do Implicit Motives Add to Our Understanding of Psychological and Behavioral Outcomes Within and Across Cultures?

Jan Hofer[*] and Michael Harris Bond[†]

*University of Osnabrück, Osnabrück, Germany
†Chinese University of Hong Kong, Shatin, New Territories, Hong Kong

> "There are more things in heaven and earth, Horatio, than are
> dreamt of in your philosophy"
> —Shakespeare, *Hamlet*

Our position is simple: If we are to do a better job at predicting behavior both within and across cultural groups, we need to supplement our typical reliance on explicit measures of personality with implicit measures of motivation, beliefs, and values. Despite the extra training required for their measurement, despite their complex relationship with the social situations in which these concepts become operative, despite the struggles to make these measures cross-culturally equivalent, they add power to our armamentarium of predictive tools in psychology.

In this chapter, we will try to make a case for using implicit measures in cross-cultural psychology. Implicit measures may be even more useful in such investigations because they rely less heavily on the sophisticated cognitive processes that compromise the validity of explicit measures when used cross-culturally. Implicit measures alert psychologists to the power of situations in evoking the constructs being implicitly tapped, so our cross-cultural consideration of implicit measures leads into a closing discussion of culture's role in infusing situations with shared meaning, the very stuff of social psychology. This shared meaning interacts with the personalities of cultured carriers of that meaning to yield predictable behavior, the Golden Fleece of our labors as psychologists.

ELEMENTS OF PERSONALITY

As psychologists, our scientific goal is to describe, explain, and predict people's mental processes and their observable behaviors that arise out of the interplay of these mental processes and the situations people confront in daily living. As psychologists, we pursue our objectives by relying on different theoretical perspectives and concepts and, closely connected with it, by employing different types of strategies and measurements to assess and evaluate the scientific impact of those approaches and constructs. In contemporary research at least, three main components may be distinguished that are considered to constitute special and significant elements of personality affecting and shaping an individual's mental processes and public acts: (1) personality traits and temperaments (2) cognitions such as attitudes, beliefs, goals, and values, and (3) motivations (see Winter, 1996).

Each of these concepts has been developed and elaborated by its own theoretical school, inspiring countless empirical studies, thereby contributing to our growing understanding of the relationships between personality and individuals' thinking, feeling, and, to a lesser extent, acting. Unfortunately, these different components of the individual have led more or less separate lives with little opportunity for interaction and stimulating exchange. Furthermore, theorizing and empirical research on motivation, which we regard as the third significant element of personality, has tended more and more to ignore the conception of motivation as implicit in favor of an almost exclusively explicit approach. Such abandonment seems to be premature (McClelland, 1985), because, as we shall argue, implicit motivations predict important outcomes and supplement explicit measures of motivation in understanding human behavior. It is also scientifically shortsighted, because of the increasingly powerful role played by concepts of automaticity and implicit processes, of mental activations of which we are unaware and that help to explain the complex pattern of human functioning. Together, these lines of evidence support the idea that conscious and/or unconscious psychological forces have profound effects on our behavior (e.g., Bargh & Chartrand, 1999; Kuhl, 2001; Kihlstrom, 2002).

In our chapter, we wish to take the opportunity of presenting empirical evidence as well as theoretical considerations regarding the significance of including implicit measurements of motives along with other psychological constructs when studying and predicting people's thinking, feeling, and acting. We also will stress the impact of the socio-cultural context on individuals' behavior. In particular, theorizing and empirical research related to individual differences in psychological and behavioral outcomes across cultures emphasize the significance of social contexts (e.g., Markus & Kitayama, 1991; Smith et al., 2006) vital when considering motivation as an element of personality.

CULTURE AS CONTEXT

Culture is a nebulous concept, one that has mesmerized and bedeviled social scientists for centuries. It probably emerged out of economic exchanges between members of different social groups to help laypersons explain the often-inappropriate and bizarre behavior of persons from the other group, leading to a mystique about "the Stranger" (Simmel, 1950). As Berger (1987) has argued, humans have a basic need to reduce uncertainty about social life in order to better achieve their social goals through communication and coordination. Understanding the other is key to achieving greater certainty, and considerable attributional effort is expended to achieve greater clarity. "Culture" was a term coined in the initial struggle to figure out strange and difficult others.

We must put social scientific teeth into this suggestive, polysemous, but imprecise construct. Bond (2004) has provided yet another definition of culture, but one that may be especially useful for psychologists:

> A shared system of beliefs (what is true), values (what is important), expectations, especially about scripted behavioral sequences, and behavior meanings (what is implied by engaging in a given action) developed by a group over time to provide the requirements of living (food and water, protection against the elements, security, social belonging, appreciation and respect from others, and the exercise of one's skills in realizing one's life purpose) in a particular geographical niche. This shared system enhances communication of meaning and coordination of actions among a culture's members by reducing uncertainty and anxiety through making its members' behavior predictable, understandable, and valued (p. 62).

This definition focuses us behavioral scientists upon the individual outcomes, what Hofstede (1980) termed "the programming of the mind", that enable persons socialized into one cultural group to interact effectively with fellow group members. Even within a given cultural group, there will be different programming outcomes arising from different profiles of individual temperaments blending with individual differences in socialization histories. But generally, within-culture interactions proceed effortlessly, even "mindlessly" (Langer, 1989), because enculturation has created "sharedness", and are less problematic than across-culture interactions. In this sense, persons effectively socialized into a given cultural system become part of its social capital (Bourdieu, 1986). By extension of this logic, persons who are cross-culturally competent can serve as a bridging function across cultures and become "inter-cultural capital" as they can reduce the incidence of cross-cultural misunderstanding and conflict.

What are the sources of such differences in programming? Bond (2004) argued that,

> A broad conceptualization of what forces conduce towards shaping a cultural system would include the ecological characteristics of a group's physical environment, such as temperature, humidity and their variability, the type and depth of the resource base of the territory it occupies or shares with other groups, and the group's vulnerability to natural disaster (see Berry's, 1979, eco-social model of culture). These factors predispose a group towards certain political, economic, legal, social, educational, and familial patterns which in turn make socialization for certain norms, role expectations, values, beliefs, personality dispositions, and efficacies more likely (p. 63).

This orientation towards the operation of cultural influences on member programming requires fleshing out, so that we can better understand the impact of different social institutions and socialization inputs on culture group members. Our discipline needs to know how the folkways of a cultural system turn in to the self-ways of its members, the focus of most personality researchers. Smith et al. (2006, Chapter 5) provide a current summary of our knowledge about these socialization processes.

Regardless of how this necessary social outcome is effected, it happens as a result of multiple inputs both directly and implicitly reinforced across a culture member's lifespan. Some of the resulting self-ways, including motivations, will be consciously available to the individual, some not. As Markus and Kitayama (2003) put it, "Meanings and values may not be cognized and stored in memory at all. Instead, they may be so deeply ingrained in the everyday mundane practices of the culture that they are 'lived' rather than being 'known' or 'cognized.'" (p. 283). This claim reinforces an earlier observation by Cohen (1997) that:

> The scripts, the motivations, the expectations are all in our heads. But because they are either so overlearned (or were never explicitly taught in the first place), they may bypass conscious processing altogether. Our verbal reports and judgments are most clearly tied to conscious levels of processing, and so they may never get connected with the cultural rules embedded in our preconscious. Cultural patterns may get their power precisely because they work through this more basic level of processing and are not subject to conscious, rational analyses (pp. 126–127).

So, given the pervasiveness of culture's influences, its taken-for-grantedness, and its daily reinforcement by members of one's proximal social groups, much of culture's impact will be unconscious to the actor. We will then need to develop and test alternative measures for tapping into unconscious processes in order to assess their impact on routine functioning and observed differences in behavioral outcomes across cultural groups.

WHAT MOVES PEOPLE TO ACT?

Research on motivation deals particularly with the issue of what it is that moves people to act under certain situational conditions and why they pursue their activities with a certain intensity for a certain period of time (Atkinson, 1958; Heckhausen, 1977). Beyond this general definition of motivation, there exists little consensus on construing and explaining the phenomenon. For more than a century, academics have wrestled with this problem and a number of psychological constructs have been proposed as the force which energizes, selects, and directs an individual's behavior. In principle, two camps of scholars may be distinguished by their view of motivation as primarily affective with hardly any conscious representation (e.g., McClelland, 1985) or as a cognitive phenomenon of which people are aware and can accurately report (e.g., Carver & Scheier, 1981). While cognitive models of motivation became very popular in the course of the so-called cognitive revolution (e.g., Neisser, 1967), research interest on motivational processes that are difficult to access by introspection has clearly abated since the fifties, partly as a consequence of harsh criticism about the scientific quality of implicit measurements (e.g., Entwisle, 1972). Advocates of thematic apperception methods have successfully refuted a number of objections raised by critics (e.g., Lundy, 1985; see also Winter, 1998), and it seems that recent years have witnessed a resurgence of interest in implicit motives: Indicative of this trend are well-elaborated motivational theories (e.g., Kuhl, 2001) and a growing number of empirical studies integrating implicit motivational processes (e.g., Woike et al., 2003). We suggest that evidence on the insufficient (ecological) validity of self-report measurements (e.g., Nisbett & Wilson, 1977; Greenwald & Banaji, 1995) combined with a renewed interest in unconscious processes in other areas of psychology has helped restore researchers' curiosity about implicit motivational processes.

In this regard, developments in neuro-/bio-psychology (e.g., LeDoux, 2002) and cognitive psychology have to be mentioned in particular. Kihlstrom (2002) argued that this rediscovery of unconscious processes might be a reaction to a purely cognitive view of social interaction and other human behavior which inappropriately stressed conscious, rational, cognitive processes at the expense of the unconscious, irrational, emotive, and conative. More and more, psychologists are willing to consider that experiences, thoughts, and actions can be influenced by mental contents (e.g., percepts, memories, thoughts, feelings, and desires) or by some event in the current stimulus environment of which we are unaware (see also Reber, 1967; Schacter, 1987).

TWO MOTIVATIONAL SYSTEMS

David McClelland and colleagues (McClelland, 1987; McClelland et al., 1989) developed a comprehensive theoretical framework that may help to overcome the fragmentation within the field of (social) motivation (cf., Brody, 1980). It can do so because it offers a promising integration of diverse findings, concepts, and theories by considering biological, learned, and cognitive components of motivation. McClelland and his associates propose that goal-directed behavior is caused by two types of qualitatively different motives, namely implicit motives (e.g., need for power) and explicit (self-attributed) motives (e.g., motivational orientation towards power and dominance). They argue that implicit and explicit motives are acquired and shaped at different times in ontogenesis, are linked to different classes of behaviors, and, crucially, must be assessed by different methods.

Implicit (social) motives reflect humans' biological heritage as shaped by evolutionary forces, i.e., they direct and energize adequate (life-sustaining) behaviors, such as seeking contact or closeness to others. They represent a disposition to have a particular affectively toned, goal-centered associative network aroused (Winter & Stewart, 1978). Such anticipatory goal states are activated by natural incentives in the environment attendant upon performing an activity, which then allows the actor to enjoy the associated pleasant affect (Weinberger & McClelland, 1990). By experience and learning, implicit motives are, thus, primarily shaped during the early stages of cognitive development when language mastery has not yet been established (McClelland & Pilon, 1983). In consequence, implicit motives are likely to operate outside of conscious awareness and control, and are difficult to verbalize.

However, they are measurable by indirect means because researchers in this tradition believe that these foundational motivations clearly express themselves in individuals' fantasy (McClelland, 1987). Today, primarily experimentally derived scoring systems, which may be regarded as modifications of the classical Thematic Apperception Test (TAT) (Morgan & Murray, 1935), have been established as instruments for the measurement of implicit needs/motives (see Winter, 1998). Typically, participants are asked to tell stories about picture or sentence cues; these stories are then coded for themes or images related to a given motive domain. Using such instruments, researchers have provided substantial evidence that implicit motives guide individuals' long-term behavior in unconstrained or free-ranging situations (e.g., McAdams & Vaillant, 1982; Winter et al., 1998).

The second motivational system evolves later in ontogeny when cognitive structures have developed further and sufficiently. Above all, the mastery of language seems to be crucial for children to acquire advanced access to and control over their mental processes. More complex learning mechanisms less saturated with emotions allow the taking into account of immediate environmental pressures, demands, incentives, and expectations. These sophisticated cognitive mechanisms are decisive for the emergence of the second motivational system that reflects itself in individuals' consciously available values, goals, beliefs, attitudes, and self-concepts. There is evidence that explicit teaching by parents and others with respect to what is important for the child (e.g., to pursue particular goals, to follow certain rules) shapes the explicit motivational system. It is clear that this type of instruction can take place only after children have acquired an advanced mastery of language, which enables them to grasp the significance of the linguistic information, and to organize its meaning into such constructs as self, others, and socio-cultural norms (McClelland et al., 1989).

We expect that implicit motives are affected by their cultural context of acquisition, just as explicit motives are (Smith et al., 2006, Chapter 7). However, motivational constituents of the explicit system are more normative because, even if they are individually held conceptions, they are more influenceable by cultural productions requiring language and hence likely to be shared by most members of a given cultural or social group. As such, they reflect what is socially desirable and good or socially undesirable and bad (Phalet & Lens, 1995).

As people can volitionally and consciously reflect on their intentions, projects, and choices, and are able to manipulate goal states, they can report on the presence of explicit motives in interviews or personality questionnaires. There is substantial evidence that explicit motives, which are more apt to be stimulated by social-extrinsic incentives (e.g., social demands and expectations; Weinberger & McClelland, 1990; Brunstein & Maier, 2005), influence immediate actions and choice behavior in constrained situations in which individuals cognitively (have to) decide on a course of action (Ajzen & Fishbein, 1970; Patten & White, 1977). In other words, explicit motives seem to affect behavior and actions that are under conscious control and thus can (or must) be aligned with an individual's self-concept.

It is hypothesized that explicit motives provide meaningful outlets for personal implicit motivation; an individual's motivational self-perceptions may be able to channel the expression of implicit motives and may help to identify behavioral correlates of implicit motives (French & Lesser, 1964). However, it seems that many people developed implicit motives that are unrelated to or at odds with prevailing socio-cultural orientations. No significant relationship between these two types of motives has been verified in empirical research (e.g., Biernat, 1989), suggesting that, under normal circumstances of motive acquisition, cognitive mechanisms enabling the transfer across the two motive systems do not exist.

Evidence in favor of two systems of human motivation is also provided by empirically founded multi-coding theories of information processing (e.g., Epstein, 1994). In this context, Schultheiss (2001) suggests that the two types of motives, which are responsive to different incentives in the environment, are linked to different kinds of information processing:

> Implicit motives are considered to be part of the (emotionally driven) experiential system that automatically, rapidly, effortlessly, and efficiently processes information. The cognitive form of motivations, however, is associated with the verbal-symbolic/rational system that is best characterized in terms of a deliberative, effortful, abstract process that operates primarily through the medium of language (see also Kuhl, 2001).

In light of the above arguments and supportive evidence, we propose that humans' goal-oriented behavior is more adequately explainable by considering two motivational systems. Even if the explicit motivational system with its relatively short evolutionary history still has to prove its long-term usefulness (see Epstein, 1994), its enhanced openness to learning and its efficiency at reacting to changes in environmental demands are of advantage by giving the individual more freedom in planning, monitoring, and realizing behavioral strategies.

Yet, the more "primitive" system of human motivation, represented by a small number of biologically based and emotionally saturated implicit motives, is still not considered an essential constituent in many contemporary theories of human behavior (e.g., Bandura, 1997). However, a growing number of scientists argue that automaticity and priming completely dominates our behavior so that the assumption of conscious control may be an illusion (see Kihlstrom, 2002). By subscribing to either position, however, a significant element of personality is possibly neglected and sidelined from theoretical and empirical consideration. There is a large body of evidence supporting the conclusion that *both* unconscious and conscious forces are real and active. By excluding either type of motive, we ignore a basic element of personality. Thus, it seems indispensable to consider both types of motivational sources to understand the nature of humans' goal-oriented behavior and strategies within as well as across cultural contexts.

COMBINING BOTH MOTIVE SYSTEMS

Supporting this proposition is the finding from various researchers exploring various topics that by measuring both implicit and explicit motives, they can increase their ability to predict a given outcome. For example, implicit motives moderate the well-established positive link between commitments to goals, successful realization of goals, and subjective well-being. The pursuance of goals that are aligned to one's implicit motives and contribute to the satisfaction of implicit motives when realized is related to enhanced levels of well-being (Brunstein et al., 1998). In other words, consciously represented commitments to motive-congruent strivings and their behavioral implementation seem to yield an enhanced feeling of personal fulfillment.

However, there are pronounced differences between individuals in how far both types of motives are aligned with each other. In particular, self-regulatory processes, such as self-awareness, self-focusing, and self-consciousness, seem to affect integrative processes in the alignment of implicit and explicit motives (Schultheiss & Brunstein, 1999). Having a strong sense of leading a self-determined life, and testing commitments to goals and values for personal fit is associated with an engagement in need-congruent strivings (Thrash & Elliot, 2002; Hofer et al., 2006a). In contrast, an obstructed access to self-representations such as needs and feelings and emotional dependence on external sources of action control (motivation) and affect regulation (relaxation) relates to an increased tendency to mistake others' expectations, goals, and preferences for one's own (Brunstein, 2001).

EXPANDING THE PREDICTIVE AMBIT OF
IMPLICIT MOTIVES

Recent findings also indicate how fruitful it is to examine the influence of implicit motives on psychological processes that were previously not considered as a topic in the field of human motivation. For example, Woike and colleagues established a link between motivational dispositions and autobiographical memory, showing that implicit motives are associated with accessibility of emotional experiences (Woike et al., 2003). Zurbriggen (2000) examined the relationship between social cognition (power-sex associations) and implicit needs in predicting self-reports of sexual aggression. Furthermore, the idea of a link between implicit motivation and hormonal/psycho-physiological processes proposed by McClelland (1989) was taken up and elaborated by Schultheiss and associates, resulting in a number of studies that demonstrated a relationship between need for power, hormonal processes, and (non-conscious) instrumental learning (e.g., Schultheiss & Rohde, 2002; Schultheiss et al., 2005). Although McClelland (1985) already reported that differences in individuals' behavior can be explained by considering motives, values, and skills at the same time, only now does there seem to be growing interest in how far different elements of personality affect each other and, in the end, determine perception and behavior. For example, even if personality traits, i.e., conscious entities representing stable qualities of social significance that people have (McAdams, 1995), seem to be related to important life outcomes, such as divorce and occupational attainment (Roberts et al., 2007), Winter and colleagues have provided striking longitudinal evidence that motives and traits interact in the prediction of behavior: Whereas motives are describing the goals for which individuals strive, traits are describing how individuals act (see also Winter et al., 1998, for a discussion of conceptions of trait and motive). In consequence, both constructs are needed in explaining behavior.

To summarize, the meaningfulness of implicit motives in predicting individuals' psychological experience and real life behavior has been supported by numerous empirical studies which were conducted in Euro-American cultures. It might be, however, that many of these studies focused primarily on personal characteristics affecting the realization of needs and to a lesser extent on contextual determinants for motive realization because in Western cultures behavior and actions are typically interpreted as an outcome of an individual's personality rather than the socio-cultural environment (Sampson, 1981). We believe that our socialization into culture involves extended training about the relevance and enforcement probabilities of behavioral norms (Pepitone, 1976). They are essential inclusions in a cross-cultural model of behavior because beliefs about the relevant norms in a situation, which might be regarded as social incentives, will interact with aspects of personality to yield behavior (Hogan & Bond, in press).

CULTURAL CONTEXT AND MOTIVATED BEHAVIOR

Henry Murray (1938) was the first to develop an elaborated theory of human motivation involving both internal and external factors. He distinguished between *needs*, i.e., internal states that drive people's behavior, and *presses*, i.e., either real or perceived environmental forces which play a significant role in the manifestation of the needs. Probably due to the *Zeitgeist* dominating the Western psychological scene of that era, only needs became a major focus for research (Dana, 1999). However, the concept of presses already underlined the significance of socio-cultural contexts in predicting and understanding implicit motivational processes. Atkinson (1982) particularly emphasized the role of incentives *in context*. He emphasized how the interplay of dispositional motives and various situational cues and their associated incentives determines arousability and realization of implicit motives. In line with such reasoning, a number of studies conducted in Western cultures show that different situational contexts affect how far implicit and/or explicit motives are related to behavior (e.g., Andrews, 1967; Brunstein & Maier, 2005).

Cultures differ not only with respect to ecological and socio-economic conditions, but also in child-rearing practices, socialization patterns, dominant belief systems, values, and social rules for sanctioning and rewarding individuals' behavior (e.g., Keller & Greenfield, 2000). Thus, the socio-cultural context represents a crucial factor for the prediction of thoughts and behavioral acts because a culture's shared (early) socialization process shapes and reshapes basic human needs and cognitions leading to a readiness to act (or not to act) in particular and appropriate ways. Even if there is latitude for variation in motivation among members of a given cultural group arising from biological and educational variations, dominant socialization patterns may result in culture-bound motives, habits, roles, and models which guide one's behavior and are helpful to explain the behavior of others (see Bond, 2005).

In Western cultures, people's concrete acts are typically interpreted as reflecting one's personality; in non-Western cultures, behavior seems to be much more readily interpreted as responsive to the requirements of a particular situation (Choi et al., 1998). Thus, cultural peculiarities may not only shape the formation of implicit motives in early childhood, but may also channel the realization of motives by defining situations and incentives through which the motive is aroused as well as instrumental means by which it can be satisfied in a culturally appropriate way. As Winter (1996) concluded, even if a motive in its original form is probably an evolved innate aspect of our biological heritage, as an adult social motive, it represents a complex learned pattern of eliciting stimuli, emotional responses, and behaviors.

CROSS-CULTURAL RESEARCH ON IMPLICIT MOTIVES

Widely used personality constructs have generally been developed in Western contexts (cf., Cheung et al., 2003). Thus, cross-cultural research is indispensable to evaluate the generalizability of psychological theories or constructs because in other cultures other constructs might be important (see e.g., Zhang & Bond,

1998). For example, research on personality in China has provided evidence for an additional dimension beyond the Big-Five Model, labeled *Interpersonal Relatedness* (Cheung, 2006). Indeed, these newly unearthed constructs may be useful in other cultural traditions, too. So, Kwan et al. (1997) found that relationship harmony was an equally strong predictor of life satisfaction for both Hong Kong Chinese and Americans. Although there is a clear trend towards detection of differences across cultures (Brouwers et al., 2004), it is equally important to reveal similarities (Brown, 1991) and to discover whether, despite cultural variations, psychological constructs and hypothesized relationships between psychological constructs can be identified in humans universally. In research on implicit motives, both lines of research have proved to be fruitful for our understanding of human motivation.

TYPES OF MOTIVATION STUDIED

Probably the single most researched need is the achievement motive, i.e., the desire to do things well, to overcome obstacles, to do things better (McClelland, 1987), and available research represents a good example of the advantage of assuming a cross-cultural approach to human motivation. McClelland and associates were criticized for neglecting situational and contextual determinants of human motivation and, in line with such arguments, a number of studies point to a qualitatively differing type of achievement motivation which in non-Western societies is characterized by a pronounced, socially oriented element (e.g., Kagan & Knight, 1981; Doi, 1982). The concept of social-oriented achievement is based on a need for social approval by meeting expectations of significant persons and groups, rather than on an effort to solely strive towards self-enhancement. Findings reported by Sorrentino (1974; Sorrentino & Shepphard, 1978) for US-American samples support the argument for a link between relational concerns (i.e., need for affiliation), social approval, and effort in an achievement-oriented activity. In particular, scholars studying Chinese culture emphasized that pushing oneself ahead of others, setting one's own goals and actively seeking individual success is not universally valued (Bond & Hwang, 1986; Yu & Yang, 1994; Yu, 1996). Thus, even if a kind of mastery motive (a general desire for agency and control) is to be seen as universal, the disparity of experiences, rewards, and punishments across cultures may lead to the development of different concerns for achievement, different releasing stimuli, different domains of action, and different standards of evaluation.

Interestingly, Phalet and Lens (1995) identified both types of achievement motivation in Western and non-Western samples. Thus, it might be that individuals develop ego-oriented and social-oriented achievement standards in all cultures. However, recurrent contexts in given cultures may differ in their claim for a particular realization of the achievement motive and consequently lead to observed differences in achievement-oriented behavior. Cultures may be conceived of psychologically as salience-inducing contexts, making certain aspects of a general phenomenon more apparent and more responsive to certain stimulus conditions. Constructs salient in one culture, and forming a focus for psychological investigation in that cultural tradition may nonetheless be useful complements to any pan-cultural theory of motivated behavior. Their discovery constitutes one of the key legitimations for cross-cultural research (Bond, 1999).

Cross-cultural work on the need for power, i.e., the desire or need to impact on other people, to control, or to hold influential and prestigious positions (Winter, 1973), and the need for affiliation-intimacy, i.e., a need for warm, close relations with others, and a concern for establishing, maintaining, or restoring a positive affective relationship with another person or group of people (Heyns et al., 1958; McAdams, 1980), is less available. Recent cross-cultural research on needs for power and affiliation-intimacy, however, points to both differences in levels of motive strength and similarities of motive correlates (e.g., well-being).

CONFRONTING CULTURAL BIAS

Keeping in mind that meaningful comparisons between cultural groups can only be made if sources of bias are addressed and successfully ruled out, Hofer and colleagues implemented an integrated examination of construct, method, and item bias in their cross-cultural research on implicit needs for power and affiliation-intimacy (Hofer et al., 2005). Construct bias is present when the definition of a construct under investigation only partially overlaps across cultures. Depending on its source, it is useful to differentiate three types of method bias: administration bias (e.g., communication problems between test administrator and participants), instrument bias (e.g., differential familiarity with test settings and methods of assessment), and sample bias (e.g., sampling differences in test-relevant background characteristics of the participants).

Finally, item bias or differential item functioning is based on characteristics of single items (e.g., their content or wording is not equivalent). An item is considered to be biased when subjects with the same underlying psychological construct (e.g., strength of power motivation) from different cultural samples react diversely to a given item (e.g., picture card of a man speaking to a woman). Neglecting issues of equivalence in cross-cultural research leads to interpretation problems because alternative explanations such as differences in construct definition cannot be eliminated (for an overview of methodological issues in cross-cultural research see, e.g., van de Vijver & Leung, 1997).

Hofer and colleagues were able to establish construct equivalence of needs for power and affiliation-intimacy by scrutinizing cross-cultural meaningfulness of established motive indicators in samples from Cameroon, Costa Rica, and Germany (Hofer et al., 2005). These cultures were selected because of reported differences in self-construal: People in Cameroon seem to be best characterized as holding an interdependent construal of their self – defined as comprising heteronomy and relatedness – which is adaptive in rural populations with lower socio-economic and educational status; people in Germany seem to be best characterized as holding an independent self – defined as comprising autonomy and separateness – which is adaptive in a culture characterized by great wealth, mass and elite education as well as a long democratic tradition. Finally, samples from Costa Rica were chosen because an autonomous-related self is adaptive for individuals who live in a traditionally interdependent society characterized by increasing urbanization, education, and affluence (see Keller et al., 2004; Kağitçibaşi, 2005).

Various precautions were set in the study design to prevent the occurrence of method bias in data collection, such as balancing cultural samples with regard to important background characteristics (e.g., level of education), extensive training of local test administrators, use of fixed scoring rules, and examination of inter-rater agreements. Furthermore, group differences in familiarity with the stimulus material and the testing situation, both representing a recurrent problem in cross-cultural studies, were minimized by giving participants from all cultural groups a detailed and vivid introduction to picture-story tests.

Due to theoretical considerations on culture-bound situational incentives for motive pull, namely item/picture bias, the study further aimed to identify contexts (picture cards depicting various scenes) which elicit motive imagery to an equal extent among participants, regardless of their culture of origin. For example, Ng (2006) recently reported differences in the arousal of power motivation between the US American and Chinese students. Whereas Chinese participants (from both Beijing and Hong Kong) were primarily motivated by the status aspect of power, the US American students were mainly motivated by the decision-making aspect of power. Similarly, the study conducted by Hofer and colleagues demonstrates that marked cross-cultural differences exist concerning picture cards depicting various scenes which are cross-culturally comparable with respect to motive pull for power and affiliation-intimacy (see also Hofer & Chasiotis, 2004). In pretests, half of the picture cards had to be removed because they triggered motives differently across cultures. For example, one of the cards depicted a ship captain talking to another man. Stories by Cameroonian respondents scored much higher for the power motive than stories written by Costa Rican and German participants. In other words, even if individuals have a general desire for affiliation and power, contexts for motive realization, as depicted in the picture cards, differ to some extent across cultures.

It is noticeable that our knowledge concerning reasons why a particular item turned out to be biased is often limited. There is growing awareness that, even if the elimination of biased items is crucial from a methodological point of view, a close scrutiny of biased items may be very interesting from a psychological perspective because it may help us to understand sources of differences between cultures (van de Vijver, 2000). The discipline of social psychology has been struggling to define situations in scientifically useable ways (Seeman, 1997), and cross-cultural work needs to integrate our understanding of the "pull-power" of different types of situations into our prediction of behavior across cultural groups (Bond, 2005).

After removing such biased pictures, bias-free stimulus sets for the assessment of implicit motives (power and affiliation-intimacy) across cultural groups could be statistically identified in the study by Hofer and colleagues. Thus, a contextual analysis of motive-related imagery (behavior) across cultures seems to be promising for identifying situations which are universally characterized by cues that signal positive or negative incentives (e.g., acceptance or rejection) and result in observable behavioral realizations of implicit motives (see Fyans et al., 1983).

DISCOVERING PAN-CULTURAL RELATIONSHIPS

Applying such psychometrically sound measurements cross-culturally, researchers have recently revealed a number of universal relationships between implicit motives and psychological and behavioral correlates. Not only do conscious and non-conscious forms of motivation operate independently and add to the prediction of subjective well-being (Zeldow et al., 1988; McAuley et al., 2004), but they can interact to conjointly shape individuals' phenomenal experience related to well-being. Hofer et al. (2006b) showed for the domain of affiliation that, even if differences in the strength of motives are present across three diverse cultural groups, participants with a pronounced implicit need for affiliation-intimacy experience higher levels of life satisfaction when their conscious benevolence values (see Schwartz, 1992) are aligned with the strength of their implicit need (see also Hofer & Chasiotis, 2003).

Also, the proposed developmental link between the presence of younger siblings and a pro-social realization of the power motive, i.e., an implicit desire to have a positive impact on other people's emotions or behaviors (e.g., Winter & Barenbaum, 1985), has been supported by cross-cultural research (Chasiotis et al., 2006), and may constitute a cross-cultural universal: A developmental pathway assuming that the interactional context of having younger siblings during childhood shapes the development of an implicit pro-social motivation which in turn influences the verbalized, explicit articulation of parenting attitudes finally leading to becoming a parent was confirmed among cultural samples from Latin-America, sub-Saharan Africa, and Europe. In another cross-cultural study, a linkage between implicit power motivation and generativity, i.e., the concern in establishing and guiding the next generation (Erikson, 1950), could be verified. It was found that a pronounced pro-social realization of the power motive is turned into a generative disposition which itself has important consequences: It determines to what extent the individual develops generative goals, and this generative disposition has a direct link to global life satisfaction (Hofer et al., 2008). Again, this is a demonstration of a possibly pan-cultural universal related to Erikson's (1950) earlier speculations about a key developmental concern, viz., whether the final stages of one's life are characterized by generativity or stagnation and despair.

NEXT STEPS

The scoring of implicit motives is time-consuming, thought-intensive work, be it TAT coding of stimulus cards or other computer-assisted methodologies for assessing other key motivational constructs, like self-esteem (Greenwald & Banaji, 1995). Much of the cross-cultural research already described gives hope that the research is doable, and also provides methodological templates for executing the work, but we are still left with the question, "Why would anyone take this work across cultures where equivalence issues add to the already daunting challenge of assessing implicit motivations?"

A first reason is the capacity of implicit measurements to obviate methodological problems of self-reports in mono- and multi-cultural research. The questions, to which extent measurements are equally appropriate for different (cultural) groups, and whether test scores can be interpreted in the same way across populations, are relevant for all types of measurements. While proponents of self-report measures generally recognize the need to establish equivalence of verbal meaning, the problem of establishing equivalence of response categories is less recognized. Also, a substantial body of evidence shows that individuals of higher age, lower education, and lower socio-economic status are more likely to show response bias, particularly social desirability and acquiescence (Grimm & Church, 1999). Thus, implicit measurement may add to our understanding of psychological and behavioral processes across individuals of various demographic backgrounds and cultures (Smith, 2004) by permitting meaningful insights about facets of personality uncompromised by these distortions in responding.

Let us accept this argument as well as the assumption that psychological functioning and behavior are affected by (cultural) influences that are automatically processed and do not reach the level of cognitive representation. It then seems promising to go beyond the assessment of implicit motives and place increased emphasis on implicit measurements of additional psychological constructs. Findings on implicit social cognition (e.g., Greenwald & Banaji, 1995), on need for uncertainty (e.g., Shuper et al., 2004; Sorrentino et al., this volume), and on the role of implicit measurements of activity inhibition on stress and mood (Langens & Stucke, 2005) represent only some examples of the advantages gained by considering implicit processes. Similarly, implicit measures of constructs that are currently ignored in research, such as Feffer's (1959) scoring system for spontaneous interpersonal decentering (i.e., consideration of another person's ideas, thoughts, feelings, or actions for subsequent modification of one's own behavior) and future generations of indirect, implicit measurements, might add to our understanding of non-normative psychological processes and social behavior. Thereby, our knowledge of the extent to which different measures of the same (motivational) domain do (or do not) overlap will be continuously broadened. A core issue in this context, of course, is how these measures have been developed, that is, whether they are experimentally (as Winter, 1998, elegantly demonstrates for thematic apperception measures in a McClellandian tradition) or theoretically derived. An intensified focus on the integration of implicit and explicit measurements in research is important from a theoretical point of view too; active research on this topic enables a scientifically sound decision to be made on whether the distinction between implicit and explicit motivation as two separate motive systems is appropriate, thus helping to explain the intricate puzzle of human motivation and actions (Bilsky & Schwartz, in press).

A second reason for working with implicit motives cross-culturally is to supplement current theoretical and empirical approaches, with their focus on traits and attitudes, by considering an additional central aspect when measuring personality and its correlates across cultures. Taking implicit measurements into account would also help in realizing recurrent claims for integrative approaches combining input from different methods and cultures, and would enable us to develop more comprehensive models for explaining social behavior (e.g., Bornstein, 2002; Bond, 2005).

A third reason is to establish developmental universals of the sort described with the example of generativity. If nomological networks of constructs in which each motivation is embedded are socialized in the same way, implicit motivations will be similarly powerful pan-culturally. Such findings would support many theories of human development and social behavior that are presumed to be universal in their applicability, but whose status as universals has not been tested empirically.

A fourth reason is to examine cultural differences (and similarities) in the process whereby behavior "gets done". Such an increased focus on behavioral outcomes and a consideration of the full range of factors leading to those outcomes would be beneficial for psychological research, as the prediction of social behavior represents a litmus test for our cross-cultural discipline (Bond, 2005). Even if there are a number of psychological constructs that are supposed to drive individuals' behavior, the prominence of implicit motives for social behavior is well documented (e.g., Winter et al., 1998). Consequently, non-consideration of implicit motives clearly runs the risk of neglecting a basic and decisive factor.

CONCEPTUALIZING A ROLE FOR CULTURE

There might be further reasons in favor of using implicit measurements, but let us first determine if we are able to predict individuals' psychological functioning and social behavior across cultures by including measurements of implicit motives: How might aspects of culture, such as power distance (Hofstede, 1980) or social cynicism (Leung & Bond, 2004) as "psychological" dimensions of culture, and human rights observance (Humana, 1992) or income inequality (Wilkinson, 1996) as "societal" dimensions of culture, affect the processes involved in translating motives into behavior? Is situational context relatively more important than internal motivations in generating behavior in collectivist cultural groups, as is often alleged (Triandis, 1995)? Do implicit motives carry relatively greater weight than explicit motives in some cultures than others, for what outcomes, and why? Will the use of implicit measures reveal more about culture than we have so far managed with our more explicit measures that are easier to use, but so limited in their applicability to many cultural populations?

Do implicit measures hold the key to unlocking some of our more intractable, practical problems in the psychology of living, such as violence (Bond, 2007)? In short, do we have a general framework that considers all these factors which conjointly shape the psychological outcomes of interest, be they internal processes or the observable behaviors that they drive and guide?

Even if it is widely accepted among scholars that culture has a pervasive reach into individuals' mental processes and behavioral acts, a common theoretical frame for research on personality and behavior across cultures is missing. Recurrent calls to make culture vital to theory and research in psychology (e.g., Pepitone, 1976; Cole, 1996) are still realized by highly different approaches based on two different traditions in defining culture: Whereas one views psychological phenomena as being inseparably linked to their cultural context (culture as a molar Gestalt), the second views culture as a set of antecedent variables that are associated with psychological functioning (molecular view of culture, see Segall, 1984). We propose a theoretical model that essentially includes all significant elements of personality enabling us to disentangle the impact of psychological and social factors on psychological outcomes and to explore and predict social behavior across cultural groups.

Basically, our model emanates from the claim for a multi-variate approach in psychological (cross-cultural) research and posits that an individual's inner experience and observable behavior are both determined by an interplay of different facets of personality, namely relatively stable personal characteristics such as traits, dispositions, temperament, cognitions, and motivations. These facets interact with social situations, defined in terms of their normative constitution, to yield the observable differences we attribute to cultural influence.

The cultural context plays a prominent role in our considerations: On the one hand, the cultural context affects the shaping of personality and, on the other hand, it affects an individual in a given situation by representing a major source of behavioral determinants that have their locus outside the individual (Pepitone, 1976). Referring to personality, people who grow up in a similar socio-cultural context are likely to have similar learning experiences and, thus, are likely to develop similar beliefs, value orientations, and dispositions concerning meaning and consequences of behavior (see Bond, 2004). According to Koltko-Rivera (2004), they are likely to develop similar worldviews, i.e., a set of conscious beliefs about physical and social reality. These constitute a normative social order which then becomes legitimized (Berger, 1967), and within which individuals from that culture function (Pepitone, 1976).

Culture is not only reflected in consciously represented psychological constructs, but shapes the forming of implicit motives via cultural models of parenting and socialization in early childhood. Such culture-bound patterns of socialization, which are, for example, characterized by different emphasis which is placed on obedience or early autonomy (see Keller, 2007), may lead to distinct levels of motive dispositions and will define contexts and behavioral expressions that are embedded in the cultural context (Hofer et al., 2006b).

Referring to the social determinants of behavior, Pepitone (1976) argued that it is crucial to understand the role of norms. As he argues,

> "... the social phenomena of interest to social psychologists in the real world, as well as the dependent variables investigated in the field and laboratory, tend to be wholly or partly 'normative' By normative is meant that such social behavior is more characteristic (e.g., more uniform) of some socio-cultural collective unit than of individuals observed at random" (p. 642).

It is rather unlikely that people are simply or directly realizing their conscious intentions. Instead, their behavior is affected by normative socio-cultural demands such as role obligations, communication styles, or norms for displaying (or not) certain behaviors in a given situation. For example, observed differences in behavior across cultures may be a function of different role demands, rather than of personality variables (Bond, 2005) or of different general display rules for the expression of emotions (Matsumoto et al., 2005).

RESEARCHING INTO THE FUTURE

With this proposed model the basic sources of social behavior can be examined to develop a more comprehensive understanding of behavior within and across cultures. Linkages between psychological constructs and outcomes may then be identified and their universality assessed. For example, the relationship between motives and behavior may be moderated or mediated by additional factors such as the individual's worldview. Socio-cultural contexts differ from each other in prevalent worldviews and consequently in how far they allow individuals to choose from a number of behavioral alternatives. Such individually held expectancies interact with implicit and explicit motives to orient behavior in a given cultural context (Bond, 2005). Thus, associations between an implicit motivational impulse and behavioral acts may, for example, differ across cultures as dominant value orientations and beliefs constrain thoughts and behavior of those who are psychologically part of these collective entities (Pepitone, 1976).

The answer to the question, "What it is that moves one to act?" is neither personality nor culture. Rather, the person has to be considered as acting in a given socio-cultural context to answer this question. It would be shortsighted only to examine personal or contextual factors; a combined examination of person and context will lead to findings that will enhance our knowledge of cultural peculiarities and universal phenomena in psychological functioning and social behavior. Past and current social contexts are part of our personalities, affecting forms of expression of all the other parts (Winter, 2005).

We claim that implicit motives are a decisive part of the model for research on personality and behavior, as they represent a fundamental source of human behavior and psychological features. It is assumed that implicit motives represent the first motivational system to be shaped in a human being's ontogeny. They have far reaching consequences for individuals' development, their feelings and actions in everyday life.

Not only do implicit motives affect how frequently individuals enter certain social contexts, but findings reported by Schultheiss and colleagues (e.g., Schultheiss & Hale, 2007) provide further evidence for the claim that situations and persons are differently perceived by individuals depending on their strength of implicit motives. Culture enters here, too, as it shapes the development of implicit motives through early acculturation, a central determinant of both perception and behavior. Hence, it is essential to examine how motives are elicited by distinctive features of the situation, because, as Mischel and Shoda (1995) pointed out, the way in which a personality disposition is realized in behavior depends on the psychologically apprehended features of situations.

> "Great lords, wise men ne'er sit and wail their loss, but cheerily seek to redeem their harms."
>
> Shakespeare, *Henry VI*

ACKNOWLEDGMENT

We are grateful to David Winter and James Pennebaker for their helpful comments and suggestions on an earlier version of this manuscript.

REFERENCES

Ajzen, I., & Fishbein, M. (1970). The prediction of behavior from attitudinal and normative variables. *Journal of Experimental Social Psychology, 6,* 466–487.

Andrews, J. D. W. (1967). The achievement motive and advancement in two types of organizations. *Journal of Personality and Social Psychology, 6,* 163–168.

Atkinson, J. W. (1958). *Motives in fantasy, action, and society.* Princeton, NJ: Van Nostrand.

Atkinson, J. W. (1982). Motivational determinants of thematic apperception. In A. J. Stewart (Ed.), *Motivation and society* (pp. 3–40). San Francisco, CA: Jossey-Bass Publishers.

Bandura, A. (1997). *Self-efficacy: The exercise of control.* New York: Freeman.

Bargh, J. A., & Chartrand, T. L. (1999). The unbearable automaticity of being. *American Psychologist, 54,* 462–479.

Berger, C. R. (1987). Communicating under uncertainty. In M. E. Roloff & G. R. Miller (Eds.), *Interpersonal processes* (pp. 39–62). Newbury Park, CA: Sage.

Berger, P. L. (1967). *The sacred canopy: Elements of a sociological theory of religion.* New York: Anchor.

Berry, J. W. (1979). A cultural ecology of social behavior. In L. Berkowitz (Ed.), *Advances in experimental social psychology* (Vol. 12, pp. 177–206). New York: Academic Press.

Biernat, M. (1989). Motives and values to achieve: Different constructs with different effects. *Journal of Personality, 57,* 69–95.

Bilsky, W., & Schwartz, S.H. (in press). Measuring motivations: Integrating content and method. *Personality and Individual Differences.*

Bond, M. H. (1999). The psychology of the Chinese people: A Marco Polo returns to Italy. *Psychologia Italiana, 17,* 29–33.

Bond, M. H. (2004). Culture and aggression – from context to coercion. *Personality and Social Psychology Review, 8,* 62–78.

Bond, M. H. (2005). A cultural-psychological model for explaining differences in social behavior: Positioning the belief construct. In R. M. Sorrentino, D. Cohen, J. M. Olson, & M. P. Zanna (Eds.), *Culture and social behavior* (Vol. 10, pp. 31–48). Manwah, NJ: Lawrence Erlbaum.

Bond, M.H. (2007). Culture and collective violence: How good people, usually men, do bad things. In B. Drozdek & J.P. Wilson (Eds.), *Voices of trauma: Treating survivors across cultures* (pp. 27–57). New York: Springer.

Bond, M. H., & Hwang, K. K. (1986). The social psychology of Chinese people. In M. H. Bond (Ed.), *The psychology of the Chinese people* (pp. 213–264). Hong Kong: Oxford University Press.

Bornstein, M. H. (2002). Toward a multiculture, multiage, multimethod science. *Human Development, 45*, 257–263.

Bourdieu, P. (1986). The forms of capital. In J. E. Richardson (Ed.), *Handbook of theory and research for the sociology of education* (pp. 241–258). New York: Greenwood.

Brody, N. (1980). Social motivation. *Annual Review of Psychology, 31*, 143–168.

Brouwers, S. A., Van Hemert, D. A., Breugelmans, S. M., & van de Vijver, F. J. R. (2004). A historical analysis of empirical studies published in the Journal of Cross-Cultural Psychology 1970–2004. *Journal of Cross-Cultural Psychology, 35*, 251–262.

Brown, D. E. (1991). *Human universals*. New York: McGraw-Hill.

Brunstein, J. C. (2001). Persönliche Ziele und Handlungs- versus Lageorientierung. Wer bindet sich an realistische und bedürfniskongruente Ziele?. *Zeitschrift für Differentielle und Diagnostische Psychologie, 22*, 1–12.

Brunstein, J. C., & Maier, G. W. (2005). Implicit and self-attributed motives to achieve: Two separate but interacting needs. *Journal of Personality and Social Psychology, 89*, 205–222.

Brunstein, J. C., Schultheiss, O. C., & Grässmann, R. (1998). Personal goals and emotional well-being: The moderating role of motive dispositions. *Journal of Personality and Social Psychology, 75*, 494–508.

Carver, C. S., & Scheier, M. F. (1981). *Attention and self-regulation: A control theory approach to human behavior*. New York: Springer.

Chasiotis, A., Hofer, J., & Campos, D. (2006). When does liking children lead to parenthood? Younger siblings, implicit prosocial power motivation, and explicit love for children predict parenthood across cultures. *Journal of Cultural and Evolutionary Psychology, 4*, 95–123.

Cheung, F. M. (2006). A combined emic-etic approach to cross-cultural personality test development: The case of the CPAI. In Q. Jing, H. Zhang, & K. Zhang (Eds.), *Psychological science around the world* (Vol. 2, pp. 91–103). London: Psychology Press.

Cheung, F. M., Cheung, S. F., Wada, S., & Zhang, J. (2003). Indigenous measures of personality assessment in Asian countries: A review. *Psychological Assessment, 15*, 280–289.

Choi, I., Nisbett, R. E., & Norenzayan, A. (1998). Causal attribution across cultures: Variation and universality. *Psychological Bulletin, 125*, 47–63.

Cohen, D. (1997). Ifs and thens in cross-cultural psychology. In R. S. Wyer,, Jr. (Ed.), *The automaticity of everyday life* (pp. 121–131). Manwah, NJ: Erlbaum.

Cole, M. (1996). *Cultural psychology*. Cambridge, MA: Harvard University Press.

Dana, R. H. (1999). Cross-cultural, multicultural use of the thematic apperception test. In L. Gieser & M. I. Stein (Eds.), *The thematic apperception test and the art of projection* (pp. 177–190). Washington, DC: American Psychological Association.

Doi, K. (1982). A two dimensional theory of achievement motivation: Affiliative and non-affiliative. *Japanese Journal of Psychology, 52*, 344–350.

Entwisle, D. R. (1972). To dispel fantasies about fantasy-based measures of achievement motivation. *Psychological Bulletin, 77*, 377–391.

Epstein, S. (1994). Integration of the cognitive and the psychodynamic unconscious. *American Psychologist, 49*, 709–724.

Erikson, E. H. (1950). *Childhood and society*. New York: Norton.

Feffer, M. H. (1959). The cognitive implications of role-taking behavior. *Journal of Personality, 27*, 152–158.

French, E. G., & Lesser, G. S. (1964). Some characteristics of the achievement motive in women. *Journal of Abnormal and Social Psychology, 68*, 119–128.

Fyans, L. J.,, Jr., Salili, F., Maehr, M. L., & Desai, K. A. (1983). A cross-cultural exploration into meaning of achievement. *Journal of Personality and Social Psychology, 44*, 1000–1013.

Greenwald, A. G., & Banaji, M. R. (1995). Implicit social cognition: Attitudes, self-esteem, and stereotypes. *Psychological Review, 102*, 4–27.

Grimm, S. D., & Church, T. A. (1999). A cross-cultural investigation of response biases in personality measures. *Journal of Research in Personality, 33*, 415–441.

Heckhausen, H. (1977). Achievement motivation and its constructs: A cognitive model. *Motivation and Emotion, 4*, 283–329.

Heyns, R. W., Veroff, J., & Atkinson, J. W. (1958). A scoring manual for the affiliation motive. In J. W. Atkinson (Ed.), *Motives in fantasy, action, and society* (pp. 205–218). Princeton, NJ: Van Nostrand.

Hofer, J., Busch, H., Chasiotis, A., Kärtner, J., & Campos, D. (2008). Concern for generativity and its relation to implicit pro-social power motivation, generative goals, and satisfaction with life: A cross-cultural investigation. *Journal of Personality, 76*, 1–30.

Hofer, J., Busch, H., Chasiotis, A., & Kießling, F. (2006a). Motive congruence and interpersonal identity status. *Journal of Personality, 74*, 511–541.

Hofer, J., & Chasiotis, A. (2003). Congruence of life goals and implicit motives as predictors of life satisfaction: Cross-cultural implications of a study of Zambian male adolescents. *Motivation and Emotion, 27*, 251–272.

Hofer, J., & Chasiotis, A. (2004). Methodological considerations of applying a TAT-type picture-story-test in cross-cultural research: A comparison of German and Zambian adolescents. *Journal of Cross-Cultural Psychology, 35*, 224–241.

Hofer, J., Chasiotis, A., & Campos, D. (2006b). Congruence between social values and implicit motives: Effects on life satisfaction across three cultures. *European Journal of Personality, 20*, 305–324.

Hofer, J., Chasiotis, A., Friedlmeier, W., Busch, H., & Campos, D. (2005). The measurement of implicit motives in three cultures: Power and affiliation in Cameroon, Costa Rica, and Germany. *Journal of Cross-Cultural Psychology, 36*, 689–716.

Hofstede, G. (1980). *Culture's consequences: International differences in work-related values.* Beverly Hills, CA: Sage.

Hogan, R., & Bond, M. H. (in press). Culture and personality. In P. Corr & G. Matthews (Eds.), *The Cambridge handbook of personality.* Cambridge, UK: Cambridge University Press.

Humana, C. (1992). *World human rights guide.* New York: Oxford University Press.

Kagan, S., & Knight, G. P. (1981). Social motives among Anglo American and Mexican American children: Experimental and projective measures. *Journal of Research in Personality, 15*, 93–106.

Kağitçibaşi, C. (2005). Autonomy and relatedness in cultural context: Implications for self and family. *Journal of Cross-Cultural Psychology, 36*, 403–422.

Keller, H. (2007). *Cultures of infancy.* Mahwah, NJ: Erlbaum.

Keller, H., & Greenfield, P. M. (2000). History and future development in cross-cultural psychology. *Journal of Cross-Cultural Psychology, 31*, 52–62.

Keller, H., Yovsi, R., Borke, J., Kärtner, J., Jensen, H., & Papaligoura, Z. (2004). Developmental consequences of early parenting experiences: Self-recognition and self-regulation in three cultural communities. *Child Development, 75*, 1745–1760.

Kihlstrom, J. F. (2002). The unconscious. In V. S. Ramachandran (Ed.), *Encyclopedia of the human brain* (Vol. 4, pp. 635–646). San Diego, CA: Academic.

Koltko-Rivera, M. E. (2004). The psychology of worldviews. *Review of General Psychology, 8*, 3–58.

Kuhl, J. (2001). *Motivation und persönlichkeit. Interaktionen psychischer systeme.* Göttingen: Hogrefe.

Kwan, V. S. Y., Bond, M. H., & Singelis, T. M. (1997). Pan-cultural explanations for life satisfaction: Adding relationship harmony to self-esteem. *Journal of Personality and Social Psychology, 73*, 1038–1051.

Langens, T. A., & Stucke, T. S. (2005). Stress and mood: The moderating role of activity inhibition. *Journal of Personality, 73,* 47–78.

Langer, E. (1989). *Mindfulness.* Reading, MA: Addison-Wesley.

LeDoux, J. E. (2002). *The synaptic self.* New York: Viking Press.

Leung, K., & Bond, M. H. (2004). Social axioms: A model for social beliefs in multi-cultural perspective. In, *Advances in experimental social psychology* (Vol. 36, pp. 119–197). San Diego, CA: Elsevier Academic Press.

Lundy, A. (1985). The reliability of the thematic apperception test. *Journal of Research in Personality, 49,* 141–145.

Markus, H. R., & Kitayama, S. (1991). Culture and the self: Implications for cognition, emotion, and motivation. *Psychological Review, 98,* 224–253.

Markus, H. R., & Kitayama, S. (2003). Culture, self, and the reality of the social. *Psychological Inquiry, 14,* 277–283.

Matsumoto, D., Yoo, S. H., Anguas-Wong, A. M., Arriola, M., Ataca, B., Bond, M. H., et al. (2008). *Mapping expressive differences around the world: Journal of Cross-Cultural Psychology, 39,* 55–74.

McAdams, D. P. (1980). A thematic coding system for the intimacy motive. *Journal of Research in Personality, 14,* 413–432.

McAdams, D. P. (1995). What do we know when we know a person? *Journal of Personality, 63,* 365–396.

McAdams, D. P., & Vaillant, G. E. (1982). Intimacy, motivation and psycho-social adjustment: A longitudinal study. *Journal of Personality Assessment, 46,* 586–593.

McAuley, P. C., Bond, M. H., & Ng, I. W.-C. (2004). Antecedents of subjective well-being in working Hong Kong adults. *Journal of Psychology in Chinese Societies, 1,* 25–49.

McClelland, D. C. (1985). How motives, skills, and values determine what people do. *American Psychologist, 40,* 812–825.

McClelland, D. C. (1987). *Human motivation.* New York: Cambridge University Press.

McClelland, D. C. (1989). Motivational factors in health and disease. *American Psychologist, 44,* 675–683.

McClelland, D. C., Koestner, R., & Weinberger, J. (1989). How do self-attributed and implicit motives differ?. *Psychological Review, 96,* 690–702.

McClelland, D. C., & Pilon, D. A. (1983). Sources of adult motives in patterns of parent behavior in early childhood. *Journal of Personality and Social Psychology, 44,* 564–574.

Mischel, W., & Shoda, Y. (1995). A cognitive-affective system theory of personality: Reconceptualizing situations, dispositions, dynamics, and invariance in personality structure. *Psychological Review, 102,* 246–268.

Morgan, C. D., & Murray, H. H. (1935). A method for investigating fantasies: The thematic apperception test. *Archives of Neurology and Psychiatry, 34,* 289–306.

Murray, H. A. (1938). *Explorations in personality.* New York: Oxford University Press.

Neisser, U. (1967). *Cognitive Psychology.* Englewood Cliffs, NJ: Prentice Hall.

Ng, I. (2006). *A cross-cultural study of power and power motivation in China and the United States.* Unpublished Doctoral Dissertation, University of Michigan, Ann Arbor.

Nisbett, R. E., & Wilson, T. D. (1977). Telling more than we can know: Verbal reports on mental processes. *Psychological Review, 84,* 231–259.

Patten, R. L., & White, L. A. (1977). Independent effects of achievement motivation and overt attribution on achievement behavior. *Motivation and Emotion, 1,* 39–59.

Pepitone, A. (1976). Toward a normative and comparative biocultural social psychology. *Journal of Personality and Social Psychology, 34,* 641–653.

Phalet, K., & Lens, W. (1995). Achievement motivation and group loyalty among Turkish and Belgian Youngsters. In M. L. Maehr & P. R. Pintrich (Eds.), *Advances in motivation and achievement: Culture, motivation and achievement* (Vol. 9, pp. 31–72). Greenwich, CT: JAI Press.

Reber, A. S. (1967). Implicit learning of artificial grammars. *Journal of Verbal Learning and Verbal Behavior, 6,* 855–863.

Roberts, B. W., Kuncel, N. R., Shiner, R., Caspi, A., & Goldberg, L. R. (2007). The power of personality: The comparative validity of personality traits, SES, and cognitive ability for important life outcomes. *Perspectives on Psychological Science, 2*, 313–345.

Sampson, E. E. (1981). Cognitive psychology as ideology. *American Psychologist, 36*, 730–733.

Schacter, D. L. (1987). Implicit memory: History and current status. *Journal of Experimental Psychology: Learning, Memory, and Cognition, 13*, 501–518.

Schultheiss, O. C. (2001). An information processing account of implicit motive arousal. In M. L. Maehr & P. R. Pintrich (Eds.), *Advances in motivation and achievement: New directions in measures and methods* (Vol. 12, pp. 1–41). Greenwich, CT: JAI Press.

Schultheiss, O. C., & Brunstein, J. C. (1999). Goal imagery: Bridging the gap between implicit motives and explicit goals. *Journal of Personality, 67*, 1–38.

Schultheiss, O. C., & Hale, J. A. (2007). Implicit motives modulate attentional orienting to facial expressions of emotion. *Motivation and Emotion, 31*, 13–24.

Schultheiss, O. C., & Rohde, W. (2002). Implicit power motivation predicts men's testosteron changes and implicit learning in a contest situation. *Hormones and Behavior, 41*, 195–202.

Schultheiss, O. C., Wirth, M. M., Torges, C. M., Pang, J. S., Villacorta, M. A., & Welsh, K. M. (2005). Effects of implicit power motivation on men's and women's implicit learning and testosterone changes after social victory or defeat. *Journal of Personality and Social Psychology, 88*, 174–188.

Schwartz, S. H. (1992). Universals in the content and structure of values: Theoretical advances and empirical tests in 20 countries. In M. Zanna (Ed.), *Advances in experimental social psychology* (Vol. 25, pp. 1–65). Orlando, FL: Academic Press.

Seeman, M. (1997). The neglected, elusive situation in social psychology. *Social Psychology Quarterly, 60*, 4–13.

Segall, M. H. (1984). More than we need to know about culture, but are afraid to ask. *Journal of Cross-Cultural Psychology, 15*, 153–162.

Shuper, P. A., Sorrentino, R. M., Otsubo, Y., Hodson, G., & Walzer, A. M. (2004). A theory of uncertainty orientation: Implications for the study of individual differences within and across cultures. *Journal of Cross-Cultural psychology, 35*, 460–480.

Simmel, G. (1950). The stranger. In K. Wolff (Ed. and trans.), *The sociology of George Simmel* (pp. 402–408). New York: Free Press.

Smith, P. B. (2004). Acquiescent response bias as an aspect of cultural communication style. *Journal of Cross-Cultural Psychology, 35*, 50–61.

Smith, P. B., Bond, M. H., & Kagitcibasi, C. (2006). *Understanding social psychology across cultures*. London: Sage.

Sorrentino, R. M. (1974). Extending initial and elaborated theory of achievement motivation to the study of group processes. In J. W. Atkinson & J. O. Raynor (Eds.), *Motivation and achievement* (pp. 255–267). Washington, D.C.: Winston.

Sorrentino, R. M., & Shepphard, B. H. (1978). Effects of affiliation-related motives on swimmers in individual versus group competition: A field experiment. *Journal of Personality and Social Psychology, 36*, 704–714.

Thrash, T. M., & Elliot, A. J. (2002). Implicit and self-attributed achievement motives: Concordance and predictive validity. *Journal of Personality, 70*, 729–755.

Triandis, H. C. (1995). *Individualism and collectivism*. Boulder, CO: Westview.

van de Vijver, F. J. R. (2000). The nature of bias. In R. H. Dana (Ed.), *Handbook of cross-cultural and multi-cultural personality assessment* (pp. 87–106). Mahwah, NJ: Lawrence Erlbaum.

van de Vijver, F. J. R., & Leung, K. (1997). *Methods and data analysis for cross-cultural research*. Newbury Park, CA: Sage.

Weinberger, J., & McClelland, D. C. (1990). Cognitive versus traditional motivational models. Irreconcilable or complementary?. In E. T. Higgins & R. M. Sorrentino (Eds.), *Handbook of motivation and cognition: Vol. 2. Foundations of social behavior* (pp. 562–597). New York: Guilford Press.

Wilkinson, R. G. (1996). *Unhealthy societies: The afflictions of inequality*. London: Routledge.

Winter, D. G. (1973). *The power motive*. New York: Free Press.

Winter, D. G. (1996). *Personality: Analysis and interpretation of lives*. New York: McGraw-Hill.

Winter, D. G. (1998). "Toward a science of personality psychology": David McClelland's development of empirically derived TAT measures. *History of Psychology, 1*, 130–153.

Winter, D. G. (2005). Things I've learned about personality from studying political leaders at a distance. *Journal of Personality, 73*, 557–584.

Winter, D. G., & Barenbaum, N. B. (1985). Responsibility and the power motive in women and men. *Journal of Personality, 53*, 335–355.

Winter, D. G., John, O. P., Stewart, A. J., Klohnen, E. C., & Duncan, L. E. (1998). Traits and motives: Toward an integration of two traditions in personality research. *Psychological Review, 105*, 230–250.

Winter, D. G., & Stewart, A. J. (1978). The power motive. In H. London & J. E. Exner (Eds.), *Dimensions of personality* (pp. 391–447). New York: Wiley.

Woike, B., McLeod, S., & Goggin, M. (2003). Implicit and explicit motives influence accessibility to different autobiographical knowledge. *Personality and Social Psychology Bulletin, 29*, 1046–1055.

Yu, A.-B. (1996). Ultimate life concerns, self, and Chinese achievement motivation. In M. H. Bond (Ed.), *The handbook of Chinese psychology* (pp. 227–246). Hong Kong: Oxford University Press.

Yu, A.-B., & Yang, K. S. (1994). The nature of achievement motivation in collectivist societies. In U. Kim, H. C. Triandis, C. Kağitçibaşi, S. C. Choi, & G. Yoon (Eds.), *Individualism and collectivism: Theory, method, and applications* (pp. 239–250). Thousand Oaks, CA: Sage.

Zeldow, P. B., Daugherty, S. R., & McAdams, D. P. (1988). Intimacy, power, and psychological well-being in medical students. *The Journal of Nervous and Mental Disease, 176*, 182–187.

Zhang, J., & Bond, M. H. (1998). Personality and filial piety among college students in two Chinese societies: The added value of indigenous constructs. *Journal of Cross-Cultural Psychology, 29*, 402–417.

Zurbriggen, E. L. (2000). Social motives and cognitive power-sex associations: Predictors of aggressive sexual behavior. *Journal of Personality and Social Psychology, 78*, 559–581.

6

A CROSS-CULTURAL ANALYSIS OF SELF-VERIFICATION MOTIVES

TAMMY ENGLISH*, SERENA CHEN* AND WILLIAM B. SWANN, JR.†

*Department of Psychology, University of California, Berkeley, USA
†Department of Psychology, University of Texas, Austin, USA

Self-verification theory (Swann, 1983, 1990) focuses on people's desire to be known and understood by others. It proposes that once people develop firmly held beliefs about themselves, they come to prefer that others see them as they see themselves. The research literature offers robust evidence that people do indeed make systematic efforts to obtain self-confirming feedback. In both laboratory studies (e.g., Swann et al., 1992a; Hixon & Swann, 1993) and naturally occurring settings (Swann & Pelham, 2002a), people demonstrate a preference for others who confirm their self-views. However, one limitation of existing research on self-verification theory is that thus far it has been conducted primarily with North American samples. The goal of this chapter is to assess the likelihood that self-verification is a culture general phenomenon. To this end, we first provide an overview of self-verification theory and research, and then discuss whether the roots of self-verification extend to cultures outside of North America and, if so, what form self-verification strivings would take in these cultures. Ultimately, we propose that self-verification strivings are universal, although cross-cultural differences in conceptions of the self may result in cultural variation in the ways they are pursued.

SELF-VERIFICATION THEORY

Self-verification theory proposes that people are motivated to be seen by others as they see themselves, or to obtain appraisals from others that confirm their firmly held self-conceptions. The theory enjoys over 2 decades of support. For example, research has repeatedly shown that people prefer both evaluations and interaction partners that confirm their enduring self-views (e.g., Swann et al., 1990; Robinson & Smith-Lovin, 1992; Swann et al., 1992b; Hixon & Swann, 1993). Importantly, people who hold negative views of the self seek and receive self-verification, just as do people who hold positive views (e.g., Swann et al., 1989; McNulty & Swann, 1994), thus demonstrating that self-verification motives may at times override well-documented, self-enhancing tendencies to seek flattering appraisals of the self.

EPISTEMIC AND PRAGMATIC ROOTS

Why do people seek self-verification? Self-verification theory has origins in self-consistency theory (e.g., Lecky, 1945; Festinger, 1957; Secord & Backman, 1965), but its focus is primarily on people's desire for psychological coherence in the self-concept rather than consistency per se. According to the theory, people strive for verification in an effort to arrive at and maintain stable views of the self, as such enduring self-views confer a "crucial source of coherence, an invaluable means of defining their existence, organizing experience, and guiding social interaction" (Swann et al., 2003, p. 369). In other words, stable, coherent self-views provide a sense of order and understanding in people's lives. They reassure people that they can predict and control their future outcomes, which in turn helps them navigate their social environments. Whereas consistency strivings may lead existing self-views to be updated or even abandoned in the face of new, self-relevant information or events, the coherence strivings that define self-verification work to maintain self-views, assimilating even contradictory, self-relevant information and events into the existing self-system. Stable, coherent self-views are so crucial that people will fight to maintain them even when doing so causes them discomfort. For example, people prefer feedback that confirms their negative self-views despite the fact that such feedback arouses negative affect in the short term (e.g., Swann et al., 1987; Swann et al., 1989).

There are both epistemic and pragmatic roots to the desire for psychological coherence, and the prediction and control such coherence allows, that fuel self-verification strivings (Swann, 1990). On an epistemic level, being verified assures people that their self-views accurately reflect social reality, and thus that they can rely on their beliefs about the self to anticipate and exert control over their outcomes. Further, it is psychologically comforting for people to feel that they know themselves and to have the sense of unity and meaning that stable self-views offer. In contrast, self-disconfirmatory feedback frustrates the search for psychological coherence, and therefore can be unsettling and may even result in anxiety (Wood et al., 2005).

Pragmatically speaking, self-verifying appraisals bolster people's sense of prediction and control by assuring them that others hold appropriate expectations of them and thus that their interactions with others will proceed smoothly. In relationships, by allowing people to maintain stable self-views, self-verifying appraisals offer mutual predictability to relationship partners (Swann et al., 2007). Conversely, self-discrepant appraisals may invite conflict and misunderstanding, leading to decreased interpersonal harmony and perhaps relationship dissolution. Indeed, self-verification processes have been shown to have significant implications for relationship satisfaction and longevity. For example, spouses and roommates who do not verify each other's central self-views are less satisfied in their relationship and more likely to end the relationship than those who do verify each other (Swann et al., 1994; Swann & Pelham, 2002a). In small groups, people experience stronger feelings of connection to the group when group members verify one another's self-views (e.g., Swann et al., 2000). Connection, intimacy, and perceptions of caring depend on feeling understood (Reis & Shaver, 1988), so if individuals are not verified by their relationship and group partners, negative relationship and group outcomes are likely to result.

To assess why people seek self-verification, Swann and colleagues (Swann et al., 1992a) asked people to indicate their reasons for choosing a self-verifying over a non-verifying interaction partner. Supporting the epistemic and pragmatic roots of self-verification strivings, these researchers found that the most common reasons given were epistemic (e.g., "I'd feel more at ease with someone who can judge me for what I am") and pragmatic (e.g., "Seeing as he knows what he's dealing with we might get along better") in nature.

SELF-VERIFICATION STRATEGIES

The desire for self-verification leads people to work to create a social environment that allows for a relatively effortless, self-perpetuating confirmation of their self-views (Swann, 1983). That is, people gravitate toward, and strive to create, environments that foster stability in their self-views and that insulate them from disconfirming appraisals. For instance, in everyday life people often unconsciously display markers of their self-views that may be used as the basis of others' appraisals of them. Along these lines, research has shown that some characteristics (e.g., extraversion) are reliably predicted from the appearance of a person (Naumann et al., 2006) and the physical structure of their living space (e.g., bedroom, office; Gosling et al., 2002). In addition, people can control others' appraisals of them through their interaction style, including amount of eye contact and frequency of interrupting conversation. Finally, individuals tend to approach self-confirming partners and avoid disconfirming partners (Swann et al., 1994; Swann & Pelham, 2002a). For example, Swann (1992) showed that participants with negative self-views chose to interact with a negative evaluator over participating in another study, yet opted to be in another study rather than interact with a positive evaluator. Such interaction partner preferences should decrease the likelihood that people are faced with partners who hold disconfirming appraisals of them (Swann et al., 1992c).

Beyond efforts to create a self-confirmatory social environment, people have a number of cognitive strategies at their disposal in their pursuit of self-verification.

For example, to maintain a sense of psychological coherence when confronted with non-verifying feedback, it is not uncommon for people to engage in biased processing of the disconfirming feedback so that it is disregarded, not encoded, or misconstrued as confirming. People judge self-verifying information to be more valid than non-verifying information (Swann et al., 1987), and attend more to, and thus better remember, the former kind of information (Swann & Read, 1981). In sum, people can elicit self-verification from others by displaying signs and symbols associated with their self-perceived identities, interacting in such a manner so as to demonstrate that they embody a given quality, selectively interacting with individuals who confirm their self-views, and selectively processing information in a self-verifying manner.

MODERATORS OF SELF-VERIFICATION

Self-verification motives stand alongside a variety of other possible self-evaluative motives, among them self-enhancement, self-assessment, and self-improvement (e.g., Swann & Schroeder, 1995; Taylor et al., 1995). Research has identified moderating variables that render self-verification more or less likely to predominate over these other motives. For example, self-verification is more likely when people have the cognitive capacity to introspect (Hixon & Swann, 1993), and when they have just received feedback indicating that an evaluator views them in a manner discrepant from their own self-view (Swann & Read, 1981). Other work suggests that the more committed one is to a source of self-evaluation, the more one seeks verification from this source. For instance, marital partners are more likely than dating partners to seek self-verification from one another (Swann et al., 1994). These findings could be driven by either or both a tendency to view the opinions of committed partners as more reliable and valid (i.e., epistemic concerns) or a stronger desire to maintain orderly interactions with these partners (i.e., pragmatic concerns).

Finally, self-verification strivings are especially likely for personally important or central self-views, as well as self-views that are held confidently (e.g., Pelham & Swann, 1994; Chen et al., 2004). For example, Swann and Pelham (2002a) showed that only college students who deemed their self-views personally important or were certain of them showed a preference for roommates who confirmed these self-views. The moderating impact of self-view centrality and certainty makes sense from both epistemic and pragmatic standpoints. Highly central and highly certain self-conceptions are core to a person's identity (Pelham, 1991); thus, when they are not verified, the person's sense of knowing the self is seriously challenged, and the potential for interpersonal misunderstandings and conflicts looms large.

CULTURE AND SELF-VERIFICATION

Having described existing theory and research on self-verification, the vast majority of which is based on North American samples, we now turn to a cross-cultural analysis of self-verification motives. Our analysis is grounded in two major propositions. First, we propose that the epistemic and pragmatic roots of self-verification are likely universal, implying that self-verification may be pursued across cultures. Second, however, we propose that the form of self-verification strivings may differ across cultures depending on the nature of the stable self-views that are most dominant and central in a given culture. In elaborating on these two propositions, our analysis will emphasize East Asian cultures because they have been the focus of most cross-cultural research to date, thus providing the largest evidentiary basis on which to make predictions regarding the extent and precise nature of self-verification strivings. However, our examination of East Asian cultures may offer hints as to how self-verification motives would operate in other cultures to the extent that these cultures are characterized by similar beliefs and values. That is, our predictions regarding self-verification among East Asians are not based on East Asian cultures per se, but rather on cultural dimensions (e.g., interdependence) that characterize these cultures, and that may potentially characterize others as well (e.g., Latin American and African cultures). Thus, East Asian cultures are the starting point for our cross-cultural analysis of self-verification motives, but ultimately we suggest that they offer a springboard for a broader analysis.

EPISTEMIC AND PRAGMATIC CONCERNS UNDERLYING SELF-VERIFICATION STRIVINGS

Is the desire for self-verification – for coherent and stable self-views – universal? As noted, self-verification theory assumes that the desire for confirmation of one's enduring self-views, and the sense of prediction and control that such verification confers, has both epistemic and pragmatic roots. Our first major proposition is that these epistemic and pragmatic underpinnings of self-verification strivings are universal. We consider the possible universality of each in turn, and then focus on their presence in East Asian cultures.

Universality of Epistemic Needs

Wide-ranging theory and research suggest that the epistemic need for psychological coherence may be universal (Popper, 1963; Guidano & Liotti, 1983; Swann, 1990; Heine et al., 2006). Basic social cognition research clearly implies the universal importance of meaning making (e.g., Heider, 1944, 1958; Bruner et al., 1956), even if the nature of meaning making processes differ across cultures (e.g., Nisbett et al., 2001). In addition, theories of human psychological needs have often recognized the intrapsychic importance of having a sense of stability and coherence. For instance, the universal importance of maintaining a sense of order and prediction in the world is suggested by the need for security in Maslow (1954) motivational hierarchy, and Epstein (1990) need for self-concept consistency. Other examples of motives related to epistemic needs for coherence include the need for closure (Kruglanski, 1990), or the desire to avoid ambiguity, and the need for structure (Neuberg & Newsom, 1993), or the desire to cognitively structure the world in ways that reduce complexity. Although the need for closure and need for structure are thought to vary across individuals, research has demonstrated such individual variations in not only North America, but also in, for example, countries in Eastern and Western Europe, as well as in Australia, Korea, and China, suggesting that these motivational constructs are meaningful cross-culturally.

Researchers have also highlighted the fundamental need for psychological coherence – for a sense of prediction, order, and understanding – in the self-concept specifically. In early thinking about the nature of the self-concept, James (1890) suggested that although individuals hold different selves across relationships and roles, a sense of unity in the self-concept is crucial. Later, Erikson (1963) argued that during identity development individuals search for a "sense of continuity and sameness" (p. 261). More recently, Vignoles et al., (2006) have suggested that the motivations to maintain continuity and meaning in the self-concept are universally important, although culture may shape how these motivations are satisfied. As a final example, the narrative approach to identity (McAdams, 1985, 1993, 2001) is strongly rooted in the assumption that individuals strive for coherence in their self-concept. Specifically, identity is thought to take the form of a story that integrates self-relevant experiences into a unified, meaningful form. People's identity stories are influenced by the norms and values of their specific social environment (Thorne, 2000; McAdams, 2001). Thus, there may be cultural differences in the nature of people's stories, but all seek to construct a coherent and meaningful identity.

Universality of Pragmatic Needs

As noted, beyond satisfying epistemic needs, self-verification is desired because it addresses pragmatic, interpersonal concerns. Namely, by providing interaction partners with mutual predictability, self-verification fosters harmonious interactions and lasting relationships. To the extent that relationships play a fundamental role in human functioning, this pragmatic facet of the desire for self-verification may well be universal. Indeed it has long been argued that the need to maintain relationships with others is of primary importance for human beings. For instance, attachment theory (Bowlby, 1969, 1973) suggests that we rely on others for comfort and support in order to be able to survive in and learn about the world. More recently, self-determination theory (Deci & Ryan, 2000) and cognitive experiential self-theory (Epstein, 1990) have proposed that a feeling of connection to others is universally essential for well-being and optimal psychological functioning. Similarly, both Maslow (1954) and Baumeister and Leary (1995) argue that humans have a fundamental need to belong, suggesting that harmonious relationships with others are a necessary condition for humans to thrive. Finally, from an evolutionary perspective, the mutual predictability that self-verification provides would have helped to maintain social bonds (e.g., mate relationships, coalitions) that were crucial to survival and that reap reproductive benefits (e.g., hunting large animals, protection, sharing food, care giving; Brewer & Caporael, 2006; Stevens & Fiske, 1995; North & Swann, in press).

Research supports the assertion that humans need healthy social bonds for optimal physical and psychological functioning. Being embedded in healthy social relationships is a key determinant of subjective well-being (Ryff & Keyes, 1995; Diener & Seligman, 2002). For example, Diener and Diener (1995) report that life satisfaction is linked to relationship satisfaction in many cultures, such as Australia, Brazil, Korea, South Africa, and the United States. In addition, social support has positive physical implications in terms of the cardiovascular, endocrine, and immune systems (Uchino et al., 1996). Conversely, the negative psychological consequences (e.g., abnormal emotional and social behavior) of lacking healthy social bonds have been demonstrated in, for instance, both socially isolated animals (Suomi & Harlow, 1972) and human infants who receive inadequate attention (Belsky, 1990).

Epistemic and Pragmatic Concerns in East Asian Cultures

The above theory and evidence suggest that the epistemic and pragmatic roots of self-verification strivings may be universal, but how well does this first proposition hold up in cultures outside of North America? More specifically, are the epistemic and pragmatic concerns driving self-verification applicable to members of East Asian cultures? This cultural group is a particularly interesting one to explore in terms of self-verification strivings because East Asians are thought to value, and are often characterized by, flexibility, or a seeming lack of consistency (e.g., Peng & Nisbett, 1999; Choi & Choi, 2002; Suh, 2002). For instance, East Asians' theories about personality characterize traits as malleable (Chiu et al., 1997), and their self-reported emotions vary more across relationship contexts than do North Americans' (Oishi et al., 2004). Self-verification is seemingly at odds with such flexibility, because seeking verification of self-views is in the service of stability, or maintaining existing self-views. Therefore, self-verification strivings might not only be muted, but they may actually be discouraged, in East Asian cultures.

As noted earlier, however, the focus of self-verification theory is on psychological coherence rather than on consistency per se. Consistency involves the logical relationship between two psychological elements, such as the persona one assumes in the workplace and at home. To maintain such consistency, incoming information or events may be accommodated, leading to change in the self-system. In contrast, coherence refers to a broader sense of order among the elements of one's psychological universe, including aspects of one's enduring self-concept. To maintain coherence, incoming information and events are assimilated, thus preserving the self-system. Indeed, it is possible for individuals to maintain a sense of coherence even in the face of inconsistency. For example, people may construct narratives that explain the inconsistency and that integrate disparate aspects of the self, thereby achieving unity and meaning – that is, a sense of coherence – within an overarching theory of self (McAdams, 2001;

Vignoles et al., 2006). The distinction between consistency and coherence suggest that although East Asians may be characterized by a seeming disregard for consistency, it is still possible for them to seek coherence.

Indeed, there is some evidence to support the idea that even if East Asians value consistency less than North Americans, they impute as much value to psychological coherence. For instance, East Asians' attributional tendencies suggest they have an epistemic need to make sense of events and people in the world (Heider, 1958; Jones et al., 1972). Dispositional attributions are particularly useful in satisfying epistemic needs, and thereby conferring a sense of prediction and control, because they refer to the enduring qualities of a person, and thus allow predictions to be made about others' behavior across time and situations. Although East Asians often use situational factors to explain events, they also make use of dispositional attributions, sometimes to the same extent as North Americans do (Choi et al., 1999). For example, Choi and Nisbett (1998) found that East Asians only used more situational attributions than North Americans when the situation was made highly salient. Otherwise, both groups were just as likely to explain events using dispositional, personality attributes.

Turning to the pragmatic roots of self-verification, there is a vast array of evidence to suggest that the interpersonal concerns fueling self-verification extend to East Asian cultures. In fact, Sheldon et al. (2001) found that although the need for relatedness is considered to be important among both Koreans and North Americans, it is rated as more important among Koreans. Members of interdependent cultures, such as East Asian ones, are particularly concerned with the pragmatic elements of prediction and control because of the emphasis placed on relationship maintenance in these cultures (Triandis, 1989; Markus & Kitayama, 1991). In interdependent cultures the self is inextricably tied to others and emphasis is placed on meeting in-group members' expectations in order to maintain harmony in one's relationships. Accordingly, East Asians are more likely than North Americans to, for instance, include relational markers in their spontaneous self-descriptions (Cousins, 1989) and experience interpersonally engaged (e.g., shame) rather than disengaged (e.g., anger) emotions (Kitayama et al., 2000).

SELF-VERIFICATION OF DIFFERENT FORMS OF SELF-VIEWS

If our first proposition is correct, that the epistemic and pragmatic concerns underlying self-verification are indeed universal, then self-verification motives are likely pursued at least to some degree across all cultures. However, one important question that arises is whether the form of self-verification strivings is the same across different cultures. As noted, research suggests that self-verification efforts are focused on self-views that are stable and personally important (Pelham & Swann, 1994). The bulk of past self-verification research has focused on global, cross-situationally stable self-views, which are tacitly or explicitly assumed to be among the most important conceptions of the self in North American cultures (e.g., Greenwald, 1980; Markus, 1977; McCrae & Costa, 1996). In our second proposition, we suggest that the same principle may hold for other forms of self-views. That is, people strive to verify the self-views that are stable and most central or core to their self-definition, in whatever form these self-views take. After elaborating on this proposition, we review supportive evidence showing that self-verification strivings can be directed at various types of self-views, global and otherwise, provided these self-views are stable and important to one's self-definition. Finally, we examine whether our second proposition holds in East Asian cultures in particular.

As stated, our second proposition is that the form of self-views that individuals work to verify may vary across cultures according to different cultural values and lay beliefs about the self. More to the point, there may be cultural variation in the dominant target of self-verification efforts depending on the type of self-views that are fostered within a given culture and internalized by its members as core to their self-definition. At the same time, we recognize that although individuals typically define themselves in culturally normative ways, they may nonetheless possess some self-views of a non-normative form that are stable and personally important to their self-definition (e.g., Brewer & Gardner, 1996), and accordingly, that they strive to verify. For instance, North Americans' self-verification efforts may focus on global self-views because, on average, such self-views tend to be the most salient or chronic form of self-definition in North American culture, but these individuals may nonetheless possess some stable and personally important context-specific self-views and seek to confirm them as well.

Although context-specificity of self-views implies instability in the self-concept across contexts, it is still possible for contextualized self-views to be the target of self-verification efforts if they are stable over time. According to interactionist, Person x Situation views of the self and personality (e.g., Mischel & Shoda, 1995), coherence and continuity in the self can be derived from maintaining conceptions of the self that vary across different contexts, but that are nonetheless stable within similar situations over time. From this perspective, each individual is thought to have a distinct behavioral signature, or "if ... then ..." profile, wherein the "if" refers to the situation and the "then" refers to the individual's response in the situation (Shoda et al., 1993; Mischel & Shoda, 1995; Mendoza-Denton et al., 2001; Mendoza-Denton & Mischel, in press). Supporting the above analysis, research with North American samples indicates that, in addition to global self-views, people may hold stable, contextualized self-views that reflect the self in a particular physical situation or setting (e.g., English & Chen, 2007), the self in relation to specific relationship partners, or relational self-views (e.g., Andersen & Chen, 2002; Chen et al., 2006a), and the self as a group member, or collective self-views (e.g., Tajfel & Turner, 1986).

Furthermore, there is evidence that self-verification strivings may be directed at these different forms of contextualized self-views. For example, Chen et al. (2006b) showed that individuals who tend to define themselves in situation-specific terms were more likely to prefer confirming over disconfirming feedback about personally important, situationally contextualized attributes (e.g., outgoing at parties) than were individuals who tend to define themselves in more global terms. Similarly, Swann et al., (2002) found that people were motivated to verify relationship-specific self-views, and were successful in eliciting feedback from their relationship partners that verified such self-views. More specifically, participants were asked how they would ideally like to be seen by their partner and how accurate their partner would be if they saw them in such a manner, with a close association being interpreted as evidence of strategic self-verification. Other studies examining self-verification at a relationship-specific level have shown that some individuals prefer feedback that confirms rather than disconfirms personally important aspects of their relational selves (e.g., bossy with sibling; Chen et al., 2006b) and are more likely to desire verifying over non-verifying feedback about personally important, relationship-specific attributes from new interaction partners (Kraus & Chen, 2007). Moreover, the accuracy of people's context specific perceptions of their relationship partners is positively associated with relationship quality (Gill & Swann, 2004).

Similar effects have been reported for verification of core collective self-views. For example, in a series of studies Chen et al. (2004) showed that participants preferred to interact with a partner who verified a negative, collective self-view over a non-verifying partner when the self-view in question was confidently held and the partner was an ingroup member. Another study found that participants reported a greater desire for collective self-verification from an ingroup member on attribute dimensions that were highly central to defining their group compared to low-centrality attributes. This centrality effect was particularly apparent among participants who were highly identified with the group. In a similar vein, other work has shown that participants' self-proclaimed group memberships predicted their reflected categorizations (i.e., perceptions of being categorized by others into their self-proclaimed groups), and that this effect was stronger when initial, self-proclaimed group memberships were high in importance (Lemay & Ashmore, 2004).

THE FORM OF SELF-VERIFICATION IN EAST ASIAN CULTURES

Having proposed that self-verification efforts will focus on whichever stable self-views are most central or personally important, and reviewed some evidence in support of this proposition in North American cultures, we now turn to a discussion of how this proposition may apply in East Asian cultures. In predicting the form that self-verification will take in a specific culture, we have suggested that one needs to consider the nature of the core self-conceptions that are fostered in the particular culture. Thus, we first review some major theories and relevant findings concerning the nature of the self-concept among members of East Asian cultures, and then discuss how self-verification motives might operate in these cultures. To preview our argument, we suggest that although the kind of global, cross-situationally stable self-views that the literature shows people seek to self-verify appear to be less central to the self-concepts of East Asian relative to Westerners, self-verification strivings may be directed at other forms of stable self-views.

The Nature of East Asians' Self-Concept

Cultural psychologists have taken various approaches to understanding how conceptions of the self may differ across cultures. The most attention has been given to individualism and collectivism (Triandis, 1989, 1990), independent and interdependent self-construals (Markus & Kitayama, 1991), and dialectical lay beliefs (Morris & Peng, 1994). Although the details of these theories vary to some degree, they all suggest that East Asians' self-concepts are more flexible and responsive to the social context than are those of Westerners.

Individualistic cultures (e.g., United States, Australia) promote the value of independence from others and emphasize individual needs, goals, and rights. In contrast, collectivistic cultures (e.g., East Asia, Latin America) value interdependence and focus on in-group goals, needs, and obligations. In such cultures, it is particularly crucial to attend to others' perspectives due to the focus on meeting the expectations of in-group members and maintaining interpersonal harmony (Heine et al., 1999). Individualistic cultures encourage an independent self-construal by emphasizing forming and maintaining a unique, coherent identity that is stable across situations. In contrast, collectivistic cultures encourage an interdependent self-construal by emphasizing the possession of a more relational, flexible self-concept that adjusts to fit the demands of in-group members in order to maintain interpersonal harmony. Accordingly, the dominant, core self-construal in individualistic cultures tends to be more independent, whereas in collectivistic cultures it tends to be more interdependent (Markus & Kitayama, 1991; Gardner et al., 1999). At a basic level, individuals with an independent self-construal aim to distinguish themselves from others, whereas those with an interdependent self-construal aim to foster connection with others.

Dialecticism, thought to arise from Eastern philosophical, religious, and epistemological traditions, is a system of thought characterized by acceptance of contradiction, expectation of change and dynamism, and holistic perception (Peng & Nisbett, 1999). Applied to the self-concept, dialectical lay beliefs suggest the self is flexible and inextricably linked to the social context, and allow for the acceptance of fluctuations and inconsistency in the self as a natural part of life, rather than as a precursor to psychic tension. By contrast, Western traditions give rise to a linear system of thought that stresses rational, analytical thinking, and the synthesis of information to create internal coherence. Accordingly, individuals in Western cultures should be bothered by contradictions and ambiguity related to the self and work to maintain an internally consistent self-concept.

Supporting the above theoretical distinctions between cultures, considerable evidence suggests that the self-views of East Asians are more dynamic and context-dependent than those of Westerners. Relative to North Americans,

East Asians have a less clearly defined global self-concept (Campbell et al., 1996) and, more broadly, tend to view personality as open to change, rather than fixed (Chiu et al., 1997). When describing themselves, East Asians tend to endorse semantically opposite self-views (Choi & Choi, 2002; Spencer-Rodgers et al., 2004), and to provide ambivalent or contradictory statements about themselves in free-response formats (Cousins, 1989; Spencer-Rodgers et al., 2004). Rather than holding primarily globally consistent self-views, East Asians tend to tailor their self-views to fit the social context. For example, compared to North Americans, East Asians are less likely to describe themselves in terms of abstract traits, and are more likely to use descriptions that include references to social roles and other contextual markers (Bond & Cheung, 1983; Cousins, 1989; Rhee et al., 1995; Choi & Choi, 2002). Accordingly, East Asians show lower cross-situational stability in their self-descriptions (Kanagawa et al., 2001; Suh, 2002). In sum, East Asians' self-concept is largely defined in terms of roles and relationships, characterized by multiple, context-specific selves that flexibly respond to changes in the social environment, whereas Westerners' self-concept is composed primarily of traits that are consistent across situations.

The Nature of East Asians' Self-Verification Efforts

Based on theory and evidence suggesting that the epistemic and pragmatic roots of self-verification are universal, we proposed that East Asians have the motivation to verify their core, pre-existing self-views. That is, they desire psychological coherence, and the prediction and control it affords, just as North Americans do, so they should be similarly motivated to confirm their self-views. However, self-verification efforts primarily focus on core, important self-views that are stable, because these are the type of self-views most strongly tied to epistemic and pragmatic concerns. If East Asians lack consistently held global self-views relative to Westerners, is there anything stable in the self for them to verify? Although interdependence encourages East Asians to tailor themselves to suit different relationship partners, we maintain that it is still possible, and important, to strive for stability in the self in some form. Specifically, we suggest that East Asians elaborate stable, meaningful, and distinct, context-specific selves, and they will seek to confirm them just as North Americans seek confirmation of their most cherished global self-views.

Drawing on interactionist views of the self and personality (e.g., Mischel & Shoda, 1995), we argue there can still be stability and coherence in the East Asian self-concept despite contextual variability. Specifically, East Asians may tailor their self-views to fit the expectations of a given role or relationship partner in an if-then manner, and subsequently seek to maintain these contextualized self-views. In other words, cross-situational variability in East Asians' self-concept does not preclude temporal stability, as long as such temporal stability is understood to be contextualized. Indeed, recent research suggests that individuals with an East Asian cultural background tend to hold stable, context-specific selves, as shown by the inconsistency of their self-views across relational contexts (e.g., with

Mom), but stability of their specific relational selves (i.e., me-with-mom) over time (English & Chen, 2007). Accordingly, East Asians, and other individuals who define themselves in stable, if-then terms, may seek to verify more context-specific self-views than those who define themselves in more global terms. In contrast, individuals from North American cultures tend to possess stable self-views at the global level, largely by filtering out contextual information, so their self-verification efforts will focus more on global self-views. The above being said, recall that although the self-verification efforts of individuals within a given culture tend to focus on the level of self-definition dominant within that culture, individuals may also show self-verification at another level if these self-views are stable and important. Accordingly, although we propose that the self-verification efforts of East Asians will generally target contextualized self-views, self-verification at the global level may also occur at times for East Asians because they likely hold at least some core, global self-views.

Existing Evidence of Self-Verification in East Asian Cultures

A handful of initial studies suggest that self-verification motives do indeed operate in East Asian cultures. For instance, Numazaki and Kudo (1995) found that Japanese were more likely to prefer tasks that are diagnostic of their global self-views (on a personality dimension akin to extraversion) when they were confident of their standing on this attribute. In addition, in a short-term longitudinal study Hasegawa and Ura (1999) found that target's self-rated self-esteem predicted a friend's rating of the target's self-esteem 3 months later (i.e., the target elicited self-verification). However, these self-verification effects only emerged when the target's rating of their self-esteem was originally more negative than their friend's appraisal.

Although the above studies are an important first step in understanding self-verification in East Asian cultures, they are limited in a number of ways. First, they do not include a cross-cultural comparison group to test how the strength of global self-verification in their East Asian samples measure up to that in a Western sample. As proposed above, we expect that East Asians are less likely to verify global self-views than are North Americans. Indeed, a study by Heine and Renshaw (2002) that included both East Asians and North Americans provides preliminary support for this assertion. Specifically, while North Americans preferred people who agree with their pre-existing global self-views, Japanese liking was unrelated to others' level of agreement with their global self-views. Second, the previous studies of self-verification in East Asian cultures have focused primarily on self-verification at the global level, ignoring the possibility of self-verification at the context-specific level.

There are some hints, however, that East Asians are likely to verify context-specific self-views. For instance, Taniguchi (in press) found that Japanese participants wanted their romantic partner to see them more positively than they saw themselves, especially if they had negative self-views. However, they deemed the overly positive appraisals they expected from their partners as accurate, suggesting that they may be verifying more positive, relationship-specific selves (cf. Swann et al., 2002; Gill & Swann, 2004). In addition, dialectical beliefs about the self, prevalent in East Asian cultures, are associated with a stronger preference for evaluations that confirm personally important aspects about situation-specific selves (Chen et al., 2006b).

Of course, future research that directly tests our proposition about how self-verification strivings operate in East Asian cultures is needed. For example, researchers might compare self-verification strivings targeted at global and relationship-specific self-views in the United States and China. After assessing participants' self-views, a potential interaction partner could provide feedback that either confirms their self-views or not. We would predict that Chinese participants would rate feedback and evaluators who confirm their core relationship-specific self-views to be more credible and appealing than those who do not confirm them, or who confirm their global self-views. In contrast, participants in the United States should view feedback and evaluators who confirm their core global self-views more favorably than those who do not confirm them or who confirm their relationship-specific self-views.

SELF-VERIFICATION STRIVINGS IN OTHER CULTURES

Thus far, our cross-cultural analysis of self-verification motives has focused on East Asian cultures. However, as we suggested at the outset, our analysis of the nature of self-verification strivings in East Asian cultures might be extended to other cultures that hold values and beliefs similar to those seen in East Asia (e.g., interdependence). That is, our propositions are tied to values and beliefs that could characterize a number of different cultures. For instance, Latin American and African cultures, which are also thought to be relatively interdependent (Markus & Kitayama, 1991) and collectivist (Oyserman et al., 2002), may also tend to focus their self-verification efforts on more relational aspects of the self, instead of on global self-views.

More broadly, according to our analysis, researchers might first identify the stable, central self-views of members of any culture, and then test whether self-verification efforts target this type of self-view just as they have been shown to do in North American samples. In this vein, Spanish culture is thought to be relatively collectivistic, implying that members of this culture place considerable value on maintaining their relationships and group memberships and, accordingly, strive to confirm associated self-views. Consistent with this, recent research conducted in Spain has shown that participants were more interested in interacting with others who verified rather than disconfirmed their group identity (Gomez et al., 2006). Moreover, when participants perceived that their group identity was verified, they felt more understood, that they could be themselves, and that they were seen as they saw themselves. These findings were similar regardless of whether the group identity involved positive or negative traits. In fact, there was a tendency for self-verification strivings to override self-enhancement strivings in that people preferred interacting with evaluators who were verifying and negative over those who were positive and non-verifying.

QUESTIONS, IMPLICATIONS, AND FUTURE DIRECTIONS

In this final section, we consider several questions raised by our cross-cultural analysis of self-verification motives, as well as potential implications it may have. In doing so, we identify several directions for future research.

SELF-VERIFICATION AND OTHER SELF-EVALUATIVE MOTIVES

Our proposition that self-verification strivings are universal, although taking potentially different forms across different cultures, should not be taken to imply that we believe that self-verification motives routinely prevail over other possible self-evaluative motives across cultures. Rather, our proposition is that self-verification motives operate under certain conditions regardless of culture – for example, when the self-view in question is stable and highly central to one's self-definition. Under other circumstances, other self-evaluative motives may predominate. Indeed, it is widely assumed that the self is multiply motivated (e.g., Swann & Schroeder, 1995; Taylor et al., 1995; Sedikides & Strube, 1997). Some other self-evaluative motives of note include self-enhancement and self-improvement. Whereas self-verification focuses on confirming pre-existing self-views in the service of psychological coherence, self-enhancement serves to maintain or boost self-esteem by dwelling on or exaggerating positive aspects of the self (Taylor & Brown, 1988; Taylor et al., 2003), and self-improvement highlights negative aspects of the self that one needs to change to meet social standards (Taylor et al., 1995; Heine, 2001; Heine et al., 2001).

Research suggests that culture may influence the relative prevalence of the varying self-evaluative motives. For example, some researchers have argued that self-enhancement is less prevalent, and self-improvement more so, in East Asian relative to Western cultures (e.g., Heine et al., 1999, 2001; Kitayama & Markus 1999; cf. Sedikides et al., 2003, 2005). Where self-verification motives weigh in relative to these other motives is an open empirical question. Nevertheless, given the theoretical and empirical reasons to believe in the cross-cultural generality of the epistemic and pragmatic concerns underlying self-verification strivings that we described earlier, it would seem likely that the desire for verification of one's stable, core self-views would be fairly universal.

More broadly, we suggest that it may be more fruitful for future research to examine how individuals may find ways to balance their different self-evaluative needs, than to focus on which self-evaluative motive is the dominant one in a given culture or across cultures. Indeed, some research conducted in North America has shown that people strike an optimal balance between their desire for self-verification and self-enhancement – namely, by seeking appraisals that are neither completely self-verifying nor excessively self-enhancing (Morling & Epstein, 1997). Along similar lines, Swann et al. (1987) found support for a cognitive-affective crossfire, such that speedy, affective responses are aligned with self-enhancement, while more thoughtful cognitive responses are aligned with self-verification (see also Chang-Schneider & Swann, in press). People may also be able to balance their motivation for coherent self-views with their desire for positivity by verifying self-views that are confidently held or central to their self-concept and enhancing those that are not (e.g., Pelham & Swann, 1994). And there is also evidence that people prefer and seek positive appraisals early in relationships and verifying appraisals once the relationship is established (e.g., Swann, et al., 1994). Future research is needed to explore the potentially different forms of interplay among different self-evaluative motives across cultures.

Finally, because our cross-cultural analysis of self-verification motives focused largely on East Asian cultures, it is important to consider our propositions in light of evidence suggesting that self-criticism, which is thought to be in the service of self-improvement, is especially prevalent in such cultures (e.g., Kitayama et al., 1997; Heine & Lehman, 1999; Heine, et al., 2001). More specifically, it may be useful to distinguish self-criticism from self-verification in East Asian cultures. Just as a preference for verifying feedback about positive, subjectively accurate, aspects of the self may be interpreted in terms of either self-verification or self-enhancement, preferring feedback that verifies negative self-views might be interpreted as either self-verification or self-criticism. Of course, a key difference between self-verification and self-criticism is that whereas the former is about maintaining self-views, the latter is driven by a desire to change self-views for the better. Researchers may be able to tease apart these two constructs by measuring the certainty of self-views. That is, because self-criticism is likely to be focused on attributes on which people are less certain of their standing (and therefore on which they are open to change), self-verification efforts tend to be directed at self-views held with high certainty (Pelham, 1991; Swann & Pelham, 2002a). In addition, whereas self-verification may occur more for attributes that are personally important, self-criticism tendencies may be focused more on attributes that are important to relationship partners and thus are particularly important to improve on for the sake of relationship harmony.

IDENTITY NEGOTIATION PROCESSES

As noted, self-verification theory maintains that targets do not passively accept others' appraisals, but rather actively attempt to bring others' perceptions in line with their own self-views and selectively interpret feedback in a self-confirming manner. However, it may be adaptive for individuals to flexibly negotiate their identity with relationship partners at least to some degree. Indeed, self-verification strivings are considered to be part of a broader identity negotiation process.

The process of identity negotiation involves coming to a working consensus about the identity each person will assume in a given relationship (Swann, 2005; Swann & Bosson, in press). During this interactive process, both the self-views of the target and the appraisals of their interaction partner are considered. That is, targets influence perceivers and perceivers influence targets, although not necessarily equally. For instance, McNulty and Swann (1994) found that for some individuals their initial self-views predicted changes in their roommates' appraisals of them over the course of a semester, whereas for others roommates' initial appraisals predicted changes in their self-views. Other studies suggest that often the person who is more invested in or certain of his or her position will be more influential in the identity negotiation process (Swann & Ely, 1984).

Differences in cultural values and beliefs about the self may tip the balance in the identity negotiation process. For example, the value placed on connection and belonging in interdependent cultures, such as East Asian ones, could influence the relative impact of self-views and others' perceptions. In such cultures, it is especially important to attend to feedback from others in order to meet their expectations, so one's own self-views may have less impact in the identity negotiation process. On the other hand, although adjusting to others is crucial in maintaining interpersonal harmony, self-verification also confers relationship benefits in the form of smoother interactions by virtue of relationship partners knowing what to expect from one another. From this perspective, one's own self-views would be expected to influence others' perceptions. We speculate that the amount of influence perceivers and the self have in the identity negotiation process changes over time. Early on in relationships, when identities are first being negotiated, others' appraisals may have more weight in interdependent cultures, but once formed, the desire for self-verification will rise such that the self-views that East Asians have tailored to their specific relationships will take precedence.

AUTHENTICITY

Self-verification strivings have often been characterized in authenticity terms (Swann et al., 1994; Swann & Pelham, 2002b). When others confirm or reinforce our self-views, feelings of authenticity are bolstered as we gain confidence that we know and are acting in accord with our "true" self, or that our behavior is congruent with our inner attitudes, feelings, and beliefs. Subjective feelings of authenticity are vital to psychological well-being (e.g., Swann & Pelham, 2002b; Gross & John, 2003; Kernis, 2003; North & Swann, in press). For instance, Sheldon et al. (1997) reported that authenticity within a specific role predicted greater satisfaction with and preference for that role (e.g., student), while average authenticity across roles was associated with less anxiety, depression, and perceived stress, as well as higher self-esteem.

Our proposition that self-verification strivings target whatever form of self-views prevail in a given culture implies that authenticity may be grounded in feeling known along these same self-view dimensions. Thus, there may be cultural differences in the meaning or source of authenticity to the extent that the form of an individual's true self varies across cultural groups. For instance, for East Asians and others who define themselves in relational terms, authenticity may derive from honoring the identities negotiated with specific others, whereas for North Americans it may be more important to maintain a single, global self across contexts and time (Schlenker, 1984; Swann et al., 2002). In line with this, research suggests that cross-situational consistency in the self is less linked to feelings of authenticity among highly relational people (Cross et al., 2003; see also Kanagawa et al., 2001) and to the sense of having a "true" self among Japanese (Kashima et al., 2004).

CONCLUSION

In this chapter, we presented a cross-cultural analysis of self-verification motives. After summarizing self-verification theory and some of the research supporting it, we discussed the potential universality of the epistemic and pragmatic concerns underlying self-verification and the form that self-verification strivings might take in cultures outside North America. We proposed that self-verification motives are universal, but the nature of the self-views that each cultural group typically strives to verify is likely to vary depending on the dominant form of self-definition in that culture. That is, people will seek verification of their stable, core self-views in whatever form these self-views tend to exist. After presenting these propositions in general terms, we applied them to East Asian cultures. Specifically, we suggested that self-verification motives operate in these cultures, but will often target more context-specific self-views because these self-view are fostered and therefore salient in interdependent cultures. In closing, although we focused on self-verification strivings in North American and East Asian cultures, we hope our analysis will contribute to researchers' predictions about self-verification in a multitude of cultures.

REFERENCES

Andersen, S. M., & Chen, S. (2002). The relational self: An interpersonal social-cognitive theory. *Psychological Review, 109*, 619–645.

Baumeister, R., & Leary, M. (1995). The need to belong: Desire for interpersonal attachments as a fundamental human motivation. *Psychological Bulletin, 117*, 497–529.

Belsky, J. (1990). Parental and nonparental child care and children's socioemotional development: A decade in review. *Journal of Marriage and the Family, 52*, 885–903.

Bond, M. H., & Cheung, T. (1983). College students' spontaneous self-concept: The effect of culture among respondents in Hong Kong, Japan, and the United States. *Journal of Cross-cultural Psychology, 14*, 153–171.

Bowlby, J. (1969). *Attachment and loss: Vol. 1. Attachment*. New York: Basic Books.

Bowlby, J. (1973). Attachment and loss: Vol 2, Separation anxiety and anger. New York: Basic Books.

Brewer, M. B., & Caporael, L. R. (2006). An evolutionary perspective on social identity: Revisiting groups. In M. Schaller, J. A. Simpson, & D. T. Kenrick (Eds.), *Evolution and social psychology: Frontiers of social psychology* (pp. 143–161). Madison, CT, US: Psychosocial Press.

Brewer, M. B., & Gardner, W. (1996). Who is this "we"? Levels of collective identity and self representations. *Journal of Personality and Social Psychology, 71*, 83–93.

Bruner, J. S., Goodnow, J. J., & Austin, G. A. (1956). *A study of thinking*. Oxford, England: Wiley.

Campbell, J. D., Trapnell, P. D., Heine, S. J., Katz, I. M., Lavalle, L. F., & Lehman, D. R. (1996). Self-concept clarity: Measurement, personality correlates, and cultural boundaries. *Journal of Personality and Social Psychology, 70*, 141–156.

Chang-Schneider, C., & Swann, W. B. Jr. (in press). The role of uncertainty in self-evaluative processes: Another look at the cognitive-affective crossfire. In R. M. Arkin, K. C. Oleson, & P. J. Carroll (Eds.), *The uncertain self: A handbook of perspectives from social and personality psychology*. Laurence Erlbaum Associates, Inc.: New Jersey.

Chen, S., Boucher, H. C., & Tapias, M. P. (2006a). The relational self revealed: Integrative conceptualization and implications for interpersonal life. *Psychological Bulletin, 132*, 151–179.

Chen, S., English, T., & Peng, K. (2006b). Self-verification and contextualized self-views. *Personality and Social Psychology Bulletin, 32*, 930–942.

Chen, S., Chen, K. Y., & Shaw, L. (2004). Self-verification motives at the collective level of self-definition. *Journal of Personality and Social Psychology, 86*, 77–94.

Chiu, C., Hong, Y., & Dweck, C. S. (1997). Lay dispositionism and implicit theories of personality. *Journal of Personality and Social Psychology, 73*, 19–30.

Choi, I., & Choi, Y. (2002). Culture and self-concept flexibility. *Personality and Social Psychology Bulletin, 28*, 1508–1517.

Choi, I., & Nisbett, R. E. (1998). Situational salience and cultural differences in the correspondence bias and actor-observer bias. *Personality and Social Psychology Bulletin, 24*, 949–960.

Choi, I., Nisbett, R. E., & Norenzyan, A. (1999). Causal attribution across cultures: Variation and universality. *Psychological Bulletin, 125*, 47–63.

Cousins, S. D. (1989). Culture and self-perception in Japan and the United States. *Journal of Personality and Social Psychology, 56*, 124–131.

Cross, S. E., Gore, J. S., & Morris, M. L. (2003). The relational-interdependent self-construal, self-concept consistency, and well-being. *Journal of Personality & Social Psychology, 85*, 933–944.

Deci, E., & Ryan, R. (2000). The "what" and "why" of goal pursuits: Human needs and the self-determination of behavior. *Psychological Inquiry, 11*, 227–268.

Diener, E., & Diener, M. (1995). Cross-cultural correlates of life satisfaction and self-esteem. *Journal of Personality and Social Psychology, 68*, 653–663.

Diener, E., & Seligman, M. E. P. (2002). Very happy people. *Psychological Science, 13*, 81–84.

English, T., & Chen, S. (2007). Culture and self-concept stability: Consistency across and within contexts among Asian Americans and European Americans. *Journal of Personality and Social Psychology, 93*, 478–490.

Epstein, S. (1990). Cognitive-experiential self-theory. In L. A. Pervin (Ed.), *Handbook of personality: Theory and research* (pp. 165–192). New York: Guilford Press.

Erikson, E. H. (1963). *Childhood and society* (2nd ed.). New York: Norton.

Festinger, L. (1957). *A theory of cognitive dissonance*. Oxford: Row, Peterson.

Gardner, W. L., Gabriel, S., & Lee, A. Y. (1999). "I" value freedom, but "we" value relationships: Self-construal priming mirrors cultural differences in judgment. *Psychological Science, 10*, 321–326.

Greenwald, A. G. (1980). The totalitarian ego: Fabrication and revision of personal history. *American Psychologist, 35*, 603–618.

Gill, M. J., & Swann, W. B., Jr. (2004). On what it means to know someone: A matter of pragmatics. *Journal of Personality and Social Psychology, 86*, 405–418.

Gomez, A., Seyle, D. C., Huici, C., & Swann W. B., Jr. (2006). *Seeking verification of one's group identity*. Unpublished manuscript, University of Texas, Austin.

Gosling, S. D., Ko, S. J., Mannarelli, T., & Morris, M. E. (2002). A room with a cue: Personality judgments based on offices and bedrooms. *Journal of Personality and Social Psychology, 82*, 379–398.

Gross, J. J., & John, O. P. (2003). Individual differences in two emotion regulation processes: Implications for affect, relationships, and well-being. *Journal of Personality and Social Psychology, 85*, 348–362.

Guidano, V. F., & Liotti, G. (1983). *Cognitive processes and emotional disorders: A structural approach to psychotherapy.* New York: Guilford Press.

Hasegawa, K., & Ura, M. (1999). An examination of the relationship between identity negotiation process and well-being. *Japanese Journal of Experimental Social Psychology, 38,* 151–163.

Heider, F. (1958). *The psychology of interpersonal relations.* New York: Wiley.

Heider, F. (1944). Social perception and phenomenal causality. *Psychological Review, 51,* 358–374.

Heine, S. J. (2001). Self as a cultural product: An examination of East Asian and North Americans selves. *Journal of Personality, 69,* 881–906.

Heine, S. J., & Lehman, D. R. (1999). Culture, self-discrepancies, and self-satisfaction. *Personality and Social Psychology Bulletin, 25,* 915–925.

Heine, S. J., & Renshaw, K. (2002). Interjudge agreement, self-Enhancement, and liking: Cross-cultural divergences. *Personality and Social Psychology Bulletin, 28,* 578–587.

Heine, S. J., Lehman, D. R., Markus, H. R., & Kitayama, S. (1999). Is there a universal need for positive self-regard?. *Psychological Review, 106,* 766–794.

Heine, S. J., Kitayama, S., Lehman, D. R., Takata, T., Ide, E., Leung, C., & Matsumoto, H. (2001). Divergent consequences of success and failure in Japan and North America: An investigation of self-improving motivations and malleable selves. *Journal of Personality and Social Psychology, 81,* 599–615.

Heine, S. J., Proulx, T., & Vohs, K. D. (2006). The meaning maintenance model: On the coherence of social motivations. *Personality and Social Psychology Review, 10,* 88–110.

Hixon, J. G., & Swann, W. B., Jr. (1993). When does introspection bear fruit? Self-reflection, self-insight, and interpersonal choices. *Journal of Personality and Social Psychology, 64,* 35–43.

James, W. (1890). *The principles of psychology, Vol I.* New York, NY, US: Henry Holt and Co.

Jones, E. E., Kanouse, D., Kelley, H. H., Nisbett, R. E., Valins, S., & Weiner, B. (1972). *Attribution: Perceiving the causes of behavior.* Morristown, N.J.: General Learning Press.

Kanagawa, C., Cross, S., & Markus, H. (2001). "Who am I?" The cultural psychology of the conceptual self. *Personality and Social Psychology Bulletin, 27,* 90–103.

Kashima, Y., Kashima, E., Farsides, T., Kim, U., Strack, F., Werth, L., & Yuki, M. (2004). Culture and context-specific self: The amount and meaning of context-sensitivity of phenomenal self differ across cultures. *Self & Identity, 3,* 125–141.

Kernis, M. H. (2003). Toward a conceptualization of optimal self-esteem. *Psychological Inquiry, 14,* 1–26.

Kitayama, S., & Markus, H. R. (1999). Yin and Yang of the Japanese self: The cultural psychology of personality coherence. In D. Cervone & Y. Shoda (Eds.), *The coherence of personality: Social cognitive bases of personality consistency, variability, and organization* (pp. 242–302). New York: Guilford.

Kitayama, S., Markus, H. R., Matsumoto, H., & Norasakkunkit, V. (1997). Individual and collective processes in the construction of the self: Self-enhancement in the United States and self-criticism in Japan. *Journal of Personality and Social Psychology, 72,* 1245–1267.

Kitayama, S., Markus, H., & Masaru, K. (2000). Culture, emotion, and well-being: Good feelings in Japan and the United States. *Cognition & Emotion, 14,* 93–124.

Kraus, M. W., & Chen, S. (2007). *Automatic activation of self-evaluative goals in relationship contexts: Striving to be known by significant others.* Unpublished manuscript, University of California, Berkeley.

Kruglanski, A. W. (1990). Motivations for judging and knowing: Implications for causal attribution. In E. T. Higgins & R. M. Sorrentino (Eds.), *The handbook of motivation and cognition: Foundation of social behavior* (Vol. 2, pp. 333–368). New York: Guilford Press.

Lecky, P. (1945). *Self-consistency: A theory of personality.* New York: Island Press.

Lemay, E. P., & Ashmore, R. D. (2004). Reactions to perceived categorization by others during the transition to college: Internalization and self-verification processes. *Group Processes & Intergroup Relations, 7,* 173–187.

Markus, H. (1977). Self-schemata and processing information about the self. *Journal of Personality and Social Psychology, 35,* 63–78.

Markus, H., & Kitayama, S. (1991). Culture and the self: Implications for cognition, emotion, and motivation. *Psychological Review, 98,* 224–253.

Maslow, A. (1954). *Motivation and personality*. New York: Harper & Row.

McAdams, D. P. (1985). *Power, intimacy, and the life story: Personological inquiries into identity*. New York: Guilford Press.

McAdams, D. P. (1993). *The stories we live by: Personal myths and the making of the self*. New York: Morrow.

McAdams, D. P. (2001). The psychology of life stories. *Review of General Psychology, 5*, 100–122.

McCrae, R. R., & Costa, P. T. (1996). Toward a new generation of personality theories: Theoretical contexts for the five-factor model. In J. S. Wiggins (Ed.), *The five-factor model of personality: Theoretical perspectives* (pp. 51–87). New York: Guilford.

McNulty, S. E., & Swann, W. B., Jr. (1994). Identity negotiation in roommate relationships: The self as architect and consequence of social reality. *Journal of Personality and Social Psychology, 67*, 1012–1023.

Mendoza-Denton, R., & Mischel, W. (2007). Integrating system approaches to culture and personality: The Cultural Cognitive-Affective Processing System (C-CAPS). In: S. Kitayama, & D. Cohen (Eds.), *Handbook of cultural psychology*. (pp. 175–195). New York: Guilford.

Mendoza-Denton, R., Ayduk, O., Mischel, W., Shoda, Y., & Testa, A. (2001). Person x situation interactionism in self-encoding (*I Am…When…*): Implications for affect regulation and social information processing. *Journal of Personality and Social Psychology, 80*, 533–544.

Mischel, W., & Shoda, Y. (1995). A cognitive-affective system theory of personality: Reconceptualizing situations, dispositions, dynamics, and invariance in personality structure. *Psychological Review, 102*, 246–268.

Morling, B., & Epstein, S. (1997). Compromises produced by the dialectic between self-verification and self-enhancement. *Journal of Personality and Social Psychology, 73*, 1268–1283.

Morris, M., & Peng, K. (1994). Culture and cause: American and Chinese attributions for social and physical events. *Journal of Personality and Social Psychology, 67*, 949–971.

Naumann, L. P., Vazire, S., Rentfrow, P. J., & Gosling, S. D. (2006). *Judgments of personality based on clothing and appearance*. Unpublished manuscript, University of California, Berkeley.

Neuberg, S. L., & Newsom, J. T. (1993). Personal need for structure: Individual differences in the desire for simpler structure. *Journal of Personality and Social Psychology, 65*, 113–131.

Nisbett, R. E., Peng, K., Choi, I., & Norenzayan, A. (2001). Culture and systems of thought: Holistic versus analytic cognition. *Psychological Review, 108*, 291–310.

North, R. J., & Swann, W. B., Jr. (2008). Self-Verification 360°: Illuminating the light and dark sides. Unpublished Manuscript, University of Texas, Austin.

Numazaki, M., & Kudo, E. (1995). Determinants of task preferences when performance is indicative of individual characteristics: Self-assessment motivation and self-verification. *The Japanese Journal of Psychology, 66*, 52–57.

Oishi, S., Diener, E., Scollon, C. N., & Biswas-Diener, R. (2004). Cross-situational consistency of affective experiences across cultures. *Journal of Personality and Social Psychology, 86*, 460–472.

Oyserman, D., Coon, H. M., & Kemmelmeier, M. (2002). Rethinking individualism and collectivism: Evaluation of theoretical assumptions and meta-analyses. *Psychological Bulletin, 128*, 3–72.

Pelham, B. W. (1991). On confidence and consequence: The certainty and importance of self-knowledge. *Journal of Personality and Social Psychology, 60*, 518–530.

Pelham, B. W., & Swann, W. B., Jr. (1994). The juncture of intrapersonal and interpersonal knowledge: Self-certainty and interpersonal congruence. *Personality and Social Psychology Bulletin, 20*, 349–357.

Peng, K., & Nisbett, R. E. (1999). Culture, dialectics, and reasoning about contradiction. *American Psychologist, 54*, 741–754.

Popper, K. R. (1963). *Conjectures and refutations*. London: Routledge.

Reis, H., & Shaver, P. (1988). Intimacy as an interpersonal process. In S. Duck, D. F. Hay, S. F. Hobfoll, W. Ickes, & B. Montgomery (Eds.), *Handbook of personal relationships: Theory, research and interventions* (pp. 367–389). Oxford, England: John Wiley & Sons.

Rhee, E., Uleman, J. S., Lee, H. K., & Roman, R. J. (1995). Spontaneous self-descriptions and ethnic identities in individualistic and collectivistic cultures. *Journal of Personality and Social Psychology*, *69*, 142–152.

Robinson, D. T., & Smith-Lovin, L. (1992). Selective interaction as a strategy for identity maintenance: An affect control model. *Social Psychology Quarterly*, *55*, 12–28.

Ryff, C. D., & Keyes, C. L. M. (1995). The structure of psychological well-being revisited. *Journal of Personality and Social Psychology*, *69*, 719–727.

Schlenker, B. R. (1984). Identities, identifications, and relationships. In V. Derlega (Ed.), *Communication, intimacy, and close relationships* (pp. 71–104). New York: Academic Press.

Secord, P. F., & Backman, C. W. (1965). An interpersonal approach to personality. In B. Maher (Ed.), *Progress in experimental personality research* (Vol. 2, pp. 91–125). New York: Academic Press.

Sedikides, C., & Strube, M. J. (1997). Self evaluation: To thine own self be good, to thine own self be sure, to thine own self be true, and to thine own self be better. In M. P. Zanna (Ed.), *Advances in experimental social psychology* (Vol. 29, pp. 209–269). San Diego, CA: Academic Press.

Sedikides, C., Gaertner, L., & Toguchi, Y. (2003). Pancultural self-enhancement. *Journal of Personality and Social Psychology*, *84*, 60–79.

Sedikides, C., Gaertner, L., & Vevea, J. L. (2005). Pancultural self-enhancement reloaded: A meta-analytic reply to Heine. *Journal of Personality and Social Psychology*, *89*, 539–551.

Sheldon, K. M., Ryan, R. M., Rawsthorne, L. J., & Ilardi, B. (1997). Trait self and true self: Cross-role variation in the Big-Five personality traits and its relations with psychological authenticity and subjective well-being. *Journal of Personality and Social Psychology*, *73*, 1380–1393.

Sheldon, K. M., Elliot, A. J., Kim, Y., & Kasser, T. (2001). What is satisfying about satisfying events? Testing 10 candidate psychological needs. *Journal of Personality and Social Psychology*, *80*, 325–339.

Shoda, Y., Mischel, W., & Wright, J. C. (1993). The role of situational demands and cognitive competencies in behavior organization and personality coherence. *Journal of Personality and Social Psychology*, *65*, 1023–1035.

Spencer-Rodgers, J., Boucher, H. C., Mori, S. C., Wang, L., & Peng, K. (2004). *The dialectical self-concept: Contradiction, change, and holism in East Asian cultures.* Submitted manuscript, University of California, Berkeley.

Stevens, L. E., & Fiske, S. T. (1995). Motivation and cognition in social life: A social survival perspective. *Social Cognition*, *13*, 189–214.

Suh, E. M. (2002). Culture, identity consistency, and subjective well-being. *Journal of Personality and Social Psychology*, *83*, 1378–1391.

Suomi, S. J., & Harlow, H. F. (1972). Social rehabilitation of isolate-reared monkeys. *Developmental Psychology*, *6*, 487–496.

Swann, W. B., Jr. (1983). Self-verification: Bringing social reality into harmony with the self. In J. Suls & A. G. Greenwald (Eds.), *Psychological perspectives on the self* (Vol. 2, pp. 33–66). Hillsdale, NJ: Erlbaum.

Swann, W. B., Jr. (1990). To be adored or to be known: The interplay of self-enhancement and self-verification. In R. M. Sorrentino & E. T. Higgins (Eds.), *Handbook of motivation and cognition* (Vol. 2, pp. 408–448). New York: Guilford.

Swann, W. B., Jr. (2005). The self and identity negotiation. *Interaction Studies*, *6*, 69–83.

Swann, W. B., Jr. & Bosson, J. K. (in press). Identity negotiation: A theory of self and social interaction. Chapter to appear in O. John, R. Robins, & L. Pervin (Eds.), *Handbook of personality psychology: Theory and Research.* New York: Guilford.

Swann, W. B., Jr., & Ely, R. J. (1984). A battle of wills: Self-verification versus behavioral confirmation. *Journal of Personality and Social Psychology*, *46*, 1287–1302.

Swann, W. B., Jr., & Read, S. J. (1981). Self-verification processes: How we sustain our self-conceptions. *Journal of Experimental Social Psychology*, *17*, 351–372.

Swann, W. B., Jr., & Pelham, B. W. (2002a). Who wants out when the going gets good? Psychological investment and preference for self-verifying college roommates. *Self & Identity*, *1*, 219–233.

Swann, W. B., Jr., & Pelham, B. W. (2002b). The truth about illusions: Authenticity and positivity in social relationships. In C. R. Snyder & S. J. Lopez (Eds.), *Handbook of positive psychology* (pp. 366–381). New York: Oxford.

Swann, W. B., Jr., & Schroeder, D. G. (1995). The search for beauty and truth: A framework for understanding reactions to evaluations. *Personality and Social Psychology Bulletin, 21,* 1307–1318.

Swann, W. B., Jr., Griffin, J. J., Predmore, S. C., & Gaines, B. (1987). The cognitive-affective crossfire: When self-consistency confronts self-enhancement. *Journal of Personality and Social Psychology, 52,* 881–889.

Swann, W. B., Jr., Pelham, B. W., & Krull, D. S. (1989). Agreeable fancy or disagreeable truth? Reconciling self-enhancement and self-verification. *Journal of Personality and Social Psychology, 57,* 782–791.

Swann, W. B., Jr., Hixon, J. G., Stein-Seroussi, A., & Gilbert, D. T. (1990). The fleeting gleam of praise: Behavioral reactions to self-relevant feedback. *Journal of Personality and Social Psychology, 59,* 17–26.

Swann, W. B., Jr., Stein-Seroussi, A., & Giesler, B. (1992a). Why people self-verify. *Journal of Personality and Social Psychology, 62,* 392–401.

Swann, W. B., Jr., Wenzlaff, R. M., Krull, D. S., & Pelham, B. W. (1992b). The allure of negative feedback: Self-verification strivings among depressed persons. *Journal of Abnormal Psychology, 101,* 293–306.

Swann, W. B., Jr., Wenzlaff, R. M., & Tafarodi, R. W. (1992c). Depression and the search for negative evaluations: More evidence of the role of self-verification strivings. *Journal of Abnormal Psychology, 101,* 314–317.

Swann, W. B., Jr., De La Ronde, C., & Hixon, J. G. (1994). Authenticity and positivity strivings in marriage and courtship. *Journal of Personality and Social Psychology, 66,* 857–869.

Swann, W. B., Jr., Milton, L. P., & Polzer, J. T. (2000). Should we create a niche or fall in line? Identity negotiation and small group effectiveness. *Journal of Personality and Social Psychology, 79,* 238–250.

Swann, W. B., Jr., Bosson, J. K., & Pelham, B. W. (2002). Different partners, different selves: The verification of circumscribed identities. *Personality and Social Psychology Bulletin, 28,* 1215–1228.

Swann, W. B. Jr., Chang-Schneider, C. & Angulo, S. (2007). Self-verification in relationships as an adaptive process. J. Wood, A. Tesser & J. Holmes (Eds.), *Self and relationships.* Psychology Press: New York.

Swann, W. B., Jr., Rentfrow, P. J., & Guinn, J. (2003). Self-verification: The search for coherence. In M. Leary & J. Tagney, *Handbook of self and identity* (pp. 367–383). New York: Guilford.

Tajfel, H., & Turner, J. C. (1986). The social identity theory of intergroup behavior. In S. Worchel & W. G. Austin (Eds.), *Psychology of intergroup relations* (pp. 7–24). Chicago: Nelson-Hall.

Taniguchi, J. (in press). Koibitokankei ni okeru jikoteiji ha jikokakushotekika jikokouyouka [Are the self-presentations in dating relationships self-verifying or self-enhancing?]. *Shakaishinrigaku Kenkyu [Research in Social Psychology].*

Taylor, S. E., & Brown, J. D. (1988). Illusion and well-being: A social psychological perspective on mental health. *Psychological Bulletin, 103,* 193–210.

Taylor, S. E., Neter, E., & Wayment, H. A. (1995). Self-evaluation processes. *Personality and Social Psychology Bulletin, 21,* 1278–1287.

Taylor, S. E., Lerner, J. S., Sherman, D. K., Sage, R. M., & McDowell, N. K. (2003). Are self-enhancing cognitions associated with healthy or unhealthy biological profiles?. *Journal of Personality and Social Psychology, 85,* 605–615.

Thorne, A. (2000). Personal memory telling and personality development. *Personality and Social Psychology Review, 4,* 45–56.

Triandis, H. C. (1989). The self and behavior in different cultural contexts. *Psychological Review, 96,* 506–520.

Triandis, H. C. (1990). Cross-cultural studies of individualism and collectivism. In J. J. Berman (Ed.), *Nebraska Symposium on Motivation, 1989* (pp. 41–133). Lincoln: University of Nebraska Press.

Uchino, B. N., Cacioppo, J. T., & Kiecolt-Glaser, J. K. (1996). The relationship between social support and physiological processes: A review with emphasis on underlying mechanisms and implications for health. *Psychological Bulletin, 119*, 488–531.

Vignoles, V. L., Regalia, C., Manzi, C., Golledge, J., & Scabini, E. (2006). Beyond self-esteem: Influence of multiple motives on identity construction. *Journal of Personality and Social Psychology, 90*, 308–333.

Wood, J. V., Heimpel, S. A., Newby-Clark, I., & Ross, M. (2005). Snatching defeat from the jaws of victory: Self-esteem differences in the experience and anticipation of success. *Journal of Personality and Social Psychology, 89*, 764–780.

7

AN ATTRIBUTION THEORIST ADDRESSES THE CO-EXISTENCE OF THEORETICAL GENERALITY AND CULTURAL SPECIFICITY

BERNARD WEINER

Department of Psychology, University of California, Los Angeles, USA

In the publication of my last research study testing attribution theory, I did more than conclude that the hypotheses were confirmed for my University of California at Los Angeles freshman and sophomore subjects, living in the city of Los Angeles on September 28, 2006. Rather, it was assumed that the findings and conclusions transcend time, place, and research population demographics including culture and ethnicity. I certainly am not alone in making research generalizations; expectations of specificity, when carried to the extreme, render the idea of scientific laws meaningless.

But behavior and its determinants do vary across time, place, and culture. How can this knowledge be reconciled with the search for, and acceptance of, general laws? Let us see if we can reason this through with the use of a motivation theory (and one with which I am not identified).

Consider, for example, Expectancy/Value theory, linked with Kurt Lewin, Edward Tolman, John Atkinson, and many others. This conception certainly has been, and remains, one of the dominant approaches to motivation. Expectancy/ Value theorists state that motivation is determined by the value (i.e., incentive magnitude or worth) of an anticipated goal and by the likelihood of reaching that goal. The more positive the incentive and the higher the goal expectancy, the greater is the motivation to approach that goal object. In common sense language, what one does depends on what one is going to get and the likelihood of getting it.

Now let us assume that an individual is engaged in cross-cultural motivation research. It is noted that Person A in Culture A is often sitting with friends and smiling during the conversation, whereas Person B in Culture B typically is alone in a room, intensely focused on completing a task. Observation of the two individuals (who we assume are typical representatives of their cultures) is likely to promote the belief that the motivational laws in the two cultures differ. However, a phenotype, that is, a detectable and visible behavioral observation, must be distinguished from a genotype, or the underlying dynamics or determinants of an expression. Presume that Culture A values friendships, maintenance of interpersonal relationships, an absence of interpersonal conflict, and interdependence. On the other hand, Culture B values personal success and independence. It then could be argued by Expectancy/Value theorists that in both cultures individuals are engaging in their highest valued activity. The same underlying principle thus accounts for the behaviors in both cultures, even though the observed behaviors across the cultures markedly differ. That is, the motivational law regarding value as a determinant of behavior generalizes across the cultures.

To test this hypothesis more systematically, a measure is devised to assess the values held in different cultures. This test is administered and it is found that indeed Person A in Culture A highly values interdependence and social activities, and that Person B in Culture B highly values independence and achievement behavior. Thus, the predictions of the theory are upheld when observing the behaviors of these two individuals (and others of their ilk).

But then an obstacle is faced. Person C in Culture C also has been observed spending some of her time alone in a room, working on a task, making sure rivals do not steal her insights, yet other times she is leisurely interacting with others. Yet on the reliable and valid test of cultural values, she scores high only in interdependence. What should we then say about the generality of Expectancy/Value theories across cultures?

1. It could be concluded that Expectancy/Value theory does not generalize to Culture C inasmuch as the reported value does not correspond to the observed behavior. On the one hand, this may be regarded as a fatal blow to the theory. On the other hand, perhaps Culture C is so remote, so small, and so different that the theorist is willing to accept this exclusion without calling the theory into question. I recall a study in which attribution theory was questioned when the findings of a small number of participants from a remote Indian village did not seem to conform to the predictions of the theory. Even if the study was not flawed, I

cannot honestly report that I was deterred in my research direction. Would one give up a theory found promising in the United States and Europe and Asia given this apparent contradiction? I certainly did not.

2. It could be reasoned that the behavior in Culture C conforms to the predictions of Expectancy/Value theory, but not to as great extent as for persons in Cultures A and B. That is, culture is a moderator variable that effects the relation between value and action. Of course, a key unknown is what properties of the cultures make them more or less confirming of the general rule. This approach maintains the general theory in the face of evidence that differs in the strength of support of the theory, and requires moderators to be incorporated into the theory.

In sum, my position regarding the search for general laws, laws that generalize across cultures, is

a. Differences in observed behaviors across cultures are not evidence of the absence of conceptual generality.
b. Some real or apparent contradictions are more important than others.
c. Some inconsistency can be reconciled with the acceptance of theoretical generality by incorporating culture as a moderator between theoretical concepts.

I now turn to attribution theory in cultural contexts and apply these rules as I contend that attribution theory generalizes across cultures. By attribution theory I mean my specific approach to this field, which is as a motivation psychologist. I therefore do not address issues related solely to the determinants of causal beliefs, which has generated a great deal of cross-cultural interest. Rather, here I focus on the consequences of causal thinking. I first introduce two attribution theories that have been developed, and then turn to issues related to cultural generality.

ATTRIBUTION THEORY

Imagine, for example, a student has just received a poor grade on an exam and we, as psychologists and educators, want to accurately predict if she or he will continue in school or will drop out. Among the likely predictors that I identify are the subjective expectancy of future success, previously mentioned as a component of Expectancy/Value theory, as well as emotions related to self-esteem, guilt, and shame. These self-directed thoughts and feelings comprise what I label an *intrapersonal* theory of motivation.

Now consider that, following the poor exam performance, significant others including peers, teachers, and parents evaluate or judge this person. They consider her good or bad, responsible or not responsible for the low-test score, moral or immoral, and she is the target of emotions including anger and sympathy. These thoughts and emotions, in turn, give rise to help or neglect, positive or negative feedback, and the like. These other-directed thoughts and feelings comprise what I label an *interpersonal* theory of motivation. The boundaries between the intrapersonal and interpersonal motivational systems at times are fuzzy, but nevertheless this distinction is important and, albeit overlapping, the theories are separately presented.

INTRAPERSONAL MOTIVATION FROM THE ATTRIBUTIONAL PERSPECTIVE

My approach to intrapersonal motivation is guided by the metaphor that people are scientists, trying to understand themselves and their environment, and then they act on the basis of this knowledge (see Weiner, 1992). This approach begins with an event that has been completed, such as a success or failure at an exam or acceptance or rejection for a date (see Figure 7.1). At the end of this sequence there is a behavioral reaction, which might be dropping out of school or not engaging in further social activities. In between is the remainder of the motivational process, guided by attributional inferences and their consequences, which fill the gap between the stimulus (the exam outcome) and the response (dropping out).

In the far left of Figure 7.1, it can be seen that following the outcome there is an affective reaction – one feels happy following goal attainment and unhappy when there is nonattainment of a goal. These general affective reactions are not antedated by a great deal of cognitive work and are labeled "outcome-dependent" emotions. Then individuals are presumed to ask: "Why did this happen? What caused this outcome?" Because of cognitive limits, search is not undertaken following all events, and is particularly likely when the outcome is negative, unexpected, and/or important. Thus, if one expects to succeed at something trivial and does, then *why* questions are not likely to follow. In contrast, unexpected failure at an important exam surely will evoke attributional processes (see Weiner, 1986; Gendolla & Koller, 2001).

The answer to this *why* question, which is a causal attribution, is influenced by many sources of evidence, including past personal history of success and failure (covariation information), social norms pertaining to the performance of others (covariation information), rules about the relations between causes (causal schemata), viewer perspective (actor or observer), hedonic biasing, and on and on (see Figure 7.1). More specifically, for example, if the person has always failed in the past, then the current failure is likely to be attributed to the self; if others succeed when that person fails, then again failure is more likely to be attributed to the self (rather than to the task); if one thinks that failure requires multiple causality, then even given knowledge of lack of effort, one is likely nevertheless to derogate personal ability and/or also ascribe the failure to some environmental factors; and so on.

Guided by these sources of information, a cause is selected, such as lack of ability, lack of effort, or bad luck given failure. Similarly, if one is rejected for a date, then again as shown in Figure 7.1, an array of causes is possible, including

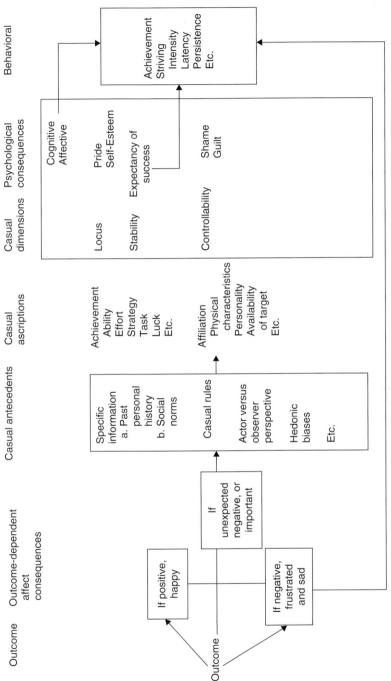

FIGURE 7.1 An intrapersonal attributional theory of motivation.

unattractive physical characteristics, poor personality, and so forth. Let us assume for purposes of clarity that there is only one phenomenological cause, although life is not that simple. This sets the stage for the next step in the process, which concerns the underlying characteristics or properties of that cause. These so-called causal dimensions are the very heart and soul of my attributional approach to motivation.

To understand the motivational consequences of causal beliefs, it is necessary that the qualitative differences between causes such as effort and ability be altered to quantitative differences, and for this to occur the causes must be comparable on some psychological dimensions. A great deal of research has documented that there are three, and indeed only three, underlying causal properties that have cross-situational generality (see Weiner, 1986). These properties are labeled locus, stability, and controllability. Locus refers to the location of a cause, which is either within or outside of the actor. For example, ability and effort are considered internal causes of success, whereas chance and help from others are construed as external causes. Causal stability refers to the duration of a cause. Some causes, such as math aptitude, are perceived as constant, whereas causes such as chance are considered unstable or temporary. Finally, a cause like effort is subject to volitional alteration and is personally controllable, whereas others cannot be willfully changed and are therefore regarded as uncontrollable. Luck and aptitudes have this property.

All causes can be located within this three-dimensional causal space. Although there may be disagreements regarding how a cause is dimensionalized because this depends on "how it seems to me," there also is a great deal of agreement that, for example, aptitude is internal, stable, and uncontrollable, whereas chance, while also uncontrollable, is external to the actor and unstable. Indeed, the dimensions define the very meanings of aptitude and chance.

The significance of these causal properties is that they map into what are considered by some to be the two main determinants of motivated action – namely, expectancy and value. Expectancy refers to the subjective likelihood of future success, while value in this context is considered to be the emotional consequences of goal attainment or nonattainment (see Atkinson, 1964). Turning first to expectancy, it has been documented that if a cause is regarded as stable then the same outcome will be anticipated again following a success or a failure. Hence, if failure is perceived as due to lack of aptitude or to an unfair teacher, then taking another exam from this teacher will be anticipated to result in continued failure. To the contrary, failure perceived as due to unstable factors, such as bad luck or lack of preparation because of the flu, is not an indicator that there will be further failure (see review in Weiner, 1992).

Locus and controllability relate to feeling states, or to the "value" of achievement outcomes. Note that I do not use the concept locus *of* control, but rather speak of locus *and* control. These are two independent dimensions. A cause may be internal to the person but quite uncontrollable, such as lack of height as the cause of not being selected for the basketball team.

Locus influences feelings of pride in accomplishment and self-esteem. Pride and increments in self-esteem require internal causality for success. One might be happy following a high grade on an exam (an outcome-dependent feeling) but pride would not be experienced if it were believed that the teacher gave only high grades. Controllability, in conjunction with locus, determines whether guilt or shame is experienced following nonattainment of a goal (although in research studies these two affects are highly correlated, so that I have somewhat shaky confidence in the conclusions that follow). Assuming a desire to succeed, attribution of failure to insufficient effort, which is internal and controllable, often elicits guilt. On the other hand, an ascription of failure to lack of aptitude, which is internal but uncontrollable, tends to evoke feelings of shame, embarrassment, and humiliation. The controllability dimension influences other affects as well, including regret, but they are not considered here. Finally, expectancy of success, along with the emotions of pride, guilt, and shame, are believed to determine subsequent behavior. That is, behavior is a function of thoughts and feelings.

Let me illustrate the logic of this analysis by examining motivation in an affiliative, rather than an achievement, context. Assume that Bill is rejected by Mary when asking her for a date. We now want to correctly predict whether Bill will seek further dates or will "hide in his shell" and withdraw. The attributional framework contends that to make this prediction accurately, Bill's perceived cause for rejection must be determined (which may or may not be the "real" cause). Assume Bill believes he was rejected because he is too short. This aspect of physical appearance refers to an internal, stable, and uncontrollable cause. Hence, Bill should suffer a decrement in self-esteem (mediated by personal causality); he will expect to be rejected again (mediated by causal stability); and feel ashamed, humiliated, and embarrassed (mediated by internal causality that is uncontrollable). This analysis leads to the prediction that Bill will drop out of (or decrease his activity in) the social world of seeking dates.

Conversely, assume Bill thinks that he was rejected because the girl already has a date. Inasmuch as this is an external cause, self-esteem is maintained; since this prior engagement presumably is unstable, expectancy of future acceptance is not reduced; and given that having a prior date is uncontrollable by him as well as external, neither shame nor guilt is experienced. Hence, motivation should not be dampened and Bill will seek out further dating opportunities. And still other predictions are generated if Bill believes the rejection was because of his height, but that others are prejudiced so there is deflection from internal to external causality.

INTERPERSONAL MOTIVATION FROM THE ATTRIBUTIONAL PERSPECTIVE

The interpersonal conception of motivation from an attribution perspective is shown in Figure 7.2. For the moment, concentrate on the top row of that figure. It can be seen that the motivation sequence again is initiated by an achievement

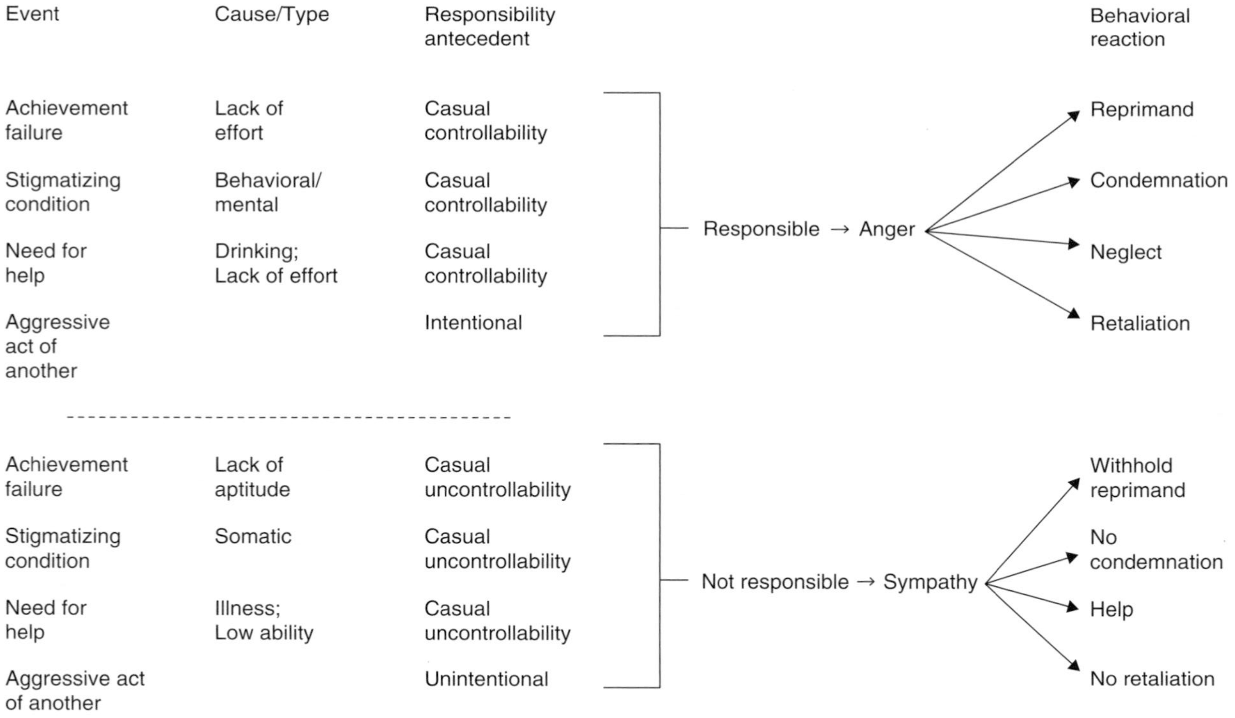

Event	Cause/Type	Responsibility antecedent		Behavioral reaction
Achievement failure	Lack of effort	Casual controllability		Reprimand
Stigmatizing condition	Behavioral/mental	Casual controllability	Responsible → Anger	Condemnation
Need for help	Drinking; Lack of effort	Casual controllability		Neglect
Aggressive act of another	Intentional	Intentional		Retaliation
Achievement failure	Lack of aptitude	Casual uncontrollability		Withhold reprimand
Stigmatizing condition	Somatic	Casual uncontrollability	Not responsible → Sympathy	No condemnation
Need for help	Illness; Low ability	Casual uncontrollability		Help
Aggressive act of another	Unintentional	Unintentional		No retaliation

FIGURE 7.2   An interpersonal attributional theory of motivation.

outcome, exam failure. Once more there is a causal search (not shown in Figure 7.2), in this case not by the actor but by an observer, such as a teacher or parent. And again, based on a variety of factors not included in the figure, a causal explanation is reached. This may or may not be the same inference made by the failing student.

This cause is then placed in the previously described dimensional space, with the dimension of causal controllability of prime importance. That is, thoughts about control versus not control are at the center of the interpersonal theory. As shown in the top row of Figure 7.2, failure is ascribed to a lack of effort, which is subject to volitional change and therefore regarded a controllable cause. If a cause (and also the linked negative event) "could have been otherwise," then the actor is perceived as responsible for the outcome (for greater detail regarding the link between controllability and responsibility, and a discussion of mitigating factors, see Weiner, 1995, 2006). Hence, the motivation process is proposed to proceed from a causal decision to an inference about the person. Responsibility for a negative event, in turn, gives rise to anger. One is mad when one's child fails an exam because of not studying, just as one is angry with a roommate for leaving the kitchen dirty following a meal (unless he or she became sick, which then mitigates the relation between control and responsibility). Anger, in turn, gives rise to a variety of anti-social responses, including punishment and reprimand.

Now consider the sequence when achievement failure is caused by lack of ability, which is depicted a few lines lower in Figure 7.2. Ability, conceived of here as akin to aptitude, is typically regarded an uncontrollable cause. Because the cause (and the linked exam outcome) cannot be volitionally altered, the failing student is not held personally responsible (able-to-respond). Lack of responsibility for a negative achievement outcome tends to elicit sympathy. We feel sorry for the mentally handicapped who cannot perform cognitive tasks and for the physically handicapped who cannot perform motor tasks. Sympathy, in turn, evokes pro-social reactions. Note that in the interpersonal theory inferences of responsibility play a major role, whereas the effects of causal locus and causal stability, as well as self-esteem and expectancy of success, are de-emphasized.

This interpersonal approach to classroom experience is not confined to an explanation of achievement-related behaviors. A number of other phenomena have been examined within the same conceptual framework. Figure 7.2 shows that, in addition to achievement-related evaluation, reactions to the stigmatized, help giving, and aggression also are subject to a responsibility-mediated analysis. If a person is responsible for being in a stigmatized state, for needing help, or for a harmful act, then anger is experienced and the reaction is negative. On the other hand, stigmatization because of noncontrollable causes such as being blind at birth, needing help because of missing school when ill, and perhaps even aggression against someone by accident (e.g., stepping on toes in a crowded subway) elicit sympathy and pro-social behaviors (see Rudolph et al., 2004).

In these situations, an appropriate metaphor to capture the reactions of the involved observer is that he or she is a judge presiding in a courtroom. The judge has the right to determine if others are responsible or not responsible for a transgression and then passes a sentence based on these beliefs and other factors, particularly the severity of the transgression. Indeed, life may be considered a courtroom where dramas related to transgressions are played out. The observer is a scientist in making causal decisions, but then also acts in a Godlike manner by reaching moral conclusions regarding right and wrong, good and bad, and behavior is in part guided by these moral thoughts and the emotions they elicit.

INTERRELATIONS OF THE THEORIES

The two motivational systems have been presented as though they are quite separate. In fact, they are closely intertwined and interactive. Consider, for example, a student whom others believe performed poorly because of a lack of aptitude. Inasmuch as aptitude is construed an uncontrollable cause, some involved observers may communicate sympathy and pity to this pupil following failure. These communications provide evidence to the person that he or she "cannot," which then increase the likelihood of personal feelings of shame and humiliation. That is, if sympathy and pity are "accepted," then this is an antecedent for a low-ability self-ascription. On the other hand, if the student is thought by others (e.g., the teacher) to have failed because of lack of effort, then that teacher may communicate anger. Anger is a cue that the pupil is responsible for the failure, which need not have taken place. Inasmuch as expressed anger is used to infer causality (see Weiner, 1995), the student is more likely to ascribe his or her personal failure to lack of effort. This, in turn, increases guilt. In sum, the two motivational theories overlap and are involved in the thoughts, feelings, and actions of both the actor and the observer within the same behavioral episode.

A CONCLUDING INTRODUCTORY REMARK

An attributional approach to motivation includes thoughts related to causal beliefs, expectancy of success, inferences of responsibility, and so on. Also incorporated are affects, including happiness and unhappiness (outcome-dependent) and pride, self-esteem, guilt, anger, shame, and sympathy (attribution-dependent). These thoughts and feelings then provide the foundation for an understanding of achievement performance, such as trying harder versus dropping out of school (intrapersonal motivation), as well as aiding in the explanation of achievement evaluation, reactions to the stigmatized, help giving, and aggression (interpersonal motivation). And that is not by any means the full range of the conception but rather captures the theoretical foci. Thus, I regard attribution theory as quite rich – integrating thinking, feeling, and doing both for an actor and for the observers of that action, and providing the "deep-structure" for motivational explanation. But is it rich enough to incorporate cultural variability, or is it impoverished by not addressing or having the capability of addressing diversity?

THE CULTURAL CHALLENGE

My position regarding whether this theory can fit diverse cultures can be summarized as follows. The basic structure of the theory, that is, the concepts and their sequential ordering, are so entrenched in my mind as to make them near inviolable. Thus, postulating that attainment and nonattainment of a goal respectively give rise to happiness and unhappiness; that unexpected, important, and negative outcomes result in attribution search; that there is an attempt to reach a causal explanation; that causes have properties of locus, stability, and control; that these respectively relate to self-esteem, expectancy of success, and the affects of guilt, shame, anger, and sympathy; and that attributional beliefs and emotions influence action, I regard as (near) universal principles (subject to cognitive limitations). Included among the broader universals are more general beliefs incorporated by these relations, such as thinking gives rise to feelings (the appraisal approach to emotions) and thinking and feeling together determine action. That is, behavior is a function of cognition and affect (rather than, or in addition to, the Lewinian notion that behavior is a function of the person and the environment).

I personally have not undertaken cross-cultural research to prove these principles, nor is there a body of cross-cultural literature to support the position espoused here. Nonetheless, a meta-analysis performed regarding the determinants of help giving and aggression provides very supportive data (Rudolph et al., 2004). In this research endeavor that tested the interpersonal theory, the authors gathered all the studies they were able to uncover that included an attribution variable (i.e., controllability, responsibility); at least one emotion and/or behavioral variable, with anger and sympathy as possible emotions and some help- or aggression-related variable as a possible behavior; and first-order or raw correlations between two of these variables.

Following a thorough search process, 39 studies were retrieved that met the above criteria for help giving and 25 studies were obtained for aggression. The total number of participants involved in the investigation of help giving was 7954, with an average of 204 participants per study. In regard to aggression, the number of participants was 4598, with an average of 184 participants per study. Thus, the data of more than 12,000 respondents were included in the analysis.

The general pattern of results was highly supportive of the theory shown in Figure 7.2. A notable finding was that for helping, there were direct relations between thinking, feeling, and doing, as hypothesized. However, for aggression, feeling was related to thinking, while behavior was jointly determined by thinking and feeling. That is, for aggression an additional path in the model went directly from thinking to acting. In sum, helping was entirely a matter of the heart (degree of sympathy), while aggression was determined by anger as well as beliefs about responsibility. This difference had not been anticipated. The models fitting these paths were highly significant and will not be discussed in further detail here.

What is important in this context is the role (or lack of same) of culture in effecting the results. Culture was tested as a moderator (along with a number of other possible moderators such as publication status, date of the publication, using real versus simulation data, and so on). It was found that culture (differentiating American subjects from those in other cultures) did not play any role in effecting the results and proved insignificant as a moderator variable.

A reasonable question to ask is whether there was there sufficient data from other cultures to allow for a fair testing of this variable. For the helping meta-analysis, 16 of the 39 reported studies (nearly 40%) were conducted in foreign cultures. The number of respondents not from the United States was 3482, a bit more than 40% of the total. These respondents came from cultures regarded as close to American (Canada, $N = 816$), somewhat American (Germany, $N = 1646$; Netherlands, $N = 143$), and far from American (Japan, $N = 463$; Nigeria, $N = 414$). For the aggression study sample, 12 of the 25 research investigations (almost 50%) were not conducted in America, including 2984 participants (more than 60%). Of these, nearly two third (2029) were from Germany. The other cultures represented included Australia ($N = 457$), Canada/Britain ($N = 240$), and Portugal ($N = 258$).

This surely is not my ideal analysis, nor the best set of data, to document that the deep structures represented in the theory have cross-cultural generality. Nevertheless, I certainly am satisfied with the findings. I can't imagine a more mundane statement than "more research is needed …," but this does seem appropriate.

Although culture, demographics, personal history and the like are presumed not to influence the basic principles of the theory, they do determine, for example, the goals for which one is striving; the definition of a success and a failure; what is unexpected and important; what information is used to determine causality; the causes salient to the person; where a cause is placed in dimensional space; and so on. That is, the antecedents and the determinants of the constructs and their magnitudes may differ between cultures and individuals within those cultures. Attribution theory embraces phenomenology and constructs have a subjective definition and meaning. For example, in one culture success is defined as a good crop of yams; in another, it is attaining the position of corporate head. Similarly, for one individual or representative of a cultural group a "B" at an exam is defined as a success, whereas for another it is regarded as a failure. And for some the grade of "A" is considered a success by the school but may be regarded as a failure by the student because it results in exclusion from the group. Further, for some a grade of "B" is anticipated and will not result in causal search; for others, the "B" is unexpected and a search is initiated. In some cultures and for some individuals, the search might start with internal causes; for others, the search starts externally; in some instances, the cause of success is thought to be a favor from God; for others, the main perceived cause of success is innate ability. In sum, attributional content is specific. However, the attribution process and the structure of the theory are general and transcend the specific determinants.

There is not a systematic literature documenting these beliefs, although some data about cultural disparities that also show cultural generality do exist. For example, Betancourt and Weiner (1982) report that both Chileans and participants in the United States are able to understand the three postulated causal dimensions and rate causes on these properties. Although there was great agreement on the dimensional ratings of causes, the Chileans perceived the external causes as more external, the stable causes as less stable, and the controllable causes as less controllable than did the Americans. This is the type of research needed to investigate cultural disparities in the face of shared cultural understanding (the underlying causal structure; see also Bar-Tal et al., 1984, for similar comparisons between Israeli children from Asian-African families versus European-American families).

In addition to affecting the antecedents or the operationalizations of any particular construct, culture and personal history at times act as moderators between the specified associations in the theory. For example, lack of effort is under personal control, so that failure due to this factor will result in anger followed by reprimand and punishment. But some cultures (e.g., Japan) regard achievement outcomes as more controllable than do other cultures (e.g., America), and stress effort as a determinant of success more than do others. Hence, Japanese teachers may punish lack of effort more than do American teachers. That is, group beliefs are recognized within the theory as functioning as moderators of particular relations. I believe I have been remiss in the past by not sufficiently emphasizing this point because I have been primarily focused on motivational mediators rather than moderators and have paid most attention to the general motivation process.

Two specific content areas provide helpful illustrations of my beliefs: differences between African-American and White students in school dropout rates (to which the intrapersonal theory is applied) and disparities between Mexicans and Americans in reaction to obesity (to which the interpersonal theory is applied). A conceptual analysis of both observations will convey how diversity, or cultural differences, can be captured within attribution theory.

ETHNIC DIFFERENCES IN SCHOOL DROPOUT RATES

It is widely recognized that African-Americans fare poorly relative to Whites on many indicators of academic performance. They have lower grade point averages and drop out of college at a higher rate than do White students (see Van Laar, 2000). How might attribution theory address these facts, and specifically the differential dropout rates between the races?

Applying the intrapersonal theory to the African-American data and mirroring the analysis of affiliative withdrawal presented earlier, attribution theory might suggest the following process. After initial failures in the challenging college environment, African-Americans ascribe their poor performance to lack of ability (aptitude). This is because others in the class are succeeding whereas they receive low grades (covariation information). Being an internal cause, an ascription to lack of aptitude lowers their self-esteem; since aptitude is perceived as stable, expectancy of success becomes low; and inasmuch as aptitude is perceived as uncontrollable, the failing students experience shame and humiliation. Low self-esteem, low expectancy of success, and feelings of shame and humiliation combine to reduce academic motivation and result in dropping out. This analysis can be depicted as follows:

This appears to be a reasonable conceptual analysis, generating a number of worthy hypotheses that deserve to be true. Indeed, this type of thinking is implicitly behind the movement to raise the self-esteem of students, thereby increasing motivation. But it unfortunately meets with an immediate empirical disconfirmation. African-American students do not have lower self-esteem than their White counterparts (see Graham, 1988, 1991; Van Laar, 2000). One might contend this is because self-esteem has many components in addition to achievement performance. However, African-American students also score as high as (or, higher than) White students in academic self-esteem (see Graham, 1988, 1991; Van Laar, 2000). Does the equivalence in self-esteem between the racial groups, which attribution theory posits is in part a function of success and failure and the attributions for these outcomes, point to a theoretical shortcoming?

Van Laar (2000) did not think so, and offered a different attributional interpretation for the high dropout rates of African-Americans. This explanation was guided by the insights and Crocker and Major (1989), who noted that stigmatized groups typically do not experience deficiencies in self-esteem, even though this is predicted by a number of different theories of the self. Crocker and Major (1989) contend that a variety of mechanisms are activated to protect individuals in the face of negative outcomes and evaluations. One widely used strategy or device is to attribute failure externally to, for example, the prejudice of others. Even a self-perception of low ability (internal causality) can be traced back to inadequate educational opportunities because of discrimination (external causality). External ascriptions maintain self-esteem in the face of failure and prevent the self-directed emotions of shame and embarrassment. Thus, here we have a situation where, given the same outcome (failure), members of diverse ethnic groups may differ in their attributions, in part because of disparities between the groups in their perceptions regarding the social system.

However, although the attribution for failure is now external for the African-American students, prejudice also is likely to be perceived as stable, so that again future success is not anticipated. That is, although the specific attribution has been altered from internal to external, the stability of the cause remains unchanged. Low expectations, Van Laar (2000) suggests, result in dropping out even when self-esteem is high.

In addition, the attribution of prejudice that is the cause of the failure is perceived as controllable by others, who "need not" act in a discriminatory manner. This now activates elements of the interpersonal model, so instead of shame-related emotions the affective experience of the failing minority students is anger. Anger, in turn, gives rise to anti-social and system blaming activities. The theoretical analysis pertinent to attributions for failure proposed by Van Laar (2000) can be depicted as follows:

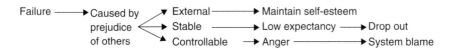

This conceptualization has a number of virtues. First, it enables high academic self-esteem and dropping out to co-exist, solving a difficult explanatory barrier. Second, it generates some interesting hypotheses. For example, among African-Americans achievement performance should be relatively unrelated to self-esteem, inasmuch as failure does not produce esteem decrements. On the other hand, among White pupils, it might be hypothesized that failure generates internal ascriptions (prejudice is not an available causal explanation), so that success and failure will give rise to large disparities in self-esteem. Therefore, among Whites performance in school would be highly related to academic self-esteem. Note that finding racial differences in the magnitude of the relation between achievement performance and self-esteem does not invalidate the attribution conception, but rather points out that the theory can be used to shed light on between-group differences.

Why, then, do African-American and White students not differ more substantially in academic self-esteem (and in a direction opposite to common sense), given that Whites are more likely to make internal attributions for failure than are African-Americans? One speculative answer is that Whites have fewer failures than African-Americans. The combination of fewer failures-more internal ascriptions (White students) versus more failures-fewer internal ascriptions (African-American students) could result in no significant self-esteem differences between these two groups. I doubt that I would bet on this explanation, although it logically follows from the discussion, Rather, I use it to show how attributional analyses can be applied to all the students, although not in a rigid or static manner.

Does, then, attribution theory provide an adequate explanation of the higher dropout rates among African-Americans as opposed to Whites, with the stability of the perceived cause of failure and its linkage with expectancy of success the crucial factor? I do not think so. The theory offered by Van Laar (2000) does implicate low expectancy of success as causing the achievement motivation and performance differences between the ethnic groups. Yet even in the face of poor performance, expectancy of success remains high among African-Americans in college and is as high as or higher than that of Whites (see Graham, 1988, 1991; Van Laar, 2000). The theory therefore again falls short. It apparently does not have the conceptual tools to handle ethnic differences in dropout rates inasmuch as neither self-esteem nor expectancy of success differentiates between the African-American students and their White counterparts.

Are other attributional interpretations available that might be more useful? I question this also. One might speculate, for example, that African-Americans do not perceive low grades in school as a failure inasmuch as high grades are not a goal for them. Hence, the attribution process is not even activated by poor grades. Or, perhaps African-American students have a lower grade threshold when defining failure, so that again attribution search is more limited. But these so-called explanations do not address the basic issues of why achievement is not a goal or why there may be lower standards for success for the African-Americans students. I suspect that answers to these questions are important for the dropout issue and they are not attributional issues.

In sum, it seems likely that dropout differences between the two racial groups are not mediated by (or, are only weakly related to) causal beliefs. As intimated above, this leaves many other concepts available to explain racial differences in school performance, ranging from innate intelligence to learned values, from the influence of peer groups to familial socialization, and from the perception of group belonging to teacher warmth and school climate. It is not my goal here to understand achievement differences between racial groups, nor to point out some of the important disparities in achievement performance that seem to fall beyond the range of attribution theory. Rather, I have tried to illustrate how to apply attribution theory to classroom diversity issues. The theory has remained intact, even though cultural differences were postulated for White and African-American students.

The prior analysis is not the only road for attribution theorists to take when addressing diversity. I now turn to a totally different phenomenon to expand my position – the differential reactions to obesity exhibited by Mexicans versus Americans.

ETHNIC DIFFERENCES IN REACTIONS TO OBESITY

I now shift from primarily the intrapersonal theory to the interpersonal theory and from achievement performance to reactions to the stigmatized. The observation I examine concerns reactions to obesity, specifically the finding that Mexicans react less negatively to obesity in females than do Americans (Crandall, 1995; Crandall & Martinez, 1996).

Guided by Figure 7.2, the following motivational analysis seems to fit these data. For Americans, obesity is perceived to be caused by overeating and/or exercising too little. These are controllable causes, so that the outcome of obesity

"could have been otherwise." Perceptions of controllability give rise to the inference that the overweight (daughter) is personally responsible for her "failed"
condition. This, in turn, evokes anger. Anger, along with responsibility as either
a direct or an indirect influence, results in an anti-social response such as some
form of punishment.

But Mexicans do not react as negatively to obesity. According to attribution
theory, why might this be the case (more generally, how does attribution theory
handle cultural diversity and differences in responses between ethnic groups)?
Here are some possible answers to that question (although not necessarily agreed
with by Crandall, 1995):

1. Mexicans do not regard obesity as a "failure." That is, thinness does not
represent a goal for which they strive and/or the definition of obesity starts at a
higher weight than it does for Americans. Therefore, among Mexicans the attribution process is not activated by a "heavy" daughter and negative emotions and
their linked behaviors do not follow.

2. Mexicans regard obesity as a personal "failure" but the causes are external and/or uncontrollable rather than internal and controllable. For example, the
perceived causes may be poverty, which results in the ingestion of fatty and less
nutritional food; lack of education regarding the adverse consequences of being
overweight; lack of time to engage in exercise and other healthy activities; and
on and on.

3. Even given the same perceived causes as Americans (eating too much and
exercising too little); these nonetheless are regarded as less controllable by the
Mexicans than by the Americans (see above).

4. Controllable causes among the Mexicans are less likely to give rise to anger
and other negative emotions than among the Americans. That is, even given the
identical causal analysis, their emotional reactions are more muted.

5. Given the presence of anger, Mexicans are less likely than are Americans
to react with punitive responses. Perhaps their anger takes other forms.

In sum, culture not only alters the operational definition of the constructs in
the theory, but also acts as a moderator between some of the linkages specified
in the theory. Again, then, the overall conception does not vary across the ethnic
groups: there are outcomes, causal antecedents, selected causes, dimensional
placement, affective and further cognitive reactions, and behavioral responses
among both ethnic groups. But nonetheless diversity can be captured within the
theoretical framework. This deep structure analysis is assumed to be generalizable
across cultures.

A FINAL NOTE

I started this chapter by exclaiming that few theorists limit the applicability
of their theories to a particular culture, or time, or place in history, or gender.

I certainly am among those who might be faulted for this rigidity. I have contended in this chapter that attribution theory as a theory, that is, as a set of inter-related constructs, is not in need of alteration. But one must be very careful in the assumptions being made when contrasting ethnic groups, cultures, genders, and so on. Success for one may be failure for another; causal information for one may be perceived as useless for another; causes salient to one group may be in the far background for the other; and so on. That is, content must be distinguished from process inasmuch as content may be culturally specific whereas process is culturally general. This means that the theorist must be alert for differences between cultures. However, one must be equally alert to convert phenotypic disparities into genotypic similarities. What appears to be a qualitative difference between cultures may be subject to a similar conceptual analysis. That is, the unique is nonetheless included within more general laws. That is the theoretical goal guiding my thinking.

REFERENCES

Atkinson, J. W. (1964). *An introduction to motivation*. Princeton, NJ: Van Nostrand.

Bar-Tal, D., Goldberg, M., & Knaani, A. (1984). Causes of success and failure and their dimensions as a function of SES and gender: A phenomenological analysis. *British Journal of Educational Psychology, 54*, 51–61.

Betancourt, H., & Weiner, B. (1982). Attributions for achievement-related events, expectancy, and sentiments: A study of success and failure in Chile and the United States. *Journal of Cross-Cultural Psychology, 13*, 362–374.

Crandall, C. S. (1995). Do parents discriminate against their own heavyweight daughters? *Personality and Social Psychology Bulletin, 21*, 724–735.

Crandall, C. S., & Martinez, R. (1996). Culture, ideology, and anti-fat attitudes. *Personality and Social Psychology Bulletin, 22*, 1165–1176.

Crocker, J., & Major, B. (1989). Social stigma and self-esteem: The self-protective properties of stigmas. *Psychological Review, 96*, 608–630.

Gendolla, G. H. E., & Koller, M. (2001). Surprise and causal search: How are they affected by outcome valence and importance? *Motivation and Emotion, 25*, 237–250.

Graham, S. (1988). Can attribution theory tell us something about motivation in Blacks? *Educational Psychologist, 23*, 3–21.

Graham, S. (1991). A review of attribution theory in achievement contexts. *Educational Psychology Review, 3*, 5–39.

Rudolph, U., Roesch, S. C., Greitemeyer, T., & Weiner, B. (2004). A meta-analytic review of help giving and aggression from an attributional perspective. *Cognition and Emotion, 18*, 815–848.

Van Laar, C. (2000). The paradox of low academic achievement but high self-esteem in African-American students: An attributional account. *Educational Psychology Review, 12*, 33–61.

Weiner, B. (1986). *An attributional theory of motivation and emotion*. New York: Springer-Verlag.

Weiner, B. (1992). *Human motivation: Metaphors, theories, and research*. Newbury Park, CA: Sage Publications.

Weiner, B. (1995). *Judgments of responsibility: A foundation for a theory of social conduct*. New York: Guilford.

Weiner, B. (2006). *Social motivation, justice, and the moral emotions*. Mahwah, NJ: Erlbaum.

8

RE-THINKING CULTURE AND PERSONALITY: HOW SELF-REGULATORY UNIVERSALS CREATE CROSS-CULTURAL DIFFERENCES

E. TORY HIGGINS[*], ANTONIO PIERRO[†] AND ARIE W. KRUGLANSKI[‡]

*Psychology Department, Columbia University, New York, USA
†Department of Development and Socialization, University of Rome, La Sapienza, Rome, Italy
‡Department of Psychology, University of Maryland, College Park, USA

INTRODUCTION

Historically, it has been commonplace for people to associate the members of different nations, cultures and ethnic groups with different personality characteristics, such as Germans being "scientific-minded," Americans being "materialistic," Italians being "artistic," and Canadians being "compliant" (e.g., Katz & Braly, 1933; Inkeles & Levinson, 1969; Peabody, 1985; Terracciano et al., 2005; McCrae & Terracciano, 2006). Cultural anthropologists have referred to the perceived common traits that members of a cultural community share with one another as the "modal personality" (Bidney, 1953; Inkeles & Levinson, 1969). Although self and other perceptions of "national character" do not always agree, often the members of a nation see themselves similarly to how members of other nations see them (McCrae & Terracciano, 2006). Despite both inside and outside consensus on differences in "national character," there is considerable debate as to whether such perceptions are accurate perceptions (e.g., Terracciano et al., 2005) or are just stereotypes without any "kernel of truth." The simplistic "national character" idea that whole nations of people possessed particular traits, such as Americans being "materialistic" or Japanese being "fanatical" (a WWII creation), was increasingly seen as stereotyping the members of different nations or cultures and, by the 1960s, this notion was rejected.

Although the earlier notion of "national character" has continued to be rejected, interest in "culture and personality" re-emerged and steadily grew in the 1990s (for reviews, see Benet-Martinez & Oishi (in press); Church, 2001). A broad range of viewpoints on "culture and personality" have been proposed – from a cultural psychology viewpoint that questions the existence of universal personality traits because personality is revealed in culture-specific situations (e.g., Markus & Kitayama, 1998; see also Markus et al., 1996) to a genotypic view of universal personality traits (e.g., extraversion; conscientiousness) that are biologically based and where cultural differences in such universal traits indicate genetic differences between the cultural communities (McCrae, 2000).

Put simply, these and other viewpoints raise two basic issues. First, are there cross-cultural universals in personality traits? Second, when there are differences between nations or cultures in the relative strength of universal personal traits, how can these differences be explained? Regarding the first issue, McCrae (2000) reports that the so-called Big-Five personality trait dimensions – *agreeableness*, *extroversion, conscientiousness, openness*, and *neuroticism* (see John, 1990; John & Srivastava, 1999) – have been identified in most cultures in which the factor structure has been examined (see also Benet-Martinez & Oishi (in press)). Notwithstanding that the specific responses associated with these trait dimensions could show cross-cultural variability as a function of additional culture-related situational forces of the kind discussed by Markus and Kitayama (1998), one could reasonably treat these trait dimensions as reflecting action-emotional tendencies that vary within every culture. Then the issue would be how to explain any cultural differences that are found in the strength of these tendencies. As noted earlier, the genotypic view would explain cultural differences in trait strength in terms of genetic differences in the cultural communities. A second approach would be to identify differences in cultural values that could account for differences in trait strength, such as cultural emphasis differences along the value dimension of individualism–collectivism (Triandis, 1990; but see also Oyserman et al., 2002). A third approach would be to identify differences in cultural knowledge (including procedural knowledge) that could produce the differences in trait strength as a function of universal cognitive principles, such as the knowledge priming and activation principles of accessibility, salience and applicability (e.g., Higgins, 1990, 2000b; Hong et al., 2000; Hong & Chiu, 2001; Morris et al., 2001).

With respect to the above two issues, our position in this chapter is to treat trait dimensions as reflecting universal action-emotional tendencies that vary within every culture, and to suggest an additional approach for explaining any cultural differences that are found in the strength of these tendencies (see also Higgins, 2008). In order to account for cultural differences in trait strength, we believe that it is necessary to consider general motivational principles (see, e.g., Heine, 2004; see also, Higgins, 2008). In fact, general motivational principles may be critical because of their major role in bridging the gap between thought and action (see Higgins & Kruglanski, 2000). Although the effects of universal motives on revealing culture are attracting increasing attention, such as the effects of need for closure (see Kruglanski, 1990) on cultural conformity (e.g., Fu et al., 2007), the possible role of universal self-regulatory principles in accounting for cultural differences, and especially differences in trait strength, has received relatively little attention (but see Lee et al., 2000; Heine et al., 2001).

The purpose of this chapter is to consider how the regulatory focus distinction between promotion concerns with accomplishment and aspirations and prevention concerns with safety and responsibilities (Higgins, 1997), and the regulatory mode distinction between locomotion concerns with movement from state to state and assessment concerns with making comparisons (Higgins et al., 2003; see also Kruglanski et al., 2000), could provide a new perspective on cultural differences in trait strength. From this *self-regulatory perspective*, traits like extraversion or conscientiousness are conceptualized as *strategic conduits or channels* in the service of promotion, prevention, locomotion, or assessment orientations. That is, rather than themselves reflecting something basic about individuals' motivational predispositions, such traits are considered as providing support for more fundamental and general self-regulatory concerns. This is not to say that these trait dimensions are not important. They can provide a general language for summarizing stable behaviors of individuals within many cultures.

Our approach to the issue of cross-cultural differences in trait strength is generally consistent with the recommendations of Inkeles and Levinson (1969) in their thoughtful and critical review of early research on "national character." They recommend defining "national character" in terms of relatively enduring personality characteristics, such as traits and conceptions of the self. To address the issue of culture and personality in these terms, we will consider four of the Big-Five trait dimensions – *agreeableness, extroversion, conscientiousness,* and *openness* (see John, 1990; John & Srivastava, 1999) – as reflecting the relative strength of different kinds of *traits* that serve as strategic channels for regulatory focus and regulatory mode orientations. [Because our studies also included the remaining Big Five dimension, *neuroticism*, we present our findings for this variable in a footnote. From our perspective, however, neuroticism is an emotional outcome characteristic rather than a strategic channel in the service of self-regulation, and thus is less germane to the thrust of this chapter.] Taking a perspective similar to that of Leary et al., (1995) sociometer perspective on *self-esteem*, we will also treat self-esteem (Rosenberg, 1979) as another kind of strategic channel.

Our objective in this chapter is to review evidence from our recent research that supports three conclusions. First, there are clear *cross-cultural differences* in the relative strength or predominance of different basic self-regulatory orientations – promotion focus versus prevention focus, locomotion mode versus assessment mode. Second, there are clear *cross-cultural similarities* (i.e., universals) in how these self-regulatory orientations relate to such central traits as extraversion, conscientiousness, openness, agreeableness, and self-esteem, with these relations generally being consistent with what regulatory focus theory and regulatory mode theory would predict. Third, previously identified cross-cultural differences in traits, such as United States being generally higher in both self-esteem and extraversion than Japan, could be explained by combining the former cross-cultural differences with the latter cross-cultural universals.

Our selection of regulatory mode and regulatory focus as the self-regulatory principles to consider in our cross-cultural studies was no accident. True, we could be biased by the fact that these are principles that relate to two theories that we ourselves developed earlier – regulatory focus theory (Higgins, 1997) and regulatory mode theory (Higgins et al., 2003; see also Kruglanski et al., 2000). But this is not the primary reason why we selected these systems. One reason we selected them is that there is substantial research evidence about how these self-regulatory principles function, both strategically and tactically, and about the cognitive, affective, and behavioral consequences of their functioning. Some of this evidence will be reviewed below.

A second reason we selected these self-regulatory principles is that each of them concerns more than personality per se. Because promotion, prevention, locomotion, and assessment refer to self-regulatory states, they vary across situations as well as across persons. A promotion concern with accomplishment, for example, can be situationally induced through priming a person's ideals or framing a task in terms of gains and non-gains as well as being a chronic predisposition of a person. Thus, it will be easier ultimately to relate a culture's institutionalized social situations (education, law, business) and socialization situations (family, community) to the likelihood of particular motivational systems developing among cultural members, while also considering how modal situations encountered day-to-day by cultural members influence current motives and strategies (both directly and in interaction with members' chronic orientations). In this way, both the prolonged influence of chronic situations (institutions; socialization) and the temporary influence of momentary situations on individuals' chronic predispositions and momentary tendencies for trait-related states can be characterized and examined with the same set of self-regulatory principles – a "common language" for person and situation influences (see Higgins, 1990, 1999, 2000a, b).

A final reason why we chose the self-regulatory principles of regulatory focus and regulatory mode in particular is our belief that they are basic to all self-regulation (not only for humans but for many other animals as well). Regulatory focus theory (Higgins, 1997) assumes that the hedonic principle of approaching pleasure and avoiding pain operates differently when serving fundamentally different needs, such as the distinct survival needs of *nurturance* (e.g., nourishment) and *security* (e.g., protection). Human survival requires adaptation to the surrounding environment, especially the social environment (see Buss, 1996). To obtain the nurturance and security they need to survive, children must establish and maintain relationships with caretakers who provide them with nurturance and security by supporting, encouraging, protecting, and defending them (see Bowlby, 1969, 1973). As the hedonic principle suggests, children must learn how to behave in order to approach pleasure and avoid pain. But what is learned about regulating pleasure and pain is different for nurturance and security needs. Regulatory focus theory proposes that nurturance-related regulation and security-related regulation differ in *regulatory focus*. Nurturance-related regulation involves a *promotion focus* whereas security-related regulation involves a *prevention focus*.

Regulatory focus theory, then, considers both promotion focus self-regulation and prevention focus self-regulation to be necessary for human survival. It considers both promotion and prevention to be orientation states. It assumes that all individuals in every society will have times when they are self-regulating in the promotion system and times when they are self-regulating in the prevention system. Everyone has both systems available to them. However, regulatory focus theory also assumes that individuals can differ chronically (i.e., personality) and situationally in the likelihood that the promotion system is more accessible than the prevention system (i.e., the promotion system currently dominates) or the reverse (i.e., the prevention system currently dominates). (For a discussion of the availability versus accessibility distinction and its relation to persons and situations, see Higgins, 1996). Given all this, we expected to find that both the promotion system and the prevention system functioned in each culture (and functioned in similar ways), but that the relative strength of each system would vary across culture.

Let us now consider regulatory mode. When people self-regulate, they decide what they want that they do not currently have; they figure out what they need to do to get what they want; and then they do it. Two key functions of self-regulation are captured in this conception. First, people *assess* both the different goals to pursue and the different means to pursue them. Second, people *locomote* or "move" from their current state in pursuit of some alternative goal pursuit state. All major models of self-regulation contain some version of these two functions (e.g., Wiener, 1948; Miller et al., 1960; Kuhl, 1984; Heckhausen & Gollwitzer, 1987; Carver & Scheier, 1990).

Regulatory mode theory (Kruglanski et al., 2000; Higgins et al., 2003) makes similar assumptions as regulatory focus theory. It considers both locomotion self-regulation and assessment self-regulation to be necessary for human survival. It considers both locomotion and assessment to be orientation states. This theory also assumes that everyone has both orientations available to them, and that all individuals in every society will have times when they are self-regulating with a locomotion orientation and times when they are self-regulating with an assessment orientation. It also assumes that individuals can differ chronically (i.e., personality) and situationally in the likelihood that locomotion system is more accessible than assessment (i.e., the locomotion orientation currently dominates) or the reverse (i.e., the assessment orientation currently dominates). Regulatory focus theory and regulatory mode theory are also similar in assuming that, generally speaking, promotion and prevention are independent of one another, and locomotion and assessment are independent of one another. That is, individuals can be high in both promotion and prevention, or low in both, or high in one and low in the other. Likewise, individuals can be high in both locomotion and assessment, or low in both, or high in one and low in the other.

We will begin our chapter by providing more details about the nature and consequences of regulatory focus and regulatory mode. This is critical for understanding the rationale behind our predictions relating promotion, prevention, locomotion, and assessment to the Big-Five trait dimensions and self-esteem as strategic conduits or channels. We will then present evidence of cross-cultural differences in the predominance of promotion, prevention, locomotion, and assessment. Next, we present evidence of cross-cultural similarities in the functional relations between these regulatory focus and regulatory mode dimensions and the Big-Five trait dimensions and self-esteem. Finally, in the "General Discussion" we compare Japan and United States to illustrate how cross-cultural differences in traits – levels of self-esteem and extraversion – can be accounted for in terms of cross-cultural differences in the relative strength of self-regulatory orientations (e.g., promotion; locomotion) combined with cross-cultural *similarities* (i.e., universals) in self-regulatory functioning.

REGULATORY FOCUS DIMENSIONS OF PROMOTION AND PREVENTION

Regulatory focus theory posits two separate and independent self-regulatory orientations, promotion and prevention (Higgins, 1997; Higgins et al., 2001). A promotion focus emphasizes hopes, accomplishments, and advancement needs. Goals are viewed as ideals. There is a strategic concern with gains (the presence of positives) versus non-gains (the absence of positives). A prevention focus, on the other hand, emphasizes safety, the fulfillment of responsibility and security needs. Goals are seen as oughts. There is a strategic concern with non-losses (the absence of negatives) versus losses (the presence of negatives). Regulatory focus may be chronic (a personality variable) or momentary (situationally induced).

Each self-regulatory orientation has its own preferred strategy or means of goal pursuit (Higgins, 1997; Crowe & Higgins, 1997; Higgins, 2000a, b). An eager strategy ensures the presence of positives (gains) and ensures against the absence of positives (non-gains). A promotion focus and an eager strategy both operate in terms of gains and non-gains, and are especially sensitive to the difference between "0" and "+1" (attainment). A vigilant strategy ensures the absence of negatives (non-losses) and ensures against the presence of negatives (losses). A prevention focus and a vigilant strategy both operate in terms of non-losses and losses, and are especially sensitive to the difference between "0" and "−1" (maintenance). Thus, someone who is chronically or situationally promotion-focused prefers an eager strategy, and someone who is chronically or situationally prevention-focused prefers a vigilant strategy (Crowe & Higgins, 1997; Higgins, 2000a, b).

Regulatory focus has been studied both as a temporary, situationally induced orientation and as a chronic, individual difference variable. When studied as an individual difference variable, regulatory focus has been assessed by using the self-guide strength measure (e.g., Higgins, 1997; Higgins et al., 1997), which measures the chronic accessibility of people's ideals and oughts (Higgins, 1997), and by using the Regulatory Focus Questionnaire (RFQ; Higgins et al., 2001). The RFQ measure was used in our cross-cultural studies. Because of its centrality to the methodology of our studies, the next section describes this measure in some detail (see Higgins & Spiegel, 2004; Molden et al., 2007 for complete reviews of regulatory focus differences).

THE REGULATORY FOCUS QUESTIONNAIRE

The RFQ was developed to measure individuals' subjective histories of success in promotion and prevention regulation (Harlow et al., 1997; Higgins et al., 2001). It was found that participants with a subjective history of success in either promotion or prevention experienced a sense of achievement pride. Where they differed was that high *promotion pride* participants were strategically inclined to use eagerness means to attain their goals, whereas high *prevention pride* participants were inclined to use vigilance means. Prevention items in the RFQ relate to ought self-regulation and the prevention of negative outcomes, and promotion items relate to ideal self-regulation and the promotion of positive outcomes. Both of these sets of items exhibited good internal reliability ($\alpha = .73$ for the Promotion scale; $\alpha = .80$ for the Prevention scale). Table 8.1 presents the RFQ as it is administered (called the Event Reaction Questionnaire when administered), along with the method for scoring Promotion Pride and Prevention Pride. The Promotion Pride items are # 1, 3, 7, 9, 10, & 11; and the Prevention Pride items are # 2, 4, 5, 6, & 8. Studies have consistently found either a modest positive correlation or no significant correlation between the promotion and prevention scales. A test–retest reliability study found that over a period of 2 months the RFQ Promotion scale had a .79 correlation ($p < .0001$) and the RFQ Prevention scale had a .81 correlation ($p < .0001$) (Harlow et al., 1997).

Harlow et al. (1997) and Higgins et al. (2001) also report that the RFQ showed good convergent and discriminant validity. They found that experiencing a history of promotion effectiveness was generally related to being eager, risky, and oriented toward the future presence of positive outcomes (toward accomplishments and advancements), whereas experiencing a history of prevention effectiveness was generally related to being careful, cautious, organized, and oriented toward ensuring against negative outcomes (toward being responsible

TABLE 8.1   The Regulatory Focus Questionnaire and Scoring Method

Event Reaction Questionnaire

This set of questions asks you HOW FREQUENTLY specific events actually occur or have occurred in your life. Please indicate your answer to each question by circling the appropriate number below it.

1. Compared to most people, are you typically unable to get what you want out of life?

1	2	3	4	5
Never or seldom		Sometimes		Very often

2. Growing up, would you ever "cross the line" by doing things that your parents would not tolerate?

1	2	3	4	5
Never or seldom		Sometimes		Very often

3. How often have you accomplished things that got you "psyched" to work even harder?

1	2	3	4	5
Never or seldom		Sometimes		Very often

4. Did you get on your parents' nerves often when you were growing up?

1	2	3	4	5
Never or seldom		Sometimes		Very often

5. How often did you obey rules and regulations that were established by your parents?

1	2	3	4	5
Never or seldom		Sometimes		Very often

6. Growing up, did you ever act in ways that your parents thought were objectionable?

1	2	3	4	5
Never or seldom		Sometimes		Very often

7. Do you often do well at different things that you try?

1	2	3	4	5
Never or seldom		Sometimes		Very often

8. Not being careful enough has gotten me into trouble at times.

1	2	3	4	5
Never or seldom		Sometimes		Very often

9. When it comes to achieving things that are important to me, I find that I don't perform as well as I ideally would like to do.

1	2	3	4	5
Never or seldom		Sometimes		Very often

10. I feel like I have made progress toward being successful in my life.

1	2	3	4	5
Never or seldom		Sometimes		Very often

11. I have found very few hobbies or activities in my life that capture my interest or motivate me to put effort into them.

1	2	3	4	5
Never or seldom		Sometimes		Very often

(continues)

TABLE 8.1 (*continued*)

Scoring Method

I. *Promotion Pride*

1. Place a tick next to items # 1, 3, 7, 9, 10, & 11

2. Reverse score items # 1, 9, & 11 [For these items, if you circled 1, change it to 5; 2 change to 4; 3 stays 3; 4 change to 2; 5 change to 1]

3. Add up the scores

4. Divide by 6. This is your *Promotion Pride* score.

II. *Prevention Pride*

1. Place an X next to items # 2, 4, 5, 6, & 8

2. Reverse score items # 2, 4, 6, & 8 [For these items, if you circled 1, change it to 5; 2 change to 4; 3 stays 3; 4 change to 2; 5 change to 1]

3. Add up the scores

4. Divide by 5. This is your *Prevention Pride* score.

and faultless). As expected, these different histories did not relate differently to achievement motivation. The promotion scale and the prevention scale each had modest, significantly positive relations to the Jackson (1974) Personality Research Form (PRF) Achievement scale. Thus, individuals with high promotion pride and individuals with high prevention pride differ in the quality of their experiences and in their strategic inclinations (i.e., eager versus vigilant) but not in the amount of their achievement motivation.

MOTIVATIONAL CHARACTERISTICS OF CHRONIC PROMOTION AND CHRONIC PREVENTION ORIENTATION

Several studies have used the RFQ to investigate the distinct motivational characteristics of individuals with high promotion versus prevention pride. In one study by Higgins et al. (2001), participants first imagined themselves in a situation where they are on a diet and are tempted by a pizza. They were then asked what tactics they would use in this situation, including tactics that would *advance* the diet goal (e.g., the "health/appearance benefits") and tactics that would *impede* the diet goal (e.g., "...[thinking] about how yummy the pizza is..."). RFQ Promotion scores were positively related to using tactics that advance the diet goal (approaching a match to the goal), while, independently, higher RFQ Prevention scores were negatively related to tactics that impede the diet goal (avoiding a mismatch to the goal).

Grant and Higgins (2003) used the RFQ to study the relation among regulatory focus, optimism, and quality of life. They found that optimism was more strongly related to promotion pride than prevention pride (controlling for the effects of neuroticism). Promotion pride also uniquely predicted having a sense of purpose in life or goal-directedness. Their findings supported the notion that the anticipation of success (optimism) increases the eagerness motivation characteristic of promotion regulation and thus sustains promotion, but it decreases the vigilance motivation characteristic of prevention regulation and thus disrupts prevention (see also Idson et al., 2004). Thus, optimism as a strategic tool should be used more by high promotion than high prevention individuals.

The Grant and Higgins (2003) findings suggest that in addition to the fundamental difference between promotion focus and prevention focus in their strategic inclinations (i.e., eagerness versus vigilance), there is also a critical difference in what strengthens and weakens these inclinations. Specifically, there is a regulatory focus difference in the effects of success and failure (actual or anticipated) on motivational strength. Generally speaking, success maintains the eagerness that sustains the orientation of promotion-focused people toward accomplishment and hopes [ideals]), but it reduces the vigilance that sustains the orientation of prevention-focused people toward security and responsibilities [oughts]). This difference is reflected in the different emotions that are experienced (see Higgins, 1997; Idson et al., 2000) after success in promotion versus prevention. Promotion success produces high intensity cheerfulness-related emotions (e.g., "happy") whereas prevention success produces low intensity quiescence-related emotions (e.g., "relaxed"). On the other hand, failure maintains the vigilance that sustains the orientation of prevention-focused people, but it reduces the eagerness that sustains the orientation of promotion-focused people. Again, this difference is reflected in the different emotions that are experienced after failure in promotion versus prevention. Prevention failure produces high intensity agitation-related emotions (e.g., "tense"), whereas promotion failure produces low intensity dejection-related emotions (e.g., "sad").

Consistent with this regulatory focus difference in the effects of success and failure, receiving success versus failure feedback on early attempts at goal attainment has been found to have different effects on the motivational systems and strategic behavior of people with subjective histories of promotion- versus prevention-related success (i.e., those with high "promotion pride" versus "prevention pride"). Idson and Higgins (2000), e.g., found that people with high promotion pride improved their performance on an anagram task over time after success feedback, but showed a decline in performance after failure feedback. In contrast, people with high prevention pride improved their performance on an anagram task over time after failure feedback, but showed a decline in performance after success feedback. In a similar study, Spiegel and Higgins (2001) found that promotion-focused participants performed better on the second round of an anagram task after receiving success feedback on the first round of the task, compared to prevention or control participants; whereas prevention-focused participants performed better on the second round of the task after receiving failure feedback on the first round of the task, compared to promotion or control participants. In another success/failure feedback study, Forster et al. (2001) found that the classic "goal looms larger" effect of motivational strength increasing as individuals move closer to the goal was highest for measures of eager motivation when the participants were promotion-focused and received success feedback, and was highest for measures of vigilant motivation when the participants were prevention-focused and received failure feedback.

REGULATORY MODE DIMENSIONS OF LOCOMOTION AND ASSESSMENT

Most deliberate human behaviors comprise activities in the regulatory modes of assessment and locomotion. Assessment "constitutes the comparative aspect of self-regulation concerned with critically evaluating entities or states, such as goals or means in relation to alternatives in order to judge relative quality" (Kruglanski et al., 2000, p. 794). "Which alternative is best?" "How did I do in the past?" Individuals strong in assessment mode are preoccupied with these kinds of critical evaluations (see Higgins et al., 2003). By contrast, the locomotion mode "is the self-regulatory aspect concerned with movement from state to state and with committing the psychological resources that will initiate and maintain goal-directed progress in a straightforward manner, without undue distractions or delays" (Kruglanski et al., 2000, p. 794). In the locomotion mode, individuals emphasize "getting on with it," "making something happen" (see Higgins et al., 2003) rather than critical evaluation. Indeed, individuals strong in locomotion mode might refrain from critical evaluation if such "stopping to reflect" halted steady movement from state to state. Whereas classic control theory (cf. Kuhl, 1985; Gollwitzer, 1990; Carver & Scheier, 1990) conceives of assessment and locomotion as inseparable and interdependent components of any action, regulatory mode theory (Kruglanski et al., 2000; Higgins et al., 2003) proposes that these functions are independent and can be differentially emphasized by individuals.

THE REGULATORY MODE QUESTIONNAIRE

Because the Regulatory Mode Questionnaire (RMQ) was central to the methodology of our cross-cultural studies, we provide some details about it in this section and in Table 8.2 (for a fuller review of the psychometric construction and testing of the RMQ scales, see Kruglanski et al., 2000). The RMQ constitutes two separate 12-item self-report measures designed to tap individual differences in both locomotion and assessment. Table 8.2 presents the RMQ as it is administered (called the Attitude, Belief and Experience Survey when administered), along with the method for scoring Locomotion and Assessment. Respondents rate the extent to which they agree with self-descriptive statements reflecting *locomotion* or *assessment*. Across different samples, the coefficient alphas for each scale range from .76 to .86, the temporal stability (test–retest correlations) for each scale is around $r = .75$ on average, and the intercorrelation of the two scales is only slightly positive (typically $r < .15$).

TABLE 8.2   The Regulatory Mode Questionnaire and Scoring Method

Attitude, Belief, and Experience Survey
Read each of the following statements and decide how much you agree with each according to your beliefs and experiences. Please respond according to the following scale.

1. Strongly disagree	4. Slightly agree
2. Moderately disagree	5. Moderately agree
3. Slightly disagree	6. Strongly agree

__1. I don't mind doing things even if they involve extra effort.

__2. I never evaluate my social interactions with others after they occur.

__3. I am a "workaholic."

__4. I feel excited just before I am about to reach a goal.

__5. I enjoy actively doing things, more than just watching and observing.

__6. I spend a great deal of time taking inventory of my positive and negative characteristics.

__7. I like evaluating other people's plans.

__8. I am a "doer."

__9. I often compare myself with other people.

__10. I don't spend much time thinking about ways others could improve themselves.

__11. I often critique work done by myself or others.

__12. When I finish one project, I often wait awhile before getting started on a new one.

__13. I often feel that I am being evaluated by others.

__14. When I decide to do something, I can't wait to get started.

__15. I am a critical person.

__16. I am very self-critical and self-conscious about what I am saying.

__17. By the time I accomplish a task, I already have the next one in mind.

__18. I often think that other people's choices and decisions are wrong.

__19. I am a "low energy" person.

__20. Most of the time my thoughts are occupied with the task I wish to accomplish.

__21. I rarely analyze the conversations I have had with others after they occur.

__22. When I get started on something, I usually persevere until I finish it.

__23. I am a "go-getter."

__24. When I meet a new person I usually evaluate how well he or she is doing on various dimensions (e.g., looks, achievements, social status, clothes).

Scoring Method

I. *Locomotion*
1. Place an "L" next to items # 1, 3, 4, 5, 8, 12, 14, 17, 19, 20, 22, 23
2. Reverse score items # 12 & 19 [For these items, change 1 to 6; 2 to 5; 3 to 4; 4 to 3; 5 to 2; 6 to 1]
3. Add up the scores
4. Divide by 12. This is your *Locomotion* score.

II. *Assessment*
1. Place an "A" next to items # 2, 6, 7, 9, 10, 11, 13, 15, 16, 18, 21, 24
2. Reverse score items # 2, 10, & 21 [For these items, change 1 to 6; 2 to 5; 3 to 4; 4 to 3; 5 to 2; 6 to 1]
3. Add up the scores
4. Divide by 12. This is your *Assessment* score.

MOTIVATIONAL CHARACTERISTICS OF CHRONIC ASSESSMENT AND CHRONIC LOCOMOTION ORIENTATION

Using the RMQ, several specific motivational characteristics have been identified that have distinct relations to chronic individual differences in assessment orientation and chronic individual differences in locomotion orientation (Kruglanski et al., 2000; Higgins et al., 2003). We will not review all of them here, but instead highlight those that are most relevant to the cross-cultural findings that we discuss later.

Distinct characteristics related to chronic differences in assessment.

Assessment involves making comparisons. An especially important comparison in self-regulation is comparing the self to some standard, where the standard could be another person or some valued end state. Thus, higher assessment should be associated with stronger self-evaluative concerns. Higher assessors should be *more self-critical.* There is substantial evidence consistent with this prediction. Kruglanski et al. (2000) measured self-consciousness with Fenigstein et al.'s (1975) scales of public and private self-consciousness. Public self-consciousness refers to a "general awareness of self as a social object," and private self-consciousness refers to "attending to one's inner thoughts and feelings" (p. 523). Comparison with standards was measured with the need for social comparison subscale of Hill's (1987) Interpersonal Orientation Scale. As predicted, assessment was strongly and positively associated with public self-consciousness, private self-consciousness, and need for social comparison. In contrast, locomotion had little or no relation to these variables.

Continuous self-evaluation is also likely to involve a wide range of standards. Thus, even individuals doing quite well are likely to compare themselves sometimes to standards that make them feel like relative failures. Continuous self-evaluation, then, is a vulnerability factor to experience failures. Combined with their greater sensitivity to social criticism described earlier, this would make high assessors vulnerable to negative affect, lower self-esteem, and lower optimism. Consistent with these predictions, Kruglanski et al. (2000) found that higher assessment had significant positive correlations with both social anxiety and depression, and significant negative correlations with self-esteem and optimism, whereas higher locomotion had the opposite relations.

Distinct Characteristics Related to Chronic Differences in Locomotion

People in a strong locomotion orientation do not like to stand still, to do nothing. They like to move along, to flow. Locomotion involves initiating and maintaining movement, changing from state to state. In order to initiate movement or change, it is important to be decisive in decision making because decisiveness allows action to proceed. Thus, higher locomotion should be associated with *higher decisiveness.* Again, there is substantial evidence consistent with this prediction. Using several different indicators of decisiveness, measuring commitment to prompt action, time spent on preactional decision processes before taking action, the decisiveness of respondents' judgments and choices, and so on, Kruglanski et al. (2000) that higher locomotion was associated with more decisiveness whereas higher assessment had the opposite relation.

One socially important form of decisive movement is the ability to cope with organizational change. Kruglanski et al. (2007) examined coping with organization change in various organizations in Italy, employing both contemporaneous and longitudinal designs. They examined diverse organizational settings, different populations, and different types of organizational change. They also used different measures of coping with change. Their studies consistently found that higher locomotion positively predicted coping with change, and that more successful coping with change predicted better post-change work attitudes.

Locomotion involves not only the initiation of movement or change but also its maintenance. Thus, locomotion needs not only decisiveness during the preactional phase (see Gollwitzer, 1990) to proceed with action but also commitment during the actional phase (Gollwitzer, 1990) to maintain action and avoid interruptions and obstacles. Higher locomotion, then, should be associated with greater attention, persistence, and vitality when engaging activities, with increased level of experiential involvement and efficiency; i.e., with greater flow (e.g., Csikszentmihalyi, 1975). Consistent with this prediction, Kruglanski et al. (2000) used several indictors of flow, measuring attentional control (e.g., "I tend to be quite wrapped up and interested in whatever I am doing,") conscientiousness (e.g., "I'm pretty good about pacing myself so as to get things done on time"), and vitality (e.g., "I feel alive and vital"), and found that higher locomotion had a strong positive association with each of the measures of flow, whereas higher assessment had a small or a negative relation to them (see also Pierro et al., 2006).

The above two sections have described regulatory focus theory and regulatory mode theory and have presented evidence of both the distinct motivational characteristics of promotion focus and prevention focus and the distinct motivational characteristics of locomotion mode and assessment mode. These theories will provide the basis for our discussion of cross-cultural differences and similarities. When discussing criteria for studying "national character" effectively, Inkeles and Levinson's (1969) state (p. 429):

> Ideally, the personality theory used in this field should have certain basic characteristics. Its assumptions and concepts should comprise an explicitly formulated, coherent whole… The variables in the analytic scheme should be *psychologically significant*, in the sense that they represent intrapersonal characteristics that play an important part in determining the individual's thought and behavior; and *socially relevant*, in the sense that they influence the individual's readiness to maintain or change the existing sociocultural system.

We believe that the evidence we have reviewed above concerning the implications of regulatory focus and regulatory mode for people's thoughts, judgments and decision making are a step forward in meeting these criteria. Given that regulatory focus and regulatory mode orientations are important in several ways, it is of interest to know whether cultures differ in the strength and the predominance of them. The next section reviews evidence that they do.

CROSS-CULTURAL DIFFERENCES IN SELF-REGULATORY ORIENTATIONS

We should note from the beginning that the participants in all of our studies are college students. Thus, the bad news is that no claim can be made that our samples are representative of the general population of each nation. The good news is that potentially confounding factors such as age and education level (and, to some extent at least, socioeconomic status) are better controlled for than might otherwise be the case. We believe that restricting our samples to college students represents a conservative test of our predictions because, if anything, it narrows the range of participants within each nation. In all nations where English was not the first language of the participants, the Regulatory Focus, Regulatory Mode, self-esteem (Rosenberg), and Big Five questionnaire items were translated and back translated for accuracy.

REGULATORY FOCUS DIFFERENCES

The nations for which we obtained measures of promotion pride and prevention pride were Australia, China, India, Israel, Italy, Japan, and United States. In our first analysis, we checked for regulatory focus predominance by subtracting each participant's prevention pride score from his or her promotion pride score (i.e., promotion minus prevention). The participants were classified as predominant promotion if they had a positive difference score, and as predominant prevention if they had a negative difference score. In United States and in Italy, there was a significantly higher percentage of predominant promotion than predominant prevention individuals. In Japan, there was a significantly higher percentage of predominant prevention than predominant promotion individuals.

In a test of homogeneity for the promotion pride scores, United States had higher promotion scores than any other nation except Israel, and Japan had lower promotion scores than any other nation. In a test of homogeneity for the prevention pride scores, China was relatively high and Italy was relatively low. Finally, in a test of homogeneity for the promotion pride minus prevention pride difference scores, Italy, and United States formed one cluster of nations that were relatively more predominant promotion, whereas Japan, India, China, and Australia formed another cluster of nations that were relatively less predominant promotion. Tables 8.3–8.5 summarize the homogeneity analyses.

In sum, for cross-cultural differences in regulatory focus, there was convergent evidence indicating that in Italy and in United States, and to a lesser extent in Israel, the regulatory focus orientation of promotion was stronger than prevention. In contrast, in Japan, the regulatory focus orientation of prevention was stronger than promotion. Promotion was weakest in Japan and prevention was

TABLE 8.3 Test post hoc of Duncan: Homogeneity Sets for *Promotion*

	Homogeneity sets for $\alpha = .05$				
Samples	1	2	3	4	5
Japan	3.14				
India		3.32			
Australia		3.32			
China			3.53		
Italy			3.57		
Israel			3.63	3.63	
USA				3.76	3.76

TABLE 8.4 Test post hoc of Duncan: Homogeneity Sets for *Prevention*

	Homogeneity sets for $\alpha = .05$			
Samples	1	2	3	4
Italy	3.13	3.13		
Japan		3.25	3.25	
Australia		3.25	3.25	
India		3.30	3.30	3.30
Israel			3.40	3.40
USA			3.44	3.44
China				3.48

TABLE 8.5 Test post hoc of Duncan: Homogeneity Sets for *Index of Promotion – Prevention Difference*

	Homogeneity sets for $\alpha = .05$			
Samples	1	2	3	4
Japan	− .11			
India	.02	.02		
China	.05	.05		
Australia	.07	.07		
Israel		.22	.22	
USA			.32	.32
Italy				.44

weakest in Italy. In India, China, and Australia, promotion and prevention were more equal in strength, with China being relatively high in both.

REGULATORY MODE DIFFERENCES

The nations for which we obtained measures of locomotion and assessment were England, India, Korea, Israel, Italy, Japan, Poland, Spain, and United States. In our first analysis, we checked for regulatory mode predominance by subtracting each participant's assessment score from his or her locomotion score (i.e., locomotion minus assessment). The participants were classified as predominant locomotion if they had a positive difference score, and as predominant assessment if they had a negative difference score. In Italy, Spain, India, Poland, United States, and England, there was a significantly higher percentage of predominant locomotion than predominant assessment individuals. In Japan and Korea, there was a significantly higher percentage of predominant assessment than predominant locomotion individuals.

In a test of homogeneity for the locomotion pride scores, Italy had higher locomotion scores than any other nation except Spain (which did not differ from India, Israel, and United States). Japan had lower locomotion scores than any other nation and Korea had the second lowest locomotion scores (lower than any other nation except Japan). In a test of homogeneity for the assessment pride scores, Israel had higher assessment scores than any other nation. Korea, United States, and Japan had the next highest assessment scores, higher than the remaining countries. Italy had relatively low assessment scores, lower than any other nations except Spain and India. Finally, in a test of homogeneity for the locomotion pride minus assessment pride difference scores, Italy was higher than any other nation on this difference score. Spain and India had the next highest difference score and differed from all the remaining nations. Japan and Korea had the lowest difference score – a negative difference score – and differed from all the other nations. Tables 8.6–8.8 summarize the homogeneity analyses.

In sum, for cross-cultural differences in regulatory mode, there was convergent evidence indicating that in Italy and in Spain, and to a lesser extent in India, the regulatory mode orientation of locomotion was stronger than assessment. In contrast, in Japan and in Korea, the regulatory focus orientation of assessment was stronger than locomotion. Locomotion was weakest in Japan and assessment was weakest in Italy. In Israel, locomotion and assessment were more equal in strength and both were relatively high.

CROSS-CULTURAL SIMILARITIES IN RELATIONS BETWEEN ORIENTATIONS AND TRAITS

Let us turn now to the evidence for there being clear *cross-cultural similarities* in how regulatory focus and regulatory mode orientations relate to the traits of

TABLE 8.6   Test post hoc of Duncan: Homogeneity Sets for *Locomotion*

Samples	Homogeneity sets for $\alpha = .05$						
	1	2	3	4	5	6	7
Japan	3.58						
Korea		3.76					
Poland			4.05	4.05			
England				4.12	4.12		
USA					4.19	4.19	
Israel						4.28	
India						4.28	
Spain						4.33	4.33
Italy							4.46

TABLE 8.7   Test post hoc of Duncan: Homogeneity Sets for *Assessment*

Samples	Homogeneity sets for $\alpha = .05$			
	1	2	3	4
Italy	3.56			
Spain	3.62	3.62		
India	3.69	3.69		
Poland		3.77		
England		3.77		
Japan			3.97	
USA			4.01	
Korea			4.04	
Israel				4.28

TABLE 8.8   Test post hoc of Duncan: Homogeneity Sets for *Index of Locomotion – Assessment Difference*

Samples	Homogeneity sets for $\alpha = .05$				
	1	2	3	4	5
Japan	− .39				
Korea	− .27				
Israel		− .01			
USA		.18	.18		
Poland			.28		
England			.35		
India				.59	
Spain				.71	
Italy					.90

extraversion, openness, agreeableness conscientiousness, and self-esteem as strategic channels. In this section, we will also discuss how these relations between the different self-regulatory orientations and the different traits are generally consistent with what regulatory focus theory and regulatory mode theory would predict. Tables 8.9 and 8.10 summarize the findings discussed in this section.[1] Note that in the following discussion of the results, all the correlations reported for a self-regulatory distinction (e.g., regulatory focus) are partial correlations where

TABLE 8.9 Partial Correlations Between Regulatory Focus (Each Focus Controlling for the Other) and Self-Esteem and Big Five

	Self-esteem	Extraversion	Neuroticism	Openness/Intel	Agreeableness	Conscientiousness
Promotion						
Australia	+	+	−	+	0	0
Italy	+	+	−	+	0	+
USA	+	+	−	+	+	+
India	+	+	0	+	+	+
Japan	+	+	−	+	+	+
Israel	+	+	−	0	0	+
Prevention						
Australia	0	−	0	−	+	+
Italy	0	0	0	0	+	+
USA	0	−	0	0	0	+
India	0	0	0	0	+	+
Japan	0	−	0	−	+	+
Israel	0	−	0	0	0	+

+: Partial correlation significantly positive; −: Partial correlation significantly negative; 0: Partial correlation non-significant.

[1]Neuroticism differs from the other Big-Five characteristics in being more of an emotional outcome characteristic than a self-regulatory strategic channel. Thus, it is less germane to the issue of what self-regulatory mechanisms underlie the relation between culture and personality. Overall, for *regulatory focus*, there was some tendency for neuroticism to be higher for predominant prevention than predominant promotion individuals. An alternative measure of regulatory focus, such as the chronic accessibility strength measure (e.g., Higgins et al., 1997), might reveal this effect more strongly given that the RFQ measures predominant prevention individuals who are relatively successful in their vigilant self-regulation (i.e., high prevention pride). It is notable, however, that there were significant negative correlations between promotion pride and neuroticism in every nation studied except India, whereas for prevention pride there were no significant correlations (see Table 8.9). Overall, for *regulatory mode*, the neuroticism scores of predominant assessment individuals were significantly higher than the neuroticism scores of predominant locomotion individuals in most nations. Also, in every nation there was a significant positive correlation between assessment and neuroticism, whereas the correlation between locomotion and neuroticism tended to be non-significantly negative (see Table 8.10).

TABLE 8.10   Partial Correlations Between Regulatory Mode (Each Mode Controlling for the Other) and Self-Esteem and Big Five

	Self-Esteem	Extraversion	Neuroticism	Openness/Intel	Agreeableness	Conscientiousness
Locomotion						
USA	+	+	−	+	+	+
India	+	+	0	+	+	+
Italy	+	+	0	+	+	+
Japan	+	+	−	+	+	+
Israel	+	+	0	0	0	+
Assessment						
USA	−	−	+	+	−	0
India	0	0	+	+	0	0
Italy	0	0	+	0	−	0
Japan	−	0	+	+	−	0
Israel	−	0	+	0	−	−

+: Partial correlation significantly positive; −: Partial correlation significantly negative; 0: Partial correlation non-significant.

the relation between an orientation (e.g., promotion) and a trait (e.g., extroversion) statistically controls for the alternative orientation (e.g., prevention).

EXTRAVERSION

For *regulatory focus*, in every nation studied there was a stronger positive correlation between promotion pride and extroversion – significantly positive in each case – than between prevention pride and extroversion (which were negative in every nation and significantly so in most nations). In addition, in every nation studied the extroversion scores of predominant promotion pride individuals were significantly higher than the extroversion scores of predominant prevention pride individuals. This cross-cultural similarity in stronger promotion pride yielding higher extroversion than stronger prevention pride is consistent with what regulatory focus theory would predict. Specifically, because extroversion relates to sociability, eagerness to meet new people, and being enthusiastic and carefree, extroverted behaviors and responses would support a promotion orientation more than a prevention orientation. Thus, one would expect that extroversion would be higher for predominant promotion individuals than predominant prevention individuals.

For *regulatory mode*, in every nation studied there was a stronger positive correlation between locomotion and extroversion – significantly positive in each case – than between assessment and extroversion (generally negative but not significantly). In addition, in every nation studied the extroversion scores of predominant locomotors were higher than the extroversion scores of predominant assessors, with this difference being significant in all but one nation. This cross-cultural similarity in stronger locomotion yielding higher extroversion than stronger assessment is consistent with what regulatory mode theory would predict. Specifically, because extroverted behaviors and responses to social situations would support entering and engaging in situations, moving ahead without hesitation or care, they would support a locomotion orientation more than an assessment orientation. Thus, one would expect that extroversion would be higher for predominant locomotors than predominant assessors.

OPENNESS

For *regulatory focus*, in every nation studied there was a stronger positive correlation between promotion pride and openness – significant in each case but one – than between prevention pride and openness (mostly non-significantly negative). In addition, in every nation studied the openness scores of predominant promotion pride individuals were higher than the openness scores of predominant prevention pride individuals, with this difference being significant in all but one nation. This cross-cultural similarity in stronger promotion pride yielding higher openness than stronger prevention pride is consistent with what regulatory focus theory would predict. Specifically, because openness relates to imaginative, original, wide interests, curious, and ingenious, one would expect that openness would be higher for predominant promotion than predominant prevention individuals.

For *regulatory mode*, there was a positive correlation between locomotion and openness in every nation studied, and they were significantly positive in every nation except one. In most (but not all) of the nations, there was also a significant positive correlation between assessment and openness. In every nation studied, the openness scores were moderately high for both predominant locomotion and predominant prevention individuals, producing no significant difference in any nation. Regulatory mode theory would not predict a priori this cross-cultural similarity of no difference in openness between locomotors and assessors. However, because openness relates to imaginative, original, wide interests, curious, and ingenious, it would be useful as a strategic channel for both locomotion and assessment. Having wide interests and high curiosity would motivate engagement in a broad range of activities and provide new opportunities for movement, which fits the locomotion orientation. Imagination and curiosity also provide opportunities for making multiple comparisons and evaluations, which fits the assessment orientation. Because openness as a strategic channel is useful for both locomotion and assessment, it is reasonable that locomotors and assessors would not differ on openness.

AGREEABLENESS

For *regulatory focus*, in every nation studied there was a positive correlation between promotion pride and agreeableness (significant in most cases) and between prevention pride and agreeableness (significant in most cases). Overall, agreeableness tended to be moderately high for both predominant promotion and predominant prevention individuals in most nations, yielding a general pattern of no significant difference in agreeableness between predominant promotion and predominant prevention individuals. Regulatory focus theory would not predict a priori this cross-cultural similarity of no difference between promotion and prevention. However, because agreeableness relates to being sympathetic, appreciative, warm, trusting, and forgiving (rather than faultfinding), it would be useful for both orientations as a strategic channel for effective self-regulation – and predominant prevention pride and predominant promotion pride individuals are both effective self-regulators. Thus, it would be reasonable that predominant prevention pride and predominant promotion pride individuals would not differ on agreeableness.

For *regulatory mode*, there was a positive correlation between locomotion and agreeableness in every nation studied, which was significant in all but one nation. In contrast, the correlation between assessment and agreeableness was significantly negative in every nation but one. In every nation studied, the agreeableness scores of predominant locomotion individuals were significantly higher than the agreeableness scores of predominant assessment individuals. This cross-cultural similarity in stronger locomotion yielding higher agreeableness scores than stronger assessment is consistent with what regulatory mode theory would predict. Being forgiving of the past and trusting others in the future supports locomotion concerns with moving on to the next project, whereas, if anything, being faultfinding rather than forgiving or trusting is supportive of assessment individuals' concerns with critical evaluation.

CONSCIENTIOUSNESS

For *regulatory focus*, there was a significantly positive correlation between promotion pride and conscientiousness in every nation studied, and also a significantly positive correlation between prevention pride and conscientiousness in every nation studied except one. This cross-cultural similarity of both promotion pride and prevention pride being positively related to conscientiousness was reflected in there being no significant difference between predominant promotion and predominant prevention in every nation studied. Regulatory focus theory would not predict a priori this cross-cultural similarity of no difference in conscientiousness between promotion and prevention. However, because conscientiousness relates to being practical, organized, thorough, planful, efficient, and responsible, it would be useful for individuals high in prevention pride because it would support their concerns with preventing future mistakes and fulfilling their responsibilities. It would also be useful for individuals high in promotion pride because it would facilitate advancement and making future progress. Thus, it is reasonable that predominant prevention pride and predominant promotion pride individuals would not differ on conscientiousness.

For *regulatory mode*, there was a significant positive correlation between locomotion and conscientiousness in every nation studied, whereas the correlation between assessment and conscientiousness was generally negative (non-significantly) in every nation. In addition, in every nation studied the conscientiousness scores of predominant locomotion individuals were significantly higher than the conscientiousness scores of predominant assessment individuals. This cross-national similarity in stronger locomotion yielding higher conscientiousness than stronger assessment is consistent with what regulatory mode theory would predict. Specifically, being organized, planful, practical and efficient allows the goal pursuit process to flow smoothly, and thus tactical conscientiousness supports the concerns of locomotors, but assessors are more concerned with critical evaluation than efficiency or practicality per se.

SELF-ESTEEM

For *regulatory focus*, in every nation studied there was a stronger positive correlation between promotion pride and self-esteem – significantly positive in each case – than between prevention pride and self-esteem (which was basically zero in each case except Japan, where it was significant but smaller than for promotion pride). In addition, in every nation studied the self-esteem scores of predominant promotion pride individuals were higher than the self-esteem of predominant prevention pride individuals, with this difference being significant in all but one nation. This cross-national similarity in stronger promotion pride yielding higher self-esteem than stronger prevention pride is consistent with what regulatory focus theory would predict. Specifically, because eagerness sustains or fits promotion whereas vigilance sustains or fits prevention, it makes sense from a self-regulatory maintenance perspective that predominant promotion individuals would tactically boost their optimism and confidence to remain eager, whereas predominant prevention individuals would tactically dampen their optimism and confidence to remain vigilant. Thus, self-esteem as a tactic for self-regulatory maintenance should be higher for predominant promotion than predominant prevention individuals.

For *regulatory mode*, there was a significant positive correlation between locomotion and self-esteem in every nation studied, whereas the correlation between assessment and self-esteem was negative in every country (and significantly so in most nations). In addition, in every nation studied the self-esteem scores of predominant locomotion individuals were significantly higher than the self-esteem of predominant assessment individuals. This cross-national similarity in stronger locomotion yielding higher self-esteem than stronger assessment is consistent with what regulatory mode theory would predict. Specifically, because predominant locomotors tactically use their confidence about the future to get themselves moving forward, whereas predominant assessors tactically engage in critical, post-action self-evaluation (experiencing regret when they believe that they could have performed better), it makes sense that self-esteem would be higher for predominant locomotors than predominant assessors.

GENERAL DISCUSSION AND CONCLUSIONS

On the basis of the results of our studies, we can draw two conclusions. First, there are clear *cross-cultural differences* in the relative strength or predominance of different basic self-regulatory orientations – promotion focus versus prevention focus, locomotion mode versus assessment mode. Second, there are clear *cross-cultural similarities* in how these self-regulatory orientations relate to such central traits as extraversion, conscientiousness, openness, agreeableness, and self-esteem, and these relations are generally consistent with what regulatory focus theory and regulatory mode theory would predict.

Among all of the traits reviewed above, cross-cultural differences in levels of self-esteem (or positive view of the self) have received the most attention in the literature. The contrast between United States and Japan has received particular attention. When we compared the self-esteem scores in our US sample with the self-esteem scores in our Japanese sample, we replicated the typical finding in the literature – the US sample had significantly higher self-esteem scores than the Japanese sample. A common explanation in the literature for this difference in self-esteem scores is that individuals in United States generally have an independent or individualistic character whereas individuals in Japan generally have an interdependent or collectivistic character (e.g., Markus & Kitayama, 1991). One notion is that people with an independent or individualistic character care about their personal self-esteem and have strong motives for personal self-enhancement, whereas people with an interdependent or collectivistic character do not care as much about their personal self-esteem and have strong motives to enhance the group through self-sacrifice and self-denial. According to this viewpoint, it is this difference that yields the self-esteem difference (but see also Kitayama et al., 1997).

Our findings suggest a quite different mechanism, or at least an additional mechanism, underlying the self-esteem difference. Rather than United States and Japan differing in their underlying self-esteem motives, we found the *same self-esteem relations* in *both* nations: self-esteem as a strategic conduit or channel was higher for predominant promotion than predominant prevention individuals, and was higher for predominant locomotors than predominant assessors. What *did* differ between these nations was whether the individuals within each nation were more likely to be predominant promotion or predominant prevention, and whether they were more likely to be predominant locomotion or predominant assessment. In United States, individuals were more likely to be predominant promotion and predominant locomotion than predominant prevention and predominant assessment, and the reverse was true in Japan. Because self-esteem is higher for predominant promotion and predominant locomotion than for predominant prevention and predominant assessment, self-esteem scores should be higher in United States than Japan.

Thus, one need not conclude that the difference in self-esteem levels between United States and Japan derives from a basic difference between an American personality and a Japanese personality. Rather, each culture has individuals with promotion, prevention, locomotion, and assessment orientations, but the relative distribution of such individuals in each nation varies. Of course, why regulatory focus and regulatory mode distributions vary across culture is itself an interesting question – a question that is beyond the scope of the current chapter but is addressed in Higgins (2008). Together with other cross-cultural perspectives, we believe that an important determinant of culture and personality are ecological/geographical factors and economic factors that place demands, set problems, introduce pressures and provide opportunities for people who live in the area. Resolving the specific demands or problems set by a particular region, or responding to the opportunities, can produce cultural differences (see, e.g., Nisbett, 2003). A fascinating question for future research is which kinds of regional demands, problems, pressures, and opportunities are likely to increase promotion, prevention, locomotion, or assessment concerns.

If the difference between United States and Japan in self-esteem levels is due, at least in part, to the differences between United States and Japan in the distributions of regulatory focus and regulatory mode, then one might expect United States and Japan to differ in other trait-related strategic channels that are associated with regulatory focus and regulatory mode. Consider, for example, *extroversion*. We have described above how extroversion across nations is higher for predominant promotion and predominant locomotion than for predominant prevention and predominant assessment. Thus, given that (for our samples) individuals in United States were more likely to be predominant promotion and predominant locomotion than predominant prevention and predominant assessment, whereas the reverse was true for individuals in Japan, one would expect that the extroversion scores would be higher in United States than Japan. Indeed, we found (for our samples) that the extroversion scores *were* significantly higher in United States than Japan!

The take-away point here is that cultural differences in some trait, like self-esteem or extraversion, need not imply some correspondent difference in the basic personality of the people from that culture. That is, one should not assume that when there is a cross-cultural difference in the level of "X," where "X" might be extroversion, there must be a correspondent basic dispositional difference in "X" between the people from those cultures, such as a genetic difference in "X." Such an assumption would be like the "correspondence bias" in person perception (Jones, 1979) where the "person" is a culture. Our findings demonstrate how the fundamental motivational mechanisms that underlie a difference in "X" levels need not themselves correspond to "X." Indeed, a difference in "X" levels could have *more than one non-correspondent source*, such as either a strong promotion orientation or a strong locomotion orientation or both orientations being the source of higher extroversion.

FINAL COMMENTS

It is precisely the cross-national *universality* in how basic self-regulatory ori-entations function that creates trait-related strategic differences from the cross-cultural differences in predominant orientations. Given cross-national differences in the predominance of different self-regulatory orientations (e.g., promotion; prevention; locomotion; assessment), then cross-national similarity in basic self-regulatory functioning *should* produce cross-national differences in traits (e.g., self-esteem; extroversion). The challenge for the future is to discover *how* the basic self-regulatory orientations produce the trait differences. It is tempting to think in terms of simple main effects. That is, if self-esteem as a strategic conduit or chan-nel is increased by strong promotion and by strong locomotion, then cultures with both strong promotion and strong locomotion individuals should have very high levels of self-esteem; and if self-esteem is decreased by strong assessment, then cultures with strong promotion and strong assessment individuals should have only moderate levels of self-esteem. Indeed, in our above discussion, we took this approach in order to simplify our presentation. But it is quite possible, even likely, that there are interactive patterns among the self-regulatory orientations. We do not know whether all logically possible patterns (e.g., 16 patterns for the 4 differ-ent orientations and high/low levels of each) are necessarily distinct in their moti-vational implications. Nonetheless, it is these patterns, and not just the separate dimensions, that ultimately must be examined (cf. Higgins et al., 1990). This will be one of the major challenges for cross-cultural research in the future.

Finally, we should note that our research was restricted to measuring the strength of self-regulatory orientations (promotion; prevention; locomotion; assessment) in the participants from the different nations we studied, and then relating these "person" variables to the strength of different traits in the same participants. As we mentioned in the beginning of this chapter, however, the reg-ulatory focus and regulatory mode orientations concern more than personality per se. Because promotion, prevention, locomotion, and assessment refer to self-regulatory states, they vary *across situations* as well as across persons. Some sit-uations are more likely to induce promotion than prevention whereas the reverse is true for other situations (cf. Kitayama et al., 1997). Similarly, some situations are more likely to induce locomotion than assessment whereas the reverse is true for other situations. Cultures also vary in the relative distribution of these dif-ferent situations, and this will also contribute to the magnitude of trait-related responses, both directly and in interaction with a culture's distribution of indi-viduals who are chronically strong in the different orientations. These direct and interaction effects need to be examined in future research.

ACKNOWLEDGMENTS

This chapter has benefited from discussions with and comments by Michael Morris, Dick Nisbett, and Shige Oishi. The authors are grateful to Poonam

Arora, Jennifer Boldero, Yumi Endo, Ran Hassin, Nira Liberman, C.-Y Chiu, Ying-Yi Hong, and Abby Scholer, for providing data for some of the nations that are discussed in the present chapter. The writing of the chapter was supported by National Mental Health Grant MH39429 to the first author.

REFERENCES

Benet-Martinez, V., & Oishi, S. (in press). Culture and personality. In O. P. John, R. W. Robins, & L. A. Pervin (Eds.), *Handbook of personality: Theory and research* (3rd ed.,). New York: Guilford Press.

Bidney, D. (1953). *Theoretical anthropology*. New York: Columbia University Press.

Bowlby, J. (1969). *Attachment* (attachment and loss, Vol. 1) New York: Basic Books.

Bowlby, J. (1973). *Separation: Anxiety and anger* (Attachment and loss, Vol. 2) New York: Basic Books.

Buss, D. (1996). The evolutionary psychology of human social strategies. In E. T. Higgins & A. W. Kruglanski (Eds.), *Social psychology: Handbook of basic principles* (pp. 3–38). New York: Guilford.

Carver, C. S., & Scheier, M. F. (1990). Origins and functions of positive and negative affect: A control process view. *Psychological Review*, 97, 19–35.

Church, A. T. (2001). Personality measurement in cross-cultural perspective. *Journal of Personality*, 69, 979–1006.

Crowe, E., & Higgins, E. T. (1997). Regulatory focus and strategic inclinations: Promotion and prevention in decision making. *Organizational Behavior and Human Decision Processes*, 69, 117–132.

Csikszentmihalyi, M. (1975). *Beyond boredom and anxiety*. San Francisco, CA: Jossey-Bass.

Fenigstein, A., Scheier, M. F., & Buss, A. H. (1975). Public and private self-consciousness: Assessment and theory. *Journal of Consulting and Clinical Psychology*, 43, 522–527.

Forster, J., Grant, H., Idson, L. C., & Higgins, E. T. (2001). Success/failure feedback, expectancies, and approach/avoidance motivation: How regulatory focus moderates classic relations. *Journal of Experimental Social Psychology*, 37, 253–260.

Fu, J., Morris, M. W., Lee, S., Chao, A., Chiu, C., & Hong, Y. (2007). Epistemic motives and cultural conformity: Need for closure, culture, and context as determinants of conflict judgments. *Journal of Personality and Social Psychology*, 92, 191–207.

Gollwitzer, P. M. (1990). Action phases and mind-sets. In E. T. Higgins & R. M. Sorrentino (Eds.), *Handbook of motivation and cognition: Foundations of social behavior* (Vol. 2, pp. 53–92). New York: Guilford press.

Grant, H., & Higgins, E. T. (2003). Optimism, promotion pride, and prevention pride as predictors of quality of life. *Personality and Social Psychology Bulletin*, 29, 1521–1532.

Harlow, R., Friedman, R. S., & Higgins, E. T. (1997). *The regulatory focus questionnaire*. Unpublished manuscript, Columbia University.

Heckhausen, H., & Gollwitzer, P. M. (1987). Thought contents and cognitive functioning in motivational versus volitional states of mind. *Motivation and Emotion*, 11, 101–120.

Heine, S. J. (2004). Positive self-views: Understanding universals and variability across cultures. *Journal of Cultural and Evolutionary Psychology*, 2, 109–122.

Heine, S. J., Kitayama, S., Lehman, D. R., Takata, T., Ide, E., Leung, C., & Matsumoto, S. (2001). Divergent consequences of success and failure in Japan and North America: An investigation of self-improving motivations and malleable selves. *Journal of Personality and Social Psychology*, 81, 599–615.

Higgins, E. T. (1990). Personality, social psychology, and person-situation relations: Standards and knowledge activation as a common language. In L. A. Pervin (Ed.), *Handbook of personality* (pp. 301–338). New York: Guilford Press.

Higgins, E. T. (1996). Knowledge activation: Accessibility, applicability, and salience. In E. T. Higgins & A. W. Kruglanski (Eds.), *Social psychology: Handbook of basic principles* (pp. 133–168). New York: Guilford.

Higgins, E. T. (1997). Beyond pleasure and pain. *American Psychologist, 52,* 1280–1300.

Higgins, E. T. (1999). Persons and situations: Unique explanatory principles or variability in general principles?. In D. Cervone & Y. Shoda (Eds.), *The coherence of personality: Social-cognitive bases of consistency, variability, and organization* (pp. 61–93). New York: Guilford.

Higgins, E. T. (2000a). Making a good decision: Value from fit. *American Psychologist, 55,* 1217–1230.

Higgins, E. T. (2000b). Does personality provide unique explanations for behavior?: Personality as cross-person variability in general principles. *European Journal of Personality, 14,* 391–406.

Higgins, E. T. (2008). Culture and personality: Variability across universal motives as the missing link. *Social and Personality Psychology Compass, 2.*

Higgins, E. T., Friedman, R. S., Harlow, R. E., Idson, L. C., Ayduk, O. N., & Taylor, A. (2001). Achievement orientations from subjective histories of success: Promotion pride versus prevention pride. *European Journal of Social Psychology, 31,* 3–23.

Higgins, E. T., & Kruglanski, A. W. (2000). Motivational science: The nature and functions of wanting. In E. T. Higgins & A. W. Kruglanski (Eds.), *Motivational science: Social-personality perspectives* (pp. 1–20). Philadelphia, PA: Psychology Press.

Higgins, E. T., Kruglanski, A. W., & Pierro, A. (2003). Regulatory mode: Locomotion and assessment as distinct orientations. In M. P. Zanna (Ed.), *Advances in experimental social psychology* (Vol. 35, pp. 293–344). New York: Academic Press.

Higgins, E. T., Shah, J., & Friedman, R. (1997). Emotional responses to goal attainment: Strength of regulatory focus as moderator. *Journal of Personality and Social Psychology, 72,* 515–525.

Higgins, E. T., & Spiegel, S. (2004). Promotion and prevention strategies for self-regulation: A motivated cognition perspective. In R. F. Baumeister & K. D. Vohs (Eds.), *Handbook of self-regulation: Research, theory, and applications* (pp. 171–187). New York: Guilford Press.

Higgins, E. T., Tykocinski, O., & Vookles, J. (1990). Patterns of self-beliefs: The psychological significance of relations among the actual, ideal, ought, can, and future selves. In J. M. Olson & M. P. Zanna (Eds.), *Self-inference processes: The Ontario Symposium* (Vol. 6, pp. 153–190). Hillsdale, NJ: Erlbaum.

Hill, C. A. (1987). Affiliation motivation: People who need people…. but in different ways. *Journal of Personality and Social Psychology, 52,* 1008–1018.

Hong, Y. Y., & Chiu, C. Y. (2001). Toward a paradigm shift: From cross-cultural differences in social cognition to social-cognitive mediation of cultural differences. *Social Cognition, 19,* 181–196.

Hong, Y., Morris, M., Chiu, C., & Benet-Martinez, V. (2000). Multicultural minds: A dynamic constructivist approach. *American Psychologist, 55,* 709–721.

Idson, L. C., & Higgins, E. T. (2000). How current feedback and chronic effectiveness influence motivation: Everything to gain versus everything to lose. *European Journal of Social Psychology, 30,* 583–592.

Idson, L. C., Liberman, N., & Higgins, E. T. (2000). Distinguishing gains from nonlosses and losses from nongains: A regulatory focus perspective on hedonic intensity. *Journal of Experimental Social Psychology, 36,* 252–274.

Idson, L. C., Liberman, N., & Higgins, E. T. (2004). Imagining how you'd feel: The role of motivational experiences from regulatory fit. *Personality and Social Psychology Bulletin, 30,* 926–937.

Inkeles, A., & Levinson, D. J. (1969). National character: The study of modal personality and sociocultural systems. In G. Lindzey & E. Aronson (Eds.), *The handbook of social psychology* (pp. 418–506). Reading, MA: Addison-Wesley.

Jackson, D. N. (1974). *The Personality Research Form.* Port Huron, MI: Research Psychologists Press.

John, O. P. (1990). The "big five" factor taxonomy: Dimensions of personality in the natural language and in questionnaires. In L. A. Pervin (Ed.), *Handbook of personality: Theory and research* (pp. 66–100). New York: Guilford Press.

John, O. P., & Srivastava, S. (1999). The big-five taxonomy: History, measurement, and theoretical perspectives. In L. A. Pervin & O. P. John (Eds.), *Handbook of personality: Theory and research* (2nd ed., pp. 102–138). New York: Guilford Press.

Jones, E. E. (1979). The rocky road from acts to dispositions. *American Psychologist, 34*, 107–117.

Katz, D., & Braly, K. W. (1933). Racial stereotypes of 100 college students. *Journal of Abnormal and Social Psychology, 28*, 280–290.

Kitayama, S., Markus, H. R., Matsumoto, H., & Norasakkunkit, V. (1997). Individual and collective processes in the construction of the self: Self-Enhancement in the United States and self-criticism in Japan. *Journal of Personality and Social Psychology, 72*, 1245–1267.

Kruglanski, A. W. (1990). Lay epistemic theory in social-cognitive psychology. *Psychological Inquiry, 1*, 181–197.

Kruglanski, A. W., Pierro, A., Higgins, E. T., & Capozza, D. (2007). "On the move", or "staying put": Locomotion, need for closure and reactions to organizational change. *Journal of Applied Social Psychology, 37*, 1305–1340.

Kruglanski, A. W., Thompson, E. P., Higgins, E. T., Atash, M. N., Pierro, A., Shah, J. Y., & Spiegel, S. (2000). To "do the right thing" or to "just do it": Locomotion and assessment as distinct self-regulatory imperatives. *Journal of Personality and Social Psychology, 79*, 793–815.

Kuhl, J. (1984). Volitional aspects of achievement motivation and learned helplessness: Toward a comprehensive theory of action control. In B. A. Maher (Ed.), *Progress in experimental personality research* (Vol. 12, pp. 99–170). New York: Academic Press.

Kuhl, J. (1985). Volitional mediation of cognition-behavior consistency: Self-regulatory processes and action versus state orientation. In J. Kuhl & J. Beckman (Eds.), *Action control: From cognition to behavior* (pp. 101–128). Berlin, Germany: Springer-Verlag.

Leary, M. R., Tambor, E. S., Terdal, S. K., & Downs, D. L. (1995). Self-esteem as an interpersonal monitor: The sociometer hypothesis. *Journal of Personality and Social Psychology, 68*, 518–530.

Lee, A. Y., Aaker, J. L., & Gardner, W. L. (2000). The pleasures and pains of distinct self-construals: The role of interdependence in regulatory focus. *Journal of Personality and Social Psychology, 78*, 1122–1134.

Markus, H., & Kitayama, S. (1991). Culture and the self: Implications for cognition, emotion, and motivation. *Psychological Review, 98*, 224–253.

Markus, H. R., & Kitayama, S. (1998). The cultural psychology of personality. *Journal of Cross-Cultural Psychology, 29*, 63–87.

Markus, H. R., Kitayama, S., & Heiman, R. (1996). Culture and "basic" psychological principles. In E. T. Higgins & A. W. Kruglanski (Eds.), *Social Psychology: Handbook of basic principles* (pp. 857–913). New York: Guilford.

McCrae, R. R. (2000). Trait psychology and the revival of personality and culture studies. *American Behavioral Scientist, 44*, 10–31.

McCrae, R. R., & Terracciano, A. (2006). National character and personality. *Current Directions in Psychological Science, 15*, 156–161.

Miller, G. A., Galanter, E., & Pribram, K. H. (1960). *Plans and the structure of behavior*. New York: Holt, Rinehart, & Winston.

Molden, D. C., Lee, A. Y., & Higgins, E. T. (2007). Regulatory focus. In J. Y. Shah & W. L. Gardner (Eds.), *Handbook of motivation science* (pp. 169–187). New York: Guilford Press.

Morris, M. W., Menon, T., & Ames, D. R. (2001). Culturally conferred conceptions of agency: A key to social perception of persons, groups, and other actors. *Personality and Social Psychology Review, 5*, 169–182.

Nisbett, R. E. (2003). *The geography of thought: How Asians and Westerners think differently…and why*. New York: Free Press.

Oyserman, D., Coon, H. M., & Kemmelmeier, M. (2002). Rethinking individualism and collectivism: Evaluation of theoretical assumptions and meta-analyses. *Psychological Bulletin, 128*, 3–72.

Peabody, D. (1985). *National characteristics*. New York: Cambridge University Press.

Pierro, A., Kruglanski, A. W., & Higgins, E. T. (2006). Regulatory mode and the joys of doing: Effects of "locomotion" and "assessment" on intrinsic and extrinsic task motivation. *European Journal of Personality, 20*, 355–375.

Rosenberg, M. (1979). *Conceiving the self*. Malabar, Florida: Robert E. Krieger.

Spiegel, S., & Higgins, E. T. (2001). *Regulatory focus and means substitution in strategic task performance*. Unpublished manuscript, Columbia University.

Terracciano, A. et al. (2005). National character does not reflect mean personality trait levels in 49 cultures. *Science, 310*, 96–100.

Triandis, H. C. (1990). Cross-cultural studies of individualism and collectivism. In J. Berman (Ed.), *Nebraska Symposium on Motivation* (pp. 41–133). Lincoln: University of Nebraska Press.

Wiener, N. (1948). *Cybernetics: Control and communication in the animal and the machine*. Cambridge, MA: MIT Press.

9

GOAL PURSUIT IN THE CONTEXT OF CULTURE

GABRIELE OETTINGEN[*,†], A. TIMUR SEVINCER[†] AND PETER M. GOLLWITZER[*,‡]

[*]Department of Psychology, New York University, New York, USA
[†]Department of Psychology, Universität Hamburg, Germany
[‡]Department of Psychology, Universität Konstanz, Germany

> To one who comes from Germany, the degree of freedom and independence of children and adolescents in the United States is very impressive. Especially the lack of servility of the young child toward adults or of the student toward his professor is striking.
>
> —Lewin, 1936, p. 269

Goal pursuit implies that people have the freedom to set themselves goals they want and can reach, and that they can strive for at their own pace using their own means. As cultures and political systems vary widely regarding the freedom they allow for such goal setting and goal striving, socio-cultural contexts should influence whether and how goal setting and goal striving occurs. For example, in a culture with binding norms of social reciprocity, accepting a dinner invitation implies that the guest will reciprocate in a form that matches the original event. To the contrary, in a culture where such norms have been fading, accepting such an invitation leaves the guest with the freedom to invite the host back or not; and even if she commits to returning the favor, she still has full freedom of when, where, and how to enact it.

The role of culture in goal pursuit may thus be discussed at various levels of analysis. First, cultural norms and values might affect the determinants of goal setting and goal striving, desirability, and feasibility. Does culture affect what future outcomes and behaviors are perceived as desirable and thus qualify as potential aspired to goal states? And does culture affect how people perceive the feasibility of realizing these desired futures? One also wonders whether and how culture influences the processes that lead people to commit to goals, and whether it influences the translation of set goals into action (i.e., goal striving). In the present chapter, we will address these questions starting with research on perceived desirability and feasibility, and ending with a focus on the role of culture in the formation of goal commitments and in the translation of set goals into action.

CULTURE AND THE DETERMINANTS
OF GOAL PURSUIT

Goal pursuit starts by committing oneself to goals or adopting goals suggested by others. Most theories of motivation (e.g., Atkinson, 1957; Gollwitzer, 1990; Locke & Latham, 1990; Bandura, 1997; see Oettingen & Gollwitzer, 2001, for review) assume that people prefer to commit to or adopt goals they perceive as desirable and feasible. Perceived desirability is commonly determined by the estimated attractiveness of likely short-term and long-term consequences of goal attainment. Such consequences may pertain to anticipated self-evaluations, evaluations of significant others, progress toward some higher order goal, external rewards of having attained the goal, and the joy/pain associated with moving toward the goal (Heckhausen, 1977). Perceived feasibility depends on people's judgments of their capabilities to perform relevant goal-directed behaviors (i.e., self-efficacy expectations, Bandura, 1997), their beliefs that these goal-directed behaviors will lead to the desired outcome (i.e., outcome expectations, Bandura, 1997; instrumentality beliefs, Vroom, 1964), or the judged likelihood of attaining the desired outcome (i.e., general expectations, Oettingen & Mayer, 2002). It is assumed that perceived feasibility and desirability may not only affect what goal a person commits to pursuing, but also the intensity of subsequent striving for goal attainment (i.e., the intensity of goal striving is assumed to be stronger the higher the respective feasibility and desirability beliefs).

CULTURE AND DESIRABILITY

Members of different cultures are attracted to different goals. For instance, people in individualist cultures prefer to pursue goals that are directed at achieving personal success, seeking social independence, and influencing and persuading others, whereas people in collectivist cultures prefer to pursue goals that are directed at achieving success of one's group, seeking social interdependence, fitting in, and finding social harmony (Triandis, 1989; Hofstede, 2001; Oishi & Diener, 2001; Kitayama et al., 2008). It has long been assumed that the values and motives that are prevalent in a given culture inform the desirability of goals (Benedict, 1934). Reviewing literature on cross-cultural differences in goal-content, Nurmi

(1991) reports that adolescents in societies that emphasize modern values set goals relating to personal happiness, future family, and leisure activities, whereas adolescents from cultures that emphasize traditional values set goals relating to their parents' family, the health and marriage of others, and to societal topics (Gillespie & Allport, 1955).

As motive dispositions such as achievement, affiliation, and power affect the kind of goals a person chooses (i.e., understanding issues, getting close to others, influencing others; Brunstein et al., 1998), cultures may affect what kind of goals their people commit to by fostering some motive dispositions and hampering others during socialization (McClelland, 1965). Moreover, growing up in a given culture may affect how a certain motive disposition is expressed (Bond, 1986; Heine et al., 1999). For example, individuals in Asian cultures can be expected to express an achievement motive in terms of interpersonally oriented achievements (i.e., achievements that meet expectations of others), but less so in terms of personally oriented achievement (i.e., achievement that meet one's own expectations), whereas the reverse is true for Western cultures.

CULTURE AND FEASIBILITY

Even though there is ample research suggesting that the values prevalent in a given culture determine which goals the members of this culture consider to be desirable (e.g., Markus & Kitayama, 1991), few studies have examined the role of cultural variables for appraising the feasibility of desired outcomes. Examining how culture affects perceived feasibility is important, because successful goal attainment requires that people commit to goals in line with their feasibility in that they commit to goals that can be attained and refrain from committing to futile goals.

Perceived feasibility of goals primarily depends on whether one expects to be capable of performing actions that are instrumental to goal attainment (efficacy expectations; Bandura, 1997). Thus in order to understand how culture might affect perceived feasibility of goals it is necessary to take a closer look at how individuals appraise their efficacy. Individuals rely on mainly four information sources in forming their efficacy beliefs. First, individuals' *performance experiences* are most influential. Successes foster a strong sense of efficacy, whereas failures result in a weak sense of efficacy. Second, people use *vicarious experiences*, in which they model achievements of similar others, in forming their efficacy beliefs. Successes attained by similar others raise the observer's sense of efficacy, whereas failures diminish it. Third, *verbal persuasions* by others also influence one's sense of efficacy. Others trusting one's capabilities can strengthen one's sense of efficacy, whereas doubt expressed by others can diminish it. A fourth information source results from the *physiological reactions* that one experiences when confronted with difficult performance situations. For example, feeling one's heart beating during an important test would indicate a weak sense of efficacy, whereas "staying cool" would indicate a strong sense of efficacy.

When appraising their efficacy, individuals attend to, sample, weigh, and integrate the information available in their preferred manner. For instance, individuals may differ in the extent to which they attend to attempts of verbal persuasion by others and how much they weigh these attempts in comparison to their own performance experiences. In sum, forming efficacy beliefs is a complex appraisal process which entails attending to, selecting, weighing, and integrating information from multiple sources. We assume that it is in this appraisal process that culture may play its influential role.

But how does culture affect this complex efficacy appraisal process? Culture may be defined as "a meaning and information system shared by a group and transmitted across generations" (Matsumoto & Yoo, 2006, p. 235). Cultural meaning systems are largely transmitted through social institutions, such as child-rearing and educational systems (e.g., families, school), that exist in virtually all human societies. These institutions may influence how individuals attend to, sample, weigh, and integrate efficacy relevant information by (a) differentially emphasizing the four sources of efficacy formation (e.g., valuing personal attainments more than evaluation by others), and (b) differing in the information that is provided (e.g., providing individual performance feedback rather than group feedback).

Cultural Values and Efficacy Appraisal

Past research has identified various dimensions of values by which cultures can be differentiated (e.g., individualism/collectivism, power differential, uncertainty avoidance; Hofstede, 2001). These dimensions are not dichotomous classifications of cultures but rather represent a continuum along which cultures can be classified. In the following, we explore how the cultural values of collectivism versus individualism, high versus low power differential, and strong versus weak uncertainty avoidance might influence the formation of efficacy beliefs.

In *collectivist* cultures individuals are bound and mutually obligated in groups. Because collectivist cultures value behavior that conforms to the norms of the in-group (Kim & Markus, 1999), social institutions in these cultures should emphasize evaluation by in-group members and modelling of in-group members (van Baaren et al., 2003) as important sources of efficacy formation. Furthermore, because members of collectivist cultures focus on playing their role in the society (Markus & Kitayama, 1991), performance outcomes in educational systems are often public and evaluated by the collective. Such public performance feedback by in-group members permits less leeway for personal interpretation than private performance feedback (Janis, 1968) and thus prevents self-enhancing interpretations (Taylor, 1989). Therefore, members of collectivist cultures should closely follow the evaluations of their in-group members, and relatively low efficacy beliefs should be observed.

Individualist cultures focus on the personal and marginalize the social (Oyserman et al., 2002). Because individualist cultures adhere to values that promote personal success, personal uniqueness, and personal control, these cultures should emphasize personal performance attainments as a source for efficacy formation. Furthermore, because social institutions focus on teaching individuals to realize their own potential rather than to play their role in society or to meet the approval of their in-group, performance feedback is often personal and private. Such private performance feedback allows for personal and self-enhancing interpretations. Therefore, by basing their efficacy appraisal on personal performance histories, members of individualist cultures should only loosely follow the evaluations of others and relatively high efficacy beliefs should be observed.

The cultural value of power distance may also affect efficacy appraisal. Members of cultures with *large power differential* accept inequality of power and respect authorities and rarely question them (Hofstede, 2001). Thus, performance evaluations by authorities such as parents and teachers should be especially selected and weighed in efficacy appraisal and these authorities should be readily modelled. Moreover, performance evaluations by these authorities should rarely be contradicted or criticized. Unquestioned performance evaluations by authorities, however, permit less personal and self-enhancing interpretations. Therefore, members of cultures with large power differential should tightly link their efficacy appraisal to the evaluations provided by the clearly identified and highly respected authorities, and be characterized by relatively low efficacy beliefs.

Members of cultures with *small power differential* value a more equal distribution of power. In these cultures it is more common to question authorities. In educational contexts students are expected to initiate communication, speak up, criticize, and express their own opinions. Individuals who sample information comparatively free of authorities' influences have more leeway for personal interpretation than do individuals who readily accept performance evaluations by authorities. Therefore, members of cultures with a small power differential should only loosely base their efficacy appraisal on the evaluations of the authority which is perceived as questionable, and thus efficacy beliefs should be relatively high.

Lastly, uncertainty avoidance may affect efficacy appraisal as well. Members of cultures of *strong uncertainty avoidance* are easily distressed by new, unstructured, unclear, or unpredictable situations. They try to avoid such situations by maintaining strict codes of conduct and a belief in absolute truths. In the educational contexts of these cultures, regular and frequent feedback on the same assignments is given. Highly structured, unidimensional teaching strategies (Rosenholtz & Rosenholtz, 1981) where materials are predefined and explicit are prevalent. These teaching strategies entail unambiguous feedback that allows for an exact comparison of performance on the same tasks (Simpson, 1981; Mac Iver, 1987), thereby permitting little personal interpretation. Therefore, members of cultures with strong uncertainty avoidance should base their efficacy appraisal on performance feedback that entails unambiguous information, and thus relatively low efficacy beliefs should be observed.

Members of cultures of *weak uncertainty avoidance* tend to be open to new experiences, tolerant, risk-accepting, and comparatively relaxed when confronted with unpredicted situations. Educational institutions in these cultures often use multidimensional teaching strategies that entail only partially structured learning materials, general instructions, and flexible, individualized pacing. Feedback from these teaching strategies is often highly ambiguous because performance on multiple different tasks cannot directly be compared. Ambiguous performance feedback permits individuals more personal interpretation. Therefore, members of cultures with weak uncertainty avoidance, by basing their efficacy appraisal on ambiguous performance feedback, should evidence relatively high efficacy beliefs.

In sum, values of collectivism, large power differential, and strong uncertainty avoidance should be associated with relatively low efficacy beliefs that are strongly based on unambiguous performance evaluations by a defined in-group and respected authorities, whereas values of individualism, small power distance, and weak uncertainty avoidance should be associated with relatively high efficacy beliefs that are only loosely based on the ambiguous evaluations of peers and authorities.

Differences in Efficacy Beliefs between East and West Berlin Children

Oettingen et al. (1994) tested these assumptions by comparing efficacy beliefs in two societies located at the opposite poles of the three cultural dimensions (individualism/collectivism, power distance, uncertainty avoidance): East Berlin versus West Berlin in 1990, right after the fall of the wall and before reunification. The socialist–totalitarian system of the former East Germany was collectivist, large in power differential, and strong in uncertainty avoidance. Specifically, it emphasized the community of the people, inequality of power between party officials and common citizens (i.e., citizens had limited human rights, e.g., they had little freedom of speech), and its economic system adhered to long-term economical plans that the government determined in advance. The citizens' professional and social perspectives were clearly spelled out with limited freedom of choice.

To the contrary, the capitalist–democratic system of West Germany was comparatively individualistic, small in power differential, and weak in uncertainty avoidance. As a capitalist system, it relies on values such as autonomy, self-fulfilment, and personal success. In democratic systems, citizens have comparatively more rights and possibilities to influence government policy. Furthermore, the government only remotely controls the economy, and it allows citizens to decide their own professional and interpersonal pathways. According to the reasoning above, individuals in East Germany should have mapped their efficacy expectations more closely to the evaluations of authorities and the in-group, and thus should have evidenced weaker efficacy beliefs than individuals in West Germany.

In June 1990, before unification of the two Germanys, Oettingen and colleagues assessed efficacy beliefs of more than 300 East Berlin children from two schools, grades 2–6. The data were compared to a matched sample in West Berlin, involving over 500 children. Children's sense of academic efficacy was operationalized as their judgments pertaining to whether they thought they could try hard, be smart, and have luck when it came to their school performance (Control, Agency, Means-Ends Instrument, CAMI, by Skinner et al., 1988).

Indeed, efficacy beliefs correlated stronger with course grades in East Berlin than in West Berlin students, reflecting the consensual construction of self-efficacy in the East Berlin rather than in the West Berlin school system. Already in the second grade-level correlations in East Berlin students ($r = 0.79$) were stronger than in West Berlin students ($r = 0.61$). At the same time, East Berlin children had a lower sense of academic efficacy than West Berlin children. That is, they had less confidence in their ability to exert effort in school, they considered themselves to be less smart, and they thought they would attract less luck. The lower sense of efficacy of the East Berlin children started in third grade and was pervasive throughout the sixth grade.

East and West Berlin Children of Varying Raven Scores

In 1991, 1 year after the first assessment, but still before the East Berlin school system adopted West Berlin's educational policies, Oettingen and Little (1993) returned to the East Berlin schools in an effort to replicate the original findings. At this point, they also administered Raven's Progressive Matrices test. They hypothesized that the observed differences between East and West Berlin children's self-efficacy and conformity would be driven by the children with lower Raven scores because once these children entered school, they were more frequently confronted with negative performance feedback that contradicted the naïve optimism with which children typically enter school. Therefore, the children with lower scores on the mental measure may have needed to revise their initial naïve performance optimism to a greater extent than would the children who obtained higher scores. Moreover, because of the initial negative performance feedback, lower scoring children should have more readily accepted future failure feedback than higher scoring children. Most importantly, this effect should have been particularly pronounced in school systems aiming at "adequate" self-evaluation, that is, more in East Berlin than in West Berlin. These hypotheses were confirmed: The differences in mean levels of self-efficacy and in conformity of efficacy appraisal were particularly due to the children with lower Raven scores.

Differences in efficacy beliefs between East and West Germany were also found in other samples and when using different instruments. For instance, students with low academic performance from various schools in East Germany were less convinced of their academic potential than their counterpart comparison group from West Germany, whereas there was no difference among students with strong academic performance (Hannover, 1995); also, East German school children conformed more readily to their teachers' evaluations than did the West German children. These differences in efficacy expectations were found in adults as well. A representative sample of adults in Dresden (East Germany) scored lower in work-related efficacy expectations than a matched sample from Mainz (West Germany, Frese et al., 1996).

Differences in Explanatory Style between East and West Berlin

Perceived feasibility may also be affected by general expectations, that is, expectations whether certain positive and negative events will occur in the future or not. One indirect way to assess such expectations is to measure optimism versus pessimism in explanatory style (Abramson et al., 1978). Optimism versus pessimism in explanatory style was extracted from East and West Berlin newspaper reports of the 1984 Olympic Games. There was more pessimism in East Berlin than in West Berlin newspapers, despite East Germany having achieved many more Olympic victories than West Germany (Oettingen & Seligman, 1990).

Pessimism in East Germany was not restricted to the cognitive side of expectations. In the mid-1980s, bar patrons in East Berlin showed more behavior consistent with depressive affect (i.e., turned-down mouths, hunched posture, sheltered bodies, as well as lack of expressive behavior and lack of smiles and laughs) than those in West Berlin (Oettingen & Seligman, 1990). Seven years later, in 1991, with the changing political system in East Germany the behavior consistent with depressive affect had waned in East Berlin to the level of West Berlin (Oettingen, 1995a).

Differences in Efficacy Beliefs Across Cultures: How Political System and Cultural Values Interact

Because for centuries East and West Berlin shared their historical, linguistic, philosophical, and religious background, the observed differences in efficacy beliefs, explanatory style, and depressive affect most likely resulted from the different political systems (socialist–totalitarian versus capitalist–democratic). However, both the political system and the original cultural values of a society as they are reflected in its historical, linguistic, philosophical, and religious background should influence the social institutional context that determines the formation of perceived feasibility. The values emphasized by a political system and the cultural values originally adhered to may either concur or collide in their impact on perceived feasibility. Thus, societies that are governed by a capitalist–democratic system and at the same time emphasize cultural values of individualism, small power distance, and weak uncertainty avoidance should especially foster the emergence of high perceived feasibility. In contrast, societies that are governed by a socialist/communist–totalitarian system and at the same time emphasize cultural values of collectivism, large power differential, and strong uncertainty avoidance, should foster low perceived feasibility. Finally, in societies where political system and cultural values oppose each other, a moderate level of perceived feasibility should emerge (Oettingen, 1995b; Oettingen & Maier, 1999).

These predictions were tested (Little et al., 1995) by comparing efficacy beliefs in a society in which both political system and cultural values should foster strong efficacy beliefs (i.e., the United States) with a society in which both the values of the political system and the cultural values should foster weak efficacy beliefs (i.e., East Germany). In addition, two societies were selected in which political system and cultural values collide and thus should produce efficacy beliefs lying in between (e.g., West Germany and USSR).

We chose the USSR as a comparison to East Germany, and the United States as a comparison to West Germany, because the USSR matched East Germany in political system but not in cultural values, while the United States matched West Germany in political system but not in cultural values. Thus to investigate the role of cultural values in light of similar political systems, the USSR is a valid comparison group to East Germany, and the United States is a valid comparison group to West Germany.

As for the comparison of the United States and West Germany, cultural values in the United States are more individualist, show smaller power differential, and weaker uncertainty avoidance than in Germany (Hofstede, 2001; Kitayama et al., 2007). Indeed, already in 1936, Lewin observed "The natural relation of adult and child is in the United States not considered that of a superior (*Herr*) to the subordinate (*Untergebener*) but that of two individuals with the same right in principle" (p. 269). These differences may partly originate in the history of voluntary settlement of the United States. According to the voluntary settlement hypothesis (Lewin, 1936; Kitayama et al., 2006), people who aspire to take challenges and seek wealth and freedom choose to immigrate to an unsettled country.

As for the comparison of the USSR and East Germany, cultural values in Eastern Europe (including the USSR) are more individualist, and they show less power differential and less uncertainty avoidance than in Germany. For instance, in comparison to East Germany, countries of the former Eastern Bloc and the USSR scored considerably higher on utilitarian involvement, an indicator for individualism and small power distance (Smith et al., 1996). This finding is supported by anecdotal and historical evidence. For example, Heinrich Mann in his novel *The Subject* or Carl Zuckmayer in his play *The Captain of Köpenick* vividly describe the readiness with which the German society complied to the power structures of the Wilhelmina period. A similar spirit did not exist in Russia where poems, novels, and proverbs tended to express disrespect for authority and low willingness to obey. For example, Alexander Puschkin in his poems or Nikolai Gogol in his novel *Dead Souls* ridicule governmental authorities. Low obedience is also expressed in the popular proverb *The sky is high and the Tsar is far!* In sum, cultural values of individualism, low power distance, and low uncertainty avoidance characterized both the USA and the USSR as compared to Germany.

Based on the considerations above, Little et al. (1995, summary by Oettingen & Maier, 1999) hypothesized that school children in Los Angeles (capitalist–democratic political system concurs with values of the culture) have the highest efficacy beliefs and the least conformity with the teachers' evaluations, whereas those in East Berlin have the lowest efficacy beliefs and most conformity (socialist–totalitarian political system concurs with the values of the culture). School children in West Berlin (democratic–capitalist political system collides with the values of the culture) and Moscow (communist–totalitarian political system collides with the values of the culture) were assumed to range in between. By testing 2000 school children from grades 2–6 in Los Angeles, Moscow, and East and West Berlin, Little et al. (1995) confirmed their hypotheses.

Further evidence that the interplay of collectivist values and a socialist–totalitarian system fosters the formation of especially low efficacy beliefs was provided by Oettingen and Maier (1999). When efficacy beliefs of more than 700 children from Prague and almost 200 children from Warsaw were compared to the children from East Berlin, children in Prague and Warsaw had a stronger sense of efficacy and lower conformity with their teachers' evaluations than children in East Berlin.

Summary

Perceived feasibility differs across cultures in line with political system and cultural values. Whereas the cultural values of collectivism, large power differential, and strong uncertainty avoidance are associated with low efficacy beliefs, the cultural values of individualism, small power distance, and weak uncertainty avoidance are associated with high efficacy beliefs. Most of the presented studies investigated efficacy expectations in school children. Here, low efficacy beliefs strongly impede scholastic performances (Schunk, 1991; Zimmerman & Kitsantas, 2005). Low scholastic performance in turn will hamper professional success, and thus may even suppress economic success on a societal level, as a nation's wealth is also based on its people's skills (Heckman, 2006). But it is not only academic and professional skill development that should be diminished by low efficacy beliefs but also non-cognitive skills such as perseverance and tenacity. Accordingly, individuals with low efficacy beliefs should be more reluctant to commit to challenging long-term goals geared at economic success (e.g., opening one's own business, persistently pursuing a professional career) and thus further deprive a society from a vital motor of economic development.

One may argue that the high efficacy beliefs, especially those in West Berlin children with low Raven scores may be simply unrealistic and thus detrimental in their effects on people's everyday lives. However, Taylor (1989) has convincingly argued and observed that optimism, even if illusory, benefits motivation and success in the central life domains, such as achievement, interpersonal relations, and health. The latter findings imply that children who need support by strengthened efficacy beliefs the most (e.g., children with low Raven scores) gain this essential motivational support to a greater extent in the cultures and political systems that tend toward individualism, low power distance, and weak uncertainty avoidance (e.g., in West Berlin more than in East Berlin). Supporting our finding of less optimism in cultures with relatively more collectivism, power distance, and uncertainty avoidance, other researchers also observed less illusory optimism in Eastern cultures than in Western cultures (e.g., Shuper et al., 2004; summary by Heine & Lehman, 1995).

CULTURE AND THE PROCESSES
OF GOAL PURSUIT

Recent research has moved away from the analysis of the determinants of goal pursuit, such as desirability and feasibility, to exploring the underlying psychological processes. Specifically, processes underlying goal setting and processes underlying goal implementation have been distinguished. Regarding goal setting, it was discovered that the way in which people mentally approach goal setting affects the strength of goal commitment. More specifically, whether perceived feasibility will affect the strength of goal commitment depends on the person's mode of thinking about the desired future (Oettingen, 2000). Process-focused research on goal implementation showed that strong goal commitments do not yet guarantee successful goal attainment as a host of problems may be encountered on the way to the goal (e.g., failing to get started, becoming derailed by distractions). Whether these problems will be ameliorated depends on people's efforts to plan out goal implementation in advance (Gollwitzer, 1999). In the following, we will first present the recent research on the processes of goal pursuit (i.e., goal setting and goal implementation) before we turn to discussing potential cultural influences on these processes.

COMMITTING TO GOALS: MENTAL CONTRASTING
OF FUTURE AND REALITY

As outlined before, self-efficacy expectations are an important determinant of goal setting as they facilitate goal commitment. However, the commitment-facilitating role of self-efficacy expectations depends on people's self-regulatory thought. Specifically, the model of fantasy realization by Oettingen et al. (2001) differentiates three self-regulatory modes of thought. When people engage in the mode of thought called mental contrasting, they first imagine a desired future (e.g., improving in math, becoming a lawyer) and then reflect on the respective negative reality (e.g., being easily distracted; having yet to take the LSAT). The conjoint elaboration of the positive future and the negative reality makes both future and reality simultaneously accessible and it activates the relational construct of negative reality standing in the way of realizing the desired future. Consequently, a necessity to change the present reality into the desired future emerges that activates perceived feasibility (efficacy expectations, outcome expectations, or general expectations of success). When expectations of success are high, people will strongly commit to attaining the goal of changing the status quo toward the desired future, when expectations of success are low they form a weak goal commitment or none at all.

Using the terminology of Newell and Simon's (1972) theory of problem solving, the problem space of the mentally contrasting person is objective as it entails both the positive future to be reached and the negative reality to be over-come. As a consequence, the person will recognize that she needs to act on the status quo in order to reach the desired future. Therefore, perceived feasibility (expectations) of turning the present reality into the desired future will determine the person's goal commitment. However, if the subjective problem space entails only part of the objective problem – either only the positive future (indulging) or only the negative reality (dwelling) – the person will fail to recognize that she needs to improve the status quo in order to arrive at the desired future. As a consequence, expectations are not consulted and goal commitments stemming from solely focusing on either the positive future or the negative reality fail to be expectancy-dependent. The level of goal commitment is determined by the a priori commitment that the person holds with respect to attaining the desired future. Thus it is only mental contrasting that succeeds in strengthening com-mitment when expectations of success are high and in weakening commitment when expectations of success are low.

A series of experimental studies measuring goal commitment as the depend-ent variable supports these hypotheses. In these experiments, participants are ran-domly assigned to one of three conditions. They either mentally elaborate both the desired future and negative reality (mental contrasting condition), only the desired future (indulging condition), or only the negative reality (dwelling con-dition). In one experiment (Oettingen et al., 2001, Study 4), adolescent students had to mentally contrast the positive future of excelling in math (participants imagined, e.g., feelings of pride, increasing job prospects) with the respective negative reality (participants reflected on, e.g., being distracted by peers, feel-ing lazy). Two weeks after the experiment, students in the mental contrast con-dition who initially had high expectations that they could improve the present reality in the direction of the desired future (i.e., of excelling in math) received better course grades and teachers rated them as exerting more effort than those in the indulging (positive fantasy only) and in the dwelling (negative reality only) conditions.

The same pattern of results emerged with individuals who wished to learn a foreign language (Oettingen et al., 2000, Study 1), to solve an interpersonal prob-lem (Oettingen et al., 2001, Studies 1 and 3), to get to know an attractive stranger (Oettingen, 2000, Study 1), to self-actualize (Oettingen et al., 2005, Study 1), to communicate with foreigners (Oettingen et al., 2005, Study 2), to reduce cigarette consumption, to obtain the help of others, and with pediatric intensive care nurses who wished to improve the relations with their patients' relatives (Oettingen & Thorpe, 2006).

In these experiments, goal commitment was assessed by cognitive (e.g., mak-ing plans), affective (e.g., feeling responsible for the wished for ending), motiva-tional (e.g., feelings of energization), and behavioral indicators (e.g., effort and achievements). The indicators were measured via self-report or observations either immediately or weeks after the experiment. Throughout, mental contrasting proved to be an effective problem solving strategy of translating expectations of success into goal commitment and subsequent goal striving. Importantly, in line with the theory, mental contrasting, indulging, and dwelling did not differentially affect the mean level of expectations. Rather, the self-regulatory modes of goal setting affected the degree to which participants respected expectations of success in forming their goal commitments (summary by Oettingen & Thorpe, 2006).

The notion that mental contrasting is a problem-solving strategy is also supported from a neuro-cognitive point of view: A study which examined the neural correlates of mental contrasting and indulging via continuous magnetoencephalographic activity (MEG; Achtziger et al., in press) evinced greater activity during mental contrasting (but not indulging) compared to resting in prefrontal, frontal, parietal, and temporal areas, indicating that mental contrasting involves strong intention formation, working memory, and episodic memory. In addition, heightened activity of occipital areas was observed during mental contrasting compared to resting and indulging, suggesting that mental contrasting more so than indulging and resting entails purposefully creating mental images. Taken together, these findings indicate that mental contrasting is indeed a purposeful problem-solving strategy respecting one's performance history.

IMPLEMENTING GOALS: MAKING IF–THEN PLANS

Having discussed modes of self-regulatory thought related to forming goal commitment, we will now turn to self-regulatory thought that facilitates goal implementation. The model of action phases (Heckhausen & Gollwitzer, 1987; Gollwitzer, 1990) assumes that getting started on one's goals and bringing goal-directed behavior to successful completion is facilitated by planning. Gollwitzer (1999) has referred to such planning as forming implementation intentions that link a critical situational cue with an intended goal-directed behavior: "If situation x is encountered, then I will perform behavior y!" Implementation intentions refer to the realization of the goal as people plan to respond to an anticipated critical situation in a certain goal-directed manner. They are distinguished from goal intentions (goals) that only specify a desired goal (outcome or behavior) and have the format of: "I intend to reach z!" or "I intend to perform behavior z!"

Implementation intentions have been found (meta-analysis of 94 independent studies by Gollwitzer & Sheeran, 2006) to facilitate the attainment of all kinds of goals that are difficult to control (e.g., writing a research report during Christmas break), easy to forget (e.g., taking of vitamin pills), or unpleasant to perform (e.g., performing cervical smear tests). They also facilitate the shielding of one's goal pursuit from unwanted influences (e.g., temptations, bad habits, adverse self-states). Implementation intentions seem to achieve their beneficial effects on goal attainment by delegating action control to the specified situational cues thus creating ad hoc or instant habits. For instance, Webb and Sheeran (2003) observed that the facilitation of goal attainment by implementation intentions is achieved without depleting a person's self-regulatory resources. Participants who used implementation intentions to achieve a difficult task goal (i.e., high performance on the Stroop task) showed no deficits in the successful regulation of a subsequent demanding cognitive task (i.e., tracing puzzles). Moreover, the initiation of the responses specified in the then-component of an implementation intention was found to be immediate (e.g., Gollwitzer & Brandstätter, 1997, Study 3), efficient (e.g., Brandstätter et al., 2001, Studies 3 and 4; Parks-Stamm et al., 2007), and did not require a further conscious intent (e.g., Webb & Sheeran, 2007).

By forming implementation intentions one can strategically switch from top-down control of one's actions by set goals to bottom-up control through specified situational cues as is typical of habitual or automatic behavior. In a recent fMRI study conducted by Gilbert et al. (2008), brain activity in the lateral area 10 was observed to move toward the medial area 10 when participants switched from performing an executive functions task by the guidance of a goal intention to performing the very same type of task by the guidance of an implementation intention; on the basis of an extensive meta-analysis on various executive function tasks it is known that lateral and medial area 10 are implicated in top-down and bottom-up action control, respectively (Burgess et al., 2007).

Moderators of the effects of implementation intentions on goal attainment pertain to characteristics of the superordinate goal, the implementation intention itself, and the individual. For instance, as implementation intentions are subordinate to goal intentions, the strength of implementation intention effects depends on the strength of commitment to and activation state of the goal (Sheeran et al., 2005). Further, commitment to the implementation intention itself also matters; when people do not commit to the pre-decided way of implementing the goal as laid down in an implementation intention (because they want to stay open to unexpectedly arising opportunities and means; Seehausen et al., 1994), no goal attainment enhancing effects are observed. Characteristics of the individual moderate the relationship between if–then planning and goal attainment as well: A recent implementation intervention study geared to help college students' class attendance (Webb et al., 2007) showed that students low in conscientiousness benefited from the intervention, but not the high conscientious students who showed perfect class attendance to begin with. In sum, characteristics of the goal (e.g., difficulty, commitment, activation), the implementation intention (commitment), and the individual (e.g., conscientiousness) all manage to moderate implementation intention effects on goal attainment.

What, however, spurs the formation of implementation intentions? More research is needed to explore the circumstances under which people are most likely to form if–then plans. It seems reasonable to assume that the anticipation of difficulties in striving for one's goal will influence whether people can and want to make plans (i.e., whether implementation intentions are formed or not). Indeed, Oettingen et al. (2001) observed that high expectancy individuals induced to engage in mental contrasting as compared to indulging and dwelling spontaneously produced more if–then plans regarding the implementation of the desired future.

SUMMARY: MENTAL CONTRASTING AND IMPLEMENTATION INTENTIONS

Findings supporting the model of fantasy realization show that perceiving the envisioned future as desirable (positive attitude or high incentive value) and feasible (e.g., high efficacy expectations) are just prerequisites for the emergence of strong goal commitments. To create strong goal commitments, people need to translate these positive attitudes and high expectations into binding goals, a process which is facilitated by mentally contrasting the positive future with negative reality. Such mental contrasting has been found to benefit behavior change in widely different life domains (e.g., interpersonal, achievement, and health), and it has been linked to brain activity typical for purposeful problem solving based on one's past performance history.

Similarly, findings supporting the model of if–then planning show that binding goal commitments are only a prerequisite for goal attainment. To facilitate goal attainment, people may form if–then plans that link instrumental responses to anticipated critical situations. By an act of will (i.e., making an if–then plan), action control is strategically delegated to these specified situations and thus acquires features of automaticity that are commonly observed only with habitual action control. In numerous studies, such if–then plans have been found to effectively increase rate of goal attainment.

MENTAL CONTRASTING AND IMPLEMENTATION INTENTIONS ACROSS CULTURES

As mental contrasting solves the problem of discriminating between feasible and unfeasible goals, we speculate that cultures that demand such "discriminative facility" (Mischel, 1973, p. 258) foster the readiness to use mental contrasting over indulging and dwelling. Similarly, because if–then planning solves the problem of strategically automating goal-directed actions, we speculate that cultures that demand such strategic automation should foster the readiness to generate implementation intentions. In sum, cultures should differ in the extent they foster self-regulation of goal setting (mental contrasting) and goal implementation (if–then planning).

These ideas go beyond the traditional claim that cultural values affect the key determinants of goal pursuit, desirability and feasibility, as they highlight that cultural values may also affect the way in which people commit to goals and implement them. Cultural variables that qualify may be manifold, though variables that relate to "the space of free movement" (Lewin, 1936, p. 268) should again be of particular importance here. According to Lewin, and as noted before, too many restrictions in the form of social prohibitions will limit the space of free movement. In light of such social prohibitions, goals should not be formed and self-regulatory strategies of goal pursuit should not be needed (Oettingen, 1997). In the following, we want to consider a cultural variable that affects the space of free movement: strong versus weak norm-orientation (tightness versus looseness; Triandis, 1989; Chan et al., 1996).

Norm-Orientation

In traditional cultures, myths and other cultural symbols favor norm-oriented rituals which then serve as the basis for action (Boesch, 1982). Norm-orientation functions as the basis for action because of two reasons: norm-oriented rituals provide the necessary assurance for action and they lay down the boundaries for action (i.e., they inform the person when and where to interact with whom in what way). However, norm-oriented rituals are fading in modern societies. The myths and symbols of modern societies, even if they sound scientific (e.g., eat healthy, be friendly, save energy), are by and large abstract ideologies without creating a basis for forming strong goal commitments and engaging in subsequent action (Ryder, 1965; Boesch, 1982; Sennett, 2005).

Therefore, in *non-normative (loose)* cultures the individual is forced to seek alternative guidance that substitutes for the lost support by rituals and prohibitions. As perceived feasibility (efficacy expectations, outcome expectations, general expectations of success) reflects an individual's personal experience and performance history, it can provide the necessary assurance to act and show the boundaries of acting. Assuming that perceived feasibility is a major determinant of a person's goal commitment in non-normative societies, mental contrasting as a mode of self-regulatory thought should be in high demand. As mental contrasting allows people to solve the problem of translating perceived feasibility into respective goal commitments with subsequent goal striving, it should help people to invest in promising projects and stay away from futile ones.

Moreover, in non-normative cultures where norms fail to provide guidance, implementation intentions should be a welcome tool for enacting one's set goals. People may benefit much from using implementation intentions when preparing for upcoming difficulties and temptations during goal striving, as norms do not guide their way. Also, because mental contrasting should be prevalent and mental contrasting leads to scrutinizing obstacles to the enactment of the desired future, people should find it easy to make if–then plans; they can use these obstacles to specify the if-component of their implementation intentions (Oettingen et al., 2001). These speculations are in line with the finding that low conscientious college students benefited from forming implementation intentions, while high conscientious students showed successful goal implementation no matter whether they formed implementation intentions or not (Webb et al., in press).

In contrast, in *normative (tight)* cultures turning to perceived feasibility is less necessary, and mental contrasting as the respective problem-solving strategy should be less in demand. If anything, indulging in the desired future should flourish. A high prevalence of indulging should have a stabilizing function for the individual's well-being and the cultural environment, because indulging helps to live with the experience of normative constraints in the present by providing hope for a better future. Indeed, in light of low feasibility, indulging in a positive future has been shown to help people "to stay in the field" (Lewin, 1936; Oettingen et al., 2001). Disregard of perceived feasibility and respective endurance is also facilitated by dwelling on the negative reality. In sum, cultures that adhere to myths and symbols which favor norm-oriented rituals should encourage indulging in positive futures and allow extensive dwelling on the current dreary reality. They should discourage mental contrasting of a positive future with negative reality that induces feasibility-guided goal pursuit.

Because highly normative cultures do not provide much space of free movement, there should be relatively little need to form implementation intentions either. Action in normative cultures is highly ritualized and thus automated by default. A strategic automaticity produced by if–then planning is superfluous. For example, people in normative cultures have been taught to tackle barriers in a pre-specified way (e.g., how to be polite to an unfriendly person). This prespecification is the purpose of if–then planning and if this purpose is fulfilled by the guidance of norms, implementation intentions are not needed to begin with. Finally, in normative cultures, as people preferably indulge and dwell rather than mentally contrast, they lack the cognitive preparation (i.e., thinking of obstacles) that facilitates the explication of the if-component of implementation intentions.

Summary

Socio-cultural contexts can be differentiated by whether they grant what Kurt Lewin has called "the space of free movement." We have operationalized this variable by pointing to the cultural value of norm-orientation (i.e., tightness versus looseness; Triandis, 1989) and reasoned that loose cultures should foster the use of mental contrasting and forming implementation intentions, while in tight cultures these modes of thought are not needed to effectively control one's actions. Moreover, we argued that indulging and dwelling should be prevalent in tight cultures, as these modes of thought facilitate endurance and positive affect in situations that do not allow for "free movement" (i.e., situations where a person's actions are determined by societal prohibitions or situations which are not escapable in the sense that they can neither be resolved nor escaped). Certainly, each individual member of a loose or tight culture should at times entertain a typical self-regulatory thought. Also, there should be individual differences in preferred self-regulatory thought within a given culture. However, the socio-cultural contexts outlined above should selectively favor the prevalence of specific types of self-regulatory thought in their members.

CONCLUSION

In the first part of this chapter, we discussed how culture may affect people's goal pursuits via determining the perceived desirability and feasibility of potential goals. With respect to perceived feasibility, we reported a line of research showing that political system and cultural variables conjointly inform people's self-efficacy beliefs. In the second part of the chapter, we raised the question of how cultural values might affect people's preferential use of certain self-regulation strategies when committing to and acting on goals. We pointed to the cultural dimensions of weak versus strong norm-orientation (looseness versus. tightness, Triandis, 1989), and reasoned that strong norm orientation reduces the space of free movement. Accordingly, there should be relatively little demand for mental contrasting or implementation intentions as people know a priori how to act (i.e., with whom, when, where, and how). To the contrary, in cultures of weak norm orientation people have to set goals and find ways of implementing them. Therefore, it is vital to develop discriminative ability in goal setting (by mental contrasting) and strategic automaticity in goal implementation (by forming implementation intentions). Future research may turn to testing the hypotheses we have developed, or start exploring their implications. For instance, one wonders whether mental contrasting and forming implementation intentions are to be preferred when people in a given culture are opting toward change and the political and economic situation allows for such a change, whereas indulging in a positive future is the proper self-regulatory strategy when people in a given culture have to endure a dismal situation until the political and economic developments allow for change toward the better.

REFERENCES

Abramson, L. Y., Seligman, M. E. P., & Teasdale, J. D. (1978). Learned helplessness in humans: Critique and reformulation. *Journal of Abnormal Psychology, 87*, 49–74.
Achtziger, A., Fehr, T., Oettingen, G., Gollwitzer, P. M., & Rockstroh, B. (in press). Strategies of intention formation are reflected in continuous MEG activity. *Social Neuroscience*.
Atkinson, J. W. (1957). Motivational determinants of risk-taking behavior. *Psychological Review, 64*, 359–372.
Bandura, A. (1997). *Self-efficacy: The exercise of control*. New York: Freeman.
Benedict, R. (1934). *Patterns of culture*. Boston: Houghton Mifflin.
Boesch, E. E. (1982). Ritual und Psychotherapie. *Zeitschrift für klinische Psychologie und Psychotherapie, 30*, 214–234.
Bond, M. H. (1986). *The psychology of the Chinese people*. New York: Oxford University Press.
Brandstätter, V., Lengfelder, A., & Gollwitzer, P. M. (2001). Implementation intentions and efficient action initiation. *Journal of Personality and Social Psychology, 81*, 946–960.
Brunstein, J. C., Schultheiss, O. C., & Grassman, R. (1998). Personal goals and emotional well-being: The moderating role of motive dispositions. *Journal of Personality and Social Psychology, 75*, 494–508.
Burgess, P. W., Simons, J. S., Dumontheil, I., & Gilbert, S. J. (2007). The gateway hypothesis of rostral prefrontal cortex (area 10) function. In J. Duncan, L. Phillips, & P. McLeod (Eds.), *Measuring the mind: Speed, control, and age* (pp. 217–248). Oxford: Oxford University Press.
Chan, D. K. S., Gelfand, M. J., Triandis, H. C., & Tzeng, O. (1996). Tightness-looseness revisited: Some preliminary analyses in Japan and the United States. *International Journal of Psychology, 31*, 1–12.

Frese, M., Kring, W., Soose, A., & Zempel, J. (1996). Personal initiative at work: Differences between East and West Germany. *Academy of Management Journal, 39*, 37–63.

Gilbert, S. J., Gollwitzer, P. M., Cohen, A.-L., Oettingen, G., & Burgess, P. W. (2008). *Separable brain systems supporting realization of future goals versus if-then plans.* Manuscript submitted for publication.

Gillispie, J. M., & Allport, G. W. (1955). *Youth's outlook on the future (a cross-national study).* New York: Doubleday & Company.

Gollwitzer, P. M. (1990). Action phases and mind-sets. In E. T. Higgins & R. M. Sorrentino (Eds.), *The handbook of motivation and cognition: Foundations of social behavior* (Vol. 2, pp. 53–92). New York: Guilford Press.

Gollwitzer, P. M. (1999). Implementation intentions: Strong effects of simple plans. *American Psychologist, 54*, 493–503.

Gollwitzer, P. M., & Brandstätter, V. (1997). Implementation intentions and effective goal pursuit. *Journal of Personality and Social Psychology, 73*, 186–199.

Gollwitzer, P. M., & Sheeran, P. (2006). Implementation intentions and goal achievement: A meta-analysis of effects and processes. *Advances in Experimental Social Psychology, 38*, 69–119.

Hannover, B. (1995). Self-serving biases and self-satisfaction in East versus West German students. *Journal of Cross-Cultural Psychology, 26*, 176–188.

Heckhausen, H. (1977). Achievement motivation and its constructs: A cognitive model. *Motivation and Emotion, 1*, 283–329.

Heckhausen, H., & Gollwitzer, P. M. (1987). Thought contents and cognitive functioning in motivational versus volitional states of mind. *Motivation and Emotion, 11*, 101–120.

Heckman, J. J. (2006). Skill formation and the economics of investing in disadvantaged children. *Science, 312*, 1900–1902.

Heine, S. J., & Lehman, D. R. (1995). Cultural variation in unrealistic optimism: Does the west feel more invulnerable than the east? *Journal of Personality and Social Psychology, 68*, 595–607.

Heine, S. J., Lehman, D. R., Markus, H. R., & Kitayama, S. (1999). Is there a universal need for positive self-regard? *Psychological Review, 106*, 766–794.

Hofstede, G. H. (2001). *Culture's consequences: Comparing values, behaviors, institutions and organizations across nations* (2nd ed.). Thousand Oaks, CA: Sage Publications.

Janis, I. L. (1968). Attitude change via role playing. In R. Abelson, E. Aronson, W. McGuire, T. Newcomb, M. Rosenberg, & P. Tennebaum (Eds.), *Theories of cognitive consistency: A sourcebook* (pp. 810–818). Chicago, IL: Rand-McNally.

Kim, H., & Markus, H. R. (1999). Deviance or uniqueness, harmony or conformity? A cultural analysis. *Journal of Personality and Social Psychology, 85*, 373–382.

Kitayama, S., Ishii, K., Imada, T., Takemura, K., & Ramaswamy, J. (2006). Voluntary settlement and the spirit of independence: Evidence from Japan's "Northern frontier". *Journal of Personality and Social Psychology, 91*, 369–384.

Kitayama, S., Park, H., Sevincer, A. T., Karasawa, M., & Uskul, A. (2008). *A cultural task analysis of implicit independence: Comparing North America, West Europe, and East Asia.* Manuscript submitted for publication.

Lewin, K. (1936). Some social psychological differences between the United States and Germany. *Character and Personality, 4*, 265–293.

Little, T. D., Oettingen, G., Stetsenko, A., & Baltes, P. B. (1995). Children's action-control beliefs about school performance: How do American children compare with German and Russian children? *Journal of Personality and Social Psychology, 69*, 686–700.

Locke, E. A., & Latham, G. P. (1990). *A theory of goal setting and task performance.* Englewood Cliffs, NJ: Prentice Hall.

Mac Iver, D. (1987). Classroom factors and student characteristics predicting students' use of achievement standards during self-assessment. *Child Development, 58*, 1258–1271.

Markus, H. R., & Kitayama, S. (1991). Culture and the self: Implications for cognition, emotion, and motivation. *Psychological Review, 98*, 224–253.

Matsumoto, D., & Yoo, S. H. (2006). Toward a new generation of cross-cultural research. *Perspectives on Psychological Science, 1*, 234–250.

McClelland, D. C. (1965). *The achieving society*. Princeton, NJ: Van Nostrand.

Mischel, W. (1973). Toward a cognitive social learning reconceptualization of personality. *Psychological Review, 80*, 252–283.

Newell, A., & Simon, H. A. (1972). *Human problem solving*. Englewood Cliffs, NJ: Prentice-Hall.

Nurmi, J. E. (1991). How do adolescents see their future? A review of the development of future orientation and planning. *Developmental Review, 11*, 1–59.

Oettingen, G. (1995a). Explanatory style in the context of culture. In G. M. Buchanan & M. E. P. Seligman (Eds.), *Explanatory style* (pp. 209–224). Hillsdale, NJ: Erlbaum.

Oettingen, G. (1995b). Cross-cultural perspectives on self-efficacy. In A. Bandura (Ed.), *Self-efficacy in changing societies* (pp. 149–176). New York: Cambridge University Press.

Oettingen, G. (1997). Culture and future thought. *Culture and Psychology, 3*, 353–381.

Oettingen, G. (2000). Expectancy effects on behavior depend on self-regulatory thought. *Social Cognition, 18*, 101–129.

Oettingen, G., & Gollwitzer, P. M. (2001). Goal setting and goal striving. In A. Tesser & N. Schwarz (Eds.), *The Blackwell Handbook of Social Psychology*. Oxford: Blackwell.

Oettingen, G., Hönig, G., & Gollwitzer, P. M. (2000). Effective self-regulation of goal attainment. *International Journal of Educational Research, 33*, 705–732.

Oettingen, G., & Little, T. D. (1993). Intelligenz und Selbstwirksamkeitsurteile bei Ost- und Westberliner Schulkindern [Intelligence and self-efficacy beliefs in East and West Berlin school children]. *Zeitschrift für Sozialpsychologie [German Journal of Social Psychology], 24*, 186–197.

Oettingen, G., Little, T. D., Lindenberger, U., & Baltes, P. B. (1994). Causality, agency, and control-beliefs in East versus West Berlin children: A natural experiment on the role of context. *Journal of Personality and Social Psychology, 66*, 579–595.

Oettingen, G., & Maier, H. (1999). Where political system meets culture: Effects on efficacy appraisal. In Y. T. Lee, C. R. McCauley, & J. G. Draguns (Eds.), *Personality and person perception across cultures*. Mahwah, NJ: Erlbaum.

Oettingen, G., & Mayer, D. (2002). The motivating function of thinking about the future: Expectations versus fantasies. *Journal of Personality and Social Psychology, 83*, 1198–1212.

Oettingen, G., Mayer, D., Thorpe, J. S., Janetzke, H., & Lorenz, S. (2005). Turning fantasies about positive and negative futures into self-improvement goals. *Motivation and Emotion, 29*, 237–267.

Oettingen, G., Pak, H., & Schnetter, K. (2001). Self-regulation of goal-setting: Turning free fantasies about the future into binding goals. *Journal of Personality and Social Psychology, 80*, 736–753.

Oettingen, G., & Seligman, M. E. P. (1990). Pessimism and behavioural signs of depression in East versus West Berlin. *European Journal of Social Psychology, 20*, 207–220.

Oettingen, G., & Thorpe, J. S. (2006). Fantasy realization and the bridging of time. In L. A. Sanna & E. C. Chang (Eds.), *Judgments over time: The interplay of thoughts, feelings, and behaviours* (pp. 120–142). Oxford: Oxford University Press.

Oishi, S., & Diener, E. (2001). Goals, culture, and subjective well-being. *Personality and Social Psychology Bulletin, 27*, 1674–1682.

Oyserman, D., Coon, H. M., & Kemmelmeier, M. (2002). Rethinking individualism and collectivism: Evaluation of theoretical assumptions and meta-analyses. *Psychological Bulletin, 128*, 3–72.

Parks-Stamm, E. J., Gollwitzer, P. M., & Oettingen, G. (2007). Do implementation intentions lead to rigid goal pursuit? Cue detection versus response selection. *Social Cognition, 25*, 248–266.

Rosenholtz, S. J., & Rosenholtz, S. H. (1981). Classroom organization and the perception of ability. *Sociology of Education, 54*, 132–140.

Ryder, N. B. (1965). The cohort as a concept in the study of social change. *American Sociological Review, 30*, 841–861.

Schunk, D. H. (1991). Self-efficacy and academic motivation. *Educational Psychologist, 26*, 207–231.

Seehausen, R., Bayer, U., & Gollwitzer, P. M. (1994, September). *Experimentelle Arbeiten zur vorsätzlichen Handlungsregulation* [Experimental studies on the intentional control of behavior]. Paper presented at the *39th convention of the German Psychological Society*, Hamburg, Germany.

Sennett, R. (2005). *The culture of the new capitalism*. London: Yale University Press.

Sheeran, P., Webb, T. L., & Gollwitzer, P. M. (2005). The interplay between goal intentions and implementation intentions. *Personality and Social Psychology Bulletin, 31*, 87–98.

Shuper, P., Sorrentino, R. M., Otsubo, Y., Hodson, G., & Walker, A. M. (2004). A theory of uncertainty orientation: Implications for the study of individual differences within and across cultures. *Journal of Cross-Cultural Psychology, 35*, 460–481.

Simpson, C. (1981). Classroom structure and the organization of ability. *Sociology of Education, 54*, 120–132.

Skinner, E. A., Chapman, M., & Baltes, P. B. (1988). Control, means-ends, and agency beliefs: A new conceptualization and its measurement during childhood. *Journal of Personality and Social Psychology, 54*, 117–133.

Smith, P. B., Dugan, S., & Trompenaars, F. (1996). National culture and the values of organizational employees: A dimensional analysis across 43 nations. *Journal of Cross-Cultural Psychology, 27*, 231–264.

Taylor, S. E. (1989). *Positive illusions: Creative self-deception and the healthy mind*. New York: Basic Books.

Triandis, H. C. (1989). The self and social behavior in differing cultural contexts. *Psychological Review, 96*, 506–520.

Van Baaren, R. B., Maddux, W. W., Chartrand, T. L., De Bouter, C., & Van Knippenberg, A. (2003). It takes two to mimic: Behavioral consequences of self-construals. *Journal of Personality and Social Psychology, 84*, 1093–1102.

Vroom, V. H. (1964). *Work and motivation*. New York: Wiley.

Webb, T. L., & Sheeran, P. (2003). Can implementation intentions help to overcome ego-depletion? *Journal of Experimental Social Psychology, 39*, 279–286.

Webb, T. L., & Sheeran, P. (2007). How do implementation intentions promote goal attainment? A test of component processes. *Journal of Experimental Social Psychology, 43*, 295–302.

Webb, T. L., Christian, J., & Armitage, C. J. (2007). Helping students turn up for class: Does personality moderate the effectiveness of an implementation intention intervention? *Learning and Individual Differences, 17*, 316–327.

Zimmerman, B. J., & Kitsantas, A. (2005). Homework practices and academic achievement: The mediating role of self-efficacy and perceived responsibility beliefs. *Contemporary Educational Psychology, 30*, 397–417.

10

UNVEILING AGENCY: A MOTIVATIONAL PERSPECTIVE ON ACCULTURATION AND ADAPTATION

MICHELLE GEZENTSVEY AND COLLEEN WARD

School of Psychology, Victoria University of Wellington, Wellington, New Zealand

Acculturation refers to the changes arising from sustained, firsthand intercultural contact. Originally of primary interest to anthropologists, acculturation was first studied as a group phenomenon (Redfield et al., 1936); more recently, however, it has been investigated by psychologists at the individual level (Graves, 1967; Berry, 1997). Acculturation occurs in a wide range of socio-cultural contexts. While it is most often examined in relation to those who make international relocations, such as sojourners, immigrants, and refugees, acculturative experiences are also relevant to sedentary groups, including indigenous peoples and established ethno-cultural communities (Berry & Kim, 1988).

Early psychological research on acculturation was largely based on medical models. It emphasized the relationship between migration and psychopathology and interpreted negative psychological outcomes in terms of "culture shock" (Furnham & Bochner, 1986). Cross-cultural travelers were often seen as victims of culture change with minimal control or influence over their transition experiences. More modern approaches have situated an agentic self at their core, a self dynamically engaged in reflection and development, active coping and culture learning. The shift from a passive view of acculturation where the individual is acted upon by external forces to an agentic view where the individual actively engages in shaping acculturation outcomes is bound up with the application of more contemporary theoretical frameworks to the study of acculturation.

THE ABCS OF ACCULTURATION

THE ABC MODEL

In recent years three broad theoretical approaches have emerged as guiding forces in the psychological study of acculturation. The first is linked to psychological models of stress and coping and applied specifically to the study of cross-cultural transition and adaptation. The second reflects a culture-learning approach, which highlights the social psychology of the intercultural encounter and the processes involved in learning the culture-specific skills required to thrive and survive in a new milieu or to operate effectively in culturally diverse settings. The third is associated with social identification and cognition and is concerned with the way people perceive and think about themselves and others, including how they process information about their own group (in-groups) and other groups (out-groups). The theoretical underpinnings of the three approaches have been largely derived from mainstream social, experimental, and health psychology. Their application to the study of culture contact over recent years has resulted in the development of an impressive body of empirical research on sojourners, immigrants, and refugees as well as indigenous peoples and established ethno-cultural communities (Ward et al., 2001).

The stress and coping approach conceptualizes cross-cultural transition as a series of stress-provoking life changes that draw on adjustive resources and require coping responses. This approach has been strongly influenced by Lazarus and Folkman's (1984) work on stress, appraisal and coping, as well as earlier theory and research on life events (Holmes & Rahe, 1967). The analytical framework is broad and incorporates both characteristics of the individual and characteristics of the situation that may facilitate or impede adjustment to a new cultural milieu. Accordingly, researchers seeking to identify the factors that affect cross-cultural adjustment, particularly psychological well-being and satisfaction, have examined many of the same variables as those who investigate stress and coping in other domains. These include life changes, cognitive appraisal of change, and coping strategies. A range of resources and deficits are seen as affecting the core coping process, including individual differences, such as personality, and situational factors such as social support. With respect to more "culture-embedded" variables, cultural identity, cultural distance, and acculturation strategies have been examined (Ward, 1996, 2001; Berry, 2006a).

Culture-learning theory has its roots in social and experimental psychology and has been strongly influenced by Argyle's (1969) work on social skills and interpersonal behaviors. This approach is based on the assumption that intercultural problems arise because cultural novices have difficulties managing everyday social encounters. Adaptation, therefore, comes in the form of learning the culture-specific skills that are required to negotiate a new cultural milieu (Bochner, 1972, 1986). Both personal and situational factors exert influence on the acquisition and performance of culturally appropriate skills. Individual differences in cultural intelligence (CQ) and self-efficacy are important as are personal assets such as language fluency. Factors that facilitate the learning process, such as intercultural contact and training, as well as those that hinder skills acquisition, such as cultural distance, also receive attention in the culture-learning framework (Earley & Ang, 2003; Masgoret & Ward, 2006). More recent developments have seen the application of the Theory of Planned Behavior (TPB) (Azjen, 1991) to the acquisition of cultural skills and behavioral changes in acculturating persons.

The final approach has been influenced and unified by contemporary theory and research on social identity and social cognition. This approach reflects greater diversity than the culture learning and stress and coping paradigms and draws on a range of theories. It includes the measurement, development, and maintenance of identity; the relationship between identity and acculturation strategies; and the cognitive processes underlying intergroup perceptions and relations. Tajfel's (1978) Social Identity Theory (SIT), which views ethnocentrism as inevitable and considers individual and group-level means for functional status enhancement, is one of the most commonly used frameworks for examining these issues although Berry's (1984, 2006b) multicultural assumption provides a more optimistic alternative. Also central to social identification approaches is Berry's (1974, 1994) model of acculturation, which addresses issues of cultural maintenance and participation in the wider society. The relative importance of maintenance and participation determine and distinguish four acculturation strategies: integration (both are important), separation (only maintenance is important), assimilation (only participation is important), and marginalization (neither is important). Of key importance and cutting across the range of perspectives on social identification and intergroup relations is the issue of perceived discrimination (Ward & Leong, 2006). While the processes underlying identity and intergroup relations are important in their own right, their relationship to adaptive outcomes is of particular interest in the acculturation literature.

ACCULTURATION AND ADAPTATION

Acculturation itself is a neutral construct in that it refers merely to changes resulting from intercultural contact; however, research in the field has been very much directed toward understanding the relationship between acculturation and adaptation. More specifically, attention has been paid to identifying factors that lead to positive outcomes for acculturating persons. Although adaptation can and has been defined in a variety of ways, the distinction proposed by Ward and colleagues is used in this chapter (Searle & Ward, 1990; Ward, 1996, 2001; Ward et al., 2001). Ward argues that there are two adaptation domains that are relevant for all acculturating persons – psychological and socio-cultural. The first refers to psychological well-being and satisfaction while the second refers to social competencies or the ability to operate effectively in a new and different cultural milieu. Put in another way, psychological adaptation refers to the affective dimensions of acculturative experiences while socio-cultural adaptation is linked to behaviors and skills.

Ward et al. (2001) have synthesized contemporary theory and research on acculturation in their ABC model (Figure 10.1). Affective components of culture contact are highlighted in the stress and coping approach, Behavioral elements are featured in the culture-learning approach, and Cognitive variables are emphasized in the social identity approach. The model combines the major theoretical approaches and incorporates the basic components of adaptation – psychological and socio-cultural – which represent central concerns to cross-cultural travelers such as sojourners, immigrants, and refugees, but may also be relevant to individuals interacting across ethno-cultural divides within culturally plural societies. The figure positions the adaptational outcomes in relation to underlying

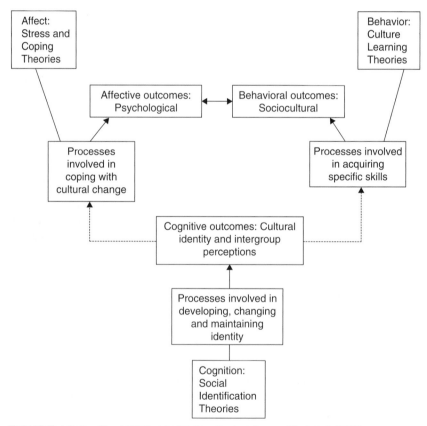

FIGURE 10.1   The ABC Model of Culture Contact. *Source*: Ward et al. (2001).

theoretical constructs and illustrates how the affective, behavioral, and cognitive perspectives merge to describe and explain culture contact and adaptation.

BEYOND THE ABC MODEL

What is noticeably absent in the ABC model of acculturation is reference to motivation. Although motivational elements permeate aspects of each of the guiding frameworks, they have not been examined in a thorough or systematic fashion. The remainder of this chapter extracts, elaborates, and synthesizes research on motivational dimensions of the acculturation experience. This is achieved through the identification, integration, and analysis of the motivational concept of agency in acculturation. As such, the chapter superimposes a motivational interpretation on the ABC model, providing a new perspective on acculturation. We believe this synthesis can benefit both motivation and acculturation researchers.

INTRODUCING AGENCY AS A COGNITIVE–MOTIVATIONAL PHENOMENON

DEFINING AGENCY

The psychological literature on motivation has examined agency over the life span, expounding that "Individuals construct their own life course through the choices and actions that they have taken within the constraints and opportunities of history and social circumstances" (Shanahan & Elder Jr., 2002, p. 150). This definition paints a picture of individuals actively engaged in creating their future, albeit within the boundaries preset by environmental constraints. Relevant constructs that tap into a sense of personal agency include beliefs about one's capabilities, such as control and self-efficacy; goal setting; self-regulation; and strategies of coping with environmental stressors (Crockett, 2002).

To interpret acculturative experiences and outcomes in terms of agency a working definition must first be formulated. Thus, agency is the active engagement of individuals in the acculturation process, that (a) encompasses the belief in one's capability of reaching selected meaningful acculturative goals; the ethno-cultural and civic navigation skills necessary to achieve those goals; and the management of environmental stressors with effective coping strategies within the social, cultural, and historical constraints of the larger society; and (b) has positive consequences for individuals' psychological and socio-cultural adaptation. In other words, agency is the active, positive engagement of individuals in the acculturation process.

In terms of individual engagement, a worthy note of caution by Markus and Kitayama (2003) is that while traditional Western models of agency assume that behavior originates from independent and autonomous selves, Eastern models encompass behavior that emanates from interdependent selves. Thus the researchers distinguish between disjoint and conjoint agency, where disjoint refers to agentic behavior that serves the independent self and conjoint refers to behavior that takes into consideration socially significant others. Thus, when we discuss individual agency in acculturation, it can encompass both kinds of agency, where acculturating individuals from more collectivist cultures may be likely to engage in conjoint agentic behavior while those from more individualistic cultures will potentially engage in disjoint agentic behavior.

In contrast, there is a further type of agency which is only experienced at a group level, the key elements of which may be discussed under the rubric of empowerment. In the context of acculturation, collective agency or empowerment can be defined as the active engagement of ethno-cultural groups in the acculturation process of long-term duration that (a) encompasses the belief in their capability of reaching selected meaningful acculturative goals; the ethno-cultural and civic navigation skills necessary in achieving those goals; the effective coping strategies in the face of external stressors; and the resolve in bringing about socio-political change in the larger society; and (b) has positive consequences for ethno-cultural vitality. In other words, empowerment is the active engagement of ethno-cultural groups in the acculturation process that has positive consequences for ethno-cultural vitality. With these definitions in hand, we can proceed to examine the nature of agency and empowerment in the context of acculturation.

AGENCY AND THE ACCULTURATION CONTEXT

While the emphasis in this chapter is on the role of agency in the experiences of acculturating individuals and groups, it must be remembered that acculturation occurs in a wider socio-cultural context. Aspects of this context may enhance or limit agency and, in turn, affect adaptive outcomes. Is the wider society relatively homogeneous or heterogenous? Is it open and receptive to cultural diversity? Is there support for multiculturalism? Do citizens endorse integration or assimilation? Are prejudice and discrimination common?

Bourhis et al. (1997) have highlighted contextual issues in their Interactive Acculturation Model, which draws attention to the significance of host community ideologies and policies and their consequences for immigrant groups. Dominant ideologies can limit and constrain the options of minority migrant and ethnic groups, undermining a sense of agency and leading to poorer adaptation. Indeed, Bourhis et al. (1997) argue that dissimilar acculturation attitudes lead to problematic or conflictual outcomes between host and migrant groups. This has been borne out in research by Jasinskaja-Lahti et al. (2003) that linked discordant acculturation preferences to greater perceived discrimination and increased psychological distress in ethnic repatriates in Finland, Germany, and Israel.

The implications of cultural heterogeneity and diversity policies for acculturation have been recently examined in the 13-nation International Comparative Study of Ethno-Cultural Youth (ICSEY; Berry et al., 2006). Participating countries were first rated on constructed indices of cultural heterogeneity, based on objective demographic factors, and diversity policies, based on the extent to which countries promote cultural diversity as a national goal. Researchers then examined the relationship between national and ethnic identity in ethno-cultural youth across these countries. Findings revealed a positive relationship between national and ethnic identity in countries such as New Zealand ($r = +0.32$), characterized by a relatively high index of cultural diversity and strong support for culturally plural policies. In contrast, a negative relationship between ethnic and national identity was found in countries such as Germany ($r = -0.28$) with a very low index of cultural diversity and weak policy support for cultural diversity. As the same project found that immigrant youth across all countries and all ethnic groups expressed a preference for integration (cultural maintenance and participation in the wider society) over assimilation, separation or marginalization, the findings lend support to the notion that context may enhance or diminish agency in reaching desired acculturative goals.

The influence of context can also be demonstrated in studies of perceived discrimination where research has shown that separation and marginalization are more likely to occur and assimilation less likely to be adopted under conditions of greater perceived discrimination (Barry & Grilo, 2003). Furthermore, studies have linked perceived discrimination to a variety of negative outcomes including increased stress, lowered self and group esteem, impaired health, antisocial behaviors such as drug use and delinquency, identity conflict and poorer work adjustment and job satisfaction in sojourner, migrant, and ethnic groups (see Ward et al., 2001). Recent research has demonstrated that the effects of perceived discrimination on mental health outcomes are mediated by agency. More specifically, perceived discrimination has been shown to lead to a reduced sense of personal control and environmental mastery and, in turn, to greater psychological distress in both Latina/o and Arab Americans (Moradi & Hasan, 2004; Moradi & Risco, 2006).

Agentic aspects of the acculturation process can also be influenced by perceived similarities or differences between the cultures in contact. In the acculturation literature this has been discussed under the rubric of cultural distance. Large differences between cultures pose more challenges to acculturating individuals; not only do they require adaptation to a greater number and wider variety of life changes, but they also demand more extensive culture-learning for psychological and socio-cultural adaptation. We suggest that cultural distance exerts a direct negative influence on a sense of agency as research has linked it to lower self-efficacy (Nesdale & Mak, 2003), higher stress (Redmond, 2000), and poorer psychological and socio-cultural adaptation (Ward & Searle, 1991; Ward & Kennedy, 1999). Cultural distance may also exert an indirect effect on agency, as it has been associated with greater perceived discrimination in acculturating persons (Sodowsky & Plake, 1992). All of these contextual factors should be borne in mind while examining agency in individual and group acculturation processes.

AGENCY IN STRESS AND COPING WITH
ACCULTURATIVE CHANGES

The stress and coping framework highlights the processes involved in coping with cultural change. Its basic premise is that any change, whether positive or negative, whether arising from cross-cultural transition or within-society intercultural contact, is intrinsically stressful in that it requires readjustment (Holmes & Rahe, 1967; Lazarus & Folkman, 1984). As such, the core stress and coping process involves change, cognitive appraisal, coping strategies, and their consequences, including psychological and social adaptation. The sequence incorporates a feedback loop where coping strategies may be evaluated for their effectiveness and altered to produce more adaptive outcomes. On the periphery of this core process is a range of mediating and moderating variables, including cognitive factors and personality domains, that affects the dynamics and outcomes of stress and coping (Berry, 1997).

COPING STRATEGIES

As a key component of agency involves the capacity to manage stressors, the coping strategies used to deal with culture contact and change merit priority attention. Chataway and Berry (1989) were the first to consider this in their research with Hong Kong Chinese students at a Canadian university. Their findings indicated that students who used withdrawal and wishful thinking were less satisfied with their ability to cope and those who adopted a detached coping style experienced greater psychological distress. The latter finding was replicated in Ward and Kennedy's (2001) study of British expatriates in Singapore where those who employed "avoidant" coping strategies, such as mental disengagement and venting, experienced more depression. In contrast, direct "approach-oriented" strategies, such as active coping and planning, resulted in more positive psychological outcomes. Research with international students in both the United States and New Zealand has highlighted the positive consequences of direct or problem-focused strategies and the negative consequences of emotion-focused strategies for reduction in perceived stress and depressive symptomatology (Cross, 1995; Berno & Ward, 1999).

COPING AND CONTROL

The choice and implementation of coping strategies to deal with culture contact and change are underpinned by a sense of agency and linked to expectations about and skills for achieving positive psychological and social outcomes. Intertwined with agency are notions of control. Along these lines, there is a substantial body of acculturation research that has documented the link between psychological adjustment and locus of control in both short and long-term migrants. More specifically, an external locus of control has been associated with more depression, anxiety, mood disorders, psycho-somatic complaints, and psychiatric symptoms (Hung, 1974; Kuo et al., 1976; Dyal et al., 1988; Ward & Kennedy, 1992, 1993). It has also been linked to decrements in migrants' life satisfaction (Seipel, 1988; Neto, 1995).

Despite the widespread use of Rotter's (1966) internal–external distinction of locus of control in the acculturation literature, scholars have suggested that this conceptualization may not adequately capture the complexity of perceived control on a cross-cultural basis (Yamaguchi, 2001). Accordingly, a body of theory and research on primary and secondary control is emerging in the cross-cultural context. Primary control resembles an internal locus, changing the situation, circumstances or environment to suit individuals' needs and preferences or to facilitate their goals. With respect to coping strategies, primary control is associated with active coping, planning and direct, problem-focused initiatives. In contrast, secondary control involves accommodation, changing individuals to fit the situation, circumstances or environment. In terms of coping responses, secondary control is linked to cognitive reframing, such as positive reinterpretation and acceptance. Ward et al.'s (2007) research on coping with cross-cultural transitions found that secondary coping strategies exerted a direct effect on reducing perceived stress and, in turn, led to fewer symptoms of depression. Furthermore, the influence of primary strategies on perceived stress and psychological adaptation was mediated by secondary coping. This pattern was observed in Asian and Western international students in both Singapore and Australia.

Reflecting control perceptions and beliefs and aligned to the notion of agency is the concept of hardiness (Kobasa, 1979). Hardiness has been conceptualized as a constellation of personality traits that function to alleviate the negative effects of stressful life events and is composed of three domains: control, commitment, and challenge. Control is expressed as a tendency to behave as if one is influential, rather than helpless; commitment is expressed as a tendency to involve oneself rather than to become alienated; and challenge is expressed in the belief that change is normative and interesting rather than unusual and threatening. Decades of research have demonstrated that hardiness affects health outcomes both directly and indirectly by buffering the effects of stressful life events (e.g., Kobasa et al., 1982). In the context of acculturation, research studies have also shown that hardiness predicts lower levels of stress in migrants and that it alleviates their psychological symptoms (Ataca & Berry, 2002; Lopez et al., 2004; Mak et al., 2005).

AGENCY AND CULTURE LEARNING

The culture-learning approach to acculturation highlights the processes involved in the acquisition of the appropriate culture-specific skills necessary to interact effectively across cultural boundaries and/or to engage successfully in the wider society (Masgoret & Ward, 2006). The processes involve the motivation to learn new skills and behavioral repertoires; the confidence or belief in one's capacity for culture learning and skills acquisition; the goal setting and self-regulation to achieve cultural competence; and ultimately the culturally appropriate display of competent behaviors. All of these elements contribute to the socio-cultural adaptation of acculturating persons. Accordingly, this section discusses theory and research on the antecedents of culture learning, such as cultural intelligence, self-efficacy, and goal-setting behavior to elucidate how agency impacts learning and the display of culture-appropriate skills.

AGENTIC ANTECEDENTS OF CULTURE LEARNING

Cultural Intelligence

Arising from contemporary theorizing on intelligence and situated in the literature on expatriate effectiveness, Earley and Ang (2003) have recently advanced the construct of cultural intelligence (CQ) to explain individual differences in the "capability to adapt effectively to new cultural contexts" (p. 59). CQ is a multi-dimensional concept; it has four basic components – cognitive, meta-cognitive, behavioral, and motivational – and both process and content features.

Underpinned by Bandura's (1997) Self-efficacy Theory and Locke and Latham's (1990) Goal-setting Theory, motivational CQ has been described as a drive and interest in learning about and functioning in new and different cultural settings (Ang et al., 2004), highlighting individual agency in the acculturation process. Individuals with high Motivational CQ have a strong desire to experience cultural novelty; they enjoy interacting with people from diverse backgrounds and set their goals accordingly; and they have a strong sense of self-efficacy in cross-cultural contexts. Earley and Ang maintain that individuals who are high in motivational aspects of CQ not only have a strong sense of personal efficacy, but also that they will tend to set challenging goals for achieving cultural competence.

As CQ is a relatively new construct, there has been limited empirical research to date on its role in the prediction of psychological and socio-cultural adaptation. Preliminary evidence, however, appears promising with the motivational domain proving to be the most robust predictor of positive outcomes. Over a series of studies, Ang et al. (2004) reported that Motivational CQ was linked to general adjustment and that the four CQ factors explained variance in general adjustment and task performance over and above that accounted for by a test of cognitive ability. More recent research has confirmed that Motivational CQ predicts work and general adjustment in expatriate employees and psychological and socio-cultural adaptation in international students (Templer et al., 2006; Ward & Fischer, 2008; Ward et al., in press).

Self-efficacy

Also serving as a personal resource and a key component of agency is self-efficacy, the "beliefs in one's capabilities to organize and execute the courses of action required to produce given attainments" (Bandura, 1997, p. 3). If individuals do not believe that they have the ability to create desired outcomes, there remains little or no motivation to act. In contrast, people who have a high sense of self-efficacy behave intentionally to reach desired goals. Thus, in the acculturation process, self-efficacy beliefs aid in achieving desired outcomes, including cultural competence and adaptation.

Regarding efficacy beliefs of migrants and members of established ethno-cultural communities, LaFromboise et al. (1993) speak of bicultural efficacy as one of six basic competencies, encompassing the belief that one can live effectively and with satisfaction within their own ethno-cultural group and the wider society without compromising a sense of cultural identity. The researchers maintain that a person's level of bicultural efficacy will influence the ability to develop cultural skills, perform appropriate behaviors, cope with acculturative stress and maintain affiliations in both cultures. Empirical evidence has certainly borne out the positive influences of self-efficacy on acculturation and adaptation. Self-efficacy has been related to better psychological (Mak & Nesdale, 2001) and socio-cultural (Tsang, 2001) adaptation of short and long-term migrants. It has also been a significant predictor of academic adaptation among migrant students in Australia (Leung, 2001) and higher educational goals for Mexican American students (Flores et al., 2006).

GOAL SETTING, SELF-REGULATION, AND THE THEORY OF PLANNED BEHAVIOR

As agency encompasses the beliefs and capabilities of reaching selected meaningful acculturative goals, it is important to examine the process of goal attainment. In this respect, goal-setting theory provides a valuable framework (Locke & Latham, 1994), emphasizing that individuals and groups consciously endeavor to shape their life paths through setting goals and engaging in behaviors necessary to reach desired outcomes. Goals are cognitive representations of desired states that lend significance and purpose to life. The pursuit of goals, as a concrete expression of one's sense of agency, requires perceived self-efficacy to perform the behaviors essential to reach desired end states. The process of goal attainment generally involves evaluation of progress and feedback on success and failure en route to the desired outcome. In this regard, self-monitoring is a useful skill (Gangestad & Snyder, 2000) and has been related to cross-cultural adaptability (Montagliani & Giacalone, 1998), general adjustment (Harrison et al., 1996), and both socio-cultural and psychological adaptation (Kosic et al., 2006) in short and long-term migrants.

It is also important to examine the nature and domains of acculturative goals. The Relative Acculturation Extended Model (RAEM) has identified seven spheres relevant to acculturating persons: political, work, economic, family, social, religious beliefs and customs, and principles and values (Navas et al., 2005). Thus, goals may entail such diverse activities as working toward national language proficiency, establishing social club networks, attaining appropriate employment, retaining religious practices, and accepting different values. The ability to achieve goals such as these has repercussions not only for goal-directed culture learning, but for adaptation more broadly as research has consistently shown that behavioral competencies are related to enhanced psychological well-being in acculturating persons (Ward & Kennedy, 1999).

A useful framework for elucidating these processes is the Theory of Planned Behavior (TPB), which examines agentic behavioral expression and incorporates the concept of self-efficacy as perceived behavioral control (Azjen, 1991). Intentions are the central motivational tenet of TPB, with stronger behavioral intentions increasing the likelihood of performance. These intentions are predicted by domain-specific attitudes (positive or negative feelings regarding the behavior), subjective norms (individual perceptions regarding the domain-specific views of important others) and perceived behavioral control (self-efficacy).

Despite its apparent utility, there has been limited research that explicitly tests the TPB in the acculturation context. An exception to this is work by Abrams et al. (1999) that examined intentions to emigrate from Hong Kong. The study revealed that attitudes toward leaving and normative beliefs and motivations were significant predictors of emigration intentions, but that perceived control did not exert a significant influence on plans. TPB has also been successfully used to predict and explain job-seeking behaviors amongst Turkish immigrants in the Netherlands (Hooft et al., 2006). For the most part, however, TPB has been examined in highly specific contexts such as intentions toward future substance abuse in Latino adolescents (Carvajal et al., 1997) and dietary changes in Chinese immigrants (Liou, 2000) rather than the acquisition of broad cultural competencies.

AGENCY AND GOAL SETTING ACROSS ACCULTURATING GROUPS

Acculturating groups may be distinguished on at least three dimensions: mobility, permanence, and voluntariness (Berry & Sam, 1997). First, people who have made cross-cultural relocations, such as refugees and immigrants, may be distinguished from members of sedentary groups, such as native peoples and established ethno-cultural communities. Secondly, cross-cultural travelers who resettle temporarily, such as sojourners, differ from those, like immigrants, whose move is more permanent. Finally, those who voluntarily engage in intercultural contact (e.g., immigrants and sojourners) may be distinguished from those who are forced by necessity into involuntary interactions (e.g., refugees, indigenous peoples). When the voluntary–involuntary distinction is applied specifically to those who have crossed international borders, the former may be described as having been drawn or "pulled" toward a new country, usually in hopes of a better lifestyle, while the latter is more commonly seen as "pushed" from their homeland into an alien environment. This section considers variations in agency and goals across acculturating groups.

Sojourners

"The term sojourner refers to individuals who travel abroad to attain a particular goal within a specified period of time. The expectation is that these culture travelers will return to their country of origin after completing their assignment [...] sojourners have a finite perspective and this influences how they acculturate to their host society" (Bochner, 2006, p. 181). The definition clearly states that there are specific aims of a sojourner's journey that intend to be fulfilled. Goals vary according to the type of sojourner: while tourists aim to amuse themselves at their chosen destination, international students intend to attain levels of academic excellence and complete chosen qualifications, and finally expatriates aim to conduct selected commercial or professional activities. Sojourners are generally perceived to exert agency over the duration and location of their acculturation experiences; however, Speiss and Wittmann (1999) have noted that employees are often expatriated more in response to market forces than in relation to career development or satisfaction issues, and there has been developing expatriate literature on the challenges faced by accompanying spouses and children (Shaffer & Harrison, 2001).

Asylum Seekers and Refugees

Both asylum seekers and refugees have experienced disruptive events in their homelands – natural disasters, famine, war, political upheaval, and human rights violations – associated with trauma and often resulting in negative psychological consequences (Allen et al., 2006). Migration is typically forced rather than voluntary with refugees and asylum seekers generally "pushed" rather than "pulled" to a new country of settlement. As such, agency is diminished. Indeed, Tran (1993) reported that pre-migration stressors reduced a sense of self-efficacy and led to depression in Vietnamese refugees in the United States. However, the goals set by refugees are likely to change over time. Immediate goals may be underpinned by a self-preservation motive (Tartakovsky & Schwartz, 2001) and focused on escape from unbearable circumstances while longer-term goals may include dealing with the loss of home and acquiring the skills and resources to settle in a new environment.

Migrants

Immigrants voluntarily relocate to a new country to establish a permanent home, attracted or pulled by various personal and socio-political factors. They have specific expectations that they wish to fulfill in their new country, including the attainment of higher economic status, professional satisfaction, and family reunification (van Oudenhoven, 2006). Overall, migrants are high in achievement and power motivation (Boneva & Frieze, 2001); seek improvement in their quality of life (Furnham & Bochner, 1986); and typically exert agency in fulfilling these motives and pursuing these goals (Cooke, 2007), although this may be diminished by social factors such as prejudice and discrimination.

Ethno-cultural Communities

Members of ethno-cultural groups set goals and exert agency on both the individual and group level and in terms of present and future orientation by navigating through their heritage culture and that of the larger society. Some may aim to accomplish this by combining the best of both worlds. This has been referred to as additive biculturalism and described in Chinese migrants to the Netherlands who select the more valuable features of their heritage culture and blend it with the preferred aspects of the national Dutch society (Verkuyten & de Wolf, 2002). Similar goals may be achieved through the alternation model of biculturalism, where individuals have affinity to two cultures, are knowledgeable in both and actively change their behavior to suit the cultural context (LaFromboise et al., 1993).

A more long-term, group-oriented goal found in members of established ethno-cultural communities involves cultural continuity over generations. This issue has been examined by Gezentsvey (in progress) under the rubric of the *Motivation for Ethno-cultural Continuity*. Her research revealed that the motive for ethno-cultural continuity is shared by Maori, Chinese, and Jews in New Zealand and that it demonstrates incremental validity in the prediction of selective dating and behavioral intentions for endogamy in Jews and Maori over and above the influence of similarity, attraction, and social network approval. Her research is effective in portraying the significance of agency and its role and consequences for both immediate behaviors and long-term, group-oriented goals.

Indigenous Peoples

Indigeneity encompasses the recognition of original occupancy as the basis for entitlement to land and cultural and political resources (Maaka & Fleras, 2000). Indigenous scholars have argued that the continued existence of indigenous peoples is dependent upon their ability to influence their own fate and to live in accordance with their own cultural patterns, social institutions, and legal systems (Kvernmo, 2006). Forced to undergo culture contact that extends in the long term, they have similar vested interests as ethno-cultural groups in transmitting their culture and seeing their group survive in the future. Unfortunately, one has difficulties speaking of cultural maintenance, as policies of segregation and assimilation have led to severe cultural loss or deculturation (Berry & Sam, 1997). Rather, revitalization processes have begun over the last decades through the process of empowerment. The reclaiming of cultural traditions, ancestral lands, and rights of self-determination are unique to indigenous peoples, with special emphasis on native language proficiency as a concrete manifestation of collective identity (Taylor, 1997). The goals of gaining political rights are central to the acculturative journey of indigenous peoples, as the distinguished Maori scholar Mason Durie has written, "without any sense of control, independence, or autonomy, endurance is probably best called existence" (Durie, 2005, p. 235).

AGENCY, SOCIAL IDENTITY AND ADAPTATION

The social identification approach deals with the ways in which people perceive and think about themselves and others, including how they process information about their in-groups and out-groups. Ethnic and cultural identity forms the core of the conceptual framework, directly linking self-definition to group membership; however, intergroup processes and dynamics are also considered. A wide range of theories and social psychological processes is encompassed within the social identification approach to acculturation; however, of primary interest here are the ways in which people exert agency in the protection of individual and collective self-esteem and the consequences of these activities for adaptation. Tajfel's (1978) Social Identity Theory (SIT), Berry's (1974) model of acculturation strategies and Phinney's (2003) work on ethnic identity and national identity are central to the exploration of these issues.

INDIVIDUAL AND COLLECTIVE ACTION: AGENCY AND EMPOWERMENT

According to SIT (Tajfel, 1981), human beings tend to strive for positive distinctiveness through their membership in a particular social category. To achieve this objective, individuals engage in a process of *self-categorization*, relying on salient or contextually relevant cues that will define membership in the in-group and out-group. They then strive to enhance personal self-esteem through *social identification* with members of their in-group. These processes are followed by *social comparison*, where in-group members compare their group's status and performance with a relevant out-group. If the comparison favors the in-group, a sense of positive distinctiveness emerges. However, if the comparison places the in-group in an unfavorable position, individuals may engage in either social mobility or social change strategies to improve their relative status.

Individual agency via social mobility is likely to occur when intergroup boundaries are seen as permeable. The same is true for assimilation (Verkuyten, 2005). In either case, individual members of lower status groups are able to dissociate from their negatively distinctive in-group and "cross-over" to become a member of a higher status group. "Switching" group membership takes place at the individual level, but the relative position of lower and higher status groups remains unchanged.

Collective agency, empowerment, and social change are more likely to arise when the boundaries between dominant and non-dominant groups appear to be relatively stable and impermeable. The limitations imposed on lower status group members by institutional and psychological constraints encourage them to rely on collective strategies to change the status quo in order to achieve a sense of positive distinctiveness. Changes may result by successfully competing with members of the dominant group or by reframing evaluative aspects of group identity. In either event, collective strategies are used to improve the relative standing of all members of the non-dominant group. This works most efficiently in political systems characterized by multiculturalism (Verkuyten, 2005).

Moghaddam et al. (1987) investigated these strategies in their study of Iranian immigrants in Canada. They observed the use of both an individualistic approach, concerned primarily with personal social mobility rather than maintenance of cultural heritage and collectivist tactics, including reliance upon the support of Iranian cultural organizations and the larger Iranian community to help with social advancement. The groups using these strategies differed on a number of salient characteristics, including willingness to remain in Canada and the perceived necessity of liaisons with the Iranian community. Most importantly, however, those who adopted collectivist strategies had a stronger belief in the justice and fairness of the Canadian system. Later research with Indian, Caribbean, Italian, and Greek migrants to Canada suggested that members of visible minorities are more likely to prefer collectivist strategies (Lalonde & Cameron, 1993). The use of collectivist strategies is also associated with greater perceived group, as opposed to personal, discrimination (Moghaddam & Perreault, 1991).

AGENCY, ACCULTURATION CHOICES AND ADAPTIVE OUTCOMES

The most commonly used framework for linking acculturation strategies and adaptive outcomes in cross-cultural psychology has been Berry's (1974, 1994) model of integration, separation, assimilation, and marginalization. Over a series of studies, Berry and colleagues found that integration is associated with the most positive adaptive outcomes, marginalization with the most negative outcomes and separation and assimilation falling in between (Berry et al., 1989). Subsequently, an abundance of evidence has been produced corroborating the link between integration and both psychological and socio-cultural dimensions of adaptation (e.g., Ward & Kennedy, 1992; Berry, 1997), and this has most recently been borne out in the ICSEY project (Berry et al., 2006).

The ICSEY project also combined Berry's conceptualization and measurement of acculturation strategies with Phinney and Devich-Navarro's (1997) approach to ethnic and national identity in their survey of young migrants (Berry et al., 2006). Factor analysis of data generated by over 5000 immigrant youth identified four acculturation profiles: integrated, ethnic, national, and diffuse. The Integrated profile was most common with 36% of the adolescent sample exhibiting high ethnic and national identities. While lower proficiency was reported for their ethnic language than the national language, language use was balanced. Similarly, peer contacts were established in both groups. The Ethnic profile, in which individuals preferred the separation strategy, comprised 23% of the adolescent sample, with high levels of ethnic identity, ethnic language preference, and strong links with ethnic peers. The National profile, found in 19% of the sample, was associated with a tendency toward assimilation, strong national identity, proficiency in the national language and ties with peers from the larger society. Finally, the Diffuse profile emerged in 22% of the youth. Adolescents in this category endorsed assimilation, separation and marginalization; however, they were low in both national and ethnic identity, had high proficiency in ethnic language but low proficiency in the national language and had few national peer contacts. The researchers acknowledged that this profile was not easily interpreted, but suggested that it described young people who are uncertain about their place in society, wanting to be a part of the larger society but lacking the requisite skills to do so. In addition, the diffuse group reported more perceived discrimination than did the ethnic, national and integrated groups. In short, the diffuse profile reflects a lack of agency.

MARGINALIZATION: THE ANTITHESIS OF AGENCY

The absence of agency has been discussed in the social science literature in connection with various terms and categories: marginalization, anomie, alienation, and diffusion. Common to all of these discussions is the notion that individuals are unwilling or unable to be actively and meaningfully engaged, whether this is at the personal, group, or societal level. In the personality and developmental literature, identity diffusion is described in terms of lacking commitment to a direction or purpose in life, often in connection with social isolation (Marcia, 1994). In sociological accounts, anomie is characterized by non-conformity and a breakdown of norms due to the disjuncture of socially acceptable goals and the means for obtaining them (Merton, 1957). In acculturation theory and research, marginalization is encapsulated by lack of involvement and participation, little interest in cultural maintenance (often for reasons of enforced cultural loss) and little interest in maintaining relations with other groups (often for reasons of exclusion). Berry and Sam (1997) make it clear that marginalization is not a chosen strategy, but one that results from the absence of other viable options. Bourhis and colleagues have further refined Berry's (1974, 1994) concept of marginalization, distinguishing volitional detachment (individualism) from anomie (Bourhis et al., 1997). Common to all of these analyses is that marginalization is the antithesis of agency and that it has negative consequences for individuals, groups, and societies.

CONCLUSION

This chapter has attempted to synthesize theory, concepts, and models from two domains of psychological research: motivation and acculturation. From the cross-cultural vantage point, a motivational analysis offers a new perspective on the acculturation process. From the motivational vantage point, the chapter has demonstrated that key theoretical constructs and processes can be extended to a new area of investigation – culture contact and change.

Our representation of the motivation–acculturation synthesis can be seen in Figure 10.2. Agency is situated at its core, underpinning and influencing critical aspects of the acculturation process that are represented in the center triangle: A – stress and coping, B – culture learning, and C – identity and intergroup relations. It influences the adaptation (represented by the inner circle) of five different acculturating groups: S – sojourners, R – refugees, M – migrants, E – ethno-cultural groups, and I – indigenous peoples that live in the wider society (represented by the darkened, all-encompassing circle).

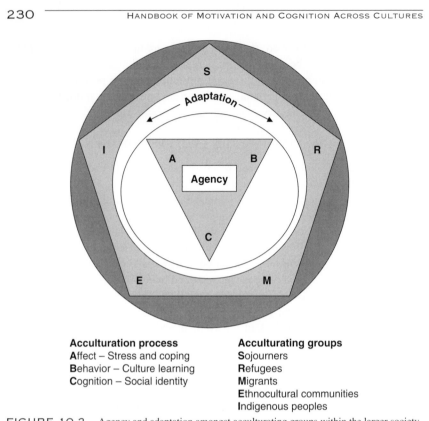

Acculturation process
Affect – Stress and coping
Behavior – Culture learning
Cognition – Social identity

Acculturating groups
Sojourners
Refugees
Migrants
Ethnocultural communities
Indigenous peoples

FIGURE 10.2   Agency and adaptation amongst acculturating groups within the larger society.

In concluding our discussion of agency, acculturation, and adaptation, we make two suggestions. To acculturation researchers we recommend more frequent, systematic, and explicit investigation of agency. We believe it holds future promise for understanding and explaining culture contact and change. To motivational researchers we note that in an age of increasing international migration, globalization and growing within-society diversity, acculturation provides an excellent context to extend motivational theories and test their external validity. To both groups of researchers we recommend the application of findings on agency and adaptation to enable individuals and empower groups in the acculturation process.

REFERENCES

Abrams, D., Hinkle, S., & Tomlins, M. (1999). Leaving Hong Kong?: The roles of attitude, subjective norm, perceived control, social identity and relative deprivation. *International Journal of Intercultural Relations, 23*(2), 319–338.

Allen, J., Basilier Vaage, A. B., & Hauff, E. (2006). Refugees and asylum seekers in societies. In D. L. Sam & J. W. Berry (Eds.), *The Cambridge handbook of acculturation psychology* (pp. 198–217). New York: Cambridge University Press.

Ang, S., Van Dyne, L., Koh, C., & Ng, K. Y. (2004). The measurement of cultural intelligence. Paper presented at the *Academy of Management Meeting's Symposium on Cultural Intelligence in the 21st Century*. New Orleans, LA.

Argyle, M. (1969). *Social interaction*. London: Methuen.

Ataca, B., & Berry, J. W. (2002). Psychological, sociocultural and marital adaptation of Turkish immigrant couples in Canada. *International Journal of Psychology, 37*, 13–26.

Azjen, I. (1991). The theory of planned behavior. *Organizational Behavior and Human Decision Processes, 50*, 179–211.

Bandura, A. (1997). *Self-efficacy: The exercise of control*. New York: W. H. Freeman and Co..

Barry, D. T., & Grilo, C. M. (2003). Cultural, self-esteem and demographic correlates of perception of personal and group discrimination among East Asian immigrants. *American Journal of Orthopsychiatry, 73*, 223–229.

Berno, T., & Ward, C. (1999). Psychological and social adjustment of foreign students in New Zealand. Paper presented at the *Society of Australasian Social Psychologists Annual Conference*. Christchurch, New Zealand.

Berry, J. W. (1974). Psychological aspects of cultural pluralism. *Topics in Culture Learning, 2*, 17–22.

Berry, J. W. (1984). Cultural relations in plural societies. In N. Miller & M. Brewer (Eds.), *Groups in contact* (pp. 11–27). New York: Academic Press.

Berry, J. W. (1994). Acculturation and psychological adaptation. In A.-M. Bouvy, F. J. R. van de Vijver, P. Boski, & P. Schmitz (Eds.), *Journeys into cross-cultural psychology* (pp. 129–141). Lisse, Netherlands: Swets & Zeitlinger.

Berry, J. W. (1997). Immigration, acculturation and adaptation. *Applied Psychology: An International Review, 46*, 5–34.

Berry, J. W. (2006a). Stress perspectives on acculturation. In D. L. Sam & J. W. Berry (Eds.), *The Cambridge handbook of acculturation psychology* (pp. 43–57). Cambridge: Cambridge University Press.

Berry, J. W. (2006b). Mutual attitudes among immigrants and ethno-cultural groups in Canada. *International Journal of Intercultural Relations, 30*, 719–734.

Berry, J. W., & Kim, U. (1988). Acculturation and mental health. In P. Dasen, J. W. Berry, & N. Sartorius (Eds.), *Health and cross-cultural psychology* (pp. 207–236). London: Sage.

Berry, J. W., & Sam, D. L. (1997). Acculturation and adaptation. In J. W. Berry, M. H. Segall, & C. Kagitcibasi (Eds.), *Handbook of cross-cultural psychology* (Vol. 3, pp. 291–326). Boston: Allyn & Bacon.

Berry, J. W., Kim, U., Power, S., Young, M., & Bujaki, M. (1989). Acculturation attitudes in plural societies. *Applied Psychology, 38*, 185–206.

Berry, J. W., Phinney, J. S., Sam, D. L., & Vedder, P. (2006). *Immigrant youth in cultural transition*: *Acculturation, identity, and adaptation across national contexts*, New Jersey: Lawrence Erlbaum.

Bochner, S. (1972). Problems in culture learning. In S. Bochner & P. Wicks (Eds.), *Overseas students in Australia* (pp. 65–81). Sydney: University of New South Wales Press.

Bochner, S. (1986). Coping with unfamiliar cultures: Adjustment or culture learning?. *Australian Journal of Psychology, 38*, 347–358.

Bochner, S. (2006). Sojourners. In D. L. Sam & J. W. Berry (Eds.), *The Cambridge handbook of acculturation psychology*. New York: Cambridge University Press.

Boneva, B. S., & Frieze, I. H. (2001). Toward a concept of a migrant personality. *Journal of Social Issues, 57*(3), 477–491.

Bourhis, R. Y., Moise, C., Perreault, S., & Senecal, S. (1997). Towards an interactive acculturation model: A social psychological approach. *International Journal of Psychology, 32*, 369–386.

Carvajal, S. C., Photiades, J. R., Evans, R. I., & Nash, S. G. (1997). Relating a social influence model to the role of acculturation in substance use among Latino adolescents. *Journal of Applied Psychology, 27*(18), 1617–1628.

Chataway, C. J., & Berry, J. W. (1989). Acculturation experiences, appraisal, coping and adaptation: A comparison of Hong Kong Chinese, French and English students in Canada. *Canadian Journal of Behavioral Science, 21*, 295–301.

Cooke, D. (2007). Agency and uncertain resettlement: Perspectives of migrants and teachers. *BRCSS New Settler Researchers Network National Conference*. Auckland, New Zealand.

Crockett, L. J. (2002). Agency in the life course: Concepts and processes. In R. A. Dienstbier & L. Crockett (Eds.), *Agency, motivation and the life course* (pp. 1–29). Lincoln: University of Nebraska Press.

Cross, S. (1995). Self-construals, coping, and stress in cross-cultural adaptation. *Journal of Cross-cultural Psychology, 26*, 673–697.

Durie, M. (2005). *Nga tai matatu: Tides of Maori endurance*. Melbourne: Oxford University Press.

Dyal, J. A., Rybensky, L., & Somers, M. (1988). Marital and acculturative strain among Indo-Canadian and Euro-Canadian women. In J. W. Berry & R. Annis (Eds.), *Ethnic psychology: Research and practice with immigrants, refugees, native peoples, ethnic groups, and sojourners* (pp. 80–95). Lisse, Netherlands: Swets & Zeitlinger.

Earley, C., & Ang, S. (2003). *Cultural intelligence: Individual interactions across cultures*. Stanford: Stanford University Press.

Flores, L. J., Ojeda, L., Gee, D., Lee, S., & Huang, Y. P. (2006). The relation of acculturation, problem solving appraisal and career decision-making self-efficacy to Mexican American high school students' educational goals. *Journal of Counseling Psychology, 53*(2), 260–266.

Furnham, A., & Bochner, S. (1986). *Culture shock: Psychological reactions to unfamiliar environments*. London: Methuen.

Gangestad, S., & Snyder, M. (2000). Self-monitoring: Appraisal and reappraisal. *Psychological Bulletin, 126*, 530–555.

Gezentsvey, M.A. (2008). Journeys of ethno-cultural continuity: Comparing the long-term acculturation of Jews with Maori and Chinese. Unpublished Ph.D. thesis, Victoria University of Wellington, New Zealand.

Graves, T. D. (1967). Psychological acculturation in a tri-ethnic community. *Southwestern Journal of Anthropology, 23*, 337–350.

Harrison, J. K., Chadwick, M., & Scales, M. (1996). The relationship between cross-cultural adjustment and the personality variables of self-efficacy and self-monitoring. *International Journal of Intercultural Relations, 20*(2), 167–188.

Holmes, T. H., & Rahe, R. H. (1967). The social readjustment rating scale. *Journal of Psychosomatic Research, 11*, 213–218.

Hooft, E. A. J., Born, M., Taris, T. W., & Flier, H. (2006). The cross-cultural generalizability of the theory of planned behavior: A study on job seeking in the Netherlands. *Journal of Cross-Cultural Psychology, 37*(2), 127–135.

Hung, Y. Y. (1974). Socio-cultural environment and locus of control. *Psychologica Taiwanica, 16*, 187–198.

Jasinskaja-Lahti, I., Liebkind, K., Horenczyk, G., & Schmitz, P. (2003). The interactive nature of acculturation: Perceived discrimination, acculturation attitudes and stress among young ethnic repatriates in Finland, Israel and Germany. *International Journal of Intercultural Relations, 27*, 79–97.

Kobasa, S. (1979). Stressful life events, personality and health: An enquiry into health. *Journal of Personality and Social Psychology, 37*, 1–11.

Kobasa, S. C., Maddi, S. R., & Kahn, S. (1982). Hardiness and health: A prospective study. *Journal of Personality and Social Psychology, 42*(1), 168–177.

Kosic, A., Mannetti, L., & Sam, D. L. (2006). Self-monitoring: A moderating role between acculturation strategies and adaptation of immigrants. *International Journal of Intercultural Relations, 30*, 141–157.

Kuo, W. H., Gray, R., & Lin, N. (1976). Locus of control and symptoms of distress among Chinese-Americans. *International Journal of Social Psychiatry, 22*, 176–187.

Kvernmo, S. (2006). Indigenous peoples. In D. L. Sam & J. W. Berry (Ed.), *The Cambridge handbook of acculturation psychology*. New York: Cambridge University Press.

LaFromboise, T., Coleman, H., & Gerton, J. (1993). Psychological impact of biculturalism: Evidence and theory. *Psychological Bulletin, 114*, 395–412.

Lalonde, R. N., & Cameron, J. E. (1993). An intergroup perspective on immigrant acculturation with a focus on collective strategies. *International Journal of Psychology, 28*(1), 57–74.

Lazarus, R. S., & Folkman, S. (1984). *Stress, coping and appraisal*. New York: Springer.

Leung, C. (2001). The psychological adaptation of overseas and migrant students in Australia. *International Journal of Psychology, 36*(4), 251–259.

Liou, D. (2000). Psychosocial correlates of fat-related dietary behavior in Chinese immigrants by degree of acculturation. *Dissertation Abstracts International: Section B: The Sciences and Engineering, 61*(2-B), 790.

Locke, E. A., & Latham, P. G. (1990). *A theory of goal-setting and task performance*. Englewood Cliffs, NJ: Prentice Hall.

Locke, E. A., & Latham, P. G. (1994). Goal setting theory. In H. F. O'Neil & M. Drillings (Eds.), *Motivation: Theory and research* (pp. 13–29). Hillsdale, NJ: Lawrence Erlbaum Associates.

Lopez, O., Haigh, C., & Burney, S. (2004). Relationship between hardiness and perceived stress in two generations of Latin American migrants. *Australian Psychologist, 39*, 238–242.

Maaka, R., & Fleras, A. (2000). Engaging with indigeneity: Tino rangatiratanga in Aotearoa. In D. Ivison, P. Patton, & W. Sanders (Ed.), *Political theory and the rights of indigenous peoples* (pp. 89–109). Melbourne: Cambridge University Press.

Mak, A. S., & Nesdale, D. (2001). Migrant distress: The role of perceived racial discrimination and coping resources. *Journal of Applied Social Psychology, 31*, 2632–2647.

Mak, W. W. S., Chen, S. X., Wong, E. C., & Zane, N. W. C. (2005). A psychosocial model of stress–distress relationship among Chinese Americans. *Journal of Social and Clinical Psychology, 24*, 422–424.

Marcia, J. (1994). The empirical study of ego identity. In H. Bosma, T. Graafsma, H. Grotevant, & D. de Levita (Eds.), *Identity and development: An interdisciplinary approach* (pp. 67–80). Thousand Oaks, CA: Sage.

Markus, H. R., & Kitayama, S. (2003). Models of agency: Sociocultural diversity in the construction of action. *Nebraska Symposium on Motivation, 49*, 1–57.

Masgoret, A.-M., & Ward, C. (2006). Culture learning approach to acculturation. In D. L. Sam & J. W. Berry (Eds.), *The Cambridge handbook of acculturation psychology* (pp. 58–77). Cambridge: Cambridge University Press.

Merton, R. (1957). *Social theory and social structure*. New York: Free Press.

Moghaddam, F. M., & Perreault, S. (1991). Individual and collective mobility strategies among minority group members. *Journal of Social Psychology, 132*, 343–357.

Moghaddam, F. M., Taylor, D. M., & Lalonde, R. N. (1987). Individualistic and collective integration orientations among Iranians in Canada. *International Journal of Psychology, 22*, 301–313.

Montagliani, A., & Giacalone, R. (1998). Impression management in cross-cultural adaptation. *Journal of Social Psychology, 138*, 598–608.

Moradi, B., & Hasan, N. T. (2004). Arab American persons reported experiences of discrimination and mental health: The mediating role of personal control. *Journal of Counseling Psychology, 51*(4), 418–428.

Moradi, B., & Risco, C. (2006). Perceived discrimination experiences and mental health of Latina/o American persons. *Journal of Counseling Psychology, 53*(4), 411–421.

Navas, M., Garcia, M. C., Sanchez, J., Rojas, A. J., Pumares, P., & Fernandez, J. S. (2005). Relative acculturation extended model (RAEM): New contributions with regard to the study of acculturation. *International Journal of Intercultural Relations, 29*(1), 21–37.

Nesdale, D., & Mak, A. S. (2003). Ethnic identification, self-esteem and immigrant psychological health. *International Journal of Intercultural Relations, 27*, 23–40.

Neto, F. (1995). Predictors of satisfaction with life satisfaction among second generation migrants. *Social Indicators Research, 35*, 93–116.

Phinney, J. S. (2003). Ethnic identity and acculturation. In K. M. Chun, P. Balls Organisa, & G. Marin (Eds.), *Acculturation: Advances in theory, measurement, and applied research* (pp. 63–81). Washington, DC: American Psychological Association.

Phinney, J. S., & Devich-Navarro, M. (1997). Variations in bicultural identification among African American and Mexican American adolescents. *Journal of Research on Adolescence, 7*, 3–32.

Redfield, R., Linton, R., & Herskovits, M. J. (1936). Memorandum for the study of acculturation. *American Anthropologist, 38*, 149–152.

Redmond, M. V. (2000). Cultural distance as a mediating factor between stress and intercultural communication competence. *International Journal of Intercultural Relations, 24*, 151–159.

Rotter, J. B. (1966). Generalized expectancies for internal vs. external control of reinforcement. *Psychological Monographs, 80*. (1, Whole No. 609).

Searle, W., & Ward, C. (1990). The prediction of psychological and sociocultural adjustment during cross-cultural transitions. *International Journal of Intercultural Relations, 14*, 449–464.

Seipel, M. M. O. (1988). Locus of control as related to life experiences of Korean immigrants. *International Journal of Intercultural Relations, 12*, 61–71.

Shaffer, M. A., & Harrison, D. A. (2001). Forgotten partners of international assignments: Development and test of a model of spouse adjustment. *Journal of Applied Psychology, 86*(2), 238–254.

Shanahan, M. J., & Elder, G. H., Jr (2002). History, agency and the life course. In R. A. Dienstbier & L. Crockett (Eds.), *Agency, motivation and the life course* (pp. 145–186). Lincoln: University of Nebraska Press.

Sodowsky, G. R., & Plake, B. S. (1992). A study of acculturation differences among international people and suggestions for sensitivity to within-group differences. *Journal of Counseling and Development, 71*, 53–59.

Speiss, E., & Wittmann, A. (1999). Motivational phases associated with the foreign placement of managerial candidates: An application of the Rubicon model of action phases. *International Journal of Human Resource Management, 10*, 891–905.

Tajfel, H. (1978). *Differentiation between social groups: Studies in the psychology of intergroup relations*. London: Academic Press.

Tajfel, H. (1981). *Human groups and social categories*. Cambridge: Cambridge University Press.

Tartakovsky, E., & Schwartz, S. H. (2001). Motivation for emigration, values, wellbeing and identification among young Russian Jews. *International Journal of Psychology, 36*(2), 88–99.

Taylor, D. M. (1997). The quest for collective identity: The plight of disadvantaged ethnic minorities. *Canadian Psychology, 28*, 174–190.

Templer, K., Tay, C., & Chandrasekar, N. A. (2006). Motivational cultural intelligence, realistic job preview, realistic living conditions preview and cross-cultural adjustment. *Group and Organization Management, 31*(3), 154–171.

Tran, T. V. (1993). Psychological traumas and depression in a sample of Vietnamese people in the United States. *Health and Social Work, 18*(3), 184–194.

Tsang, E. (2001). Adjustment of mainland Chinese academics and students to Singapore. *International Journal of Intercultural Relations, 25*(4), 347–372.

Van Oudenhoven, J. P. (2006). Immigrants. In D. L. Sam & J. W. Berry (Eds.), *The Cambridge handbook of acculturation psychology* (pp. 163–180). New York: Cambridge University Press.

Verkuyten, M. (2005). Ethnic group identification and group evaluation among minority and majority groups: Testing the multiculturalism hypothesis. *Journal of Personality and Social Psychology, 88*(1), 121–138.

Verkuyten, M., & de Wolf, A. (2002). Being, feeling and doing: Discourses and ethnic self-definitions among minority group members. *Culture and Psychology, 8*(4), 271–299.

Ward, C. (1996). Acculturation. In D. Landis & R. Bhagat (Eds.), *Handbook of intercultural training* (2nd ed., pp. 124–147). Thousand Oaks, CA: Sage.

Ward, C. (2001). The ABCs of acculturation. In D. Matsumoto (Ed.), *The handbook of culture and psychology* (pp. 411–445). New York: Oxford University Press.

Ward, C., & Fischer, R. (2008). Personality, cultural intelligence and cross-cultural adaptation: A test of the mediation hypothesis. In S. Ang & L. Van Dyne (Eds.), *Cultural intelligence: Theory measurement and applications*. Armonk, NY: M. E. Sharpe.

Ward, C., & Kennedy, A. (1992). Locus of control, mood disturbance and social difficulty during cross-cultural transitions. *International Journal of Intercultural Relations, 16,* 175–194.

Ward, C., & Kennedy, A. (1993). Where's the culture in cross-cultural transition? Comparative studies of sojourner adjustment. *Journal of Cross-cultural Psychology, 24,* 221–249.

Ward, C., & Kennedy, A. (1999). The measurement of sociocultural adaptation. *International Journal of Intercultural Relation, 56,* 1–19.

Ward, C., & Kennedy, A. (2001). Coping with cross-cultural transition. *Journal of Cross-cultural Psychology, 32,* 636–642.

Ward, C., & Leong, C.-H. (2006). Intercultural relations in plural societies. In D. L. Sam & J. W. Berry (Eds.), *The Cambridge handbook of acculturation psychology* (pp. 484–503). Cambridge: Cambridge University Press.

Ward, C., & Searle, W. (1991). The impact of value discrepancies and cultural identity on psychological and socio-cultural adjustment of sojourners. *International Journal of Intercultural Relations, 15,* 209–225.

Ward, C., Bochner, S., & Furnham, A. (2001). *The psychology of culture shock.* London: Routledge.

Ward, C., Fischer, R., Lam, F. S. Z., & Hall, L. (in press). The convergent, discriminant and incremental validity of scores on a self-report measure of cultural intelligence. *Educational and Psychological Measurement.*

Ward, C., Masgoret, A.-M., & Leong, C. H. (2007). *Primary and secondary coping during cross-cultural transition.* Manuscript submitted for publication.

Yamaguchi, S. (2001). Culture and control orientations. In D. Matsumoto (Ed.), *The handbook of culture and psychology* (pp. 223–244). New York: Oxford University Press.

11

A SITUATED COGNITION PERSPECTIVE ON CULTURE: EFFECTS OF PRIMING CULTURAL SYNDROMES ON COGNITION AND MOTIVATION

DAPHNA OYSERMAN* AND SPIKE W. S. LEE*

*School of Social Work and Department of Psychology, University of Michigan, Ann Arbor, MI, USA

When the term *culture* is used, it refers to something that is both fixed and fluid, both situated and mobile. That is, culture is fixed enough that at least some parts of it are transmitted over generations, but also fluid enough that at least some parts of it are always evolving and changing as features of the environment change; situated enough that we often think of a "culture" as strongly associated with the population in a specific region, but also mobile enough that immigrants can bring their "own culture" to a "different culture." With these caveats, culture can be operationalized as a set of structures and institutions, values, traditions, and ways of engaging with the social and nonsocial world used in a certain time and place and transmitted across generations (e.g., Shweder & LeVine, 1984). Culture can be thought of as a set of societal-level processes (e.g., legal systems, languages, religions) with societal-level outcomes (e.g., suicide rates, divorce rates, fertility rates) (Oyserman & Uskul, 2008). Just as importantly, as cross-cultural psychologists have noted, these societal-level processes can produce average effects at the individual-level. Our current focus is on this latter part, examining culture-relevant *contents*, *procedures*, and *motivations* at the individual-level. Thus, by culture we mean culturally characteristic content (what is relevant, moral, central, of consequence), culturally characteristic ways of thinking and making sense of oneself, others and the world, and culturally characteristic motivations (e.g., to self-enhance or self-improve, to assert confidence and leadership or not to offend). These elements together constitute that which "goes without saying," that which feels transparent, right, and logical in context.

While this feeling of fluency is a telltale marker that culture is at work, it also makes it difficult to systematically model all that "culture" is and reduces social scientists' ability to make predictions about when and how culture matters. To take on this challenge, cultural psychologists have developed a number of potentially useful basic organizing constructs to describe and distinguish cultural "syndromes." These simplifying models are not meant to provide detailed descriptions of any particular culture, but rather to highlight systematic patterns that characterize clusters of cultures. Such models are useful to the extent that they set the stage for specific and testable predictions about culture's consequences.

Proposed cultural syndrome models include contrasts between "individualistic" and "collectivistic" (e.g., Hofstede, 1980), "tight" and "loose" (Triandis, 1995), "horizontal" and "vertical" (Triandis & Gelfand, 1998), "masculine" and "feminine" (Hofstede, 1980), "survival values" and "self-expression values" (Inglehart, 1997), and "honor-modesty" and "shame" (e.g., Gregg, 2005; see also Cohen, 2001) focused cultural syndromes. Each of these models sets up a contrast between prototypes of opposing cultural processes and has provided some predictive insights. Perhaps because it captures salient Western values and has some overlap with the other models, the cultural syndrome model that has received most research attention is individualism and its assumed opposite collectivism (e.g., Triandis, 1995, 2007; Hofstede, 1980, 2001; Kagitçibasi, 1997; Kashima et al., 2001; Oyserman et al., 2002a).

Although the correlational evidence supports the claims made by individualism and collectivism models of culture, without experimental evidence, the process by which culture matters remains hidden. In this chapter, our goal is to illuminate at least part of this hidden process, focusing on *how* individualism and collectivism as cultural syndromes are likely influence how we think – cognitive content, procedures, and motivations. The chapter is divided into three main parts. To set the stage, we first provide a brief summary of the mostly correlational evidence that operationalizing culture in terms of individualism and collectivism captures some important aspects of cross-cultural difference, drawing on the review of Oyserman et al. (2002a). This literature focuses mostly on content differences, with less emphasis on process and motivation. To address gaps in causal reasoning that this correlational evidence cannot address, a situated cognition approach to culture is outlined in the second part, and evidence for this model is presented, drawing on Oyserman and Lee's (2007, 2008) review and meta-analysis of the culture-priming research. The priming literature has focused on both content and process, but has not really examined culturally characteristic motivations. Therefore, in the third part of this chapter, we step beyond integrative summary to ask what a situated cognition approach to culture says about how culture influences cognitive content (what), cognitive process (how), and motivation (for what purpose), drawing on the model presented by Oyserman and Sorensen (in press).

INDIVIDUALISM AND COLLECTIVISM

OPERATIONALIZATION

A main contention of cultural and cross-cultural psychology is that societies differ in individualism and collectivism and that these differences have consequences for what has meaning and value, what is worthy of persistent effort and how we make sense of ourselves and others (e.g., Schwartz, 1994; Inglehart & Oyserman, 2004). While much cultural and cross-cultural psychology has emphasized differences in content of thinking, embedded in this description are differences in both content, and motivation and style of thinking. More broadly, individualism and collectivism can be described as cultural syndromes that place differential emphasis on individuals versus social groups (e.g., Triandis, 1995). Individualism as a cultural syndrome focuses on the individual as the basic unit of analysis; societal structures are valued to the extent that they support individual happiness; from an individualistic perspective, groups serve individuals. Collectivism as a cultural syndrome focuses on the group as the basic unit of analyses; societal structures are valued to the extent that they support preservation and enhancement of group resources; from a collectivistic perspective, individuals serve groups. This initial operationalization suggests differences between collective cultural values of group solidarity, social obligation, connection and integration and individualistic cultural values of individual freedom, personal fulfillment, autonomy and separation – either as directly assessed at the individual-level or as implied by examining themes in cultural products such as advertisements, newspapers, text books, fiction, or proverbs. Thus, operationalizations of individualism and collectivism clearly emphasize content of thinking, but as will be evident in this chapter, cognitive processes and motivations are also implicated in these cultural syndromes.

IMPLICATIONS OF INDIVIDUALISM AND COLLECTIVISM

Content

Rather than assess individualism and collectivism directly, researchers often rely on prior cross-national typologies, especially that of Hofstede (1980). Alternatively, they assess differences in individualism values and/or collectivism values directly in their samples (however, see Oyserman et al., 2002a; Oyserman & Uskul, 2008, for a detailed critique of both of these methods). Willingness to use these methods implies that individualism and collectivism as cultural syndromes are assumed to most directly implicate differences in content – chronically salient values and norms.

As outlined by Oyserman et al. (2002a), in addition to differences in values, other content differences – in relationality, self-concept, well-being, and process differences, in motivational or cognitive style, can also be deduced from how individualism and collectivism have been operationalized. With regard to the impact of cultural syndromes on how relationships are construed, individualism is assumed to scaffold the feeling that relationships are chosen, voluntary and changeable, can be worked on and improved or left when costs outweigh benefits (e.g., Triandis, 1995; Sayle, 1998; Morris & Leung, 2000). Collectivism is assumed to scaffold the feeling that important group memberships are ascribed and fixed "facts of life" to which people must accommodate; both in-groups and boundaries between in- and out-groups are experienced as stable, impermeable, and important.

Cultural syndromes are also assumed to influence how the self is typically construed (e.g., Markus & Kitayama, 1991). Theorists assume that individualism sets up the expectation that a basic self-goal is to feel good about oneself as a unique and distinctive person and to define these unique features in terms of abstract traits. Collectivism, on the other hand, sets up the expectation that a basic self-goal is to attain and maintain group membership, so that the self is defined both in terms of one's social roles (e.g., middle daughter) and group memberships (e.g., Hong Kong Chinese) and the traits and abilities relevant for maintaining these (e.g., loyalty, energetic perseverance).

With regard to well-being, individualism implies that open emotional expression and attainment of one's personal goals are important sources of well-being and life satisfaction (e.g., Diener & Diener, 1995). Collectivism implies that successfully carrying out social roles and obligations and avoiding gaffs or failures in these domains are important sources of well-being and life satisfaction, making emotional restraint important as a way to successfully carry out one's social obligations (Markus & Kitayama, 1991; Kim et al., 1994; Kwan et al., 1997).

Cognitive Processes

With regard to cognitive style or chronically salient cognitive procedures, because the de-contextualized self is assumed to be a stable, causal nexus, individualism implies that focus is generally oriented toward the person rather than the situation or social context (see also Miller, 1984; Newman, 1993; Morris & Peng, 1994; Choi et al., 1999). Thus, individualism promotes a de-contextualized reasoning style that assumes social information is not bound to social context. This has been described as a "separate-and-pull-apart" style as opposed to a situation-specific relational "embed-and-connect" style (Markus & Oyserman, 1989; Oyserman et al., 2002b). In contrast, collectivism as a cultural syndrome generally implies that social context, situational constraints and social roles figure prominently in person perception and causal reasoning (Miller, 1984; Morris & Peng, 1994); that meaning is contextualized and memory is likely to contain richly embedded details.

Motivation

While less prominent in the literature, a number of cross-cultural researchers also emphasized motivation differences. A number of studies have focused on differential salience of self-concept goals (e.g., self-enhancement or self-improvement, Heine, 2005). An emerging focus is on difference in the salience of relationality goals (e.g., modesty or "not offend others," Yamagishi & Suzuki, in press).

EVIDENCE FROM CROSS-CULTURAL RESEARCH

VALUES

Prior research used values as a key to the operationalization of "culture", assuming that individualistic cultural groups should endorse more individualistic values and collectivist cultural groups should endorse more collectivist values. As shown in a recent thorough review and meta-analytic synthesis (Oyserman et al., 2002a), there is consistent evidence for such difference. With regard to cultural differences in chronically accessible basic values, their meta-analysis shows significant differences in endorsement of individualism values (e.g., personal independence and uniqueness) and collectivism values (e.g., group membership and group processes). On average Anglo Americans endorse values of individualism more and values of collectivism less than Africans, Eastern Europeans, Asians, and Asian Americans. Results are integrated and displayed graphically in Figure 11.1.

In addition to this generally confirming picture, Oyserman et al. (2002a) reported some interesting caveats. The meta-analysis suggests that although Anglo Americans and individuals from other English-speaking countries do not differ in individualism and collectivism, they differ from Western Europeans. Anglo Americans are *lower* in collectivism than Western Europeans, with effects similar to those found in comparisons with Asians. However, while differences between Anglo Americans and Asians of Chinese heritage (including Asian Americans) are robust, differences between Anglo Americans and other Asians are often small and sensitive to differences in scale content and reliability. Moreover, Anglo Americans and African Americans do not differ in collectivism and African Americans are higher in individualism, suggesting that African Americans are in some important ways quintessential Americans. These results challenge the notion of a single "Western" culture, the simplistic approach of contrasting "East vs. West," and the assumption that high individualism and low collectivism is part of a Western European tradition brought to America and most accessible to Anglo Americans. Rather there seems to be a uniquely Anglo and American way of being (high individualism and low collectivism) common to Americans whether claiming Anglo-European or African descent. These results

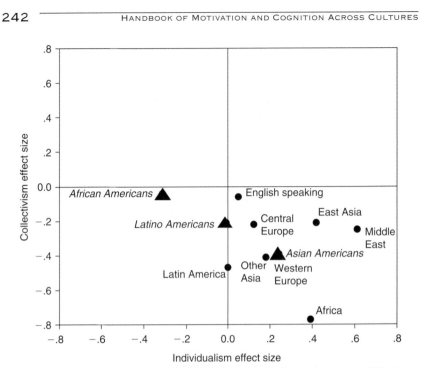

FIGURE 11.1   Are Americans more individualistic and less collectivistic than others? Simultaneous mapping of effects sizes of comparisons between Anglo Americans, African Americans, Latino Americans and other regions of the world on individualism and collectivism. *Source*: Adapted with permission from Oyserman et al. (2002a). Rethinking individualism and collectivism: Evaluation of theoretical assumptions and meta-analyses. *Psychological Bulletin, 128*, 3–73. Copyright 2002 American Psychological Association. Positive effect sizes reflect higher Anglo American individualism and collectivism; negative effect sizes reflect lower Anglo American individualism and collectivism. Circles denote regional international comparisons, triangles denote within US comparisons.

thus suggest a pressing need for a more nuanced approach to understanding how individualism and collectivism matter both within as well as between societies. This need to unpack process raises the next question, which is to what extent differences in values of individualism and collectivism matter for how individuals connect and relate to others, how they make sense of themselves, what constitute their bases of well-being, their motivations and how they process information about the world. Each of these issues is addressed briefly in the next section.

RELATIONALITY

Quality of close relationships (family, intimate relationships), in-group–out-group interactions (social behavior, communication style, conflict resolution style), and groups in work or organizational contexts (working in groups, organizational conflict management) were assessed in 71 studies (Oyserman et al., 2002a). Effects were moderate-to-large in size, though variable. Broadly speaking, these studies suggest that individualism and collectivism as cultural syndromes are associated with differences in relationality and group relations: individualism is associated with ease of interacting with strangers, preference for direct rather than indirect communication style; collectivism is associated with in-group preference in relationships and some forms of face saving.

SELF-CONCEPT

A total of 30 studies assessed self-concept related constructs (self-esteem, self-concept, or personality), and associated these with individualism and/or collectivism. Research typically compared groups within United States or made comparisons between United States and another country group. In these studies, when cross-group differences were found, they were assumed to be due to individualism and collectivism, but individualism and collectivism were not directly assessed. This is clearly a weak inferential basis. However, large effects were found in studies that did assess individualism and/or collectivism and then correlated levels of individualism and collectivism with content of self-concept, especially content describing the self in terms of in-group and collective memberships. Because research in this area is either correlational or lacks direct assessment of individualism and collectivism, it remains open to criticism and awaits a more critical assessment of the claim that individualism and collectivism have a causal influence on content of self-concept.

WELL-BEING

Evidence from 29 studies on well-being and/or emotional expressiveness suggested that Hofstede's (1980) individualism ratings for various countries tend to moderate the correlations between sources of satisfaction and general life satisfaction, with higher correlations in higher individualism countries. However, individualism has an effect primarily in research that does *not* control for country-level differences on other variables (e.g., national wealth, civil rights, social comparison of income). Research controlling for these confounds shows smaller effect sizes attributable to individualism (Arrindell et al., 1997). In terms of emotional expression, effect sizes were generally large and positively associated with individualism. Other emotion-related analyses did not provide enough information to calculate effect sizes.

COGNITIVE PROCESS

While research on content of self-concept and relationality support the notion that individualism and collectivism as cultural syndromes matter in everyday life, potential impact of culture on cognitive process is particularly intriguing (as noted by Nisbett et al., 2001; Norenzayan et al., 2007). In their review, Oyserman et al. (2002a) summarized 40 studies on this topic, with 29 focusing on explanations,

6 on persuasion, and 5 on attributions about obligations. Americans were consistently more likely to focus on dispositions than on situations in providing rationales for behavior or explaining causality than were participants from non-Western countries. Where measured, individualism and collectivism appeared to mediate between-country effects, thus among Americans, individualism correlated with increased use of trait-based inference and decreased use of situation-cued recall (Newman, 1993, Studies 1 and 2; Duff & Newman, 1997, Studies 1 and 2). Where calculable, orthogonal and medium to large effect sizes were found for the influences of individualism and collectivism on social cognition. In the past few years, evidence of cross-national differences between the United States, China (Nisbett, 2003), and Japan (Kitayama et al., 2003) in non-social cognitive processes has emerged as well. This emerging research suggests that Americans are faster and more accurate in recall of abstract and central information, Chinese more accurate with details, background and elements of the whole, Japanese more accurate with proportions between elements (see Norenzayan et al., 2007, for a review).

MOTIVATION

Different cultural groups also appear to differ in chronic motivations. This has been assessed particularly in terms of differential salience of basic self-concept goals and relational goals, comparing the United States and Canada with Japan, Korea, and China (between-countries) and comparing Anglo Americans with Asian Americans (within-U.S., between-ethnicities). Results suggest that self-consistency (being the same in different contexts) and self-enhancement (perceiving the self as positively as one can) are more salient self-motives in North American contexts than in these other contexts but that effects may be due in part to a more salient relational goal of "not offending others" in these contexts. Specifically, compared to European Americans, Koreans are more likely to describe themselves differently in different contexts (Suh, 2002) and mainland Chinese and Asian Americans are less interested in reducing these inconsistencies (Spencer-Rodgers et al., 2004). US and Canadian self-images are systematically biased toward the positive end so that participants from these societies generally view themselves as better than others, but such self-enhancement bias is much weaker among Japanese participants (Heine et al., 1999). This latter effect may be due to a relational motivation – to fit in, be modest (Heine, 2007), or not offend others (Suzuki & Yamagishi, 2004). Thus, US and Japanese respondents equally demonstrate implicit self-regard as revealed by semantic associations between positive evaluative judgment and the self (Kitayama & Uchida, 2003). However, positive self-evaluations are more suspect in Japanese contexts, so that Japanese participants do not explicitly report better-than-average self-ratings unless concern about offending others is overridden by research-induced incentives (e.g., payment for accurate self-estimates, Suzuki & Yamagishi, 2004).

SOCIETIES VARY IN SALIENCE OF INDIVIDUALISM AND COLLECTIVISM IN VARIOUS SITUATIONS

How are these results to be interpreted? One possibility is that cultural syndromes are based in distal cultural features such as philosophy, religion, or language and that these features directly influence values, relationality, self-concept, well-being, cognitive style, and characteristic motivations. While initially plausible and certainly congruent with some approaches to cross-cultural difference (e.g., Nisbett, 2003), a number of studies suggest that distal features do not have a direct effect in and of themselves. Rather, features of the immediate situation are critical in turning on individualistic versus collectivistic cultural syndromes. In other words, empirical findings suggest that culture may be better understood as *situated* cognition.

For example, a number of studies have used language as a proximal cue, with results of these studies suggesting that what language cues is dependent on the meaning of using that language in the particular experimental context. The same language can cue a more collective or a more individualistic response, depending on subjective meaning in context. Thus, two studies conducted in Hong Kong while it was still under British rule demonstrated higher endorsement of Chinese cultural values in Hong Kong Chinese students randomly assigned to fill out the questionnaire in English rather than in Chinese (Yang & Bond, 1980; Bond & Yang, 1982). These studies suggest that feeling forced to use the out-group's language can intensify in-group feelings. Conversely, two studies with immigrants and international students suggest that in contexts in which out-group language is felt to be chosen (rather than forced by colonial power), language used cues congruent cultural syndrome. Thus, when Russian immigrants to the United States are randomly assigned to an all-English response format rather than an all-Russian response format, they are more likely to generate self- rather than other-focused memories (Marian & Kaushanskaya, 2004). Similarly, Chinese students studying in Canada do not differ in their responses to values and self-concept questions from European heritage Canadians when both groups are randomly assigned to respond in English, but do differ when randomly assigned to an all-Chinese response format (Ross et al., 2002).

These results together suggest that cultural syndromes can be situationally primed in the moment, and that what comes to mind in the moment is that working subset of content and process knowledge relevant to the task at hand (see also Oyserman et al., 2002b). Rather than thinking of language or heritage or history as directly determining culturally characteristic content, cognitive, or motivational style, it is more plausible to think of these distal differences as influencing cognitive content, cognitive style and motivation indirectly, through their effect on the social structures and social situations individuals are likely to encounter. Social structures and situations likely in a society cue meaning for individual participants (e.g., "this is about separation, being unique"; "this is about connection, being part of a group").

Because all cultures are rooted in evolutionary and natural selection and have the same adaptive needs, all societies likely provide sufficient experience of both individualism and collectivism to allow either cultural syndrome to be primed when situationally relevant (see Cohen, 2001; Oyserman et al., 2002b). A society that did not have the potential to invoke group loyalty would not be likely to survive as a coherent whole over time, nor would a society that did not provide spaces for individual choice when group needs were met. Given the universality of both a basic sense of bodily and spatial-symbolic separateness (Burris & Rempel, 2004) and a sense of social connectedness and need to belong (Baumeister & Leary, 1995), it seems plausible that human minds are structured to see both separation and connection.

A graphic presentation of a working process model linking distal and proximal features of culture and their effects on psychologically meaningful outcomes – affect, behavior, and cognition – is displayed in Figure 11.2. As can be seen, distal culture is assumed to influence social structures, social situations and the norms and values likely to be internalized. But these are *not* the proximal sources of influence on the subset of values, ways of understanding relationships, making meaning of the self, attitudes, judgments and style of thinking, and motivational goals likely to be on-line at any particular moment. Rather, as will be detailed below, these outcomes are most proximally influenced by how the situation is construed and this construal cues both content and process knowledge.

The notion that societies include both individualism and collectivism cultural syndromes differs from the initial view that societies high in individualism are necessarily low in collectivism and those high in collectivism are necessarily low in individualism. Though conceptualizing societies as including both individualism and collectivism seems novel, quite a few scholars have advanced the idea that individualism and collectivism are not opposing ends of the same unidimensional cultural syndrome (e.g., Kagitçibasi, 1987; Triandis et al., 1988; Bontempo, 1993; Oyserman, 1993; Singelis, 1994; Sinha & Tripathi, 1994; Rhee et al., 1996; Lehman et al., 2004). Each of the previously cited social scientists noted that a unidimensional model simply does not fit the experience of living in a culture. Some suggest that individualism increases while collectivism remains viable in traditional societies that modernize (e.g., Kagitçibasi, 1987). Others suggest that individuals have both collectivist and individualist cognitive "bins" that function separately (e.g., Triandis et al., 1988).

From a situated cognition perspective, all societies incorporate *both* individualism and collectivism so that both individualism and collectivism are enough part of the general cultural socialization process that when cued, each can come to mind. What differs across societies or cultures is the extent that individualism or collectivism is likely to be made accessible or cued by proximal situations. This situated model is a better fit to the evidence than a distal fixed feature model and also allows for the use of experimental methods to gain insight into

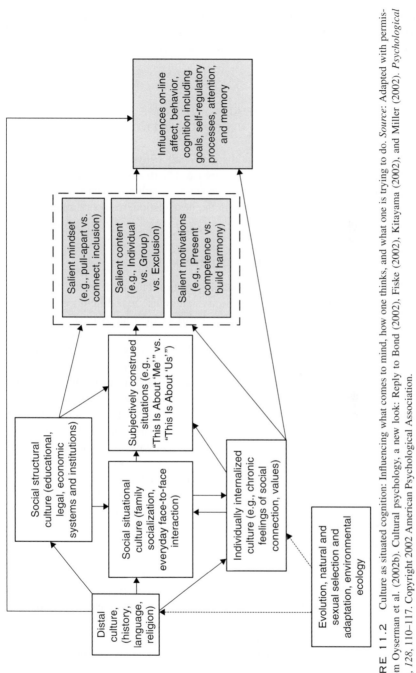

FIGURE 11.2 Culture as situated cognition: Influencing what comes to mind, how one thinks, and what one is trying to do. *Source:* Adapted with permission from Oyserman et al. (2002b). Cultural psychology, a new look: Reply to Bond (2002), Fiske (2002), Kitayama (2002), and Miller (2002). *Psychological Bulletin, 128,* 110–117. Copyright 2002 American Psychological Association.

situations that evoke cultural syndromes as well as the implications of evoking these syndromes. Such experimental evidence has been generated by a good number of studies that primed or made salient individualism and collectivism. We now turn to these studies.

PRIMING CULTURAL SYNDROME: CULTURE AS SITUATED COGNITION

The literature on priming has distinguished between conceptual priming, mindset priming, and goal priming (Bargh & Chartrand, 2000). In this section we first ask why priming is useful in the study of culture. Then we briefly outline each category of priming so that in the next section, results of culture-priming studies can be better understood.

WHY USE PRIMING?

Cross-national comparisons and studies using bilingual or bicultural participants provide a feel of ecological validity – they use real differences in where one lives and the language one speaks, and document an association between these differences and how individuals make sense of themselves and their social worlds and how they think more generally. However, these comparisons make it difficult to answer questions about the psychological mechanisms through which culture exerts its effects. Cross-national comparisons are difficult to interpret when differences are assumed to be due to cultural syndrome without measurement; any and all differences may be attributed to "culture" reducing the term to unwieldy vagueness. The alternative of using of bilingual or bicultural participants is also not satisfying. When comparisons focus on distinct subgroups – those who are bilingual and/or bicultural, they do not allow clear generalization about the fluidity of culture as a situated process; rather, they subtly reinforce the focus on culture as an "in-the-head" within-person variable like other traits or personality factors. Equally importantly, studies with bilingual and bicultural participants are mute as to whether individualism and collectivism are the active ingredients in observed differences and if so, which aspects of individualism and collectivism make a difference.

To answer these situated-process questions, it is necessary to experimentally manipulate the salience of components of individualism and collectivism and to compare effects of bringing active ingredients of these syndromes to mind. Indeed, an emerging body of literature involves the use of experimental techniques based in social cognition research to prime aspects of individualism or collectivism. By studying specifically primed active ingredients of cultural syndrome, the priming method can isolate particular effects on outcome measures of interest.

Generally, priming involves making content, procedures, and/or motivations temporarily accessible. The influence of construct accessibility on social perception is well documented (Higgins et al., 1977; Higgins & Bargh, 1987). Accessibility can be the temporary result of priming (Srull & Wyer, 1979, 1980) or a more chronic result of routine or habitual activation of a construct in one's everyday environment (Bargh, 1984, 2006; Higgins, 1989, 1996). Temporary and chronic accessibility effects on social judgments are comparable in nature and additive in quantity (Bargh et al., 1986; Rudman & Borgida, 1995). Recent priming and chronic activation are both predictive of construct accessibility.

In the laboratory, priming typically involves having participants engage in a series of tasks. Participants are not made aware of the researchers' intent to influence them. Unbeknownst to participants, the semantic content, procedural knowledge and goals cued by the first task (prime) carries or "spills" over to subsequent tasks (outcome measures). This spillover effect can be studied by comparing groups exposed to different first tasks (priming stimuli). By comparing spillover effects to cross-national differences, it is possible to test hypothesized models of cultural influence on content, cognitive process and motivational style.

Priming studies create an experimental analog of chronic differences between cultural groups by temporarily focusing participants' attention on culture-relevant content (declarative knowledge), mindsets (procedural knowledge), and goals. By using a priming technique, culture-relevant values, norms, goals, beliefs, attitudes, cognitive and motivational styles can be cued automatically, simply because they were brought to mind by the previous task and without participants' awareness. Rather than simply compare groups, priming requires an a priori commitment to an active ingredient of individualistic and/or collectivistic cultural syndrome to be cued. By comparing responses to individualism- versus collectivism-primed conditions against hypothesized differences between individualism and collectivism, researchers can examine the extent that hypothesized differences between cultures are actually due to the primed active ingredients of cultural syndrome. Experiments also provide the possibility of studying whether effects associated with one society (e.g., individualism and the United States) can just as well occur in another when primed (e.g., effects of priming individualism in China).

Of course, priming can only make accessible that which is available in mind. Like all priming methods, cultural-syndrome priming tasks can only be effective if semantic content, procedural mindset knowledge and motivations relevant to each construct is available to be primed. One cannot be individualism-primed if one has available in memory only collectivism-relevant semantic and procedural knowledge and goals; similarly one cannot be collectivism-primed if one has available in memory only individualism-relevant semantic and procedural knowledge and goals. Thus, for cultural syndrome priming to be effective, a basic assumption is that across societies and cultures, individuals are capable of thinking about themselves and the world as both separate and independent and as connected and interdependent even if they are typically likely to focus on one or the other and likely to be habitually motivated to self-present or self-efface.

CONCEPTUAL PRIMING

Conceptual priming involves activation of specific mental representations such as traits, values, norms, or goals which then serve as interpretive frames in the processing of subsequent information (Higgins, 1996). Once a concept is primed, other concepts associated with it in memory are activated through spreading activation (Neely, 1977). Following this line of reasoning, average between-society or between racial-ethnic group differences attributed to differences in cultural syndrome may be due to differences in the conceptual networks primed in everyday situations. Objects and practices continually activate corresponding culturally meaningful thoughts. Different cultural syndromes may therefore prime different cognitive contents by creating differing content and associative networks that together influence what we think about ourselves, about others, and about the world.

MINDSET PRIMING

Mindset priming involves activation of a previously stored mental procedure or way of making sense of the world in one context that is carried over into another (Bargh & Chartrand, 2000). For example, when primed to think either about *whether* to engage in a goal or *how* to engage in a goal, participants later use this same thinking style in a second unrelated task (e.g., Gollwitzer et al., 1990). Mindset priming is consistent with the general assumption that processing strategies are situated and tuned to meet current situational requirements (for a review, see Schwarz, 2002, 2006). These processing strategies or procedures can be thought of as part of a procedural toolkit used to structure thinking and reasoning about the world.

MINDSETS AND CULTURE

Markus and Oyserman (1989) proposed that women and individuals from non-Western societies are more likely to view themselves as importantly connected and that, in contrast, men and individuals from Western societies are more likely to view themselves as importantly separate from others. They argued that basic cognitive procedures are associated with these divergent basic self-schemas: connected self-schemas cue a connecting and integrating cognitive style; separated self-schemas cue a separating and distinguishing cognitive style. These arguments were refined by Markus and Kitayama (1991) in their follow-up review in which connected self-schemas were termed interdependent self-construals and separate self-schemas were termed independent self-construals, with the proposal that this difference in self-concept is true of average differences between Eastern and Western self-construals. Cross and Madson (1997) made the same argument for gender (for a different perspective on gender and culture, see Kashima et al., 1995).

Following these initial reviews of the literature, empirical work demonstrating the association of "separate" and "connected" self-schemas with preference for "separating" and "connecting" cognitive processes was carried out by Woike, Lavezzary, and Barksy (Woike, 1994; Woike et al., 2001) and by Hannover, Kühnen, and colleagues (e.g., Kühnen et al., 2001; Kühnen & Oyserman, 2002; Hannover & Kühnen, 2004). Woike and her colleagues follow the terminology of Bakan (1966) and describe connected self-schemas as communion self-concepts and separate self-schemas as agency self-concepts and term the relevant preferred cognitive processes integration and distinction, respectively. The cognitive procedure chronically preferred by those with an agentic self-schema is to distinguish or separate while the cognitive procedure chronically preferred by those with a communal or connected self-schema is to connect and integrate. Hannover, Kühnen, and colleagues (e.g., Kühnen et al., 2001; Kühnen & Oyserman, 2002; Hannover & Kühnen, 2004) describe differences in procedures associated with independent and interdependent self-representations using priming procedures to demonstrate effects on cognitive process.

GOAL PRIMING

Motivations or goals can also be primed. The priming literature has not consistently separated priming of goals or motivation from priming of content. This makes sense because a goal is a representation of a desired end state and in that sense includes content (Bargh, 1990). However, goals can also be thought of as processes, in that strategies and a general array of procedures are necessary to attain the end state represented in a goal (e.g., Gollwitzer & Moskowitz, 1996; Kruglanski, 1996). Thus, goals can be thought of as a mix of content and meta-procedures. Indeed, goals-and-means networks overlap with semantic networks (Bargh & Chartrand, 2000; Förster et al., 2007). Like content and procedures, once stored in memory, goals can be primed without explicit, conscious intention formation (Chartrand & Bargh, 1996). For example, Bargh et al. (1995) and Chen et al. (2001) exposed participants in the lab to words associated with possession of power and found that this manipulation activated specific, individualized goals associated with power which influenced participants' perception and behavior. Priming power made salient sexualized images of women among men chronically likely to sexually harass (Bargh et al., 1995). But priming power made salient social responsibility among individuals high in communal orientation (Chen et al., 2001).

EFFECTS HYPOTHESIZED BY A SITUATED COGNITION MODEL OF CULTURE

The proposed culture-as-situated-cognition model suggests that priming individualism will evoke individualism-relevant content, mindset, and goals in both men and women across diverse societies. Five broad areas of content knowledge are proposed to be cued when individualism, rather than collectivism is primed. Priming individualism will

1. Enhance endorsement of individualistic values and dampen endorsement of relational or collective values.
2. Make unique traits and attribute-based elements of self-concept more accessible and social or relational-based elements of self-concept less accessible.
3. Dampen felt closeness and obligation to in-group others and reduce sensitivity to their needs and goals.
4. Enhance the accessibility of well-being based in happiness, self-fulfillment, and personal success and dampen the accessibility of well-being based in fulfilling social obligations and commitments, providing reflectable glory for in-group members and basking in the reflected glory of other in-group members.
5. Make messages focused on the self, difference, and uniqueness more believable and persuasive than messages focused on the group, similarity and connection.

Effects on cued procedural knowledge are also posited when individualism rather than collectivism is primed. Priming individualism will

1. Enhance the accessibility of pull-apart and separate processing strategies.
2. Dampen accessibility of connect and integrate processing strategies.

Finally, effects on cued motivations are posited when individualism rather than collectivism is primed. Priming individualism will

1. Make certain self-goals (self-enhancement and self-consistency) and relational goals (be competent, be equitable) more salient.
2. Make other self-goals (self-deprecation) and relational goals (don't offend others, maintain harmony) less salient.

META-ANALYSES OF CULTURAL SYNDROME PRIMING LITERATURE

Oyserman and Lee (2008) reviewed the priming literature through January 1, 2005, obtaining 67 studies conducted in three regions (and eight countries) that prime individualism and collectivism cultural syndromes and assessed effects on values, relationality, self-concept, well-being, and cognition. They found a significant and meaningful overall effect of cultural syndrome priming (mean unweighted $d = 0.45$, mean weighted $d = 0.34$, Confidence Interval (CI) $= 0.29/0.39$). This average effect was comparable across the three most common cultural syndrome priming tasks (pronoun circling, Brewer & Gardner, 1996; thinking about similarities/differences with family and friends [SDFF] and Sumerian warrior story, Trafimow et al., 1991) and when the same priming tasks are used, effects are in the same range for both European/European American samples and for Asian (primarily Hong Kong Chinese) samples.

Among these 67 studies, Oyserman and Lee (2008) examined those that reported comparison to control condition to provide an estimate of whether priming moves responses of those primed with individualism, those primed with collectivism, or both groups equally. They found 14 studies that included a comparison with control, reporting small-to-moderate effect sizes in both directions when individualism was compared with control, $d = 0.35$, CI $= 0.23/0.48$; when collectivism was compared with control, $d = 0.34$, CI $= 0.21/0.46$. They also note that in currently used individualism and collectivism primes there seems to be a trade-off in priming effectiveness. Primes that involve relational priming tasks such as SDFF or pronoun circling task, are not as effective in cuing collectivism ($d = 0.23$) as they are in cuing individualism ($d = 0.43$), at least among the samples tested so far. Similarly, priming tasks that include both relational and collective-group collectivism primes (e.g., Trafimow et al.'s Sumerian Warrior task) are not as effective at cuing individualism ($d = 0.25$) as they are at cuing collectivism ($d = 0.48$). Unfortunately, results are sample-dependent and not all primes have been used in every society. However, results are promising as they provide support to the situated cognition model's prediction that both individualism and collectivism can be activated and influence psychological outcomes. Though to be sure, they also call for an expanded set of priming tasks in order to better understand active ingredients of both individualism and collectivism.

In their final set of analyses, Oyserman and Lee (2007b) also examined results from 32 other studies that primed individualism or collectivism (but not both) and compared the primed groups to various control or comparison groups. Taken as a whole these additional studies show effects consistent with those found in the main meta-analysis comparing both individualism and collectivism. This suggests that results are robust to differences in methodology and study quality.

Cultural syndrome primes are diverse in task type, content, and transparency (i.e., the likelihood that what is being primed is plausibly clear to the participant). In combination with the general stability of findings across primes, this diversity is helpful because it constitutes strong evidence that effects are due to an underlying process rather than due to the specifics of a particular prime. The only priming task that produced widely varying results was use of language as a prime (with effects in the hypothesized direction in some studies and effects in the opposite direction in others, overall $d = 0.10$). As noted by recent reviews (e.g., Chiu et al., 2007; Norenzayan et al., 2007; Wang & Ross, 2007), language is related to culture, memory, and cognition. While studies using language are limited to participants who are bi- or multilingual, potential effects of language can be operationalized and studied with other primes, thus disentangling language from other culture-relevant factors. Our interpretation of the near zero average effect of language-priming is that the meaning of language is highly contextualized (see earlier discussion in *Societies Vary in Salience of Individualism and Collectivism in Various Situations* section).

EFFECTS OF PRIMING CULTURAL SYNDROMES ON CULTURE-RELEVANT CONTENT

Effects in the priming literature are consistent with those in the cross-national literature, in the expected direction across outcome domains, with moderate effects on both relationality and cognition, and small effects on values, well-being and self-concept. Effects for values are stronger when known measures of individualism or collectivism are used. With regard to self-concept, effects are stronger when effects on private or collective self-concept are examined; no effect on relational self-concept content was found. Effects are particularly robust for relationality, not only are effects large in size, but they are also internally homogeneous across various priming tasks and outcome measures. This robust finding is important because, along with values, how one relates to others is central to many operationalizations of cultural difference. Therefore the large and homogeneous effect size suggests that priming cultural syndrome systematically shifts which way of engaging others is cued.

EFFECTS OF PRIMING CULTURAL SYNDROMES ON COGNITIVE PROCESS

Each of the priming tasks Oyserman and Lee (2008) describe clearly involves a conceptual prime, that is, the task and task instructions prime words related to individualism and collectivism. These are likely to bring to mind relevant content in the form of values, ways of being a self, ways of engaging with others and ways of making sense of the world. None of the tasks or instructions is explicitly process oriented – participants are *not* told to connect or pull apart, assimilate or contrast. Two key questions then are: Do these tasks nonetheless prime procedural knowledge – separating out and focusing on a main object versus connecting, integrating, and focusing on the whole. And second, does priming procedural knowledge influence *how* (not only *what*) we think, feel and act. Thus when words like *separate, different, dissociate*, or words like *similar, connect, together* are used in instructions or in the task itself, do they prime mindsets rather than simply content knowledge? And if mindsets are primed, is there evidence that they influence cognition, affect and behavior? In the next section, we summarize Oyserman and Lee's (2008) results as relevant to this question.

Of the 28 studies Oyserman and Lee (2008) coded as focused on cognition, about a third focused on cognitive content (attitudes and judgment) and the remaining two thirds focus on cognitive process in social and nonsocial domains. Across each domain, effect size was moderate ($d \geq 0.50$). These results suggest that priming cultural syndrome does prime a style of thinking in both social and non-social domains. These results were not moderated by gender or region. Priming collectivism made it more likely that men and women,

Europeans/European Americans and Asians would use a "connect and relate" mindset; priming individualism made it more likely that men and women, Asians and Europeans would use a "pull-apart and separate" mindset. For example, collectivism priming improves recall for spatial position of a random array of objects and speed of recognition of a big letter made up of little letters (Kühnen & Oyserman, 2002); individualism priming improves accuracy in an embedded figures task (Kühnen et al., 2001).

In addition, a number of studies examine microprocesses within the cultural syndrome priming tasks. Following up on their initial finding that collectivism priming cues assimilation and individualism priming cues contrast, Stapel and Koomen (2001, Study 4) asked why contrast effects were significant only when the contrast favored self-enhancement. They decomposed the effect of their prior priming using first person pronouns and showed that first person pronouns cues self-enhancement among Dutch participants but that separation and distinction can be cued separately from self-enhancement.

EFFECTS OF PRIMING CULTURAL SYNDROMES ON GOALS

While less examined, as demonstrated in the Stapel and Koomen (2001) research summarized above, it seems plausible that priming cultural syndromes should also prime culturally relevant goals and motives. Integrating and synthesizing prior research, it seems reasonable to argue that self-enhancement and self-consistency motives (Swann, 1985; Taylor & Brown, 1988), competence and leadership goals, and relational principles that emphasize individual benefit (e.g., fairness, equality matching) and competition for success (e.g., market pricing; Fiske, 1991) should all be cued at least in some circumstances, by individualism. With the group taking primacy, collectivism should be likely to prime self-effacement and self-improvement motives (Heine, 2003, 2005), harmony-building goals and strategies (e.g., loyalty, modesty, not offending others, protecting face; Yamagishi & Suzuki, in press), as well as relational principles that emphasize collective benefit (e.g., communal sharing; Fiske, 1991). Theorizing along these lines, Oyserman et al. (1998) varied the salience of individualism and collectivism and found that both Jewish and Asian American participants were faster and more confident in choosing to help others at the cost of their own goals across a variety of scenarios when relevant cultural values were primed and endorsed. Specifically, helping in-group others increased when cultural values were primed and collectivism was highly endorsed, whereas helping broader society others increased when cultural values were primed and both collectivism and individualism were highly endorsed. Results suggest that different forms of obligation are salient when one is reminded of one's values and these values reflect individualism, collectivism, or both individualism and collectivism.

These results were conceptually replicated by Gardner et al. (1999, Study 1), who found that compared to those primed with individualism, people primed with collectivism perceive a target person as more obligated to help a close friend. Similarly, Gardner et al. (2004) found that individualism-primed participants were more oriented toward self-goals but collectivism-primed participants were more oriented toward group-goals. The effect of priming was robust across Anglo American and Asian American participants (for similar findings, see Utz, 2004a, b; Wenzel, 2002). Collectivism-primed motivation to support group goals was also found by Gardner et al. (2002),who found that mismatch between *own* and *group's* performance produced opposite effects among individualism-primed, compared with collectivism-primed, participants. Individualism-primed participants reported more positive mood when their own performance was good (and their group's was not good). Collectivism-primed participants reported more positive mood when their group's performance was good (and their own performance was not good).

The effects of priming on group-focused motivation have also been studied with regard to endorsement of social justice relevant attitudes. Kemmelmeier (2003) primed participants with individualism by having them circle singular first-person pronouns (*I, me, my, mine*, Study 1) or read and rephrase a paragraph revolving around the theme of personal freedom (Study 2) and compared results to participants primed with collectivism (Study 1, circling plural first-person pronouns *we, us, our, ours*; Study 2, read and rephrase a paragraph revolving around the theme of family commonality). In both cases, collectivism-primed participants favored affirmative action more than individualism-primed partici-pants and individualism-primed participants favored equal opportunity more than collectivism-primed participants. It is possible to interpret these results in terms of shifting relational goals, with ending in the same place being more important for those primed with collectivism and beginning at the same place being more important for those primed with individualism.

BUT WHICH GOALS ARE PRIMED?

Existing findings seem to support the general contention that cultural syndrome primes activate culturally prescribed goals and accordingly, direct motivated rea-soning and actions: individualism-primed people are more motivated for equality and individual-focused fairness; collectivism-primed people are more motivated for group benefits and helping in-group others in society. Indeed, these findings were described by the original authors in terms of goals or in similar motivational terms. However, aside from the suggestive research summarized above, the priming lit-erature has yet to provide the type of motivation-focused evidence provided in the cross-national literature (e.g., Yamagishi & Suzuki, in press). That is, while cross-national studies such as those summarized below strongly suggest differences in chronic relational motivation, priming studies have yet to demonstrate that these motivations can be turned on and have the same effects across national groups.

In their cross-national studies, Yamagishi and Suzuki (in press) demon-strate that Japan–United States differences in choices and in how modest one is in one's self reports of successes, skills, and abilities can be made to disappear when differences relational motivation is taken into account. First, they provide a conceptual replication of Kim and Markus's (1999) findings. Kim and Markus (1999) showed differences between Asian (Chinese American, Koreans, East Asian Americans) and European American participants in their choice of a common or uncommon pen in an array of pens provided as a gift. While Kim and Markus attribute choice difference to difference in preference for uniqueness, Yamgagishi and Suzuki disagree with their interpretation and argue that the difference in choice was due to difference in relational goals. They argue that Asian participants simply did not want to offend others by making a choice that would inconvenience others (taking an uncommon pen might mean that others would not have access to this choice). They demonstrate that the initial effect remains when Japanese participants are told that they are making the first choice and that others will choose later, but disappears when Japanese participants are told that they are making the last choice and no one will follow. If there is no one to be offended, that is, when they are last, they can and do take the uncommon pen.

Suzuki and Yamagishi (2004) also show that what would otherwise appear to be a goal of modesty also seems to be part of the "not offend others" goal. First, they replicate prior research showing greater modesty in Japanese than American respondents: only a third of Japanese but 70% of Americans estimate that their achievement test performance is better than average. Then they demonstrate that the Japanese but not the Americans shift their responses when told that they will be paid for accurate responses, in which case Japanese are just as self-enhancing as are Americans. Yamagishi and colleagues argue that these results suggest that the chronic "not offend others" motivation is turned off only when it is clear that others will not be offended. Their results mesh well with research by Kitayama (Kitayama & Karasawa, 1997; Kitayama & Uchida, 2003) demonstrating that Japanese do not differ in their implicit self-regard, but rather in their willingness to express positive self-regard openly. When social situations are ambiguous – as they generally are – Japanese are more likely to assume by default the presence of others and are motivated not to offend others by conforming to the majority, sharing and being modest. Conversely, in ambiguous situations, such relational motives are not cued in Americans, allowing free reign for self-enhancement and authority-asserting motivations. These results are highly relevant, but without experimental manipulation, it is impossible to tell if these effects are part of the active ingredients of individualism and collectivism or due to some other differences between Japanese and American societies. As demonstrated in these studies, if culture-congruent self or relational motivation processes are ignored, effects may be misinterpreted.

AN INTEGRATION

We have provided evidence that a situated cognition approach to culture is necessary and that a situated model highlights how culture influences cognitive content (what), cognitive process (how), and motivation (for what purpose). While cross-national comparisons can be high in ecological validity (because they demonstrate real differences between real groups), these studies are limited in other ways. Reliance on survey response leaves open questions about interpretability of comparisons and studies that lack experimental manipulation cannot illuminate the process by which culture matters, leaving as a black box the mechanism through which culture influences individuals. To address these problems, social cognition research provides content, mindset and potentially, goal priming as tools to assess the impact of some key aspects of cultural syndromes.

Oyserman et al.'s (2002a) meta-analyses of cross-national comparisons between Anglo or European Americans and others suggests a moderate sized difference in endorsement of individualism and collectivism values with some caveats. Oyserman and Lee's (2007, 2008) follow-up meta-analyses and review of the cultural syndrome priming literature suggests that expressed endorsement of individualism and collectivism values is sensitive to situational priming, and that across priming tasks, effects are moderate in size when the kinds of value scales used in the cross-national literature are employed. Priming cultural syndrome shifts salience of individualism and collectivism values with about the same magnitude of effect as is found in the cross-national literature. When studies used comparison with control, effects were found for both individualism and collectivism priming.

With regard to effects of cultural syndrome priming on content and process of thinking, we find evidence that priming cultural syndrome influences mindset. Thus, collectivism priming increases likelihood of including rather than excluding information, resulting in assimilating information about another into one's self-rating, while individualism priming increases likelihood of contrasting information about another with one's self-rating – using the other as a standard rather than as part of oneself. Moreover, cultural syndrome priming shifts use of pull-apart versus integrate-and-connect processes even for non-social cognitive tasks. Thus, collectivism priming relative to individualism priming shifts speed of recognition of embedded figures, of letters made up of other letters and speed in the Stroop Task (e.g., Kühnen & Oyserman, 2002; Oyserman et al., 2008). These effects parallel cross-national effects found by Norenzayan et al. (2007), Nisbett (2003), and Kitayama et al. (2003).

Both cross-national and priming literatures suggest moderate-to-large effects of individualism and collectivism on ways of engaging with others. Some of these studies seem to be priming culturally relevant relational goals such as desire for personal achievement, relationship building, and collective success. While the cross-national literature documented apparent goal differences between a good number of countries, the cultural syndrome priming literature on relationality is mostly limited to Western samples. We found only one study assessing effects of cultural syndrome priming on relationality using an Asian

American sample (Gardner et al., 2004), suggesting a need for further research in other regions of the world. That said, the fact that effects of cultural syndrome priming on both individualism-collectivism values and social-relational engagement parallels cross-national differences affords important ecological validity to priming as a way of isolating the active ingredients of cultural syndrome (Oyserman & Sorensen, in press).

Our review supports the cross-cultural psychological contention that culture matters – influencing how the self is defined, how relationships with others are imagined, what is of value and how the mind works – and more importantly, moves beyond this general framework by suggesting that culture matters *because it situates cognition*. Culture makes certain ways of being in the world "go without" saying because they have been brought to mind without conscious awareness. That is, priming culture-relevant content shows a clear impact on accessible cultural knowledge resulting in shifting values, altered self-descriptions, and differences in understanding about one's social obligations and relations with others. These findings suggest that culture is a conceptual prime, activating relevant knowledge. Perhaps more intriguingly, priming influences situated cognitive processes as well. That is, priming different cultural syndromes makes accessible different procedural knowledge. The mindset of individualism is to pull apart and separate, to contrast figure from ground, self from other. The mindset of collectivism is to connect and integrate, to assimilate figure with ground, self with other. These findings suggest that culture is also a procedural prime, activating relevant naïve theories as to how to make meaning.

Evidence thus supports a situated cognition model of culture that is applicable to both "East" and "West." Far from being immutable, cultural differences are malleable in the moment. Because cultural syndrome priming can be understood as setting up a situation that cues isolated active ingredients of culture, the evidence that cultural syndrome priming is effective suggests that in everyday life such malleability is also plausible. Subtle priming evokes subjective construals that afford and elicit culturally meaningful and relevant thoughts, feelings, and behaviors. Thus, despite the phenomenal experience of culture as natural, real, and immutable, cultural meanings and cultural differences are likely to be fluid. Such fluidity is grounded in the notion that culturally situated reasoning is action based, that is, the situation cues what is relevant to making meaning and taking action in the moment (see Smith & Semin, 2004). The finding that cultural syndrome priming influences both content and process is particularly important because procedural knowledge or naïve theories about how to process information and make meaning of meta-cognitive experience matter for the sense we make of ourselves and others, goal-pursuit and inter-group dialogue.

Clearly there is much to be done. Priming research does not yet include regions of the world such as Latin America, Africa, and the Middle East. To understand more about the underlying process, to make predictions with regard to differences in real groups (other than college students) and population, it will be necessary to conduct at least some priming research off college campuses. Good cultural syndrome primes should provide the ability to test effects within and across countries and to test effects with non-college student participants. Use of varied primes is recommended as none alone should be assumed to fully embody the latent construct of "culture" or even its active ingredients. The general argument that cultural syndromes are situated cognition – that cultural syndromes work by cuing cognitive content and cognitive style, which in turn influence what and how we think – is greatly strengthened by robustness of findings across tasks, regions, and outcome variables.

Taken together, evidence suggests that the situated cognition model provides an excellent starting point for future research: Expanding beyond individualism and collectivism is likely to provide new insights by providing additional ways of identifying active ingredients of culture. As we have argued, meanings in situation matter because culture is a form of situated cognition that provides cues as to who one is, what is meaningful and desirable, and how to process information about the world. While not initially salient, research on motivational processes is beginning to emerge. This work promises to better situate what content and processes come to mind when active ingredients of culture are primed. By articulating what turns on culturally characteristic motivations and studying the extent that these motivations map on to individualism and collectivism or other cultural syndrome models, research on the interface between culture and motivational processes provides a new frontier on cultural psychology.

REFERENCES

Arrindell, W. A., Hatzichristou, C., Wensink, J., Rosenberg, E., van Twillert, B., Stedema, J. et al. (1997). Dimensions of national culture as predictors of cross-national differences in subjective well-being. *Personality and Individual Differences, 23*(1), 37–53.

Bakan, D. (1966). *The duality of human existence: An essay on psychology and religion.* Oxford, England: Rand Mcnally.

Bargh, J. A. (1984). Automatic and controlled processing of social information. In R. S. J. Wyer & T. K. Srull (Eds.), *Handbook of social cognition* (pp. 1–41). Hillsdale, NJ: Erlbaum.

Bargh, J. A. (1990). Auto-motives: Preconscious determinants of social interaction. In E. T. Higgins, & R. M. Sorrentino (Eds.), *Handbook of motivation and cognition* (Vol. 2, pp. 93–130). New York: Guilford Press.

Bargh, J. A. (2006). Agenda 2006: What have we been priming all these years? On the development, mechanisms, and ecology of nonconscious social behavior. *European Journal of Social Psychology, 36*(2), 147–168.

Bargh, J. A., & Chartrand, T. L. (2000). In H. T. Reis, & C. M. Judd (Eds.), *The mind in the middle: A practical guide to priming and automaticity research.* New York: Cambridge University Press.

Bargh, J. A., Bond, R. N., Lombardi, W. J., & Tota, M. E. (1986). The additive nature of chronic and temporary sources of construct accessibility. *Journal of Personality and Social Psychology, 50*(5), 869–878.

Bargh, J. A., Raymond, P., Pryor, J. B., & Strack, F. (1995). Attractiveness of the sex association and its consequences for sexual → underling: An automatic power harassment and aggression. *Journal of Personality and Social Psychology, 68*(5), 768–781.

Baumeister, R. F., & Leary, M. R. (1995). The need to belong: Desire for interpersonal attachments as a fundamental human motivation. *Psychological Bulletin*, *117*(3), 497–529.

Bond, M. H., & Yang, K. S. (1982). Ethnic affirmation versus cross-cultural accommodation: The variable impact of questionnaire language on Chinese bilinguals from Hong Kong. *Journal of Cross-Cultural Psychology*, *13*(2), 169–185.

Bontempo, R. (1993). Translation fidelity of psychological scales: An item response theory analysis of an individualism-collectivism scale. *Journal of Cross-Cultural Psychology*, *24*(2), 149–166.

Brewer, M. B., & Gardner, W. (1996). Who is this 'we'? Levels of collective identity and self representations. *Journal of Personality and Social Psychology*, *71*(1), 83–93.

Burris, C. T., & Rempel, J. K. (2004). 'It's the end of the world as we know it': Threat and the spatial-symbolic self. *Journal of Personality and Social Psychology*, *86*(1), 19–42.

Chartrand, T. L., & Bargh, J. A. (1996). Automatic activation of impression formation and memorization goals: Nonconscious goal priming reproduces effects of explicit task instructions. *Journal of Personality and Social Psychology*, *71*(3), 464–478.

Chen, S., Lee-Chai, A. Y., & Bargh, J. A. (2001). Relationship orientation as a moderator of the effects of social power. *Journal of Personality and Social Psychology*, *80*(2), 173–187.

Chiu, C., Leung, A. K., & Kwan, L. (2007). Language, cognition, and culture: Beyond the Whorfian hypothesis. In S. Kitayama & D. Cohen (Eds.), *Handbook of cultural psychology* (pp. 668–689). New York: Guilford Press.

Choi, I., Nisbett, R. E., & Norenzayan, A. (1999). Causal attribution across cultures: Variation and universality. *Psychological Bulletin*, *125*(1), 47–63.

Cohen, D. (2001). Cultural variation: Considerations and implications. *Psychological Bulletin*, *127*(4), 451–471.

Cross, S. E., & Madson, L. (1997). Models of the self: Self-construals and gender. *Psychological Bulletin*, *122*(1), 5–37.

Diener, E., & Diener, M. (1995). Cross-cultural correlates of life satisfaction and self-esteem. *Journal of Personality and Social Psychology*, *68*(4), 653–663.

Duff, K. J., & Newman, L. S. (1997). Individual differences in the spontaneous construal of behavior: Idiocentrism and the automatization of the trait inference process. *Social Cognition*, *15*(3), 217–241.

Fiske, A. P. (1991). *Structures of social life: The four elementary forms of human relations: Communal sharing, authority ranking, equality matching, market pricing.* New York: Free Press.

Förster, J., Liberman, N., & Friedman, R. S. (2007). Seven principles of goal activation: A systematic approach to distinguishing goal priming from priming of non-goal constructs. *Personality and Social Psychology Review*, *11*(3), 211–233.

Galinsky, A. D., Gruenfeld, D. H., & Magee, J. C. (2003). From power to action. *Journal of Personality and Social Psychology*, *85*(3), 453–466.

Gardner, W. L., Gabriel, S., & Lee, A. Y. (1999). 'I' value freedom, but 'we' value relationships: Self-construal priming mirrors cultural differences in judgment. *Psychological Science*, *10*(4), 321–326.

Gardner, W. L., Gabriel, S., & Hochschild, L. (2002). When you and I are 'we,' you are not threatening: The role of self-expansion in social comparison. *Journal of Personality and Social Psychology*, *82*(2), 239–251.

Gardner, W. L., Gabriel, S., & Dean, K. K. (2004). The individual as 'melting pot': The flexibility of bicultural self-construals. *Cahiers de Psychologie Cognitive/Current Psychology of Cognition*, *22*(2), 181–201.

Gollwitzer, P. M., Heckhausen, H., & Steller, B. (1990). Deliberative and implemental mind-sets: Cognitive tuning toward congruous thoughts and information. *Journal of Personality and Social Psychology*, *59*(6), 1119–1127.

Gollwitzer, P. M., & Moskowitz, G. B. (1996). In E. T. Higgins, & A. W. Kruglanski (Eds.), *Goal effects on action and cognition*. New York: Guilford Press.

Gregg, G. S. (2005). *The middle east: A cultural psychology*. New York: Oxford University Press.

Hannover, B., & Kühnen, U. (2004). Culture, context, and cognition: The semantic procedural interface model of the self. *European Review of Social Psychology, 15*, 297–333.

Heine, S. J. (2003). In V. Murphy-Berman, & J. J. Berman (Eds.), *An exploration of cultural variation in self-enhancing and self-improving motivations*. Lincoln, NE: University of Nebraska Press.

Heine, S. J. (2005). In R. M. Sorrentino, D. Cohen, J. M. Olson & M. P. Zanna (Eds.), *Constructing good selves in Japan and North America*. Mahwah, NJ: Lawrence Erlbaum Associates Publishers.

Heine, S. J. (2007). Culture and motivation: What motivates people to act in the ways that they do?. In S. Kitayama & D. Cohen (Eds.), *Handbook of cultural psychology* (pp. 714–733). New York: Guilford Press.

Heine, S. J., Lehman, D. R., Markus, H. R., & Kitayama, S. (1999). Is there a universal need for positive self-regard?. *Psychological Review, 106*(4), 766–794.

Higgins, E. T. (1989). In J. S. Uleman, & J. A. Bargh (Eds.), *Knowledge accessibility and activation: Subjectivity and suffering from unconscious sources*. New York: Guilford Press.

Higgins E. T., & Kruglanski A. W. (Eds.) (1996). *Knowledge activation: Accessibility, applicability, and salience*. New York: Guilford Press.

Higgins, E. T., & Bargh, J. A. (1987). Social cognition and social perception. *Annual Review of Psychology, 38*, 369–425.

Higgins, E. T., Rholes, W. S., & Jones, C. R. (1977). Category accessibility and impression formation. *Journal of Experimental Social Psychology, 13*(2), 141–154.

Hofstede, G. (1980). *Culture's consequences*. Thousand Oaks, CA: Sage.

Hofstede, G. (2001). *Culture's consequences: Comparing values, behaviors, institutions and organizations across nations* (2nd ed.). Thousand Oaks, CA: Sage.

Inglehart, R. F. (1997). *Modernization and postmodernization: Cultural, economic, and political change in 43 societies*. Princeton, NJ: Princeton University Press.

Inglehart, R. F., & Oyserman, D. (2004). Individualism, autonomy, and self-expression: The human development syndrome. In H. Vinken, J. Soeters, & P. Ester (Eds.), *Comparing cultures: Dimensions of culture in a comparative perspective* (pp. 76–96). Leiden, The Netherlands: Brill.

Kagitçibasi, Ç. (1987). *Growth and progress in cross-cultural psychology*. Berwyn, PA: Swets North America.

Kagitçibasi, Ç. (1997). Whither multiculturalism?. *Applied Psychology: An International Review, 46*(1), 44–49.

Kashima, Y., Yamaguchi, S., Kim, U., Choi, S., Gelfand, M. J., & Yuki, M. (1995). Culture, gender, and self: A perspective from individualism-collectivism research. *Journal of Personality and Social Psychology, 69*(5), 925–937.

Kashima, Y., Kashima, E., & Aldridge, J. (2001). In C. Sedikides, & M. B. Brewer (Eds.), *Toward cultural dynamics and self-conceptions*. New York: Psychology Press.

Kemmelmeier, M. (2003). Individualism and attitudes toward affirmative action: Evidence from priming experiments. *Basic and Applied Social Psychology, 25*(2), 111–119.

Kim, H., & Markus, H. R. (1999). Deviance or uniqueness, harmony or conformity? A cultural analysis. *Journal of Personality and Social Psychology, 77*(4), 785–800.

Kim, U., Triandis, H. C., Kâgitçibasi, Ç., Choi, S., & Yoon, G. (1994). *Individualism and collectivism: Theory, method, and applications*. Thousand Oaks, CA: Sage Publications, Inc.

Kitayama, S., & Karasawa, M. (1997). Implicit self-esteem in Japan: Name letters and birthday numbers. *Personality and Social Psychology Bulletin, 23*(7), 736–742.

Kitayama, S., & Uchida, Y. (2003). Explicit self-criticism and implicit self-regard: Evaluating self and friend in two cultures. *Journal of Experimental Social Psychology, 39*(5), 476–482.

Kitayama, S., Duffy, S., Kawamura, T., & Larsen, J. T. (2003). Perceiving an object and its context in different cultures: A cultural look at new look. *Psychological Science, 14*(3), 201–206.

Kruglanski, A. W. (1996). In E. T. Higgins, & A. W. Kruglanski (Eds.), *Motivated social cognition: Principles of the interface*. New York: Guilford Press.

Kühnen, U., & Oyserman, D. (2002). Thinking about the self influences thinking in general: Cognitive consequences of salient self-concept. *Journal of Experimental Social Psychology*, *38*(5), 492–499.

Kühnen, U., Hannover, B., & Schubert, B. (2001). The semantic-procedural interface model of the self: The role of self-knowledge for context-dependent versus context-independent modes of thinking. *Journal of Personality and Social Psychology*, *80*(3), 397–409.

Kwan, V. S. Y., Bond, M. H., & Singelis, T. M. (1997). Pancultural explanations for life satisfaction: Adding relationship harmony to self-esteem. *Journal of Personality and Social Psychology*, *73*(5), 1038–1051.

Lehman, D. R., Chiu, C., & Schaller, M. (2004). Psychology and culture. *Annual Review of Psychology*, *55*, 689–714.

Marian, V., & Kaushanskaya, M. (2004). Self-construal and emotion in bicultural bilinguals. *Journal of Memory and Language*, *51*(2), 190–201.

Markus, H. R., & Kitayama, S. (1991). Culture and the self: Implications for cognition, emotion, and motivation. *Psychological review*, *98*(2), 224–253.

Markus, H. R., & Oyserman, D. (1989). Gender and thought: The role of the self-concept. In M. Crawford & M. Gentry (Eds.), *Gender and thought: Psychological perspectives* (pp. 100–127). New York: Springer-Verlag.

Miller, J. G. (1984). Culture and the development of everyday social explanation. *Journal of Personality and Social Psychology*, *46*(5), 961–978.

Morris, M. W., & Leung, K. (2000). Justice for all? progress in research on cultural variation in the psychology of distributive and procedural justice. *Applied Psychology: An International Review*, *49*(1), 100–132.

Morris, M. W., & Peng, K. (1994). Culture and cause: American and Chinese attributions for social and physical events. *Journal of Personality and Social Psychology*, *67*(6), 949–971.

Neely, J. H. (1977). Semantic priming and retrieval from lexical memory: Roles of inhibition-less spreading activation and limited-capacity attention. *Journal of Experimental Psychology: General*, *106*(3), 226–254.

Newman, L. S. (1993). How individualists interpret behavior: Idiocentrism and spontaneous trait inference. *Social Cognition*, *11*(2), 243–269.

Nisbett, R. E. (2003). *The geography of thought: How Asians and Westerners think differently... and why*. New York: Free Press.

Nisbett, R. E., Peng, K., Choi, I., & Norenzayan, A. (2001). Culture and systems of thought: Holistic versus analytic cognition. *Psychological Review*, *108*(2), 291–310.

Norenzayan, A., Choi, I., & Peng, K. (2007). Perception and cognition. In S. Kitayama & D. Cohen (Eds.), *Handbook of cultural psychology* (pp. 569–594). New York: Guilford Press.

Oyserman, D. (1993). The lens of personhood: Viewing the self and others in a multicultural society. *Journal of Personality and Social Psychology*, *65*(5), 993–1009.

Oyserman, D., & Lee, S. W. S. (2007). Priming "culture": Culture as situated cognition. In S. Kitayama & D. Cohen (Eds.), *Handbook of cultural psychology* (pp. 255–279). New York: Guilford Press.

Oyserman, D., & Lee, S. W. S. (2008). *Does culture influence what and how we think? Effects of priming individualism and collectivism*. Psychological Bulletin, *134*, 311–342.

Oyserman, D., & Uskul, A. K. (2008). Individualism and collectivism: Societal-level processes with implications for individual-level and society-level outcomes. In: F. J. R. Van de Vijver, D. A. van Hemert, Y. H. Poortinga (Eds.), *Individuals and cultures in multilevel analysis* (pp. 145–1730). Mahwah, NJ: Erlbaum.

Oyserman, D., Coon, H. M., & Kemmelmeier, M. (2002a). Rethinking individualism and collectivism: Evaluation of theoretical assumptions and meta-analyses. *Psychological Bulletin*, *128*(1), 3–72.

Oyserman, D., Kemmelmeier, M., & Coon, H. M. (2002b). Cultural psychology, a new look: Reply to bond (2002), Fiske (2002), Kitayama (2002), and Miller (2002). *Psychological Bulletin*, *128*(1), 110–117.

Oyserman, D., Sakamoto, I., & Lauffer, A. (1998). Cultural accommodation: Hybridity and the framing of social obligation. *Journal of Personality and Social Psychology, 74*(6), 1606–1618.

Oyserman, D. & Sorensen, N. (in press). Understanding cultural syndrome effects on what and how we think: A situated cognition model. To appear in C-y Chiu, R. Wyer, & Y-y Hong (Eds). *Problems and solutions in cross-cultural theory, research and application.* NY: Psychology Press.

Oyserman, D., Sorensen, N., Reber, R., Sannum, P. & Chen, S. X. (2008). Connecting and separating: A situated cognition model to understand effects of priming individualism and collectivism on processing of visual and auditory information. Under editorial review. University of Michigan, Ann Arbor.

Rhee, E., Uleman, J. S., & Lee, H. K. (1996). Variations in collectivism and individualism by ingroup and culture: Confirmatory factor analysis. *Journal of Personality and Social Psychology, 71*(5), 1037–1054.

Ross, M., Xun, W. Q. E., & Wilson, A. E. (2002). Language and the bicultural self. *Personality and Social Psychology Bulletin, 28*(8), 1040–1050.

Rudman, L. A., & Borgida, E. (1995). The afterglow of construct accessibility: The behavioral consequences of priming men to view women as sexual objects. *Journal of Experimental Social Psychology, 31*(6), 493–517.

Sayle, M. (1998). The social contradictions of Japanese capitalism. *Atlantic Monthly, 281,* 84–94.

Schwartz, S. H. (1994). In Kim U., Triandis H. C., Kâgitçibasi Ç, Choi S. and Yoon G. (Eds.), *Beyond individualism/collectivism: New cultural dimensions of values.* Thousand Oaks, CA: Sage Publications, Inc.

Schwarz, N. (2002). In L. F. Barrett, & P. Salovey (Eds.), *Situated cognition and the wisdom in feelings: Cognitive tuning.* New York: Guilford Press.

Schwarz, N. (2006). Attitude research: Between ockham's razor and the fundamental attribution error. *Journal of Consumer Research, 33*(1), 19–21.

Shweder, R. A., LeVine, R. A. (Eds.) (1984). *Culture theory: Essays on mind, self, and emotion.* New York: Cambridge University Press.

Singelis, T. M. (1994). The measurement of independent and interdependent self-construals. *Personality and Social Psychology Bulletin, 20*(5), 580–591.

Sinha, D., & Tripathi, R. C. (1994). In U. Kim, H. C. Triandis, Ç. Kâgitçibasi, S. Choi, & G. Yoon (Eds.), *Individualism in a collectivist culture: A case of coexistence of opposites.* Thousand Oaks, CA: Sage Publications, Inc.

Smith, E. R., & Semin, G. R. (2004). In M. P. Zanna (Ed.), *Socially situated cognition: Cognition in its social context.* San Diego, CA: Elsevier Academic Press.

Spencer-Rodgers, J., Peng, K., Wang, L., & Hou, Y. (2004). Dialectical self-esteem and east-west differences in psychological well-being. *Personality and Social Psychology Bulletin, 30*(11), 1416–1432.

Srull, T. K., & Wyer, R. S. (1979). The role of category accessibility in the interpretation of information about persons: Some determinants and implications. *Journal of Personality and Social Psychology, 37*(10), 1660–1672.

Srull, T. K., & Wyer, R. S. (1980). Category accessibility and social perception: Some implications for the study of person memory and interpersonal judgments. *Journal of Personality and Social Psychology, 38*(6), 841–856.

Stapel, D. A., & Koomen, N. (2001). I, we, and the effects of others on one: How self-construal level moderates social comparison effects. *Journal of Personality and Social Psychology, 80,* 766–781.

Suh, E. M. (2002). Culture, identity consistency, and subjective well-being. *Journal of Personality and Social Psychology, 83*(6), 1378–1391.

Suzuki, N., & Yamagishi, T. (2004). An experimental study of self-effacement and self-enhancement among the Japanese. *Japanese Journal of Social Psychology, 20*(1), 17–25.

Swann, W. B. J. (1985). The self as architect of social reality. In B. Schlenker (Ed.), *The self and social life* (pp. 100–125). New York: McGraw-Hill.

Taylor, S. E., & Brown, J. D. (1988). Illusion and well-being: A social psychological perspective on mental health. *Psychological Bulletin, 103*(2), 193–210.

Trafimow, D., Triandis, H. C., & Goto, S. G. (1991). Some tests of the distinction between the private self and the collective self. *Journal of Personality and Social Psychology*, *60*(5), 649–655.

Triandis, H. C. (1995). *Individualism and collectivism*. Boulder, CO: Westview Press.

Triandis, H. C. (2007). Culture and psychology: A history of the study of their relationship. In S. Kitayama & D. Cohen (Eds.), *Handbook of cultural psychology* (pp. 59–76). New York: Guilford Press.

Triandis, H. C., Bontempo, R., Villareal, M. J., Asai, M., & Lucca, N. (1988). Individualism and collectivism: Cross-cultural perspectives on self-ingroup relationships. *Journal of Personality and Social Psychology*, *54*(2), 323–338.

Triandis, H. C., & Gelfand, M. J. (1998). Converging measurement of horizontal and vertical individualism and collectivism. *Journal of Personality and Social Psychology*, *74*(1), 118–128.

Utz, S. (2004a). Self-activation is a two-edged sword: The effects of I primes on cooperation. *Journal of Experimental Social Psychology*, *40*(6), 769–776.

Utz, S. (2004b). Self-construal and cooperation: Is the interdependent self more cooperative than the independent self?. *Self and Identity*, *3*(3), 177–190.

Wang, Q., & Ross, M. (2007). Culture and memory. In S. Kitayama & D. Cohen (Eds.), *Handbook of cultural psychology* (pp. 645–667). New York: Guilford Press.

Wenzel, M. (2002). What is social about justice? Inclusive identity and group values as the basis of the justice motive. *Journal of Experimental Social Psychology*, *38*(3), 205–218.

Woike, B. A. (1994). The use of differentiation and integration processes: Empirical studies of 'separate' and 'connected' ways of thinking. *Journal of Personality and Social Psychology*, *67*(1), 142–150.

Woike, B., Lavezzary, E., & Barsky, J. (2001). The influence of implicit motives on memory processes. *Journal of Personality and Social Psychology*, *81*(5), 935–945.

Yamagishi, T., & Suzuki, N. (in press). An institutional approach to culture. In M. Schaller, S. J. Heine, A. Norenzayan, T. Yamagishi, & T. Kameda (Eds.), *Evolution, culture, and the human mind*. Mahwah, NJ: Erlbaum.

Yang, K. S., & Bond, M. H. (1980). Ethnic affirmation by Chinese bilinguals. *Journal of Cross-Cultural Psychology*, *11*(4), 411–425.

12

THE FUNDAMENTAL TOOLS, AND POSSIBLY UNIVERSALS, OF HUMAN SOCIAL COGNITION

BERTRAM F. MALLE

Department of Psychology, University of Oregon, Eugene, USA

Social cognition is the capacity to perceive and interpret the behavior of social agents. It has a bright side, which includes the ability to understand others' intentional actions, infer their mental states, and share experiences; and it has a dark side, which includes misunderstanding, stereotypes, and prejudice. A large portion of social-psychological research over the past 20 years has focused on this dark side; undoubtedly, it has a pressing impact on human social behavior. However, of equal importance is the study of those fundamental capacities that can bridge the gap between two minds and enable social communities to flourish through joint action, close relationships, and an intelligible social structure. This brighter side of social cognition has received increasing attention in recent years and is the focus of this chapter.

Early writers on social perception (e.g., Cantril, 1947; Asch, 1952; Heider, 1958; Tagiuri & Petrullo, 1958; Ostrom, 1984) emphasized the unique features of *persons* that make them objects of social cognition: that they have motives, thoughts, and feelings; that they have a capacity to act intentionally; and that they perceive the perceiver back, so that humans engage in a process of mutual or reciprocal cognition (Hastorf et al., 1970; Fiske & Taylor, 1991).

This mutual recognition of humans as mental, intentional beings lies at the very core of social cognition (Wellman, 1990; Perner, 1991; Mitchell, 1997; Malle & Hodges, 2005).

In response to the variety of tasks and demands in social life, humans have evolved a suite of interrelated subsystems that together form what may be called the social-cognitive toolbox (Ames, 2004; Cloutier et al., 2005; Malle, 2005; Mitchell, 2006). This toolbox contains abstract concepts (e.g., *agency* and *intentionality*); processes of gaze following, automatic empathy, mimicry, and joint attention; and increasingly complex functions of imaginative simulation and mental state inference. These tools belong together not because they form a module or are implemented in the same brain areas; what unites them is their responsiveness to the social environment with its challenges of ambulant intentional agents – minded, intelligent, and unique individuals.

In what follows I will discuss extant knowledge on each social-cognitive tool and ask whether there are compelling data for or against universality of that tool. However, systematic data on this question are scarce and answers must remain tentative, so I will encourage research more often than review it and rely more on theoretical arguments than empirical demonstrations. However, making theory the starting point of future cross-cultural research may be a valuable complement to the more common documentation of broad cultural group differences.

THE SOCIAL-COGNITIVE TOOLBOX

CONCEPTUAL FRAMEWORK

Humans perceive people, and interactions among them, through a framework that conceptualizes behavior as fundamentally linked with mental states. This framework, variously called *common-sense psychology, folk psychology,* or *theory of mind* consists of two parts: (1) systems that filter, group, and integrate certain stimulus inputs into such concepts or categories as *agent, intention, belief,* and *reason* (D'Andrade, 1987; Leslie, 1995; Malle & Knobe, 1997; Kashima et al., 1998; Malle, 2004); and (2) assumptions about these categories and their relationships (Fodor, 1983; Morton, 1996). For example, coordinated movements of agents are classified into the category *intentional action* (Wellman & Phillips, 2001; Woodward et al., 2001), and the concept of intentional action relies on the interplay of multiple mental state categories, including *belief* and *desire* (Malle & Knobe, 1997).

The system of folk concepts begins to develop early in childhood, aided by an either innate or very early-developing sensitivity to certain stimulus configurations in streams of behavior (Baird & Baldwin, 2001). Between the second and seventh year of life, this sensitivity grows into a network of sophisticated conceptual assumptions about mind and action (Wellman, 1990; Woodward et al., 2001; Gergely & Csibra, 2003).

Even though this framework is typically labeled a "theory" (as in *theory of mind*; Premack & Woodruff, 1978; Wellman, 1990; Flavell, 1999), there is some debate over exactly what this theory encompasses (e.g., inferences, experience-based simulations) and whether it is a *theory* in the first place. I suggest that *theory of mind*, or its cognate terms, refer to a conceptual framework and be kept separate from the variety of debated psychological processes, such as action parsing, simulation, and inference, that operate within this framework (Malle, 2004, 2005). The entire package of a conceptual framework and the suite of psychological processes then make up the larger phenomenon of human social cognition.

The central categories of the folk theory of mind are arguably *agent, intentionality*, and *mind*, and they are closely related to one another (Smedslund, 1997). Agents are entities that can act intentionally, intentional actions require a particular involvement of the mind, and only agents have minds. At first glance seeming circular, this web of concepts is anchored by specific perceptual-cognitive processes. For example, objects perceived as self-propelled and behaving contingently are classified into the category *agent* (Premack, 1990; Johnson, 2000). Having identified an agent, the human perceiver is sensitive to face, gaze, and motion patterns that reveal whether the agent's behavior is *intentional* (Dittrich & Lea, 1994; Phillips et al., 2002), and further analyses of behavior and context lead to inferences of specific goals, beliefs, and emotions. Agents are also assumed to be rational, acting in efficient ways to achieve their goals (Heider, 1958; Malle, 1999; Gergely & Csibra, 2003). Specifically, agents integrate beliefs and desires to form an intention to act, and those beliefs and desires are seen as the agent's *reasons* (Davidson, 1963). When explaining intentional behaviors, people indeed offer what they infer to be the agent's reasons (Malle, 1999, 2004). According to the folk-conceptual framework, only intentional actions emerge from this structure of reason-based causality, whereas unintentional behaviors are produced "mechanically," through an interplay of numerous causes inside and outside the person (Heider, 1958; Searle, 1983; Mele, 1992; Malle, 1999).

The intentionality concept represents the hub of the folk-conceptual framework because it separates the entire realm of behavior into intentional and unintentional events, for perceptual and cognitive purposes just as much as for evaluative purposes, most notably in the judgments of praise, blame, and moral as well as legal culpability (Shaver, 1985; Weiner, 1995; Malle & Nelson, 2003; Malle, 2006). Developmental change in the folk-conceptual framework also occurs primarily as a differentiation of the intentionality concept. Infants recognize intentionality first as a behavioral category of object-directedness (Wellman & Phillips, 2001; Gergely & Csibra, 2003), and only in subsequent years does the concept becomes richly mentalistic (Malle & Knobe, 1997). The first mental concept appears to be desire, followed by belief (Wellman & Woolley, 1990). Then intentions are differentiated from desires (Astington, 2001; Baird & Moses, 2001; Schult, 2002), a distinction that becomes quite fine-grained among adults (Malle & Knobe, 2001). At least by late adolescence, we also see skill and awareness of fulfilling one's intention as additional requirements of full-fledged intentional actions (Malle & Knobe, 1997).

Questions of Universality

Some research suggests East–West differences in how much perceived agency is ascribed to groups and individuals (Menon et al., 1999; Kashima et al., 2005), but such studies presuppose existence of a similar concept of intentional agency while delineating possible differences in thresholds of its application (see also Oerter et al., 1996; Edge & Suryani, 2002). Other authors have claimed to observe different "agency conceptions" in Eastern and Western cultures (e.g., Hernandez & Iyengar, 2001), but the evidence speaks only to variation in what motivates people from different cultures to act (e.g., personal effort versus collective endeavors).

In favor of universality, many linguists count the concepts of *agent* and *intentionality* as fundamental to the way humans see the world, and linguistic forms of these concepts have been found across all known languages (Givón, 1975; Bybee, 1994; Wierzbicka, 1996). Developmental evidence similarly finds the concept of intentional agent across all studied cultures (Wellman & Miller, 2006). A few studies have even explored cultural stability of intentionality judgments and their conceptual underpinnings (see Malle & Knobe, 1997), and so far we see striking convergence between Western and Eastern cultures/languages, even across diverse age groups (Zaw, 2006; Ohtsubo, 2007).

Constituents of the intentionality concept (belief, desire, intention, control/skill, and awareness) appear to be themselves good candidates for universality. Wierzbicka (1996) indeed lists all of them, except intention, among the cross-linguistically derived universal conceptual primitives. Bybee (1994) complements this analysis with a convincing case for the universality of the intention concept. One specific concept, that of (false) belief, shows a reliable trajectory of development in 3- to 5-year-old children across many cultures and languages (Wellman et al., 2001). There was an initial indication of slightly different onset times of false-belief development across, for example, African Baka, Peruvian Indian, and US children. But a more recent study suggests that even onset times may be strikingly similar when children from different cultures (Canada, India, Peru, Samoa, and Thailand) complete exactly the same false-belief test (Callaghan et al., 2005). Similarly, Sabbagh et al. (2006) found that a variety of theory of mind tasks as well as executive function showed virtually identical onset and age development in Chinese and US preschool children, though the Chinese children showed significantly higher levels of executive function.

Among other specific mental state concepts, emotions have most extensively been studied as candidates for universality. The evidence on universal recognition of a core set of facially expressed emotions is good (Ekman, 1973; Brown, 1991). Many emotion concepts also appear to be perceived and experienced quite similarly on such dimensions as valence, expectedness, attention direction, and goal-obstructiveness (Wallbott & Scherer, 1988; Mauro et al., 1992). However, linguistic labels (e.g., *joy, fear, anger, disgust, sadness* in English) do not cut experience at exactly the same boundaries across diverse languages. Instead, the universal ingredient in emotions may be such conceptual primitives as intention, belief, and desire (Wierzbicka, 1996). The adaptive value of emotion expressions

TABLE 12.1   Layers of Concepts and Processes in Social Cognition

Conceptual framework
— Agent, intentionality, desire, belief, intention, and so on
Foundational processes
— Identifying agents
— Face processing
— Gaze following
— Parsing behavior streams
— Mimicry and imitation
— Automatic empathy
— Recognizing goals
— Joint attention
Mediating processes
— Self-other discrepancies
— Inhibitory control
— Self-awareness
— Simulating other minds
Explicit mental state inference
Inference of stable attributes

and concepts arguably lies in its communicative functions: to provide the interaction partner with information about mental states that disambiguate an interpersonal situation (Fridlund, 1994; Chovil, 1997).

FOUNDATIONAL PROCESSES

A conceptual framework could not by itself meet the fundamental challenges of social cognition; it only categorizes stimuli but does not interpret them. Moreover, concepts are too abstract to provide any explanation, prediction, or guide for a response. Knowing that there is an agent who performs some action with some desire is better than seeing only blobs of different wavelengths, but the perceiver must infer what specific action was performed (e.g., stretching out hand) with what specific motive (e.g., greeting).

The human mind recruits many psychological processes that rely on and interact with the conceptual framework of mind and behavior. Table 12.1 lists processes that have been identified in the literature so far, ranging from relatively basic person and behavior processing to simulation and explicit inferences of mental states and stable attributes. I begin the discussion with the most elementary processes that are presumably available soon after birth.

Identifying Agents

For adults, the concept of *agent* is defined by the capacity to act intentionally whereas for infants it begins as a broad distinction that emerges out of a responsiveness to diagnostic features – including having a face, moving in a self-propelled manner, "rationally" bringing about outcomes, and responding contingently to the infant's own behavior (Premack, 1990; Bertenthal, 1993; Johnson et al., 1998; Király et al., 2003). Within a few weeks after birth, infants respond favorably to contingently interacting persons but retreat from noninteracting persons (Watson, 1985; Legerstee et al., 1987), and 3-month-old babies discriminate between light point arrays that move randomly and those that are attached to a moving body (Bertenthal, 1993). In adults, there is also suggestive evidence for a region of the visual cortex that responds selectively to images of the human body (Downing et al., 2001). During the first year of life, infants refine their discrimination of self-propelled objects by paying attention to the ensemble of faces, body parts, and articulated motion (Markson & Spelke, 2006). Contingent interaction (the other acts in response to one's own actions) becomes the central feature for identifying agents (Johnson, 2000), reflecting perhaps the parallel between infants' own discovery of intentional action control and their recognition of such control in others (Russell, 1996; Hauf & Prinz, 2005).

Questions of Universality

Currently, no cross-cultural data directly speak to the psychological processes of agency detection. However, the very early-developing responsiveness to particular features (self-propelledness, contingent interaction) and the fact that those features are arguably diagnostic of actual agentic behavior make substantial cultural variation unlikely. Culture can certainly constrain or expand whether particular unobservable entities fall under the agent concept broadly speaking – such as gods, ghosts, and forces of nature – but the feature-sensitive processes of agency detection apply to observable entities only, and for those, universality can be assumed until contradictory data emerge.

Face and Gaze Processing

One of the critical features of agents is that they have faces – or so the human brain expects. The human sensitivity to faces has been well documented, from the behavioral to the cognitive to the neural level (Kanwisher, 2000). Sensitivity to faces may be a prerequisite for the newborn's ability to imitate adult facial behaviors (Meltzoff & Moore, 1977) and to affectively engage with them in mutual smiling. It also allows for the later-developing tendency of emotional contagion (Hatfield et al., 1994), for automatic extraction of categorical information such as sex (Cloutier et al., 2005), and for efficient memory of one's preferred social partners. The sensitivity to eyes is especially notable, as the remarkable speed at which faces are recognized is lost when eyes are removed (Rousselet et al., 2004).

But we must distinguish between the processing of two aspects of faces: the structural and the dynamic (Posamentier & Abdi, 2003). Structural processing can be easily done with static faces and allows for fast (100–200 ms) identity recognition, relying considerably on the target's eyes (Mason et al., 2004). Dynamic processing responds to change of gaze or of facial expressions that indicate the target's altered emotional state. Here too, they eyes play a central role (Bassilli, 1978; Buchan et al., 2007). The distinction between structural and dynamic face processing is also borne out by data at the neural level. Structural features are heavily computed in the fusiform face area (FFA), and a lesion to this area is associated with impaired recognition of facial identity (Damasio et al., 1982). Eye direction and especially gaze change are heavily computed in a posterior part of the superior temporal sulcus (STS), as both patient studies and single-cell recordings in monkeys indicate (Campbell et al., 1990). On the whole, however, the processing of face and gaze are distributed over a number of brain regions that typically serve other functions as well. In particular, the more dynamic the stimulus processing, the less evidence we find for dedicated modules that are anatomical correlates of function (Farah & Aguirre, 1999). Whereas the FFA is a circumscribed region sensitive to static face perception, the STS also processes language stimuli and is involved in general visual attention. Moreover, other brain areas besides the STS process gaze as well. For example, the amygdala is activated by moving eyes, and amygdala lesions impair gaze perception (Young et al., 1995; Kawashima et al., 1999).

Gaze Following

When people follow another person's gaze, they recognize or extrapolate direction and target of the person's looking behavior. Gaze following plays important roles in goal inference, joint attention, and social coordination (Frischen et al., 2007), but it typically operates quite reflexively. Adults automatically orient toward the target of a facing partner's gaze even if there is an incentive to look in the opposite direction (Driver et al., 1999). Gaze following is also present in other animals, such as dogs (Hare & Tomasello, 1999), and chimpanzees can compute the object of a target's gaze even when that object is not directly visible to them. For example, they look around a barrier to locate the apparent target of the other's gaze (Brauer et al., 2005).

Gaze following by itself does not constitute a mental state inference, as following another person's line of sight is a process distinct from constructing the person's actual mental perspective. We know this because visual perspective taking, but not mere gaze following, allows the perceiver to quickly determine whether an object is to the right or to the left of a target person (Michelon & Zacks, 2006). Gaze following is essentially an eye-behavior monitoring and prediction process, and many other, more mind-sensitive processes have to fall into place before such monitoring delivers mental state inferences. If the perceiver does try to infer mental states, gaze information is readily used (Castiello, 2003).

Questions of Universality

The low-level basis of face processing, its availability in neonates, and the absence of any known cultural variation in this sensitivity suggests a universal capacity. Similarly, gaze following is partially reflexive and evolutionarily old, making it a strong candidate for universality as well. The biological function of an agent's gaze obviously lies in orientation and regulation of locomotive and manipulative behavior in a three-dimensional world. As observers, many organisms take gaze as reliable predictor of action, but humans build on their expanded conceptual capacities to interpret gaze as a signal of mental states as well (e.g., interest, distraction, discomfort) even in the absence of any anticipated action. Humans' universal experience of the link between their own gaze and such basic states as attention and intention may facilitate such finer interpretation, but culture also assigns differential meaning to some of these signals, such as looking down as boredom or bashfulness.

Parsing Behavior Streams

One of the most basic (but certainly not easiest) tasks for humans is to properly parse the continuous stream of behavior observed in other people (Baird & Baldwin, 2001). Even though behavior is varied, unpredictable, and interactive, there are plenty of regularities in its production that allow humans to segment the behavior stream into meaningful units. Indeed, by 11 months, babies form clear expectations about the boundaries between action units (Baldwin et al., 2001). But what are those units? An ideal system would parse the perceived stream into the very units that underlie the production of the observed behavior in the first place (Prinz, 1990; Wilson, 2001). From what we know about action control, intentions play a fundamental role in structuring behavior production (Wolpert et al., 2003). And intentions indeed serve as a fundamental unit of behavior perception. This match between production and perception can be found at a very basic level, in what has been termed the "mirror neuron system." Rizzolatti et al. (1996) discovered that single neurons in the macaque monkey's brain fire selectively both when the monkey performs a certain action and when it observes that same action being performed by another agent. Among humans, that same matching capacity is implemented in a far more distributed manner, and neuroimaging studies have found extended brain areas that are highly active both in the production and the perception of certain actions (e.g., Decety, 2002; Decety & Grèzes, 2006). With a link between produced and perceived actions, finding the units in the behavior stream becomes easier through practice of performing certain behaviors, and even 3-month olds appear to benefit from such practice transfer (Sommerville et al., 2005).

Sensitivity to intention-based units in the behavior stream does not entail a full understanding of intentionality. It does, however, present an opportunity – through much repetition – for becoming familiar with prototypical characteristics of intentional action. These features include smooth movement execution, a clear beginning and end, as well as appropriate body, head, and face orientations. Armed with this sensitivity for detecting intentional action, children develop a strong preference for imitating those actions (Carpenter et al., 1998) and a tendency to learn words that refer to intentional, not accidental behaviors (Tomasello & Barton, 1994).

Universality

The process of behavior parsing appears to be neurally quite basic and a requirement for simple forms of imitation found in other animals (Byrne, 2006). Cultures may single out certain actions to be significant that are therefore parsed more efficiently by members of that culture. However, nothing in the process itself is open to cultural modulation because cultural influences presuppose the very mechanism of parsing (no social learning and communication would be possible without it).

Imitation and Mimicry

Humans are the only species in which members instruct each other by demonstrating a novel behavior and inviting the other to perform it in turn. Complementarily, humans are exceptional observational learners, capable of picking up even complex sequences of action after observing them performed only once. This capacity to learn by imitation has great advantages for the helpless human infant who is born with a third of the adult's brain size and has very few functions hardwired from the start. Imitation is also rewarding because it aligns oneself with valued others in reciprocal interaction and imitative play, amply illustrated by the smile game or that of ceaselessly rolling a ball back and forth (Nadel-Brulfert & Baudonnière, 1982).

Where do those more intentional and sophisticated forms of imitation and instruction come from? In part they build on a simpler copying mechanism called mimicry, which is evolutionary much older (e.g., found in monkeys, birds, even octopi). Reviews by Hatfield et al. (1994) and Chartrand and Bargh (1999) document that social mimicking of gestures, postures, and mannerisms often occurs automatically, without the interactants' awareness or intention. However, in humans this rather automatic type of imitation has important social functions: it both expresses feelings of social affiliation and can increase affiliation and rapport among mimicking partners (Bernieri, 1988; Chartrand & Bargh, 1999). One way to explain mimicry is with the "mirror system" mentioned above, which transforms perceptions of the other's behavior into corresponding motor patterns. These patterns have to be preexisting and are primed by their perceptual representations. When these primed patterns are actually executed, we have a case of mimicry (Byrne, 2006). Surprisingly, however, contagious yawning – what one would consider a prototype of automatic mimicking – does not selectively involve activation of the mirror neuron system (Schürmann et al., 2005). We may have to distinguish between two kinds of mimicry. A low-level one relies on reflexive stimulus-response connections and explains phenomena such as contagious yawning and the coordination of flocks of birds. A higher-level one involves action parsing and processing with a sensitivity to context and function (Chartrand & Bargh, 1999). The significant step from such higher-level mimicry to full-blown imitation is the role of novelty: apparently only humans can imitate and teach truly novel behaviors – for which no preexisting neural program exists (Byrne, 2004).

Universality

All the current evidence points to mimicry and imitation to exist and function universally across cultures. Forms of imitation have been demonstrated in newborns (Meltzoff & Moore, 1977), and mimicry at various levels of sophistication exist in many other species. Just like behavior parsing, imitation, and social teaching are prerequisites for human culture itself, ranging from manufacturing tools to establishing social norms to the acquisition of language (e.g., Gergely & Csibra, 2004; Norenzayan et al., 2006).

Automatic Empathy

Mimicry is a tool of behavior matching. Closely related is a mechanism of matching mental states, which has been called *automatic empathy* or *emotional contagion* (Hatfield et al., 1994; Hodges & Wegner, 1997; Levenson & Ruef, 1997; Stueber, 2006). It involves a target person having a feeling F, expressing that feeling in characteristic ways, and the perceiver feeling $\approx F$ as a result. Simple forms of such contagion have been observed in nonhuman primates (Preston & de Waal, 2002), in 3-month-old infants (Haviland & Lelwica, 1987), and even in 34-hour-old newborns who are more likely to cry when other newborns cry (Simner, 1971). How does it work? A plausible model suggests that the perceiver observes the target's expressive behaviors, something akin to a mirror system activates (but does not execute) the perceiver's own copy of those behaviors, and feelings associated with this behavior program are activated in the perceiver as well (Hatfield et al., 1994). Thus, mimicry may be at the heart of the loop, but both the target's behavior and the mimicker's behavior must be reliably associated with certain emotions, and those are then synchronized (Bavelas et al., 1987).

Automatic empathy would in principle allow perceivers to read off the other person's emotions from their own emotions. However, perceivers typically do not appreciate that their own emotions may originate in the other's emotions. As a result, emotional contagion can increase rapport in some cases (La France, 1982) but escalate conflict or instigate crowd violence in others (Levenson & Gottman, 1983; Patten & Arboleda-Flórez, 2004). A skillful social agent could therefore manipulate another person who is in the perceiver role and experiences emotional empathy, just like good actors can cause us to clench our fists, shed tears, and suffer complex emotions (Coplan, 2006).

Universality

The capacity to "catch" another person's emotion is a convincing candidate for universality, especially considering that Levenson and Ruef (1997) identified varieties of contagion that reach deep into the autonomous nervous system and even into the hormonal system. Kokkinaki (2003) provided cross-cultural evidence (though limited to Crete and Scotland) for a reliable interplay between imitation and emotions, involving contagion as well as more systematic affect attunement, and Hatfield et al. (1994) identified cross-cultural evidence for contagion in Malaysia, Africa, and the Yakut territory in northern Asia. Because emotional contagion requires a reliable link between the target's emotional state and the manifested expressive behavior and another reliable link between the perceiver's mimicking behavior and this person's emotional state, there is some room for cultural variation. For one thing, automatic empathy may be less pronounced in cultures that have tighter display rules. For another, expressive behaviors may not be exactly the same from culture to culture, so even if a perceiver mimics the other's expressions, he or she may not have an associative link from those expressions to the *same* emotion that generated the target's expressions in the first place. Even though such a situation would involve behavioral mimicking, the perceiver does not catch the other person's actual emotion.

Recognizing Goals and Intentions

When parsing the stream of behavior into meaningful units, humans do not attend to behavior by itself but to another person's acting upon the world. This process requires an understanding of self-propelled agents being *directed to* objects in the world (Wellman & Phillips, 2001). Directedness reveals itself in simple cues (head turn, gaze orientation) and predicts characteristic actions (e.g., grasp, show) as well as emotions (e.g., satisfaction of reaching the goal). In this way, infants who are 6- to 12-months old begin to appreciate that behaviors can be directed at something (Woodward, 1998; Gergely & Csibra, 2003), and this is their first concept of intentional action. The direction is typically toward a physical object, and the actions toward it are basic, such as grasping, placing, or moving (Woodward et al., 2001). Such behaviors trigger the infant's notion of goal-directedness most reliably when performed by a human arm and hand, not by a mechanical device (Woodward, 1998). However, even a gloved hand is interpreted as acting in a goal-directed manner if the hand has been previously associated with the whole person (Guajardo & Woodward, 2004). This pattern illustrates quite powerfully the relationships among conceptual components of the human theory of mind (here, between *agent* and *action*).

Intentions as Action Contents

It is one thing to recognize an action as intentional; it takes additional processing to recognize the content of the action – *what* the person is trying to do. Adults, who have accumulated experience with many actions, show a remarkable capacity to recognize both intention and details of the planning process revealed in the kinematics of human behavior (Runeson & Frykholm, 1983). For example, if a target person knows from previous lifts how heavy a given object is and prepares to lift that object again, perceivers can judge the object's weight merely from the (point-light) outlines of the target's body as it prepares the movement. Remarkably, if the target intends to pretend lifting a heavy object that is actually quite light, people recognize the deceptive intention as well as the object's true weight. Inferring intentions from minimal behavioral clues is well illustrated by athletes who are sensitive to the other person's tiniest indication of what they are trying to do – defensive players in football trying to read the offensive players' intentions from looks or body twitches or soccer keepers trying to kill a penalty kick.

The origins of this remarkable capacity can be seen in the 9- to 12-month old's understanding of simple goal-directed actions such as grasping or handing something over. However, these actions are transparent – they form a perceivable unit with their observable goal. Other behaviors, such as pulling a rectangular object out of one's pocket and putting green paper on the counter, require considerable world knowledge to understand. This world knowledge grows rapidly during the second year of life, and it allows children to infer an agent's intention even if the corresponding goal object is not visible. In a study by Meltzoff (1995), 18-month olds who watched an adult try but fail to perform certain acts on an unfamiliar object imitated what they saw the actor do but also continued on with actions that the adult had never performed but apparently had intended to perform. Thus, children were able to infer the actor's goal or intention from the behavior. This, however, occurred only when the failed attempts were performed by an agent, not when the "other" was a mechanical device (Meltzoff, 1995). In the same vein, Russell and Danish (2007) found that children imitate an incomplete action (and achieve completion) only when the action was performed by a human hand, not when it was performed by an arrow.

In each of these studies, children may infer the actor's intentions without necessarily conceptualizing them as genuinely mental states. However, they do go beyond the observable behavior as they infer a complex goal object – an action sequence or an action outcome – that is itself not observable. Perhaps the child's own experiences of attention, planning, and voluntary action control, as they get increasingly sophisticated, provide the template for eventually inferring a *mental* state (Russell, 1996; Rochat, 2002).

Universality

The world knowledge involved in goal and intention inference brings culture strongly into play. Cultures provide and demand practice of certain scripts and schemas that are immediately understandable for members of the given culture but mysterious to those outside. Just consider the variation across cultures and languages in the bodily signals that represent "yes," "no," or certain insults. Despite this variability of specific scripts, the general capacity to infer goals and intentions does not appear to be culturally variable. No cross-cultural data speak to 18- to 24-month-old children performing the abovementioned goal and inference tasks. However, evidence on older children shows no relevant cultural variation. Tardif and Wellman (2000) replicated in Chinese children the pattern found in American children (Bartsch & Wellman, 1995) that the onset of using desire verbs (during the third year) precedes the onset of using belief verbs (during the fourth year). Likewise, using experimental theory of mind tasks, Wellman et al. (2006) showed that both mainland Chinese and American children ages 3 to 5 understood concepts of desire before they understood concepts of belief. Simpson (2003) compared European American and Mexican American children 4- to 9-years old and found no differences in their use of desires to explain behavior. Finally, Barrett et al. (2005) showed that German adults and 4- to 5-year-old children as well as Shuar adults from Amazonian Ecuador performed similarly in using abstract motion cues to correctly to infer such intentions as chasing, fighting, courting, and playing.

Joint Attention

Humans enter situations of joint attention when both participants attend to an object and are also aware of each other's attending to that object. This is a deeply social process because the two individuals form a higher unit, a "we," that delivers affective, cognitive, and behavioral benefits. Like no other animal, people seek out and enjoy sharing thoughts, emotions, attitudes, perceptions, and knowledge (Higgins & Pittman, in press). Having the same thought or emotion is deeply rewarding, validating, and bonding. Human language is the best vehicle to achieve such acts of sharing, as in disclosure, gossip, and story telling. Communication itself is an act of sharing as well: Speakers establish a common ground of what is mutually known, what each speaker's symbols refer to, and what the overarching purpose of the communicative exchange is (Clark, 1996). And language acquisition already depends on the capacity to share attention to objects, because learning the name of an object requires that the new speaker and the established speaker both know to what object a linguistic term refers (Baldwin, 1995).

Joint attention develops in the 9- to 18-month-old child, originating from two important patterns. The first pattern is the child's affective tuning to the adult's attitude toward objects (Hobson, 2005). For example, when the child registers the adult's directedness to an object, the child tends to take on the adult's attitude toward that object, exhibiting emotional contagion. The second pattern is the adult's inclination to attend to whatever the *child* happens to be attending to at the moment, thereby facilitating alignment between attention foci (Franco, 2005). For example, the child grasps a ball, and the adult comments: "Yeah, look at the ball."

Together, these two tendencies cover a large number of situations: when the child already attends to an object, adults align their attention with the child's; when the child is not yet attending to something, the adult's expression of interest can draw the child into aligned attention to a particular object. During the second year of life, the child begins to point to objects that are out of reach, thus inviting the rewarding state of joint attention and attitude sharing. The child also checks the adult's attention before pointing, showing clear signs of appreciation for the fact that people can attend to different things. Children also look to the other's facial and bodily cues to determine the appropriate attitude toward an object or action (what is called *social referencing*), and they use attentional cues to determine toward *which object* the other is showing a certain attitude (Repacholi, 1998; Moses et al., 2001).

The affective alignment we see in the earliest forms of joint attention continues far into adulthood in the process of social convergence, famously demonstrated in Sherif's (1935) autokinetic studies. There, people jointly perceived an ambiguous stimulus – the apparent movement of a light dot in a pitch-dark room – and spontaneously arrived at a consensual judgment (the width of the movement) within just a few trials of the experiment. Their convergence manifested not only cognitively but in an affective alignment as well. They jointly agreed on what was "right," and they defended that stance in subsequent rounds of making judgments in the presence of other people. Thus, adult norm formation may derive from the fundamental human tendency to align one's attitudes with those of others.

Universality

Current knowledge of joint attention nurtures confidence in the assumption of its universality. The joint attention capacity appears to be a necessary or at least highly facilitative ingredient in language learning (Tomasello & Farrar, 1986; Baldwin, 1995), and if it is compromised, as in autistic children, linguistic and social behaviors are severely compromised as well (Mundy, 1995). The universal adaptive value of joint attention for social living is also compelling in light of its connection to norm formation and moral judgment, two universals in their own right. So until we discover new data, joint attention should be considered a fundamental human (perhaps primate) process of social and cognitive relatedness without which neither language nor culture could exist.

MEDIATING PROCESSES: EN ROUTE TO MENTAL STATE INFERENCES

Out of all the discussed foundational concepts and processes, humans weave an explicit understanding of mental states that enables them to read emotions, desires, and interests, detect deceiving intentions, and actively take even a stranger's perspective. One of the greatest puzzles for social-cognitive science is to delineate exactly how humans develop, at both the process and conceptual level, from sensitive *behavior* readers to perceivers of the *mind*, forming explicit and verbalizable representations of the large variety of human mental states (Coricelli, 2005). The puzzle has not yet been solved, but existing evidence allows us to identify three contributors that will have to be part of the final analysis: the experience of discrepancies between self and other; the capacity for inhibitory control; and the maturing of self-awareness. Finally, the process of *simulating* other minds encompasses all three of these capacities (as well as earlier ones) and is perhaps the central bridging mechanism between foundational processes and full-blown mental state inferences.

Self-Other Discrepancies

By the beginning of the second year, toddlers move independently and begin to experience conflict between their own desires of touching, moving, and swallowing objects and caretakers' desires (Biringen et al., 1995). The child learns, sometimes through clashes of will, that people differ in interest and desire, and these experiences of mismatch may well force the development of concepts that distinguish different mental states in different people. In one study (Repacholi & Gopnik, 1997), 18-month olds understood that an adult apparently disliked (showed a disgust face toward) an object that the child liked (goldfish cracker), and they understood that the adult liked (showed a happy face toward) an object that the child disliked (raw broccoli). When the adult said, "Give me some," the 18-month-old children handed the adult the object that *the adult* liked (raw broccoli), whereas a comparison group of 14-month olds handed the adult the object that they *themselves* liked.

Considerable evidence shows that the desire concept is the first mental concept that children master reliably (Wellman, 1990; Perner, 1991), and mental state verbs of desire indeed appear in children's speech just around 18 months (Bartsch & Wellman, 1995). Increasingly during the preschool years, children use mental state talk to negotiate conflict (Howe et al., 1998), and it might be in part these conflicts – with parents, siblings, and peers – that demand the understanding of others' mental states. Indirect evidence also comes from studies in which the presence of siblings predicts accelerated theory of mind development (Lewis et al., 1996; Peterson, 2001). Even though these studies typically measure theory of mind as false-belief understanding, the importance of conflict remains, because explicitly recognizing another people's distinct beliefs represents the experience of epistemic conflict.

The experience and regulation of conflicts may thus help shift the early tendency toward self-other convergence (e.g., in emotional contagion) to a more flexible process in which the child's own internal state may be a starting point, but differences between self and other are simulated and predicted as well (Gordon, 1992; Goldman, 2006). Of course, the self-other distinction is not perfect: the stronger the child's own desire, for example, the less likely the other person's distinct desire will be appreciated (Moore et al., 1995). The same holds in adults, for whom the salience and intensity of an internal state can distort, slow, or prevent inferences about the other person's internal state (e.g., Malle & Pearce, 2001; Van Boven & Loewenstein, 2003; Barr & Keysar, 2005; Birch, 2005). Thus, it takes a corrective mechanism to bring the other person's mind into the foreground; and that mechanism is inhibitory control.

Inhibitory Control

The child's experience of conflicting desires (and later beliefs) challenges, I argued, the earlier processes of self-other attunement and matching (e.g., in imitation and joint attention). That earlier stage is characterized by a "like-me" assumption (Meltzoff & Brooks, 2001), a form of naïve realism in which the child's own emotional, motivational, and epistemic states are assumed to be shared by others. To break up this equation and appreciate conflicting states the child must inhibit its own mental state just enough to recognize the alternative – somebody wanting, liking, feeling, or thinking something else. The facilitative role of inhibitory control in developing theory of mind performance is well documented, though primarily for the classic false-belief test (Leslie & Polizzi, 1998; Carlson et al., 2002; Lang & Perner, 2002). Already earlier, from about 16 months on, inhibitory control may enable children's capacity for pretense (Bosco et al., 2006), which can be considered an inhibition of a default interpretation (e.g., of actions and objects) in favor of new interpretation, while keeping both interpretations to some extent active. Also, inhibitory control supports emotion regulation, such as suppressing a momentary urge to receive a larger reward later on (Metcalfe & Mischel, 1999), and it is needed for deception (Hughes, 1998) and irony (Lucariello & Mindolovich, 1995). Not surprisingly, then, inhibitory control skills correlate with mental state inference skills even in adulthood (Chasiotis & Kiessling, 2004). Inhibition strengthens both the emergence of explicit mental state inferences in the child and the instigation of such inferences in the adult (Epley et al., 2004).

Self-Awareness

A third process that supports the emergence of mental state inferences is the child's increasingly sophisticated self-awareness. For if the mind can discriminate among its own states (which are computationally and experientially easily accessible) it can also learn to discriminate those of others. Inhibitory control is already a type of self-awareness in that it operates on an intention (later on other representations) and is thus a mental state regulating another mental state.

The more general capacity for self-awareness is often indexed by the mirror self-recognition test (Gallup, 1970). Children pass the test if, while watching their mirror image, they detect and remove a color dot from their face that the experimenter had unobtrusively placed there. This bodily self-recognition emerges at around 14 months (Brooks-Gunn & Lewis, 1984), and with it comes a more reliable discrimination between one's own and other people's behaviors. Synchronous imitation of another person's behavior, for example, emerges only among children who pass the self-recognition test (Asendorpf et al., 1996). Visual self-recognition also predicts the child's joint attention at 18 months (Nichols et al., 2005), which itself predicts later social-cognitive functioning (Charman et al., 2001). However, 2-year-old children with autism pass the self-recognition test but fail most joint attention tests (Mundy, 1995), so joint attention capacities rely on more than self-recognition.

Simulating Other Minds

According to the well-known simulation theory of human mentalizing, social perceivers use their own faculties of perceiving, feeling, and thinking "off-line" to interpret other people's perceptions, feelings, and thoughts. They pretend, as it were, to be in the target's particular situation and recruit their own situation-appropriate mental states to attribute to the other person (Gordon, 1992). However, many phenomena have been related to or subsumed under the term *simulation* (Goldman, 2006). In the simplest case, a perceiver's motor system *mirrors* another person's action but does not perform the relevant action (Wilson, 2001); rather, the goal state that normally goes along with that type of action is activated and the perceiver understands the target person's action in terms of that goal state. A related second phenomenon is *projection* (Ross et al., 1977; Ames, 2004). The social perceiver assumes that "other = like me" and therefore ascribes his or her own (simulated or experienced) mental states to the other person (Meltzoff & Brooks, 2001). When failing to take into account the other's distinctness, perceivers who merely project display a naïve realism (Ross & Ward, 1996) or egocentrism (Barr & Keysar, 2005). The third variant of simulation is the sophisticated attempt to *construct a model* of the other person's situation and of his or her most likely mental states from all available data: observed actions, empathic responses, general knowledge, inference, and so on. Perceivers may still assume some degree of similarity with the target person but patch mere projection and actively try to identify the target's mental states that differ from their own (Gordon, 1992; Epley et al., 2004).

Even though many precursors to mentalizing, such as motor mirroring, automatic empathy, and imitation, have been adduced as evidence for the fundamental nature of simulation (e.g., Gallese & Goldman, 1998; Goldman, 2006), I consider it most prudent to use the term *simulation* only for the process of more or less explicitly constructing a model of the other person's mental states. Some of the precursors share with this more sophisticated simulation process the involvement of the perceiver's *own* internal states – action programs, associated goals, contagious emotions, and the like. But as the earlier discussion showed, the precursors that somehow involve "the self" are manifestly distinct, and subsuming, say, motor mimicry, projection, and model construction under one broad notion of simulation is not fruitful. A more specific conception of simulation also connects well to simulation processes that have been described in the decision-making literature, in which the agent simulates possible future states and makes a decision according to the value of those simulated outcomes (Klein & Crandall, 1995). The specific conception of simulation also goes beyond the classically warring factions of simulation theory. When constructing another person's mental states, the perceiver makes use of all available knowledge, rules, theories, and his or her own mental states, real or imagined (Nichols & Stich, 2003). Simulation is thus one important process in the social-cognitive toolbox – alongside knowledge retrieval, inference, and even some foundational processes that may resemble modular systems.

Universality

Of the mediating mechanisms that facilitate the young human's transition from intelligent behavior reading to genuine mind reading, all are good candidates for universality, though, as usual, the evidence is scarce. Self-other discrepancies, defined as clashes between two people's goals (or preferences or attitudes) are bound to exist across all cultures, even though there will be variations in the specific goals over which, say, parents and children most readily collide. The culturally preferred resolution of such discrepancies may vary as well, with possible consequences for the speed with which children appreciate the distinctness of mental states. Inhibitory control has been identified cross-culturally both in studies of individual differences (Rothbart et al., 2001) and as a predictor of theory of mind development (Chasiotis et al., 2006). Self-awareness as a principled capacity is unlikely to vary cross-culturally (in fact, it has been shown in other primates and in dolphins), but culturally variable parenting styles appear to influence the time of onset for self-recognition and self-regulation (Keller et al., 2004). Simulation, finally, is hardly in question as a universal human capacity (Goldman, 2006), though the frequency and value of simulating other minds and possible worlds may well vary across cultures.

EXPLICIT MENTAL STATE INFERENCES

Perhaps the hallmark of the social-cognitive toolbox is the capacity to make explicit mental state inferences. This tool allows the social perceiver to consciously represent the other person's mental state as a distinct fact of the world – but one that has a unique point of view and a subjective experiential quality. Sometimes called perspective taking, this capacity yields an understanding of the multiplicity of visual, affective, and interpretive views vis-à-vis the same reality. Typically developing children ad adults not only appreciate the variability of desires, beliefs, intentions, and emotions but are also motivated to find out what specific mental state another person might have.

The famous indicator for whether a child has mastered explicit perspective taking is the false-belief test. In a classic paradigm (Wimmer & Perner, 1983), the child participant and one other person see the experimenter hide an object in container 1, next to an empty container 2. The other person than leaves the scene and the experimenter switches, in the child's plain view, the object from container 1 to container 2. The other person returns and the child is asked where the other person will look for the object (or, more difficult, where the other person thinks the object is). The correct answer is of course "In container 1," but the child's own knowledge of reality is a powerful default response (Birch, 2005; Nickerson, 1999). Most children master this difficult inference at age 4, though some changes in the task or question formulation can lower this threshold (e.g., Siegal & Beattie, 1991; Freeman, & Lacohée, 1995). By contrast, genuinely mentalistic desire inferences emerge 1–2 years earlier.

The greater difficulty of belief over desire inferences can be seen in adults as well. When people explain intentional actions, they primarily use *reasons*, which are typically the beliefs and desires the agent had when deciding to act (Malle, 1999). However, when we compare people's explanations for their own actions (the "actor" perspective) and their explanations for other people's actions (the "observer" perspective), we reliably find that actors use more belief reasons, and fewer desire reasons, than observers do (Malle et al., 2007). Moreover, intimate observers use more belief reasons than stranger observers do (Malle et al., 2007). In recent research we also found that when people watch short video clips of agents performing a variety of everyday actions, they more readily infer the agents' goals (desires) than their beliefs, and they are also faster in making these goal inferences (Holbrook, 2006).

Research on perspective taking in adults has shown that efforts to understand the other person's mental states lead to a number of positive outcomes, such as greater perceived similarity with the person, reduced stereotyping, greater sympathy, forgiveness, and helping, though it can also lead to personal distress (for a review, see Davis, 2005). Accuracy of explicit mental state inferences has been described as moderate, though only one paradigm has been used so far to provide such accuracy estimates (Ickes, 1993). Very little research has been devoted to the actual psychological processes underlying explicit mental state inferences – either the integration of conceptual connections, simulations, and knowledge retrieval, or the relationship between more implicit, lower-level tools (e.g., emotional empathy, joint attention) and the explicit form of mental state inferences. The dearth of work on these issues is a result of the emphasis in developmental research on the performance of such inferences (and the methodological limitations to studying processes in children) and the emphasis in social-psychological research on people's inferences of personality traits. This type of inference is discussed below.

Universality

The cross-cultural evidence speaks strongly for the existence of false-belief inferences and their developmental order as succeeding desire inferences. Both analyses of speech patterns (Tardif & Wellman, 2000) and numerous experiments support the existence and natural order of desire and belief inferences (Wellman et al., 2001; Callaghan et al., 2005; Wellman et al., 2006). More generally, however, cultures may vary in the effort and readiness with which their members explicitly infer other people's mental states (Lillard, 1998; Wu & Keysar, 2007). Unfortunately, the patterns of results are by no means clear (and sometimes contradictory), as cultural differences can occur at many different levels. It may be more or less appropriate to publicly utter mental state ascriptions; it may be more or less difficult to gather behavior cues as indicators of mental states (e.g., because of display rules); and there may be more or less impact of status, power, and practice in performing certain inferences. For example, in hierarchical societies, those lower in power are likely to exert more effort and gain more practice in making such inferences. Despite the interesting dynamics revealed by such differences, the universality of mental state inferences in general should not be in question.

INFERENCES OF STABLE ATTRIBUTES

Human social perceivers ascribe not only momentary mental states to others; they also infer abstract and stable attributes, including status, personality traits, attitudes, and abilities. Social-psychological research has uncovered a considerable amount of knowledge on the inference of attitudes and personality traits, and many reviews of this research are available (Gilbert & Malone, 1995; Uleman et al., in press). Here I will briefly relate these stable attribute inferences to mental state inferences.

Function

Whereas the primary function of the social-cognitive tools described above is to make sense of immediate events (such as actions and mental states), the primary function of attribute inferences is to accumulate more general information about the *person*. This information is useful for predicting future behavior tendencies, so attribute inferences will be frequent when encountering strangers – in a job interview, at a party, on a first date. In interactions with familiar others, by contrast, attribute inferences will be rare whereas mental state inferences are still continuously needed. To illustrate, in folk explanations of behavior, mental states are cited about 65% of the time, whereas stable person attributes are cited no more than 5% of the time (Malle, 2004; Malle et al., 2007; see also Lewis, 1995).

Accuracy

Research has shown that people are capable of inferring stable attributes from behavior even without any awareness of making those inferences (Uleman et al., in press). Other work suggests that people may be all too willing to make such inferences (Ross, 1977; Gilbert & Malone, 1995). At the same time, evidence exists that people's tendency to infer traits from minimal information comes with noteworthy, though certainly not perfect, accuracy (Funder, 1999), and having such an inclination to infer traits appears to be associated with positive, not negative social adaptation (Block & Funder, 1986). Overall, questions of accuracy and adaptive value are difficult to assess as long as no ecologically sensitive data sets are available that would document the frequency of spontaneous attribute inferences, the relative frequency of correct and incorrect ones, and the costs and benefits of these inferences in social life.

Inference Hierarchy

Inferences about specific mental states can be informed by knowledge about the target person's stable attributes, such as when a person's desire is inferred from her presumed temperament. More typically, the dependence goes in the opposite direction, such that people build stable attribute inferences from more specific mental state inferences. For example, when people observe a behavior and infer that the agent's motive is to help another person, they are more likely to infer that the agent is generous and helpful than when they either infer a different motive or cannot figure out the motive at all (Read et al., 1990; Fein, 1996; Reeder et al., 2004). Hoffman et al. (1981) also showed that people who process behavioral information in goal-based categories remember that information better than those who form impressions of the person in trait-based categories. We also know from the developmental literature that children learn to infer traits and use them to explain behavior after they learn to ascribe and use mental states (Yuill & Pearson, 1998). The primacy of mental state inferences over trait inferences is even more directly reflected in recent data from my lab. Holbrook (2006) found that people who watch short video clips of a variety of behaviors are far more likely to make goal inferences than trait inferences, and their goal inferences are considerably faster.

Universality

Folk conceptions of personality have been most thoroughly studied within the framework of lexical studies, with recent work beginning to explore the stability of personality constructs across many languages and cultures (Saucier & Goldberg, 2001). A few dimensions emerge as remarkably stable (e.g., dynamism and social propriety), but variation increases once abstract factors break into more specific facets. In addition, some cultures or languages put more emphasis on some dimensions than on others. However, cultural differences in the frequency of using certain trait dimensions do not cast doubt on the universal human proclivity to infer stable attributes in the first place. Previously reported claims of a weaker proclivity in Eastern cultures have not stood up to empirical tests (Choi et al., 1999; Krull et al., 1999). And even though individual differences appear to exist within and across cultures in the conviction of how stable certain traits, abilities and skills really are (Dweck et al., 1993), no extant research suggests that some cultures have no conception of personality – are radical situationists, for example.

CONCLUSION

To survive in complex social communities humans have evolved, and develop from birth on, a remarkable set of psychological tools that range from fundamental concepts to simple processes and complex inferences. Social living demands the use of all of these tools, and they in turn enable communication, relationships, and culture. The current evidence base suggests considerable universality of these social-cognitive tools, though research has also documented variations in their relative use. No less universal than this bright side of social cognition is the dark side that includes stereotyping, prejudice, and hostile intergroup perception. However, to triumph over this darker side, humans can only nurture their capacities to be cognitively engaged and emotionally moved by others, to appreciate and simulate their distinct mental states, and infer as best they can their values and character. That, and nothing less, makes us human.

REFERENCES

Ames, D. R. (2004). Inside the mind reader's tool kit: Projection and stereotyping in mental state inference. *Journal of Personality and Social Psychology*, *87*, 340–353.

Asendorpf, J. B., Warkentin, V., & Baudonniere, P. (1996). Self-awareness and other-awareness. II: Mirror self-recognition, social contingency awareness, and synchronic imitation. *Developmental Psychology*, *32*, 313–321.

Asch, S. E. (1952). *Social psychology*. Englewood Cliffs, NJ: Prentice-Hall.

Astington, J. W. (2001). The paradox of intention: Assessing children's metarepresentational understanding. In B. F. Malle, L. J. Moses, & D. A. Baldwin (Eds.), *Intentions and intentionality: Foundations of social cognition* (pp. 85–104). Cambridge, MA: MIT Press.

Baird, J. A., & Baldwin, D. A. (2001). Making sense of human behavior: Action parsing and intentional inference. In B. F. Malle, L. J. Moses, & D. A. Baldwin (Eds.), *Intentions and intentionality: Foundations of social cognition* (pp. 193–206). Cambridge, MA: MIT Press.

Baird, J. A., & Moses, L. J. (2001). Do preschoolers appreciate that identical actions may be motivated by different intentions?. *Journal of Cognition and Development*, *2*, 413–448.

Baldwin, D. A. (1995). Understanding the link between joint attention and language. In C. Moore & P. J. Dunham (Eds.), *Joint attention: Its origins and role in development* (pp. 131–158). Hillsdale, NJ: Erlbaum.

Baldwin, D. A., Baird, J. A., Saylor, M. M., & Clark, M. A. (2001). Infants parse dynamic action. *Child Development*, *72*, 708–717.

Barr, D. J., & Keysar, B. (2005). Mindreading in an exotic case: The normal adult human. In B. F. Malle & S. D. Hodges (Eds.), *Other minds: How humans bridge the divide between self and others* (pp. 271–283). New York: Guilford Press.

Barrett, H. C., Todd, P. M., Miller, G. F., & Blythe, P. (2005). Accurate judgments of intention from motion cues alone: A cross-cultural study. *Evolution and Human Behavior, 26*, 313–331.

Bartsch, K., & Wellman, H. M. (1995). *Children talk about the mind.* New York: Oxford University Press.

Bassilli, J. N. (1978). Facial motion in the perception of faces and of emotional expressions. *Journal of Experimental Psychology: Human Perception and Performance, 4*, 373–379.

Bavelas, J. B., Black, A., Lemery, C. R., & Mullett, J. (1987). Motor mimicry as primitive empathy. In N. Eisenberg & J. Strayer (Eds.), *Empathy and its development* (pp. 317–338). New York: Cambridge University Press.

Bernieri, F. J. (1988). Coordinated movement and rapport in teacher-student interactions. *Journal of Nonverbal Behavior, 12*, 120–138.

Bertenthal, B. I. (1993). Infants' perception of biomechanical motions: Intrinsic image and knowledge-based constraints. In C. Granrud (Ed.), *Visual perception and cognition in infancy* (pp. 175–214). Hillsdale, NJ: Lawrence.

Birch, S. A. J. (2005). When knowledge is a curse: Children's and adults' reasoning about mental states. *Current Directions in Psychological Science, 14*, 25–29.

Biringen, Z., Emde, R. N., Campos, J. J., & Appelbaum, M. I. (1995). Affective reorganization in the infant, the mother, and the dyad: The role of upright locomotion and its timing. *Child Development, 66*, 499–514.

Block, J., & Funder, D. C. (1986). Social roles and social perception: Individual differences in attribution and error. *Journal of Personality and Social Psychology, 51*, 1200–1207.

Bosco, F. M., Friedman, O., & Leslie, A. M. (2006). Recognition of pretend and real actions in play by 1- and 2-year-olds: Early success and why they fail. *Cognitive Development, 21*, 3–10.

Brauer, J., Call, J., & Tomasello, M. (2005). All great ape species follow gaze to distant locations and around barriers. *Journal of Comparative Psychology, 119*, 145–154.

Brooks-Gunn, J., & Lewis, M. (1984). The development of early visual self-recognition. *Developmental Review, 4*, 215–239.

Brown, D. (1991). *Human universals.* San Francisco: McGraw-Hill.

Buchan, J. N., Paré, M., & Munhall, K. G. (2007). Spatial statistics of gaze fixations during dynamic face processing. *Social Neuroscience, 2*, 1–13.

Bybee, J. (1994). *The evolution of grammar: Tense, aspect, and modality in the languages of the world.* Chicago: The University of Chicago Press.

Byrne, R. W. (2004). Detecting, understanding, and explaining imitation by animals. In S. Hurley & N. Chater (Eds.), *Perspectives on imitation: From neuroscience to social science* (Vol. 1, pp. 225–242). Cambridge, MA: MIT Press. Mechanisms of imitation and imitation in animals.

Byrne, R. W. (2006). Parsing behaviour. A mundane origin for an extraordinary ability? In N. Enfield, & S. Levinson (Eds.), *The roots of human sociality* (pp. 478–505). New York: Berg.

Callaghan, T., Rochat, P., Lillard, A., Claux, M. L., Odden, H., Itakura, S., Tapanya, S., & Singh, S. (2005). Synchrony in the onset of mental-state reasoning: Evidence from five cultures. *Psychological Science, 16*, 378–384.

Campbell, R., Heywood, C. A., Cowey, A., Regard, M., & Landis, T. (1990). Sensitivity to eye gaze in prosopagnosic patients and monkeys with superior temporal sulcus ablation. *Neuropsychologia, 28*, 1123–1142.

Cantril, H. (1947). *Understanding man's social behavior: Preliminary notes.* Princeton, NJ: Office of Public Opinion Research.

Carlson, S. M., Moses, L. J., & Breton, C. (2002). How specific is the relation between executive function and theory of mind? Contributions of inhibitory control and working memory. *Infant and Child Development, 11*, 73–92.

Carpenter, M., Akhtar, N., & Tomasello, M. (1998). Fourteen- through 18-month-old infants differentially imitate intentional and accidental actions. *Infant Behavior and Development, 21*, 315–330.

Castiello, U. (2003). Understanding other people's actions: Intention and attention. *Journal of Experimental Psychology: Human Perception and Performance, 29,* 416–430.

Charman, T., Baron-Cohen, S., Swettenham, J., Baird, G., Cox, A., & Drew, A. (2001). Testing joint attention, imitation, and play infancy precursors to language and theory of mind. *Cognitive Development, 15,* 481–498.

Chartrand, T. L., & Bargh, J. A. (1999). The chameleon effect: The perception-behavior link and social interaction. *Journal of Personality and Social Psychology, 76,* 893–910.

Chasiotis, A., & Kiessling, F. (2004). Does the specifity of theory of mind and inhibitory control persist over the life-span? The relation of mentalistic and self-regulatory competence in adult age. *Zeitschrift fur Entwicklungspsychologie und Padagogische Psychologie, 36,* 105–114.

Chasiotis, A., Kiessling, F., Hofer, J., & Campos, D. (2006). Theory of mind and inhibitory control in three cultures: Conflict inhibition predicts false belief understanding in Germany, Costa Rica and Cameroon. *International Journal of Behavioral Development, 30,* 249–260.

Choi, I., Nisbett, R. E., & Norenzayan, A. (1999). Causal attribution across cultures: Variation and universality. *Psychological Bulletin, 125,* 47–63.

Chovil, N. (1997). Facing others: A social communicative perspective on facial displays. In J. A. Russell & J. M. Fernandez-Dols (Eds.), *The psychology of facial expression* (pp. 321–333). New York: Cambridge University Press.

Cloutier, J., Mason, M. F., & Macrae, C. N. (2005). The perceptual determinants of person construal: Reopening the social-cognitive toolbox. *Journal of Personality and Social Psychology, 88,* 885–894.

Coplan, A. (2006). Catching characters' emotions: Emotional contagion responses to narrative fiction film. *Film Studies, 8,* 26–38.

Coricelli, G. (2005). Two-levels of mental states attribution: From automaticity to voluntariness. *Neuropsychologia, 43,* 294–300.

D'Andrade, R. (1987). A folk model of the mind. In D. Holland & N. Quinn (Eds.), *Cultural models in language and thought* (pp. 112–148). New York: Cambridge University Press.

Damasio, A. R., Damasio, H., & Van Hoesen, G. W. (1982). Prosopagnosia: Anatomic basis and neurobehavioral mechanisms. *Neurology, 32,* 331–341.

Davidson, D. (1963). Actions, reasons, and causes. *Journal of Philosophy, 60,* 685–700.

Davis, M. H. (2005). A "constituent" approach to the study of perspective taking: What are its fundamental elements? In B. F. Malle & S. D. Hodges (Eds.), *Other minds: How humans bridge the divide between self and others* (pp. 44–55). New York, NY: Guilford Press.

Decety, J. (2002). Is there such a thing as functional equivalence between imagined, observed, and executed action?. In A. N. Meltzoff & W. Prinz (Eds.), *The imitative mind: Development, evolution, and brain bases* (pp. 291–310). Cambridge: Cambridge University Press.

Decety, J., & Grèzes, J. (2006). The power of simulation: Imagining one's own and other's behavior. *Brain Research, 1079,* 4–14.

Edge, H., & Suryani, L. K. (2002). A cross-cultural analysis of volition. *Florida Philosophical Review, 2,* 56–72.

Dittrich, W. J., & Lea, S. E. G. (1994). Visual perception of intentional motion. *Perception, 23,* 253–268.

Downing, P. E., Jiang, Y., Shuman, M., & Kanwisher, N. (2001). A cortical area selective for visual processing of the human body. *Science, 293,* 2470–2473.

Driver, J., Davis, G., Ricciardelli, R., Kidd, P., Maxwell, E., & Baron-Cohen, S. (1999). Gaze perception triggers reflexive visuospatial orienting. *Visual Cognition, 6,* 509–540.

Dweck, C. S., Hong, Y., & Chiu, C. (1993). Implicit theories: Individual differences in the likelihood and meaning of dispositional inference. *Personality and Social Psychology Bulletin, 19,* 644–656.

Ekman, P. (Ed.) (1973). *Darwin and facial expression: A century of research in review.* New York: Academic Press.

Epley, N., Keysar, B., Van Boven, L., & Gilovich, T. (2004). Perspective taking as egocentric anchoring and adjustment. *Journal of Personality and Social Psychology, 87,* 327–339.

Farah, M. J., & Aguirre, G. K. (1999). Imaging visual recognition: PET and fMRI studies of the functional anatomy of human visual recognition. *Trends in Cognitive Sciences, 3,* 179–186.

Clark, H. H. (1996). *Using language.* New York: Cambridge University Press.

Fein, S. (1996). Effects of suspicion on attributional thinking and the correspondence bias. *Journal of Personality and Social Psychology, 70,* 1164–1184.

Fiske, S. T., & Taylor, S. E. (1991). *Social cognition* (2nd Ed.). New York: McGraw-Hill.

Flavell, J. H. (1999). Cognitive development: Children's knowledge about the mind. *Annual Review of Psychology, 50,* 21–45.

Fodor, J. A. (1983). *Modularity of the mind.* Cambridge, MA: MIT Press.

Franco, F. (2005). Infant pointing: Harlequin, servant of two masters. In N. Eilan, C. Hoerl, T. McCormack, & J. Roessler (Eds.), *Joint attention: Communication and other minds: Issues in philosophy and psychology* (pp. 129–164). New York: Oxford University Press.

Freeman, N. H., & Lacohée, H. (1995). Making explicit 3-year-olds' implicit competence with their own false beliefs. *Cognition, 56,* 31–60.

Fridlund, A. J. (1994). *Human facial expression: An evolutionary view.* San Diego, CA: Academic Press.

Frischen, A., Bayliss, A. P., & Tipper, S. P. (2007). Gaze cueing of attention: Visual attention, social cognition, and individual differences. *Psychological Bulletin, 133,* 694–724.

Funder, D. C. (1999). *Personality judgment: A realistic approach to person perception.* San Diego, CA: Academic Press.

Gallese, V., & Goldman, A. (1998). Mirror neurons and the simulation theory of mind-reading. *Trends in Cognitive Sciences, 2,* 493–501.

Gallup, G. G. (1970). Chimpanzees: Self-recognition. *Science, 167,* 86–87.

Gergely, G., & Csibra, G. (2003). Teleological reasoning in infancy: The naive theory of rational action. *Trends in Cognitive Sciences, 7,* 287–292.

Gergely, G., & Csibra, G. (2004). The social construction of the cultural mind: Imitative learning as a mechanism of human pedagogy. *Interaction Studies: Social Behaviour and Communication in Biological and Artificial Systems, 6,* 463–481.

Gilbert, D. T., & Malone, P. S. (1995). The correspondence bias. *Psychological Bulletin, 117,* 21–38.

Givón, T. (1975). Cause and control: On the semantics of interpersonal manipulation. *Syntax and Semantics, 4,* 59–89.

Goldman, A. I. (2006). *Simulating minds: The philosophy, psychology, and neuroscience of mind-reading.* Oxford: Oxford University Press.

Gordon, R. M. (1992). The simulation theory: Objections and misconceptions. *Mind and Language, 7,* 11–34.

Guajardo, J. J., & Woodward, A. L. (2004). Is agency skin deep? Surface attributes influence infants' sensitivity to goal-directed action. *Infancy, 6,* 361–384.

Hare, B., & Tomasello, M. (1999). Domestic dogs (*Canis familiaris*) use human and conspecific social cues to locate hidden food. *Journal of Comparative Psychology, 113,* 173–177.

Hastorf, A. H., Schneider, D. J., & Polefka, J. (1970). *Person perception.* Reading, MA: Addison-Wesley.

Hatfield, E., Cacioppo, J., & Rapson, R. L. (1994). *Emotional contagion.* New York: Cambridge University Press.

Hauf, P., & Prinz, W. (2005). The understanding of own and others' actions during infancy: "You-like-Me" or "Me-like-You"?. *Interaction Studies, 6,* 429–445.

Haviland, J. M., & Lelwica, M. (1987). The induced affect response: 10-week-old infants' responses to three emotion expressions. *Developmental Psychology, 23,* 97–104.

Heider, F. (1958). *The psychology of interpersonal relations.* New York: Wiley.

Hernandez, M., & Iyengar, S. S. (2001). What drives whom? A cultural perspective on human agency. *Social Cognition, 19,* 269–294.

Higgins, E. T., & Pittman, T. S. (2008). Motives of the human animal: Comprehending, managing, and sharing inner states. *Annual Review of Psychology, 59,* 361–385.

Hobson, R. P. (2005). What puts the jointness into joint attention?. In N. Eilan, C. Hoerl, T. McCormack, & J. Roessler (Eds.), *Joint attention: Communication and other minds: Issues in philosophy and psychology* (pp. 185–204). New York: Oxford University Press.

Hodges, S. D., & Wegner, D. M. (1997). Automatic and controlled empathy. In W. J. Ickes (Ed.), *Empathic accuracy* (pp. 311–339). New York: Guilford.

Hoffman, C., Mischel, W., & Mazze, K. (1981). The role of purpose in the organization of information about behavior: Trait-based versus goal-based categories in person cognition. *Journal of Personality and Social Psychology*, *40*, 211–225.

Holbrook, J. (2006). *The time course of social perception: Inferences of intentionality, goals, beliefs, and traits from behavior*. Unpublished doctoral dissertation, University of Oregon.

Howe, N., Petrakos, H., & Rinaldi, C. M. (1998). "All the sheeps are dead. He murdered them": Sibling pretense, negotiation, internal state language, and relationship quality. *Child Development*, *69*, 182–191.

Hughes, C. (1998). Executive function in preschoolers: Links with theory of mind and verbal ability. *British Journal of Developmental Psychology*, *16*, 233–253.

Ickes, W. (1993). Empathic Accuracy. *Journal of Personality*, *61*, 587–610.

Johnson, S. C. (2000). The recognition of mentalistic agents in infancy. *Trends in Cognitive Sciences*, *4*, 22–28.

Johnson, S. C., Slaughter, V., & Carey, S. (1998). Whose gaze will infants follow? Features that elicit gaze-following in 12-month-olds. *Developmental Science*, *1*, 233–238.

Kanwisher, N. (2000). Domain specificity in face perception. *Nature Neuroscience*, *3*, 759–763.

Kashima, Y., McIntyre, A., & Clifford, P. (1998). The category of the mind: Folk psychology of belief, desire, and intention. *Asian Journal of Social Psychology*, *1*, 289–313.

Kashima, Y., Kashima, E., Chiu, C.-Y., Farsides, T., Gelfand, M., Hong, Y.-Y., Kim, U., Strack, F., Werth, L., Yuki, M. et al. (2005). Culture, essentialism, and agency: Are individuals universally believed to be more real entities than groups?. *European Journal of Social Psychology*, *35*, 147–169.

Kawashima, R., Sugiura, M., Kato, T., Nakamura, A., Hatano, K., Ito, K., Fukuda, H., Kojima, S., & Nakamura, K. (1999). The human amygdala plays an important role in gaze monitoring: A PET study. *Brain*, *122*, 779–783.

Keller, H., Yovsi, R., Borke, J., Kartner, J., Jensen, H., & Papaligoura, Z. (2004). Developmental consequences of early parenting experiences: Self-recognition and self-regulation in three cultural communities. *Child Development*, *75*, 1745–1760.

Király, I., Jovanovic, B., Prinz, W., Aschersleben, G., & Gergely, G. (2003). The early origins of goal attribution in infancy. *Consciousness and Cognition: An International Journal*, *12*, 752–769.

Klein, G., & Crandall, B. W. (1995). The role of mental simulation in problem solving and decision making. In P. Hancock, J. M. Flach, J. Caird, & K. J. Vicente (Eds.), *Local applications of the ecological approach to human-machine systems* (Vol. 2, pp. 324–358). Hillsdale, NJ: Erlbaum.

Kokkinaki, T. (2003). A longitudinal, naturalistic and cross-cultural study on emotions in early infant-parent imitative interactions. *British Journal of Developmental Psychology*, *21*, 243–258.

Krull, D. S., Loy, M. H., Lin, J., Wang, C., Chen, S., & Zhao, X. (1999). The fundamental fundamental attribution error: Correspondence bias in individualist and collectivist cultures. *Personality and Social Psychology Bulletin*, *25*, 1208–1219.

La France, M. (1982). Posture mirroring and rapport. In M. Davis (Ed.), *Interaction rhythms: Periodicity in communicative behavior* (pp. 279–298). New York: Human Sciences Press.

Lang, B., & Perner, J. (2002). Understanding of intention and false belief and the development of self control. *British Journal of Developmental Psychology*, *20*, 67–76.

Legerstee, M., Pomerleau, A., Malcuit, G., & Feider, H. (1987). The development of infants' responses to people and a doll: Implications for research in communication. *Infant Behavior and Development*, *10*, 81–95.

Leslie, A. M. (1995). A theory of agency. In A. J. Premack, D. Premack, & D. Sperber (Eds.), *Causal cognition: A multidisciplinary debate* (pp. 131–149). Oxford: Clarendon Press.

Leslie, A. M., & Polizzi, P. (1998). Inhibitory processing in the false-belief task: Two conjectures. *Developmental Science*, *1*, 247–254.

Levenson, R. W., & Gottman, J. M. (1983). Marital interaction: Physiological linkage and affective exchange. *Journal of Personality and Social Psychology, 45*, 587–597.

Levenson, R. W., & Ruef, A. M. (1997). Physiological aspects of emotional knowledge and rapport. In W. Ickes (Ed.), *Empathic accuracy* (pp. 44–72). New York: Guilford.

Lewis, C., Freeman, N., Kyriakidou, C., Maridaki-Kassotaki, K., & Berridge, D. (1996). Social influences on false belief access: Specific sibling influences or general apprenticeship? *Child Development, 67*, 2930–2947.

Lewis, P. T. (1995). A naturalistic test of two fundamental propositions: Correspondence bias and the actor-observer hypothesis. *Journal of Personality, 63*, 87–111.

Lillard, A. (1998). Ethnopsychologies: Cultural variations in theories of mind. *Psychological Bulletin, 123*, 3–32.

Lucariello, J., & Mindolovich, C. (1995). The development of complex metarepresentational reasoning: The case of situational irony. *Cognitive Development, 10*, 551–576.

Malle, B. F. (1999). How people explain behavior: A new theoretical framework. *Personality and Social Psychology Review, 3*, 21–43.

Malle, B. F. (2004). *How the mind explains behavior: Folk explanations, meaning, and social interaction.* Cambridge, MA: MIT Press.

Malle, B. F. (2005a). Folk theory of mind: Conceptual foundations of human social cognition. In R. Hassin, J. S. Uleman, & J. A. Bargh (Eds.), *The new unconscious* (pp. 225–255). New York: Oxford University Press.

Malle, B. F. (2006). The relation between judgments of intentionality and morality. *Journal of Cognition and Culture, 6*, 61–86.

Malle, B. F., Hodges, S. D. (Eds.) (2005). *Other minds: How humans bridge the divide between self and other.* New York: Guilford Press.

Malle, B. F., & Knobe, J. (1997a). The folk concept of intentionality. *Journal of Experimental Social Psychology, 33*, 101–121.

Malle, B. F., & Knobe, J. (2001). The distinction between desire and intention: A folk-conceptual analysis. In B. F. Malle, L. J. Moses, & D. A. Baldwin (Eds.), *Intentions and intentionality: Foundations of social cognition* (pp. 45–67). Cambridge, MA: MIT Press.

Malle, B. F., & Nelson, S. E. (2003). Judging *mens rea:* The tension between folk concepts and legal concepts of intentionality. *Behavioral Sciences and the Law, 21*, 563–580.

Malle, B. F., & Pearce, G. E. (2001). Attention to behavioral events during social interaction: Two actor-observer gaps and three attempts to close them. *Journal of Personality and Social Psychology, 81*, 278–294.

Malle, B. F., Knobe, J., & Nelson, S. (2007). Actor-observer asymmetries in behavior explanations: New answers to an old question. *Journal of Personality and Social Psychology, 93*, 491–514.

Markson, L., & Spelke, E. S. (2006). Infants' rapid learning about self-propelled objects. *Infancy, 9*, 45–71.

Mason, M. F., Hood, B. M., & Macrae, C. N. (2004). Look into my eyes: Gaze direction and person memory. *Memory, 12*, 637–643.

Mauro, R., Sato, K., & Tucker, J. (1992). The role of appraisal in human emotions: A cross-cultural study. *Journal of Personality and Social Psychology, 62*, 301–317.

Mele, A. R. (1992). *Springs of action: Understanding intentional behavior.* New York: Oxford University Press.

Meltzoff, A. N. (1995). Understanding the intentions of others: Re-enactment of intended acts by 18-month-old children. *Developmental Psychology, 31*, 838–850.

Meltzoff, A. N., & Brooks, R. (2001). "Like me" as a building block for understanding other minds: Bodily acts, attention, and intention. In B. F. Malle, L. J. Moses, & D. A. Baldwin (Eds.), *Intentions and intentionality: Foundations of social cognition* (pp. 171–191). Cambridge, MA: MIT Press.

Meltzoff, A. N., & Moore, M. K. (1977). Imitation of facial and manual gestures by human neonates. *Science, 198*, 75–78.

Menon, T., Morris, M. W., Chiu, C.-Y., & Hong, Y.-Y. (1999). Culture and the construal of agency: Attribution to individual versus group dispositions. *Journal of Personality and Social Psychology, 76*, 701–717.

Metcalfe, J., & Mischel, W. (1999). A hot/cool-system analysis of delay of gratification: Dynamics of willpower. *Psychological Review, 106*, 3–19.

Michelon, P., & Zacks, J. M. (2006). Two kinds of visual perspective taking. *Perception and Psychophysics, 68*, 327–337.

Mitchell, J. P. (2006). Mentalizing and Marr: An information processing approach to the study of social cognition. *Brain Research, 1079*, 66–75.

Mitchell, P. (1997). *Introduction to theory of mind: Children, autism, and apes.* New York: St. Martin's Press.

Moore, C., Jarrold, C., Russell, J., Lumb, A., Sapp, F., & MacCallum, F. (1995). Conflicting desire and the child's theory of mind. *Cognitive Development, 10*, 467–482.

Morton, A. (1996). Folk psychology is not a predictive device. *Mind, 105*, 119–137.

Moses, L. J., Baldwin, D. A., Rosicky, J., & Tidball, G. (2001). Evidence for referential understanding in the emotions domain at 12 and 18 months. *Child Development, 3*, 718–735.

Mundy, P. (1995). Joint attention and social–emotional approach behavior in children with autism. *Development and Psychopathology, 7*, 63–82.

Nadel-Brulfert, J., & Baudonnière, P. M. (1982). The social function of reciprocal imitation in 2-year-old peers. *International Journal of Behavioral Development, 5*, 95–109.

Nichols, K. E., Fox, N., & Mundy, P. (2005). Joint attention, self-recognition, and neurocognitive function in toddlers. *Infancy, 7*, 35–51.

Nichols, S., & Stich, S. (2003). *Mindreading: An integrated account of pretence, self-awareness, and understanding other minds.* Oxford University Press.

Nickerson, R. S. (1999). How we know – and sometimes misjudge – what others know: Imputing one's own knowledge to others. *Psychological Bulletin, 125*, 737–759.

Norenzayan, A., Schaller, M., & Heine, S. J. (2006). Evolution and culture. In M. Schaller, J. A. Simpson, & D. T. Kenrick (Eds.), *Evolution and social psychology: Frontiers of social psychology* (pp. 343–366). New York: Psychology Press.

Oerter, R., Agostiani, H., Kim, H., & Wibowo, S. (1996). The concept of human nature in East Asia: Etic and emic characteristics. *Culture and Psychology, 2*, 9–51.

Ohtsubo, Y. (2007). Perceived intentionality intensifies blameworthiness of negative behaviors: Blame-praise asymmetry in intensification effect. *Japanese Psychological Research, 49*, 100–110.

Ostrom, T. (1984). The sovereignty of social cognition. In R. S. Wyer, Jr. & T. K. Srull (Eds.), *Handbook of social cognition* (pp. 1–38). Hillsdale, NJ: Erlbaum.

Patten, S. B., & Arboleda-Flórez, J. A. (2004). Epidemic theory and group violence. *Social Psychiatry and Psychiatric Epidemiology, 39*, 853–856.

Perner, J. (1991). *Understanding the representational mind.* Cambridge, MA: MIT Press.

Peterson, C. C. (2001). Influence of siblings' perspectives on theory of mind. *Cognitive Development, 15*, 435–455.

Phillips, A. T., Wellman, H. M., & Spelke, E. S. (2002). Infants' ability to connect gaze and emotional expression to intentional action. *Cognition, 85*, 53–78.

Posamentier, M. T., & Abdi, H. (2003). Processing faces and facial expressions. *Neuropsychology Review, 13*, 113–143.

Premack, D. (1990). The infant's theory of self-propelled objects. *Cognition, 36*, 1–16.

Premack, D., & Woodruff, G. (1978). Does the chimpanzee have a 'theory of mind'? *Behavioral and Brain Sciences, 1*, 515–526.

Preston, S. D., & de Waal, F. (2002). Empathy: Its ultimate and proximate bases. *Behavioral and Brain Sciences, 25*, 1–20.

Prinz, W. (1990). A common coding approach to perception and action. In O. Neumann & W. Prinz (Eds.), *Relationships between perception and action* (pp. 167–201). Berlin: Springer-Verlag.

Read, S. J., Jones, D. K., & Miller, L. C. (1990). Traits as goal-based categories: The importance of goals in the coherence of dispositional categories. *Journal of Personality and Social Psychology*, *58*, 1048–1061.

Reeder, G. D., Vonk, R., Ronk, M. J., Ham, J., & Lawrence, M. (2004). Dispositional attribution: Multiple inferences about motive-related traits. *Journal of Personality and Social Psychology*, *86*, 530–544.

Repacholi, B. M. (1998). Infants' use of attentional cues to identify the referent of another person's emotional expression. *Developmental Psychology*, *34*, 1017–1025.

Repacholi, B. M., & Gopnik, A. (1997). Early reasoning about desires: Evidence from 14- and 18-month-olds. *Developmental Psychology*, *33*, 12–21.

Rizzolatti, G., Fadiga, L., Fogassi, L., & Gallese, V. (1996). Premotor cortex and the recognition of motor actions. *Cognitive Brain Research*, *3*, 131–141.

Rochat, P. (2002). Ego function of early imitation. In A. N. Meltzoff & W. Prinz (Eds.), *The imitative mind: Development, evolution, and brain bases* (pp. 85–97). Cambridge: Cambridge University Press.

Ross, L. (1977). The intuitive psychologist and his shortcomings: Distortions in the attribution process. In L. Berkowitz (Ed.), *Advances in experimental social psychology* (Vol. 10, pp. 174–221). New York: Academic Press.

Ross, L., & Ward, A. (1996). Naïve realism in everyday life: Implications for social conflict and misunderstanding. In E. Reed, E. Turiel, & T. Brown (Eds.), *Values and knowledge* (pp. 103–135). Hillsdale, NJ: Erlbaum.

Ross, L., Greene, D., & House, P. (1977). The "false-consensus effect:" An egocentric bias in social perception and attribution processes. *Journal of Experimental Social Psychology*, *13*, 279–301.

Rothbart, M. K., Ahadi, S. A., Hersey, K. L., & Fisher, P. (2001). Investigations of temperament at three to seven years: The Children's Behavior Questionnaire. *Child Development*, *72*, 1394–1408.

Rousselet, G. A., Macé, M. J.-M., & Fabre-Thorpe, M. (2004). Animal and human faces in natural scenes: How specific to human faces is the N170 ERP component? *Journal of Vision*, *4*, 13–21.

Runeson, S., & Frykholm, G. (1983). Kinematic specification of dynamics as an informational basis for person-and-action perception: Expectation, gender recognition, and deceptive intention. *Journal of Experimental Psychology: General*, *112*, 585–615.

Russell, J. (1996). *Agency: Its role in mental development*. Hove, England: Erlbaum.

Russell, J., & Danish, D. (2007). The role of 'action effects' and perceived agency in infant imitation. *Cognitive Development*, *22*, 69–76.

Sabbagh, M. A., Xu, F., Carlson, S. M., Moses, L. J., & Lee, K. (2006). The development of executive functioning and theory of mind: A comparison of U.S. and Chinese preschoolers. *Psychological Science*, *17*, 74–81.

Saucier, G., & Goldberg, L. R. (2001). Lexical studies of indigenous personality factors: Premises, products, and prospects. *Journal of Personality*, *69*, 847–879.

Schult, C. A. (2002). Children's understanding of the distinction between intentions and desires. *Child Development*, *73*, 1727–1747.

Schürmann, M., Hesse, M. D., Stephan, K. E., Saarela, M., Zilles, K., Hari, R., & Fink, G. R. (2005). Yearning to yawn: The neural basis of contagious yawning. *NeuroImage*, *24*, 1260–1264.

Searle, J. R. (1983). *Intentionality: An essay in the philosophy of mind*. Cambridge, England: Cambridge University Press.

Shaver, K. G. (1985). *The attribution of blame: Causality, responsibility, and blameworthiness*. New York: Springer.

Sherif, M. (1935). A study of some social factors in perception. *Archives of Psychology*, *27*, 1–60.

Siegal, M., & Beattie, K. (1991). Where to look first in children's knowledge of false beliefs. *Cognition*, *38*, 1–12.

Simner, M. L. (1971). Newborn's response to the cry of another infant. *Developmental Psychology*, *5*, 136–150.

Simpson, D. L. (2003). *The role of culture and gender in children's development of display rules and theory of mind.* Unpublished Dissertation, Claremount Graduate University.

Smedslund, J. (1997). *The structure of psychological common sense.* Mahwah, NJ: Erlbaum.

Sommerville, J. A., Woodward, A. L., & Needham, A. (2005). Action experience alters 3-month-old infants' perception of others' actions. *Cognition, 96,* B1–B11.

Stueber, K. (2006). *Rediscovering empathy: Agency, folk psychology, and the human sciences.* Cambridge, MA: MIT Press.

Tagiuri, R., & Petrullo, L. (Eds.) (1958). *Person perception and interpersonal behavior.* Stanford: Stanford University Press.

Tardif, T., & Wellman, H. M. (2000). Acquisition of mental state language in Mandarin- and Cantonese-speaking children. *Developmental Psychology, 36,* 25–43.

Tomasello, M., & Barton, M. E. (1994). Learning words in nonostensive contexts. *Developmental Psychology, 30,* 639–650.

Tomasello, M., & Farrar, M. J. (1986). Joint attention and early language. *Child Development, 57,* 1454–1463.

Uleman, J. S., Adil Saribay, S., & Gonzalez, C. M. (2008). Spontaneous inferences, implicit impressions, and implicit theories. *Annual Review of Psychology, 59,* 329–360.

Van Boven, L., & Loewenstein, G. (2003). Social projection of transient drive states. *Personality and Social Psychology Bulletin, 29,* 1159–1168.

Wallbott, H. G., & Scherer, K. R. (1988). How universal and specific is emotional experience? Evidence from 27 countries. In K. R. Scherer (Ed.), *Facets of emotion: Recent research* (pp. 31–56). Hillsdale, NJ: Erlbaum.

Watson, J. S. (1985). Contingency perception in early social development. In T. M. Field & N. A. Fox (Eds.), *Social perception in infants* (pp. 157–176). Norwood, NJ: Ablex.

Weiner, B. (1995). *Judgments of responsibility: A foundation for a theory of social conduct.* New York: Guilford.

Wellman, H. (1990). *The child's theory of mind.* Cambridge, MA: MIT Press.

Wellman, H. M., & Miller, J. G. (2006). Developing conceptions of responsive intentional agents. *Journal of Cognition and Culture, 6,* 27–55.

Wellman, H. M., & Phillips, A. T. (2001). Developing intentional understandings. In B. F. Malle, L. J. Moses, & D. A. Baldwin (Eds.), *Intentions and intentionality: Foundations of social cognition* (pp. 125–148). Cambridge, MA: MIT Press.

Wellman, H. M., & Woolley, J. D. (1990). From simple desires to ordinary beliefs: The early development of everyday psychology. *Cognition, 35,* 245–275.

Wellman, H. M., Cross, D., & Watson, J. (2001). Meta-analysis of theory-of-mind development: The truth about false belief. *Child Development, 72,* 655–684.

Wellman, H. M., Fang, F., Liu, D., Zhu, L., & Liu, G. (2006). Scaling of theory-of-mind understandings in Chinese children. *Psychological Science, 17,* 1075–1081.

Wierzbicka, A. (1996). *Semantics: Primes and universals.* Oxford: Oxford University Press.

Wilson, M. (2001). Perceiving imitatible stimuli: Consequences of isomorphism between input and output. *Psychological Bulletin, 127,* 543–553.

Wimmer, H., & Perner, J. (1983). Beliefs about beliefs: Representation and constraining function of wrong beliefs in young children's understanding of deception. *Cognition, 13,* 103–128.

Wolpert, D. M., Doya, K., & Kawato, M. (2003). A unifying computational framework for motor control and social interaction. *Philosophical Transactions of the Royal Society of London (Biological Sciences), 358,* 593–602.

Woodward, A. L. (1998). Infants selectively encode the goal object of an actor's reach. *Cognition, 69,* 1–34.

Woodward, A. L., Sommerville, J. A., & Guajardo, J. J. (2001). How infants make sense of intentional action. In B. F. Malle, L. J. Moses, & D. A. Baldwin (Eds.), *Intentions and intentionality: Foundations of social cognition* (pp. 149–170). Cambridge, MA: MIT Press.

Wu, S., & Keysar, B. (2007). The effect of culture on perspective taking. *Psychological Science, 18,* 600–606.

Young, A. W., Aggleton, J. P., Hellawell, D. J., Johnson, M., Broks, P., & Hanley, J. R. (1995). Face processing impairments after amygdalotomy. *Brain*, *118*, 15–24.

Yuill, N., & Pearson, A. (1998). The development of bases for trait attribution: Children's understanding of traits as causal mechanisms based on desire. *Developmental Psychology*, *34*, 574–586.

Zaw, G. (2006). *The attribution of intentionality in relation to culture and self.* Unpublished Doctoral Dissertation, Loma Linda University, California.

13

CROSS-CULTURAL DIFFERENCES VERSUS UNIVERSALITY IN COGNITIVE DISSONANCE: A CONCEPTUAL REANALYSIS

BERTRAM GAWRONSKI*, KURT R. PETERS* AND FRITZ STRACK†

*Department of Psychology, University of Western Ontario, London, Ontario, Canada
†Department of Psychology, University of Würzburg, Würzburg, Germany

INTRODUCTION

Festinger's (1957) theory of cognitive dissonance is probably one of the most significant and influential theories in the history of social psychology. The central tenet of Festinger's theory is that inconsistency between cognitive elements elicits aversive feelings of dissonance, which in turn promote actions aimed at reducing these feelings.[1] According to Festinger, such reductions can be achieved

---

[1]Somewhat ironically, Festinger (1957) himself was inconsistent in his use of the term *dissonance*, in that it was sometimes used to describe the inconsistency between cognitive elements and sometimes to refer to the aversive feelings arising from inconsistency. For the sake of conceptual clarity, we will use the term *inconsistency* to describe the relation between cognitive elements, and the term *dissonance* to describe the aversive feelings arising from inconsistency.

either by changing one of the inconsistent cognitive elements or by adding a new cognitive element that reconciles the existing inconsistency. More specifically, cognitive dissonance can be reduced by (a) changing one's attitudes, (b) changing one's behavior, (c) searching for consonant information, or (d) trivializing the importance of inconsistency. Whereas the first two cases represent examples of the aforementioned change strategy, the latter two represent examples of the addition strategy.

Even though Festinger (1957) was convinced that the need for cognitive consistency in humans is as basic as hunger and thirst, the universality of cognitive dissonance has recently been challenged by cross-cultural researchers (e.g., Heine & Lehman, 1997; Kitayama et al., 2004; Hoshino-Browne et al., 2005). For example, Heine and Lehman (1997) claimed that "cognitive dissonance, as it has been investigated in the literature, is more likely to be experienced by North Americans" (p. 391). This assumption is based on earlier theorizing by Markus and Kitayama (1991) who argued that dissonance arising from counterattitudinal behavior may not be experienced by individuals with interdependent self-construals. According to these authors, interdependent self-construals, which are common in East Asian cultures, are characterized by lower importance of internal attributes (e.g., attitudes) as self-defining characteristics compared to external attributes (e.g., social roles). As such, inconsistency between attitudes and behavior may be regarded as less significant in Eastern compared to Western cultures, thereby limiting the generality of dissonance arising from counterattitudinal behavior. More recently, Hoshino-Browne et al. (2005) claimed that both Easterners and Westerners experience aversive feelings of cognitive dissonance, even though cultural differences may shape the particular situations in which dissonance is aroused. Specifically, these researchers argued that dissonance is aroused whenever important aspects of one's self-concept are threatened (see Steele et al., 1993). Thus, to the extent that there is cultural variation in the relative importance of a given self-attribute, the particular instances that elicit dissonance experiences may be different for Easterners and Westerners.

In this chapter, we provide a conceptual reanalysis of inconsistency processes that aims at specifying different sources of cross-cultural differences in dissonance-related phenomena. The central claim of our reanalysis is that the general *processes* associated with cognitive inconsistency are universal, even though cross-cultural differences pertaining to the *contents* of belief systems may function as important moderators of the outcomes of these processes. For this purpose, we will first review our conceptualization of cognitive consistency as an inherently propositional phenomenon (Gawronski & Strack, 2004; Gawronski et al., in press-a). Drawing on the distinction between associative and propositional processes (Strack & Deutsch, 2004; Gawronski & Bodenhausen, 2006a), we argue that the contents of the cognitive elements described by Festinger (1957) have to be regarded as either true or false in order to acquire the potential for being consistent or inconsistent with each other. Based on this specification of inconsistency, we propose a three-stage model of inconsistency processes that distinguishes between (a) the identification of inconsistency, (b) the elicitation of dissonance experiences, and (c) the resolution of inconsistency to reduce dissonance experiences. This three-stage model is then used as an organizing framework for our discussion of cross-cultural differences in dissonance-related phenomena. Specifically, we argue that the proposed processes are culturally universal, even though cross-cultural differences may moderate the respective outcomes of each of the three stages. From this perspective, cross-cultural differences in dissonance-related phenomena (e.g., dissonance-related attitude change) often remain nondiagnostic as to whether they are due to (a) differences in the inconsistency of culturally diverging systems of beliefs (i.e., *inconsistency identification*), (b) differences in the experiences elicited by an inconsistent belief system (i.e., *dissonance elicitation*), or (c) differences in the employed strategy to resolve inconsistency (i.e., *inconsistency resolution*). The implications of this conclusion are further addressed in the last section of this chapter, which discusses some directions for future research based on the present reanalysis.

THE PROPOSITIONAL NATURE OF COGNITIVE CONSISTENCY

Before addressing cross-cultural differences in cognitive dissonance, it seems essential to specify its underlying precursor: cognitive inconsistency. According to Festinger (1957), two cognitions are inconsistent with each other if, considering these two alone, one of them follows from the opposite of the other. Festinger further specified this definition in a formal manner, stating that "x and y are dissonant if not-x follows from y" (p. 13). We argue that such logical relations play a crucial role in the definition of (in)consistency. Specifically, we claim that the relation between two cognitive elements cannot even be defined without reference to the syllogistic rules of logic (Gawronski & Bodenhausen, 2006a). Thus, any claim regarding consistency or inconsistency between cognitive elements makes (implicit or explicit) reference to the abstract notion of logical implication (see also Jones & Gerard, 1967; Kruglanski, 1989).

Even though the crucial role of logical implication tended to disappear in recent reformulations of dissonance theory (Greenwald & Ronis, 1978), it has important implications for the psychological nature of cognitive consistency. In a general sense, logical implication is defined as the deductive transfer of truth values from one proposition to another. For instance, to say that "not-x follows from y" simply means that, if y is true, then not-x must be true as well. If the truth value of y is unknown, nothing can be said about not-x. From this perspective, logical implication – and thus cognitive consistency – essentially depends on the assignment of truth values. In that sense, the *subjective* nature of personal beliefs supplements the *objective* nature of logical implication, such that (in)consistency within an individual's system of beliefs is determined by the application of logical principles to what this individual believes to be true or false (Quine & Ullian, 1978).

This dependency on truth values led Gawronski and Strack (2004) to conclude that cognitive dissonance is an inherently propositional phenomenon (see Strack & Deutsch, 2004; Gawronski & Bodenhausen, 2006a), such that the cognitive elements involved in dissonance have to be regarded as either true or false (cf. Sakai, 1999). Specifically, Gawronski and Strack (2004) argued that dissonance emerges when two propositions are regarded as true, and one follows from the opposite of the other. Moreover, dissonance can be reduced by either (a) changing the (subjective) truth value of one proposition (resembling Festinger's strategy of changing cognitions) or (b) searching for an additional proposition that resolves the inconsistency (resembling Festinger's strategy of adding cognitions). The dependency on truth values that characterizes propositional reasoning stands in contrast to the nature of associative processes, which can be defined as mere activation independent of subjective truth or falsity (Strack & Deutsch, 2004; Gawronski & Bodenhausen, 2006a). That is, associations can be activated in memory irrespective of whether one considers these associations as accurate or inaccurate (cf. Sakai, 1999). Thus, the qualitatively distinct nature of associative and propositional processes (see Gawronski & Bodenhausen, 2006b) can lead to dissociations between the two when the content of activated associations is rejected as a valid basis for a propositional judgment (Gilbert, 1991; Deutsch et al., 2006a). In support of these claims, Gawronski and Strack (2004) demonstrated that dissonance arising from counterattitudinal behavior (Festinger & Carlsmith, 1959) influenced only propositional evaluations reflected in explicit measures, but not associative evaluations reflected in implicit measures (in this case, the Implicit Association Test; Greenwald et al.,1998). Moreover, ("implicit") associative and ("explicit") propositional evaluations were highly correlated under control conditions and when participants had a situational explanation for their counterattitudinal behavior (and thus relied on activated evaluative associations). However, correlations significantly dropped – and even showed a tendency for negative relations – when participants did not have a situational explanation for their counterattitudinal behavior (and thus rejected the content of activated associations as invalid). Taken together, these results support the assumption that cognitive dissonance is an inherently propositional phenomenon, requiring the assignment of truth values to the involved cognitive elements.

Notwithstanding the supportive evidence for these claims, one could object that dissonance-related attitude changes have also been shown for participants who did not have any explicit memory for the behavior that has caused these changes in the first place. Specifically, Lieberman et al. (2001) found that amnesic participants who did not have any recollection of an earlier decision showed the same spreading-of-alternatives effects in the post-decisional dissonance paradigm (Brehm, 1956) that have previously been shown for participants with full memory for their decision. These findings seem difficult to explain in terms of the present framework, which requires a conscious assignment of truth values to the relevant cognitive elements. Obviously, it does not make sense to argue that Lieberman et al.'s amnesic participants consciously reflected on their behavior despite the lack of any memory for that behavior. However, in contrast to Lieberman et al.'s interpretation in terms of post-decisional dissonance, a recent study by Gawronski et al. (2007) suggests that post-decisional attitude changes in amnesic participants may not be driven by cognitive dissonance, but by an alternative, low-level process of associative self-anchoring (see also Gawronski et al., in press-a). Specifically, Gawronski et al. (2007) showed that the act of choosing an object creates a mental association between the chosen object and the self. By virtue of this association, associative evaluations of the self tend to transfer to the chosen object, such that attitudes toward the chosen object depend on associative evaluations of the self. Given that associative self-evaluations tend to be highly positive (Bosson et al., 2000; Greenwald & Farnham, 2000; Koole et al., 2001) and given that new associations to the self are created rapidly during the act of choosing an object, this process of associative self-anchoring can lead to post-decisional attitude change without requiring conscious recollection of the decision or the type of higher-order propositional processes implied by dissonance reduction (for a more detailed discussion, see Gawronski et al., in press-a).

A THREE-STAGE MODEL OF INCONSISTENCY PROCESSES

Once cognitive dissonance is specified as an inherently propositional phenomenon, the psychological dynamics proposed by Festinger (1957) can be incorporated into a general three-stage model of inconsistency processes. Specifically, we argue that inconsistency processes involve the following three sequential steps: (a) the identification of inconsistency, (b) the elicitation of dissonance experiences, and (c) the resolution of inconsistency to reduce dissonance experiences (see Figure 13.1).

INCONSISTENCY IDENTIFICATION

The first important step in the sequence of inconsistency processes is the identification of inconsistency. People often hold various inconsistent beliefs, but they may not realize the inconsistency between these beliefs when they are

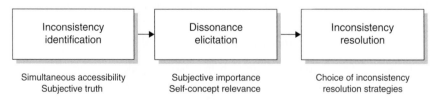

FIGURE 13.1   Three-stage model of inconsistency processes. Identification of inconsistency within one's system of beliefs is assumed to elicit aversive feelings of dissonance, which in turn motivate agents to resolve the inconsistency that has led to these feelings. General variables influencing the three steps are depicted below the respective boxes.

not activated simultaneously (McGregor et al., 1999). For instance, many of our attitudes may be inconsistent with our behavior. Nevertheless, we may fail to experience any dissonance resulting from this inconsistency, if we fail to think about one of the two elements. That is, there will be no inconsistency identified if we fail to think about our behavior every time we reflect on our attitudes; and there will be no inconsistency identified if we fail to think about our attitudes every time we reflect on our behavior. For inconsistency to arise, both types of thoughts need to be accessible simultaneously.

However, even though simultaneous accessibility is *necessary* for inconsistency to occur, it is *not sufficient*. As outlined above, the contents of the relevant cognitions have to be regarded as true or false in order to acquire the potential of being (in)consistent with each other (Gawronski & Bodenhausen, 2006a). For instance, negative stereotypic associations pertaining to a disadvantaged minority group may not result in inconsistency with explicitly endorsed egalitarian goals when accessible stereotypic associations are rejected as inaccurate or false (Gawronski et al., in press-b). Hence, the two major determinants of inconsistency identification are (a) the simultaneous accessibility of potentially inconsistent cognitions (McGregor et al., 1999) and (b) the assignment of truth values that makes these cognitions factually inconsistent (Gawronski & Strack, 2004).

The relevance of these determinants can be illustrated with the experimental situation in the hypocrisy paradigm (e.g., Stone et al., 1994; Fried & Aronson, 1995; Stone et al., 1997). In this paradigm, participants are first asked to indicate their general opinion about a specific issue in a pro-attitudinal manner (e.g., advocating the importance of safe sex), and are then made aware of past failures to behave in line with their attitudes (e.g., past failures to use condoms). The common finding in this paradigm is that the inconsistency between personal attitudes and past behavior influences subsequent behavior in a manner consistent with the endorsed attitude (e.g., buying more condoms). In other words, the inconsistency between participants' attitudes and their cognitions about past behavior leads them to change the cognitions about their behavior, in this case by actually changing their behavior.[2] However, for this behavioral change to occur, it seems necessary that (a) the attitude and the cognitions about past behavior are made simultaneously accessible by the experimental procedure and (b) both of them are explicitly endorsed as valid. If one of the two conditions is not met, there will be no inconsistency identified in the first place and thus no dissonance-related changes in behavior.

DISSONANCE ELICITATION

If inconsistency in one's system of beliefs has been identified, this inconsistency may arouse aversive feelings of cognitive dissonance. However, according

---

[2]An alternative means of changing cognitions about behavior that does not imply actual changes in behavior would be a reinterpretation of the meaning of past behavior to make it consistent with one's attitude. To our knowledge, this possibility has not yet been investigated empirically.

to Festinger (1957), the relative magnitude of dissonance experiences depends on the subjective importance of the involved elements. In line with this claim, several reformulations of dissonance theory state that inconsistency between cognitions elicits uncomfortable feelings of dissonance only when these cognitions involve aversive consequences (Cooper & Fazio, 1984; but see Harmon-Jones et al., 1996) or threatens important aspects of one's self-concept (Aronson, 1968; Steele & Liu, 1983; Steele et al., 1993). For instance, Aronson (1968) claimed that people generally strive to maintain a sense of self that is both consistent and positive. Thus, if self-consistency is violated by negative behaviors, people's positive self-image will be threatened, thereby resulting in particularly high levels of dissonance experiences (compared to behaviors that are irrelevant to one's self-concept).

Applied to the present question of cross-cultural differences, a particularly important reformulation of dissonance theory is Stone and Cooper's (2001) self-standards model. This model asserts that cognitive dissonance depends on the type of standard that is used to evaluate one's behavior. Specifically, Stone and Cooper argued that people compare their behavior to either personal or normative standards. Which of the two kinds of standards is used in a given situation depends on their relative accessibility. The discrepancy between the behavior and the employed standard then determines the relative magnitude of dissonance experiences, which may therefore differ as a function of the momentarily accessible standards.

Despite significant differences between different reformulations of dissonance theory (for a discussion, see Stone & Cooper, 2003), most of them share the assumption that aversive feelings of dissonance are aroused only for particular types of inconsistencies. As noted above, some of these boundary conditions have been anticipated by Festinger (1957), who argued that the magnitude of dissonance experiences depends on the subjective importance of the involved elements. Applied to the present question of cross-cultural differences, it suffices to note that not all types of inconsistency are created equal. Rather, people may differ in terms of what types of cognitions they regard as important, which in turn can lead to differences in the magnitude of dissonance experiences elicited by the same inconsistency. In addition, people may differ in terms of the relative importance they attribute to personal versus normative standards they habitually employ to evaluate their behavior (Stone & Cooper, 2001), which may further contribute to cross-cultural differences in cognitive dissonance.

Notwithstanding these potential sources of inter-individual differences in the elicitation of dissonance experiences, it is important to note that empirical studies guided by the aforementioned reformulations primarily focused on dissonance-related attitude change. Specifically, these studies investigated whether a given moderator increased or decreased dissonance-related attitude change in a manner consistent with the predictions derived by a given reformulation (e.g., Cooper & Fazio, 1984; Aronson, 1997; Stone & Cooper, 2003). If dissonance-related attitude change occurred, this outcome has typically been taken as evidence for the arousal of dissonance experiences. If, however, no attitude change occurred, this outcome is often interpreted as indicating absence of dissonance experiences. From the perspective of our three-stage model, such interpretations seem premature as long as dissonance experiences are not directly assessed (for notable exceptions, see Croyle & Cooper, 1983; Losch & Cacioppo, 1990; Elliot & Devine, 1994; Harmon-Jones, 2000; see also Zanna & Cooper, 1974). Specifically, we argue that any moderating effect on dissonance-related attitude change may also be due to the changes in the employed strategy to reduce inconsistency, thereby remaining nondiagnostic about the actual elicitation of dissonance experiences. This issue represents the tenet of the final stage of our three-stage model.

INCONSISTENCY RESOLUTION

If inconsistency has been identified within one's system of beliefs and if this inconsistency has indeed aroused aversive feelings of cognitive dissonance, these feelings are assumed to motivate people to resolve the inconsistency that gave rise to dissonance experiences. According to Festinger (1957), there are two general strategies to resolve inconsistency. First, people may resolve inconsistency by changing one of the involved elements. Second, people may add a cognitive element that resolves the inconsistency. As outlined above, the first strategy can be descried as a change in the (subjective) truth value of one of the involved propositions, whereas the second strategy can be regarded as the search for an additional proposition that resolves the momentary inconsistency (Gawronski & Strack, 2004). Examples of the first strategy include changes in attitudes or behavior; examples of the second strategy include the search for consonant information or trivializing the importance of inconsistency (Festinger, 1957).

A useful example to illustrate the significance of these strategies is Festinger & Carlsmith's (1959) induced compliance paradigm. In this paradigm, participants are first asked to engage in some obviously counterattitudinal behavior (e.g., writing a counterattitudinal essay). In one condition, participants are implicitly provided with a situational explanation for their counterattitudinal behavior (e.g., high situational pressure); in another condition, they are implicitly given the impression that they have freely chosen to engage in the counterattitudinal behavior (e.g., low situational pressure). The well-replicated finding is that participants tend to change their original attitudes when they do not have a situational explanation for their counterattitudinal behavior, but not when they do have a situational explanation. According to Festinger (1957), these changes are driven by aversive feelings of cognitive dissonance arising from attitude–behavior inconsistency, which motivates participants to reduce this inconsistency by means of changing their original attitudes.

The interpretation of attitude changes under low situational pressure is widely accepted and relatively uncontroversial among dissonance researchers. What has received less attention is the underlying mechanism in the high situational pressure condition. Even though researchers tend to regard this condition as a simple control condition, an implicit assumption seems to be that there is no inconsistency in the first place, and therefore no arousal of dissonance experiences. Alternatively, however, one could argue that counterattitudinal behavior *generally* gives rise to inconsistency, thereby eliciting dissonance experiences under both high and low situational pressure. From this perspective, the primary difference between the two conditions is whether the dissonance-arousing inconsistency is resolved by means of either (a) attitude change or (b) consonant information, in this case a situational explanation for the counterattitudinal behavior. Hence, it remains an open question whether the availability of a situational explanation for one's counterattitudinal behavior prevents inconsistency – and thus the elicitation of dissonance experiences – in the first place (i.e., *inconsistency identification*) or whether the availability of a situational explanation simply provides an alternative means to resolve the present inconsistency (i.e., *inconsistency resolution*). Even though the available evidence tends to support the former interpretation (e.g., Croyle & Cooper, 1983; Harmon-Jones, 2000; see also Zanna & Cooper, 1974), the important message of these considerations is that inconsistency can be resolved in multiple ways, which implies that any factor that influences the use of inconsistency resolution strategies may influence the emergence of dissonance-related attitude change (see also Steele et al., 1993; Simon et al., 1995; Gosling et al., 2006). In other words, the mere absence of dissonance-related attitude change remains nondiagnostic as to whether there was a lack of dissonance arousal in the first place, or whether participants simply used a different strategy to resolve inconsistency. As we will outline in the next section, this ambiguity has important implications for the interpretation of cross-cultural differences in dissonance-related attitude change.

CROSS-CULTURAL DIFFERENCES VERSUS UNIVERSALITY IN COGNITIVE DISSONANCE

The proposed three-stage model of inconsistency processes seems particularly useful for identifying potential sources of cross-cultural differences in dissonance-related phenomena. As outlined in the introduction, we argue that the general processes involved in cognitive inconsistency are culturally universal, even though cross-cultural differences pertaining to the contents of the involved elements may moderate the respective outcomes of each of the three stages, thereby leading to corresponding differences in dissonance-related phenomena.

DIFFERENCES IN INCONSISTENCY IDENTIFICATION

A central assumption of our three-stage model is that inconsistency depends on the assignment of truth values, such that the contents of potentially inconsistent cognitive elements have to be regarded as true or false (Gawronski & Strack, 2004). Thus, a relatively trivial source of inter-individual differences in dissonance-related phenomena resides in diverging opinions about the same state of affairs.

In the domain of science, for example, empirical evidence challenging the validity of a scientific theory may produce inconsistent cognitions in researchers who
believe in the accuracy of that theory, but not in those who rejected that theory
in the first place (Kruglanski, 1989). Needless to say, similar differences may
emerge at the level of cultural traditions. For instance, the cognitions "I love my
wife" and "I am attracted to another woman" will be inconsistent in cultures
with monogamous relationship norms, but they may be perfectly consistent in
cultures with polygamous relationship norms. As already outlined by Festinger
(1957), any difference in the sets of culturally accepted beliefs can determine
whether or not the acceptance of a particular proposition results in inconsistency,
thereby leading to corresponding differences in dissonance experiences.

Aside from this rather trivial cause, there is a somewhat deeper source that
may account for cross-cultural differences in the identification of inconsistency.
As outlined above, inconsistency essentially depends on the truth values assigned
to a given set of propositions. A common finding in cross-cultural research is that
Eastern cultures differ from Western cultures in their relative emphasis of situational contexts (Markus & Kitayama, 1991; Choi et al., 1999). Applied to the
notion of truth values, this difference can result in a contextualized interpretation
of truth, such that whether or not a given statement about an object is regarded
as true depends on the particular context of that object. This interpretation stands
in contrast to the predominantly decontextualized way of thinking in Western
cultures, implying that the truth or falsity of a given statement about an object
is determined by the inherent properties of that object, rather than by the particular context in which it is encountered. Thus, what may appear as inconsistent
from a Western, decontextualized point of view may be perfectly consistent from
an Eastern, contextualized point of view (Peng & Nisbett, 1999). For instance,
a decontextualized negative attitude toward abortion may be inconsistent with
any kind of behavior favoring abortion, whereas a contextualized attitude may be
sensitive to particular circumstances, thereby leading to a positive evaluation in
some contexts and a negative evaluation in others (see Schwarz, 2007). From this
perspective, decontextualized attitudes have a much stronger potential to result in
inconsistency than contextualized attitudes, thereby increasing the likelihood of
dissonance experiences. Thus, to the extent that Eastern cultures have a stronger
tendency to contextualize attitudes and beliefs (Markus & Kitayama, 1991; Choi
et al., 1999), inconsistency in belief systems – and thus dissonance experiences
– may be less likely in Eastern compared to Western cultures.

This decontextualized assignment of truth values resembles the notion of dialectical reasoning that is often attributed to East Asian cultures. According to
Peng and Nisbett (1999), East Asian ways of reasoning can be characterized by
their willingness to accept the truth of two inconsistent views, thereby tolerating
apparent contradictions. Instead of discounting, differentiating, or denying the
involved elements, East Asian philosophy regards such contradictions as an inherent feature of our world, which tends to be "in constant flux" (Peng & Nisbett,
1999, p. 742). This ontology is often contrasted to Western conceptualizations

of the world as constant and stable. From our point of view, these divergent perspectives can be described in terms of the aforementioned contextualization of truth, such that East Asian philosophy implies a contextualized assignment of truth values, whereas Western cultures tend to decontextualize the assignment of truth values. Thus, as outlined above, what may appear as inconsistent from a Western, decontextualized point of view may be perfectly consistent from an Eastern, contextualized point of view. Importantly, the proposed contextualization of truth values does not imply that consistency is completely irrelevant in East Asian cultures. Rather, inconsistency is simply less likely to occur given that the truth value of a proposition is always considered in relation to its context.

DIFFERENCES IN DISSONANCE ELICITATION

If inconsistency is identified, this inconsistency is assumed to elicit aversive feelings of dissonance. However, as outlined by Festinger (1957), the relative magnitude of these feelings depends on the subjective importance of the involved elements. Such differences in subjective importance can also function as the source of cross-cultural differences. In support of this assumption, Hoshino-Browne et al. (2005) found that European Canadians tended to rationalize choices more when these choices were made for themselves than when they were made for a friend. Conversely, Asian Canadians tended to rationalize choices more when they were made for a friend than when they were made for themselves. In Festinger's (1957) terms, these results can be explained with the higher importance of social relations compared to individual needs in East Asian cultures, which tends to be the opposite in North American cultures. In a nutshell, relative importance influences the magnitude of dissonance aroused by a given inconsistency, and relative importance often depends on cultural norms and traditions.

Another source of cross-cultural differences at the dissonance elicitation stage may be the standard employed to evaluate one's behavior. As outlined above, Stone and Cooper (2001) argued that people compare their behavior to either personal or normative standards and that the magnitude of dissonance experiences is determined by the discrepancy between one's behavior and the momentarily employed standard. Thus, to the extent that Westerners show a stronger emphasis of personal standards, whereas East Asians tend to exhibit a stronger emphasis of normative standards, the differential importance of personal and normative standards for evaluating one's behavior could affect the magnitude of dissonance experiences elicited by a given behavior. For instance, making a career-related decision that is in line with the expectations of one's parents but inconsistent with one's personal preferences may elicit more dissonance in Westerners compared to Easterners. Conversely, deciding for a career that is in line with one's personal preferences, but inconsistent with the expectations of one's parents may elicit more dissonance in Easterners than Westerners.

DIFFERENCES IN INCONSISTENCY RESOLUTION

If inconsistency has been identified and if this inconsistency has elicited aversive feelings of dissonance, people will typically try to resolve the inconsistency that gave rise to these feelings. According to Festinger (1957), inconsistency can be resolved either by changing one of the involved elements or by adding a cognitive element that resolves the inconsistency. Whereas the first strategy can be described as a change in the (subjective) truth value of one of the involved propositions, the second strategy can be regarded as the search for an additional proposition to resolve the momentary inconsistency (Gawronski & Strack, 2004). Examples of the first strategy include changes in attitudes or behavior; examples of the second strategy include the search for consonant information or trivializing the importance of inconsistency (Festinger, 1957).

As outlined in the general description of inconsistency resolution, the presence versus absence of dissonance-related attitude change is often equated with the presence versus absence of dissonance experiences. Given Festinger's (1957) emphasis on different inconsistency resolution strategies, this equation seems premature. In fact, any change in the chosen strategy to resolve inconsistency is likely to affect the emergence of dissonance-related attitude change (e.g., Simon et al., 1995; Gosling et al., 2006). From this perspective, reductions in dissonance-related attitude change often remain nondiagnostic as to whether these reductions are due to a lack of dissonance experiences or a change in the strategy to resolve inconsistency.

These considerations have important implications for cross-cultural differences in dissonance-related attitude change. For instance, in their overview of cross-cultural studies on cognitive dissonance, Heine and Lehman (1997) cited several studies that failed to show any effect of induced compliance (Festinger & Carlsmith, 1959) in East Asian participants (e.g., Hiniker, 1969; Kudo & Mitsui, 1974; Mondon, 1980; Hirose & Kitada, 1985). Heine and Lehman (1997) interpreted these findings as preliminary evidence showing that East Asians may not experience cognitive dissonance and that cognitive dissonance may be a phenomenon that is limited to Western cultures (but see Sakai, 1981). From the perspective of our three-stage model, this conclusion seems premature. Rather, the obtained differences may also be due to differences in the strategy to resolve inconsistency, such that Westerners may be more likely to reduce inconsistency via attitude change, whereas Easterners may be more likely to reduce inconsistency by means of one of the other three strategies. In our opinion, the most plausible candidate for such strategy differences is the differential tendency to explain behavior in situational terms (Choi et al., 1999). A number of cross-cultural studies on causal attribution have shown that Easterners have a stronger tendency to explain behavior in situational terms than Westerners (e.g., Miller, 1984; Morris & Peng, 1994). Thus, Easterners may explain their counterattitudinal behavior in situational terms regardless of whether situational pressure is high or low (e.g., "the experimenter asked me to do it"), whereas Westerners may explain their counterattitudinal behavior in situational terms only when situational pressure is high (e.g., "I got a lot of money for doing it"), but not when situational pressure is low. As situational explanations for counterattitudinal behavior can function as additional cognitions that resolve inconsistency (Stalder & Baron, 1998), a potential lack of attitude change obtained for Easterners remains nondiagnostic as to whether it is due to a complete lack of dissonance experiences or to the use of a different strategy to resolve inconsistency. This question can be answered only by including measures of dissonance experiences (e.g., Croyle & Cooper, 1983; Elliot & Devine, 1994; Harmon-Jones, 2000; Losch & Cacioppo, 1990), but not by the mere presence or absence of dissonance-related attitude change. Moreover, even if there is no evidence for dissonance-related affect in East Asians, this lack of aversive feelings could also be related to the identification of inconsistency, such that the enhanced tendency for situational explanations in East Asians could prevent the emergence of inconsistency in the first place (see Harmon-Jones, 2000). In other words, the mere emergence of cross-cultural differences in dissonance-related attitude change does not provide any information as to whether these differences are due to (a) differences in the inconsistency of culturally diverging systems of beliefs, (b) differences in the experiences elicited by an inconsistent belief system, or (c) differences in the employed strategy to resolve inconsistency.

IMPLICATIONS

Our conceptual reanalysis suggests that the general *processes* involved in cognitive dissonance may indeed be universal, as proposed by Festinger (1957), even though cross-cultural differences pertaining to the *contents* of belief systems may function as important moderators of the respective outcomes of these processes. Drawing on a conceptualization of cognitive dissonance as an inherently propositional phenomenon (Gawronski & Strack, 2004), we proposed a three-stage model of inconsistency processes that distinguishes between (a) the identification of inconsistency, (b) the elicitation of dissonance experiences, and (c) the resolution of inconsistency to reduce dissonance experiences (see Figure 13.1). We further argued that the respective outcomes of these steps depend on several important factors. The first step, identification of inconsistency, depends on the simultaneous accessibility of potentially inconsistent cognitions (McGregor et al., 1999), and the assignment of truth values that makes these cognitions factually inconsistent (Gawronski & Strack, 2004). The second step, elicitation of dissonance experiences, depends on the subjective importance of the involved cognitive elements (Festinger, 1957) and the particular standards employed to evaluate one's behavior (Stone & Cooper, 2001). Finally, the third step, inconsistency resolution, depends on the particular strategy used to resolve inconsistency (Festinger, 1957).

Several of these determinants can be related to well-established differences between Eastern and Western cultures. As such, culture may function as an important moderator of the outcomes of each of the three steps, even though the general processes may be universal. With regard to the first step, identification of inconsistency, we argued that cultural differences in accepted beliefs can determine whether or not the acceptance of a particular proposition results in inconsistency. In addition, the contextualized nature of evaluations and beliefs in East Asian cultures may reduce the general likelihood of inconsistency compared to the decontextualized way of thinking in Western cultures. With regard to the second step, elicitation of dissonance experiences, we argued that cultural norms and traditions influence the relative importance of a particular cognition, thereby affecting the relative magnitude of dissonance experiences elicited by the same inconsistency. In addition, the differential use of personal versus normative standards can lead to cross-cultural differences in dissonance experiences arising from the same inconsistency. Finally, with regard to the third step, inconsistency resolution, we argued that culturally transmitted habits may influence the strategies employed to resolve inconsistency, with East Asian cultures showing a stronger tendency to explain counterattitudinal behavior in situational terms, thereby reducing the likelihood of dissonance-related attitude change.

These conclusions have important implications for the study of cross-cultural differences in cognitive dissonance. Specifically, our reanalysis suggests that accurate interpretations of cross-cultural differences require a consideration of the particular mechanisms that underlie these differences. For instance, simply showing that Easterners exhibit less attitude change in the induced compliance paradigm (Festinger & Carlsmith, 1959) than Westerners does not say anything about whether such cultural variations are due to (a) differences in the identification of inconsistency, (b) differences in the dissonance experiences elicited by cognitive inconsistency, or (c) differences in the employed strategy to resolve inconsistency. To address this question, researchers would need to include additional measures tapping into the relevant components of each of the three steps. For instance, measures assessing the aversive feelings arising from inconsistency may provide important information about the elicitation of dissonance experiences (e.g., Croyle & Cooper, 1983; Losch & Cacioppo, 1990; Elliot & Devine, 1994; Harmon-Jones, 2000). Such evidence seems particularly important for current controversies regarding the universality versus cultural dependency of cognitive dissonance (e.g., Sakai, 1981; Heine & Lehman, 1997; Kitayama et al., 2004; Hoshino-Browne et al., 2005; see also Norenzayan & Heine, 2005). Future research distinguishing between the three steps of inconsistency resolution may provide a deeper understanding of cross-cultural differences in cognitive dissonance.

Aside from cross-cultural differences, our conceptual reanalysis of inconsistency processes also has important implications for dissonance research in general. Thirty years ago, Greenwald and Ronis (1978) complained that the notion of logical consistency got lost in modern reformulations of dissonance theory, which in their view have more similarities to theories of self-esteem maintenance compared to Festinger's (1957) original formulation. As such, these reformulations seem unable to integrate many of the original studies and illustrations that Festinger used to specify his definition of cognitive dissonance. Our three-stage model of inconsistency processes captures Greenwald and Ronis' (1978) concern by emphasizing the crucial role of logical relations in the definition of inconsistency. This emphasis has led to the discovery that dissonance arising from counterattitudinal behavior (Festinger & Carlsmith, 1959) influences ("explicit") propositional evaluations, but not ("implicit") associative evaluations (Gawronski & Strack, 2004; see also Wilson et al., 2000). Notwithstanding this reintegration of logical consistency, our three-stage model seems flexible enough to incorporate many of the assumptions made by reformulations of dissonance theory (e.g., Aronson, 1968; Cooper & Fazio, 1983; Steele & Liu, 1983; Steele et al., 1993; Stone & Cooper, 2001). In fact, our model may even help to refine these assumptions by specifying the particular stage of inconsistency processes that is affected by a given variable. Thus, future research relating the three steps to the variables identified in modern reformulations of dissonance theory may help to further clarify the interplay between cognitive and motivational processes in cognitive dissonance. Such research may also provide deeper insights into the sources of cross-cultural differences pertaining to these variables (e.g., Heine & Lehman, 1997; Kitayama et al., 2004; Hoshino-Browne et al., 2005).

CONCLUSION

In summary, we argued that the general *processes* related to cognitive inconsistency – and thus cognitive dissonance – may indeed be universal, even though cross-cultural differences pertaining to the involved *contents* may function as important moderators of dissonance-related phenomena (e.g., dissonance-related attitude change). This assumption echoes theoretical considerations by Harmon-Jones and Harmon-Jones (2002), who claimed that the motivating force in the resolution of cognitive inconsistency is the dysfunctional effect of inconsistent cognitions on effective action. In line with this notion, we believe that inconsistency may function as a cue to inaccurate components in one's system of beliefs (Quine & Ullian, 1978). Thus, to the extent that inaccurate belief systems can undermine effective action, inconsistency acquires an important function from a pragmatic point of view. As William James (1890, p. 333) described it: "My thinking is first and last and always for the sake of my doing." In our view, cognitive consistency plays a significant role in this regard by facilitating context-appropriate action – a requirement that we deem universal.

ACKNOWLEDGEMENT

Preparation of this article was supported by grants from the Canada Research Chairs program, the Social Sciences and Humanities Research Council of Canada, the Academic Development Fund of the University of Western Ontario, and the TransCoop Program of the Alexander-von-Humboldt Foundation. We are grateful to Haruki Sakai, Jeff Stone, Mark Zanna, and the Editors for valuable comments on an earlier version of this chapter.

REFERENCES

Aronson, E. (1968). Dissonance theory: Progress and problems. In R. P. Abelson, E. Aronson, W. J. McGuire, T. M. Newcombe, M. J. Rosenberg, & P. H. Tannenbaum (Eds.), *Theories of cognitive consistency: A sourcebook* (pp. 5–27). Skokie, IL: Rand-McNally.

Aronson, E. (1997). The theory of cognitive dissonance: The evolution and vicissitudes of an idea. In C. McGarty & S. A. Haslam (Eds.), *The message of social psychology* (pp. 20–35). Cambridge, MA: Blackwell.

Brehm, J. W. (1956). Postdecision changes in the desirability of alternatives. *Journal of Abnormal and Social Psychology*, *52*, 384–389.

Bosson, J. K., Swann, W. B., & Pennebaker, J. W. (2000). Stalking the perfect measure of implicit self-esteem: The blind men and the elephant revisited?. *Journal of Personality and Social Psychology*, *79*, 631–643.

Choi, I., Nisbett, R. E., & Norenzayan, A. (1999). Causal attribution across cultures: Variation and universality. *Psychological Bulletin*, *125*, 47–63.

Cooper, J., & Fazio, R. H. (1984). A new look at dissonance theory. In L. Berkowitz (Ed.), *Advances in Experimental Social Psychology, Vol. 17* (pp. 229–266). San Diego, CA: Academic Press.

Croyle, R. T., & Cooper, J. (1983). Dissonance arousal: Physiological evidence. *Journal of Personality and Social Psychology*, *45*, 782–791.

Deutsch, R., Gawronski, B., & Strack, F. (2006). At the boundaries of automaticity: Negation as reflective operation. *Journal of Personality and Social Psychology*, *91*, 385–405.

Elliot, A. J., & Devine, P. G. (1994). On the motivational nature of cognitive dissonance: Dissonance as psychological discomfort. *Journal of Personality and Social Psychology*, *67*, 382–394.

Festinger, L. (1957). *A theory of cognitive dissonance*. Evanston, IL: Row Peterson.

Festinger, L., & Carlsmith, J. M. (1959). Cognitive consequences of forced compliance. *Journal of Abnormal and Social Psychology*, *58*, 203–210.

Fried, C. B., & Aronson, E. (1995). Hypocrisy, misattribution, and dissonance reduction. *Personality and Social Psychology Bulletin*, *21*, 925–933.

Gawronski, B., & Bodenhausen, G. V. (2006a). Associative and propositional processes in evaluation: An integrative review of explicit and implicit attitude change. *Psychological Bulletin*, *132*, 692–731.

Gawronski, B., & Bodenhausen, G. V. (2006b). Associative and propositional processes in evaluation: Conceptual, empirical, and meta-theoretical issues. Reply to Albarracín, Hart, and McCulloch (2006), Kruglanski and Dechesne (2006), and Petty and Briñol (2006). *Psychological Bulletin*, *132*, 745–750.

Gawronski, B., Bodenhausen, G. V., & Becker, A. P. (2007). I like it, because I like myself: Associative self-anchoring and post-decisional change of implicit evaluations. *Journal of Experimental Social Psychology*, *43*, 221–232.

Gawronski, B., & Strack, F. (2004). On the propositional nature of cognitive consistency: Dissonance changes explicit, but not implicit attitudes. *Journal of Experimental Social Psychology*, *40*, 535–542.

Gawronski, B., Strack, F., & Bodenhausen, G. V. (in press-a). Attitudes and cognitive consistency: The role of associative and propositional processes. In: R. E. Petty, R. H. Fazio & P. Briñol (Eds.), *Attitudes: Insights from the new implicit measures*. Mahwah, NJ: Erlbaum.

Gawronski, B., Peters, K. P., Brochu, P. M., & Strack, F. (in press-b). Understanding the relations between different forms of racial prejudice: A cognitive consistency perspective. *Personality and Social Psychology Bulletin*.

Gilbert, D. T. (1991). How mental systems believe. *American Psychologist, 46,* 107–119.

Gosling, P., Denizeau, M., & Oberlé, D. (2006). Denial of responsibility: A new mode of dissonance reduction. *Journal of Personality and Social Psychology, 90,* 722–733.

Greenwald, A. G., & Farnham, S. D. (2000). Using the Implicit Association Test to measure self-esteem and self-concept. *Journal of Personality and Social Psychology, 79,* 1022–1038.

Greenwald, A. G., McGhee, D. E., & Schwartz, J. K. L. (1998). Measuring individual differences in implicit cognition: The Implicit Association Test. *Journal of Personality and Social Psychology, 74,* 1464–1480.

Greenwald, A. G., & Ronis, D. L. (1978). Twenty years of cognitive dissonance: Case study of the evolution of a theory. *Psychological Review, 85,* 53–57.

Harmon-Jones, E. (2000). Cognitive dissonance and experienced negative affect: Evidence that dissonance increases experienced negative affect even in the absence of aversive consequences. *Personality and Social Psychology Bulletin, 26,* 1490–1501.

Harmon-Jones, E., Brehm, J., Greenberg, J., Simon, L., & Nelson, D. E. (1996). Evidence that the production of aversive consequences is not necessary to create cognitive dissonance. *Journal of Personality and Social Psychology, 70,* 5–16.

Harmon-Jones, E., & Harmon-Jones, C. (2002). Testing the action-based model of cognitive dissonance: The effect of action orientation on postdecisional attitudes. *Personality and Social Psychology Bulletin, 28,* 711–723.

Heine, S. J., & Lehman, D. R. (1997). Culture, dissonance, and self-affirmation. *Personality and Social Psychology Bulletin, 23,* 389–400.

Hiniker, P. J. (1969). Chinese reactions to forced compliance: Dissonance reduction or national character. *Journal of Social Psychology, 77,* 157–176.

Hirose, Y., & Kitada, T. (1985). Actors' and observers' attributions responsibility and attitude change in the forced compliance situation. *Japanese Journal of Psychology, 56,* 262–268.

Hoshino-Browne, E., Zanna, A. S., Spencer, S. J., Zanna, M. P., Kitayama, S., & Lackenbauer, S. (2005). On the cultural guises of cognitive dissonance: The case of Easterners and Westerners. *Journal of Personality and Social Psychology, 89,* 294–310.

James, W. (1890). *The principles of psychology* (Vol. II). New York: Henry Holt & Co.

Jones, E. E., & Gerard, H. B. (1967). *Foundations of social psychology.* New York: Wiley.

Kitayama, S., Snibbe, A. C., Markus, H. R., & Suzuki, T. (2004). Is there any "free" choice: Self and dissonance in two cultures. *Psychological Science, 15,* 527–533.

Koole, S. L., Dijksterhuis, A., & Van Knippenberg, A. (2001). What's in a name: Implicit self-esteem and the automatic self. *Journal of Personality and Social Psychology, 80,* 669–685.

Kruglanski, A. W. (1989). *Lay epistemics and human knowledge: Cognitive and motivational bases.* New York: Plenum Press.

Kudo, T., & Mitsui, H. (1974). The magnitude of incentive, timing, and attitude change. *Japanese Psychological Review, 17,* 384–402.

Lieberman, M. D., Ochsner, K. N., Gilbert, D. T., & Schacter, D. L. (2001). Do amnesics exhibit cognitive dissonance reduction? The role of explicit memory and attention in attitude change. *Psychological Science, 12,* 135–140.

Losch, M. E., & Cacioppo, J. T. (1990). Cognitive dissonance may enhance sympathetic tonus, but attitudes are changed to reduce negative affect rather than arousal. *Journal of Experimental Social Psychology, 26,* 289–304.

Markus, H., & Kitayama, S. (1991). Culture and the self: Implications for cognition, emotion, and motivation. *Psychological Review, 98,* 224–253.

McGregor, I., Newby-Clark, I. R., & Zanna, M. P. (1999). "Remembering" dissonance: Simultaneous accessibility of inconsistent cognitive elements moderates epistemic discomfort. In E. Harmon-Jones & J. Mills (Eds.), *Cognitive dissonance: Progress on a pivotal theory in social psychology* (pp. 325–353). Washington, DC: American Psychological Association.

Miller, J. G. (1984). Culture and the development of everyday social explanation. *Journal of Personality and Social Psychology, 46,* 961–978.

Mondon, K. (1980). Attitude change and attitude recall in a consonant or dissonant: An attempt to integrate cognitive dissonance theory and self-perception theory. *Japanese Journal of Psychology*, *51*, 128–135.

Morris, M. W., & Peng, K. (1994). Culture and cause: American and Chinese attributions for social and physical events. *Journal of Personality and Social Psychology*, *67*, 949–971.

Norenzayan, A., & Heine, S. J. (2005). Psychological universals: What are they and how can we know?. *Psychological Bulletin, 763-784*.

Peng, K., & Nisbett, R. E. (1999). Culture, dialectics, and reasoning about contradiction. *American Psychologist*, *54*, 741–754.

Quine, W. V. O., & Ullian, J. S. (1978). *The web of belief* (2nd ed.). New York: McGraw-Hill.

Sakai, H. (1981). Induced compliance and opinion change. *Japanese Psychological Research*, *23*, 1–8.

Sakai, H. (1999). A multiplicative power-function model of cognitive dissonance: Toward an integrated theory of cognition, emotion, and behavior after Leon Festinger. In E. Harmon-Jones & J. Mills (Eds.), *Cognitive dissonance: Progress on a pivotal theory in social psychology* (pp. 267–294). Washington, DC: American Psychological Association.

Schwarz, N. (2007). Attitude construction: Evaluation in context. *Social Cognition, 25*, 638–656.

Simon, L., Greenberg, J., & Brehm, J. (1995). Trivialization: The forgotten mode of dissonance reduction. *Journal of Personality and Social Psychology*, *68*, 247–260.

Stalder, D. R., & Baron, R. S. (1998). Attributional complexity as a moderator of dissonance-produced attitude change. *Journal of Personality and Social Psychology*, *75*, 449–455.

Steele, C. M., & Liu, T. J. (1983). Dissonance processes as self-affirmation. *Journal of Personality and Social Psychology*, *45*, 5–19.

Steele, C. M., Spencer, S. J., & Lynch, M. (1993). Self-image resilience and dissonance: The role of affirmational resources. *Journal of Personality and Social Psychology*, *64*, 885–896.

Stone, J., Aronson, E., Crain, A. L., Winslow, M. P., & Fried, C. B. (1994). Inducing hypocrisy as a means of encouraging young adults to use condoms. *Personality and Social Psychology Bulletin*, *20*, 116–128.

Stone, J., & Cooper, J. (2001). A self-standards model of cognitive dissonance. *Journal of Experimental Social Psychology*, *37*, 228–243.

Stone, J., & Cooper, J. (2003). The effect of self-attribute relevance on how self-esteem moderates attitude change in dissonance processes. *Journal of Experimental Social Psychology*, *37*, 228–243.

Stone, J., Wiegand, A. W., Cooper, J., & Aronson, E. (1997). When exemplification fails: Hypocrisy and the motive for self-integrity. *Journal of Personality and Social Psychology*, *72*, 54–65.

Strack, F., & Deutsch, R. (2004). Reflective and impulsive determinants of social behavior. *Personality and Social Psychology Review*, *8*, 220–247.

Wilson, T. D., Lindsey, S., & Schooler, T. Y. (2000). A model of dual attitudes. *Psychological Review, 107*, 101–126.

Zanna, M. P., & Cooper, J. (1974). Dissonance and the pill: An attribution approach to studying the arousal properties of dissonance. *Journal of Personality and Social Psychology*, *29*, 703–709.

MOTIVATION AND COGNITION FROM A CULTURAL PERSPECTIVE

14

THE ROLE OF LANGUAGE IN THE PERCEPTION OF PERSONS AND GROUPS

MINORU KARASAWA[*] AND ANNE MAASS[†]

*Department of Psychology, Nagoya University, Nagoya, Japan
†Department of Developmental Psychology and Socialization, University of Padova, Padova, Italy

The role of language in culture and cognitive as well as motivational processes has been a highly popular and long-standing focus of interest in various fields. Just as psychologists are interested in the degree of universality and variations of cognition and behavior across different cultures, so are linguists often engaged in the debate over singular versus multiple bases of the linguistic system. Likewise, while psychologists investigate the "dynamic and mutual constitution" between culture and psychological processes (e.g., Fiske et al., 1998), linguists raise questions regarding the relationship between language and thought (e.g., Whorf, 1957; Lakoff, 1987; Langacker, 1987, 1991). Certainly, language constitutes an integral part of culture. First, linguistic representations are an indispensable device for humans to make sense of the environment, and transcend symbols of meaning and practices to others and over generations. Very often, positive or negative evaluative significance is attached to the transmitted communication, and hence either drives people toward, or inhibit them from, engaging in certain behavior. Furthermore, language functions as a behavioral norm. Grammatical and pragmatic rules dictate what are the right ways and what are the wrong ways to verbally express one's ideas in certain contexts, on the basis of common ground knowledge shared within the community. Whereas language exerts such prescriptive and consistent impact on behavior, it also shows a great deal of flexibility, making room for new forms of practices to develop. In this sense, the practice of language use can be seen as a distinct kind of social action, involving various cognitive and motivational processes (Holtgraves, 2002).

Despite its widely recognized importance, language has been a relatively under-investigated area in the empirical study of culture, cognition, and motivation, at least involving the social domain. One reason seems to lie in the status of the so-called Whorfian hypothesis. Whorf's (1957) somewhat counter-intuitive claim that language determines the content of cognition was highly appealing, and stimulated a substantial amount of research. The enthusiasm seemed to have waned after a series of failures in providing solid evidence for the pure Whorfian view, but there is a resurgence of interest in Whorf's original views, especially with regard to the impact of language *use* on cognition and motivation (for overviews, see Hunt & Agnoli, 1991; Gumperz & Levinson, 1996; Boroditsky, 2003). Still, it should be pointed out that evidence is relatively limited to cognition of the physical world, and even less is known about *social* cognition (for important exceptions, however, see Semin, 2001; Lau et al., 2004).

In this chapter, we will discuss three functions of language in social cognition. First, we will analyze the way in which language drives *attention*. We will argue that subtle differences in language use determine what the listeners will focus on, what will attract their attention, and also what they may overlook or ignore. Second, we will review research showing that linguistic choices of the speaker affect *inferences* that the listener is likely to draw about the speaker as well as the object of the conversation. Finally, taking an embodiment perspective, we will argue that our perception and *imagery* of social reality is, in a subtle manner, influenced by the way in which language is written.

Throughout this chapter we will report both language-specific and, where available, cross-linguistic evidence, in line with the idea that human thought is not only influenced by structural differences between languages (Whorf, 1957) but also by linguistic choices within a given language. In fact, some researchers have even emphasized that within-language analyses are more desirable than cross-linguistic analyses both theoretically and methodologically (Stapel & Semin, 2007). Although it is not our aim to provide an exhaustive review of the literature, we hope that this chapter will, through prototypical examples, illustrate some basic processes through which seemingly small differences in linguistic choices and communicative styles may affect cognition and motivation in social contexts.

LANGUAGE DRIVING ATTENTION IN THE SOCIAL WORLD

Language is at times observed to draw attention of speakers and listeners to specific properties of social objects. For instance, languages that have terms for "left" and "right" tend to direct attention to the spatial relation between objects (including the self) and the surrounding environment, thus motivating the speaker to apply a relative frame of reference. In contrast, languages that have only absolute spatial terms (such as North–South or uphill–downhill) lead people to pay attention to the absolute position of objects and to develop an absolute frame of reference (Levinson, 1996). Here, the question is whether analogous mechanisms may also operate in social cognition. Will our attention be driven to specific characteristics of the social environment as a function of the vocabulary available in a given language or of the linguistic choices made by the speaker?

PRONOUN DROP

Certain cultures seem to encourage their constituent members to pay careful attention to individually acting agents, whereas other cultures emphasize a greater significance of paying attention to the context and the relationship in which those individuals behave. The contextual factors include social environment, such as other people and social groups, and physical settings (see Menon et al., 1999; Masuda & Nisbett, 2001; Nisbett et al., 2001). Evidence shows that language plays a role, at least in part, in sustaining such practices of agent-oriented versus context-orientated emphasis. For instance, some languages necessitate a clear marker of the agent in a sentence such as a singular deictic pronoun. English, with "I" and "you" as singular first- and second-person pronouns, is a typical example of this category of languages. In contrast, other languages allow sentences void of the pronoun and require the listener (and reader) to infer the missing agent. Languages such as Italian and Spanish at times show this "pronoun drop," and some East Asian languages including Chinese, Korean, and Japanese allow the absence in more marked ways.

On the basis of a literature survey of over 39 languages from 71 countries, Kashima and Kashima (1998) demonstrated that the frequency of using first- and second-person pronouns (i.e., an inversed index of pronoun drop) was associated with the cultural value of *individualism* (i.e., the orientation to giving priority to individuals' interest over the collective's; see Hofstede ,1980) with remarkably high correlations ($r = .75$, with cultures as the unit of analysis; $r = .64$, with languages as the unit). Kashima and Kashima (1998) furthermore pointed out that some languages show a greater variety in second-person pronouns (e.g., *vous* and *tu* in French; *Lei* and *tu* in Italian; *anata, kimi, omae*, and many more in Japanese), and claimed that this reflects the speaker's sensitivity toward the social structure and interpersonal relationships. Indeed, individualism was found to be negatively correlated to the number of such multiple pronouns. In addition, Kashima and Kashima (2003) demonstrated that language exerts a substantial influence on relationships among individualism and other structural factors such as the Gross National Product per capita.

POLITENESS

Another contextual influence on language is observed with regard to politeness. Across different cultures, there appears to be a highly universal principle according to which people select language that does not threaten or offend the recipient of the communicated message (e.g., Brown & Levinson, 1978; Leech, 1983). The consideration for the recipient directs communicators' attention to particular individual characteristics as well as categorical attributes of the communication partner (e.g., gender, social status and power, etc.). On the other hand, even if the significance of politeness may be observed across diverse linguistic communities, the attributes of communication partners that draw special attention in one culture may be practically meaningless in other cultures. Age is one example of such categorical attributes of cultural significance. In East Asian societies (and in other cultures to various degrees), age carries critically important information about individuals because many social variables, such as status, power difference, expectations for respect, assistance, protection, and so forth are associated with or even determined by biological age. Importantly, the relative significance of age tends to be reflected in language. For instance, Japanese have countless rules with regard to suffices and particles to construct honorifics and intimate forms. People with such linguistic practices are predicted to encode age information at an early stage of social relationship in order to build smooth interactions. Indeed, Japanese people often mention their age when introducing oneself to others, and if they fail to do so they will be asked about their age. Also, Japanese speakers are often observed to switch their linguistic forms even toward the same person, after discovering the other person's age.

The possibility that disproportionate attention is attracted by a culturally important category was illustrated in a study by Karasawa et al. (2007). Using the "who said what paradigm" (cf. Taylor et al., 1978), these researchers examined memory errors among Italian and Japanese students in the age range between 19 and 23 years. Half of the target individuals were described as being slightly younger than the participants (i.e., 16, 17, and 18-years old), while others as slightly older (24, 25, and 26-years old). Note that Japanese language rules require speakers to use different forms of addressing the two groups, whereas slightly younger and slightly older communication partners are addressed equally in Italian language. Indeed, when the numbers associated with the target thus implied two groups of "older" and "younger" than the self, Japanese participants showed a significantly greater number of *within-category* memory confusions than *between-category* confusions in identifying the target individuals. In contrast, Italian participants did not show such memory bias, presumably because the age of the target was irrelevant to their linguistic choices. When the numbers purportedly indicated a less meaningful attribute (i.e., each individual's "favorite number"), the memory bias among Japanese disappeared. More important for the present discussion, for Japanese, memory confusions in the age condition were particularly pronounced when participants expected to communicate with the target person, suggesting that the greater attention to age information was, at least in part, driven by the need to make linguistic choices. Indeed, when analyzing the participant's responses to the target, Japanese used honorifics toward the "senior" targets and intimate forms toward the "juniors" in a differentiated manner, whereas Italians consistently used intimate forms. Together, these findings suggest that the requirements of a given language (such as the necessity to choose more or less formal language) lead people to pay close attention to relevant social cues (such as age), cues that are easily overlooked by speakers of other languages that do not make such differentiations. Thus, the grammatical requirements of a language are able to guide the speakers' attention toward relevant attributes of the social environment.

GRAMMATICAL GENDER

Yet another way in which languages differ systematically, is the presence or absence of grammatical gender. There are considerable variations in gender marking even within Indo-European languages. For example, gender marking is minimal in English as it is limited to subjects with natural gender and affects only few parts of the sentence (such as personal pronouns or possessive adjectives). In contrast, in many other languages, *all* nouns are assigned to distinct gender classes, typically two (French, Italian, etc.) or three classes (German, see also Russian). In these languages, a noun's gender generally affects many parts of speech, including the article, the adjective, and, at times, the verb. Importantly, gender assignment in these languages is largely arbitrary, as evidenced by the fact that many nouns are masculine in one and feminine in the other language, such as "tiger" and "snow" which are masculine in German but feminine in Italian, or "sun" and "cat" which are feminine in German, but masculine in Italian.

The question then arises as to whether grammatical gender affects the way in which the respective objects are perceived. Do we infer masculine or feminine characteristics in line with the grammatical gender despite the fact that gender assignment is largely arbitrary? For instance, do German–Italian bilinguals perceive a "tiger" as stronger when they think about it in German rather than in Italian? There is now evidence to suggest that this is indeed the case. Konishi (1993) asked German and Spanish speakers to judge, among others, the potency of words that are masculine in one and feminine in the other language, finding that the same object (e.g., a tiger) was perceived as more potent when marked by masculine gender in one's native language. This suggests that grammatical gender does carry meaning in line with stereotypically masculine versus feminine traits even where there is no logical reason for why a word should be marked by one or the other gender. Interestingly, conceptually similar results were also found with elementary schoolchildren of different nationalities, including Italian, Spanish, and German speakers, who tended to assign male versus female voices to objects in line with grammatical gender when asked to imagine that these objects were to appear in a cartoon (Sera et al., 2002; Agnoli & Forer, 2005). Together, these findings suggest that grammatical gender affects the perception of objects reliably, a bias already observable in middle childhood. Interestingly, this bias derived from one's native language even generalizes to second languages that have no grammatical gender (Boroditsky, Scmidt, and Phillips, 2003).

If grammatical gender is semantically informative even when unrelated to natural gender, as the above studies suggest, then there are interesting implications for those language communities in which the masculine plural is used generically to refer to both male and female components. In many languages in which nouns carry grammatical gender, the masculine form is used when the speaker intends to refer to both males and females. For example, "studente" and "Student" describe a male, "studentessa" and "Studentin" a female student in Italian and German, respectively. In the plural form, male students are referred to as "studenti" and "Studenten," female students as "studentesse" and "Studentinnen." However, when referring generically to students of *both* sexes, the speaker will need to use the masculine, rather than feminine plural. From a social-linguistic point of view, it then becomes interesting to ask whether the use of the masculine plural in a generic sense may lead people to "overlook" women subsumed under the masculine label. The extensive research project by Stahlberg and Sczesny (2001, Stahlberg et al., 2001) provides a very clear, affirmative answer to this question. In one of their studies (Braun et al., 1998), German university students read a fictitious newspaper article reporting on a scientific conference in geophysics whose participants were referred to in different linguistic forms, among which either the standard masculine generic plural ("Wissenschaftler") or a dual nomination including both the masculine and feminine plural ("Wissenschaftler und Wissenschaftlerinnen"). When asked to estimate the percentage of women participating at the conferences, female respondents indicated much lower percentage estimates when the generic masculine plural than when the dual (masculine and feminine), plural was used. In a conceptually similar study, Stahlberg et al. (2001) asked German participants to indicate their favorite writer, actor, musician, or athlete while systematically varying the linguistic formulation of the question (generic masculine, gender-neutral, or masculine-feminine dual nomination). As expected, results showed that both male and female respondents named fewer female writers, actors, and so forth when the question was formulated in the generic masculine form, suggesting that the generic masculine inhibited access to female exemplars stored in memory. Together, these and other studies suggest that the use of generic masculine plurals, that are the grammatical rule in most gender-bound languages, biases the retrieval of male versus female exemplars and decreases the visibility of women relative to men.

The three lines of research cited so far illustrate that the lexical, syntactic, and pragmatic features of a language guide the attention of both speaker and listener. Languages that allow (or prohibit) pronoun drop appear to be associated with more group-oriented (or individual oriented) focus of attention and related social values. Also, languages that have complex ways of addressing others force speakers to attend very carefully to status and age cues, needed to choose the most appropriate linguistic form. In contrast, speakers of languages with relatively simple politeness rules are unlikely to pay attention to or to process such cues simply because they are irrelevant to speech. By the same logic, the properties of a given language not only determine what we pay attention to, but also what we tend to overlook, as in the case of gender-bound languages in which women become cognitively "invisible," because they are grammatically subsumed under the masculine generic label.

The examples cited so far suggest that specific characteristics of a given language (such as personal pronoun drop, grammatical gender, etc.) guide attention to specific aspects of our social or physical environment (such as agent, gender, age etc.). Recently, Stapel and Semin (2007) have argued that language properties may also have generic effects on cognition that are not limited to any specific content domain. These authors advance the provocative idea that the meta-semantic features of linguistic categories, in particular the degree of linguistic abstraction, influence a wide range of perceptual, attentional, and cognitive processes. The more abstract the language to which people are exposed, the more global their perceptual focus will be on tasks that have little or nothing to do with language. To cite just one example from this research project (Stapel & Semin, 2007, Experiment. 2), participants were initially primed with concrete (action verbs, e.g., "A punches B") or abstract language (adjectives, e.g., "A is aggressive") and then engaged in a categorization task that allowed to see how inclusive participants were when deciding whether an exemplar fit a given category. In line with hypotheses, participants who had been exposed to abstract language were much more inclusive than those who had been exposed to concrete language. This and other studies of the same line of research suggest that general features of language affect very basic processes including perceptual focus and categorization, with more abstract predicates directing attention to more global aspects of the environment. Considering that this research is concerned with linguistic variations within a single language community, a challenging question for future research is whether such generalized effects of language on cognition may, at least in part, account for cross-cultural variations in thought processes (see Nisbett et al., 2001), assuming that languages differ systematically in their relative use of concrete versus abstract terms.

In sum, the research reviewed here illustrates that language not only produces domain-specific effects that are largely in line with Whorfian thinking, but also shapes the person's general mindset, directing his or her attention to different aspects of the environment.

LANGUAGE GUIDING SOCIAL INFERENCES

Linguistic communication presupposes that the communicators share common ground knowledge (Grice, 1975; Clark, 1996). Otherwise, communication would be a laborious activity because the message sender would have to transmit every relevant piece of information while the recipient would need to reproduce every single piece of information accurately. Instead, communicators can fill in implicated or missing information on the basis of the common ground and context information (Sperber & Wilson, 1995). The pragmatic property of language seems to be closely related to the human capacity of drawing inferences and generalizations. In this section, we will discuss how language influences social inferences (and vice versa).

IMPLICIT CAUSALITY AND DISPOSITIONISM

The study of causal attribution has been among the most productive areas in the history of social psychology (Jones et al., 1972; Hewstone, 1989; Anderson et al., 1996). Whether it is performed in a normative or a biased manner, causal inference often necessitates the mediation of linguistic representations of the target event. Empirical evidence indeed shows that language exerts subtle, and yet systematic influences on causal judgments. An example is found in the phenomenon called the "implicit verb causality effect" (Brown & Fish, 1983; Rudolph & Försterling, 1997). When people read a sentence, "Jack loves Rose," they typically perceive that Rose (i.e., the sentence *object*) is the cause. Another sentence, "Rose attracts Jack," also implies that Rose is the likely cause, but in this case, she is the *subject* of the sentence. The effect takes place, of course, not because Rose is so attractive, but because the semantic roles of the verbs are different in the respective sentences. Both "love" and "attract" are classified as "state verbs," referring to mental interactions between the protagonists, but the former verb is assumed to activate a set of knowledge (i.e., schema) indicating that the subject is the "experiencer" of the emotion whereas the object is the "stimulus." On the contrary, the verb "attract" is thought to activate a schema that the word order should represent a stimulus-experiencer sequence (Brown & Fish, 1983). The implicit causality effect is also found in another verb category called "action verbs" which refer to behavioral interactions typically involving volitional motor activities. A sentence, "Jack protects Rose" implies that the cause is now in Jack, the subject. Action verbs with this "agent-patient" word order are generally associated with causality judgment for the sentence subject (Brown & Fish, 1983; but see also Rudolph & Försterling, 1997, for a different type of action verbs).

The linguistic analysis of implicit causality was further advanced by Semin and Fiedler (1988; 1992). In their Linguistic Category Model (LCM), these authors claimed that variations in predicates carry information not only about the subject versus object locus of causal agency but also about other properties of the event such as characteristics of the actor, the situation, and the generalizability of the observed event. They further maintained that the taxonomy of predicates with regard to their level of *abstraction* represents such inferential information. According to the LCM, predicates located at the lowest level of abstraction are Descriptive Action Verbs (DAV) such as "call" and "kick." These refer to specific and physically invariant features of the act, and the valence associated with them is assumed to be minimal. At the next level, we find Interpretive Action Verbs (IAV; e.g., "help," "attack"). These verbs describe lager classes of behaviors and typically carry positive or negative value connotations. Next, State

Verbs (SV) referring to internal states of the actor, such as "care" and "hate," are more informative about the disposition of the actor[1]. Finally, at the highest level are Adjectives (ADJ) that refer to the actor's traits (e.g., helpful and aggressive). Semin and Fiedler (1988) proposed and indeed found that predicates with higher level of abstraction are perceived as more informative about the person but less telling about the situation, more enduring over time, and more difficult to verify objectively.

One advantage of taking the linguistic approach lies in the fact that the knowledge concerning the rules of implicit verb causality as well as the abstractness of sentence predicates is supposed to be *shared* by the members of the same linguistic community. It owes to this pragmatic utility that people can exchange their thoughts and ideas through linguistic communication. A series of studies using a "question and answer paradigm" developed by Semin and his colleagues has nicely demonstrated such utility in communicating causality. In one of the studies (Semin & De Poot, 1997), Dutch participants were asked to imagine different specific occasions and write down details of the behavioral episodes in each occasion. The descriptions obtained from an open-ended format were then content-analyzed. When the questions employed IAV as the predicate (e.g., "What happened when you *confided* in someone?"), the responses were constructed with predicates at lower abstraction levels, compared to when the questions were in SV form (e.g., *trusted*). Also, the described episodes placed a greater causal emphasis on the side of the sentence subject (i.e., the participant him/herself) when they were in response to the IAV questions, whereas the implied causality was reversed in the SV-question condition. More important, when an independent group of participants read the response descriptions with no knowledge about the original questions, they judged the events written in response to the SV-questions as less likely to be caused by the sentence subject, compared to those described in answering the IAV-questions. Hence, the implicit verb causality was generated between the questioner and the answerer, and was further transmitted to a third party. Interestingly, when the answerer was asked to predict the third-party observer's causal inferences, their prediction did not match the actual judgments. In other words, the transmission of implicit causality took place outside of the answerer's awareness (see also Semin et al., 1995, for similar results). These results suggest that a subtle difference in the type of predicate when asking questions can influence the verbal responses from the answerer, as well as how the answerer unknowingly appears to an independent observer. Language thus can serve as a tool to construct not only perceived but also an *actual* social relationship (Semin, 2000).

---

[1] In a revised version of LCM, another category named State Action Verbs (SAV) was proposed (e.g., surprise, excite, impress), which was comparable to "stimulus-experiencer state verb" in the terminology used by Brown and Fish (1983). However, SAV is typically treated as IAV in the practice of LCM in many studies because the properties of these two are judged to be identical in terms of the linguistic abstractness (Semin & Fiedler, 1992).

It should be noted, however, that evidence of the implicit causality effect has mainly been accumulated concerning Western European languages such as Dutch, English, and German. Further research is needed to examine whether we can find a similar effect in other languages. On the other hand, the LCM has been tested not only in Western languages but also in East Asian languages like Japanese (e.g., Karasawa & Suga, 2008; Suga & Karasawa, 2006; Tanabe & Oka, 2001), suggesting the possibility of its pan-cultural applicability. However, we will present empirical evidence in a later section, which indicates important qualifications.

VERB TRANSITIVITY AND INFERENCE OF AGENCY

Another linguistic property that is related to inferences about agency is the *transitivity* of verbs. For instance, a transitive sentence, "I broke the dish" unambiguously indicates that the sentence subject was the agent of the event, whereas an intransitive sentence, "The dish broke" does not explicitly point to the causal agent. Western languages generally have clear syntactic rules that dictate verb transitivity, such as consistent word orders (e.g., Subject–Verb–Object in English and others) and the dative and accusative cases accompanied by declension of the sentence object. In other languages, however, the definition of transitivity is less clear-cut (Hopper & Thompson, 1980). For instance, Japanese allows flexible word orders of subject and object. Certainly, inflections of verbs and suffixes attached to nouns and pronouns indicate the transitivity most of the time, but still there are some cases where help is needed from the semantic content of the sentence and the context, in order to decide whether an agentic effect on the supposed "object" word is truly expressed (Ikegami, 1991). Some languages are even known to lack transitive verbs for certain events that would easily be described as transitive in Western languages (e.g., DeLancy, 1984). Such variations can be reflected, at least in part, in linguistic transitivity.

In a study by Karasawa and Yoshinari (2007), Japanese participants read scenarios in which a protagonist caused damage to others' property. When the instruction induced an internal attribution of causality (i.e., projecting the self onto the protagonist), participants more frequently used transitive verbs in explaining the situation to the damage recipient (e.g., "I hit your car and scarred it") rather than intransitive verbs ("My car hit [against yours], and your car scarred"). In the external cause condition (e.g., projecting a friend on the protagonist), the use of intransitive verbs generally increased, in addition to an obvious change in the sentence subject (e.g., "My friend hit your car"). However, there was an interesting qualification. When the external cause was an inanimate object, the use of *first-person* transitive verbs significantly increased (e.g., "Because of a break failure, I hit your car"). This is presumably because a grammatical constraint in Japanese does not allow a sentence with an inanimate object being the sentence subject such as "A sudden break failure caused the fatal accident." This constraint likely forced the participants to substitute some animate entity for the subject, and consequently, a transitive verb accompanied it. (In fact, some participants even added "I'm sorry, but..."!) Still more important, the ratings of causality and responsibility that were made after the open-ended explanations showed that the scenario with an inanimate object as the cause resulted in high attribution of causality and responsibility to the self. Theses results demonstrate that, in addition to a straightforward effect of agency on transitivity (i.e., internal causes eliciting *first-person* transitivity), other linguistic features can also determine the use of transitive versus intransitive verbs. Furthermore, a resultant judgment of causality and responsibility may also be influenced by the language use, consistent with the main thrust of the Worfian hypothesis.

LANGUAGE AND TRAIT INFERENCES

Traits and dispositions are abstract concepts, and they are not directly observable. Instead, what we actually observe in social settings is concrete behavior. Nevertheless, perceivers instantly and spontaneously draw inferences about traits of the actor on the basis of behavioral episodes (Uleman et al., 1996). This tendency appears to be highly robust and even irrevocable. That is, it is generally easier to draw *inductive* (i.e., representing behavioral observation in an abstract trait term) rather than *deductive* inferences (i.e., deriving behavioral predictions from trait expectancy). The Induction-Deduction Asymmetry (IDA) was clearly demonstrated in a series of experiments by Maass et al. (2001). Participants received a series of descriptions of a target person, half of which were presented in adjective form (traits), half in verb form (behaviors). A subsequent recognition task was constructed so that some of the items (adjectives and verbs) had actually been seen, some were entirely new, and some were new but had been implied by the information given. Results showed that participants often falsely reported that they had seen *trait* adjectives that had not actually been present in the original stimulus information but that had been implied by a behavior. In contrast, they rarely misidentified behavior-descriptive verbs implied by a trait adjective as already seen.

In view of these findings regarding spontaneous trait inference and IDA, it may appear that seeking a stable, dispositional, and essence-like property in the character of an individual is a fundamental and universal tendency in person perception (Gilbert, 1998; Ross & Nisbett, 1991). However, recent studies suggest that this tendency is subject to cultural constraints. First of all, there is evidence that people living in cultures with so-called "holistic cognition" and those with "analytic cognition" show different patterns of information processing (Nisbett et al., 2001). Holistic cognition is characterized by a greater attention to "the context or field as a whole" and relationship among events, and experiential rather than abstract logic-based knowledge. In contrast, analytic cognition is associated with "detachment of the object from its context, a tendency to focus on attributes of the object to assign it to categories" as well as rule-based explanation and prediction of the object's behavior (p. 293). Consistent with this distinction, evidence shows that spontaneous trait inference is less prominent in East Asian culture (typically characterized by holistic cognition) than in the North-American culture (typically analytic) (e.g., Rhee et al., 1995, who compared Koreans, Korean-Americans, and Caucasian Americans; see also Zárate et al., 2001, for Hispanic data). Also, Japanese are found to use more relation-based terms in descriptions of their own attributes, compared to Americans who predominantly show trait-based self-concepts (Bond & Cheung, 1983; Cousins, 1989; Kanagawa et al., 2001).

Drawing on these previous findings, Maass et al. (2006) compared Italian and Japanese participants, predicting that IDA would be less prevalent among the latter. Even though adjectives and verbs may have similar functions in representing traits and behavioral episodes across these languages, the potential difference in analytic versus holistic cognition could be reflected in language use. The results generally confirmed the prediction. First, when participants were asked to describe social categories (i.e., men and women in general) or individuals (a male and a female friend), Italian participants used adjectives in 90% of all phrases. Japanese showed a much stronger inclination toward using verbs, resulting in a more balanced ratio of adjectives and verbs. These tendencies were the same whether the target was a category or an individual. The asymmetric preferences for adjectives and verbs were not confined to word choice in open-ended responses, but were observed in memory bias as well. In another study (Study 3), these researchers presented participants with a letter of recommendation for a fictitious target person. Half of critical pieces of information were presented in verbs (e.g., "enjoys doing sports"), whereas half-in adjective forms (e.g., "athletic"). In response to a surprise recall task, an important difference was found between the two national samples when they committed memory errors. Italian participants showed a clear IDA in that the rate of inductive errors (i.e., using adjectives when recalling information that was originally provided in verbs) was higher than that of deductive errors (i.e., using verbs in recalling trait information). On the contrary, deductive errors among Japanese were significantly more frequent than their inductive errors.

There can be multiple explanations for these cross-linguistic differences, and much more research is needed to identify the exact mechanisms responsible for the effect. An additional study by Maass et al. (2006; Study 5) provides suggestions with this regard. In this study, pairs of verbs and adjectives sharing the same word stem were prepared (e.g., aggress-aggressive, obey-obedient). Participants read one word from each pair, and rated its inferential properties. Consistent with the assumption of LCM (Semin & Fiedler, 1988), both Italian and Japanese participants judged adjectives to be more informative about the person, more enduring, and less telling about the situation than were verbs. However, differences were also found in that Italians judged adjectives to be more useful to predict future events (also consistent with the LCM), whereas Japanese rated verbs to be equally predictive. This seems to reflect a holistic orientation toward experiential, context-based predictions among Japanese. Also, Italians indicated that it was more difficult to imagine concrete situations derived from adjectives than from verbs, but the difference was not significant among Japanese. This is consistent with the deductive tendency among the latter. Together, these studies suggest that there are systematic differences in the use of verbs versus adjectives in communication, which reflect the dominant cognitive styles of the respective language community and which, in turn, contribute to the maintenance of the culturally dominant perspective on context versus focal target.

LINGUISTIC INTERGROUP BIAS AND EXPECTANCY BIAS

In daily interactions, we typically observe other people's behavior with some prior expectations. The process of accommodating expectancy-congruent and incongruent pieces of evidence is known to reflect in systematic patterns of word choices. That is, when people describe an observed behavior congruent with their expectancy, they tend to employ more abstract and dispositional predicates than when the behavior violates the expectancy. This phenomenon is called "the Linguistic Expectancy Bias" (LEB) (Wigboldus et al., 2000; for a review, see Maass, 1999). The term "level of abstractness" again draws on the LCM (Semin & Fiedler, 1988).

The significance of LEB was originally demonstrated in intergroup contexts. Because group members generally hold favorable expectations toward their fellow group members (e.g., Brewer, 1979; Tajfel, 1982), desirable behaviors of these in-group members tend to be characterized by predicates with higher levels of abstraction, whereas their undesirable behaviors are described in less abstract terms. Descriptions of acts by members from other groups (i.e., out-group) show a reversal pattern. This special form of the LEB, called the Linguistic Intergroup Bias (LIB) (Maass et al., 1989), may provoke or exasperate intergroup conflicts by enhancing biased interpretations of group members' behavior. In addition, more recent studies demonstrate that the LIB is not limited to the situation with favorable in-group and unfavorable out-groups. Consistency with prior expectations influences the level of predicate abstractness regardless of the valence of the expectancy (e.g., Maass et al., 1995, Experiment. 1), and even when the target out-group is associated with positive expectations (e.g., Karasawa & Suga, 2008). In fact, the same effect can take place when the expectancy pertains to characteristics of an *individual* target rather than group-based stereotypes (e.g., "best friend" versus "archenemy" – Maass et al., 1995; see also Karpinski & von Hippel, 1996; Wigboldus et al., 2000). Furthermore, the LEB is so powerful that it can qualify other inferential processes. For instance, Maass et al. (2005) demonstrated that the IDA discussed in the previous section was more pronounced when the inductive inference pertained to stereotype-congruent information.

Different explanations have been proposed regarding what processes are responsible for the LEB and LIB. First, abstract and dispositional terms allow generalization of observed incidents across different situations over different time points, whereas less abstract (more concrete) expressions help the observer to dispense incongruent cases as peculiar or exceptional (Semin & Fiedler, 1988; Maass & Arcuri, 1992). This may serve the general tendency among people to preserve their pre-existing beliefs even in face of disconfirming evidence (e.g., Snyder & Stukas, 1999).

Second, some researchers from an alternative perspective emphasize the communicative function of abstract versus concrete terms (e.g., Maass et al., 1995; Wigboldus et al., 2000). Verbal expressions are often communicated to a receiver of the information. Because more abstract terms contain more information about dispositions of the actor, such words are expected to promote the recipient's understanding of the characteristics of the actor. The pragmatic value of abstract words can be enhanced particularly when they are used for describing expectancy-confirming instances because of the relative ease in understanding (Karasawa & Suga, 2008). Indeed, substantial research indicates that the message recipient plays a critical role in moderating the language use (e.g., Semin et al., 2003; Wigboldus et al., 2005), and that communicators modify the abstractness of their message depending on their communication goal (e.g., Douglas & Sutton, 2003).

Third, in addition to these cognitive and pragmatic explanations, a motivational view should also be noted, particularly with regard to LIB. The inclination toward expressing in-group-positive and out-group-negative characteristics in abstract terms may reflect in-group serving motivations. The attempt to protect in-group interests and disdain the value of the out-group is among the most well-established phenomenon in the literature of social psychology (Brewer & Brown, 1998), and a variety of motivational processes that potentially underlie the ethnocentric tendency has been proposed from diverse theoretical viewpoints (Tajfel & Turner, 1986; Hogg, 2006; Yamagishi, 2007). These motivational mechanisms may well be reflected in linguistic choices, over and above the effect of expectancy. Through abstract language, positive in-group and negative out-group behaviors are portrayed as typical and enduring, whereas negative in-group and positive out-group behaviors, described concretely, appear as exceptions, thus contributing to the maintenance of a positive image of one's own group. Not surprisingly then, such motivationally driven language use mainly occurs when people's social identity is threatened (Maass et al., 1996). In line with this motivational explanation, the LIB has typically been reported in contexts involving actual intergroup contentions, such as group-based horse race competitions with fervor of community pride (Maass et al., 1989) as well as regional prejudices in Italy (Maass et al., 1995, Experiment. 1), rivalry between fans of Japanese professional baseball teams (Tanabe & Oka, 2001), Caucasians' views on African-Americans (von Hippel et al., 1997), the liberal versus conservative ideology (Karpinski & von Hippel, 1996), and military conflicts (Maass et al., 1994, Experiment. 3), or a mere comparison between "friend" and "enemy" (Maass et al., 1995).

The issue of universality and cultural variations should also be considered with respect to the LEB and LIB. These linguistic biases have been repeatedly demonstrated across different linguistic cultures, not only in Western languages (e.g., Italian, German, Dutch, and English; see Maass, 1999) but also in languages such as Chinese (Ng & Chan, 1996) and Japanese (e.g., Tanabe & Oka, 2001; Karasawa & Suga, 2008). Of course, there is a great deal of discrepancies in grammatical and pragmatic rules among these languages, and therefore, methods to accommodate certain variations have been developed (e.g., Suga & Karasawa, 2006). The success in replicating the LEB/LIB and thus validating the LCM suggest that the potentially underlying cognitive (or epistemic), pragmatic, and motivational processes outlined above may have reasonable universality.

At the same time, it should be noted that the possibility of variations, at least within a linguistic culture, has also been demonstrated. Specifically, a study by Webster et al. (1997) revealed that the size of LIB can be moderated by the level of "need for closure" (i.e., the tendency to avoid ambiguity and instead seek a definitive answer on a certain issue). The study demonstrated that people who were either chronically or situationally high in the need for closure showed a greater LIB. Representing expectancy-consistent behavior in more abstract terms was presumably consistent with the need for *quickly* reaching an understanding of the actor's enduring dispositions (cf. Kruglanski & Webster, 1996). As we discussed in the previous section, attaining an unambiguous understanding of an event and seeking consistency over time may be more strongly associated with the essentialist orientation in analytic, rather than holistic, cognition (Nisbett et al., 2001). This seems to be particularly the case with regard to judgment of dispositions of a person (Maass et al., 2006). Such potential cultural variations should be further pursued by empirical investigations.

THE SPECIAL ROLE OF NOUNS IN SOCIAL PERCEPTION

Recently, this line of research, concerning the role of language abstraction in interpersonal and intergroup contexts, has been extended to an even more general level, namely nouns. Already Allport (1954), in his seminal book on the "Nature of Prejudice," had argued that nouns, compared to adjectives, are particularly powerful linguistic devices. Once people have been classified by a noun label as in the phrase "Shira is a Jew" it becomes difficult to think about the person in any other way than her Jewishness, quite differently from adjectival statements such as "Shira is Jewish" that describe one out of many possible qualities that Shira may possess. Carnaghi et al. (in press) have tested this idea and found that, compared to adjectives, nouns lead people to draw more stereotypical as well as more essentialist inferences about the target. Nouns also inhibit alternative classifications of the same person, such that once a person is classified as an "artist" (rather than as "artistic"), people find it difficult to imagine that the same person may also belong to other social groups or have other qualities (such as "being athletic"). Thus, despite the surface similarity of nouns and adjectives, nouns are much more powerful and prognostic devices in defining social category membership, as they suggest greater essentialism and induce stronger stereotyping, while blocking alternative classifications of the same person. Although we are not aware of any cross-language comparisons, one may suspect that the preference of speakers of Germanic and Romance languages for abstract language may foster the conceptualization of social categories in essentialist and quasi-biological terms (see Rothbart & Taylor, 1992), whereas speakers of East Asian languages such as Japanese and Korean may well develop a more flexible and permeable view. Of course, in the absence of empirical studies, this remains pure speculation.

DEROGATORY LANGUAGE

So far, we have focused on variations in language that most people are unaware, but that channel the inferences of listeners in a very subtle way. However, not all language choices are so fine-grained and benign. At times language is used with the clear intent to offend specific target groups, such as when majority members talk about *fags*, *niggers*, or *kikes*. Although such offensive expressions are relatively rare when talking to members of the target group, they are not uncommon when majority members talk about (rather than to) minority members (Graumann, 1995). Besides being clearly harmful to minority targets, one may plausibly assume that such derogatory labels also induce majority listeners to form more negative impressions of the target group than neutral labels. Although intuitive, the empirical evidence for this assumption is limited to a small number of recent studies comparing derogatory labels (e.g., *fag*) with neutral category labels (e.g., *gay*) referring to the same group. The first studies showing the negative effects of derogatory labels such as *nigger* were reported by Greeenberg and collaborators (Greenberg & Pyszczynski, 1985; Kirkland et al., 1987), but in these studies the offensive term (*nigger*) was compared to a neutral label referring to a different category (*pro-debator*). More telling is a subsequent study by Simon and Greenberg (1996), in which participants were exposed to a comment containing either a derogatory ethnic label (*nigger*) or a neutral ethnic label (*Black*) referring to the same ethnic group. Participants were then asked to evaluate the target of the comment. Surprisingly, there was no evidence that the derogatory ethnic label (*nigger*) would trigger a more negative evaluation than the non-derogatory ethnic label (*Black*). If anything, there was a tendency to evaluate the target of the derogatory ethnic label more positively, although this was limited to participants with ambivalent racial attitudes. Does this mean that derogatory language is innocuous?

Recently, Carnaghi and Maass (2006, 2007, in press) have argued that the effect of derogatory labels may be less visible at an explicit level where people can easily control their responses and provide socially appropriate responses, than on an implicit level that escapes conscious control. These authors used different unobtrusive measures to assess participants' implicit attitudes (free association task, semantic priming, and approach-avoidance measures) to study ethnophaulisms (i.e., language that disparages social groups), or, more specifically, "homophaulism" (linguistic expressions derogating homosexuality). Their results consistently showed that neutral category primes (such as *gay* or *homosexual*) triggered more positive associations and evaluations of the target group than derogatory labels (such as *fag* or *queer*). Interestingly, neutral and derogatory labels did not differ in their capacity to activate stereotypic content; indeed, both made concepts that are stereotypically associated with the target group "homosexuals" highly accessible. What distinguishes neutral from derogatory labels is mainly the affective or evaluative dimension. The associations activated by derogatory labels are much less favorable than those activated by neutral category labels. In other words, people form an equally stereotypical, but much less favorable image of gays or of other minorities when they are exposed to a derogatory (rather than neutral) label. Interestingly, derogatory labels seem to affect majority members (e.g., heterosexuals) more than they affect members of the insulted minority group (e.g., homosexuals). Although both groups are equally conscious of the offensive nature of such homo- or ethnophaulisms at an explicit level, majority members are more likely to be negatively affected by derogatory terms at the implicit level. Although somewhat counter-intuitive, the greater susceptibility of majority members to disparaging speech has considerable applied relevance, considering that such language is mainly used in within-majority discourse. Thus, derogatory language seems to exert its greatest impact in social situations in which it is most likely to be used.

Considering the powerful effects of ethno- and homophaulisms on people's affective reactions, it may not be surprising that the relative number of such derogatory terms can be used as a rough index of the status that a given minority enjoyed at a given point in history. Particularly telling are the analyses of archival data by Mullen and collaborators suggesting that derogatory terms became increasingly complex and less negatively valenced, the more the relative size and familiarity of the group in society increased (Mullen & Johnson, 1993, 1995; Mullen et al., 2000, 2001). This suggests that the availability and valence of derogatory group labels provide a rough index of the status of ethnic minorities in a given society. Together, research on derogatory language suggests that (a) people's affective reactions to minority groups are greatly influenced by offensive language, especially at an implicit level, and (b) that the prevalence and negativity of such labels in a given language is indicative of a minority's status in society.

SUMMARY

The studies discussed in this section demonstrate that analyses of language can provide useful insights into how social inferences are carried out. These include both very obvious (as in the case of derogatory labels) and very subtle variations in language use (as in the case of implicit causality of verbs, language abstraction, or verb transitivity). Even seemingly minor variations in language (e.g., *confide* versus *trust*, *Jewish* versus *Jew*) can lead to remarkable differences in inferences regarding event instigation, causality, underlying traits, generality and essentialism of characteristics, valence, and many other dimensions. Also, such variations can easily influence other socially important judgments concerning responsibility, fairness, and blameworthiness. These are associated with tangible consequences. Examples include promotion versus termination of relationship, monetary compensation, and physical sanctions.

Important, the understanding of these properties of language is very likely shared within each culture, as evidenced, among others, by findings obtained with the question-answer-paradigm. Indeed, cultural characteristics in cognition are often reflected in language use. As such, language and inference may jointly play an important role in constructing social reality not only inside of the cognitive system but also in the actual and veridical world (see Semin, 2000). Unfortunately, many of the language effects on social inferences reported here have only been tested within a single language group. The few cross-language studies available suggest that some mechanisms, such as LIB/LEB, are universal as they have been shown to operate in a very similar way in different language communities. In other and possibly more interesting cases, systematic differences have emerged, suggesting that linguistic rules and preferences (e.g., for concrete versus abstract language) go hand in hand with systematic differences in inferential processes, such as trait inferences. What is missing at this point is an overarching model that can explain universal as well as culture-specific language effects on inferential processes within a single framework. To develop such a general model remains a challenging issue for future research and theorizing.

LANGUAGE AFFECTING SPATIAL IMAGING OF
SOCIAL EVENTS

So far, we have focused on the vocabulary, syntax, or grammar of a given language while ignoring a less frequently investigated aspect of language, namely the way in which it is written. Writing differs greatly across languages, not only in terms of logographic (such as Chinese characters or hieroglyphs) versus alphabetic writing systems, but also in terms of spatial trajectories. Some languages are written horizontally from left to right (such as English) or from right to left (such as Arab, Hebrew, Farsi, and Urdu), others vertically, in columns from left to right or from right to left (such as Chinese), and other languages use mixed systems (such as Japanese). It has long been argued that the way we habitually read and write languages affects our way of thinking well beyond the activity of reading and writing.

In a sense, this may not be surprising if one accepts the idea that concepts are stored in our minds, not as abstract representations, but containing perceptual cues and that even off-line processes are intrinsically linked to visual and motor behaviors (Barsalou, 1999; Barsalou et al., 2003). This general idea, now referred to as embodiment perspective, in reality entails a great number of approaches and assumptions (for a taxonomy see Wilson, 2002). Important to our argument is the fact that spatial aspects of both the object and the perceiver are likely to be involved in the reenactment process underlying memory, comprehension, reasoning, and imagery. For instance, people tend to look up when thinking about a bird, but down when thinking about a worm (Spivey et al., 2000), they are faster at recognizing the relatedness of two concepts (such as "root" and "branch") if they are arranged in the canonical way ("branch" above "root" rather than vice versa; Zwaan & Yaxley, 2003), and they imagine powerful people and groups to be up, powerless down (Schubert, 2005). Although spatial information is logically irrelevant for any of these tasks, the facilitation or inhibition observed in this kind of experiment suggests that the objects (animals, tree parts, social groups) are conceptualized in space.

If such perceptual simulations are the rule rather than the exception as suggested by embodiment theories, may writing and reading habits lead to similar "entrenched situated conceptualizations" of action (Barsalou et al., 2003). For instance, Germanic and Romance languages are written and read from left to right and, in most standard active sentences, the agent (sentence subject) tends to precede the patient or recipient of the action (generally the object). Would this predispose people from such cultures to develop a generalized scheme for action that evolves from left to right and in which the agent is perceived to the left of the receiver? Considering that adolescents and adults in developed countries spend a considerable portion of their time writing and reading, one may suspect that the predominant left–right trajectory should pervade large areas of cognition, well beyond the realm of reading and writing. For the same reason, an exactly opposite pattern can be expected for languages that are written/read from right to left, such as Arabic, Hebrew, Farsi, and Urdu.

There is now first evidence that this is, indeed, the case. For example, when asking people to draw scenes corresponding to minimal subject–verb–object phrases (e.g., *Fabio feeds the dog*) or to match pictures with such phrases, a vast majority of respondents raised in left–right languages will envisage the agent (Fabio) to the left of the receiver (dog) (Chatterjee et al., 1999), whereas respondents in right–left language communities such as Arabic will show the opposite bias (Maass & Russo, 2003). Similar asymmetries related to writing direction have been found in many basic perceptual and cognitive phenomena including inhibition of return (Spalek & Hammad, 2005), representational momentum (Morikawa & McBeath, 1992; Halpern & Kelley, 1993), the imaginary number line (Dehaene et al., 1993), as well as in drawing, exploration of art, and esthetic preferences (e.g., Nachshon, 1985; Tversky et al., 1992; Nachshon et al., 1999; Chokron & De Agostini, 2000).

Recently, writing direction has also been shown to affect social cognition in a subtle way. For example, Maass et al. (2007a) found that, in left–right writing cultures, human action is perceived as more powerful when evolving with a left–right trajectory. Violent film scenes were perceived as more aggressive and more harmful to the victim when the aggressor was positioned left of the victim than when the exact same scenes were observed with an opposite spatial arrangement. Along the same line, the same soccer goal was perceived as more powerful, faster, and more beautiful when the player was observed as acting in a left–right rather than right–left fashion. Importantly, this bias reversed for Arabic speakers who observed the same scenes.

Thus, observers seem to assign greater potency to the action and greater agency to the actor when the trajectory mirrors the direction in which language is written in a given culture. This also has interesting implications for stereotyping. Chatterjee (2002) was probably the first to propose a systematic link between stereotypes and spatial imaging, hypothesizing that, if there is a general left–right scheme for action (as appears to be in left–right writing cultures), then stereotypically more agentic targets should be portrayed facing right, less agentic targets facing left (as seen from the perspective of the observer). In line with this idea, analyses of art work generally show that men are more likely to be portrayed facing right than are women who are overwhelmingly portrayed facing left (McManus & Humphrey, 1973; Chatterjee, 2002; Suitner & Maass, 2007). In a similar vein, Maass et al. (2007b) found that, in images (i.e., paintings, photographs, cartoons, etc.) representing both a male and a female target (such as Adam and Eve), males were over-proportionally positioned to the left of females, but only for couples in which the male was perceived as more agentic. Also, lay people tend to draw males to the left of females, but only if they hold stereotypic beliefs that associate males with greater agency. Importantly, a comparison of Italian- and Arabic-speakers evidenced that, contrary to Italian speakers, Arabic-speakers positioned the more agentic groups (men and young people) to the right of less agentic groups (females and old people). These results suggest that the mental imagery of stereotypically more versus less agentic groups matches the position that agents (sentence subject) versus recipients (sentence object) occupy in a given language.

Together, these and other studies suggest that mental imagery is influenced by the way in which language is written and read within a given culture. Although these effects are subtle, of small magnitude, and, most likely, occur outside of awareness, they tend to bias thought and imagery in a reliable way, coherent with an embodiment approach to social cognition.

CONCLUDING COMMENTS

As we have reviewed in this chapter, language is found to influence various domains of social cognition and behavior. Specifically, we analyzed how language guides and influences our attention, inference and judgments, and imageries through embodiment of representations. As we noted earlier, this was not intended to be an exhaustive, encyclopedic coverage of the current literature. Rather, we attempted to highlight certain specific issues that exemplify the important role of language in our cognitive system and social life.

The studies reviewed here demonstrate that the influence of language is found at different layers of social domains. First, linguistic effects are observed on *intra*personal processes. For instance, phenomena such as implicit verb causality and the IDA in trait inferences raise a number of important research questions concerning how information processing within individuals is related to linguistic rules and representations. In this sense, language serves an important tool for sense-making in individuals. What is evident, however, is the fact that language functions as a tool for communication as well, that is, in relational processes at the *inter*personal level. Specific word choices associated with implicit causality, LEB, predicate abstractness and transitivity, among other diverse phenomena that we discussed above, can easily entail pragmatic values full of implicatures. The core essence of such pragmaticity is a mutual understanding between the communicators (i.e., sender and recipient of the message) regarding the target issue. Also, certain linguistic phenomena pertain to *intergroup* relations. The LIB and the ethnocentric languages are good examples with this regard. Not only cognitive but also affective and/or motivational processes also seem to underlie these linguistic effects. Finally, but needless to say, language constitutes an integral part of *cultural* bases of social cognition. Our analyses throughout this chapter concerning within-language variations and cross-linguistic comparisons elucidate that symbolic representations coded in language transcend and implement collectively shared meanings and practices. Collaborations between social-cognitive and linguistic approaches hence provide useful conceptual and methodological frameworks for understanding the essence of human cognition and culture.

ACKNOWLEDGMENT

The preparation of this manuscript was supported by Grant-in-Aid for Scientific Research by Japan Society for the Promotion of Science (#15330134) granted to the first author.

REFERENCES

Agnoli, F., & Forer, D. (2005). *Can objects become male or female? The influence of Italian and German grammatical gender on object classification.* Biennial Meeting of the Society for Research in Child Development, Altanta, April 7–10, 2005.

Allport, G. W. (1954). *The nature of prejudice.* Cambridge, MA: Addison-Wesley.

Anderson, C. A., Krull, D., & Weiner, B. (1996). Explanations: Processes and consequences. In E. T. Higgins & A. Kruglanski (Eds.), *Social psychology: Handbook of basic principles* (pp. 271–296). New York: Guilford Press.

Barsalou, L. W. (1999). Perceptual symbol systems. *Behavior and Brain Sciences, 22,* 577–609.

Barsalou, L. W., Niedenthal, P., Barbey, A., & Ruppert, J. (2004). Social embodiment. In B. Ross (Ed.), *The psychology of learning and motivation* (vol. 43, pp. 43–92). San Diego, CA: Academic Press.

Bond, M. H., & Cheung, T.-S. (1983). College students' spontaneous self-concept: The effect of culture among respondents in Hong Kong, Japan, and the United States. *Journal of Cross-Cultural Psychology, 14*, 153–171.

Boroditsky, L. (2003). Linguistic relativity. In L. Nadel (Ed.), *Encyclopedia of cognitive science* (pp. 917–921). London: MacMillan Press.

Boroditsky, L., Scmidt, L. A., & Phillips, W. (2003). Sex, syntax and semantics. In: S. Goldin-Meadow & D. Gentner (Eds.), *Language in mind: Advances in the study of language and thought* (pp. 61–79). Cambridge, MA: MIT Press.

Braun, F., Gottburgsen, A., Sczensny, S., & Stahlberg, D. (1998). Koennen Geophysiker Frauen sein? Generische Personenbezeichnungen im Deutschen. *Zeitschrift fuer Germanistische Linguistik, 26*, 265–283.

Brewer, M. B. (1979). In-group bias in the minimal intergroup situation: A cognitive-motivational analysis. *Psychological Bulletin, 86*, 307–324.

Brewer, M. B., & Brown, R. J. (1998). Intergroup relations. In: D. T. Gilbert, S. T. Fiske, & G. Lindzey (Eds.), *The handbook of social psychology, 4th ed.* (Vol. 2, pp. 554–594). New York: McGraw-Hill.

Brown, P., & Levinson, S. C. (1978). Universals in language usage: Politeness phenomenon. In E. N. Goody (Ed.), *Questions and politeness: Strategies in social interaction* (pp. 56–311). Cambridge, UK: Cambridge University Press.

Brown, R., & Fish, D. (1983). The psychological causality implit in language. *Cognition, 14*, 237–273.

Carnaghi, A., & Maass, A. (2006). Terrone! Culattone! Effetti delle etichette denigratorie sulle risposte comportamentali. [Redneck! Fag! Effects of derogatory labels on behavioral responses]. *Rivista di Psicologia Sociale, 1*, 121–132.

Carnaghi, A., & Maass, A. (2007). In-group and out-group perspectives in the use of derogatory group label: Gay vs fag. *Journal of Language and Social Psychology,, 26*, 142–156.

Carnaghi, A., & Maass, A. (2008). Derogatory language in intergroup context: Are "gay" and "fag" synonymous? In: Y. Kashima, K. Fiedler, & P. Freytag (Eds.), *Stereotype dynamics: Language-based approaches to stereotype formation, maintenance, and transformation* (pp. 117–134). Mahwah, NJ: Lawrence Erlbaum Associates.

Carnaghi, A., Maass, A. Gresta, S., Bianchi, M., Cadinu, M., & Arcuri, L. (2008, in press). Nomina sunt omina: On the inductive potential of nouns and adjectives in person perception. *Journal of Personality and Social Psychology*.

Chatterjee, A. (2002). Portrait profiles and the notion of agency. *Empirical Studies of the Arts, 20-1*, 33–41.

Chatterjee, A., Southwood, M. H., & Basilico, D. (1999). Verbs, events and spatial representations. *Neuropsychologia, XX*, 395–402.

Chokron, S., & De Agostini, M. (2000). Reading habits influence aesthetic preference. *Cognitive Brain Research, 10*, 45–49.

Clark, H. H. (1996). *Using language.* Cambridge, UK: Cambridge University Press.

Cousins, S. D. (1989). Culture and self-perception in Japan and the United States. *Journal of Personality and Social Psychology, 56*, 124–131.

Dehaene, S., Bossini, S., & Giraux, P. (1993). The mental representation of parity and number magnitude. *Journal of Experimental Psychology: General, 122*(3), 371–396.

DeLancy, S. (1984). Notes on agentivity and causation. *Studies in Language, 8*, 181–213.

Douglas, K. M., & Sutton, R. M. (2003). Effects of communication goals and expectancies on language abstraction. *Journal of Personality and Social Psychology, 84*, 682–696.

Fiske, A. P., Kitayama, S., Markus, H. R., & Nisbett, R. E. (1998). The cultural matrix of social psychology. In D. Gilbert, S. T. Fiske, & G. Lindzey (Eds.), *The handbook of social psychology, 4th ed.* (vol. 2, pp. 915–981). New York: McGraw-Hill.

Gilbert, D. T. (1998). Ordinary personlogy. In D. T. Gilbert, S. T. Fiske, & G. Lindzey (Eds.), *The handbook of social psychology, 4th ed.* (vol. 2, pp. 89–150). New York: McGraw-Hill.

Graumann, C. F. (1995). Discriminatory discourse. *Pattern of Prejudice, 29*, 69–83.

Greenberg, J., & Pyszczynski, T. (1985). The effect of an overheard ethnic slur on evaluations of the target: How to spread a social disease. *Journal of Experimental Social Psychology*, *21*, 61–72.

Grice, H. P. (1975). Logic and conversation. In P. Cole & J. L. Morgan (Eds.), *Syntax and semantics 3: Speech acts* (pp. 41–58). New York: Academic Press.

Gumperz, J. J., & Levinson, S. C. (Eds.) (1996). *Rethinking linguistic relativity*. Cambridge, UK: Cambridge University Press.

Halpern, A. R., & Kelley, M. H. (1993). Memory biases in left versus right implied motion. *Journal of Experimental Psychology: Learning, Memory and Cognition*, *19*, 471–484.

Hewstone, M. (1989). *Causal attribution: From cognitive processes to collective beliefs*. Oxford, UK: Blackwell.

Hofstede, G. (1980). *Culture's consequences*. Beverly Hills, CA: Sage Publications.

Hogg, M. (2006). Self-conceptual uncertainty and the lure of belonging. In R. Brown & D. Capozza (Eds.), *Social identities: Motivational, emotional and cultural influences* (pp. 33–49). Hove, England: Psychology Press / Taylor & Francis.

Holtgraves, T. M. (2002). *Language as social action: Social psychology and language use*. Mahwah, NJ: Lawrence Erlbaum Associates.

Hopper, P. J., & Thompson, S. A. (1980). Transitivity in grammar and discourse. *Language*, *56*, 251–299.

Hunt, E., & Agnoli, F. (1991). The Whorfian hypothesis: A cognitive psychology perspective. *Psychological Review*, *98*, 377–389.

Ikegami, Y. (1991). "DO-language" and BECOME-language: Two contrasting types of linguistic representation. In Y. Ikegami (Ed.), *The empire of signs: Semiotic essays on Japanese culture* (pp. 285–326). Amsterdam: John Benjamins.

Jones, E. E., Kanouse, D. E., Kelley, H. H., Nisbett, R. E., Valins, S., & Weiner, B. (1972). *Attribution: Perceiving the causes of behavior*. Morristown, NJ: General Learning Press.

Kanagawa, C., Cross, S. E, & Markus, H. R. (2001). "Who am I?" The cultural psychology of the conceptual self. *Personality & Social Psychology Bulletin*, *27*, 90–103.

Karasawa, M., & Suga, S. (2008). Retention and transmission of socially shared beliefs: The role of linguistic abstraction in stereotypic communication. In Y. Kashima, K. Fiedler, & P. Frytag (Eds.), *Stereotype dynamics: Language-based approaches to stereotype formation, maintenance, and transformation* (pp. 241–262). Mahwah, NJ: Lawrence Erlbaum Associates.

Karasawa, M., & Yoshinari, Y. (2007). *A linguistic analysis of perceived causality and responsibility: Causal attributions and verb transitivity*. Unpublished manuscript. Nagoya University.

Karasawa, M., Maass, A., Rackic, T., & Kato, A. (2007). *The emergent nature of culturally-based social categorization: Effects of spontaneous use of category information on person memory*. Manuscript in preparation.

Karpinski, A., & von Hippel, W. (1996). The role of the linguistic intergroup bias in expectancy maintenance. *Social Cognition*, *14*, 141–163.

Kashima, E. S., & Kashima, Y. (1998). Culture and language: The case of cultural dimensions and personal pronoun use. *Journal of Cross-Cultural Psychology*, *29*, 461–486.

Kashima, Y., & Kashima, E. S. (2003). Individualism, GNP, climate, and pronoun drop: Is individualism determined by affluence and climate, or does language use play a role?. *Journal of Cross-Cultural Psychology*, *34*, 125–134.

Kirkland, S. L., Greenberg, J., & Pyszczynski, T. (1987). Further evidence of the deleterious effects of overheard derogatory ethnic labels: Derogation beyond the target. *Personality and Social Psychology Bulletin*, *13*, 216–227.

Konishi, T. (1993). The semantics of grammatical gender: A cross-cultural study. *Journal of Psycholinguistic Research*, *22*, 519–534.

Kruglanski, A., & Webster, D. M. (1996). Motivated closing of the mind: "Seizing" and "freezing". *Psychological Review*, *103*, 263–283.

Lakoff, G. (1987). *Women, fire, and dangerous things: What categories reveal about the mind*. Chicago: University of Chicago Press.

Langacker, R. W. (1987). *Foundations of cognitive grammar (vol.1): Theoretical prerequisites* Stanford: Stanford University Press.

Langacker, R. W. (1991). *Foundations of cognitive grammar (vol.2): Descriptive application.* Stanford: Stanford University Press.

Lau, I. Y.-M., Lee, S.-l., & Chiu, C.-y. (2004). Language, cognition, and reality: Constructing shared meanings through communication. In M. Schaller & C. Crandall (Eds.), *The psychological foundations of culture* (pp. 77–100). Mahwah, NJ: Lawrence Erlbaum Associates.

Leech, G. N. (1983). *Principles of pragmatics.* London: Longman.

Levinson, S. (1996). Frames of reference and Molyneux's question: Cross-linguistic evidence. In P. Bloom, M. Peterson, L. Nadel, & M. Garrett (Eds.), *Language and space.* Cambridge, MA: MIT Press.

Maass, A. (1999). Linguistic intergroup bias: Stereotype perpetuation through language. In M. P. Zanna (Ed.), *Advances in experimental social psychology* (vol. 31, pp. 79–121). San Diego, CA: Academic Press.

Maass, A., & Arcuri, L. (1992). The role of language in the persistence of stereotypes. In G. R. Semin & K. Fiedler (Eds.), *Language, interaction and social cognition* (pp. 129–143). Newbury Park, CA: Sage Publications.

Maass, A., Ceccarelli, R., & Rudin, S. (1996). The linguistic intergroup bias: Evidence for ingroup-protective motivation. *Journal of Personality and Social Psychology, 71,* 512–526.

Maass, A., & Russo, A. (2003). Directional bias in the mental representation of spatial events: Nature or Culture?. *Psychological Science, 14*(4), 296–300.

Maass, A., Salvi, D., Arcuri, L., & Semin, G. (1989). Language use in intergroup contexts: The linguistic intergroup bias. *Journal of Personality and Social Psychology, 57,* 981–993.

Maass, A., Corvino, P., & Arcuri, L. (1994). Linguistic intergroup bias and the mass media. *Revue de Psychologie Sociale, 1,* 31–43.

Maass, A., Milesi, A., Zabbini, S., & Stahlberg, D. (1995). Linguistic intergroup bias: Differential expectancies or in-group protection?. *Journal of Personality and Social Psychology, 68,* 116–126.

Maass, A., Colombo, A., Colombo, A., & Sherman, S. J. (2001). Inferring traits from behaviors and behaviors from traits: The induction-deduction asymmetry. *Journal of Personality and Social Psychology, 81,* 391–404.

Maass, A., Cadinu, M., Boni, M., & Borini, C. (2005). Converting verbs into adjectives: Asymmetrical memory distortions for stereotypic and counterstereotypic information. *Group Processes & Intergroup Relations, 8,* 271–290.

Maass, A., Karasawa, M., Politi, F., & Suga, S. (2006). Do verbs and adjectives play different roles in different cultures? A cross-linguistic analysis of person representation. *Journal of Personality and Social Psychology, 90,* 734–750.

Maass, A., Pagani, D., & Berta, E. (2007a). How beautiful is the goal and how violent is the fistfight? Spatial bias in the interpretation of human behavior. *Social Cognition, 25,* 833–852.

Maass, A., Suitner, C., Favaretto, X., & Cignacchi, M. (2007b). *Groups in space.* Unpublished Manuscript, Padova University.

McManus, I., & Humphrey, N. (1973). Turning the left cheek. *Nature, 243,* 271–272.

Masuda, T., & Nisbett, R. E. (2001). Attending holistically versus analytically: Comparing the context sensitivity of Japanese and Americans. *Journal of Personality and Social Psychology, 81,* 922–934.

Menon, T., Morris, M. W., Chiu, C.-Y., & Hong, Y.-Y. (1999). Culture and the construal of agency: Attribution to individual versus group dispositions. *Journal of Personality and Social Psychology, 76,* 701–717.

Morikawa, K., & McBeath, M. (1992). Lateral motion bias associated with reading direction. *Vision Research, 32,* 1137–1141.

Mullen, B., & Johnson, C. (1993). Cognitive representation in ethnophaulisms as a function of group size: The phenomenology of being in a group. *Personality and Social Psychology Bulletin, 19,* 296–304.

Mullen, B., & Johnson, C. (1995). Cognitive representation in ethnophaulisms and illusory correlation in stereotyping. *Personality and Social Psychology Bulletin, 21,* 420–433.

Mullen, B., Rozell, D., & Johnson, C. (2000). Ethnophaulisms for ethnic immigrant groups: Cognitive representation of 'the minority' and 'the foreigner'. *Group Processes & Intergroup Relations*, *3*, 5–24.

Mullen, B., Rozell, D., & Johnson, C. (2001). Ethnophaulisms for ethnic immigrant groups: The contributions of group size and familiarity. *European Journal of Social Psychology*, *31*, 231–246.

Nachshon, I. (1985). Directional preferences in perception of visual stimuli. *International Journal of Neuroscience*, *25*, 161–174.

Nachshon, I., Argaman, E., & Luria, A. (1999). Effects of directional habits and handedness on aesthetic preference for left and right profiles. *Journal of Cross-Cultural Psychology*, *30*, 106–114.

Ng, S. H., & Chan, K. K. (1996). Biases in the description of various age groups: A linguistic category model analysis. *Bulletin of the Hong Kong Psychological Society*, *36/37*, 5–20.

Nisbett, R. E., Peng, K., Choi, I., & Norenzayan, A. (2001). Culture and systems of thought: Holistic versus analytic cognition. *Psychological Review*, *108*, 291–340.

Rhee, E., Uleman, J. S., Lee, H. K., & Roman, R. J. (1995). Spontaneous self-descriptions and ethnic identities in individualistic and collectivistic cultures. *Journal of Personality and Social Psychology*, *69*, 142–152.

Ross, L., & Nisbett, R. E. (1991). *The person and the situation: Perspectives of social psychology*. New York: McGraw-Hill.

Rothbart, M., & Taylor, M. (1992). Category labels and social reality: Do we view social categories as natural kinds?. In G. R. Semin & K. Fiedler (Eds.), *Language, interaction and social cognition* (pp. 11–36). Newbury Park, CA: Sage Publications.

Rudolph, U., & Försterling, F. (1997). The psychological causality implicit in verbs: A review. *Psychological Bulletin*, *121*, 192–218.

Schubert, T. W. (2005). Your highness: Vertical positions as perceptual symbols of power. *Journal of Personality and Social Psychology*, *89*, 1–21.

Semin, G. R. (2000). Language as a cognitive and behavioral structure resource: Question – answer exchanges. In W. Stroebe & M. Hewstone (Eds.), *European review of social psychology* (vol. 11, pp. 75–104). Chichester, UK: Wiley.

Semin, G. R. (2001). Language and social cognition. In A. Tesser & N. Schwarz (Eds.), *Blackwell handbook of social psychology: Intraindividual processes* (pp. 159–180). Oxford, UK: Blackwell.

Semin, G. R., & De Poot, C. J. (1997). The question – answer paradigm: You might regret not noticing how a question is worded. *Journal of Personality and Social Psychology*, *73*, 472–480.

Semin, G. R., & Fiedler, K. (1988). The cognitive functions of linguistic categories in describing persons: Social cognition and language. *Journal of Personality and Social Psychology*, *54*, 558–568.

Semin, G. R., & Fiedler, K. (1992). The inferential properties of interpersonal verbs. In G. R. Semin & K. Fiedler (Eds.), *Language, interaction and social cognition* (pp. 58–78). Newbury Park, CA: Sage Publications.

Semin, G. R., Rubini, M., & Fiedler, K. (1995). The answer is in the question: The effect of verb causality on locus of explanation. *Personality and Social Psychology Bulletin*, *21*, 834–842.

Semin, G. R., Gil de Montes, L., & Valencia, J. F. (2003). Communication constraints on the linguistic intergroup bias. *Journal of Experimental Social Psychology*, *39*, 142–148.

Sera, M. D., Elieff, C., Forbes, J., Burch, M. C., Rodrguez, W., & Dubois, D. P. (2002). When language affects cognition and when it does not: An analysis of grammatical gender and classification. *Journal of Experimental Psychology: General*, *131*, 377–397.

Simon, L., & Greenberg, J. (1996). Further progress in understanding the effects of derogatory ethnic labels: The role of preexisting attitudes toward the targeted group. *Personality and Social Psychology Bulletin*, *22*, 1195–1204.

Snyder, M., & Stukas, A. A., Jr. (1999). Interpersonal processes: The interplay of cognitive, motivational, and behavioral activities in social interaction. *Annual Review of Psychology*, *50*, 273–303.

Spalek, T. M., & Hammad, S. (2005). The left-to-right bias in inhibition of return is due to the direction of reading. *Psychological Science*, *16*, 15–18.

Sperber, D., & Wilson, D. (1995). *Relevance: Communication and cognition* (2nd ed.). Oxford, UK: Blackwell.

Spivey, M., Richardson, D., Tyler, M., & Young, E. (2000). Eye movements during comprehension of spoken scene descriptions, *Proceedings of the Twenty-second Annual Meeting of the Cognitive Science Society* (pp. 487–492). Mahwah, NJ: Erlbaum.

Stahlberg, D., & Sczesny, S. (2001). Effekte des generischen Maskulinums und alternativer Sprachformen auf den gedanklichen Einbezug von Frauen [Effects of the generic use of the masculine pronoun and alternative forms of speech on the cognitive visibility of women]. *Psychologische Rundschau, 52,* 131–140.

Stahlberg, D., Sczesny, S., & Braun, F. (2001). Name your favorite musician: Effects of masculine generics and of their alternatives in German. *Journal of Language and Social Psychology, 20,* 464–469.

Stapel, D. A. & Semin, G. R. (2007). *The magic spell of language: Linguistic categories and their perceptual consequences.* Unpublished manuscript, Tilburg University.

Suga, S., & Karasawa, M. (2006). Jinbutsu no zokusei hyougen ni mirareru shakaiteki sutereotaipu no eikyou. [Effects of social stereotypes on language use in the description of person disposi- tions.]. *Japanese Journal of Social Psychology, 22,* 180–188.

Suitner, C. & Maass, A. (2007). Positioning bias in portraits and self-portraits: Do female artists make different choices? *Empirical Studies of the Arts, 25,* 71–95.

Tajfel, H. (1982). Social psychology of intergroup relations. *Annual Review of Psychology, 33,* 1–39.

Tajfel, H., & Turner, J. C. (1986). The social identity theory of intergroup behaviour. In S. Worchel & W. G. Austin (Eds.), *Psychology of intergroup relations, 2nd ed* (pp. 7–24). Chicago: Nelson-Hall.

Tanabe, Y., & Oka, T. (2001). Linguistic intergroup bias in Japan. *Japanese Psychological Research, 43,* 104–111.

Taylor, S. E., Fiske, S. T., Etcoff, N. L., & Ruderman, A. J. (1978). Categorical and contextual bases of person memory and stereotyping. *Journal of Personality and Social Psychology, 36,* 778–793.

Tversky, B., Kugelmass, S., & Winter, A. (1992). Cross-cultural and developmental trends in graphic productions. *Cognitive Psychology, 23,* 515–557.

Uleman, J. S., Newman, L. S., & Moskowitz, G. B. (1996). People as flexible interpreters: Evidence and issues from spontaneous trait inference. In M. P. Zanna (Ed.), *Advances in experimental social psychology* (vol. 28, pp. 211–279). San Diego, CA: Academic Press.

von Hippel, W., Sekaquaptewa, D., & Vargas, P. (1997). The linguistic intergroup bias as an implicit- indicator of prejudice. *Journal of Experimental Social Psychology, 33,* 490–509.

Webster, D. M., Kruglanski, A. W., & Pattison, D. A. (1997). Motivated language use in intergroup contexts: Need-for-closure effects on the linguistic intergroup bias. *Journal of Personality and Social Psychology, 72,* 1122–1131.

Wigboldus, D. H. J., Semin, G. R., & Spears, R. (2000). How do we communicate stereotypes? Linguistic bases and inferential consequences. *Journal of Personality and Social Psychology, 78,* 5–18.

Wigboldus, D. H. J., Spears, R., & Semin, G. R. (2005). When do we communicate stereo- types? Influence of the social context on the linguistic expectancy bias. *Group Processes and Interpersonal Relations, 8,* 215–230.

Wilson, M. (2002). Six views of embodied cognition. *Psychonomic Bulletin and Review, 9*(4), 625–636.

Whorf, B. L. (1957). *Language, thought, and reality.* Cambridge, MA: MIT Press.

Yamagishi, T. (2007). The social exchange heuristic: A psychological mechanism that makes a sys- tem of generalized exchange self-sustaining. In M. H. B. Radford, S. Ohnuma, & T. Yamagishi (Eds.), *Cultural and ecological foundations of the mind: Mutual construction of the mind and society* (pp. 11–38). Sapporo, Japan: Hokkaido University Press.

Zárate, M. A., Uleman, J. S., & Voils, C. I. (2001). Effects of culture and processing goals on the activation and binding of trait concepts. *Social Cognition, 19,* 295–323.

Zwaan, R. A., & Yaxley, R. H. (2003). Spatial iconicity affects semantic relatedness judgments. *Psychonomic Bulletin & Review, 10,* 945–958.

15

CULTURE AND INTERGROUP RELATIONS: THE ROLE OF SOCIAL REPRESENTATIONS OF HISTORY

DENIS J. HILTON*AND JAMES H. LIU†

*Department of Psychology, University of Toulouse, Toulouse, France
†School of Psychology, Victoria University of Wellington, Wellington, New Zealand

A people's image of itself and its relation to other peoples will depend on its perceptions of history. These representations of history will in turn condition intergroup relations. For example, Hilton et al. (1996) found that attitudes to the treaty of Maastricht in 1991, which reinforced the European Union and introduced the Euro as a common currency, were predicted by historical beliefs. Thus both British and French respondents were more likely to hold favorable attitudes to European unification if they attributed Hitler's rise to power in 1933 to circumstances external to Germany, whereas Germans would be less likely to support European unification if they attributed Hitler's rise to power to the economic instability of the Weimar republic. These patterns held even controlling for other attitude-relevant beliefs (e.g. that European unification would strengthen the national economy and security) but were explicable given each culture's world view, such as British and French reluctance to share a "common house" with a nation whose Nazi past was not explained by external factors, and the historically grounded German fear that giving up their beloved Deutsche Mark would remove the financial autonomy and rigor that had guaranteed Germany's postwar economic and political stability.

Research has shown that war and politics are widespread and prominent in national groups' representations of world history (Liu et al., 2005). In particular, these studies (which we review below) show that World War II (WW II) occupies an especially significant place in representations of world history across cultures, and these representations predict important differences between cultures in attitudes to intergroup relations, whether these take the form of integration into supranational structures, managing internal diversity, or war against other nations. For example, Paez et al. (2007) show that the relative prominence of WW II in national groups' representations of world history predicts cross-cultural differences at the country level in willingness to fight for one's country.

Findings such as these raise important questions about the content, structure and function of socially shared beliefs about history, and how these representations guide intergroup behavior within, between and across cultures. In this chapter, we review how socially shared representations of history can include culture-specific "legitimizing myths" (Sidanius & Pratto, 1999) that help define a people's identity and perceived mission, which we refer to as "historical charters" following Malinowski (1926).

Below, we explicate our use of the concept of social representations of history and show how it can function with respect to group identity construction and agenda setting. We speculate that they include "charters" that serve a normative function of warranting group attitudes and actions by explaining them in terms of key events in the group's history. Charters define roles that confer legitimacy and allow groups to see themselves in a flattering light. They can be mobilized in arguments about legitimacy in dialogues between and within communities, hence may be influenced by confrontation with neighboring groups' accounts of history. When consensually accepted they anchor such debates about legitimacy in that even opponents have to refer to them by denying their relevance. We also discuss other ways in which charters can be changed or contested. Because empirical studies of social representations of national histories are currently rare, we focus our review of empirical work on large cross-national studies of social representations of world history, which are of particular relevance to understanding international relations. We conclude by reviewing studies that show the relevance of representations of history for group identities and collective emotions, such as collective guilt.

FORM AND FUNCTIONS OF SOCIAL REPRESENTATIONS OF HISTORY

SOCIAL REPRESENTATIONS OF HISTORY: DESCRIPTIVE VERSUS NORMATIVE ELEMENTS

Liu and Hilton (2005) argued that groups have social representations of history that function as "prisms" through which current historical challenges are interpreted. Collective memories of past events can be revived by present experiences: thus the significant "national and world events over the past 70 or so years" that became more prominent in the American mentality after the attacks of September 11th 2001 (9/11) all involved war or an attack against an American institution, whereas the events that lost ground included space exploration, civil rights, advances in communication and transportation, computers and internet, and the fall of communism (Schuman & Rodgers, 2004). However, collective memories may be more than just shared descriptive records of a group's experiences (e.g. Halbwachs, 1950/1980), and some function as normative "charters" (Malinowski, 1926) that define a group's identity and mission, and justify its actions. For example, while collective memories of John F. Kennedy's assassination were revived among Americans by September 11th (it was also a violent attack on a symbol of America), it is hard to see what *moral* could be drawn from this. However, many commentators cited the analogy between 9/11 and Pearl Harbor, thus renewing the significance of WW II as a template through which to evaluate the nation's response to the 9/11 attacks (Schuman & Rodgers, 2004). The analogy with Pearl Harbor shows how the WW II could thus serve as a "charter" dictating how America *should* respond; namely by seeking out and destroying the source of the aggression now matter how far from America's shores it was necessary to go.[1]

FROM *BECAUSE* TO *OUGHT*: THE EXPLANATORY AND LEGITIMIZING FUNCTIONS OF "CHARTERS"

Group histories have long been used to *explain* why current social arrangements and practices exist at the national level. Liu and Hilton (2005) give the example of Goody and Watt's (1963) account of the state of Gonja in Ghana, which is divided into a number of divisional chiefdoms, each of which are recognized as providing in turn the ruler of the whole nation. When asked to explain their system, the Gonja recounted how the founder of the state, Ndewura Jakpa, came down from the Niger Bend in search of gold, conquered the indigenous inhabitants of the area and installed himself as chief of the state and his sons as rulers of territorial divisions. When this story was first recorded at the beginning of the twentieth century, Jakpa was said to have begotten seven sons, corresponding to the seven divisions. However, some 60 years later, when there were only five divisions, due to the tribal incorporation of one division, and to boundary changes made by the British administration, Jakpa was credited with only five sons and no mention was made of the founders of the two political divisions which had since disappeared from the political map.

---

[1] Intriguingly, the only non-violent memory that increased in prominence after 9/11 was the Great Depression of the 1930s. However, this appears to be the exception that proves the rule that history must be relevant to current concerns, as the American economy was experiencing a severe downturn when the survey was taken.

The historical "charters" of modern societies share many characteristics with that of the Gonja (see for example Halbwachs, 1950/1980; Hobsbawm & Ranger, 1983). Charters are widely accepted versions of a group's history that *explain* what "we" *must* do. As an illustration, we may consider how different representations of the causes of the WW II might explain the differing reactions of European powers to the American-led war in Afghanistan following the attacks of September 11th 2001. As Liu and Hilton (2005) note, Britain, France and Germany had similar interests as stake, yet their differences in response were striking. Britain was America's principal military ally and dispatched troops immediately. While the French showed initial solidarity (as in the famous post September 11th headline from *Le Monde* "We are all Americans now"), France promised military aid but with rather more reticence. In Germany the debate about whether to send troops to Afghanistan was sufficiently serious that Chancellor Schroeder called a vote of confidence in his government (the first in Germany in over 20 years).

One reason for the differing responses to the attacks of September 11th 2001 may be the different representations of the causes of the WW II favored in each country, and in particular, the "lessons" of Munich. The British and the French might conclude that the failure in 1938 to stand up to Hitler's intransigence merely led to a later war with him on more unfavorable terms, whereas Germans who think of Munich may recall how Hitler's bellicose rhetoric led them into an unjustified war that led to Germany's ruin. From the British and French perspectives the analogy can be used to explain why their troops should intervene in a foreign war, but from the German perspective why their troops should stay out.

Such analogies do appear to be effective. Experimental activation of the Munich analogy made American participants more likely to support armed intervention against a threat in a fictitious distant country (Gilovich, 1981). Likewise, survey data showed that endorsement of the Munich analogy (as opposed to the Vietnam analogy) predicted the level of support for the first Gulf War in 1991 (Schuman & Rieger, 1992). Of course, the Vietnam analogy is habitually used by Americans to explain why their troops should stay out of foreign wars, and it is significant that scepticism concerning President Bush's decision to send more troops to Iraq in January 2007 was accompanied by widespread media comparisons to Vietnam.[2]

CHARTERS, SOCIAL IDENTITIES AND LEGITIMACY

Social representations of history can also legitimate group actions through processes of self-categorization that enable groups to see themselves in a positive light. Charters can buttress the kinds of positive distinctiveness strategies available

---

[2] Spellman and Holyoak (1993) show how perceived similarity between a source event and a target one can be affected by role perspective and judgments of representativeness (Tversky & Kahneman, 1974).

to people. For example, Hilton (1993) has shown that while the British, French and Germans all think that economic strength is important to being a great nation, only the British and French considered diplomatic position (e.g. through having permanent seats on United Nations security council) and military strength (both countries possess nuclear deterrents) important as well. The French also considered cultural distinction to be important in defining national greatness. In line with the positive distinctiveness hypothesis of social identity theory, members of each nation seemed to privilege those dimensions as important on which their own country was favorably positioned.

Being victors in the WW II "allows" Britain and France to play the role of world policemen who can send troops to trouble spots in their spheres of influence (e.g. Sierra Leone, Kosovo, Afghanistan, Ivory Coast) without asking the permission of their allies. Furthermore, charters may become formalized and incorporated into legal institutions; hence, the claims of Britain and France to be "world policemen" are institutionalized through their permanent seats on UN Security Council. Germans on the other hand can avoid their "identity deficit" due to a detested militaristic past by identifying more strongly with the supranational category of "European" (Hilton et al., 1996). Interestingly, national budgets reflect these values. Thus Britain and France allocated significantly higher budgets to national military spending than Germany during this period (Thatcher, 2002), whereas Germany was by far the largest net contributor to the European Union budget.

Given the universal salience of WW II and Hitler in representations of world history in the last 1000 years (Liu et al., 2005), Germany can ill afford to be perceived as engaging in warlike adventures on foreign soil. However, through creative re-interpretation of their history, Germans can nevertheless seek to attain a moral high ground. Thus Foreign minister Joschka Fischer repositioned Germany as "an early warning station against genocide," turning Germany's historical legacy from a burden to a strength in order to persuade his fellow Germans of the justification of deploying troops to Kosovo in 1998, Germany's first deployment of troops on foreign soil since WW II (Dresler-Hawke & Liu, 2006).

MOBILIZING CHARTERS TO JUSTIFY POLICIES

Historical events can be mobilized as charters that structure debate and justify collective courses of action. A striking example of how a historical event can serve as a charter, fall into disfavor, and then be resurrected once more is given by the Treaty of Waitangi in New Zealand, which was signed in 1840 between the indigenous Maori and the new British settlers, and served as the constitutional basis for sharing land and other rights in New Zealand. It was nevertheless considered a legal "nullity" 37 years later through colonization, only to be re-mobilised as a new social compact another hundred or so years later (see Orange, 2004). Liu (2005) argued that the revitalization of the Treaty was in part a response to the gradual withdrawal of support by Great Britain for her former colony, and the need for a new positively distinct social identity after "loyal subjects of the British Empire" had become untenable. The revitalization of this "bicultural charter" has helped legitimize Maori claims for compensation from the state for injuries and land alienation suffered during colonization (Sibley et al., 2008).

Historical events will often be mobilized as charters in order to fit with political interpretive schemes of the day (Hanson, 1989; Evans, 2003; Southgate, 2005; Sen & Wagner, 2005). Changes in group agendas may render certain aspects of their history more relevant than others for political purposes. The existence of historical records (books, recordings, memorials) and professional groups dedicated to the preservation and interpretation of historical knowledge (archaeologists, archivists, historians etc.) means that events that have effectively disappeared from public consciousness can be resurrected as part of a historical charter when the need arises. One example is the story of Masada, where Jewish "nationalists" fought to the death against encircling Roman legions. The ascent of Masada has become an integral part of the training for the Israeli Defense Force of today and serves to remind new recruits of the bravery, determination and fate of their forebears (Zerubavel, 1994). Similarly, Sen and Wagner (2005) describe how the destruction of a mosque at the supposed birthplace of mythical hero Ram was used to mobilize a new ideology of Hindu nationalism for India that has polarized Muslims and Hindus.

"ANCHORING" OF SOCIAL REPRESENTATIONS OF NATIONAL HISTORY

Some "charters" are so widely accepted within a society that they may be considered as "hegemonic" (Moscovici, 1988). Examples may be the rights asserted in the American Declaration of Independence for the United States, and the nature of the French republic founded after the 1789 for the French, which are taught as part of the general school curriculum of these countries, and treated as foundational events that explain the nature of the countries concerned. The Treaty of Waitangi in New Zealand serves as a prototypic exemplar of what we mean by an historic charter at the national level, being consensually regarded as the most important event in New Zealand history (Liu et al., 1999). It provides an "anchor" for public debate about intergroup relations which can be contested, re-interpreted or rejected, but never ignored (Liu & Sibley, 2006). Like the smile of the Cheshire cat, historical charters will be ever present in public consciousness.

Liu (2005) argued that the Treaty of Waitangi anchors a bicultural narrative for New Zealand identity that represents the Maori (indigenous Polynesians who arrived about 800 years ago) and the Pakeha (or whites, mainly British who arrived about 200 years ago) as coming together through war and peace to become partners in a sovereign state. Sibley and Liu (2007) showed the psychological power of this anchor in influencing not only the explicit level of attitudes and institutional forms, but also the level of implicit associations between Maori (brown) and Pakeha (white) faces and symbols of New Zealand. Unlike in the United States, where white participants implicitly (but not explicitly) more readily associate white than black targets with symbols of national identity (Devos & Banaji, 2005), in New Zealand Pakeha (whites) equally associate white and Maori targets with symbols of New Zealand on both explicit and implicit measures, despite manifest disadvantages for Maori in domains related to the distribution of wealth and power in society.

We argue that an anchored social representation such as the Treaty of Waitangi will always be present in New Zealanders' minds in public debates about anything to do with Maori. Liu et al. (2007a) hypothesized and found that evoking the Treaty of Waitangi in New Zealand did not change mean levels of support in issues critical to public opinion, as one might expect from a priming effect (see studies reported below on collective guilt). On the other hand, individual differences in the perceived relevance and meaning of an anchored historical representation should be predictive of attitudes and opinion (Liu & Sibley, 2006), because anchoring means that an attitude is embedded within a social and nomological network of associations grounded in daily life and discourse. Accordingly, Liu et al. (2007a) showed that perceptions of the importance and relevance of the Treaty of Waitangi, but not a less well-known historical event involving Maori and Pakeha (whites), were predictive of individual differences in levels of support for various aspects of biculturalism even after controlling for such factors measuring general social identity variables such as social dominance orientation (SDO), right-wing authoritarianism (RWA), national and ethnic identity and collective guilt.

Liu et al. further demonstrated the distinctive role of content-specific social representations of history in determining intergroup attitudes in Taiwan, where the most important event in Taiwanese history is the February 28th incident [where KuoMingTang (KMT) troops from mainland China suppressed Taiwanese civil disturbances using massive violence soon after the Japanese surrender of the island at the end of WW II. Another event of importance is the Meilidao incident (where the KMT jailed dissident political activists for publishing a magazine critical of the government, but resulted in raising dissidents' public profile and popularity). Both explained unique variance in addition to SDO, RWA and social identities), regarding the most important question facing Taiwan whether to become independent or reunify with mainland China.

INNOVATING, INTERPRETING AND IMPOSING HISTORY: CHANGING AND CONTESTING CHARTERS

History has shown that foundational charters are open to reinterpretation and renegotiation; indeed, the story of the American Civil War tells how the "inalienable" rights of man in the American Declaration of Independence were extended to blacks. Even if "anchored" charters cannot be ignored, their relevance can still be challenged. For example, in New Zealand the constitutional status of the

Treaty of Waitangi has been challenged by right-wing politicians and members of the general public who argue against Maori having "special rights" and a claim to a unique status. Sibley et al. (2008) show that "historical negation" – by which they mean the tendency to deny the relevance of past historical wrongdoings in current political debates – significantly predicted white New Zealanders' hostility toward a wide range of policy issues to do with social relations between Maori and non-Maori and the distribution of value between them.

Another way to undermine the force of a charter is to challenge its factual basis and thus challenge the legitimacy of claims based on that charter. Charters endow certain groups with rights, particularly land rights. An extremely striking case is Israel, where some Jews base their land claims on biblical accounts, some of which risk being undermined by archaeological evidence. In a clear (and undisguised) attempt to call into question the legitimacy of the state of Israel, Iranian President Mahmoud Ahmadinejad hosted a conference in Teheran in 2006 to which academics who question the existence of the Holocaust were invited.

Another example of how archaeology may undermine historical charters is illustrated by a current debate about the levels and the sophistication of Native American cultures in the Americas in 1491 (Mann, 2005). A low estimation would accredit the image of "virgin territory" that was transformed by European settlement and mechanization into a latter day Garden of Eden. A high estimation would accredit the thesis that European settlement was destructive of native civilizations. Given the importance of discovery, colonization and settlement in American history, this debate could have significant implications for the American self-image as a nation with a "manifest destiny" to expand its civilization, and undermine American confidence in policies that assume the existence of unlimited natural resources for economic expansion and the desirability of exporting its civilization through military force.

THE EXPLANATORY VALUE OF SOCIAL REPRESENTATIONS OF HISTORY FOR CROSS-CULTURAL AND INTERCULTURAL PSYCHOLOGY

To summarize, social representations of history have a descriptive function of summarizing a group's collective memories. This captures a broad consensus across the social sciences that history is an essential ingredient in constructing and maintaining the "imagined community" of nationhood (e.g., Anderson, 1983; Hobsbawm, 1990; Condor, 1996; Kohl & Fawcett, 1996; Reicher & Hopkins, 2001; Wertsch, 2002; Southgate, 2005). Although social representations of history serve the purpose of collective remembering (see Pennebaker et al., 1997 or Wertsch, 2002 for overviews of this literature), sometimes they will also include events that help define the essential identity (cf. Hamilton et al., 2002) of a "people" that have or seek to constitute a sovereign society. This is because history can provide a "warrant of antiquity" (Malinowski, 1926) describing how the group (nation, society, culture) has endured through time despite travails and the mortality of individuals (see Sani & Bowe, in press). We define an historical charter as a widely shared and iconic representation where selective elements of group history, its causes and consequences have been elaborated into a quasi-legal form that gives moral and sometimes legal implications for group action. Historical charters anchor debate by providing a common understanding through which dialogue flows (Billig, 1988; Lau et al., 2001). They can be used to justify certain privileges and social arrangements in society, and be perceived as part of the fabric of social reality (Moscovici, 1984, Hardin & Higgins, 1996). Because of their status in society, even those who contest their relevance or factuality must acknowledge their existence through debate [Liu et al. (2007a)].

More generally, social representations of history are widely-shared systems of knowledge and belief about history that are realized through communication (see Wagner & Hayes, 2005). It is important to note that this concept has several key differences to other constructs used to characterize cross-cultural differences between societies. First, social representations of a nation's history are explicitly group-level constructs that depend on the particular history of the people concerned. Their content is specific to each people and defines it in relation to and with respect to other peoples. This is consistent with Bar-Tal's (2000) position that group and intergroup processes depend on the specific *content* of societal beliefs that in turn condition general psychological functioning. In contrast, constructs such as values (Schwartz, 1992) and social axioms (Leung & Bond, 2004) are more personal and/or interpersonal in nature, and are conceptualized to have the same or similar content and structure across cultures, varying only in degree. These characteristics may explain the general failure in the literature to find a consistent relationship between dimensions of cultural variation (Hofstede, 1980) and measures of intergroup conflict, prejudice and discrimination.

Unlike values or axioms, which are relatively enduring, implicit and atomistic units of belief, social representations of history may be explicitly used in public debate to justify positions on current policy issues. Whereas values and social axioms are often taken for granted as implicit elements built into a culture and its institutions, a society's history is explicitly taught in schools and communicated through mass media and other institutional channels (Hein & Selden, 2000). Furthermore, through a process that has been described as "collective symbolic coping" (Wagner et al., 2002), social representations change as people in societies adapt to challenges fostered by new technologies (or more traumatic events such as war).

SOCIAL REPRESENTATIONS OF WORLD HISTORY: A WORLDWIDE STUDY

Given the current paucity of empirical work on social representations of national history, we focus our attention here on an extensive study of social representations of world history. Liu and his colleagues (Liu et al., 2005; Liu et al., in press)obtained survey data from university students in 24 societies representing two-thirds of the population on the planet Earth. Using open-ended questions asking participants to list the most important events and most important people in world history in the last 1000 years, they were able to ascertain the content of social representations of world history across cultures. Twelve of the most populous countries surveyed are presented here in Table 15.1, from both the 2005 paper where most of the data were collected in the mid-to-late 1990s and the 2007 paper where all of the data were collected after 2002. The top row consists of four great Western powers, while the bottom row consists of some of the largest Asian countries. The middle row depicts some of the larger Eastern European, South American and Middle-Eastern countries. Three striking features can be ascertained from the results in Tables 15.1 and 15.2 that hold true for all 24 societies surveyed.

TABLE 15.1   Most important events in world history

Rank	USA (n = 82)	(%)	Great Britain (n = 39)	(%)	France (n = 99)	(%)	Germany (n = 81)	(%)
1	WW II	86	WW II	77	WW II	64	WW II	68
2	WW I	50	WW I	64	French Rev	54	WW I	60
3	American Independence	38	Vietnam War	28	WW I	30	French Rev	49
4	Sept 11 Terrorism	27	Man on the Moon	26	US History	28	Discovery Americas	32
5	Discovery Americas	26	Birth of Christ	26	Colonization	27	German Reunification	23
6	Vietnam War	20	Industrial Rev	18	Atomic Bombing	20	Russian Rev	23
7	American Civil War	20	Discovery of America	18	German Reunification	19	Cold War	21
8	French Revolution	14	Roman Empire	18	Man on the Moon	16	Vietnam War	20
9	Birth of Christ	14	Atomic Bombing	15	Decolonization	14	Crusades	15
10	Breakup of USSR	12	Slavery	13	Nazism/Facism	12	Colonialism	15
10 =			Gulf War	13				

(continues)

TABLE 15.1 (*continued*)

Rank	Russia (*n* = 60)	(%)	Poland (*n* = 102)	(%)	Turkey (*n* = 227)	(%)	Brazil (*n* = 367)	(%)
1	WW II	57	WWII	73	WW I	44	WW II	40
2	WW I	46	WW I	54	Turkish War of Independence	42	WW I	32
3	Great Patriotic War	45	9/11 WTC	29	WW II	41	German Reunific	22
4	Christian. Of Russia	33	Fall of Communism	26	Conquest of Istanbul	35	Industrial Revolution	20
5	Chechnya War	32	Discovery of Americas	21	9/11 WTC	26	9–11 WTC	19
6	Kulikovo Battle	28	Polish Pope	14	French Revolution	22	French Rev	17
7	Fall of Soviet Union	27	Creation of EU	14	Found. Turkish Rep.	19	Both World Wars	14
8	Russian Revolution	23	Death of Polish Pope	12	Iraq War	20	Abolish Slavery	11
9	Atomic Bomb	18	Beginning of communism	12	Discovery Americas	13	Iraq War	11
10	Afganistan War	18	Birth of Christ	12	Industrial Revolution	12	Atomic Bomb	11

Rank	China (*n* = 115)	(%)	India (*n* = 100)	(%)	Japan (*n* = 75)	(%)	Indonesia (*n* = 104)	(%)
1	WW II	81	WW II	61	WW II	52	WW II	79
2	Found PR China	48	9/11 WTC	49	WW I	29	9/11 WTC	60
3	WW I	40	Indian Independence	42	French Revolution	23	Asian Tsunami	43
4	Industrial Revolution	36	WW I	37	Industrial Revolution	17	WW I	24
5	Technological Development	33	Cold War	20	Vietnam War	17	Iraq War	32
6	Fall of Communism	24	India–Pakistan War	18	Cold War	12	Crusades	24
7	Man on Moon	20	Both World Wars	15	Crusades	11	Industrial Revolution	22
8	Colonization	20	India–Pakistan Partition	15	Atomic Bombing	9	Bali Bombing	21
9	Sino-Japanese War	17	Iraq War	14	Discovery Americas	9	Israel–Palest. Conflict	21
10	Atomic Bomb	16	Asian Tsunami	14	Korean War	7	Atomic Bomb	20
10 =	Opium War	16			American Independence	7		

TABLE 15.2 Most important figures in the last 1000 years of world history

USA (n = 85)	(%)	Great Britain (n = 40)	(%)	France (n = 100)	(%)	Germany (n = 69)	(%)
Hitler	79	Hitler	100	Hitler	86	Hitler	91
Gandhi	36	M.L. King	33	Napoleon	30	Napoleon	48
M.L. King	32	Churchill	30	De Gaulle	24	Martin Luther	33
Napoleon	22	Thatcher	23	Einstein	21	Gandhi	26
Columbus	16	Einstein	23	Gandhi	19	Einstein	22
Marx	15	Princess Diana	20	Columbus	18	Stalin	22
Lincoln	14	Mandela	20	Freud	18	Gorbachev	19
Washington	14	Mother Theresa	18	Mandela	15	Bismarck	17
Einstein	13	Saddam Hussain	18	Marx	14	Lincoln	16
Kennedy	12	Kennedy	13	Kennedy	14	Kennedy	16
Stalin	12						

Russia (n = 60)	(%)	Poland (n = 102)	(%)	Turkey (n = 227)	(%)	Brazil (n = 367)	(%)
Hitler	57	Hitler	86	Kemal Ataturk	94	Hitler	43
Stalin	56	Stalin	38	Hitler	60	George Bush Jr.	35
Lenin	55	Pope John Paul II	48	Sultan Mahmed II	29	Osama bin Laden	23
Napoleon	52	Napoleon	29	Einstein	25	Lula da Silva	22
Vladimir Putin	35	Lech Walesa	19	George Bush Jr.	24	Gandhi	16
Peter the Great	33	Einstein	14	Bill Gates	10	Freud	14
Gorbachev	20	Joseph Pilsudski	13	Ismet Inonu	8	Saddam Hussain	14
Boris Yeltsin	13	Mother Teresa	11	Thomas Edison	7	Ayrton Senna	13
Mikhail Kutuzov	13	Columbus	10	Turgut Ozal	7	Che Guevara	13
Czar Ivan IV	13	Copernicus	8	Che Guevara	6	Mother Teresa	11

China (n = 115)	(%)	India (n = 100)	(%)	Japan (n = 78)	(%)	Indonesia (n = 104)	(%)
Mao	64	Gandhi	75	Hitler	54	Hitler	58
Hitler	58	Hitler	61	Napoleon	26	George Bush Jr.	30
Einstein	42	Osama bin Laden	25	Edison	19	Sukarno	30
Marx	40	Mother Teresa	22	Mao	15	Mohammed	28
Deng Xiaoping	36	Singh	19	Lincoln	15	Einstein	23
Napoleon	28	Shivaji Bhonsle	18	N. Oda	14	Mother Teresa	20
Zhou Enlai	21	Einstein	16	Kennedy	14	Gandhi	18
Newton	16	Subhas C. Bose	11	H. Toyotomi	13	Princess Diana	16
Sun Yatsen	10	Lincoln	16	Einstein	10	Thomas Edison	14
Confucius	10	George Bush Jr.	11	Columbus	10	Marx	12

THE PROMINENCE OF WAR IN REPRESENTATIONS OF HISTORY

The first is the prominence of wars in all samples studied. Indeed, the most striking feature of Table 15.1 is the extent to which WW II dominates the list of the most important events in world history across cultures. WW II together with its closely related predecessor WW I were among the only events to be named by more than 50% of the survey respondents across the 24 societies. WW I follows WW II in second place in most societies. There were only slight variations on this theme across cultures, mostly due to events of national rather than international significance. More generally, warfare is the single most mentioned category of events, exceeding the second largest category of politics by a wide margin. The building and dropping of atomic bombs was widely regarded across cultures as important, as were the Vietnam War and the Crusades. More recently, the Gulf War, the September 11 World Trade Center Attack and the Iraq War form another trio of interconnected series of events involving collective violence.

It should be noted that the second most frequently named category of events, coded as "politics" also often involved collective violence or its threat. These included the Cold War, the French Revolution, American Independence (often written in by participants as the "American War of Independence") and the Holocaust. The most frequently nominated cluster of peaceful political events involved the end of the Cold War, including German Reunification, the Fall of the Soviet Union and the Fall of Communism. These events were notable for the surprising restraint from violence exercised by rulers of the Communist block rather than being unrelated to violence. A final set of political events related to the founding of nations – such as the People's Republic of China or India – were also preceded by or followed by huge amounts of collective violence (e.g., civil war in China, the partition of India and Pakistan).

The most important economic event was the Industrial Revolution. Other important events named cross culturally were the Birth of Christ, the Discovery of the Americas, Colonization and the Man on the Moon/Space Travel. The emphasis on war was also reflected in the choice of important historical figures (Table 15.2) led by Hitler, Napoleon, then Mao, followed by a host of lesser lights, including WW II contemporaries Churchill, Roosevelt and Stalin. Overall, across samples, two-thirds of the figures named could be classified as political leaders. Among these, more than 60% played significant roles during wartime. John F. Kennedy was the most frequently nominated nonwartime political leader across cultures. But most nonwartime political leaders were regarded as important only in their nations of origin [e.g., Deng (China), Putin, Gorbachev and Yeltsin (Russia), Singh (India), Walesa (Poland), Lula (Brazil), Sukarno (Indonesia), etc.].

Some scientific and spiritual leaders achieved iconic status across cultures. After Hitler, it is Albert Einstein who was nominated most often across cultures, followed closely by Indian spiritual leader Gandhi. Martin Luther King, Nelson Mandela and Mother Teresa were also among the more positive figures nominated. Karl Marx was the most prominent social scientist, and Columbus the most prominent explorer. Although diverse, the domains of achievement of the figures nominated as a whole were dominated by politics and war.

HISTORICAL FORESHORTENING: THE FOCUS ON
RECENT EVENTS

After the preponderance of warfare, the second most salient feature is that most of the nominated events occurred in the last hundred years. Almost two-thirds were from the 20th and 21st centuries. Respondents from the great and ancient civilization of India named not a single event outside of the last hundred years; their focus was on the creation of the 20th century state of India. Mainland Chinese named three events in the 19th century related to modernization, and similarly focused on the creation of the People's Republic of China rather than ancient Chinese civilization. The lists produced by recently independent countries tended to be dominated by events related to the creation of their state (including Ukraine and East Timor, not shown here, but see Liu et al., in press).

There is also an overwhelming recency effect for nomination of historical figures. Sample means for 20th century figures in the 2005 paper ranged from 48% (Japan) to 83% (Singapore), with an overall average of 72%. Unlike the results obtained for events, in most samples 19th century figures were the second most nominated group (8–31%, across sample averages of 16%). Between them, the last two centuries accounted for almost 90% of the figures named for the 2005 data, a trend that is even stronger in the 2007 data when 21st century figures (e.g. Bush, Bin Laden) are included in the last two centuries.

It is, however, important to distinguish two kinds of recency effect. The World Wars are more recent than the French and Industrial Revolutions, yet none of these events will have been experienced in their lifetimes by our student samples. The pre-eminence of the former is likely to be due to greater prominence in family stories, school and media such as books and films. However, the impact of events have occurred in the lifetime of our student samples can be gauged by the similarities and differences between samples collected in the 1990s and in the 2000s (see Table 15.1). Thus while WW II continues to dominate representations of world histories in all countries in both samples, the Gulf War of 1991 was frequently nominated in samples collected in the mid-1990s but not at all 10 years later, being superseded by the Iraq War of 2003 (Liu et al., in press). We suspect that recency effects for such events experienced in the lifetime of respondents are likely to be due to greater availability in memory (Tversky & Kahneman, 1974), due in part to extensive media exposure (Lichtenstein et al., 1978).

However, we should conclude by noting that cognitive availability driven by media salience may not suffice *per* se for an event to be considered to be of historical significance. For example, Liu et al. (in press) found that while the Asian Tsunami received saturation mass media coverage and was prominent in word of mouth discussions, it was strikingly less frequently nominated (2 of 12 samples) than either the September 11 terrorist attack (9 of 12 samples) or the Iraq War (8 of 12 samples). The Tsunami brought with it tragic and heart-rending tales of death and destruction whose vividness would rival those of any war, yet this natural disaster was less prominent in representations of world history, perhaps because it was considered to have less political and social significance.

EUROCENTRISM VERSUS ETHNOCENTRISM IN
REPRESENTATIONS OF WORLD HISTORY

Third, and less salient, there was little systematic difference between Western and non-Western samples. The pattern of nominations was Eurocentric and Westernized for all countries, with Europe accounting for more than a third of the events named, and North America accounting for another 14%. Nonregional events (dominated by WW II) accounted for another quarter of nominations. Most non-Western countries named more events from Western regions than in their own, and events in non-Western regions involved a Western power, generally the United States, engaged in warfare on foreign soil (Iraq War, Korean War and Vietnam War). Both Western and non-Western countries treated European events such as WW I, the French Revolution and the Industrial Revolution as important.

Similar, but less Eurocentric patterns were found in the representation of the most important figures in world history. As seen in Table 15.2, Hitler is regarded as the most influential person in world history in most samples, surpassed only by national heroes Mao, Gandhi and Ataturk in China, India and Turkey, respectively. Not only was Hitler perceived as important but negative, with evaluative ratings ranging between 1.3 (do not admire at all) to 2.4 on a 7 point Likert scale for most countries. Most samples nominated leaders of national importance (especially related to state formation), but rarely were these figures perceived as important in other countries; this tempered the effect of Eurocentrism, but did not lead to regional configurations as might be expected from a "clash of civilizations."

CONCLUSIONS AND IMPLICATIONS OF SOCIAL
REPRESENTATIONS OF WORLD HISTORY

Three clear characteristics emerge from the lay representations of world history sampled across cultures. Social representations of world history are overwhelmingly about war and politics, refer mostly to events and personalities from the last two hundred years and are Eurocentric in focus. Using a different cuing technique, Pennebaker et al. (2006) were able to reduce the recency effect, but obtained a similar emphasis on war and politics, as well as a Eurocentric focus in seven samples from Europe, the United States and Japan. It is unlikely that this pattern is attributable to the student samples used. Liu et al. (2005) reported data from Taiwan from both mature and young adults and found little difference between them. In related vein, Schuman and Rodgers (2004) found that war was prominent in the collective memories of Americans of all ages. Advances in science, technology and medicine receive rather less attention than war and politics. And despite its importance for societal well-being, the hand of economics seems to be quite invisible in lay representations of history. The events during the Reagan–Thatcher years leading to and following from the "Washington consensus" (Hertz, 2001) that instituted the global hegemony of neo-liberal market capitalism, is both recent and far-reaching in its impact on all human beings, but this and other crucial economic changes receive virtually no mention from respondents in any society.

Lay representations of history seem to broadly reflect those of popular histories, such as *Days that changed the world: The 50 defining events of world history* by a British historian (Williams, 2006), in which 64% of events named were from the last 200 years, 52% were from Europe (plus another 27% from the Americas), and 46% concerned war (another 24% were about politics). Compared to our international surveys, these figures show a considerable Eurocentric focus, and only slightly less focus on war and recent events. However, it is important to note that some expert accounts of world history and societal evolution (e.g., Mann, 1986; Hobsbawm, 1994) accord far more importance to cultural, economic and social development in their representations of world history.

Level of education may influence which events are accorded most importance in lay representations. For example, Schuman and Rodgers (2004) found that, compared to less educated people, more educated people were more likely to evoke WW II but not John F. Kennedy's assassination or the Gulf War in their collective memories. This pattern may reflect a greater impact of school education on higher-educated people, as well as a motivation to privilege events such as WW II that serve as "charters" that help explain fundamental aspects of current economic, political and social arrangements.

IMPLICATIONS OF EUROCENTRISM IN WORLD HISTORY

The story of world history across cultures appears to represent Europeans (followed by Americans) as the primary actors on the world stage, with other peoples reacting to the social forces unleashed by democracy, militarization, colonization, and industrialization in idiosyncratic ways, as reflected by their frequent nomination of local heroes central to the establishment of their current state. This pattern is also evident among former Eastern block countries including Russia and Ukraine (not shown). World history appears to be constructed as an experience of globalization, a social process which emanates from the West, both historically and contemporaneously.

The only evidence of an East–West dichotomy was Mao, nominated in seven of nine Asian samples and none of the Western samples. Westerners accounted for more than almost 90% of persons nominated in the Western samples. Among Asian samples, Westerners accounted for about 50% of total nominations. Across the three Muslim nations surveyed, Turkey, Indonesia and Malaysia (not shown), there was little evidence of a pan-Islamic representation of history, as there was neither a single "culture hero" nor a single religion-based event (not even the Crusades) that transcended the national boundaries of these Muslim countries. Rather, Turkey produced a very secular representation, perhaps more characteristic of its university educated elites rather than its masses.

The Eurocentric focus of world history may reflect several factors. First, it was European explorers such as Columbus and Magellan in the 15th and 16th centuries who set out to circumnavigate the globe and thus pave the way for European colonization. The predominance of Europe and America in representations of world history thus no doubt reflects economic, military and political realities. Nevertheless, it is also important to note that the Eurocentric focus of world history may also provide Westerners with considerable symbolic capital. Liu et al. (2005) argued that "such representations of history can be used by Western powers to justify their political and military actions where they conflict with other groups... We argue that not only military and economic might, but representational resources are part of the pre-eminence of Western powers in the world today... Conversely, Germany and Japan, as the biggest losers of World War II, suffer from the 'burden of history'... Their ability to act unilaterally in international relations, especially using military might, is far more limited than their objective economic and military power would suggest." (p. 187).

WORLD WAR TWO AS A NATIONAL AND SUPRANATIONAL CHARTER

At the country level, WW II seems to serve as an historical "charter." As a striking demonstration of this, Paez et al. (2007) analyzed country-level aggregate data from the 24 societies described above. They found that percentage free-recalling WW II among the most important events in world history, evaluation of how positive or negative WW II was and being a victorious nation in WW II were all positively correlated with willingness to fight for one's country as indexed by country level scores from the World Values Survey (Inglehart et al., 2004). Interestingly, percentage recall of war in history as a whole was unrelated to willingness to fight, suggesting an effect of analogical transfer from WW II rather than a general effect of warlike collective remembering or warlike cultures (see Staub, 1988).

However, the universality of WW II in worldwide representations of world history may provide an opportunity for the development of global society. Thus WW II gave birth to a major institution, the United Nations, much of whose structure (e.g., the permanent members of the Security Council) and mandate (e.g., to prevent global war, to provide humanitarian aid to stricken areas) reflects an action orientation derived from experiences of the war. The importance of this event and the universally negative evaluation of Hitler have implications as a nascent "global charter," wherein civilized nations have a mandate to band together to combat genocide. Both Kosovo and East Timor were areas where the objective interests of Western nations were not directly threatened, and yet action was taken to defend the weaker group against the perceived genocidal intentions of the stronger.

WW II's prominence an anchor for public debate about new wars and collective violence can thus provide symbolic capital that can be used to mobilize international action. When Tony Blair talked about going to war beside America in Afghanistan and Iraq as "the right thing to do," he was making reference to the historical alliance of English-speaking peoples against tyrannical dictators most famously represented by Hitler. However, when America, Great Britain and Australia went to war in Iraq without a United Nations Security Council mandate and then subsequently found no weapons of mass destruction (the basis of their case for going to war), they violated a more fundamental tenet of the historical charter of WW II – that civilized nations have a duty to band together to not only fight against barbarism, but obey the rule of law themselves. The subsequent loss of prestige and soft power for America has been unprecedented, as the Pew Reports (2006) and our own data have shown. In our 21st century data (Liu et al., in press), George Bush Jr's evaluations were significantly *more* negative than Hitler's in a majority of the countries where they both made the top ten.

USING REPRESENTATIONS OF HISTORY: IDENTITY RELEVANCE WITHIN NATIONS

In the following section we turn to work that examines the relationship between identity and history within nations, at the individual level and using predominantly experimental rather than survey methods.

REMINDING GROUPS OF THREATS: HISTORY AND INGROUP SOLIDARITY

That the presence of an external threat facilitates ingroup solidarity and exacerbates outgroup hostility is well known to social psychologists (Sherif et al., 1961). For example, using hourly self-report data, Mehl and Pennebaker (2003) found that in the days after the September 11th attacks, Americans sought each other's company to share information and views. In a related vein, Roccas et al. (2006) note that intensification of the Israel–Palestine conflict led to a greater use of exonerating cognitions and rejection of collective guilt for Israeli transgressions against Palestinians.

Historical narratives that recount threats from the past can have analogous effects to the occurrence of conflict itself (Hong et al., 2001). Thus Wohl and Branscombe (2004) show that presenting reminders of the holocaust led Israeli respondents to reject collective guilt for Israeli wrongdoings to Palestinians, and to endorse causal attributions that exonerated the Israelis (e.g. attributions to Palestinian terrorism) and to reject attributions that laid blame at their door (Israeli oppression). Politicians are well aware of the power of representations of history to mobilize national solidarity, and many have used historical appeals to this end. An instructive example comes from Communist China, where a nationalist approach to history was downplayed in favor of a Marxist narrative that emphasized the importance of (international) class struggle following the establishment of the People's Republic (Liu & Atsumi, 2008). Tellingly, however, there has been an upsurge of mass media accounts of historical grievances against Japan (especially the Nanjing massacre) beginning in the 1980s that coincided with the liberalization of the country's economy. Liu and Atsumi (2008) suggest that this remobilization of a nationalistic account of history increases national solidarity at a time when there is considerable unrest about the degree of inequality that has emerged as a consequence of replacing the communist economic system with a market-based economy.

COLLECTIVE GUILT: DEALING WITH THE MEMORY OF INGROUP TRANSGRESSIONS

Dominant groups who are led to feel that they owe their position to historical exploitation of other groups may feel collective guilt (Wohl et al., 2006). For example, Doosje et al. (1998) presented historical narratives that were either positive or negative in their implications about Dutch colonization in Indonesia. The negative account aroused feelings of guilt and favorable attitudes to compensation among Dutch respondents, particularly those who did not strongly identify with being Dutch. This last finding points to a paradox about collective guilt in that those who feel least identified with a group may also be those who feel most responsible for its actions.

Roccas et al. (2006) have suggested that identification with a group needs to be decomposed into two separable factors, which they termed glorification and attachment. Glorification involves nationalism, vertical collectivism and blind patriotism – the endorsement of chauvinistic beliefs that one's group is better than other groups. In contrast, attachment refers to the feeling of involvement with one's group and involves horizontal collectivism and critical patriotism. Although glorification and attachment are correlated, they are sufficiently distinct that it is possible to be "critically detached," that is, to feel a deep involvement with one's group while being able to criticize it and without glorifying it in comparison with other groups. Importantly, attachment (controlling for glorification) predicted greater collective guilt and less endorsement of exonerating cognitions in Israeli students who read an account of an Israeli atrocity committed against Arabs in 1956. Glorification (controlling for attachment) showed the opposite pattern of relations.

CONFRONTING A NEGATIVE PAST: THE DUTY TO REMEMBER

Research on collective guilt reveals a paradox about modern human societies. On the one hand, it is clear that there are strong psychological pressures to rewrite history in a way that is flattering to a group's self-image. These tendencies are very clearly revealed in an experiment on the oral transmission of a fictitious (but plausible) historical atrocity conducted by Marques et al. (2006). In part of this study, Portuguese subjects were led to believe that they had listened to the soundtrack from a television documentary that included an account of a massacre and rape of defenseless Indians by Portuguese (in-group) or Spanish (out-group) mercenaries during the colonization of the Americas. Participants reported more guilt and shame in the in-group than out-group perpetrator conditions. In a communications chain procedure modeled on Allport and Postman's (1947) classic studies of rumor transmission, the end reports showed striking tendencies to produce in-group flattering histories. Whereas end narratives of the discovery of the Americas by the out-group (Spanish) mentioned massacres in 28% of cases and rapes in 54% of cases, narratives that featured the in-group (Portuguese) as protagonists only mentioned massacres in 4% of cases and rapes in 13% of cases.

Nevertheless, certain groups (or group members) do adopt a critical attitude to their past. A paradigm case is postwar Germany, which has deliberately confronted much of its Nazi past and accepted war guilt to a much greater extent than Japan (Hein & Selden, 2000). This may be for at least three reasons. First, in modern democratic societies the existence of permanent records (books, films, memorials, etc.) and of professional historians whose job is to interpret these records is likely to reduce the distortions produced by oral traditions (see Liu & Hilton, 2005 for the contrast between oral and "objective" histories). Second, globalization will lead to greater interaction between people from different groups, hence enabling outgroup members to confront group members with negative aspects of their group's past. Consistent with this reasoning, Dresler-Hawke and Liu (2006) found that feelings of collective shame were exacerbated by the regard of others from relevant outgroups. Thus young Germans reported that they would feel more shame and guilty if they were visiting memorials to atrocities committed by Germans in WW II with foreigners (especially Jews) than if they were visiting these memorials with other Germans. By contrast, Japan is an island nation firmly within the political orbit of the United States rather than accountable to its Asian neighbors (Liu & Atsumi, 2008). Finally, attitudes to history itself may determine adopting a critical attitude to an ingroup's history. For example, French participants who agreed that France had a "duty to remember" were more likely to be in favor of punishing Maurice Papon during his trial in 1998 for his role in handing over Jews to Nazi Germany in 1944 (Douchet et al., 2004). Intriguingly, "duty to remember" was significantly related to a measure of collective guilt (Branscombe et al., 2004).

REPRESENTATIONS OF HISTORY AND INTERGROUP RECONCILIATION

A significant implication of the foregoing research is that representations of history can sometimes be modified in a way that will influence intergroup relations. For example, Wohl and Branscombe (2005) demonstrated that different frames for accounts of the Holocaust influenced American Jews' attitudes to Germans and Germany. Framing these events using inclusive categorizations ("what people have suffered at the hands of other people") rather than as ingroup-outgroup categorizations ("what Jews suffered at the hands of Germans") led to less assignment of collective guilt to Germans and to more forgiveness of Germans, as well as a more favorable disposition to Germans and toward buying German products.

Liu et al. (1999) found that white (Pakeha) New Zealanders proved to be an exception to the rule of ingroup favoritism through accepting blame for the nonrespect of the Treaty of Waitangi. In addition, both Pakeha and Maori who were familiar with the other group's history were more likely to adopt moderate positions on questions such as compensation for Maoris and teaching Maori in schools. This raises interesting questions about whether changing knowledge about history can lead to intergroup reconciliation. Current work by Bar-Tal (2001) and Liu et al. (in press) suggests that historical events and accounts centrally embedded within a society's discourses and institutions will resist attempts at change, whereas more peripheral events will be more amenable to change.

CONCLUSION

Space constraints have made it impossible to include the topic of collective remembering, the interdisciplinary study of institutional forms of "remembering" (see Wertsch, 2002; Devine-Wright, 2003), or studies of historical wrongdoing outside of psychology, as exemplified by the holocaust literature, or the literature on truth and reconciliation in South Africa. Nor have we been able to explore the psychological processes involved in the construction of group narratives of history in depth (but for this see Liu & László, 2007).

A question for future research concerns social representations of national histories. A striking finding is how many events and people in lay representations of world history are relevant to the formation and status of their current nation-state. For example, Liu et al. (in press) note that the hypothesis that histories serve as charters that "warrant" the current state seems confirmed by the finding that nations as diverse as China, India, Russia, Poland, East Timor, Ukraine and Hungary (the latter three not shown in Tables 15.1 and 15.2) generally named events and people related to the formation of their current states, rather than events and people related to the origins of their (often very ancient) civilizations.

Some lay representations of national history will, like representations of world history, contain an emphasis on war and conflict. Hungarian representations of their national history showed an almost exclusive focus on war and conflict, and a focus on events from the 19th and 20th centuries that explain how Hungary came to have its current form (László et al., 2002), favoring the theory offered by experts such as Tilly (1975) that "war made the state, and the state made war" (p. 42). Bar-Tal (2001) has argued that Israel's protracted conflict with her neighbors has produced an ethos characterized by fear, deep mistrust of the outgroup and perpetual readiness for conflict, and may reflect a general tendency to privilege warfare and security issues above other elements of society necessary for well-being. But not all national histories show such an extreme focus on armed conflict, as the cases of New Zealand (Liu et al., 1999), Singapore and Malaysia (Liu et al., 2002), and to a lesser extent Taiwan (Huang et al., 2004) show. Future research is needed to address the question whether the content of national representations of history will predict political attitudes to national questions (e.g. war, the rule of law, etc.).

The social representations of world history that we have reviewed above have impressed us by their similarity, with their focus on recent wars that have originated in Europe and America. Nevertheless, WW II is interpreted differently by each people with respect to its own experience of this war (winner versus loser, lives lost, etc.), and this specificity predicts differences in national attitudes to fighting for one's country. In our view, this illustrates the importance of understanding how the content of social representations of history conditions intergroup processes. This can provide a foundation for a theory that bridges the gap between universal and culture-specific aspects of intergroup conflict in human societies. It will remain for future research to define national and global historical charters and their functions in greater detail to realize this promise of using the content of shared systems of belief to bind the general and the specific together into a societal psychology.

REFERENCES

Allport, G. W., & Postman, L. (1947). An analysis of rumor. *Public Opinion Quarterly, 10,* 501–517.

Anderson, B. (1983). *Imagined communities: Reflections on the origins and spread of nationalism.* London, England: Verso.

Bar-Tal, D. (2000). *Shared beliefs in a society: Social psychological analysis.* London, England: Sage.

Bar-Tal, D. (2001). Why does fear override hope in societies engulfed by intractable conflicts, as it does in the Israeli society? *Political Psychology, 22,* 601–627.

Billig, M. (1988). Social representation, anchoring and objectification: A rhetorical analysis. *Social Behaviour, 3,* 1–16.

Branscombe, N. R., Slugoski, B., & Kappen, D. M. (2004). The measurement of collective guilt: What it is and what it is not. In N. R. Branscombe & B. Doosje (Eds.), *Collective guilt: International perspectives* (pp. 16–34). New York: Cambridge University Press.

Condor, S., (1996). Unimagined community? Some social psychological issues concerning English national identity, In: G.M. Breakwell, E. Lyons, (Eds.), Changing European identities: Social psychological analyses of social change Oxford: Butterworth-Heinemann.

Devine Wright, P. (2003). Theoretical overview of memory and conflict. In E. Cairns & M. D. Roe (Eds.), *The role of memory in ethnic conflict.* New York: Palgrave Macmillan.

Devos, T., & Banaji, M. R. (2005). American = White? *Journal of Personality and Social Psychology, 88,* 447–466.

Doosje, B., Branscombe, N. R., Spears, R., & Manstead, A. S. R. (1998). Guilty by association: When one's group has a negative history. *Journal of Personality and Social Psychology, 75,* 872–886.

Douchet, K., Giudicelli, M.-N., & Hilton, D. J. (2002). Lay judgments of responsibility for collaboration in Vichy France: Individual or collective? Paper presented at the General meeting of the European Association for Experimental Social Psychology, San Sebastian, Spain, June.

Dresler-Hawke, E., & Liu, J. H. (2006). Collective shame and the positioning of German national identity. *Psicologia Politica, 32*, 131–153.

Evans, R. J. (2003). Redesigning the past: History in political transitions. Introduction to special issue of *Journal of Contemporary History, 38*(1), 5-12.

Gilovich, T. (1981). Seeing the past in the present: The effect of associations to familiar events on judgments and decisions. *Journal of Personality and Social Psychology, 40*, 797–808.

Goody, J., & Watt, I. (1963). The consequences of literacy. *Comparative studies in society and history, 5*, 304–345.

Halbwachs, M. (1950/1980). *The collective memory.* New York: Harper & Row.

Hamilton, D. L., Sherman, S. J., & Castelli, L. (2002). A group by any other name: The role of entitativity in group perception. *European review of social psychology, 12*, 139–166.

Hardin, C., & Higgins, E. T. (1996). Shared reality: How social verification makes the subjective objective. In R. Sorrentino & E. T. Higgins (Eds.), *Handbook of motivation and cognition, Vol 3* (pp. 28–84). New York: Guilford Press.

Hanson, A. (1989). The making of the Maori: Culture invention and its logic. *American anthropologist, 91*, 890–902.

Hein, L., & Selden, M. (2000)(eds.). *Censoring history: Citizenship and memory in Japan, Germany, and the United States.* Armonk, NY: An East Gate Book.

Hertz, N. (2001). *The silent takeover.* New York: Free Press.

Hilton. D. J. (1993). *The struggle for German history.* Unpublished manuscript.

Hilton, D. J., Erb, H-P., McDermott, M., & Molian, D. J. (1996). Social representations of history and attitudes to European unification in Britain, France and Germany. In G. M. Breakwell & E. Lyons (Eds.), *Changing European identities: Social psychological analyses of social change. International series in social psychology* (pp. 275–295). Woburn, MA, US: Butterworth-Heinemann.

Hobsbawm, E. (1990). *Nations and nationalism since 1780: Programme, myth, reality.* Cambridge: Cambridge University Press.

Hobsbawm, E. (1994). *Age of extremes: The short history of the twentieth century.* London: Michael Joseph.

Hobsbawm, E., & Ranger, T. (Eds., 1983). *The invention of tradition.* Cambridge: Cambridge University Press.

Hofstede, G. (1980). *Culture's consequences: International differences in work-related values.* Beverly Hills, CA: Sage.

Hong, Y. Y., Wong, R., & Liu, J. H. (2001). History of war enhances ethnic identification. *Journal of Psychology in Chinese Societies, 2*(1), 77–106.

Huang, L. L., Liu, J. H., & Chang, M. L. (2004). The double identity of Chinese Taiwanese: A dilemma of politics and identity rooted in history. *Asian Journal of Social Psychology, 7*(2), 149–189.

Inglehart, R., Basañez, M., Diez-Medrano, N., Halman, X., & Lüijk, X. (2004). *Human Beliefs and Values: A cross-cultural sourcebook based on the 1999–2002 values surveys.* Mexico, DF: Siglo XXI.

Kohl, P. L., & Fawcett, C. (1996) (Eds.) *Nationalism, politics, and the practice of archaeology.* New York: Cambridge University Press.

László, J., Ehmann, B., & Imre, O. (2002). Les représentations sociales de l'histoire: La narration populaire historique et l'identité nationale. In S. Laurens & N. Roussiau (Eds.), *La mémoire sociale. Identités et représentations sociales* (pp. 187–198). Rennes: Université de Rennes.

Lau, I. Y. M., Chiu, C. Y., & Lee, S. L. (2001). Communication and shared reality: Implications for the psychological foundations of culture. *Social cognition, 19*(3), 350–371.

Leung, K., & Bond, M. H. (2004). Social axioms: A model for social beliefs in a multicultural perspective. *Advances in experimental social psychology, 36*, 119–197.

Lichtenstein, S., Slovic, P., Fischhoff, B., Layman, M., & Combs, B. (1978). Judged frequency of lethal events. *Journal of Experimental Psychology: Human Learning and Memory, 4,* 551–578.

Liu, J. H. (2005). History and identity: A system of checks and balances for Aotearoa/New Zealand. In J. H. Liu, T. McCreanor, T. McIntosh, & T. Teaiwa (Eds.), *New Zealand identities: Departures and destinations* (pp. 69–87). Wellington, NZ: Victoria University Press.

Liu, J. H., & Hilton, D. J. (2005). How the past weighs on the present: Social representations of history and their impact on identity politics. *British Journal of Social Psychology, 44,* 537–556.

Liu, J. H., & Sibley, C. G. (2006). Differential effects of societal anchoring and attitude certainty in determining support or opposition to (bi)cultural diversity in New Zealand. *Papers on Social Representations, 15,* 1–15.

Liu, J. H., & Atsumi, T. (2008). Historical conflict and resolution between Japan and China: Developing and applying a narrative theory of history and identity. In: T. Sugiman, K. J. Gergen, W. Wagner, & Y. Yamada (Eds.), *Meaning in action: Constructions, narratives, and representations* (pp. 327–344). Tokyo: Springer-Verlag.

Liu, J. H., & László, J. (2007). A narrative theory of history and identity: Social identity, social representations, society and the individual. In: G. Moloney & I. Walker (Eds.), *Social representations and identity: Content, process and power* (pp. 85–107). London: Palgrave Macmillan.

Liu, J. H., Wilson, M. W., McClure, J., & Higgins, T. R. (1999). Social identity and the perception of history: Cultural representations of Aotearoa/New Zealand. *European Journal of Social Psychology, 29,* 1021–1047.

Liu, J. H., Lawrence, B., Ward, C., & Abraham, S. (2002). Social representations of history in Malaysia and Singapore: On the relationship between national and ethnic identity. *Asian Journal of Social Psychology, 5*(1), 3–20.

Liu, J. H., Goldstein-Hawes, R., Hilton, D. J., Huang, L. L., Gastardo-Conaco, C., Dresler-Hawke, E., Pittolo, F., Hong, Y. Y., Ward, C., Abraham, S., Kashima, Y., Kashima, E., Ohashi, M., Yuki, M., & Hidaka, Y. (2005). Social representations of events and people in world history across twelve cultures. *Journal of Cross-Cultural Psychology, 36*(2), 171–191.

Liu, J. H., Sibley, C. S., & Huang, L. L., (2007a). The historical anchoring of public opinion: Effects of culture specific symbols on intergroup relations. Under review.

Liu, J.H., Paez, D., Slawuta, P., Cabecinhas, R., Techio, E., Kokdemir, D., Sen, R., Vincze, O., Muluk, H., Wang, F.X., & Zlobina, A. (In press). Representing world history in the 21st century: The impact of 9-11, the Iraq War, and the nation-state on the dynamics of collective remembering. In press, *Journal of Cross-Cultural Psychology.*

Mann, M. (1986). *The Sources of Social Power.* Cambridge: Cambridge University Press.

Mann, C. (2005). *1491. The Americas before Columbus.* London: Granta Books.

Malinowski, B. (1926). *Myth in primitive psychology.* London: Kegan Paul, Trench, Trubner.

Marques, J., Paez, D., Valencia, J., & Vincze, O. (2006). Effects of group membership on the transmission of negative historical events. *Psicologia Politica, 32,* 79–105.

Mehl, M. R., & Pennebaker, J. W. (2003). The social dynamics of a cultural upheaval. *Psychological Science, 14,* 579–585.

Moscovici, S. (1984). The phenomenon of social representations. In R. M. Farr & S. Moscovici (Eds.), *Social representations* (pp. 3–70). Cambridge University Press: Cambridge.

Moscovici, S. (1988). Notes towards a description of social representations. *European Journal of Social Psychology, 18,* 211–250.

Orange, C. (2004). *An Illustrated history of the Treaty of Waitangi, (2nd ed).* Wellington, NZ: Allen & Unwin.

Paez, D., Liu, J. H., Techio, E., Slawuta, P., Zlobina, A., & Cabecinhas, R. (2007). "Remembering" world war two and willingness to fight: Sociocultural factors in the social representation of warfare across 22 societies. *Journal of Cross-Cultural Psychology* (in press).

Pennebaker, J. W., Paez, D., & Rimé, B. (1997). *Collective Memory of Political Events.* Mahwah, NJ: Lawrence Erlbaum.

Pennebaker, J., Paez, D., & Deschamps, J-C. (2006). The social psychology of history: Defining the most important events of the last 10, 100 & 1000 years. *Psicologia Politica, 32*, 15–32.

Pew Global Attitude Project (2006). America's image slips, but allies share U.S. concerns over Iran, Hamas. www.pewglobal.org.

Reicher, S., & Hopkins, N. (2001). *Self and nation*. London: Sage.

Roccas, S., Klar, Y., & Liviatan, I. (2006). The paradox of group-based guilt: modes of national identification, conflict vehemence, and reactions to the ingroup's moral violations. *Journal of Personality and Social Psychology, 91*, 698–711.

Sani, F. & Bowe, M. (in press). Perceived collective continuity: Seeing groups as temporally enduring entities. In F. Sani (Ed.). Individual and collective self-continuity: Psychological perspectives. Hillsdale, NJ: Erlbaum.

Schuman, H., & Rieger, C. (1992). Historical analogies, generational effects and attitudes towards war. *American Sociologist, 57*, 315–326.

Schuman, H., & Rodgers, W. L. (2004). Cohorts, chronology, and collective memories. *Public Opinion Quarterly, 68*, 217–254.

Schwartz, S. (1992). Universals in the content and structure of values: Theoretical advances and empirical tests in 20 countries. *Advances in Experimental Social Psychology, 25*, 1–65.

Sen, R., & Wagner, W. (2005). History, emotions and hetero-referential representations in inter-group conflict: The example of Hindu-Muslim relations in India. Papers on Social Representations, *14*, 2.1–2.23.

Sherif, M., Harvey, O. J., White, B. J., Hood, W. R., & Sherif, C. W. (1961). *The Robber's Cave experiment*. Norman, OK: University of Oklahoma Press.

Sidanius, J., & Pratto, F. (1999). *Social dominance: An intergroup theory of social hierarchy and oppression*. Cambridge: Cambridge University Press.

Sibley, C. G. & Liu, J. H. (2007). New Zealand = bicultural? Implicit and explicit associations between ethnicity and nationhood in a New Zealand context. In press, *European Journal of Social Psychology, 37*(6), 1222–1243.

Sibley, C. G., Liu, J. H., Duckitt, J. & Khan, S. (2008) Social representations of history and the legitimation of social inequality: The form and function of historical negation. In press, *European Journal of Social Psychology, 38*, 542–565.

Spellman, B. A., & Holyoak, K. J. (1993). If Saddam is Hitler then who is George Bush? Analogical mapping between systems of social roles. *Journal of Personality and Social Psychology, 62*, 913–933.

Staub, E. (1988). The evolution of caring and nonaggressive persons and societies. *Journal of Social Issues, 44*, 81–100.

Southgate, B. (2005). *What is history for?*. New York: Routledge.

Thatcher, M. (2002). *Statecraft*. London: Harper Collins.

Tilly, C. (ed.) (1975). *The formation of national states in Western Europe*. Princeton, NJ: Princeton University Press.

Tversky, A., & Kahneman, D. (1974). Judgment under uncertainty: Heuristics and biases. *Science, 185*, 1124–1131.

Wagner, W., & Hayes, N. (2005). *Everyday discourse and common sense: The theory of social representations*. New York: Palgrave Macmillan.

Wagner, W., Kronberger, N., & Seifert, F. (2002). Collective symbolic coping with new technology: Knowledge, images and public discourse. *British Journal of Social Psychology, 41*, 323–343.

Wertsch, J. V. (2002). *Voices of collective remembering*. Cambridge: Cambridge University Press.

Williams, H. (2006). *50 Days that changed the world: The 50 defining events of world history*. London: Quercus.

Wohl, M. J. A., & Branscombe, N. R. (2004). Importance of social categorization for foregiveness and collective guilt assignment for the Holocaust. In N. R. Branscombe & B. Doosje (Eds.), *Collective guilt: International perspectives* (pp. 284–306). New York: Cambridge University Press.

Wohl, M. J. A., & Branscombe, N. R. (2005). Forgiveness and collective guilt assignment to historical perpetrator groups depend on level of social category inclusiveness. *Journal of Personality and Social Psychology, 88*, 288–303.

Wohl, M. J. A., Branscombe, N. R., & Klar, Y. (2006). Collective guilt: Emotional reactions when one's group has done wrong or has been wronged. *European Review of Social Psychology, 17*, 1–37.

Zerubavel, Y. (1994). The historic, the legendary, and the incredible: Invented tradition and collective memory. In J. R. Gillis (Ed.), *Commemorations: The politics of national identity* (pp. 105–123). Princeton: Princeton University Press.

16

MOTIVATED EXPRESSION

OF SELF-ESTEEM ACROSS

CULTURES

SUSUMU YAMAGUCHI*, CHUNCHI LIN**,
HIROAKI MORIO[†] AND TAICHI OKUMURA*

*University of Tokyo, Tokyo, Japan
**University of California, Berkeley, CA, USA
[†]Faculty of Business Administration, Sapporo University, Japan

Self-esteem has been considered an indispensable ingredient of psychological health in North America (Taylor & Brown, 1988). Indeed, North Americans have been found to strive for higher self-esteem (e.g., Crocker & Park, 2004; Koch, 2006; Solomon, 2006). The huge number of studies addressed on the topic of self-esteem is evidence that self-esteem is an important part of North American culture. In the fall of 2007, when we were writing this chapter, a literature search by PsycINFO returned almost 30,000 articles.

The cultural perspective, however, challenges the well-accepted view that self-esteem is desirable both personally and socially and thus people strive for high self-esteem. Based on cross-cultural comparisons involving North Americans and Japanese, Heine et al. (1999) questioned the universality of the need for self-esteem and the importance of self-esteem. The main purpose of this chapter is to examine the validity of Heine et al.'s arguments regarding two issues: Claimed low self-esteem and insignificance of self-esteem in Japanese culture (and more generally in East Asian cultures). Because previous studies (including Heine et al.) have focused on the comparison between North America (i.e., United States and Canada) and Japan, this chapter will review studies mostly conducted in those countries, with references to studies in China, where available. Before the details of our approach are presented, what we mean by self-esteem would need to be explicated.

DEFINING SELF-ESTEEM

Self-esteem is a familiar concept both for researchers and lay people alike. However, no consensus exists over the definition of self-esteem (Mruk, 2006). More than 110 years ago, James (1890, p. 204) grouped self-esteem together with pride, conceit, vanity, arrogance, and vainglory, implying that affection for the self constitutes an important ingredient of self-esteem. Modern researchers, on the other hand, tend to prefer "drier" definitions of self-esteem. For example, Baumeister et al. (2003, p. 2) in their comprehensive review defined self-esteem as "how much value people place on themselves." According to this definition, the affective component is excluded, because self-esteem is "the evaluative component of self-knowledge" (p. 2). Other researchers have also proposed their own definitions that emphasize self-evaluation. For example, self-esteem is "a personal judgment of worthiness that is expressed in the attitudes the individual holds toward himself" (Coopersmith, 1967, pp. 4–5). Exceptionally, Raynor and McFarlin (1986, p. 329) insisted that researchers should restrict "the concept of positive and negative self-esteem to affective evaluations (i.e., distinct from the concept of the degree of possession of an attribute, set of attributes, or overall competence)." This argument resonates well with James's (1890) position that self-esteem can be grouped with affections such as pride. However, "pride" has its own place in social psychology with its definition being "'self-conscious' emotion with self-evaluative processes" (Tracy & Robins, 2007, p. 147). Obviously, this definition of pride is similar to Raynor and McFarlin's definition of self-esteem.

As this cursory review indicates, researchers have not reached an agreement about what they should mean by self-esteem. This led Mruk (2006) to propose that each author should begin by defining what the author means by self-esteem. In our view, the construct of self-esteem would be most appropriately defined here as a mixture of affect and self-evaluation. In this sense, Rosenberg's (1965, p. 30) definition appears to be most reasonable, because both affect and cognition are included when he defined self-esteem as "a positive or negative attitude toward a particular object, namely, the self." Because attitudes typically consist of three components (i.e., affection, cognition, and behavior) (Breckler, 1984), Rosenberg's definition can be interpreted as containing both affective and cognitive components with behavioral consequences. Additionally, it is practical to adopt Rosenberg's definition for this chapter because Rosenberg's scale is "by far the most popular among researchers" (Baumeister et al., 2003, p. 5). As will be shown, this is also the case in Japan. Thus, in this review, by self-esteem we refer to an individual's positive and possibly negative attitude toward the self, which consists mostly of positive self-evaluation, as well as positive affection toward the self. With this definition, we now proceed to examine the challenge against the universalistic view of self-esteem.

QUESTIONED UNIVERSALITY OF THE NEED FOR HIGH SELF-ESTEEM

As stated in the introduction, previous research has demonstrated that North Americans tend to self-enhance their abilities and desirable personality traits to maintain positive self-esteem (Taylor & Brown, 1988). On the other hand, it is widely known that East Asians score lower on self-esteem scales such as Rosenberg's (1965). The lower self-esteem scores among Japanese, coupled with other findings, have led Heine et al. (1999) to claim that Japanese have lower self-esteem and do not consider self-esteem important. They suggested furthermore that Japanese seek something other than self-esteem, such as face maintenance, to maintain their sense of positive self-regard. Because Heine et al.'s claim is multifaceted; we will examine their claim in the following two sections focusing on two issues. First, we will examine if Japanese have actually lower self-esteem relative to North Americans. For this purpose, we will examine the comparability of self-evaluation measures. Second, we will examine the importance of self-esteem in Japanese (and partially Chinese) culture by analyzing a nomological network including self-esteem both in North America and Japan (partially including China). If self-esteem is as important for Japanese (and Chinese) as it is for North Americans, a similar nomological network must be found in those cultures. On the other hand, if self-esteem is insignificant for Japanese as Heine et al. (1999) claimed, the two cultures would show different nomological networks, such that self-esteem is not related to important psychological variables such as self-confidence, mental health, life satisfaction, and so forth. We start with a critical examination of Japanese "low" self-esteem.

"LOW" SELF-ESTEEM AMONG JAPANESE (RELATIVE TO NORTH AMERICANS)

Is Japanese self-esteem lower than that of North Americans? Heine et al. (1999) presented two main lines of evidence to support their claim. First, Japanese self-esteem scores are lower than those of North Americans. Second, Japanese do not self-enhance in many situations. We agree that Japanese self-esteem scores are lower and that Japanese do not self-enhance in many situations. However, we are not convinced that these results reflect Japanese lower self-esteem as compared with North Americans, because the cross-cultural comparability (i.e., equivalence) of self-esteem measures has not been examined fully and previous findings can still be explained in terms of Japanese modesty. In the following, we will elaborate on the two competing hypotheses (i.e., the self-criticism hypothesis versus the modesty hypothesis) and examine the validity of the two hypotheses in the context of equivalence.

Two Competing Explanations

There are two competing explanations for the lower self-esteem scores and less prevalent self-enhancement among Japanese. The *self-criticism hypothesis* states that Japanese are self-critical and this self-criticism leads to lower self-evaluations and the motivation to improve themselves (Heine et al., 1999). According to this hypothesis, Japanese have lower self-esteem, because they are self-critical. This hypothesis also predicts that Japanese do not self-enhance because they have lower self-esteem and thus have little reason to self-enhance.

The chief tenet of the self-criticism hypothesis is the assumed self-improvement motive underlying Japanese self-critical attitudes. In Heine et al. (1999), self-improvement is assumed to be an inseparable component of Japanese self-criticism. Actually, if the self-criticism hypothesis did not include a self-improvement motivation, it would be equivalent to an explanation of modesty, which is prevalent in East Asian cultures. That is, if a person is modest, the person would present a self-evaluation that is lower than their actual self-evaluation, which is tantamount to being self-critical. Thus, the self-criticism hypothesis can be distinct from modesty only when self-criticism is accompanied with the self-improvement motivation.

On the other hand, according to the *modesty hypothesis*, which is favored by Yamaguchi et al. (2006), Japanese lower self-evaluation is a result of Japanese modesty, rather than a self-critical attitude. That is, Japanese present their self-evaluations as lower than they actually evaluate themselves due to the modesty norm prevalent in Japanese culture. This hypothesis also explains why Japanese do not self-enhance in many situations: The modesty norm prevents Japanese from presenting a grandiose self-view.

Self-enhancement Across Cultures

In contrast with Heine et al.'s (1999) claim that Japanese do not self-enhance, Sedikides et al. (2003) showed that Japanese self-enhance on collectivistic behaviors (i.e., conforming to group decisions) and traits (such as self-sacrifice, loyalty), which are culturally important for Japanese. The modesty hypothesis explains this finding very well. Japanese have positive self-esteem and are motivated to claim superiority as are North Americans. However, the modesty norm prevalent in Japanese culture prevents them from self-enhancing in many situations. However, when it comes to important behaviors or traits, Japanese do self-enhance, because the need for self-enhancement outweighs the modesty norm. Indeed, consistent with this line of argument, Japanese have been found to self-enhance at job interviews, in which self-enhancement is expected and culturally acceptable (Matsumoto & Kijima, 2002). In this study, undergraduate students who were seeking a job were asked to report their self-presentation strategies at their job interviews. The most important strategy for those students was to impress their interviewers with their competence, followed by the strategy to emphasize their positive attitude. It would be easy to imagine that self-critical attitudes (stressing one's shortcomings) would not create a favorable impression on the interviewer.

As is the case with most controversies in our field, the controversies over the universality of the self-enhancement motivation are not easily settled. Debates continue regarding how results of previous studies can be summarized by meta-analysis (Heine et al., 2007a, b, Sedikides et al., 2005, 2007a, b). We will not get into the details in this chapter. Instead, we would like to point out that the conceptual relationship between self-esteem and self-enhancement remains vague. Although Heine et al. (1999) assume that high self-esteem is always accompanied by the self-enhancement motivation, high self-esteem individuals do not necessarily need to self-enhance in order to maintain self-esteem, as long as they are confident about their self-worth (i.e., secure high self-esteem). On the other hand, defensive high self-esteem individuals, who have nagging doubts about their self-worth, tend to self-enhance on highly unlikely positive qualities (Lambird & Mann, 2006).

Assumed Comparability of Self-esteem Scores

The comparability of self-esteem scores was also assumed in Heine et al. (1999). With this assumption, the Japanese low self-esteem scores (relative to North Americans) was attributed to Japanese low self-esteem. In other words, they assumed that self-esteem scales (such as Rosenberg's) yield scores comparable across cultures. The cross-cultural comparability of self-esteem scales, however, has not been examined, to the authors' best knowledge.

The cross-cultural comparability of a scale is called *full score equivalence*. If a self-esteem scale has *full score equivalence*, people who have the same position on the latent variable (i.e., self-esteem) earn exactly the same scale score independent of their culture (Berry, 1992; Fontaine, 2005; Fischer et al., this volume). Thus, a score from one culture can be validly compared with a score from another culture. On the other hand, the modesty hypothesis questions the full score equivalence of self-esteem scales, because Japanese are expected to express lower self-esteem as compared to their North American counterparts even when both Japanese and North American subjects have the same position on the latent variable (i.e., self-esteem). Thus, the modesty hypothesis posits that the requirement of full score equivalence is not satisfied and thus cross-cultural comparisons of self-esteem scale scores are not justifiable. According to this view, the lower self-esteem scores earned by Japanese cannot be considered as the results of Japanese low self-esteem as advocated by Heine et al. (1999).

It should be noted here that Heine et al. (1999, p. 785) denied the full score equivalence of self-esteem scales when they argued that "positive self-regard, as it is conceptualized, operationalized, and measured, is not as prevalent, significant, or sought after, discussed, functional, elaborated on, or desired in Japan as it is in North America." This contention obviously questions the cross-cultural equivalence of self-esteem measures developed and validated in North America. The foregoing argument would call on researchers to examine full score equivalence, or cross-cultural comparability, of the self-esteem scales. As elaborated in Fischer et al.'s chapter (this volume), full score equivalence is the highest level of equivalence required for cross-cultural comparisons and its confirmation requires multiple approaches. Probably for this reason, no attempts have ever been made to confirm full score equivalence of a self-esteem scale. We can examine full score equivalence, however, when it comes to self-evaluation of specific abilities (such as math ability), for which objective standardized tests are available.

Testing the Full Score Equivalence of Specific Self-evaluations

In the case of math ability, we can compare students' math test score with their self-evaluation of math ability if a standardized test to measure students' math ability across cultures is available. If full score equivalence of the test holds, Japanese and North American students with the same test score will evaluate their own math ability as the same. The modesty hypothesis, however, predicts that this will not happen. That is, Japanese students are expected to report lower self-evaluation on math ability than are their North American counterparts with the same test score. Thus, full score equivalence of self-evaluation scale in the above example will disconfirm the modesty hypothesis.

On the other hand, quite paradoxically, the self-criticism hypothesis does not predict that the study described above would confirm full score equivalence (Heine et al., 1999). No matter what kind of self-evaluation measures (specific or global) are used, the self-criticism hypothesis would predict that self-critical attitudes among Japanese make them report lower self-evaluations of math ability, relative to North Americans with the same score. Thus, proponents of the self-criticism hypothesis can claim that full score equivalence should be confirmed by other means. For this reason, the absence of full score equivalence in this case does not disconfirm the self-criticism hypothesis.

The two hypotheses can be pitted against each other in terms of self-improvement motivation, even when full score equivalence is not confirmed. Remember, the operation of the self-improvement motivation among self-critical individuals is the chief tenet of the self-criticism hypothesis. The self-criticism hypothesis with the self-improvement motivation would make the counterintuitive prediction that lower self-evaluation is associated with higher achievement motivation and thus with higher performance. On the other hand, the modesty hypothesis does not predict that lower self-evaluation is accompanied by higher performance.

To test the full score equivalence and the competing predictions derived from the two hypotheses, we used data from the Trends in International Mathematics and Science Study in 2003 (TIMSS2003) (Yamaguchi et al., 2008). As we describe in the next section, TIMSS2003 allows us to compare students' self-evaluation of math and science abilities with their actual performance on these subjects, exactly as we described above.

Self-Evaluation and Performance: A Case of TIMSS2003

TIMSS2003 is a world-wide study of students' math and science achievement. Since 1995, the International Association for the Evaluation of International Achievement (IEA) has been conducting a series of studies on cross-national achievement in mathematics and science every 4 years. In the most recent study in 2003, fourth graders and eighth graders in 51 countries/regions participated in the Trends in International Mathematics and Science Study (TIMSS2003). An important feature of this study for our purpose is that the students' self-evaluations of their math and science abilities were measured, in addition to the administration of standardized math and science questions. Specifically, the students were asked to answer four questions about their math and science ability, respectively, using a four-point scale (1. Agree a lot; 2. Agree a little; 3. Disagree a little; 4. Disagree a lot):

1. I usually do well in mathematics (science).
2. Mathematics (Science) is more difficult for me than for many of my classmates (reversed item).
3. Mathematics (Science) is not one of my strengths (reversed item).
4. I learn things quickly in mathematics (science).

Data on the self-evaluations and achievement in math and science were downloaded from the website of the International Association for the Evaluation of Achievement (IEA) (http://timss.bc.edu/timss2003i/userguide.html).

Country Level Analysis

Previous research emphasized country level differences, typically those between Japan and North America, such that Japanese on the average express lower self-evaluations (e.g., Heine et al., 1999; Kitayama, 2006). Thus, for comparison, we examined correlations between self-evaluation in math and science abilities and actual scores at the country level. In doing so, however, we decided to go beyond the Japan–North America comparison, taking advantage of the world-wide scale of the study. For eighth graders, self-evaluation and achievement scores on math and science were available for 222,336 students in 51 countries/regions and 149,107 students in 32 countries/regions, respectively. If the self-criticism hypothesis is valid throughout the world, *lower* self-evaluation (which can be a reflection of a self-critical attitude) must be associated with *higher* achievement scores. Consistent with this expectation, countries/regions with *lower* self-evaluations in math and science earned *higher* scores on both math and science tests. This result apparently fits very well with the argument that people in self-critical cultures are motivated to improve themselves, resulting in higher math and science scores. This finding further suggests that this may be the case above and beyond Japan and North America.

The global analysis of the relation between self-evaluation and achievement, however, may not be appropriate to test the modesty hypothesis because East Asian cultures are supposed to be characterized with modesty but little is known about modesty in, say, African cultures. Thus, in the next step, we narrowed the focus of our analysis on the difference between East Asia and the West. One would expect that the negative relation between self-evaluation and achievement score is even more prominent between people in East Asian cultures compared to those in North American cultures. Because this chapter is mainly concerned with the contrast between two East Asian cultures (i.e., Japanese and Chinese) and North American cultures, country/regional means for self-evaluation and achievement scores in math and science in those countries/regions are plotted in Figures 16.1 and 16.2, respectively. The eighth graders' response on each of the

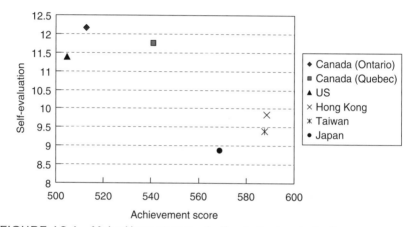

FIGURE 16.1   Math achievement score and self-evaluation (country level).

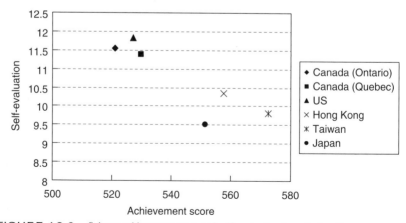

FIGURE 16.2   Science achievement score and self-evaluation (country level).

four self-evaluation questions was summed to yield the Self-Evaluation of Math (Science) Ability Score, so that the larger means indicate higher self-evaluations of math ability or science ability. As can be seen in those figures, there is a clear tendency for the eighth graders in those countries/regions with low self-evaluation (i.e., Japan and China) to score higher on both math and science. There is a negative correlation between self-evaluation and achievement score both for math and science: $r(N = 6) = -0.84$, $p < 0.05$ and $r(N = 6) = -0.88$, $p < 0.05$, respectively. This result appears consistent with the contention that the Japanese (and Chinese) self-critical attitudes are accompanied by the motivation to improve and thus result in higher academic performance. Based on the results of the country level analyses, a researcher may well argue that East Asian students' high scores on math and science are a consequence of their self-criticism. Indeed, previous arguments in support of the self-criticism hypothesis have been largely based on such country level results, which are often very impressive as we have shown here. However, such argument did not take into account the possibility of ecological fallacy (see below).

Ecological Fallacy

No matter how impressive the results of country level analyses, they are vulnerable to faulty interpretations. This is because country level variables cannot always explain individual level processes. Robinson (1950) termed this kind of misinterpretation an *ecological fallacy*. He illustrated the fallacy very clearly using data on illiteracy and ethnicity (Caucasian Americans versus African Americans) in 1930. Because the education level of African Americans was much lower than that of Caucasians at that time, illiteracy was expected to be related to ethnicity. Actually, the illiteracy rate in nine geographic divisions of the United States was almost perfectly correlated with the rate of African American population ($r = 0.946$), indicating that a geographic division with more African American residents had a higher rate of illiterate residents. However, the individual level correlation between illiteracy and ethnicity was much lower ($r = 0.203$), indicating that the correlation at the aggregate level was exaggerated. Furthermore, his second example demonstrated that correlation at the two levels (aggregate level versus individual level) can be in the opposite direction. He examined the relationship between nativity (the foreign born versus native born) and illiteracy at the aggregate and individual levels. The correlation between the rate of the foreign born population and illiteracy rate at the state level was negative ($r = -0.619$), meaning that a state with a higher foreign born population had a lower rate of illiterate people. Given the lower education level of the foreign born at that time, this result may be surprising. However, he further showed that the individual level correlation was in the opposite direction ($r = 0.118$), indicating that foreign birth was associated with higher possibility of illiteracy.

The lesson of ecological fallacy is that aggregate level correlations cannot be valid substitutes for individual level correlations (Robinson, 1950). Thus, we should not interpret aggregate level results with individual level constructs.

In the case of the relationship between ethnicity and illiteracy, poorer geographic divisions (in which more households could not afford to send their children to school) had higher population of African Americans, which resulted in higher illiteracy rates. Also, in the case of the relationship between the nativity and illiteracy, the state level correlation could be explained by a state level variable, i.e., economic situation of the state. Immigrants may well prefer to live in affluent states, where foreign workers are needed and thus are welcomed. In affluent states, it is very likely that more parents can afford to send their children to school and consequently those states had a lower illiteracy rate.

Thus, in the present case, we should not solely depend on the results of the country level analyses to test individual level hypotheses. It would be an ecological fallacy if individual level analyses do not yield a negative relationship between self-evaluation and achievement, which was obtained at the country level. To examine this possibility, we conducted a multi-level modeling analysis, which allows us to examine the relationship between self-evaluation both at the country level and individual level simultaneously. Specifically, the multi-level modeling analysis addressed two questions. First, is there any difference in self-evaluation at the country level between East Asian and Western eighth graders? This question is concerned with self-enhancement among Westerners (or self-effacement among Asians). The multi-level analysis will confirm the lower self-evaluations among East Asian students, as compared with North American students. The second question, which is critical for the present purpose, is concerned with the relationship between self-evaluation and achievement among East Asian and North American eighth graders at the individual level. If the self-criticism hypothesis is valid, the relationship between self-evaluation and achievement will be negative. On the other hand, the modesty hypothesis predicts otherwise, as has been explained above.

The multi-level analyses yielded significant results, confirming that the eighth graders in North America express higher self-evaluations about their ability both in math and science. This indicates that Japanese and Chinese students in the TIMSS2003 study expressed lower self-evaluations relative to their counterparts in North America, like those in past research.

However, the expressed lower self-evaluations were *not* negatively related to achievement in math and science at the individual level. Contrary to the results of the country level analysis, self-evaluation and achievement were positively correlated in East Asian cultures as well as in the North American cultures. Because our focus in this chapter is on Japanese and Chinese self-esteem as contrasted with North Americans, we conducted a separate analysis for those countries/regions. The results of the separate analysis are presented in Figures 16.3 and 16.4. These results fail to confirm the self-criticism hypothesis at the individual level. Self-critical attitude did not facilitate performance. Rather, the positive relationship between self-evaluation and achievement among East Asians indicates that they can claim self-superiority to a greater extent with higher performance, albeit their overall level of claim is modest relative to North Americans'. This result

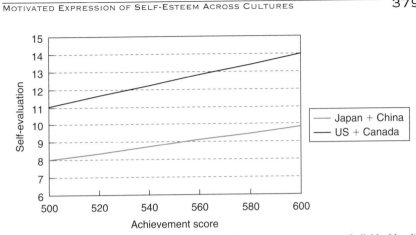

FIGURE 16.3   Relationship between self-evaluation and math achievement (individual level).

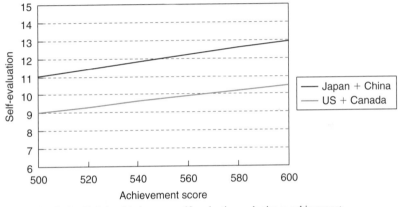

FIGURE 16.4   Relationship between self-evaluation and science achievement (individual level).

supports the modesty hypothesis that East Asians express lower self-evaluations to accord with their modesty norm.

Although largely neglected in previous research, these findings point to the generality of correspondence between self-evaluation and achievement. It is very likely that high self-evaluation is accompanied by high performance and thus is important for individuals' psychological well-being and health, although East Asians are reticent about positive self-evaluations.

In the next section, we will review empirical research on self-esteem mainly among Japanese (with occasional reference to Chinese data) and examine if self-esteem functions similarly in Japan (and China) as in North America. Is self-esteem meaningfully related to its presumed antecedents and consequences such as achievement, interpersonal relationship, and psychological well-being?

IMPORTANCE OF SELF-ESTEEM IN JAPAN RELATIVE
TO NORTH AMERICA

Heine et al. (1999, p. 785) questioned the universality of the need for positive self-regard, insisting that it is not "as prevalent, significant, or sought after, discussed, functional, elaborated on, or desired in Japan as it is in North America". This contention obviously questions the *functional equivalence* of the self-esteem construct, which is attained when a "similar network of convergent and discriminant relationships with other theoretical variables across cultural groups" is confirmed (Fontaine, 2005, p. 806). More specifically, if Heine et al.'s contention was valid, self-esteem would not function in Japan as it does in North America. Then, the relationship between self-esteem (as conceptualized in North America) and theoretically relevant variables would not be the same in Japan (and China) as that in North America.

This section reviews empirical research conducted on Japanese and Chinese self-esteem and compares it with that of North Americans. As a benchmark with which the functional equivalence of Japanese (and Chinese) self-esteem and that of North Americans is evaluated, we will rely on Baumeister et al.'s (2003) extensive review that includes 230 studies. As mentioned in the introduction, there are almost 30,000 studies conducted so far and a mega-review is required to draw a definite conclusion even for North Americans alone. However, because such an attempt has never been made, we will follow Baumeister et al.'s classification of relevant variables, although of course we will not be restrained by their review and we will extend our scope to cover other relevant studies.

School Performance

Self-esteem among North Americans has been found to be positively correlated with self-perception of ability and actual school performance, achievement motivation, and persistence in learning. Consistent with those findings, as well as the results of the TIMSS2003, self-esteem among Japanese has been reported to be positively related to school performance and motivation for learning. Self-esteem among Japanese seventh and eighth graders was found to be heightened after better school performance, especially for those students with moderate school performance (Saito et al., 1987). Similarly, self-esteem as measured by Rosenberg's (1965) Self-Esteem Scale (RSES) was positively correlated with academic performance in the previous semester of female ninth graders, suggesting that with higher academic performance students express higher self-esteem (Sato et al., 2000).

Self-esteem has also been found to be positively associated with achievement motivation. Coopersmith's Self-Esteem Scale (1967) scores among Japanese eighth graders were positively correlated with achievement motivation both among boys and girls, $r = 0.63$ and $r = 0.30$, respectively (Ogawa, 1976). Also, self-esteem among fourth graders was highly correlated with self-efficacy and achievement motivation, $r = 0.62$ and $r = 0.62$, respectively (Shiomi & Nakai, 1996).

Furthermore, high school students with high self-esteem tended to have higher expectancies about their achievement (Choi, 1985). These results are consistent with a finding in a cross-generational study on the relationship between self-esteem and self-confidence (Amagai, 1997). Amagai showed that the self-esteem of her subjects (ranging from teenagers to those in their 80s) was positively correlated with their self-confidence.

Self-esteem as measured by RSES was also negatively correlated with academic procrastination ($r = -0.26$) among female students, indicating that students with high self-esteem tend to be more persistent in learning (Ryu & Ogawauchi, 2005). If lower self-esteem is caused by self-critical attitudes, which is assumed to motivate one to improve oneself, self-esteem should be positively correlated with academic procrastination. But this was not the case.

As to the direction of causality, only weak evidence is available to support the argument that high self-esteem causes high performance in North America (Baumeister et al., 2003). In Japan, we could not locate any study that demonstrated this causality, either.

Planning fallacy is another optimistic bias prevalent in North America. People tend to hold a biased belief that their own project will proceed as planned (Kahneman & Tversky, 1979). Buehler et al. (1994) demonstrated that undergraduate students' time estimates for a variety of academic tasks, including their Honors Theses, are overly optimistic. In one study, students enrolled in the Honors Thesis course were asked to predict, as accurately as possible, when they would submit their finished thesis. The subjects were also asked to provide their optimistic (when everything went well) and pessimistic (when everything went poorly) predictions. The researchers compared the students' estimates with the actual submission date and found that fewer than 30% of their subjects finished in the time they provided as the most accurate prediction. Even their pessimistic prediction was overly optimistic. This phenomenon has been replicated in a series of experiments in North America. Japanese researchers have also successfully replicated the planning fallacy phenomenon among Japanese students, although little is known outside Japan. For example, Murata (1999a) reported that Japanese undergraduate students had predicted that they would attend more class meetings than they actually did. He also found in another study that Japanese undergraduate students predicted that they would start writing their term paper earlier than they actually did (Murata, 1999b). Furthermore, self-esteem has been shown to be related to the planning fallacy among Japanese. Female students with higher self-esteem tended to predict that they would work longer for a mid-term examination and achieve a higher score (Fujishima, 2004), indicating that higher self-esteem is related to optimistic bias – as it is in North America (Taylor & Brown, 1988).

These results clearly indicate that high self-esteem among Japanese is positively related to school performance, achievement motivation, persistence in learning, and optimistic bias in planning, exactly as it is in North America.

Interpersonal Relationship

As Battistich et al. (1993) showed in North America, Japanese college students with high self-esteem as measured by RSES tended to evaluate themselves higher on such dimensions as sociability, sports, intelligence, and physical appearance (Ito, 1999). Japanese college students with higher self-esteem also tended to rate their relationships with friends more highly (Endo et al., 2000), exactly as Keefe and Berndt (1996) showed in North America, although Japanese self-evaluations were lower than those of Canadians (Endo et al.). Endo et al. also have confirmed that self-esteem is positively correlated with self-evaluations both in Japan ($r = 0.53$) and in Canada ($r = 0.46$ for European Canadians and $r = 0.40$ for Asian Canadians). Furthermore, corresponding to the result of Buhrmester et al. (1988) in North America, self-esteem and self-reported social skills among female college students was found to be positively correlated in Japan ($r = 0.29$) (Daibo, 1991).

The self-criticism hypothesis posits that individuals with low self-esteem are self-critical in order to improve. If so, it would be reasonable that those who are motivated to self-improve do not hesitate to talk about their shortcomings. Actually, Japanese have been shown to express lower self-evaluations in many situations (Heine et al., 1999). Thus, when it comes to self-disclosure, this line of reasoning would lead one to predict that individuals with low self-esteem disclose their negative aspects more than do those with high self-esteem. This prediction, however, has not been supported by empirical evidence. Rather, contrary to the prediction of the self-criticism hypothesis, studies in Japan have shown that low self-esteem people anticipated that they would be hurt after disclosure of their negative experiences (Katayama, 1996), which is consistent with the results of Campbell et al. (1991) in North America. Indeed, among Japanese older people, low self-esteem individuals tended to disclose their distress less to their intimate other (such as a spouse), compared with those with medium or high self-esteem (Suganuma, 1997). Also, low self-esteem Japanese college students, whose self-esteem scores fall in the lowest quartile, tended to answer that they would disclose their distress to others to a lesser extent than did their counterparts in the top quartile (Kameda, 2002). These results indicate that self-esteem functions similarly in terms of its relationship to self-disclosure: higher self-esteem individuals can afford to disclose negative aspects of the self in both cultures.

As to the relationship between attachment style and self-esteem, studies in North America have shown that securely attached individuals have higher self-esteem than insecurely attached individuals (e.g., Brennan & Morris, 1997; Huntsinger & Luecken, 2004). Likewise, among Japanese females (18–52 years old), securely attached people tended to have higher self-esteem than those with avoidant or ambivalent attachment style (Takahashi, 2002).

Buhrmester et al. (1988) examined the relationship between interpersonal behaviors and self-esteem in North America. According to their results, self-esteem was positively related to the initiation of new contacts and friendships ($r = 0.38$). Consistent with this result, Shiomi and Nakai (1996) reported that self-esteem among Japanese fourth graders is positively correlated with affiliative tendencies ($r = 0.57$). Thus, both in Japan and in North America, people high in self-esteem can afford to initiate contact with other people, probably supported by confidence in their attractiveness and social skills, as Baumeister et al. (2003) suggested. Actually, self-esteem among Japanese youngsters (ranging from seventh graders to college students) is negatively correlated with anthrophobia, or the fear of other people (Okada & Nagai, 1990). Also, according to Ogawa (1976), self-esteem is negatively correlated with dependency, $r = -0.30$ for boys and $r = -0.20$ for girls. These results suggest that high self-esteem is associated with independence among Japanese, as it is among North Americans. The following study by Ikegami (2002) provides additional empirical support for this interpretation.

Ikegami's (2002) experiment is exceptional in the sense that it was concerned with determinants of self-esteem and allowed her to draw conclusions about causality. She showed that a self-enhancing task elicited a positive mood and heightened state self-esteem as measured by Heatherton and Polivy's scale (1991). In the self-enhancing task, her Japanese subjects were asked to complete self-referent sentences such as "I feel self-confident that ..." On the other hand, in the other-enhancing task, the subjects were asked to complete other-referent sentences such as "I feel gratitude towards others, when they ..." Ikegami confirmed that positive mood was elicited by the two sentence completion tasks to the same degree: no significant difference was found between the effects of the two tasks. The state self-esteem, however, was heightened only after the self-enhancing task. Most importantly, in the present context, self-esteem was heightened after the induced self-enhancement rather than other-enhancement, meaning that Japanese self-esteem is as individualistic as that of North Americans. A similar argument has been advanced by Uchida and Kitayama (2001).

Group Behavior

Although fewer studies have been conducted in Japan on the relation between self-esteem and group behavior, results are consistent with those in North America (e.g., Crocker et al., 1987): Japanese junior high school students with high self-esteem showed ingroup favoritism to a greater extent than did their low self-esteem counterparts (Namioka, 1993). The greater ingroup favoritism in evaluations can be explained in terms of self-anchoring (Cadinu & Rothbart, 1996): People rely on their self-evaluations when they evaluate their ingroup. Because this process does not occur when people evaluate outgroups, it is quite plausible that high self-esteem people evaluate their ingroup higher than outgroups. Furthermore, because this tendency is more prominent among high self-esteem people, it appears that both Japanese and North Americans with high self-esteem rely on their high self-evaluations when they evaluate their ingroup.

Antisocial Behavior

Proponents of the self-esteem movement in California expected low self-esteem to cause antisocial behavior such as aggression and delinquency (California State

Department of Education, 1990). However, North American results on antisocial behavior are mixed (Baumeister et al., 2003). On the other hand, if the self-
criticism hypothesis is valid, antisocial behavior should be less frequent among
people with low self-esteem in Japan; because those with low self-esteem are
expected to be motivated to improve their behavior after critical self-evaluations.

Empirical studies in Japan have also provided mixed results. Two thousand
and seventy-three high school students (1041 males and 1032 females) at 29
high schools in Tokyo were asked questions about their delinquent behavior
(e.g., smoking), criminal behavior (e.g., shoplifting), and hypothesized relevant
variables (such as attachment and self-esteem) (Nishimura et al., 1984). The
results of step-wise analyses indicated that self-esteem was positively related to
delinquent behavior among boys but it was not related to boys' criminal behavior or girls' delinquent and criminal behaviors. In another study, 41 delinquents
(mean age = 17 years old) were compared with 86 high school boys (Murakami,
1986). The results indicated that the delinquents were more antisocial and lower
in self-esteem than were the high school students. In yet another study, Suzuki
(1989) asked 1285 junior high school students (685 boys and 600 girls) about
their delinquent behavior, criminal behavior, and hypothesized relevant variables
(such as self-confidence and self-esteem). The results indicated that self-esteem
was not related to delinquent behaviors. But delinquent behavior was positively
related to self-confidence, suggesting that those with high self-esteem are bold
and go beyond the bounds of socially acceptable behavior.

In all, Japanese studies on the relation between self-esteem and antisocial
behavior have provided mixed evidence as have those in North America. The
mixed evidence, however, did not support the self-criticism hypothesis, because
low self-esteem was not associated with low delinquency in Japan. In the
Japanese literature, high self-esteem was either associated with low delinquency
or no relationship was found.

Mental Health

Happiness is strongly related to self-esteem not only in North America but
in countries across the five continents (Baumeister et al., 2003). According to
Diener and Diener (1995), data from 13,000 college students from 31 countries
showed that self-esteem and life satisfaction are positively correlated ($r = 0.47$).
The correlation between life satisfaction and self-esteem was positive in the
United States, Canada, and also in Japan. Life satisfaction was also similarly
correlated with finances, satisfaction with family, and satisfaction with friends,
in all three countries. Thus, although expressed happiness of Japanese was lower
than that of North Americans, it was positively correlated with self-esteem and
other relevant variables both in North America and Japan.

Furthermore, studies conducted in Japan have largely shown similar tendencies as those reported in North America. RSES scores were positively correlated
with satisfaction with physical appearance both among male and female college
students, $r = 0.57$ and $r = 0.67$, respectively (Shibata & Nobeji, 1990). In a

similar vein, self-esteem was positively correlated with satisfaction with physical appearance and negatively correlated with concern about body appearance among both male and female college students, $r = 0.44$ and $r = 0.43$, respectively for satisfaction, and, $r = -0.27$ and $r = -0.23$, respectively for concern (Ono, 1984); this tendency was replicated by Kamakura et al. (2004). Another study showed that a daily positive mood, as measured by a diary method, was found to be positively associated with daily self-esteem (Mizuma & Oshio, 2002).

Self-esteem has been found to be associated with better mental health among Japanese. Self-esteem as measured by RSES was negatively correlated with frequency of stress response such as helplessness and feelings of isolation among older people (age ranges from 58–87; $r = -0.18$) (Maehara, 2001). Reported life stress among college students was also negatively correlated with RSES scores among Japanese college students, $r = -0.61$ (Takino, 2001). RSES scores were also negatively correlated with the neuroticism score of the Big Five Scale among male and female college students, $r = -0.60$ and $r = -0.62$, respectively (Nushi, 2004). RSES scores were also positively correlated with a sense of self-efficacy among college students (Inoue et al., 2005).

RSES was negatively correlated with the translated version of the Hopelessness Scale ($r = 0.51$) among 207 female college students (Takahira, 1996). Self-esteem among Japanese high school students and college students, as measured by RSES, was negatively correlated with paranoid tendencies (Kaneko, 2000). Furthermore, this study showed that high self-esteem students tended to claim that they are more psychologically adaptive than their low self-esteem counterparts. As in North America, high self-esteem individuals tend to claim that they are psychologically healthier. Otsuka et al. (1998) report that the tendency toward suicidal ideation (as measured by their scale) is negatively correlated with self-esteem, suggesting that people with high self-esteem are less prone to commit suicide. Thus, overwhelming numbers of empirical studies in Japan point to self-esteem's positive relationship with psychological well-being and mental health in Japan, as it is in North America.

A recent review by Cai et al. (2007) revealed that self-esteem is positively related to mental health in China as well. They reviewed 45 studies in China, involving 50 independent samples of 16,275 participants with a mean age of 21.79. These studies overwhelmingly supported the universal view of self-esteem: self-esteem was positively related to subjective well-being and negatively related to depression and anxiety. More specifically, all correlations between self-esteem and subjective well-being were positive, whereas all correlations of self-esteem with depression and anxiety were negative. Statistically, all the correlations were significant except for the correlation between self-esteem and anxiety. These results obviously indicate that Chinese with high self-esteem experience more happiness, less depression, and less anxiety, exactly as do North Americans and Japanese. Thus, one can conclude that self-esteem functions similarly both in North America and in two East Asian countries when it comes to psychological well-being and mental health, as well as in those areas that we have examined in the previous sections. Self-esteem plays important personal and social functions both in Japan and China, as it does in North America.

INTEGRATIVE OVERVIEW AND FUTURE RESEARCH DIRECTIONS

We have examined the equivalence of the concept of self-esteem on two levels: functional equivalence and full score equivalence in North America and Japan (and partly included China). The results of our review indicate that self-esteem has functional equivalence, because the nomological network involving self-esteem was quite similar across the cultures. In both North America and Japan, self-esteem was positively related to school performance, motivation for learning, self-evaluations of attractiveness and intelligence, disclosure of the negative aspects of the self, secure attachment, independence, and so forth. Also, similarly positive relationships between self-esteem and measures of mental health were found in the three cultures (i.e., North America, Japan, and China). On the other hand, full score equivalence remains questionable. As the data from TIMSS2003 have shown, Japanese and Chinese eighth graders expressed lower self-evaluations relative to their North American counterparts with the same achievement scores. This fact suggests that either Japanese and Chinese self-evaluations are deflated and/or North American self-evaluations are inflated.

Implications of the present review for the controversies over East Asian self-esteem are straightforward. First, the lack of the full score equivalence of self-report measures does not justify comparing those scale scores across cultures. In this respect, implicit measures of self-esteem would be preferable because they are considered impervious to self-presentational motives. When self-esteem was measured by the Implicit Association Test (Greenwald et al., 1998), a recent cross-cultural study revealed that the implicit self-esteem of college students in Japan and China is positive and comparable to that of their counterparts in the United States (Yamaguchi et al., 2007). This result suggests that Japanese and Chinese express lower level of self-esteem than they actually feel on self-report measures. Second, the confirmed functional equivalence indicates that self-esteem in Japanese culture is as important as it is in North American culture. Because initial evidence from China also supports the functional equivalence of self-esteem, we argue that self-esteem is a legitimate topic of scientific study across cultures. Although self-esteem is not an omnipotent psychological state that solves any personal or social problems (Baumeister et al., 2003), it is no doubt an important ingredient of life satisfaction and psychological well-being.

So, what can be concluded regarding the self-criticism and modesty hypotheses? In our view, the self-criticism hypothesis, as we elaborated upon in the introduction, is not supported by the available evidence. Most importantly, lower self-esteem or self-evaluations are not associated with a heightened self-improvement motivation among Japanese. Rather, high self-esteem was found to be associated with higher achievement motivation and persistence in learning among Japanese as well as among North Americans.

At the country level, on the other hand, the cross-cultural differences in self-evaluations and self-esteem apparently fit very well with the self-criticism hypothesis: Countries with lower self-evaluations gained higher achievement scores. However, the country level differences should be interpreted in terms of country level constructs – not in terms of individual level constructs such as motivation to improve. As long as the self-criticism hypothesis is concerned with intra-individual processes, it cannot explain the country level differences. It is an interesting idea that self-criticism is associated with the motivation of self-improvement at the cultural level. But this argument cannot be differentiated from its rival hypothesis in terms of modesty. One can claim that the cultural norm of modesty is associated with another cultural norm of diligence and the two norms result in higher achievement in East Asian cultures. Indeed, Confucius emphasized modesty based on self-reflection and also self-cultivation (Kim & Park, this volume). In all, as long as the self-criticism hypothesis is concerned with intra-individual processes, the available evidence does not support it. If the self-criticism hypothesis is concerned with cultural level differences, it cannot differentiate itself from the modesty hypothesis.

There are some remaining issues that need to be addressed in future research. First, as stated in the introduction, the affective component of self-esteem has not been received much research attention in North America and thus cross-cultural research has largely ignored this issue. For a fuller understanding of the functional equivalence of self-esteem, however, it is essential to know affective antecedents and consequences of self-esteem within and across cultures. Future cross-cultural research should examine individuals' affective responses in situations in which their self-esteem is at stake. Second, the use of Western measures in most Japanese and Chinese studies may have left uniquely East Asian aspects of self-esteem untapped. In addition to the commonality of self-esteem across cultures, which was confirmed as the functional equivalence of self-esteem, there remains a possibility that self-esteem among Japanese and the other East Asians involves a uniquely East Asian component. For example, modesty can be a source of East Asian's sense of self-worth. In East Asia, if individuals behave modestly, it means that they know the culturally ascribed practice and can behave accordingly. Future research should attempt to identify sources of self-esteem that may be unique in East Asian cultures.

We argued in this chapter that cultural differences in self-esteem found in previous research can be explained in terms of modesty. It should be noted, however, that this conclusion does not exclude the possibility that cultural differences in self-esteem (and its expressions) go beyond modesty. It is very plausible that the determinants and consequences of self-esteem are different across cultures for reasons other than modesty. Hopefully, this chapter sets the stage for researchers to explore those possibilities beyond the self-criticism versus modesty controversy.

ACKNOWLEDGEMENT

Preparation of this article was partly supported by Grant-in-Aid for Scientific Research (B) (20330131) from the Japanese Society for the Promotion of Science, granted to the first author. We thank Helen Boucher and Gill Steel for their helpful comments and suggestions on an earlier version of this chapter.

REFERENCES

Amagai, Y. (1997). Self-esteem o kiteisuru youin to shiteno shinraikan: Sono shogai hattatsu teki kenkyu [The effects of trust on self-esteem: The developmental changes in the lifelong stages]. *Japanese Journal of Counseling Science, 30,* 103–111.

Battistich, V., Solomon, D., & Delucchi, K. (1993). Interaction processes and student outcomes in cooperative learning groups. *The Elementary School Journal, 94,* 19–32.

Baumeister, R. F., Campbell, J. D., Krueger, J. I., & Vohs, K. D. (2003). Does high self-esteem cause better performance, interpersonal success, happiness, or healthier lifestyles? *Psychological Science in the Public Interest, 4,* 1–44.

Berry, J. W. (1992). Introduction to methodology. In H. Triandis & J. W. Berry (Eds.), *Handbook of cross-cultural psychology, Volume 2: Methodology* (pp. 1–28). Cambridge, NY: Cambridge University Press.

Breckler, S. J. (1984). Empirical validation of affect, behavior, and cognition as distinct components of attitude. *Journal of Personality and Social Psychology, 47,* 1191–1205.

Brennan, K. A., & Morris, K. A. (1997). Attachment styles, self-esteem, and patterns of seeking feedback from romantic partners. *Personality and Social Psychology Bulletin, 23,* 23–31.

Buehler, R., Griffin, D., & Ross, M. (1994). Exploring the "planning fallacy": Why people under-estimate their task completion times. *Journal of Personality and Social Psychology, 67,* 366–381.

Buhrmester, D., Furman, W., Wittenberg, M. T., & Reis, H. T. (1988). Five domains of interpersonal competence in peer relationships. *Journal of Personality and Social Psychology, 55,* 991–1008.

Cadinu, M. R., & Rothbart, M. (1996). Self-anchoring and differentiation process in the minimal group setting. *Journal of Personality and Social Psychology, 70,* 661–677.

Cai, H., Wu, Q., & Brown, J. D. (2007). *Is self-esteem a universal need? Evidence from the People's Republic of China.* Manuscript submitted for publication.

California State Department of Education. (1990). *Toward a State of Esteem: The Final Report of the California Task Force to Promote Self-Esteem and Personal and Social Responsibility.* State of California.

Campbell, J. D., Chew, B., & Scratchley, L. S. (1991). Cognitive and emotional reactions to daily events: The effects of self-esteem and self-complexity. *Journal of Personality, 59,* 473–505.

Choi, K. S. (1985). Koukousei ni okeru gakugyo ga motarasu seika kitai ni tsuite no inshibunsekiteki kenkyu [Expectancy factors related to the academic achievement-outcome of high school students]. *Japanese Journal of Educational Psychology, 33,* 267–271.

Coopersmith, S. (1967). *The antecedents of self-esteem.* San Francisco: Freeman.

Crocker, J., & Park, E. L. (2004). The costly pursuit of self-esteem. *Psychological Bulletin, 130,* 392–414.

Crocker, J., Thompson, L. L., McGraw, K. M., & Ingerman, C. (1987). Downward comparison, prejudice, and evaluations of others: Effects of self-esteem and threat. *Journal of Personality and Social Psychology, 52,* 907–916.

Daibo, I. (1991). Gaiken inshou kanri to shakaiteki skill [Physical impression management and social skill]. In *Proceedings of the 39th Annual Conference of the Japanese Group Dynamics Association* (pp. 115–116). Sendai.

Diener, E., & Diener, M. (1995). Cross-cultural correlates of life satisfaction and self-esteem. *Journal of Personality and Social Psychology, 68*, 653–663.

Endo, Y., Heine, S. J., & Lehman, D. R. (2000). Culture and positive illusions in close relationships: How my relationships are better than yours. *Personality and Social Psychology Bulletin, 26*, 1571–1586.

Fontaine, J. R. J. (2005). Equivalence. In K. Kempf-Leonard (Ed.), *Encyclopedia of social measurement: Vol. 1* (pp. 803–813). San Diego, CA: Academic Press.

Fujishima, Y. (2004). Kadaiseiseki ni okeru higenjitsuteki rakkanshugini kyakutaiteki jikokakuchi jyoutai ga oyobosu kouka [Effects of objective self-awareness on unrealistically optimistic predictions about task performance]. *Bulletin of the Faculty of Human and Social Sciences, Showa Women's University, 761*, 106–115.

Greenwald, A. G., McGhee, D. E., & Schwartz, J. L. K. (1998). Measuring individual differences in implicit cognition: The Implicit Association Test. *Journal of Personality and Social Psychology, 74*, 1464–1480.

Heine, S. J., Lehman, D. R., Markus, H. R., & Kitayama, S. (1999). Is there a universal need for positive self-regard?. *Psychological Review, 106*, 766–794.

Heine, S. J., Kitayama, S., & Hamamura, T. (2007a). Inclusion of additional studies yields different conclusions: Comment on Sedikides, Gaertner, & Vevea (2005), *Journal of Personality and Social Psychology*. *Asian Journal of Social Psychology*, 10, 49–58.

Heine, S. J., Kitayama, S., & Hamamura, T. (2007b). Which studies test whether self-enhancement is pancultural? Reply to Sedikides, Gaertner, and Vevea, 2007. *Asian Journal of Social Psychology*, 10, 198–200.

Heatherton, T. F., & Polivy, J. (1991). Development and validation of a scale for measuring state self-esteem. *Journal of Personality and Social Psychology, 60*, 895–910.

Huntsinger, E. T., & Luecken, L. J. (2004). Attachment relationships and health behavior: The mediational role of self-esteem. *Psychology & Health, 19*, 515–526.

Ikegami, T. (2002). The role of state self-esteem in positive mood effects on person impression: When does a positive mood lead to a favorable view of others? *Japanese Psychological Research, 44*, 20–33.

Inoue, T., Mino, M., & Wanaka, Y. (2005). Daigakusei ni okeru jiko kouryokukan to shushoku katsudo ga shuugyo douki ni oyobosu eikyou [The effects of the sense of self-efficacy and job applications on work motivation among college students]. In *Proceedings of the 47th Annual Meeting of the Japanese Association of Educational Psychology* (p. 319). Ebetsu, Japan.

Ito, T. (1999). Shakaiteki hikaku ni okeru jiko kouyou keikou – heikin ijyo kouka no kentou [Self-enhancement tendency and other evaluations: An examination of "better-than-average effect"]. *Japanese Journal of Psychology, 70*, 367–374.

James, W. (1890). *The principles of psychology* (Vols. 1–2). New York: Dover.

Kahneman, D., & Tversky, A. (1979). Intuitive prediction: Biases and corrective procedures. *TIMS Studies in Management Science, 12*, 313–327.

Kamakura, T., Ando, T., & Maekawa, H. (2004). Self-esteem to shintai human, yase ganbou tono kanren ni kansuru iden to kankyo [Heredity and environment as determinants of the relationship between self-esteem and dissatisfaction with body image and wishes for weight-loss]. In *Proceedings of the 26th Annual Meeting of the Japanese Association of Educational Psychology* (p. 86). Kyoto, Japan.

Kameda, S. (2002). Hiteitekinaiyou no jikokaiji to jison kanjyo oyobi kaiji teikou no kanrensei [Relationship of disclosure of the negative aspect of the self with self-esteem and reluctance to disclose]. In *Proceedings of the 44th Annual Meeting of the Japanese Association of Educational Psychology* (p. 148). Kumamoto, Japan.

Kaneko, H. (2000). Seinenki no shinsei to shite no jiko kankeizuke [Self-reference tendency in adolescents]. *Japanese Journal of Educational Psychology, 48*, 473–480.

Katayama, M. (1996). Hiteiteki naiyouno jikokaiji eno teikoukan to jisonshin tono kanren [The relationship between self-esteem and self-disclosure of negative information]. *Japanese Journal of Psychology, 67*, 351–358.

Keefe, K., & Berndt, T. J. (1996). Relations of friendship quality to self-esteem in early adolescence. *Journal of Early Adolescence, 16*, 110–129.

Kitayama, S. (2006). Does self-esteem matter equally across cultures? In M. H. Kernis (Ed.), *Self-esteem issues and answers: A sourcebook of current perspective* (pp. 376–382). New York: Psychology Press.

Koch, E. J. (2006). Examining the role of self-esteem in psychological functioning and well-being. In M. H. Kernis (Ed.), *Self-esteem issues and answers: A sourcebook of current perspective* (pp. 260–266). New York: Psychology Press.

Lambird, K. H., & Mann, T. (2006). When do ego threats lead to self-regulation failure? Negative consequences of defensive high self-esteem. *Personality and Social Psychology Bulletin, 32*, 1177–1187.

Maehara, T. (2001). Koureisha no jisonkanjyo to sono kanren youin [Self-esteem among senior people and its relevant variables]. In *Proceedings of the 43rd Annual Meeting of the Japanese Association of Educational Psychology* (p. 533). Nagoya, Japan.

Matsumoto, Y., & Kijima, T. (2002). Shushoku katsudou ni okeru jiko-teiji no senryaku mokuhyou [Job hunters' strategic goals of self-presentation]. *Japanese Journal of Experimental Social Psychology, 41*, 111–123.

Mizuma, R., & Oshio, S. (2002). Nichijo bamenni okeru jison kanjyo (2) [Self-esteem in every-day situation (2)]. In *Proceedings of the 66th Annual Meeting of the Japanese Psychological Association* (p. 51). Hiroshima, Japan.

Mruk, J. C. (2006). Defining self-esteem: An often overlooked issue with crucial implications. In H. M. Kernis (Ed.), *Self-esteem issues and answers: A sourcebook of current perspectives* (pp. 10–15). New York: Psychology Press.

Murakami, Y. (1986). Hikoushonen to futsuu shonen no saini tsuite [The mentality differences between the delinquent and non-delinquent boys]. *Japanese Journal of Psychology, 57*, 1–7.

Murata, K. (1999a). Keikaku sakugo no jisshoteki kenkyu (1): Gakusei no nichijyouteki katsudou no chousa [Empirical study on planning fallacy (1): Survey of students' everyday activities]. In *Proceedings of the 63rd Annual Meeting of the Japanese Psychological Association* (p. 533). Nagoya, Japan.

Murata, K. (1999b). Keikaku sakugo no jisshoteki kenkyu (2): Report teishutsu no yosoku to jissai [Empirical study on planning fallacy (2): Prediction and reality of term-paper submission]. In *Proceedings of the 40th Annual Meeting of the Japanese Society of Social Psychology* (pp. 218–219). Tokyo, Japan.

Namioka, T. (1993). Jisonshin ga shudanhyoka ni oyobosu eikyo ni tsuite – chugakusei wo taishoto shite [Effect of self-esteem on group evaluation: A case of junior high students. In *Proceedings of the 35th Annual Meeting of the Japanese Association of Educational Psychology* (p. 201). Nagoya, Japan.

Nishimura, H., Suzuki, S., & Takahashi, Y. (1984). Hikou wo seigyo suru chikarato doukizukeru chikarano hikaku bunseki [Weakening of social bonds or flourishing of deviant motivation?]. *Kagakukeisatsukenkyuujyo Houkoku, 25*, 107–118.

Nushi, T. (2004). Big five to jisonkanjyo, kanjyo no kankei ni tsuite [On the relationship between big five and both self-esteem and emotion]. In *Proceedings of the 46th Annual Meeting of the Japanese Association of Educational Psychology* (p. 46). Toyama, Japan.

Ogawa, T. (1976). Test huan no chosa kenkyuu [Survey study on test anxiety]. In *Proceedings of the 40th Annual Meeting of the Japanese Psychological Association* (pp. 887–888). Nagoya, Japan.

Okada, T., & Nagai, T. (1990). Seinenki no jikohyoka to taijinkyohuteki shinsei tono kanren [Self-esteem and anthrophobic-tendency in adolescents]. *Japanese Journal of Psychology, 60*, 386–389.

Ono, K. (1984). Shintai ishiki ni kansuru ichi kenkyu (2) [A study on body image (2)]. In *Proceedings of the 48th Annual Meeting of the Japanese Psychological Association* (p. 631). Osaka, Japan.

Otsuka, A., Seto, M., Kanno, J., & Agari, I. (1998). Jisatsu nenryo shakudo no sakusei to jisatsu nenryo ni kansuru youin no kenkyu [Development of the Suicide Ideation Scale for Japanese and a study of the factors related to suicide ideation]. *Japanese Journal of Counseling Science, 31,* 247–258.

Raynor, J. O., & McFarlin, D. B. (1986). Motivation and the self-system. R. M. Sorrentino & E. T. Higgins (Eds.), (pp. 315–349). New York: Guilford.

Robinson, W. S. (1950). Ecological correlations and the behavior of individuals. *American Sociological Review, 15,* 351–357.

Rosenberg, M. (1965). *Society and the adolescent self-image.* Princeton, NJ: Princeton University Press.

Ryu, Y., & Ogawauchi, T. (2005). Jyoshigakusei no gakugyoteki enin ni oyobosu ninchisareta oyano youikutaido to jisonkanjyou no eikyou [The effects of perceived parental care and self-esteem on academic procrastination]. In *Proceedings of the Annual Meeting of the Japanese Association of Educational Psychology* (p. 158). Ebetsu, Japan.

Saito, S., Kato, T., & Tatsuno, Y. (1987). Seishohnen no self-esteem no tokushitsu to sono kiteiyouin (4) [Characteristics of adolescents' self-esteem and its determinants (4)]. In *Proceedings of the 51st Annual Meeting of the Japanese Psychological Association* (p. 528). Tokyo.

Sato, I., Sugihara, K., & Fujiu, H. (2000). Jyoshi chuugakuseino jisonkanjyou to jikohyokaishiki ni tsuiteno tanki jyudanteki kenkyuu [A short term longitudinal study of self-esteem and self-appreciation in junior high school girls]. *Japanese Journal of Counseling Science, 33,* 57–68.

Sedikides, C., Gaertner, L., & Toguchi, Y. (2003). Pancultural self-enhancement. *Journal of Personality and Social Psychology, 84,* 60–79.

Sedikides, C., Gaertner, L., & Vevea, J. L. (2005). Pancultural self-enhancement reloaded: A meta-analytic reply to Heine (2005). *Journal of Personality and Social Psychology, 89,* 539–551.

Sedikides, C., Gaertner, L., & Vevea, J. L. (2007a). Inclusion of theory-relevant moderators yield the same conclusions as Sedikides, Gaertner, and Vevea (2005): A meta-analytical reply to Heine, Kitayama, and Hamamura (2007). *Asian Journal of Social Psychology, 10,* 59–67.

Sedikides, C., Gaertner, L., & Vevea, J. L. (2007b). Evaluating the evidence for pancultural self-enhancement. *Asian Journal of Social Psychology, 10,* 201–203.

Shibata, T., & Nobeji, M. (1990). Seinenki ni okeru shintai manzokudo to jison kanjyou no kanren-sei [Relationship between satisfaction with physical fitness and self-esteem among adolescents]. In *Proceedings of the 54th Annual Meeting of the Japanese Psychological Association* (p. 68). Tokyo, Japan.

Shiomi, K., & Nakai, M. (1996). Jidou no gakugyo tassei ni okeru jiko kouryokukan to jisonkanjyou [Self-efficacy and self-esteem in children's academic achievement]. In *Proceedings of the Annual Meeting of the Japanese Association of Educational Psychology* (p. 475). Tsukuba, Japan.

Solomon, S. (2006). Self-esteem is central to human well-being. In M. H. Kernis (Ed.), *Self-esteem issues and answers: A sourcebook of current perspective* (pp. 254–259). New York: Psychology Press.

Suganuma, M. (1997). Rounenki no jikokaiji to jison kanjyou [Self-disclosure and self-esteem in old age]. *Japanese Journal of Educational Psychology, 45,* 378–387.

Suzuki, S. (1989). Chugakusei no shinri teki stress to hikou tono kanrenni kansuru kenkyu [A study on the relationship between psychological stress and deviant behavior among junior high school students]. *Kagakukeisatsukenkyuujyo Houkoku, 30,* 13–27.

Takahashi, Y. (2002). Aichaku style to jisonshin: Taijin kankei style no kanten kara [Attachment and self-esteem: From a perspective of interpersonal relationship style]. In *Proceedings of the 44th Annual Meeting of the Japanese Association of Educational Psychology* (p. 77). Kumamoto, Japan.

Takahira, M. (1996). Kakuchoban hopelessness shakudo (nihongo ban) no sakusei [Construction of an extended Hopelessness Scale (Japanese version)]. In *Proceedings of the 60th Annual Meeting of the Japanese Psychological Association* (p. 122). Tokyo, Japan.

Takino, Y. (2001). Seinen no stress level to stress no gensen [Stress level and the source of stress among adolescents]. In *Proceedings of the 65th Annual Meeting of the Japanese Psychological Association* (p. 789). Tsukuba, Japan.

Taylor, S. E., & Brown, J. D. (1988). Illusion and well-being: A social psychological perspective on mental health. *Psychological Bulletin, 103*, 193–210.

Tracy, J. L., & Robins, R. W. (2007). Emerging insights into the nature and function of pride. *Current Directions in Psychological Science, 16*, 148–150.

Uchida, Y., & Kitayama, S. (2001). Omoiyari shakudo no sakusei to datousei no kentou [Development and validation of a sympathy scale]. *Japanese Journal of Psychology, 72*, 275–282.

Yamaguchi, S., Lin, C., & Aoki, S. (2006). Self-esteem in cultural context: The case of the Japanese. In Q. Jing, M. R. Rosenzweig, G. d'Ydewalle, H. Zhang, Chen Hsuan-Chih, & K. Z. Zhang (Eds.), *Progress in psychological science around the world, Vol. 2: Social and applied issues* (pp. 319–330). New York: Psychology Press.

Yamaguchi, S., Greenwald, A. G., Banaji, M. R., Murakami, F., Chen, D., Shiomura, K. et al. (2007). Apparent universality of positive implicit self-esteem. *Psychological Science, 18*, 498–500.

Yamaguchi, S., Okumura, T., & Morio, H. (2008). Japanese self-criticism: Fact or fiction. In preparation.

17

CULTURE, NARRATIVE, AND HUMAN AGENCY

YOSHIHISA KASHIMA, KIM PETERS AND
JENNIFER WHELAN

Department of Psychology, University of Melbourne, Victoria, Australia

Meaning is centrally involved in human psychology. Culture can be thought of as a repository of meaning. Culture, therefore, is central to human psychology. Despite the undisputed importance of culture, the culture concept presents a fundamental question for psychology, and tends to polarize research orientations. One orientation regards culture as a coherent system of meaning shared among a group of people over a period of time (e.g., Triandis, 1972; Geertz, 1973); the other views culture as processes of meaning making and remaking by concrete actors in concrete situations (e.g., Cole, 1996; Rogoff, 2003). The systems view regards culture as consensual, enduring, and context-general, whereas the process view takes culture to be more fragmented, changing, and context-specific (Kashima, 2000). More recently in cultural psychology, a context-general systems view (e.g., Schwartz, 1992, 1994; Triandis, 1995; Trianids, 1996; Leung et al., 2002; Leung & Bond, 2004) and a situated process view (e.g., Trafimow et al., 1991; Hong et al., 2000; Kuhnen & Oyserman, 2002) of culture have emerged yet again, this time, as embodied by their preferred research methodologies. The former examines cross-cultural differences in beliefs, attitudes, and values; the latter experimentally activates cultural constructs by priming. In fact, this is a cultural psychological version of a master question in social science, namely, the agency-structure or micro-macro problem, which asks the fundamental question about the relationship between the individuals and the collective. Nonetheless, we take the view that culture endures as well as changes, and that culture is both context-general and situated. A critical question here is how individuals' particular meaning-making activities in specific situations collectively generate a globally enduring system of meaning. We call this dynamic stability *cultural dynamics* (Kashima, 2000, 2001).

One approach to cultural dynamics that has taken shape in recent years may be called *neo-diffusionism*, a class of theories that take the transmission (or diffusion) of cultural information as central to a theory of culture. The reason why we place a prefix *neo-* is that the idea is not new. In the early 20th century, anthropologists postulated that much of existing human culture resulted from diffusion of cultural knowledge and practices. Although these schools of thought went out of favor, there has been a resurgence of its central tenet. In the neo-diffusionist view, there exists a unit of cultural information, which is generated at one point in time and transmitted to and learned by others. There may be different types of transmission of cultural information: one may be vertical, from one generation to next, and another may be horizontal between people within the same generation. They may be transmitted by formal education or by informal "on the job" apprenticeship. Whatever form it takes, a critical feature of this approach is the assumption that cultural information is transmitted socially, rather than genetically, from one person to another, and that its distribution within populations is critical for cultural diversity.

The main objective of this chapter is to outline broad contours of the neo-diffusionist thinking and to conceptualize cultural variability in human agency within this framework. In so doing, we will highlight the role of narrative in the cultural underpinning of human agency. To put it succinctly, the social psychological question here is this: How can culturally transmitted meaning engage human agency? After all, cultural information is only secondhand information that we gain from others; it does not materially affect us in a tangible way. Yet, cultural meaning appears to engage us psychologically, and to shape our thoughts, feelings, and actions. One possible reason for this is cultural norms. People internalize culturally transmitted narratives as norms, and internalized norms drive people to behave the way they do. Perhaps social sanctions – to avoid punishment and to gain reward – may lead people to follow narratively transmitted cultural meaning. Although this must be part of the answer, to assume that cultural norms can explain all, that there is nothing more to be explained, and that culture is unproblematically internalized to compel people to act the way culture dictates is to "over-socialize" the individual (Wrong, 1961) and to oversimplify the process by which a person actively appropriates cultural meaning (e.g., Valsiner, 1989; Valsiner & Lawrence, 1997). The answer that we sketch out here is that narrative provides part of the answer because it is a cultural medium well suited to the engagement of *spontaneous* human agency, and that narrative is one of the critical psychological mechanisms that enable culturally mediated human agency. Parenthetically, in this article, we will use the concepts of cultural meaning and cultural information interchangeably. Although they differ in connotation, we believe leaving the distinction ambiguous for the time being will help us present a broad picture on hand.

NEO-DIFFUSIONIST THEORY OF CULTURAL
EVOLUTION

The basic tenet of neo-diffusionism is that there exists a unit of cultural meaning, and that it is transmitted from one person to another through a cultural medium. To illustrate, take for example the following passage from Trafimow et al. (1991, p. 652):

> Sostoras, a warrior in ancient Sumer, was largely responsible for the success of Sargon I in conquering all of Mesopotamia. As a result, he was rewarded with a small kingdom of his own to rule. About 10 years later, Sargon I was conscripting warriors for a new war. Sostoras was obligated to send a detachment of soldiers to aid Sargon I. He had to decide who to put in command of the detachment. After thinking about it for a long time, Sostoras eventually decided on Tiglath who was a talented general. This appointment had several advantages. Sostoras was able to make an excellent general indebted to him. This would solidify Sostoras's hold on his own dominion. In addition, the very fact of having a general such as Tiglath as his personal representative would greatly increase Sostoras's prestige. Finally, sending his best general would be likely to make Sargon I grateful. Consequently, there was the possibility of getting rewarded by Sargon I.

Analyzed from a neo-diffusionist perspective, this experimental material is a cultural medium communicable between English speakers. This narrative passage instantiates a unit of meaning, in this instance, the individualist conception of the person, which was succinctly summarized by Geertz (1983) as "a bounded, unique, more or less integrated motivational and cognitive universe, a dynamic center of awareness, emotion, judgment, and action organized into a distinctive whole and set contrastively both against other such wholes and against its social and natural background ...." (p. 59). The passage describes Sostoras's individual "cognitive universe" as well as Tiglath as a separate individual that is equipped with its own distinctive "cognitive universe."

In contrast, the other passage used by Trafimow et al. (1991, p. 652) instantiates a different unit of cultural meaning, a family-collectivist conception of the person.

> Sostoras eventually decided on Tiglath who was a member of his family. This appointment had several advantages. Sostoras was able to show his loyalty to his family. He was also able to cement their loyalty to him. In addition, having Tiglath as the commander increased the power and prestige of the family. Finally, if Tiglath performed well, Sargon I would be indebted to the family.

This ending expresses the construal of Sostoras as a member of his family and also in relation to another family member, Tiglath. In this unit of meaning, a person is suspended in a network of family relationships which is itself contained in the family as a collective. Neo-diffusionism would suggest that when communicated, it would result in learning or relearning of either individualist or collectivist conceptions of the person, which should have some psychological consequences. Indeed, Trafimow et al. (1991) reported that, depending on which version of the story they read, American undergraduate students described themselves with individualistic or collectivistic descriptors.

HISTORICAL BACKGROUND

Where did the idea of cultural diffusion come from? Diffusionism is a school of thought in anthropology that was popular in the early part of 20th century (Lowie, 1937; Kuklick, 1991). In *The History of Ethnological Theory*, Lowie (1937) described two diffusionist schools, one mainly espoused by British anthropologists, Smith, Perry, and Rivers, and the other by German ethnologists, Graebner and Schmidt. They were both reactions against the 19th century cultural evolutionists like Spencer, who argued for a unilinear cultural evolution from a simpler to more complex cultural system. Instead of an inevitable march towards a higher and more "sophisticated" civilization (and a tendency to explain cultural diversity in terms of levels of cultural evolution), they emphasized the process by which cultural ideas, practices, and artifacts were invented in a group of people and transmitted to others over millennia. To be sure, the idea of cultural diffusion is not unique to these schools of thought; academic anthropology's founding fathers such as Taylor and Boas acknowledged the significance of diffusion of cultural characteristics from one group to another by borrowing or by immigration. Galton's problem (e.g., Naroll et al., 1980) epitomizes the fact of cultural diffusion most starkly. Basically, similarities among the cultural characteristics of social groups may be due to cultural diffusion, rather than due to similarities in the ecological characteristics, modes of production (e.g., agriculture, hunter-gatherer, or industrial economies), and other factors.

British diffusionists, most notably Smith and Perry, took the view that most human cultural knowledge was generated in ancient Egypt and diffused to other human populations from there (e.g., Perry, 1923; Smith, 1933). Rivers (1914), well known for his leadership role in the Cambridge Expedition to Torres Straits in 1898, also tried to explain the cultural diversity in Melanesia and Oceania in terms of a succession of migratory cultural diffusions into the region over a long period of time. Although Lowie (1937) is dismissive of their contributions, it is perhaps noteworthy that Rivers influenced the early work of Bartlett (1932), who is best known for his contribution to schema theory and reconstructive memory. As we will see, this intellectual connection may have been significant in Bartlett's later research on the transmission of cultural information (see Kuklick, 1991). According to Lowie (1937), the German school of diffusionism is less extreme and more empirically grounded. They argued that several independent cultures evolved due to their isolation, rather than from a single source. However, as modes of travel improved, cultural characteristics were transmitted to other parts of the world *en masse* as a system of interrelated cultural characteristics, rather than piecemeal, element by element. When waves of diffusion collide with each other, the cultures may mix or one may dominate another, and some cultural characteristics may change, degenerate, or completely disappear. Still, cultural characteristics were largely invented in those cultural centers, and much of their current distribution depends on information diffusion. As Lowie (1937) noted, both schools of thought down played the inventiveness of humans, and the possibility that similar cultural characteristics may be produced independently of each other. This and other problems led to the eventual demise of these diffusionist theories.

A VARIETY OF NEO-DIFFUSIONISM

It was perhaps Donald Campbell (1975) who first forcefully advocated a view of culture that is best classified as neo-diffusionism. However, a recent interest in cultural diffusion may find its roots in Dawkins's (1976/1989) coinage of the term, *meme*, to signify a unit of cultural transmission, although he points his finger at Popper's evolutionary epistemology, as well as others such as Cavalli-Sforza as precursors. Neo-diffusionist theories include those put forward by Dawkins (1976/1989; see also Blackmore, 1999; Aunger, 2002), Cavalli-Sforza and Feldman (1981), Boyd and Richerson (1985), and Sperber (1996), among others. In psychology, the theoretical perspectives adopted by Hong et al. (2000), Kashima (2000), Schaller et al. (2002), and Heath et al. (2001) can be classified together under this broad banner.

In order to characterize neo-diffusionism as a broad framework, we will use generic concepts in this chapter. Generally, neo-diffusionism has the following set of assumptions:

1. There exists a unit of cultural meaning (we will use the term, cultural meaning unit, or CMU in the following);
2. a CMU is instantiated in a material form that can be communicated from a sender to a receiver;
3. the receiver learns (or relearns if the receiver has already learnt it before) a CMU via a communicated form; and
4. the distribution of a CMU within a population results in this population's group characteristics.

It is unclear what constitutes a unit of cultural meaning; as we will see, it seems to vary from one theory to another, and even within each theory, there does not seem to be a clear definition.

There is a variety of neo-diffusionist stances on offer. One may be called *Universal Darwinism* (e.g., Dawkins, 1976/1989; Cavalli-Sforza & Feldman, 1981; Boyd & Richerson, 1985). Originally used by Dawkins (1982), this phrase was meant to suggest the potential applicability of Darwinian evolutionary theory to the origin and evolution of life forms beyond Earth. However, the phrase can now refer to the intellectual stance that explores the utility of Darwinism in the biosphere as well as other domains, such as human culture (e.g., Dennet, 1995). To put it simply, it is the school of thought that a certain type of evolutionary theory based on Darwin's ideas can be similarly applicable to biological and cultural evolution. It grew out of the so-called *Modern Synthesis* (e.g., Huxley, 1942/1963; Mayr, 1980) in evolutionary biology, which integrated the Mendelian genetic inheritance and Darwinian natural selection. It takes the view that genetic variation, which gives rise to phenotypic differences, can result in differential adaptive fitness under environmental pressure. The genotypes that give rise to maladaptive phenotypes will not be passed on to the next generation, and so will be selected out. The result is not so much "the survival of the fittest" as the extinction of the unfit. When applied to cultural dynamics, common across Universal Darwinism are (1) a kind of population thinking (Mayr, 1980), where CMUs are assumed to be distributed within a population; (2) a commitment to the idea of variation, inheritance, and selection as the basic processes of cultural evolution, where selection of CMUs is a key element; and (3) an adaptation to the environment as a consequence of the selection of the CMUs. It is assumed that units of cultural meaning differ in fitness, namely, the adaptiveness of "phenotypes" that a CMU generates. In other words, CMUs are assumed to vary in degrees of adaptiveness. Those CMUs that are not adaptive are assumed to be *selected* out, so that the remaining CMUs are adaptive to the environment.

Universal Darwinism is not a single unified theory. One variant is meme theory. Dawkins (1976/1989; 1982) suggested that the Darwinian process can be conceptualized as *replicator* dynamics. He defines a replicator as "anything in the universe of which copies are made (Dawkins, 1982, p. 83)." Genes, or DNA molecules, are replicators. He suggests that memes are also replicators; they are CMUs that replicate themselves. Dawkins (1999; see also Blackmore, 1999) further suggested that memes may be best thought of as a set of instructions, or in psychological parlance, a chunk of procedural knowledge. Using origami constructions of a Chinese junk boat as an example, he suggested that meme is a set of instructions to construct a Chinese junk boat, whereas any particular Chinese junk boat constructed by following the instructions is a phenotype. A meme is a genotype; meme theory insists that what is culturally transmitted is genotype. In this theory, meme is not only a unit of cultural meaning, but also a unit that varies within a population, and a unit that is selected in the cultural evolutionary process. In other words, the selection process operates not at the level of individuals or groups, but at the level of memes. In social psychology, Heath et al. (2001) adopted this perspective to theorize about the distribution of disgusting urban legends.

Another variant of Universal Darwinism is group selectionism as put forward by Boyd, Richerson, and their colleagues (see Boyd & Richerson, 2005, for a collection of papers). They argue that in cultural evolution, the selection pressure is greater at the group level than at the individual level, despite the contrary evidence for biological evolution among non-human species. They argued that altruistic punishment (punishment of undesirable behaviors directed toward a third party) of a violation of a group-beneficial norm can sustain the group-beneficial norm, and that the group-beneficial norm may be retained under intergroup competition or when there is a tendency to imitate a successful neighbor's group-beneficial norm. Unlike meme theory, Boyd and Richerson (1995, 2000) insist that what is culturally transmitted is a phenotype, or a publicly observable behavior, practice, or activity, or its material product. A set of instructions (or rules) to generate a phenotype may not be directly transmitted along with the cultural inheritance system (see Sperber, 2000, for a related criticism). Instead of a CMU per se, it is groups that are under selective pressure.

In contrast to Universal Darwinism, which assumes that adaptation occurs only by natural selection, Sperber (1996) suggests that cultural evolution does not happen by selection, but by transformation. He argues that, in Universal Darwinism, CMUs are transmitted from one individual to another mainly by imitation; if a CMU fails to be imitated, it is selected out. While Sperber does not deny the significance of imitation, he insists that cultural evolution is more like transformation. When a representation (broadly conceived to include propositions, beliefs, and practices) is transmitted from one person to another, the receiver's representation resembles that of the sender's, but is neither identical nor completely different. Sperber calls this process of cultural evolution by transformation an attraction model, as opposed to a selection model, and Sperber and Wilson (1986) conceptualized it in terms of communication of relevant information. Sperber (1996) calls this type of theorizing of cultural evolution the *epidemiological model* (also see Urban, 2001), analogizing the process of diffusion of cultural meaning to the spread of germs and viruses.

In a similar, but more dynamic vein, Kashima and his colleagues (e.g., McIntyre et al., 2004; Kashima et al., 2007b) began to conceptualize the transmission of cultural information as collaboration between the sender and receiver. Based on the *grounding model* of communication (e.g., Clark, 1996), they argued that cultural transmission can be thought of as a joint activity between the sender and the receiver, in which they collaborate to come to a mutual understanding of cultural information. In this view, the process of cultural transmission is inherently dynamic, collaborative, and distributed. The grounding process involves the sender's presentation of cultural information, and the receiver's acceptance of it. The sender actively seeks evidence that the receiver has understood what the sender has communicated; the receiver is expected to provide evidence for his or her understanding. Evidence of mutual understanding may be simple – a nod, a simple "Uh huh" or "Yes, I see"; it may take more complex verbal exchanges such as paraphrasing of the sender's statement, relevant questions about the sender's point, or commentaries or criticisms of the sender's opinion. Whichever form it takes, as a result of the grounding of cultural information, the receiver obtains the cultural information. However, the received cultural information is not an exact replication of the sender's. In this sense, cultural transmission involves transformation as Sperber (1996) maintained; however, it may be even more collaborative and dynamic than Sperber and Wilson (1986) envisaged.

Using Bartlett's (1932) serial reproduction paradigm, Kashima and his colleagues (Kashima, 2000; Kashima & Kostopoulos, 2004; Lyons & Kashima, 2001, 2003, 2006) showed that people tend to transmit narrative information that is consistent with stereotypes that they share and believe to share. They constructed a story that contained information that was consistent or inconsistent with culturally shared stereotypes of an out-group (Kashima, 2000) or of their in-group (Kashima & Kostopoulos, 2004) and had people communicate it to another person from memory, who in turn transmitted it to another, and so on down a chain. Even if communicators at earlier positions of the chain reproduced more stereotype inconsistent than consistent information, this trend was reversed toward the end, showing that information that is consistent with culturally shared ideations within a community is more likely transmitted, contributing to the maintenance of culture. Lyons and Kashima (2003) showed that this phenomenon tends to occur when communicators share the same cultural meaning system (e.g., stereotypes) and also believe that they partially, but not completely, share the CMU.

NARRATIVE AS A MEDIUM OF CULTURAL TRANSMISSION

Cultural meaning may be transmitted by a variety of means. Clearly, language expressed in words, phrases, and sentences is used to transmit cultural information. Cultural icons such as the Great Wall of China and the Statute of Liberty also act as symbols that remind people of their cultural knowledge and practices (Hong et al., 2000). In this chapter, we focus on narrative as a medium of cultural transmission. As we will argue below, narrative is a powerful and complete medium that can pack in it both pragmatic and existential information and whose form is well suited for cognitive processing and interpersonal communication. As we humans produce and reproduce stories as we speak, we transmit our cultural meaning to whoever has ears for them.

By narrative, we roughly mean a story, a meaningful unit of actors' actions and events with a temporal closure, namely, with the beginning, the middle, and the end. Narrative has been variously defined by scholars in different disciplines. Ricoeur (1981, p. 277) gave a traditional Western characterization:

> A story describes a sequence of actions and experiences of a certain number of characters, whether real or imaginary. These characters are represented in situations which change.... These changes, in turn, reveal hidden aspects of the situations and the characters, giving rise to a new predicament which calls for thought or action or both. The response to this predicament brings the story to its conclusion.

In somewhat more abstract terms, Burke (1945/1969) suggested that a narrative requires a Pentad, five elements organized in a coherent way: actor, action, goal (or intention), scene, and instrument. An imbalance among these elements and the process of resolving it constitute a story. Nevertheless, a number of non-Western narrative traditions often do not emphasize as much dramatism (e.g., Scalise Sugiyama, 2001; Rogoff, 2003). In this regard, Labov's (1972, p. 360), definition of a minimal narrative as a sequence of two temporally ordered clauses may serve as a broad guideline.

There are several reasons why narrative is particularly useful cultural medium for transmitting cultural meaning. First of all, narrative is prevalent. It is one of the human universals that can be found in most, if not all, cultures (Murdoch, 1945; Brown, 1991). Even children as young as 3-years old can tell a story (e.g., Sutton-Smith, 1986). Among adults, narrative is surely one of the most common forms of everyday discourse. People's explanations of their actions to others often takes the form of a narrative (Harvey et al., 1990), businessmen explain their success by telling a story (Baumeister & Newman, 1994), and social scientists tell stories in their academic discourse (Greimas, 1990). Scalise Sugiyama (2001) even argued that narrative is a species-typical form of evolutionary adaptation to the need to acquire second hand information.

The usefulness of narrative as a cultural medium comes not only from its prevalence and "naturalness," but also from its typical content. Narrative often contains pragmatic information, such as information about characters' goal-directed activities (e.g., Burke (1945/1969); Greimas, 1966/1983), how the characters interact with each other (Thompson, 1957; Greimas, 1966/1983; Propp, 1968; El-Shamy, 1995), the characters' psychological states and processes associated with their goal-directed activities or social interaction (Greimas & Courtés, 1976), causal relationships among events (e.g., Trabasso & Sperry, 1985; Trabasso & van den Broek, 1985), and events and objects that people are likely to encounter in their local environment (Scalise Sugiyama, 2001). Further, narrative often contains existential information, such as information about life and death, the origin (and sometimes the end) of the world, the nature of gods and supernatural beings, and the place of humans in the universe (e.g., the Bible, origin myths around the world). In this way, narrative has informed us about our predecessors' knowledge about the world, about ourselves, and about our place in it.

COGNITION

The human psychological and communicative apparatus may be well suited to process information packaged in narrative form. A number of theorists have suggested the centrality of narrative information processing for humans (e.g., Bruner, 1990; Schank & Abelson, 1995; Wyer, 2004). Schank and Abelson (1995) are among the most explicit, asserting "[v]irtually all human knowledge is based on stories constructed around past experiences" (p. 1). Whether this extreme claim is warranted or not, it is justifiable to say that narrative is a powerful cognitive tool. Narrative helps people encode events and actions. Pennington and Hastie (1986, 1988, 1992) proposed the Story Model of jury decision making, whereby jurors construct a story from various pieces of evidence in a trial, and this story mediates their evaluation of evidence and judgments of guilt. In their program of research, multiple methods (think-aloud protocol, memory measures, and judgments) were used to gain support for their model. Other legal scholars have also made a similar point (e.g., Ewick & Silbey, 1995). Narrative helps people recall information. People tend to recall events that are expected in a story better than those that are irrelevant or unrelated to it (see Hastie et al., 1984, for a review). Although it is unclear whether people recall information that is contradictory to expectations better (e.g., Graesser et al., 1980) or worse (e.g., Bower et al., 1979), the literature generally suggests that events that are difficult to integrate into a narrative structure are likely to be forgotten (Kintsch, 1988). Taken together, narrative can play a significant role in people's comprehension and impressions about social events. For instance, when people constructed stories about their relationships, the stories that they told tended to bias their judgments about the events in the direction of the constructed stories (McGregor & Holmes, 1999).

Narrative does not only help people understand about the past, but may also help them deal with the future by facilitating problem solving and planning. Gick and Holyoak (1980, 1983) showed that reading a story about a situation analogous to a problem-facilitated people's problem solving performance. They were told that a malignant tumor needs to be treated by radioactive rays, but that a single, powerful burst will destroy the surrounding healthy tissue as well. In one condition, participants were told about a military general who captured an enemy fortress by dividing his army and having small units attack the fortress from many directions. Exposure to this story increased the probability of solving the tumor problem; the solution was to use multiple rays from many directions converging on the tumor, just like small military units converging on the fortress. The military story that captures the causal structure of the tumor problem enabled people to solve problems and make plans for action.

EMOTION

The psychological function of narrative does not stop with cognition but affect and emotion are centrally involved in narrative as well. To begin with, given that a story usually describes its characters' goal-directed activities, it often contains a description of their emotional experience as they engage with their goals and objectives, successfully or otherwise (Oatley, 1999). Successful achievements yield positive emotions; failures perhaps result in disappointment, anger, and sadness. Even if no explicit description is provided, people infer the characters' emotional states in response to their more or less successful attempts to attain their goals (Gernsbacher et al., 1992). This means that narratives are inherently about the characters' emotions. By inducing empathy or otherwise, narrative often evokes emotions in those who read, watch, or listen to them (e.g., Brewer & Ohtsuka, 1988). People often cry during movies, even if they have been instructed not to (Kraemer & Hastrup, 1988; Rottenberg et al., 2002); adults and adolescents report experiencing emotions when reading narrative extracts (Cupchick et al., 1998) and short stories (Oatley, 1998), emotions that are typically of moderate to high intensity (Axelrad, 1993, cited in Oatley, 1994); and readers have high levels of physiological arousal when reading books of their choice (Nell, 1988). Narratives are such an important source of our emotions that in one diary study (Oatley & Duncan, 1992) they accounted for about 7% of all daily emotional experiences.

This emotion arousing property of narrative may help us regulate emotions. As Baumeister et al. (1993) suggested, stories make a difference to emotional experience. When a negative event happens, it may be reinterpreted by constructing a narrative that puts a positive spin on the event (see also Josephson et al., 1996). Perhaps by constructing a story that evokes a positive emotion out of events that typically evoke negative emotions, one may be able to balance negative emotions with positive ones. For instance, Harvey et al. (1990) and Baumeister et al. (1990) showed that stories are used to diffuse the self-blame when people terminate their interpersonal relationships or commit transgressions. Murray and Holmes (1993, 1994) showed that American university students used stories to reinterpret negative attributes of their romantic partners in ways that allowed them to maintain their confidence in their relationships.

SELF

Given the cognitive and emotional functions of narrative, it is not too surprising that there is an intimate link between narrative and self. McAdams (1985, 1990, 2001) argued that people living in modern societies provide their lives with unity and purpose by constructing internalized and evolving narratives of the self. He further argued that identity takes the form of an internalized and evolving story of self that integrates intentions and various, often competing, motives into a coherent life story or coherent plan of actions. Holland et al.'s (1998) exploration of narrative construction of self and agency in Nepal points to the possibility that cultivation of self-narratives is not restricted to modern industrialized societies. More generally, Gergen and Gergen (1988) suggest that self-narrative is "the individual's account of the relationship among self-relevant events across time" (p. 19). According to Polkinghorne (1988, p. 150),

> We achieve our personal identities and self concept through the use of the narrative configuration, and make our existence into a whole by understanding it as an expression of a single unfolding and developing story. We are in the middle of our stories and cannot be sure how they will end; we are constantly having to revise the plot as new events are added to our lives. Self, then, is not a static thing not a substance, but a configuring of personal events into a historical unity which includes not only what one has been but also anticipations of what one will be.

Miller et al. (1990), Hermans (1996), and Holland et al. (1998) argued that narrative constructions of the self and identity are accomplished in social interaction, rather than an individual's solitary endeavor.

Moreover, people's self-narratives appear to matter for their self-cultivation of well-being. Bauer et al. (2005) argued that the interpretations people make of their lives in their self-narratives can lead to maturity and well-being because whether one finds meaning in an event is largely a matter of interpretation: where some people can see low points, others can see development opportunities (Bauer & Bonnano, 2001; Bluck & Gluck, 2004). For instance, people's use of redemption themes in their life stories, which transform negative events into positive outcomes, is positively associated with self-reported life satisfaction, self-esteem and a sense of life coherence, and negatively associated with depression (McAdams et al., 2001). On the other hand, the use of contamination sequences, where initially positive events take a negative turn, is negatively associated with self-reported life satisfaction, self-esteem and a sense of life coherence, and positively associated with depression (McAdams et al., 2001). This corresponds with findings that people who feel that their injuries, misfortunes, or illnesses bring some benefits tend to make a faster recovery and to have enhanced well-being (Affleck & Tennen, 1996). Therefore, people may be able to actively cultivate well-being through the interpretations that they make in their self-narratives.

COMMUNICATION

Narrative's emotional property makes for cultural transmission because emotional narratives are likely to be communicated to others. People are very likely to talk about traumatic, emotion arousing, autobiographical events, sometimes repeatedly for many years afterwards. For example, following the Loma Prieta earthquake on October 7, 1989, which killed at least 63 people in the San Francisco Bay Area, respondents reported talking about the event an average of almost eight times a day one week after the event (Pennebaker & Harber, 1993). Likewise, people who had suddenly lost a spouse or child as the result of a car accident between 4 and 7 years previously still reported speaking about the death of their spouse or child frequently (Lehman et al., 1987). The sudden loss of a spouse or child is arguably one of the most traumatic events that people can experience, but a decade of research by Rimé and his colleagues (Rimé et al., 1991; Pennebaker et al., 2001; for a review see Rimé et al., 1992) has shown that less intense, everyday emotions can facilitate the sharing of autobiographical narratives, as across age group and gender, participants report sharing between 88% and 96% of positive and negative personal emotional events through autobiographical narrative. Importantly, the more emotional the event, the more likely people are to share it.

This emotional facilitation is not limited to autobiographical narratives. Diana, the Princess of Wales, was killed in a car accident on August 30, 1997. Around the world, news of Diana's death aroused strong emotional responses, and was a frequent topic of conversation. For instance, Stone and Pennebaker (2002) found that in the day following her death, conversation about the circumstances of Diana's life and death, and the sadness and shock that people felt, consumed 48.5% of all conversation in one particular internet chat room. It is likely that people's emotional responses to her death facilitated their sharing of narratives about her life and death, as Christophe and Rimé (1997; see also Curci & Bellelli, 2004) found that participants who reported experiencing high levels of emotion in response to other's narratives shared these narratives in turn more often, with more people. In an experimental demonstration of this effect, Luminet et al. (2000) showed that participants were significantly more likely to spontaneously talk about a short film with a friend when the film aroused more intense emotions. Furthermore, there is evidence that emotion drives people to share urban legends (Heath et al., 2001), social anecdotes (Peters, Kashima, & Clark, in press), and may facilitate the sharing of gossip (Walker, 2003; Baumeister et al., 2004).

SUMMARY

Narrative pervades human life as people of all cultures and ages (except for the very young) engage in storytelling and story listening. Narrative is implicated in our cognitive lives, as we are good at comprehending, recalling, and using information narratively. Narrative is also implicated in our emotional lives, as emotionality is perhaps inherent to stories, which describe a character's movements relative to their goals and objectives. Where successful achievements may yield positive emotions; failures may result in disappointment, anger, and sadness. When we process narratives we also experience emotions in turn. In this way we can use narrative to regulate our emotions. Further, narrative is implicated in our personal lives, as we express our self-identities in narrative form. Therefore, as we relate narratives, we transmit cultural meaning, both pragmatic and existential. The emotionality of narrative magnifies this effect, as people prefer to communicate emotion arousing stories. Thus, narrative is potentially a powerful and complete medium for cultural transmission.

NARRATIVE AND HUMAN AGENCY

We believe that narrative is instrumental to culturally transmitted meaning having compelling psychological forces to engage spontaneous human agency. Narrative transmits culture and engages us psychologically. This is because narrative is closely linked to the acquisition and activation of an *ideomotor representation* (see Greenwald, 1970; James, 1890). By ideomotor representations, we mean psychological representations that have ideational and motor components, and that have symbolic expressions (e.g., narratively described actions) and molar behaviors (e.g., actual behavior enactment). We assume that an accessed ideomotor representation may be symbolically expressed by narrative or behaviorally enacted by motor activities. Like any other representations, we assume that its current accessibility is determined by its chronic and temporary accessibility (e.g., Higgins, 1996). Consistent with this, narratives are embodied (e.g., Zwaan, 2004) and psychologically represented actions are likely to have corresponding motoric representations (e.g., Prinz, 1997). Indeed, narratively represented events and actions tend to activate brain regions that are implicated in the processing of those events and actions that the narrative represents (e.g., Mar, 2004). Kashima et al. (2007a) reviewed relevant literature and proposed a connectionist model capable of acquiring such an ideomotor action orientation based on imitation learning. In this final section, we apply this general idea to argue that socially transmitted narrative can influence people's motives, which drive their actions. To put it differently, people may acquire their goals from culturally transmitted narratives, and spontaneously engage their self-regulatory processes in accordance with them. We also argue that narrative shapes human agency at both individual and collective levels, so that it engages people's individual as well as collective actions.

NARRATIVE STRUCTURE AND SELF-REGULATION

The close link between narrative and human agency can be seen in the similarity between a typical narrative structure and self-regulation as theorized by Higgins's (1987) self-discrepancy theory in particular. To illustrate, take a simple (admittedly androcentric) fairy tale: A beautiful princess is taken away by a dragon, a brave prince rescues the princess by slaying the dragon with his magic sword, and the king allows the princess to marry the prince. According to a French structuralist, Greimas (1966/1983), this type of story can be analysed in terms of its underlying narrative structure. Based on Propp's (1968) analysis of Russian folk tales, Greimas suggests that a story can be understood in terms of relations among narrative elements, which he called *actants*. One relation, axis of desire, connects *Subject* and *Object*, the prince and the princess, in this example. Another relation is called the axis of conflict, which connects *Helper* and *Opponent*, the magic sword and the dragon. *Helper* helps and *Opponent* hinders *Subject*'s approach toward *Object*. Finally, there is the axis of communication, which connects *Sender* and *Receiver*. The king is a sender in this example, and the prince, a receiver. *Sender* gives *Object* to *Receiver*. In this example, the same character, the prince, occupies the roles of *Subject* and *Receiver*. Figure 17.1 describes Greimas's analytical schema.

In Greimas's schema, the axis of desire, or *Subject*'s actions to obtain *Object*, is central to a narrative. A story then tells the protagonist's thoughts and deeds that lead up to the attainment or otherwise of the goal, namely, the acquisition of the object of desire. There is some empirical support for this conjecture. Because goals provide reasons for actions (e.g., Trabasso & Sperry, 1985), people generally remember more details about goal-action causal chains in narratives when trying to explain a character's actions (Trabasso & Suh, 1993; Wolfe et al., 2005).

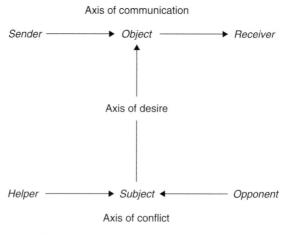

FIGURE 17.1   Greimas's narrative structure.

Related to this finding is research suggesting that people take longer to process narratives in which a protagonist's goals and actions are inconsistent (Huitema et al., 1993; Poynor & Morris, 2003). However, the goal-directed activities unfold within social and moral contexts. On the one hand, the axis of conflict locates the protagonist's movement within the social context of allies and foes, who help or hinder his or her goal-directed actions. This creates tension and drama. On the other hand, the axis of communication places the protagonist's movement within the moral context. When the king gives permission to marry, he is acting as a moral agent that sanctions the prince's heroic deed to rescue the princess. By *Sender* = king metaphorically giving *Object* = princess to *Receiver/Subject* = prince, the king gives moral approval. This way, *Sender* often acts as an embodiment of morality in Greimas's schema. In short, Greimas's analytical schema characterizes narrative as goal-directed activities in social and moral contexts.

It is interesting to note that Greimas's schema can be used to analyze a popular theory of self-regulation, Higgins's self-discrepancy theory (1987). According to him, people regulate their cognition and action in terms of the discrepancy of their *actual self*-relative to their self-guides, *ideal* and *ought self*. An ideal self represents what people want to become, whereas an ought self dictates what they feel they ought to be like, a kind of moral standard. A failure to live up to the ideal self will disappoint them, but not following the ought self would make them anxious. Higgins argues that people regulate their cognitive and behavioral activities to reduce the discrepancies between the actual self and the self-guides. Note that an ideal self in this theory is *Object*. *Subject* is the person who is self-regulating his or her thoughts and actions. An ought self takes the role of *Sender*, who dispenses moral sanctions to *Receiver/Subject*, the person who is self-regulating. That human thoughts and actions as described by self-discrepancy theory can be understood within Greimas's narratology suggests the homology, the structural similarity between narrative and self-regulation. In other words, narrative packages in itself self-regulatory information in social and moral contexts; it informs people of how to be social and moral agents.

NARRATIVE, GOALS, AND MOTIVATION

Narrative is intertwined with conceptualizations of human motivation. To begin with, motivation psychology has a tradition of using narratives to measure people's motives. The Thematic Apperception Test (TAT), developed by Murray (1938) and used extensively by McClelland et al. 1953, uses stories to assess motives. The stories that people tell about ambiguous pictures of social scenes are coded for various themes, which are assumed to reflect their underlying motives. The coding scheme developed in one culture may have cultural biases, but a more culturally sensitive coding procedure may be developed to overcome this limitation (Kornadt et al., 1980). McClelland (1989) called the motives that are inferred from people's TAT stories *implicit motives*. By contrast, he called the motives that people explicitly attribute to themselves as consciously held goals self-attributed motives; these motives are now often called *explicit motives* (e.g., Woike et al., 2003). As Sorrentino and Higgins (1986) noted, the TAT may be reinterpreted within a contemporary cognitive-motivational theoretical framework. If indeed an ideomotor representation that associates both symbolic narratives and motoric behaviors exists, such a representation is likely to contain a representation of a goal and goal-directed actions that allow one to attain the goal. As the ideo-motor representation is accessed, the associated behavioral goal is also likely to be accessed. Such accessible goals may spontaneously and even nonconsciously drive people's cognitive and behavioral activities (e.g., Bargh et al., 2001; Chartrand & Bargh, 1996; see Chartrand & Bargh, 2002, for a review).

Conceptualized this way, stories people tell about ambiguous stimuli (e.g., TAT) may reflect their chronically accessible goals, and as such, much of the research on implicit motives may be interpretable as about chronically accessible goals. In line with this, people's implicit motives can predict their life outcomes several decades in the future, such as their work achievement and marital satisfaction (McClelland, 1965; McAdams & Valliant, 1982). So, people who have high need for power, rather than affiliation or achievement, will tend to tell stories that detail the protagonist's concern for having impact on others, their influence on others through strong and forceful actions, their unsolicited helping and their status (e.g., Langner & Winter, 2001), and they are themselves more likely to attain power relevant careers and to succeed in these careers in the future (Jenkins, 1994).

Likewise, when people tell autobiographical narratives about their lives, the content of these narratives is strongly related to their implicit motives, and therefore their chronically accessible goals. For instance, when participants were instructed to recall autobiographical events, those high in power recalled more power-related experiences and those high in intimacy recalled more intimacy-related experiences (McAdams, 1982). In addition, participants high in power selected more agentic memories (describing their autonomy and instrumentality) to re-experience, and those high in intimacy selected more communal memories (describing relationships and connection with others) to re-experience (Woike, 1994; see also McAdams, 1985; McAdams et al., 1996; Woike & Polo, 2001). Similarly, when agentic and communal participants were asked to recall their most memorable life experiences, they tended to recall agentic and communal events, respectively (Woike, 1994).

Memory processes play an important role in the influence of implicit motives on the construction of narratives, particularly autobiographical narratives, because implicit motives influence the acquisition and organization of motive-related knowledge as well as modulating its accessibility (Woike et al., 2003). In particular, Woike et al. (1999) proposed that agentics should tend to favor the cognitive process of differentiation, which involves perceiving differences, in structuring motive-relevant events in memory because it will help them feel autonomous. Similarly, communals should tend to favor the cognitive process of integration, which involves perceiving relationships, in structuring motive-relevant events in memory because it will help them to feel connected. In line with this, they found that agentic and communal people used differentiation and integration respectively to encode motive-relevant information in episodic memory. Further research has shown that while agentics recalled and recognized more differentiation in an agentic story, communals recalled and recognized more integration in a communal story (Woike et al., 2001).

If the current conceptualization is true, narrative should also be able to prime goals. There is evidence that suggests this is the case. Trafimow et al. (1991) used narratives to prime either the private or the collective self in American and Chinese participants. As we showed for illustrative purposes earlier, they gave participants a story about a warrior making a decision that would bring him either great personal reward (in the private self prime) or demonstrate loyalty and bring benefit to his family (in the collective self prime). The results of two studies indicated that culture played a role in differential self-activation as people from individualistic cultures gave more individualist responses than people from collectivistic cultures. However, they also found that participants in the private self prime condition retrieved more individualistic than collectivistic self-cognitions. The authors use these findings to argue that the private/collective self distinction is meaningful and has consequences in terms of the retrieval of self-cognitions. However, the findings also indicate an important consequence of narratives – that stories can facilitate the activation of different selves.

Brewer and Gardner (1996) also used narratives to prime different representations of the collective self. Their experiment involved a more subtle priming of the self using a story in which the manipulation was embedded in the form of different collective pronouns ("us" and "we" versus "they" and "them") to describe the protagonists. Participants who read stories containing the "us" and "we" pronouns rated ambiguous statements as more similar to their own, evidencing an expansion of the self-concept (from the personal to the collective – including both interpersonal/small group and collective). Participants first read a narrative about a trip to the city containing different pronouns. They then rated a series of evaluative statements on a range of issues in terms of how similar those statements were to their own views. Participants in the "we" prime condition responded more quickly and rated the ambiguous statements as more similar to their own views compared with participants in the "they" prime conditions. In a second experiment, the authors investigated the kind of collective self being activated – interpersonal or large scale collective. They manipulated the kind of collective self being primed to include a large group context, using a story watching a football game in a large stadium. Again, the "we" prime facilitated similarity judgments of ambiguous statements, and inhibited dissimilarity judgments. Finally in a third experiment, they explored the effect of "we" primes on participant's freely generated self statements using the Twenty Statements Test (Hartley, 1970). Again, they found that participants generated more social self statements in the "we" prime condition. The authors suggest that these experiments provide evidence of the lowering of participants' threshold for similarity judgments, and an expansion of the self-concept, from the personal to the collective, under narrative priming conditions due to its effect on the accessibility of different levels of self-representations.

More direct evidence that narratives prime goals comes from Aarts et al. (2004), who looked at goal contagion, which is the automatic taking on of others' goals in automatic goal pursuit. In a series of experiments, they showed that, after reading a story about a male undergraduate seeking a casual sex (relative to reading an unrelated story), male undergraduates became more helpful towards a female (but not to a male) student (Experiment 2), and this increased helpfulness became even stronger over time (Experiment 3). Aarts et al. (2005) replicated this finding using representations of stereotyped groups that contained information about the group's goals and found that participants pursued goals congruent with those of the stereotyped group representation they had read. Similarly, Houser-Marko and Sheldon (2006) had university students read a children's story that does or does not involve the exertion of physical effort (*The Little Engine That Could* versus *Curious George and the Pizza*). Half of the participants who read either story wrote three short paragraphs about how the story applied to themselves or to a close friend in the past, present, and future. In an ostensibly unrelated task, they were asked to hold a weight above a string and to squeeze a handgrip as long as possible. After controlling for gender and exercise habits, those who read the story that involved physical exertion and effort and wrote about how the story applied to themselves spent more time holding up the weight holding and squeezing the handgrip. This shows that a narrative describing physical exertion can prime the actual physical exertion; however, if the narrative is explicitly made applicable to others, it may lose its priming effect.

NARRATIVE, COLLECTIVE IDENTITY, AND COLLECTIVE AGENCY

If narratives can inform and effect individual identity and act as a conduit for individual agency, can the same be argued of collective agency? One of the most prominent approaches to the social psychology of groups has been the social identity perspective, encompassing both social identity theory (SIT: Tajfel & Turner, 1986) and self-categorization theory (SCT: Turner, 1985). The social identity perspective describes a process whereby aggregates of individuals become social groups through their awareness of their group membership, and their sense of attachment to it. In self-categorization, the similarities between the self and other in-group members are accentuated, as are the differences between in-group and out-group members. The individual shares the same social identity with other group members, and behaves in ways, which are congruent with the group norm. Social comparisons are motivated by the desire to be confident in our beliefs about ourselves, others and the world, but are also directed by the need to have consensus with in-group members, and to positively evaluate the in-group's properties, or achieve positive distinctiveness in relation to other groups (Hogg & Abrams, 1988). This results in a tendency to maximize the differences between the in-group and out-group, and achieve positive distinctiveness for the in-group. Social identity is a statement about category membership on the basis of some shared characteristics, but it does not require direct contact between members, and exists as a subjective claim by the individual. That is, category membership only becomes a social identification when it is seen by the individual to be self-defining.

While this approach implies that collective agency is expressed through the desire to achieve positive distinctiveness for the group, it does not explore what the content of this distinctiveness is, or the reasons for its importance in relation to particular groups. Criticisms of the social identity perspective have centered on its neglect of these aspects of group function. Hopkins and Reicher (1996) have suggested that of crucial importance is how a group is defined and understood, and that a group's attitudes and behavior depend on their relations with other groups, and the perceivability of alternative constructions of the group's position (see also Huddy, 2001, for a similar point). What the social identity perspective does not address is how such beliefs about what is permissible and legitimate arise in the first place. That is, how are some categories made meaningful to self-definition in the first place? The category chosen as meaningful determines the range of relations that are relevant (i.e., class, as opposed to nation). In other words, the *meaning* of the identity-defining social category is what matters.

Taking the grounding approach in the neo-diffusionist perspective on cultural evolution, Kashima et al. (2007b) suggested that the process of social communication necessarily implies a grounding of a collective identity and a collective representation that is shared among those who share the collective identity. In this view, the transmission of cultural meaning is inherently constitutive of the cultural identity. In particular, cultural transmission of collective narratives – stories in which the protagonist is a group of people – are a significant source of a collective identity (e.g., Wertsch, 1998, 2002; Jacobs, 2002; Ashmore et al., 2004). There seems to be little in the way of empirical research on the role of narratives in the construction of a collective identity, other than Kashima and Kostopoulos's (2004) demonstration that people tend to communicate information, that is congruent with their own national stereotype. However, there has been abundant theorizing about it, though largely within disciplines other than psychology, such as sociology, history, political science, and anthropology. Imbuing the nation with a sense of history, tradition, legitimacy, and strong emotional investment on the part of the people who reside in it, appears to be a universal feature of nations. This appears to be the case regardless of whether a nation can actually claim an ancient, traditional, ethnic basis or must invent or imagine one to cloak a more recent socially constructed origin.

Regardless, the importance of symbols, tradition, myth and legend, and the language and discourse to present and represent them is crucial, and national narratives are a central aspect of this. A recent and generative view in political science argues that nations are imagined, socially constructed, and relatively recent cultural artifacts (Hobsbawm & Ranger, 1983; Anderson, 1991), and that any claim to ancient kin-based origins is engendered in shared cultural "affinities" which embody a myth of descent, or narratives of such, which enable people to make sense of their national past and present, and imagine a desirable future, and also serve the needs and interests of the elites that propagate them (Smith, 1991). This latter approach has paved the way for discursive theorists to focus on the way in which social reality is constructed around the assumption of a national concept (Sutherland, 2005). Highlighting this, Billig (1995) argued that nationalism is a banal, everyday experience, rather than the preserve of ideological extremists, and that nationalism makes nations seem natural, inevitable, and legitimate (Ricouer, 1986; Billig, 1995, 1996; Murray, 2003). This naturalization is instantiated in everyday communication, traditions, practices, histories, and continually presented and represented in the media and in political and public discourse, and engendered in imagined traditions and myths which reinforce the sense that the nation is "self-evidently natural, rooted in antiquity," when in fact it is a novel cultural artifact (Hobsbawm & Ranger, 1983). The result is that ordinary ways of speaking become suffused with nationalist assumptions, which are only possible if the nation is seen to exist as a socially real entity. It is in this context that national narratives may represent collective goals, and can be constitutive of collective agency.

For instance, American college students often construe the history of the United States as a story of a "quest for freedom," according to Wertsch (1998). Starting with the Pilgrims' quest for a religious freedom in the New World, the 13 states' fight for political freedom in the Independence War, and so on, the recurrent theme in the students' narration about their own country was the story in which the White Americans as the collective were portrayed as the protagonist that struggled for (and won) freedom. Somewhat more pejoratively, Feldman (2001) suggested that what Engelhardt (1995) called *triumphalism* is an American national narrative. It is a recurrent theme in the American movies and stories about cavalries and Indians, the World War II, and the like, in which Americans (typically White Americans) are portrayed as the main characters morally wronged by an opponent (Indians and enemies), who is eventually annihilated by the morally superior protagonist. The eventual triumph marks a moral victory. A collective narrative has also been explored in relation to the construction of British (Wallwork & Dixon, 2004) and Scottish national identity (Kearton, 2005), and illustrates the way in which elites draw on particular myths of national identity to motivate people's attitudes on contemporary issues. Kornprobst (2005) argues that national stories operate to lay out and constrain the kinds of national identities that are plausible. Thus, a collective narrative is a symbolic medium by which the moral and historical meaning of the collective is constructed and conveyed through public discourse (e.g., Bhabha, 1990; Solomon, 2004; Liu & Hilton, 2005). When thus acquired collective identity and its collective goals are activated, it may then engage collective agency. Empirical research for this conjecture, however, needs to be conducted in the future.

CONCLUDING REMARKS

Culture is part of human nature. *Homo sapiens* have evolved to construct culture. Human ontogeny presupposes cultural input; children become fully human to the extent that they are enculturated into the meaningful world of the human social reality. Whereas culture may influence genetic evolution in the long run (e.g., Cavalli-Sforza & Feldman, 1981; Boyd & Richerson, 1985), cultural evolution proceeds much more quickly than biological evolution. Much of human adaptation (or otherwise) to our natural and social environment has to be driven by cultural evolution. In this sense, human agency, either individual or collective, is fundamentally cultural. A question we tried to address in this paper, however, is how such enculturated agency is possible. After all, culturally transmitted information is secondhand information; it is not firsthand information that we gain directly and personally. Yet, culturally transmitted information seems to compel us to act not willy-nilly, because other people tell us to do so, but intrinsically and spontaneously as something that we regard as our own motives that drive us.

An answer put forward in this chapter has been that humans have a psychological architecture to acquire an ideomotor representation that combines both symbolic and motoric activities (Kashima et al., 2007a). This ideomotor representation then may be acquired by imitation, but also through narratives, and it may be narratively primed or expressed. This is because narratives symbolically represent goal-directed action sequences, which are likely embodied and engage associated motor responses though their overt expressions may be inhibited under normal circumstances. We have argued that such ideomotor representations may include behavioral goals, whose activations may give rise to implicit motives and nonconscious goal pursuit. When we reflect on our own activities driven by these psychological processes, however, we perhaps regard them as our own, spontaneous thoughts and actions (James, 1890). Through narrative transmission of cultural meaning, we may acquire and activate collective goals – goals that are attributed to our in-groups. This process then may engage our collective agency. Human agency is fundamentally enculturated. Narrative as a cultural medium may play a profound role in human agency in cultural context.

REFERENCES

Aarts, H., Gollwitzer, P. M., & Hassin, R. R. (2004). Goal contagion: Perceiving is for pursuing. *Journal of Personality and Social Psychology, 87*, 23–37.

Aarts, H., Chartrand, T., Custers, R., Danner, U., Dik, G., Jefferis, V. E. et al. (2005). Social stereotypes and automatic goal pursuit. *Social Cognition, 23*(6), 465–490.

Affleck, G., & Tennen, H. (1996). Construing benefits from adversity: Adaptational significance and dispositional underpinnings. *Journal of Personality, 64*(4), 899–922.

Anderson, B. (1991). *Imagined communities: Reflections on the origin and spread of nationalism.* London: Verso.

Ashmore, R. D., Deaux, K., & McLaughlin-Volpe, T. (2004). An organizing framework for collective identity: Articulation and significance of multidimensionality. *Psychological Bulletin, 130,* 80–114.

Aunger, R. (2002). *The electric meme: A new theory of how we think.* New York: Free Press.

Bargh, J. A., Gollwitzer, P. M., Lee-Chai, A., Barndollar, K., & Trotschel, R. (2001). The automated will: Nonconscious activation and pursuit of behavioural goals. *Journal of Personality and Social Psychology, 81,* 1014–1027.

Bartlett, F. C. (1932). *Remembering: A study in experimental and social psychology.* Cambridge: Cambridge University Press.

Bauer, J. J., & Bonnano, G. A. (2001). Doing and being well (for the most part): Adaptive patterns of narrative self-evaluation during bereavement. *Journal of Personality, 69,* 451–482.

Bauer, J. J., McAdams, D. P., & Sakaeda, A. R. (2005). Interpreting the good life: Growth memories in the lives of mature, happy people. *Journal of Personality and Social Psychology, 88*(1), 203–217.

Baumeister, R. F., & Newman, L. S. (1994). How stories make sense of personal experiences: Motives that shape autobiographical narratives. *Personality and Social Psychology Bulletin, 20,* 676–690.

Baumeister, R. F., Stillwell, A., & Wotman, S. R. (1990). Victim and perpetrator accounts of interpersonal conflict: Autobiographical narratives about anger. *Journal of Personality and Social Psychology, 59,* 994–1005.

Baumeister, R. F., Wotman, S. R., & Stillman, A. M. (1993). Unrequited love: On heartbreak, anger, guilt, scriptlessness, and humiliation. *Journal of Personality and Social Psychology, 64,* 377–394.

Baumeister, R. F., Zhang, L., & Vohs, K. D. (2004). Gossip as cultural learning. *Review of General Psychology, 8,* 111–121.

Bhabha, H. K. (1990). Introduction: Narrating the nation. In H. K. Bhabha (Ed.), *Nation and narration.* London: Routledge.

Billig, M. (1995). *Banal nationalism.* London: Sage Publications.

Billig, M. (1996). Nationalism as an international ideology: Imagining the nation, others and the world of nations. In G. Marie & E. Lyons (Eds.), *Changing European identities: Social psychological analyses of social change* (pp. 181–194). Woburn, MA: Butterworth-Heinemann.

Blackmore, S. J. (1999). *The meme machine.* Oxford, UK: Oxford University Press.

Bluck, S., & Gluck, J. (2004). Making things better and learning a lesson: Experiencing wisdom across the lifespan. *Journal of Personality, 72,* 543–572.

Bower, G., Black, J., & Turner, T. (1979). Scripts in memory for text. *Cognitive Psychology, 11,* 120–177.

Boyd, R., & Richerson, P. J. (1985). *Culture and the evolutionary process.* Chicago, IL: University of Chicago Press.

Boyd, R., & Richerson, P. J. (1995). Why does culture increase human adaptibility?. *Ethology and Sociobiology, 16,* 125–143.

Boyd, R., & Richerson, P. J. (2000). Memes: Universal acid or a better mouse trap. In R. Aunger (Ed.), *Darwinizing culture: The status of memetics as a science* (pp. 143–162). Oxford: Oxford University Press.

Boyd, R., & Richerson, P. J. (2005). Solving the puzzle of human cooperation. In S. Levinson (Ed.), *Evolution and culture* (pp. 105–132). Cambridge, MA: MIT Press.

Brewer, M., & Gardner, W. (1996). Who is this "we"? Levels of collective identity and self representations. *Journal of Personality and Social Psychology, 71,* 83–93.

Brewer, W. F., & Ohtsuka, K. (1988). Story structure, characterization, just world organization, and reader affect in American and Hungarian short stories. *Poetics, 17,* 395–415.

Brown, R. (1991). *Human universals.* Philadelphia: Temple University Press.

Bruner, J. (1990). *Acts of meaning.* Cambridge, MA: Harvard University Press.

Burke, K. (1945/1969). *Grammar of motives.* New York: Prentice-Hall.

Campbell, D. T. (1975). On the conflicts between biological and social evolution and between psychology and moral tradition. *American Psychologist, 30,* 1103–1126.

Cavalli-Sforza, L. L., & Feldman, M. W. (1981). *Cultural transmission and evolution.* Princeton: Princeton University Press.

Chartrand, T. L., & Bargh, J. A. (1996). Automatic activation of impression formation and memorization goals: Nonconscious goal priming reproduces effects of explicit task instructions. *Journal of Personality and Social Psychology, 71,* 464–478.

Chartrand, T. L., & Bargh, J. A. (2002). Nonconscious motivations: Their activation, operation, and consequences. In A. Tesser, D. A. Stapel, & J. V. Wood (Eds.), *Self and motivation: Emerging psychological perspectives* (pp. 13–41). Washington, DC: American Psychological Association.

Christophe, V., & Rimé, B. (1997). Exposure to the social sharing of emotion: Emotional impact, listener responses and secondary social sharing. *European Journal of Social Psychology, 27*(1), 37–54.

Clark, H. H. (1996). Communities, commonalities, and communication. In J. J. Gumperz & S. C. Levinson (Eds.), *Rethinking linguistic relativity* (pp. 324–355). Cambridge, UK: Cambridge University Press.

Cole, M. (1996). *Cultural psychology: A once and future discipline.* Cambridge: Harvard University Press.

Cupchick, G. C., Oatley, K., & Vorderer, P. (1998). Emotional effects of reading excerpts of short stories by James Joyce. *Poetics, 25,* 363–377.

Curci, A., & Bellelli, G. (2004). Cognitive and social consequences of exposure to emotional narratives: Two studies on secondary social sharing of emotions. *Cognition & Emotion, 18*(7), 881–900.

Dawkins, R. (1976/1989). *The selfish gene.* Oxford, UK: Oxford University Press.

Dawkins, R. (1982). *The extended phenotype: The gene as a unit of selection.* Oxford: Oxford University Press.

Dawkins, R. (1999). Forward. In S. Blackmore (Ed.), *The meme machine.* Oxford: Oxford University Press.

Dennet, D. (1995). *Darwin's dangerous idea.* New York: Simon and Schuster.

El-Shamy, H. M. (1995). *Folk traditions of the Arab world: A guide to motif classification* (Vol. 1). Indiana University Press: Bloomington.

Engelhardt, T. (1995). *End of victory culture: Cold war America and the disillusioning of a generation.* New York: University of Massachusetts Press.

Ewick, P., & Silbey, S. (1995). Subversive stories and hegemonic tales: Toward a sociology of narrative. *Law and Society Review, 29*(2), 197–226.

Feldman, C. F. (2001). Narratives of national identity as group narratives: Patterns of interpretive cognition. In J. Brockmeier & D. Carbaugh (Eds.), *Narrative and identity: Studies in autobiography, self and culture* (pp. 129–144). Amsterdam, The Netherlands: John Benjamins Publishing.

Geertz, C. (1973). *The interpretation of cultures: Selected essays.* New York: Basic Books.

Geertz, C. (1983). "From the native's point of view": On the nature of anthropological understanding. In C. Geertz (Ed.), *Local knowledge* (pp. 55–70). New York: Basic Books.

Gergen, K. J., & Gergen, M. M. (1988). Narrative and the self as relationship. In L. Berkowitz (Ed.), *Advances in experimental social psychology* (Vol. 21, pp. 17–56). New York: Academic Press.

Gernsbacher, M. A., Goldsmith, H. H., & Robertson, R. R. W. (1992). Do readers mentally represent characters' emotional states?. *Cognition and Emotion, 6,* 89–111.

Gick, M. L., & Holyoak, K. J. (1980). Analogical problem solving. *Cognitive Psychology, 12,* 306–355.

Gick, M. L., & Holyoak, K. J. (1983). Schema induction and analogical transfer. *Cognitive Psychology, 15*(1), 1–38.

Graesser, A. C., Woll, S. B., Kowalski, D., & Smith, D. A. (1980). Memory for typical and atypical actions in scripted activities. *Journal of Experimental Psychology: Human Learning and Memory, 6*(5), 503–515.

Greenwald, A. (1970). Sensory feedback mechanisms in performance control: With special reference to the ideo-motor mechanism. *Psychological Review, 77,* 73–99.

Greimas, A. J. (1966/1983). *Structural semantics: An attempt at a method.* (D. Mcdowell, R. Schleifer, & A. Velie, Trans.). Lincoln: University of Nebraska Press.

Greimas, A. J. (1990). *The social sciences: A semiotic view.* (P. Perron, & F. H. Collins, Trans.). Minneapolis: University of Minnesota Press.

Greimas, A. J., & Courtés, J. (1976). The cognitive dimension of narrative discourse. *New Literary History, 7*, 433–447.

Hartley, W. S. (1970). *Manual for the twenty statements problem.* Kansas City, MO: Greater Kansas City Mental Health Foundation.

Harvey, J. H., Weber, A. L., & Orbuch, T. L. (1990). *Interpersonal accounts: A social psychological perspective.* Oxford, UK: Blackwell.

Hastie, R., Park, B., & Weber, R. (1984). Social memory. In R. S. Wyer & T. K. Srull (Eds.), *Handbook of social cognition.* Hillsdale, NJ: Lawrence Erlbaum Associates.

Heath, C., Bell, C., & Sternberg, E. (2001). Emotional selection in memes: The case of urban legends. *Journal of Personality and Social Psychology, 81*(6), 1028–1041.

Hermans, H. J. M. (1996). Voicing the self: From information processing to dialogical interchange. *Psychological Bulletin, 119*, 31–50.

Higgins, E. T. (1987). Self-discrepancy: A theory relating self and affect. *Psychological Review, 94*, 319–340.

Higgins, E. T. (1996). Knowledge activation: Accessibility, applicability, and saliency. In E. T. Higgins & A. W. Kruglanski (Eds.), *Social psychology: Handbook of basic principles* (pp. 133–168). New York: Guilford Press.

Hobsbawm, E., & Ranger, T. (1983). *The invention of tradition.* Cambridge: Cambridge University Press.

Hogg, M. A., & Abrams, D. (1988). *Social identifications: A social psychology of inter-group relations and group processes.* Florence, KY: Taylor & Frances/Routledge.

Holland, D., Skinner, D., Lachicotte, W., & Cain, C. (1998). *Identity and agency in cultural worlds.* Cambridge: Harvard University Press.

Hong, Y., Morris, M., Chiu, C., & Benet-Martinez, V. (2000). Multicultural minds: A dynamic constructivist approach to culture and cognition. *American Psychologist, 55*, 709–720.

Hopkins, N., & Reicher, S. (1996). The construction of social categories and processes of social change: Arguing about national identities. In G. Marie & E. Lyons (Eds.), *Changing European identities: Social psychological analyses of social change* (pp. 69–96). Woburn, MA: Butterworth-Heinemann.

Houser-Marko, L., & Sheldon, K. M. (2006). Motivating behavioral persistence: The self-as-doer construct. *Personality and Social Psychology Bulletin, 32*, 1037–1049.

Huddy, L. (2001). From social to political identity: A critical examination of social identity theory. *Political Psychology, 22*, 127–156.

Huitema, J. S., Dopkins, S., Klin, C. M., & Myers, J. L. (1993). Connecting goals and actions during reading. *Journal of Experimental Psychology: Learning, Memory, and Cognition, 19*, 1053–1060.

Huxley, J. (1942/1963). *Evolution: The modern synthesis.* London: Allen and Unwin.

Jacobs, R. N. (2002). The narrative integration of personal and collective identity in social movements. In M. C. Green, J. J. Strange, & T. C. Brock (Eds.), *Narrative impact: Social and cognitive foundations* (pp. 205–228). Mahwah, NJ: Lawrence Erlbaum.

James, W. (1890). *The principles of psychology* (Vol. 1, 2). New York: Dover Publications.

Jenkins, S. R. (1994). Need for power and women's careers over 14 years: Structural power, job satisfaction, and motive change. *Journal of Personality and Social Psychology, 66*(1), 155–165.

Josephson, B. R., Singer, J. A., & Salovey, P. (1996). Mood regulation and memory: Repairing sad moods with happy memories. *Cognition and Emotion, 10*, 437–444.

Kashima, Y. (2000). Maintaining cultural stereotypes in the serial reproduction of narratives. *Personality and Social Psychology Bulletin, 26*, 594–604.

Kashima, Y. (2001). Culture and social cognition: Towards a social psychology of cultural dynamics. In D. Matsumoto (Ed.), *Handbook of culture and psychology*. New York: Oxford University Press.

Kashima, Y., & Kostopoulos, J. (2004). Unintended social influence: Interpersonal communication may inadvertently help maintaining a shared culture. *Cahiers de Psychologie Cognitive, 22*, 445–461.

Kashima, Y., Gurumurthy, A. K., Ouschan, L., Chong, T., & Mattingley, J. (2007a). Connectionism and self: James, Mead, and the stream of enculturated consciousness. *Psychological Inquiry, 18*, 73–96.

Kashima, Y., Klein, O., & Clark, A. E. (2007b). Grounding: Sharing information in social interaction. In K. Fiedler (Ed.), *Social communication* (pp. 27–77). New York: Psychology Press.

Kearton, A. (2005). Imagining the 'mongrel nation': Political uses of history in the recent Scottish nationalist movement. *National Identities, 7*, 23–50.

Kintsch, W. (1988). The role of knowledge in discourse comprehension construction-integration model. *Psychological Review, 95*, 163–182.

Kornadt, H.-J., Eckensberger, L. H., & Emminghaus, W. B. (1980). Cross-cultural research on motivation and its contribution to a general theory of motivation. In H. C. Triandis & W. Lonner (Eds.), *Handbook of cross-cultural psychology: Basic processes* (Vol. 3, pp. 223–2321). Boston: Allyn and Bacon.

Kornprobst, M. (2005). Episteme, nation-builders, and national identity: the re-construction of Irishness. *Nations and Nationalism, 11*, 403–421.

Kraemer, D. L., & Hastrup, J. L. (1988). Crying in adults: Self-control and autonomic correlates. *Journal of Social and Clinical Psychology, 6*, 53–58.

Kuhnen, U., & Oyserman, D. (2002). Thinking about the self influences thinking in general. *Journal of Experimental Social Psychology, 38*, 492–499.

Kuklick, H. (1991). *The savage within: The social history of British anthropology, 1885-1945*. Cambridge, UK: Cambridge University Press.

Labov, W. (1972). *Sociolinguistic patterns*. Philadelphia, PA: University of Pennsylvania Press.

Langner, C. A., & Winter, D. G. (2001). The motivational basis of concessions and compromise: Archival and laboratory studies. *Journal of Personality and Social Psychology, 81*(4), 711–727.

Lehman, D. R., Wortman, C. B., & Williams, A. F. (1987). Long-term effects of losing a spouse or child in a motor vehicle crash. *Journal of Personality and Social Psychology, 52*(1), 218–231.

Leung, K., & Bond, M. H. (2004). Social axioms: A model of social beliefs in multicultural perspective. *Advances in Experimental Social Psychology, 34*, 119–197.

Leung, K., Bond, M. H., de Carrasquel, S. H., Munoz, C. M., Hernández, M., Murakami, F. et al. (2002). Social axioms: The search for universal dimensions of general beliefs about how the world functions. *Journal of Cross-Cultural Psychology, 33*, 286–302.

Liu, J. H., & Hilton, D. (2005). How the past weighs on the present: Social representations of history and their role in identity politics. *British Journal of Social Psychology, 44*, 1–21.

Lowie, R. (1937). *The history of ethnological theory*. New York: Farrar and Rinehart.

Luminet, O., Bouts, P., Delie, F., Manstead, A. S. R., & Rimé, B. (2000). Social sharing of emotion following exposure to a negatively valenced situation. *Cognition and Emotion, 14*(5), 661–688.

Lyons, A., & Kashima, Y. (2001). The reproduction of culture: Communication processes tend to maintain cultural stereotypes. *Social Cognition, 19*, 372–394.

Lyons, A., & Kashima, Y. (2003). How are stereotypes maintained through communication? The influence of stereotype sharedness. *Journal of Personality and Social Psychology, 85*, 989–1005.

Lyons, A., & Kashima, Y. (2006). Maintaining stereotypes in communication: Investigating memory biases and coherence-seeking in storytelling. *Asian Journal of Social Psychology, 9*, 59–71.

Mar, R. A. (2004). The neuropsychology of narrative: Story comprehension, story production and their interrelation. *Neuropsychologica, 42*, 1414–1434.

Mayr, E. (1980). How I became a Darwinian. In E. Mayr & W. B. Provine (Eds.), *The evolutionary synthesis: Perspectives on the unification of biology* (pp. 413–423). Publisher: Harvard University Press.

McAdams, D. P. (1982). Experiences of intimacy and power: Relationships between social motives and autobiographical memory. *Journal of Personality and Social Psychology, 42,* 292–302.

McAdams, D. P. (1985). *Power, intimacy, and the life story: Personological inquiries into identity.* New York: Guilford Press.

McAdams, D. P. (1990). Unity and purpose inhuman lives: The emergence of identity as a life story. In A. I. Rabin, R. A. Zuker, R. A. Emmons, & S. Frank (Eds.), *Studying persons and their lives* (pp. 148–200). New York: Springer.

McAdams, D. P. (2001). The psychology of life stories. *Review of General Psychology, 5,* 100–122.

McAdams, D. P., & Valliant, G. E. (1982). Intimacy, motivation and psychosocial adjustment: A longitudinal study. *Journal of Personality Assessment, 46,* 586–593.

McAdams, D. P., Hoffman, B. J., Mansfield, E. D., & Day, R. (1996). Themes of agency and communion in significant autobiographical scenes. *Journal of Personality, 64,* 339–378.

McAdams, D. P., Reynolds, J., Lewis, M. L., Patten, A., & Bowman, P. T. (2001). When bad things turn good and good things turn bad: Sequences of redemption and contamination in life narrative, and their relation to psychosocial adaptation in midlife adults and in students. *Personality and Social Psychology Bulletin, 27,* 472–483.

McClelland, D. C. (1965). N achievement and entrepreneurship: A longitudinal study. *Journal of Personality and Social Psychology, 1,* 389–392.

McClelland, D. C. (1989). Motivational factors in health and illness. *American Psychologist, 44,* 675–683.

McClelland, D. C., Atkinson, J. W., Clark, R. A., & Lowell, E. L. (1953). *The achievement motive.* New York: Appleton-Century-Crofts.

McGregor, I., & Holmes, J. G. (1999). How storytelling shapes memory and impressions of relationship events over time. *Journal of Personality and Social Psychology, 76,* 403–419.

McIntyre, A., Lyons, A., Clark, A. E., & Kashima, Y. (2004). The microgensis of culture: Serial reproduction as an experimental simulation of cultural dynamics. In M. Schaller & C. S. Crandall (Eds.), *The psychological foundations of culture.* Mahwah, NJ: Lawrence Erlbaum.

Miller, P., Potts, R., Fung, H., Hoogstra, L., & Mintz, J. (1990). Narrative practices and the social construction of self in childhood. *American Ethnologist, 17*(2), 292–311.

Murdoch, G. P. (1945). The common denominator of cultures. In R. Linton (Ed.), *The science of man in the world crisis* (pp. 123–142). New York: Columbia University Press.

Murray, H. A. (1938). *Explorations in personality.* New York: Oxford University Press.

Murray, M. (2003). Narrative psychology and narrative analysis. In P. Camic, J. Rhodes, & L. Yardley (Eds.), *Qualitative research in psychology: Expanding perspectives in methodology and design* (pp. 95–112). Washington, DC: American Psychological Association.

Murray, S. L., & Holmes, J. G. (1993). Seeing virtues in faults: Negativity and the transformation of interpersonal narratives in close relationships. *Journal of Personality and Social Psychology, 65,* 707–722.

Murray, S. L., & Holmes, J. G. (1994). Storytelling in close relationships: The construction of confidence. *Personality and Social Psychology Bulletin, 20,* 650–663.

Naroll, R., Michik, G. L., & Naroll, F. (1980). Holocultural research methods. In H. C. Triandis & J. Berry (Eds.), *Handbook of cross-cultural psychology: Methodology* (Vol. 2, pp. 479–521). Boston, MA: Allyn & Bacon.

Nell, V. (1988). *Lost in a book.* New Haven and London: Yale University Press.

Oatley, K. (1994). A taxonomy of the emotions in literary response and a theory of identification in fictional narrative. *Poetics, 23,* 53–74.

Oatley, K. (1998). Meeting of minds. In S. Janssen & N. V. Dijk (Eds.), *The empirical study of literature and the media: Current approaches and perspectives* (pp. 58–72). Rotterdam: Barjesteh van Waalwijk van Doorn.

Oatley, K. (1999). Why fiction may be twice as true as fact: Fiction as cognitive and emotional simulation. *Review of General Psychology, 3*(2), 101–117.

Oatley, K., & Duncan, E. (1992). Incidents of emotion in daily life. In K. T. Strongman (Ed.), *International review on studies in emotion* (pp. 250–293). Chichester, UK: Wiley.

Pennebaker, J. W., & Harber, K. D. (1993). A social stage model of collective coping: The Loma Prieta earthquake and the Persian Gulf War. *Journal of Social Issues, 49*(4), 125–145.

Pennebaker, J. W., Zech, E., & Rimé, B. (2001). Disclosing and sharing emotion: Psychological, social, and health consequences. In M. S. Stroebe & R. O. Hansson (Eds.), *Handbook of bereavement research: Consequences, coping, and care* (pp. 517–543). Washington, DC: American Psychological Association.

Pennington, N., & Hastie, R. (1986). Evidence evaluation in complex decision making. *Journal of Personality and Social Psychology, 51*, 242–258.

Pennington, N., & Hastie, R. (1988). Explanation-based decision making: The effects of memory structure on judgment. *Journal of Experimental Psychology: Learning, Memory and Cognition, 14*, 521–533.

Pennington, N., & Hastie, R. (1992). Explaining the evidence: Tests of the story model for juror decision making. *Journal of Personality and Social Psychology, 62*, 189–206.

Perry, W. J. (1923). *The children of the sun.* London: Methuen.

Peters, K. O., Kashima, Y., & Clark, A. E. (in press). The emotional facilitation of social talk. *European Journal of Social Psychology.*

Polkinghorne, D. E. (1988). *Narrative knowing and the human sciences.* Albany: SUNY Press.

Poynor, D. V., & Morris, R. K. (2003). Inferred goals in narratives: Evidence from self-paced reading, recall, and eye movements. *Journal of Experimental Psychology: Learning, Memory, and Cognition, 29*, 3–9.

Prinz, W. (1997). Perceptioni and action planning. *European Journal of Cognitive Psychology, 9*(2), 129–154.

Propp, V. (1968). *Morphology of the folktale. (L. Scott, Trans.).* Austin: University of Texas Press.

Ricoeur, P. (1981). The hermeneutical function of distanciation. In J. B. Thompson (Ed.), *Hermeneutics and the social sciences* (pp. 131–144). Cambridge: Cambridge University Press.

Ricouer, P. (1986). *Lectures on ideology and utopia.* New York: Columbia University Press.

Rimé, B., Mesquita, B., Philippot, P., & Boca, S. (1991). Beyond the emotional event: Six studies on the social sharing of emotion. *Cognition and Emotion, 5*(5–6), 435–465.

Rimé, B., Philippot, P., Boca, S., & Mesquita, B. (1992). Long-lasting cognitive and social consequences of emotion: Social sharing and rumination. *European Review of Social Psychology, 3*, 225–258.

Rivers, W. R. H. (1914). *The history of Melanesian society.* Cambridge: The University Press.

Rogoff, B. (2003). *The cultural nature of human development.* New York: Oxford University Press.

Rottenberg, J., Gross, J. J., Wilhelm, F. H., Najmi, S., & Gotlib, I. H. (2002). Crying threshold and intensity in major depressive disorder. *Journal of Abnormal Psychology, 111*(2), 302–312.

Scalise Sugiyama, M. (2001). Food, foragers, and folklore: The role of narrative in human subsistence. *Evolution and Human Behavior, 22*, 221–240.

Schaller, M., Conway, L. G., & Tanchuk, T. L. (2002). Selective pressures on the once and future conents of ethnic stereotypes: Effects of the communicability of traits. *Journal of Personality and Social Psychology, 82*, 861–877.

Schank, R. C., & Abelson, R. P. (1995). Knowledge and memory: The real story. In R. S. Wyer (Ed.), *Knowledge and memory: The real story* (pp. 1–85). New Jersey: Lawrence Erlbaum Associates.

Schwartz, S. (1992). The universal content and structure of values: Theoretical advances and empirical tests in 20 countries. *Advances in Experimental Social Psychology, 25*, 1–65.

Schwartz, S. (1994). Beyond individualism/collectivism: New dimensions of values. In U. Kim, H. C. Triandis, C. Kagitcibasi, S. C. Choi, & G. Yoon (Eds.), *Individualism and collectivism: Theory application and methods* (pp. 85–119). Newbury Park, CA: Sage.

Smith, A. D. (1991). *National identity*. London: Penguin.

Smith, G. E. (1933). *The diffusion of culture*. London: Watts & Co.

Solomon, G. (2004). A narrative-based view of coexistence education. *Journal of Social Issues, 60*, 273–287.

Sorrentino, R. M., & Higgins, E. T. (1986). Motivation and cognition: Warming to synergism. In R. M. Sorrentino & E. T. Higgins (Eds.), *The handbook of motivation and cognition: Foundations of social behavior* (pp. 3–10). New York: Guilford.

Sperber, D. (1996). *Explaining culture: A naturalistic approach*. Oxford: Blackwell.

Sperber, D. (2000). Metarepresentations in an Evolutionary Perspective. In D. Sperber (Ed.), *Metarepresentations: A Multidisciplinary Perspective* (pp. 117–137). New York: Oxford University Press.

Sperber, D., & Wilson, D. (1986). *Relevance*. Oxford, UK: Blackwell.

Stone, L. D., & Pennebaker, J. W. (2002). Trauma in real time: Talking and avoiding online conversations about the death of Princess Diana. *Basic and Applied Social Psychology, 24*(3), 173–183.

Sutherland, C. (2005). Nation-building through discourse theory. *Nations and Nationalism, 11*, 185–202.

Sutton-Smith, B. (1986). *Toys as culture*. New York: Gardner Press, Inc.

Tajfel, H., & Turner, J. C. (1986). The social identity theory of inter-group behaviour. In S. Worchel & W. G. Austin (Eds.), *Psychology of inter-group relations* (pp. 7–24). Chicago: Nelson-Hall.

Thompson, S. (1957). *Motif index of folk literature*. Bloomington: Indiana University Press.

Trabasso, T., & Sperry, L. (1985). Causal relatedness and importance of story events. *Journal of Memory and Language, 24*, 595–611.

Trabasso, T., & Suh, S. (1993). Understanding text: Achieving explanatory coherence through on-line inferences and mental operations in working memory. *Discourse Processes, 16*, 3–34.

Trabasso, T., & van den Broek, P. (1985). Causal thinking and the representation of narrative events. *Journal of Memory and Language, 24*, 612–630.

Trafimow, D., Triandis, H., & Goto, S. (1991). Some tests of the distinction between the private and collective self. *Journal of Personality and Social Psychology, 60*, 649–655.

Triandis, H. C. (1972). *The analysis of subjective culture*. New York: Wiley-Interscience.

Triandis, H. C. (1995). *Individualism and collectivism*. Boulder, CO: Westview Press.

Trianids, H. C. (1996). The psychological measurement of cultural syndromes. *American Psychologist, 51*, 407–415.

Turner, J. C. (1985). Social categorization and the self-concept: A social cognitive theory of group behaviour. In E. J. Lawler (Ed.), *Advances in group processes: Theory and research* (Vol. 2, pp. 77–122). Greenwich, CT: JAI Press Inc.

Urban, G. (2001). *Metaculture*. Philadelphia: University of Pennsylvania Press.

Valsiner, J. (1989). *Human development and culture*. Toronto: Lexington Books.

Valsiner, J., & Lawrence, J. A. (1997). Human development in culture across the life span. In: J. W. Berry, P. R. Dasen, & T. S. Saraswathi (Eds.), *Handbook of cross-cultural psychology* (2nd ed., Vol. 2, pp. 69–106). Boston, MA: Allyn & Bacon.

Walker, C. J. (2003). *If you can't say something bad, say something good!* Paper Presented at the Society for Personality and Social Psychology, Los Angeles, California, February 8.

Wallwork, J., & Dixon, J. (2004). Foxes, green fields and Britishness: On the rhetorical construction of place and national identity. *British Journal of Social Psychology, 43*, 21–39.

Wertsch, J. V. (1998). *Mind as action*. New York: Oxford University Press.

Wertsch, J. V. (2002). *Voices of collective remembering*. New York: Cambridge University Press.

Woike, B., Gershkovich, I., Piorkowski, R., & Polo, M. (1999). The role of motives in the content and structure of autobiographical memory. *Journal of Personality and Social Psychology, 76*, 600–612.

Woike, B., Lavezzary, E., & Barsky, J. (2001). The influence of implicit motives on memory processes. *Journal of Personality and Social Psychology, 81*, 935–945.

Woike, B. A. (1994). The use of differentiation and integration processes: Empirical studies of "separate" and "connected" ways of thinking. *Journal of Personality and Social Psychology, 67*, 142–150.

Woike, B. A., & Polo, M. (2001). Motive-related memories: Content, structure and affect. *Journal of Personality, 69*, 391–415.

Woike, B. A., Mcleod, S., & Goggin, M. (2003). Implicit and explicit motives influence accessability to different autobiographical memories. *Personality and Social Psychology Bulletin, 29*, 1046–1055.

Wolfe, M. B., Magliano, J. P., & Larsen, B. (2005). Causal and semantic relatedness in discourse understanding and representation. *Discourse Processes, 39*, 165–187.

Wrong, D. H. (1961). The oversocialized conception of man in modern sociology. *American Sociological Review, 26*, 183–193.

Wyer, R. S. (2004). *Social comprehension and judgment: The role of situation models, narratives and implicit theories.* Mahwah, NJ: Erlbaum.

Zwaan, R. A. (2004). The immersed experiencer: Toward an embodied theory of language comprehension. In B. H. Ross (Ed.), *The psychology of learning and motivation* (Vol. 44), pp. 35–62. New York: Academic Press.

18

CULTURE, COGNITIONS, AND LEGAL DECISION- MAKING

JUSTIN D. LEVINSON

University of Hawaii, Honolulu, USA

The collaboration between psychological and legal scholarship is only just beginning. Recent interdisciplinary projects have demonstrated that an important accomplishment – the building of an accurate and culturally competent legal behavioral model – is within reach. Building such a model has major societal ramifications, ranging from protecting victims of racial and cultural discrimination to ensuring a behaviorally and economically efficient system of rules. This chapter brings up to date legal scholarship incorporating cognitive, social, and cultural psychology, highlights new interdisciplinary research directions, and challenges psychologists and legal scholars to increase collaborations.

Research at the intersection of cognitions and the law has focused on three main areas: implicit bias and discrimination, legal assumptions about the human mind, and behavioral economics. Implicit bias research challenges legal models of discrimination that only seek to prohibit explicit and intentional acts of prejudice. Studies on legal assumptions about the human mind demonstrate how legal reliance on psychological concepts may not only be inaccurate, but also may be culturally biased. And work in behavioral economics challenges fundamental legal assumptions of how people analyze risk, probability, and other economic decisions. Together, these areas demonstrate how psychological and legal collaboration can help eliminate bias and build more efficient and accurate legal rules.

IMPLICIT BIAS AND UNCONSCIOUS
MOTIVATIONS

Implicit social cognition research has revived legal scholarship on racial discrimination. As this new psychological research has emerged, legal scholars have slowly begun to realize that a more complete psychological model challenges fundamental legal assumptions about the nature of racial discrimination. Evidence from the Implicit Association Test ("IAT") (Banaji et al., 1993; Greenwald & Banaji, 1995) as well as from other implicit task studies (e.g., Gilbert & Hixon, 1991; Payne, 2001) highlight the pervasiveness of implicit biases in daily life. In light of this emerging research paradigm, legal scholars have begun to examine a variety of legal arenas where implicit biases challenge how the law is structured and applied.

CIVIL RIGHTS, EMPLOYMENT DISCRIMINATION,
AND UNCONSCIOUS BIAS

One divergence between racial discrimination laws and psychological reality is illustrated by the law's "intent doctrine" (Lawrence, 1987). This doctrine, which was introduced into civil rights discourse by the Supreme Court in *Washington v. Davis* (1976), requires that a person making a discrimination claim prove that the discrimination was intentional. This subjective intent standard stems from an assumption that racial discrimination is an intentional action. While it is beyond doubt that discrimination is often intentional, psychological research on implicit attitudes and biases reveals an entirely new (legal) way that discrimination may manifest. Because of this new research, proponents of a psychologically competent model of discrimination law argue that the law must protect not only against the less common instances of intentional discrimination, but also against a more subtle but systematic set of implicit attitudes, biases and stereotypes (Krieger, 1995).

Discussions of this gap between legal protections and implicit psychological reality have prospered in employment discrimination law. These discussions typically focus on the gap between unconscious discriminatory motivations and the evidentiary focus of employment discrimination laws. Under Title VII, when a terminated employee brings an action for unequal treatment based on race, sex, religion or other protected category (known as a disparate treatment claim), that employee must introduce direct or circumstantial evidence of an employer's intent to discriminate based upon race, gender, or other protected status (Krieger, 1995). After the defendant attempts to rebut this evidence by showing that there was a non-discriminatory reason for the employment decision, the employee will then try to prove that the non-discriminatory reason was simply a pretext for discrimination.

Because of Title VII's evidentiary standards, disparate treatment claims typically involve detailed discussions of employee evaluations and other human resources records. Legal commentators have argued that this evidentiary focus fails to incorporate knowledge of pervasive unconscious bias (Krieger, 1995) and ignores the facts that even the decision-maker may not even be aware of the discriminatory reason (Pollard, 1999; Green, 2005). Though most employment law scholars agree that unconscious bias evidence should be allowed in some form, they disagree as to whether a new legal standard is required to introduce evidence of unconscious bias into legal proceedings (e.g., Green, 2005; Hart, 2005).

Some scholars are hopeful that courts will eventually allow unconscious bias evidence to prove employment discrimination under the existing legal framework (see McGinley, 2000; Hart, 2005). This accommodation could happen without legislative action; judges could begin to consider unconscious bias information as part of existing Title VII standards. Proponents for this solution argue that unconscious bias information can be introduced as circumstantial evidence, a type of evidence that is already allowed under current case law (Lee, 2005). Other commentators, however, are not as optimistic. Green (2005) suggests that because much discrimination comes from a complex work culture of discrimination, the nature of the discrimination is "too intertwined with valuable social relations to be easily regulated through judicial pronouncements and direct regulation of relational behavior" (p. 629). Thus, Green advocates for a new standard of discrimination that would be based upon a discriminatory work culture. Regardless of whether creating a new standard is the best legal solution, legal commentators continue to look toward psychology for empirical evidence linking employment discrimination to unconscious or implicit cognitive processes.

COMMUNICATIONS LAW, PEREMPTORY CHALLENGES, AND AFFIRMATIVE ACTION

Legal scholars have been slower to react in discussing the importance of implicit social cognition research outside the context of discrimination law. Nonetheless, recent discourse in a communications law, jury selection law, and affirmative action has begun to examine how legal standards must become informed by research on implicit bias. These scholars recognize the early stage of psychologically competent legal work, but nonetheless advocate for a broad range of future projects that incorporate evidence of unconscious biases and implicit processes (Kang, 2005).

Communications Law

One scholar relied on implicit bias scholarship to argue that federal communications law policy may actually propagate discrimination (Kang, 2005). Before turning to his psychologically based argument, Kang described how the Federal Communications Commission ("FCC") evaluates television station ownership applications based upon the "supervening norm of 'public interest'" (p. 1549). The FCC's current practice essentially equates the norm of "public interest" with the frequency of local news broadcasts. The more local news a station offers, the more likely it is to satisfy regulatory hurdles and avoid ownership restrictions. Relying upon implicit social cognition concepts generally as well as specific studies linking local news to stereotypes, Kang argued that the FCC's interpretation of the "public interest" norm acts as a "Trojan horse" of racial stereotypes (p. 1553). That is, by essentially requiring more local news, the FCC sanctions the distribution of racial stereotypes into the public sphere.

Peremptory Challenges

Another scholar has discussed the impact of implicit biases on jury selection rules (Page, 2005). During jury selection in criminal trials, "peremptory challenges" typically allow lawyers to remove potential jurors without having to provide a rationale. Although this standard is generally quite flexible, lawyers are not allowed to remove potential jurors based upon race (*Batson v. Kentucky*, 1986). The Batson standard requires that if a challenge raises a presumption of racial exclusion, the lawyer seeking to remove the juror must convince the judge of a race-neutral justification for the removal (p. 158). While scholars have noted the potential for fabricating race-neutral justifications, until recently the social cognition implications of the Batson rule had not been discussed.

Applying social cognition studies to the peremptory challenge process, Page (2005) suggested that even well-intentioned attorneys may unknowingly base their peremptory challenges on race (p. 209). Research by Sommers and Norton (2007) supports Page's argument and lends itself to the possibility that attorneys may use unconsciously driven pretexts in determining which jurors to exclude. Though these projects support the contention that the peremptory challenge should be abolished entirely, such a legal change is very unlikely (Page, p. 261). Instead, more moderate solutions might be possible, such as alerting attorneys to the possibility of their own unconscious biases (p. 261). These second-best solutions may help reduce the problem of unconscious racism in the use of peremptory challenges. Similar to other legal areas, however, the best solutions for the problem of unconscious bias in jury exclusion will probably come from emerging interdisciplinary collaborations.

Affirmative Action

Social and cognitive psychology has also informed new discussions about affirmative action. A project by Kang and Banaji (2006), designed to begin discourse in the area of "behavioral realism," explored how social cognition research opens up new debates on affirmative action. The authors set the stage for their implicit bias discussion by discussing a near stalemate that has occurred in recent discussions of affirmative action. The stalemate has been driven by a "deadlock" over traditional affirmative action justifications, which have mostly been "historical and moral-philosophical" (p. 1064). According to Kang and Banaji, implicit social cognition research opens up the door for an entirely new type of repair called "fair measures."

The idea behind "fair measures" is to use the science and measurement techniques of implicit social cognition to determine not only what to do to eliminate racial bias, but also how long to do it. Unlike traditional affirmative action, the fair measures paradigm relies upon science to suggest potential solutions to continuing racial bias. For example, research on "countertypical exemplars" indicates that people who are briefly exposed to images of African-American exemplars or who study and learn in a counter-typical environment (such as a women's college) temporarily exhibit reduced implicit bias (Dasgupta & Greenwald, 2001; Dasgupta & Asgari, 2004). A "fair measure" response to such research might include making efforts to hire employees based upon their debiasing capacity (Kang & Banaji, p. 1108). Kang and Banaji argue that a fair measures response should continue until implicit biases are gone.

MEMORY BIAS AND LEGAL DECISION-MAKING

Recent projects have also begun to examine how unconscious cognitive processes may affect legal decision-making in racially biased ways. One such study (Levinson, 2007) examined whether judges and jurors may be influenced by implicit memory biases. Drawing from research on memory, social cognition, and legal decision-making, Levinson pieced together the process whereby an implicit memory bias may manifest and affect the decision-making of judges and jurors.

First, memory studies demonstrate that errors in recall and false memories often occur unconsciously and in ways that interact with stereotypes (Lenton et al., 2001; Macrae et al., 2002). As a result, judges and juries may unknowingly misremember trial information in racially stereotyped ways. Second, memory processes often function as a key component in decision-making (Pennington & Hastie, 1988, 1990; Weber et al., 1995; Dougherty et al., 2003). Thus, racially biased memory errors are likely to affect legal outcomes. Finally, memory errors committed by judges and jurors are unlikely to be self-corrected or improved through jury deliberation (Pritchard & Keenan, 1999, 2002). Thus, racially biased memory errors will go uncorrected during and after a trial.

Levinson followed up his hypothesis with an empirical study. In the study, participants were presented with legally relevant stories. One story described the details of a fight. An abbreviated version reads

> Tyronne first encountered James when they accidentally bumped elbows in a crowded bar... An hour after leaving the bar, Tyronne and a friend spotted James outside a local diner. They approached James slowly, and Tyronne said: 'Why did you bump into me back there?' ... James moved forward, shoved him with both hands, and said: 'Get out of my face.' ...Without hesitating, Tyronne then stepped forward and tried to shove James in the chest, but missed and hit him in the face. James fell back slightly. He then turned around, took a couple steps away from Tyronne, and appeared to reach for something in his pocket. Tyronne quickly pursued James from behind and punched him in the side of the head. James fell to the ground. Tyronne's friend stepped forward and kicked James...

There were three race conditions in the story. Participants read about either William, a Caucasian; Tyronne, an African-American; or Kawika, a Hawaiian. All other facts in the story remained the same. After reading the story and briefly being distracted, participants were given a recall task.

Results of the recall task generally confirmed the hypothesis that participants who read about Tyronne (compared to participants who read about William) had better memories of aggressive behaviors. That is, when asked to recall whether the actor had done something aggressive, participants were more likely to forget about the aggressive action when reading about a William, a Caucasian (compared to participants reading about Tyronne). False memory generation followed a similar, though less systematic pattern. Participants who read about Tyronne in particular were sometimes more likely to generate false memories of aggression.

Results also demonstrated that the memory errors were not related to explicit measures of "social dominance" (Pratto et al., 1994). Results of a social dominance orientation (SDO) task indicated that SDO generally did not predict memory errors. However, for a few individual memory tasks, the SDO score predicted memory errors in an unexpected direction. For these tasks, participants who disfavored social dominance were more likely to misremember aggressive facts in racially biased ways. These results tend to indicate that explicit measures of racial preference do not predict memory errors, but may be occasionally related. From a legal perspective, it is most important to note that people with more explicit racial preferences were not those more likely to manifest memory biases. The results indicate that traditional legal safeguards targeted at intentional acts of racism and explicitly racist discriminators are likely to overlook the harms caused by memory (and related) biases.

SUMMARY AND IMPLICATIONS

Taken together, discussions of implicit biases in legal discourse have challenged some fundamental and well regarded legal principles and processes. Employment discrimination law may rely on legal standards of proof that overlook systematic and unconscious influences on human motivation. The process of allowing peremptory challenges may be propagating discrimination in jury selection. FCC policy on the "public interest" and local news may be increasing discrimination by introducing "Trojan horses" of implicit biases. And legal decision-making itself may be subject to a systematic memory bias, whereby judges and jurors unknowingly misremember case facts in racially biased ways. These new discussions of implicit bias in the legal context illustrate both the progress of legal discourse as well as its untapped potential. Building upon these studies, future projects and collaborations have the opportunity to take even greater steps in achieving racial and social justice.

LEGAL ASSUMPTIONS ABOUT THE
HUMAN MIND

With judges and juries determining the fate of all legal actions, it is not surprising that interdisciplinary researchers frequently investigate legal decision-making. Studies focused on legal decision-making have examined an array of human cognitive processes, including how jurors evaluate information during trials (e.g., Pennington & Hastie, 1990), how judges make pretrial decisions (e.g., Dhami, 2005), and how juries deliberate (e.g., Pritchard & Keenan, 2002; Sommers, 2006). While such endeavors hold obvious importance, new law and psychology scholarship has begun to look at a traditionally under-explored area, the link between laws themselves and the human mind. Because a vast number of laws make explicit assumptions about how people think, it is surprising that only a few research endeavors have looked at how laws themselves may make incorrect assumptions about the way people perceive reality.

The fundamental legal principles of causation and intentionality illustrate how the law makes assumptions about psychological reality. Psychologists will quickly note that these two areas are central to social psychology. Attribution theory and theory of mind research are at the forefront of social psychological contributions and debates (Malle, 2004). Similarly, both causation and intentionality hold enormous legal importance. Causation acts as a prerequisite to liability. When a plaintiff brings an action against a defendant (imagine a lawsuit over a car accident or a class action against a prescription drug manufacturer), the plaintiff must always prove that the defendant's negligence caused the plaintiff's injuries.

Like causation, intentionality acts as a prerequisite to various types of legal liability. In criminal law, for example, the prosecution in a murder trial must prove not only that the defendant killed the victim (causation), but also that the killing was planned, premeditated, or otherwise deliberate. Similarly, in contract law, a party attempting to enforce the terms of a disputed deal will have to demonstrate that the parties intended to be bound by a contract.

CAUSATION AND LAW

The principle of causation helps demonstrate how the law makes psychological assumptions without considering social and cultural psychological knowledge. In the law, when a plaintiff brings a lawsuit against an allegedly negligent defendant, that plaintiff must be prepared to prove both "actual causation" and "proximate causation" (Keeton et al., 1984). Actual causation requires a "but for" counterfactual determination and ensures that a person or company will not be held liable for something that would have happened anyway. Thus, for example, if a drunk bar patron tumbles and falls to the ground solely due to intoxication, a lawsuit would fail against a person who negligently left a slippery banana peel on the ground nearby. Although a banana peel would be sufficient to cause a person to fall, if the patron would have fallen anyway, imposing liability for the patron's injuries would be inappropriate. Proximate causation is more of a policy-driven judgment and often requires jurors to determine whether harm was fore-seeable. Forseeability, like causation, is a psychological question. A jury must determine whether the defendant should have reasonably been able to foresee that harm would happen. Thus, both pieces of the causation inquiry, actual cau-sation and foreseeability, rely upon psychological principles. Yet legal standards relating to such a fundamental psychological process generally ignore psycho-logical knowledge (Levinson & Peng, 2004).

Consider a short hypothetical story: "Rick is speeding on a two-lane road. The road is wet, and a dense fog has settled upon it. Up the road, a bus has run out of gas and has attempted to pull over to the shoulder. The bus, however, is still slightly blocking the roadway. Rick's car hits the bus" (Levinson & Peng, p. 205). If Rick is sued by bus passengers who were injured in the crash, psycho-logical knowledge reveals how two potential legal policy problems policy arise. First, due to "culpable causation" (Alicke, 1992), Rick may be unfairly preju-diced by the actual causation inquiry. Second, because of systematic cultural dif-ferences in the way people perceive actions, if Rick is a cultural minority, he may be penalized for failing to think like a cultural majority member.

Culpable causation predicts that people will more frequently attribute an event's cause to a morally blameworthy party than to a morally good party (Alicke, 1992). Returning to the hypothetical story, if jurors learn that Rick was speeding in order to get home in time to hide drugs he left sitting in plain view (a variation on Alicke's study), they will be more likely to state that Rick's negligent driving is the actual cause of the accident than if Rick was speeding in order to get home to hide a present for his wife. As a result, although the law assumes that causation can be determined without regard to presumably extraneous information such as a person's morality, a morally bad person (or worse, someone incorrectly judged as morally bad) may be penalized. If, as some research suggests (e.g., Pettigrew, 1979), out-group members are more likely to be judged as morally worse people than in-group members, the actual causation inquiry may discrimi-nate against racial minorities and other societal members who are stereotyped as low moral individuals.

The second problem, cultural bias in the causation inquiry, can be illustrated by referencing cultural psychological studies on causal attributions. Cultural psychologists have proposed that attribution styles and processes systematically vary across cultures (Nisbett et al., 2001). According to this model, compared to Westerners, East Asians focus on the field rather than the object, attribute behav-iors as due to situational causes, and view the world as constantly changing. Compared to East Asians, European Americans focus on the object rather than the field, attribute behaviors as due to internal causes, and are resistant to notions of constant change. Cultural psychological studies have corroborated this model by finding systematic cultural differences in the way people attribute causation of various behaviors (e.g., Morris & Peng, 1994).

These systematic cultural differences may affect legal judgments of causation in multicultural settings. Based on cultural differences in attribution styles, Westerners (on a jury, for example) will be more likely than Easterners to find actual causation (Levinson & Peng, 2007a). If Rick, for example, is an East Asian living in the United States, unless he knows that Westerners hold more person-focused causal attribution patterns, he may underestimate the chances of incurring future liability. The law assumes that people have the ability to evaluate the likelihood of future liability and take adequate precautions against it. If, because of cultural differences, some actors predictably underestimate the potential of future liability, they will be more likely to take potentially negligent actions without taking adequate precautions. Such a system will ultimately under-encourage precaution and over-allocate liability to those cultural minorities who are unable to make a culturally competent prediction of liability.

INTENTIONALITY AND LAW

Similar to causation, intentionality is fundamental to legal decision-making. Intentionality frequently works to establish guilt or liability in a variety of legal areas, including criminal law, contract law, tort law, employment discrimination, corporate and securities law, and more. In each of these areas, legal decision-makers are required to make judgments about (typically subjective) mental states of legal actors. Legal standards of intent, like the law's causation standard, tend to overlook psychological reality and ignore cultural differences.

Psychologists have amassed great knowledge about how the human mind evaluates and understands the intents of others (Heider, 1958; Malle & Knobe, 1997; Malle, 2004). As this psychological research developed, legal scholars (and even the Supreme Court) recognized the challenges inherent in determining others' subjective mental states, but overlooked psychology as a tool for critiquing or improving legal standards (*Morissette v. U.S.*, 1952). Only recently have scholars begun to note the potential shortcomings of legal intentionality standards that make unfounded psychological assumptions (Malle & Nelson, 2003; Levinson, 2005).

Criminal Law

Homicide laws present a straightforward area in which to explore how the law's reliance on mental states can be psychologically critiqued. Depending upon the jurisdiction, legal standards vary as to the requisite mental state required in order to prove a killer's guilt. For murder (the most serious form of homicide), common mental state standards include intent to kill, purpose to kill, object to kill, knowledge, deliberation, or premeditation (Levinson, 2005). Typically, the only difference between culpability for one level of homicide versus another is the requisite mental state. A premeditated, intentional killing is viewed as more morally culpable (and therefore a more serious crime) than a reckless killing, for example.

One study (Levinson, 2005) empirically investigated how well American criminal law's mental state standards match the way people think across cultures. Participants in the study were presented with a series of state of mind ambiguous stories designed to mirror criminal cases. For example, participants read about a woman who quickly drove her car backward, hitting her boyfriend. Participants learned that immediately prior to the incident, the woman had witnessed her boyfriend kissing another woman. The scenario was designed to be state of mind ambiguous. That is, the woman may or may not have intended to hit her boyfriend with the car. After reading the stories, participants made a series of mental state judgments derived from different jurisdictions.

Results of the study indicated that some mental state judgments did not function as legal scholars have assumed (Levinson, p. 21). For example, the Model Penal Code, a set of model laws codified by many jurisdictions, assumes that a mental state hierarchy exists: "purpose" is a more culpable mental state than "knowledge," which is in turn more culpable than "reckless" (Model Penal Code, 1985). Yet participants sometimes judged the mental states as being quite similar to one another. Other mental states presumed to be analogous, such as "intent" and "purpose," were judged by participants as being significantly different from one another.

Thus, results of the study indicated that mental states legally assumed to be different were sometimes psychologically perceived to be the same, and mental states legally assumed to be the same were sometimes psychologically perceived to be different. Results also demonstrated that Chinese participants and American participants judged mental state questions in significantly different ways. Chinese participants, for example, were more likely than American participants to state that the actors had acted intentionally. A regression analysis indicated that the participants' processes of making mental state determinations also varied across cultures. Overall, the study suggests that the law must further investigate the psychological assumptions it embeds into laws. This study also demonstrates that the application of legal standards may be dependent upon the cultural perspective of the decision-maker.

Contract Law

Contract law is another area where the law makes assumptions about intentionality. Because contract law attempts to enforce the intents of people and businesses in collaborative relationships, it is important to investigate whether contract law understands human behavior and whether it is culturally competent.

Levinson et al. (2004) tested whether western legal assumptions of contract formation matched psychological judgments of intentionality in the United States and China. The results of the study revealed two main findings. First, Western legal assumptions about the parties' contractual intents were not always corroborated by psychological judgments. Participant responses regarding contractual intent sometimes yielded results opposite from legal assumptions. Second, cultural differences in the way people evaluated contractual expectations emerged systematically. For example, unlike American judgments, Chinese judgments of contractual intent were correlated with a variety of psychological measures, including immorality and guilt.

This finding of cultural differences in the evaluation of contractual intent indicates that Chinese may view contract formation as a fluid, in flux process, as cultural psychological theory would predict. Western laws assume that the immorality and psychological guilt of the seller and are irrelevant to the question of contract formation because formation occurs upon an assent to an offer or a meeting of the minds. The Chinese responses indicate that East Asians may have a more fluid concept of contracts that does not match Western legal assumptions.

SUMMARY AND IMPLICATIONS

The studies that have emerged in the past few years have repeatedly high-lighted two themes. First, legal assumptions about the human mind often do not match psychological reality. Second, people from different cultures perceive events differently based upon their cultural backgrounds. In each case, social and cultural psychological research has sounded a clear warning to legal scholars. The law, replete with psychological concepts and assumptions, must be careful not only about its tendency to deviate from psychological reality, but also about its tendency to ignore cultural differences. Whether it is the importance of building culturally competent laws for an increasingly diverse America, or the danger of implementing international laws and treaties solely based upon Western legal and psychological concepts, the law must heed these calls. Psychology has opened up a meaningful critique of legal discourse. A more complete and culturally competent model of legal standards is a needed response.

BEHAVIORAL ECONOMICS AND LAW

Of the three emerging interdisciplinary areas discussed in this chapter, the most developed area is situated at the intersection of economics, law, and psychology. This three-way collaboration builds upon the field of law and economics, which began with a splash in the early 1960s (Coase, 1960; Calabresi, 1961). Law and economics scholarship focuses on the efficient regulation of entitlements both in consensual exchanges and in competitive situations (Korobkin, 2003). Until the past decade, however, the human behavior element in law and economics meth-odology and analysis had largely been overlooked. In a field dominated by econ-omists, the behavioral assumption was frequently explicit and often wrong: an actor faced with a decision will always act in his or her economic best interests.

Although psychologists were discovering and documenting an impressive list of deviations from rational behavior beginning in the late 1970s (Kahneman & Tversky, 1979), it took legal scholars until the 1990s to think deeply about how laws crafted based upon economic assumptions might overlook meaningful

intricacies of the human mind (Jolls et al., 1998). Once this type of psychologically informed scholarship began, however, it quickly prospered (Kamin &
Rachlinski, 1995; Sunstein, 2000). These projects linking psychology, law and
economics have continued to develop at quite a fast pace, often driven by well
known legal scholars with economic (and occasionally psychological) training.
Research in this area is now frequently called "behavioral law and economics."
Despite the energy and effort placed into this area of study, quite a few
topics, including the influence of culture on behavioral economics, remain
under-explored. This under-exploration results from the simple fact that the law
has been built with a less than accurate (and culturally unaware) model of the
human mind.

HINDSIGHT BIAS AND FRAMING EFFECTS

Within behavioral law and economics, scholars have attempted to analyze
how a wide variety of cognitive biases and heuristics function in the legal realm
(Langevoort, 1998). Two notable examples, hindsight bias and framing effects,
illustrate the way the law is beginning to build a more accurate behavioral
model.

Hindsight Bias in Law

The "hindsight bias" has been well known to psychologists since Fischoff
(1975) first described it. Legal discussion of the hindsight bias and its effects,
like other work in behavioral law and economics, is a fairly new contribution to
discourse (e.g., Arkes & Schipani, 1994; Kamin & Rachlinski, 1995). Yet the
behavioral assumptions underlying the hindsight bias are not new to legal discourse. Perhaps because it is easy for laypersons to understand (consider the well
known phrase "hindsight is 20/20"), court decisions considered it even before
Fischoff documented its existence (Rachlinski, 1998).

An example of one early judicial reaction to hindsight bias, made well before
the boom in behavioral law and economics, is illustrated by corporate law's
"business judgment rule" (Rachlinski, 1998). This rule protects directors of
corporations from shareholder lawsuits based upon negligent decision-making
so long as decisions are made within a broad range of discretion. Essentially,
the business judgment rule means that a company's board of directors can make
decisions without fear of liability, even if those decisions turn out to be poor.
The business judgment rule emerged as courts recognized that allowing liability
for decisions that seem negligent in hindsight (but were not in foresight) would
be injurious to corporate success and efficiency (see *Shlensky v. Wrigley*, 1968).

More recent discussions of the hindsight bias frequently embody the
same concerns as the business judgment rule. Consider tort law, for example.
According to Rachlinski, hindsight bias can affect three types of tort law liability
determinations: "(1) judgments under objective ('should have known') standards;
(2) judgments under subjective ('did know') standards; and (3) judgments of

what was foreseeable" (p. 590). Under each of these analyses, defendants may be penalized because in hindsight their actions will seem more negligent and foreseeable than they actually were.

Behavioral law and economics scholars frequently debate how the law should (or should not) react to cognitive biases (Jolls & Sunstein, 2006). Some scholars believe that decision-makers must be guided away from their biases so that they can make efficient choices (e.g., Sunstein & Thaler, 2003). Others abhor such "paternalistic" approaches. In the case of hindsight bias in tort law, Rachlinski argued that existing safeguards are probably sufficient to avoid unfairness and inefficiency. First, courts have already taken some steps to protect against the harms of hindsight bias. For example, most jurisdictions prohibit the plaintiff from introducing evidence of remedial measures taken by the defendant after the harm occurred, such as building a fence to surround a swimming hole after a child was injured by it. Second Rachlinski argued, although hindsight bias will probably still result in liability for some actions that were not actually negligent, such a result will merely convert the law's negligence standard to a "strict liability" standard. A strict liability standard, also common in tort law, is one where proof of negligence or culpable mental state is not required; causing the harm itself is enough to trigger liability. According to Rachlinski, assuming that people can predict a judge or jury's susceptibility to hindsight bias, they will adjust their behavior to take extra precautions that are consistent with a strict liability system (p. 597). Thus, hindsight bias will simply shift the system of liability and societal actors will continue to have economic incentives to take adequate precautions. Though these precautions will be more expensive, they will still be consistent with an economically efficient system of rules.

Framing Effects in Law

Framing effects emerged as part of Kahneman and Tversky's prospect theory (1979; Tversky & Kahneman, 1986) and, like hindsight bias, have become prominent in discussions of behavioral law and economics (e.g., McCaffery et al., 1995; Zelinsky, 2005). Because of the documented influence of framing effects on risk perception, legal scholars have found it easy enough to comprehend and incorporate into mainstream legal policy discussions. One discussion of framing effects in law surrounds the debate over frivolous litigation. Legal scholars have applied the concept of framing effects not only to explain why frivolous litigation occurs, but also to propose ways to regulate it.

Scholars examining framing effects and loss aversion in litigation and settlement decisions have claimed that prospect theory can explain why frivolous litigation has become a major societal problem (Guthrie, 2000). Whereas a traditional law and economics analysis would attempt to analyze the problem of frivolous litigation by examining the economic incentives of rational litigants, behaviorally informed scholars have recognized that the traditional economic model fails to accurately predict the ways humans evaluate and perceive risk and reward. Guthrie calls this behaviorally informed model of frivolous litigation the

"Frivolous Framing Theory." This theory uses framing effects to explain why legal traditional reform efforts have failed to inhibit frivolous lawsuits.

According to the Frivolous Framing Theory, which is based on the psychological assumption that plaintiffs and defendants evaluate gains and losses differently, "plaintiffs in frivolous litigation... are psychologically inclined toward trial, while defendants in frivolous litigation are psychologically inclined toward settlement" (p. 168). Furthermore, even in settlement negotiations, frivolous plaintiffs will continue their seemingly irrational risk-seeking behavior. As a result of the disconnect between true economic incentives and frivolous plaintiffs' risk-seeking perceptions, settlements will be infrequent. Guthrie uses this psychologically informed model of incentives to argue that the legal system should change legal rules on litigation costs in order to alter the frivolous plaintiff's psychological frame. For example, requiring plaintiffs to advance their own litigation costs would introduce the prospect of loss to otherwise overoptimistic plaintiffs. By ensuring that plaintiffs face "at least some prospect of loss" (p. 210), frivolous plaintiffs would be forced to recalculate their incentives, causing them to favor settlement instead of continued litigation.

BUILDING A BETTER MODEL: CRITIQUING BEHAVIORAL ECONOMICS

Behavioral law and economics has vastly improved the accuracy of legal assumptions by incorporating scientific knowledge of the human mind. Efforts of scholars in this field have helped introduce a psychological component into the legal model of human behavior. Despite this great step, scholarship in behavioral law and economics has yet to incorporate research from two fields, cultural psychology and social cognition. Developing a truly accurate (and culturally competent) behavioral model of law and economics will require addressing these two fields. First, scholars must acknowledge the role of systematic cultural differences in economic decision-making. Current work in behavioral law and economics typically assumes that all people think alike (Levinson & Peng, 2007b). Second, behavioral law and economics typically overlooks the relationship between implicit biases and economic decision-making. Implicit social cognition research demonstrates, among other things that the way people think is affected by stereotypes. If economic decision-making is systematically altered by implicit biases, potentially reallocating entitlements in biased ways, these deviations from efficiency must be addressed. This subsection briefly explains the two-pronged critique of behavioral law and economics scholarship, as applied to the hindsight bias and framing effects.

Hindsight Bias and Stereotypes

Research indicates that the hindsight bias may work to selectively disadvantage people from stereotyped groups. A study by Bodenhausen (1990) investigated the interaction of hindsight bias and stereotypes in criminal trial outcomes.

Participants in the study read about a criminal court case. In the stereotype condition, participants read about either a stereotyped or non-stereotyped defendant. In the outcome information condition, participants either received outcome information (guilty or not guilty) or no outcome information. After reading about the case, participants were asked to estimate the likely outcome of the trial.

Not surprisingly, the study demonstrated hindsight bias in most conditions. Generally, participants who read about a defendant who was found guilty were more likely to predict a guilty outcome compared to those who read about a defendant who was found not guilty. The most interesting results, however, indicated that participants who read about not-guilty defendants from stereotyped groups did not display hindsight bias. Even when the participants had learned that the stereotyped defendant had been found not guilty, they were just as likely to predict a guilty outcome as those who read about a guilty defendant. Thus, the results of the study showed that, at least in the case of not-guilty defendants, stereotype information overcame the hindsight bias.

As Bodenhausen's (1990) study demonstrated, when hindsight bias is combined with stereotypes, members of stereotyped groups may be harmed. This stereotype-hindsight bias interaction could result in greater conviction rates for defendants from stereotyped groups. For example, suppose that a person is on trial for attempted murder. A conviction for attempted murder requires, (1) an intent to kill or commit great bodily harm combined with (2) taking actions in furtherance of the crime. Often, the only difference between a murder charge and an attempted murder charge is the outcome of the crime, whether the victim has died or not. In an attempted murder trial, the jury generally knows the outcome information, that the victim was not killed. As a result, the hindsight bias could affect jurors' judgments of whether the defendant intended to kill the victim or not. Because the victim did not die, the hindsight bias could make it less likely that a jury would believe that a defendant intended to kill the victim.

From a behavioral economic perspective, one might attempt to figure out how to minimize the effects of the hindsight bias. After all, the hindsight bias would result in the acquittal (or perhaps the conviction of a lesser offense) of some defendants that should have been convicted of attempted murder. However, of perhaps greater concern is the possibility that stereotyped defendants will be treated more harshly by the hindsight bias-stereotype interaction. In the case of stereotyped defendants, Bodenhausen's study indicates that jurors will disregard the outcome information (the fact that the victim did not die). Instead, they will be influenced by the stereotype (that the defendant is aggressive). Thus, based solely on the interaction between the hindsight bias and stereotypes, more stereotyped defendants will be convicted than non-stereotyped defendants in otherwise identical trials. Obviously such a result is at odds with the goals of the legal system. Behavioral economic scholarship should not ignore these potential stereotype effects.

Framing Effects and Cultural Differences

Discussions of framing effects in legal discourse generally ignore cultural differences. For example, Guthrie's (2000) discussion of Frivolous Framing Theory does not address whether people from different cultures may be influenced differently by framing effects. A recent study found that Americans and Chinese reacted differently to framing effects (Levinson & Peng, 2007b). In that study, participants in China not only demonstrated stronger framing effects than participants in the United States, but also exhibited framing effects that interacted with other variables, including in-group and out-group membership as well as morality information.

Like most behavioral economic theories, Frivolous Framing Theory assumes that all people display the same framing effects as they evaluate litigation and settlement possibilities. This assumption is probably accurate so long as it attempts to predict and evaluate the litigation behaviors of culturally homogenous Western actors. Yet Frivolous Framing Theory's current formulation would not accurately predict the cognitive behavioral perspective of an East Asian plaintiff, for example. Incorporating cultural differences into Frivolous Framing Theory will require further research on cultural differences in framing effects and a more sophisticated model. Like with other models based upon universalistic assumptions about cognitive biases, incorporating cultural knowledge provides the hope of an accurate and culturally competent model of behavioral economics.

SUMMARY AND IMPLICATIONS

Research in behavioral economics has triggered major advancements in legal theory. Economic models of law that previously ignored systematic deviations from rational predictions now are behaviorally competent. Scholars that tended to ignore how the human mind really works now spend significant time thinking about how humanity, law, and economics intersect. Yet this is only the first step. As interdisciplinary collaborations continue to prosper, scholars will build an accurate, unbiased, and culturally competent legal economic model of behavior. Only then will behavioral law and economics truly achieve its goals.

CONCLUSION

The incorporation of psychological knowledge into legal models has helped to dramatically improve the law's human and behavioral competence. Of the three developing areas discussed in this chapter, each one has made great strides in building an accurate legal model of human behavior. Yet big challenges remain. Despite the psychological progress, legal standards relating to discrimination still require proof of explicit discriminatory intent. Legally embedded concepts such as intentionality and causation continue to overlook psychological reality and cultural differences. And scholarship building a more psychologically accurate model of law and economics continues to assume that all people think alike. For these reasons, the need for informed collaborations between legal scholars and psychologists is as great as ever.

REFERENCES

Alicke, M. D. (1992). Culpable causation. *Journal of Personality and Social Psychology*, *63*, 368–378.

Arkes, H. R., & Schipani, C. A. (1994). Medical malpractice and the business judgment rule: Differences in hindsight bias. *Oregon Law Review*, *73*, 587–638.

Banaji, M. R., Hardin, C., & Rothman, A. J. (1993). Implicit stereotyping in person judgment. *Journal of Personality and Social Psychology*, *65*(2), 272–281.

Batson v. Kentucky, 476 U.S. 79 (1986).

Bodenhausen, G. V. (1990). Second-guessing the jury: Stereotypic and hindsight biases in perceptions of court cases. *Journal of Applied Social Psychology*, *20*, 1112–1121.

Calabresi, G. (1961). Some thoughts on risk distribution and the law of torts. *Yale Law Journal*, *70*, 499–553.

Coase, R. H. (1960). The problem of social cost. *Journal of Law and Economics*, *3*, 1–44.

Dasgupta, N., & Asgari, S. (2004). Seeing is believing: Exposure to counterstereotypic women leaders and its effect on automatic gender stereotyping. *Journal of Experimental Social Psychology*, *40*, 642–658.

Dasgupta, N., & Greenwald, A. G. (2001). On the malleability of automatic attitudes: Combating automatic prejudice with images of admired and disliked individuals. *Journal of Personality and Social Psychology*, *81*(5), 800–814.

Dhami, M. K. (2005). From discretion to disagreement: Explaining disparities in judges pretrial decisions. *Behavioral Sciences and the Law*, *23*, 367–386.

Dougherty, M. R. P., Gronlund, S. D., & Gettys, C. F. (2003). Memory as a fundamental heuristic for decision making. In S. L. Schneider & J. Shanteau (Eds.), *Emerging perspectives on judgment and decision research* (pp. 125–164). Cambridge, MA: Cambridge University Press.

Fischoff, B. (1975). Hindsight ≠ foresight: The effect of outcome knowledge on judgment under uncertainty. *Journal of Experimental Psychology: Human Perception and Performance*, *1*, 288–299.

Gilbert, D. T., & Hixon, J. G. (1991). The trouble of thinking: Activation and application of stereotypic beliefs. *Journal of Personality and Social Psychology*, *60*(4), 509–517.

Greenwald, A. G., & Banaji, M. R. (1995). Implicit social cognition: Attitudes, self-esteem, and stereotypes. *Psychological Review*, *102*(1), 4–27.

Green, T. (2005). Work culture and discrimination. *California Law Review*, *93*, 623–684.

Guthrie, C. (2000). Framing frivolous litigation: A psychological theory. *University of Chicago Law Review*, *67*, 163–216.

Hart, M. (2005). Subjective decisionmaking and unconscious discrimination. *Alabama Law Review*, *56*, 741–791.

Heider, F. (1958). *The psychology of interpersonal relations*. New York: Wiley.

Jolls, C., & Sunstein, C. (2006). Debiasing through law. *Journal of Legal Studies*, *35*, 199–241.

Jolls, C., Sustein, C., & Thaler, R. (1998). A Behavioral approach to law and economics. *Stanford Law Review*, *50*, 1471–1550.

Kahneman, D., & Tversky, A. (1979). Prospect theory: An analysis of decision under risk. *Econometrica*, *47*, 263–291.

Kamin, K. A., & Rachlinski, J. (1995). Ex post ≠ ex ante: Determining liability in hindsight. *Law and Human Behavior*, *19*, 89–104.

Kang, J. (2005). Trojan horses of race. *Harvard Law Review, 118*, 1489–1593.

Kang, J., & Banaji, M. R. (2006). Fair measures: A behavioral realist revision of "affirmative action". *California Law Review, 94*, 1063–1118.

Keeton, W. P. et al. (Eds.) (1984). Prosser and Keeton on the law of torts. St. Paul, MN: West Group.

Krieger, L. H. (1995). The content of our categories: A cognitive bias approach to discrimination and equal employment opportunity. *Stanford Law Review, 47*, 1161–1248.

Korobkin, R. (2003). Empirical legal realism: A new social scientific assessment of law and human behavior: The endowment effect and legal analysis. *Northwestern University Law Review, 97*, 1227–1293.

Langevoort, D. (1998). Behavioral theories of judgment and decision making in legal scholarship: A literature review. *Vanderbilt Law Review, 51*, 1499–1540.

Lawrence, C. (1987). The id, the ego, and equal protection: Reckoning with unconscious racism. *Stanford Law Review, 39*, 317–388.

Lee, A. (2005). Unconscious bias theory in employment discrimination litigation. *Harvard Civil Rights-Civil Liberties Law Review, 40*, 481–503.

Lenton, A. P., Blair, I. V., & Hastie, R. (2001). Illusions of gender: Stereotypes evoke false memories. *Journal of Experimental Social Psychology, 37*, 3–14.

Levinson, J. D. (2005). Mentally misguided: How state of mind inquiries ignore psychological reality and overlook cultural differences. *Howard Law Journal, 49*, 1–29.

Levinson, J. D. (2007). Forgotten racial equality: Implicit bias, decision making and misremembering. *Duke Law Journal, 57*, 345–424.

Levinson, J. D., & Peng, K. (2004). Different torts for different cohorts: A cultural psychological critique of tort law's actual cause and foreseeability inquiries. *Southern California Interdisciplinary Law Journal, 13*, 195–226.

Levinson, J. D., & Peng, K. (2007a). *Collective causal inquires: How culture-specific theories of agency affect culpable causation and legal judgments.* Unpublished manuscript.

Levinson, J. D., & Peng, K. (2007b). Valuing cultural differences in behavioral economics. *ICFAI Journal of Behavioral Finance, 4*, 32–47.

Levinson, J. D., Peng, K., & Wang, L. (2004). Let's make a deal: Understanding the cultural psychological basis of contract formation. Unpublished manuscript.

Macrae, C. N., Schloerscheidt, A. M., Bodenhausen, G. V., & Milne, A. B. (2002). Creating memory illusions: Expectancy-based processing and the generation of false memories. *Memory, 10*, 63–80.

Malle, B. F. (2004). *How the mind explains behavior: Folk explanations, meaning, and social interaction.* Cambridge, MA: MIT Press.

Malle, B. F., & Knobe, J. (1997). The Folk concept of intentionality. *Journal of Experimental Social Psychology, 33*, 101–121.

Malle, B. F., & Nelson, S. E. (2003). Judging mens rea: The tension between folk concepts and legal concepts of intentionality. *Behavioral Sciences and the Law, 21*, 563–580.

McCaffery, E. J., Kahneman, D., & Spitzer, M. L. (1995). Framing the jury: Cognitive perspectives on pain and suffering awards. *Virginia Law Review, 81*, 1341–1420.

McGinley, A. C. (2000). !Viva la evolucion! Recognizing unconscious motive in Title VII. *Cornell Journal of Law and Public Policy, 9*, 415–492.

Model Penal Code (1985). Section 2.02(4). American Law Institute.

Morissette v. U.S., 342 U.S. 246 (1952).

Morris, M., & Peng, K. (1994). Culture and cause: American and Chinese attributions for social and physical events. *Journal of Personality and Social Psychology, 67*, 949–971.

Nisbett, R. E., Peng, K., Choi, I., & Norenzayan, A. (2001). Culture and systems of thought: Holistic vs. analytic cognition. *Psychological Review, 108*, 291–310.

Page, A. (2005). Batson's blind-spot: Unconscious stereotyping and the peremptory challenge. *Boston University Law Review, 85*, 155–262.

Payne, B. K. (2001). Prejudice and perception: The role of automatic and controlled processes in misperceiving a weapon. *Journal of Personality and Social Psychology, 81*, 181–192.

Pennington, N., & Hastie, R. (1988). Explanation based decision making: Effects of memory structure on judgment. *Journal of Experimental Psychology: Learning, Memory and Cognition, 14*, 521–533.

Pennington, N., & Hastie, R. (1990). Practical implications of psychological research on juror and jury decision making. *Personality and Social Psychology Bulletin, 16*, 90–105.

Pettigrew, T. F. (1979). The ultimate attribution error: Extending Allport's cognitive analysis of prejudice. *Personality and Social Psychology Bulletin, 5*, 461–476.

Pollard, D. (1999). Unconscious bias and self critical analysis: The case for a qualified evidentiary equal employment opportunity privilege. *Washington Law Review, 74*, 913–1031.

Pratto, F., Sidanius, J., Stallworth, L. M., & Malle, B. F. (1994). Social dominance orientation: A personality variable predicting social and political attitudes. *Journal of Personality and Social Psychology, 67*, 741–763.

Pritchard, M., & Keenan, J. M. (1999). Memory monitoring in mock jurors. *Journal of Experimental Psychology: Applied, 5*, 152–168.

Pritchard, M., & Keenan, J. M. (2002). Does jury deliberation really improve jurors' memories?. *Journal of Applied Cognitive Psychology, 16*, 589–601.

Rachlinski, J. J. (1998). A positive theory of judging in hindsight. *University of Chicago Law Review, 65*, 571–625.

Shlensky v. Wrigley, 237 N.E.2d 776 (Ill. App. 1968).

Sommers, S. R. (2006). On racial diversity and group decision-making: Identifying multiple effects of racial composition on jury deliberations. *Journal of Personality and Social Psychology, 90*, 597–612.

Sommers, S. R., & Norton, M. I. (2007). Race-based judgments, race-neutral justifications: Experimental examination of peremptory use and the Batson challenge procedure. *Law and Human Behavior, 31*, 261–273.

Sunstein, C. R. (Eds.) (2000). *Behavioral Law and Economics* (Ed.). New York: Cambridge University Press.

Sunstein, C. R., & Thaler, R. H. (2003). Libertarian paternalism is not an oxymoron. *University of Chicago Law Review, 70*, 1159–1202.

Tversky, A., & Kahneman, D. (1986). Rational choice and the framing of decisions. *Journal of Business, 59*, 251–277.

Washington v. Davis, 426 U.S. 229 (1976).

Weber, E. U., Goldstein, W. M., & Barlas, S. (1995). And let us not forget memory: The role of memory processes and techniques in the study of judgment and choice. In J. R. Busemeyer, R. Hastie, & D. L. Medin (Eds.), *The psychology of learning and motivation: Decision making from a cognitive perspective* (pp. 33–82). San Diego: Academic Press.

Zelinsky, E. A. (2005). Do tax expenditures create framing effects? Volunteer firefighters, property tax exemptions, and the paradox of tax expenditure analysis. *Virginia Tax Review, 24*, 797–834.

19

THE PSYCHOLOGICAL PROCESS OF COPING WITH THREAT AND ITS CULTURAL MAINTENANCE FUNCTION

EMIKO S. KASHIMA

La Trobe University, Victoria, Australia

Adverse life events such as separation, loss of face, and unexpected life changes are unavoidable part of human life. They are instances of symbolic threat; an impairment of social motives that we implicitly and explicitly subscribe to and strive for. The ways in which symbolic threats are experienced and managed depend to some extent on the individuals and their circumstance. Some individuals react more to a certain type of threat more than others; they may gain more satisfaction when certain goals are achieved rather than others. Further, the world's major religious doctrines and folk theories across cultures construe human suffering and coping in distinct ways. In this chapter, I will consider the relationship between culture and human reactions to threats.

Culture is a collection of meanings and practices that are shared by a large group of people, making group life possible and thereby advancement of knowledge itself viable (Triandis, 1979). Throughout the evolutionary history, humans developed an immense advantage over other animal species because of their evolved characteristic to share knowledge (Boyd & Richerson, 1985, 1990;

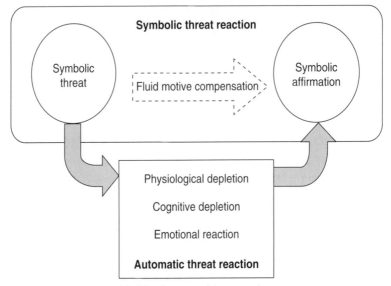

FIGURE 19.1   The individual-level process of threat reactions.

Baumeister, 2005). This enabled the more experienced and competent members of the group to impart their knowledge that had been tested and improved by themselves and their forerunners to the less experienced and less capable (Navarrete & Fessler, 2005). Perhaps, the human tendency to be subjected to and react to symbolic threats might be a part of this species-specific practice of cultural transmission.

Given the overwhelming advantage of culture for individual and group survival, a psychological mechanism that ensured the individual's adherence to, and within-group maintenance of, the shared knowledge would have been critical. While some animal species including humans physically threaten others to dominate and gain own advantages (Sapolsky, 2004) humans are unique in their ability to threaten self as well as others by using culturally shared meanings. Likewise, humans are capable of symbolically alleviating the psychological injuries experienced by self and other. In other words, culture is both an antecedent and a consequence of threat for an individual, with an important group-level implication of knowledge preservation. The more the given meaning is activated, used, and encoded in the memory of the people who participated in the event, the more likely it becomes that this meaning is used in the future of people.

To advance this view regarding culture and threat reactions, first I will briefly discuss the unique human aspect of threat reactions I refer to as *symbolic affirmation*, followed by a short discussion of non-symbolic, automatic consequences of threat which humans may share with many lower animals (see Figure 19.1). In so doing, I will highlight some of the basic principles involved in these processes of threat reaction, guided by a review of recent literature, such as compensatory satisfaction of motives, and physiological and cognitive depletions that follow threat.

I will then turn to the topic of individual differences in threat reactions. A brief review of the literature suggests that some individuals are more susceptible to certain threats than others. Furthermore, some people react to a threat more autonomously by maintaining their personal control while others in react to the same threat less autonomously by conforming and adjusting to others. These differences will be analyzed in terms of individuals' psychological resources. It will be argued that individuals with more limited psychological resource are more vulnerable to threats, consistent to the notion that cultural knowledge is transmitted from experts to novices. I will also propose that repeated resource depletions through the experiences of threat would lead the victim to be other-dependent and conforming rather than autonomous and agentic.

The view taken in this paper assumes that symbolic affirmation and automatic reactions that follow threat are universal. Nevertheless, human cultural adaptation that took place in different parts of the globe over the long human history facilitated cultural variations across groups. Cross-cultural research on values for instance has demonstrated that even though people from different cultures adopted to their diverse life problems by using similar abstract principles, cultural groups do vary in terms of which value types they find more or less important as guiding principles in their life (e.g., Schwartz & Bilsky, 1990). If values that people depend on in dealing with their major life issues differ across groups, there should also be differences in the content of the meanings that people find more or less threatening, and likewise, the content of meanings that they affirm to cope with those threats. I will thus present a brief review of research that shows cultural variability in symbolic threats. Finally, I will submit a theoretical framework that posits the relationship between culture and threat reactions, and in doing so, highlight the social processes that contribute to both individual's threat reactions and the collective maintenance of meaning.

SYMBOLIC THREATS AND REACTIONS

Threat can relate to a variety of sources such as social evaluation, situational uncertainty, physical danger to life, and various personal and interpersonal issues. In the early days of psychological research on threat, Maslow (1943) has observed threats as involving the feeling that one's basic goals and needs, or the conditions upon which they rest, are in danger of being thwarted. Allport (1943, p. 470) took a view that many of those conceptually distinct social motives indeed serve essentially a common goal and that they are therefore mutually substitutive, thus highlighting the notion of fluid compensation among motives. In doing so, Allport also emphasized the notion of ego-involvement in threat process, stating that "frustration of goal-seeking behavior or any kind of threat to the individual is very likely to engage the ego-system." Issues concerning the assumption of how one relates to the world, and more generally, how aspects of this world relate coherently to one another, are experienced as unsettling, anxiety provoking, or even painful at times. These issues are referred to as *symbolic threat*. A distinction is often drawn between threat, a focus of this paper, and demand, which reflects the stress experienced when perceived situational demand is appraised as excessive (Lazarus & Folkman, 1984; Kuhl, 2000).

Over the years, researchers have investigated various forms of threat reactions, such as self- or ego-threat, collective identity threat, social rejection and ostracism, anticipation of noxious stimuli, learned helplessness, expectation violation, worldview threat, subjective uncertainty and meaninglessness, thoughts of own death, and psychological contamination by filthy, immoral objects. Individual reactions to these threats have been observed with regard to a number of psychological processes and outcomes, such as emotional responses, physiological arousal, self-regulation and coping strategies, to name a few. It is not a goal of this paper to file those different forms of threat reactions, and readers are referred to some excellent reviews by authors such as Heine et al. (2006), Sherman and Cohen (2006), and Steele et al. (2002).

The voluminous literature has highlighted some important notions that are common to symbolic threat reactions of all forms. Threat, at the individual level, is essentially a motivational process in which an actor experiences a psychological arousal when a motive (a goal, a valued meaning, a desiderata) is thwarted or damaged. This may occur when the person's goal pursuit or a state desired by the person is blocked by other or situational circumstances. The person can be released from this psychologically unsettling state by engaging in an act that brings a closure. This process involves *symbolic affirmation* or satisfaction of the motive through reaffirming the valued meaning. Over decades, much social psychological research has evidenced, however, that motivational closure can be achieved through alternative paths, by affirming valued meanings that are distinct from the one injured. Thus, a person whose sense of personal integrity was impaired by a public blunder can regain composure by revealing his/her very integrity, or alternatively, by glorifying his/her personal hero instead, for instance. Gaining a closure via satisfaction of an alternative motive has been referred to as motive compensation (Allport, 1943; Steele et al., 1993). Research has also highlighted that affirming a certain valued meaning first protects the individual against the subsequent attack on the same or an alternative motive.

Social psychology literature in the last half century has brought to light an amalgam of social motives to be at the foundation of various social behaviors and psychological phenomena. Between the 1950s and 1970s, attitude research highlighted cognitive dissonance as a galvanizer of attitude change whereas research on social comparison, social facilitation, attribution and the like underscored the import of self-motives. Research in the 1980s and 1990s further unearthed the various forms of self-motives including self-affirmation (Steele, 1988), self-efficacy (Bandura, 1986), self-enhancement (e.g., Taylor & Brown, 1988; Kunda, 1990), self-improvement

(Taylor et al., 1995), and self-verification (e.g., Swann, 1987). Researchers in the area of close relationships stressed the needs for attachment and intimacy (Baumeister & Leary, 1995; Reis et al., 2000), whereas group researchers, the needs for affiliation, belonging, self-esteem, and epistemic certainty (Tajfel, 1981; Hogg & Abrams, 1993; Hornsey & Jetten, 2004). In contrast to these theories that focused on single types of motives, researchers also put forward the models that adopted multiple motives and posited some flexible compensatory relationships among them.

Thus, building on Allport's (1943) notion of fluid motive compensation, Steele (1988) and Steele et al. (1993) proposed that the general need for self-affirmation, rather than the more specific needs for consistency, control, competence, and personal values, to be at the core of various self-threats and to be responsible for such processes as attribution and attitude change (see Sherman & Cohen, 2006, for a more recent review). Tesser (1988, 2000) also argued that self-esteem governs social comparison, dissonance reduction, and self-affirmation processes, and more recently, Sedikides and Strube (1997) proposed the SCENT model, arguing that self-verification, self-assessment, and self-improvement all serve self-enhancement ends. By contrast, Terror Management Theory (Greenberg et al., 1997) made a claim that a dual buffering system comprised cultural worldview and self-esteem protects people from the terror of death or symbolic immortality needs. Taking a step further, Mikulincer, Shaver, and their colleagues (Mikulincer et al., 2002; Hart et al., 2005) have advanced a model of tripartite security system such that attachment, worldviews, and self-esteem flexibly guard people from the threats about symbolic immortality, cultural worldview, and self-esteem. Furthermore, Heine et al. (2006) advanced Meaning Maintenance Model, advocating that the most fundamental goal of humans amongst all is the maintenance of meaning frameworks, and that goals of maintaining self-esteem, certainty, belonging, and symbolic immortality fluidly compensate for one another to achieve this common, larger end.

In short, what seems common in these different models of fluid motive compensation is the notion that humans constantly engage in reconstruction of their meaningful world or its part, especially when they find meanings that are psychologically important are under attack. Symbolic immortality, group values, self-integrity, and the like are universal motives for people; as such, symbolic affirmation of these meanings ought to be universal and uniquely human. Interestingly, however, some of the important social motives such as attachment and affiliation not only play a vital role in the human motivational process as suggested by some theorists (e.g., Mikulincer et al., 2002), but also contribute to the adaptation of animals (Sapolsky, 2004). Research suggests, for instance, that laboratory animals that are maternally deprived show biobehavioral signs of stress and maladjustment whereas those that are maternally tended adapt better (see Taylor et al., 2000, for a review). Thus, understanding of human threat reactions should involve the knowledge of the non-symbolic side shared with other animals, which I will briefly visit in the next section.

NON-SYMBOLIC THREAT REACTIONS

Non-symbolic or automatic processes of threat reactions have also been investigated expensively over decades, spawning several distinct literatures. Recent research is beginning to bring those separate research literatures together. The knowledge concerning physiological reactions to threats, the change in cognitive resources that accompanies those reactions, the parallel attentional and affective processes is increasingly being integrated.

That stressful events trigger physiological arousals such as cardiovascular reactivities and affect neuroendocrine responses with long-term as well as short-term implications for well-being is widely accepted. Importantly, however, research suggests (e.g., Tomaka et al., 1993) that the state of threat, resulting from an appraisal of situational demands exceeding available resources, has distinct physiological consequences from the state of challenge, resulting from an appraisal of resources exceeding demands, one of the central theses of the cognitive model of stress and coping (Lazarus & Folkman, 1984). For instance, threat is negatively related to cardiac reactivity and positively related to vascular resistance, whereas challenge is positively related to cardiac reactivity and negatively related to vascular resistance (Blascovich & Tomaka, 1996). Recently, Dickerson and Kemeny (2004) quantitatively integrated over 200 experiments that examined neuroendocrine reactions to motivated cognitive tasks in laboratories and concluded that a lack of personal control and an anticipated social evaluation have reliable and independent impacts on physiological responses of individuals. Social evaluation, manipulated by anticipated performance evaluation, video-recording, or social comparison, as well as situations of low personal control, triggered an immediate increase in the salivary cortisol level and required longer to return to the normal levels. Interestingly, multiple sources of social evaluation were found to have greater impacts than a single source of social evaluation. Further, experimental studies have shown that cortisol reactions are a consequence rather than an antecedent of threats (Tomaka et al., 1997).

Research has also highlighted the high relevance of cortisol reactions to social relationships. For instance, Dickerson et al. (2004) reported that evaluation of performance by other rather than by self produced cortisol activation. Powers et al. (2006) highlighted the role of attachment in moderating stress–cortisol relationship. Blascovich et al. (2001) have shown that individuals interacting with partners who were stigmatized (versus non-stigmatized), due to their facial birthmark or minority group membership, exhibited elevated cortisol reactions as well as poorer performance. Personal and collective self-esteem, the sense of optimism, and perceived control are also linked to cortisol reactions (Matheson & Cole, 2004; see Sapolsky, 2004, concerning lower animals). Finally, cortisol reactions to threats are linked to behavioral performance (Blascovich & Tomaka, 1996, for a review). Research evidence therefore generally stresses the notion that a symbolic threat is accompanied by a pattern of physiological reactions that correspond to the "fight-or-flight" reaction (Cannon, 1914). It may be added, however, Taylor et al. (2000) propose that this picture may be somewhat modified in their new perspective that suggests female responses to threats reveal building on attachment-caregiving processes which down-regulate such fight-or-flight sympathetic responses, mediated by the "hormone of love" oxytocin.

The link between threat and depletion of cognitive resources has also been long recognized. Easterbrook (1959) in his cue utilization theory predicted that high levels of arousal will lead to attention narrowing. Wachtel (1968) found a threat slows down responses to stimuli presented at the periphery but not at the center of attention, whereas Geen (1976) also reported that evaluation apprehension leads to cognitive overload with a similar tendency. More recent work by Baumeister, Gailliot, and their colleagues has suggested that an effort to cope with threat through self-regulation of thoughts and affect consumes mental energy, causing "ego-depletion" (Baumeister et al., 2006). For instance, social rejection may lead to poorer performances in tasks such as dichotic listening (Baumeister et al., 2005). Viewing an emotion-provoking movie impairs performance of demanding cognitive tasks (Schmeichel et al., 2003) and unfamiliar self-regulation effort may produce a social blunder (Schmeichel et al., 2003; Vohs et al., 2005). Terror Management Theory also predicts that supraliminal mortality threat leads to a state of limited cognitive resource through effort to suppress death-related thoughts, producing behaviors that validate cultural worldview and self-esteem (Pyszczynski et al., 1999). Subliminal priming of death thoughts also induces this state (e.g., Arndt et al., 1997). Evidence therefore supports that the experience of symbolic threat is likely to lead to the state of limited conscious resource, which may force the individual to seek cognitive closure, using simpler structures and heuristics, reliance on implicit cognition, and exercising generally lower discriminative facility (e.g., Chiu et al., 1995; Kruglanski & Webster, 1996; Cheng, 2003; Landou et al., 2004; Gailliot et al., 2006; see also Dittes, 1961; Yang & Yang, 1973; van den Bos & Lind, 2002).

That threats generate negative emotion is also well documented, although its role in the threat coping process is controversial. Self-regulation theorists claim that a perceived discrepancy between the self and a standard for the self instigates negative emotions which in turn prompt a discrepancy-reducing behavior (Carver & Scheier, 1981; Higgins, 1987; Carver, 2001). Other researchers have suggested that affective reaction is a mere by-product of threats (e.g., Schmeichel et al., 2003; Baumeister et al., 2006), including terror management theorists who maintain that affect is unrelated to effects of mortality salience. However, research that examines implicit, non-conscious affect implies an involvement of unconscious affect in threat coping processes. One such study by Koole et al. (1999) has shown that self-affirmation led to an activation of positive affect which in turn alleviated rumination of negative thoughts. Also, Arndt et al. (2001) found by using facial electromyography (EMG) that mortality salience increases the facial expression of fear, a manifestation of negative implicit affect which, according to recent research, relates to elevated cortisol responses moderated by optimism (Lerner et al., 2005). Arndt et al. nevertheless found EMG to be unrelated to cultural worldview defense, maintaining the independence of mortality salience effects and affect. In addition, research has also highlighted the facilitative effects of emotion in attention, decision making, and learning from the negative experience (Baumeister, 2005) as well as those of positive affect during coping (e.g., Aspinwall, 1998; Isen & Shmidt, 2007).

A recent model of self-regulation also stresses the role played by negative affect in coping with threats. According to Personality Systems Integration Theory (Kuhl, 2000), negative affect triggered by threat makes the person preoccupied by the source of threat and ruminate (Koole & Jostmann, 2004; Baumann et al., 2005). To be freed from this state, individuals must access their self-memories, called extension memory in the theory, which assists down-regulating negative affect. The efficiency in engaging in this process depends on the individual difference in state versus action orientation. For example, after being exposed to a threat, it takes a longer time for state-oriented (versus action-oriented) people to remove negative affect. At the same time, they also experience more difficulty in distinguishing between what is socially imposed by other people and their own intrinsic needs, a state referred to as self-infiltration (Baumann et al., 2005). Kazen et al. (2005) demonstrated that after a mortality threat, action-oriented people were able to down-regulate their negative affect and present their negative ingroup identity in more positive light. Jostmann et al. (2005) have shown that state-oriented (versus action-oriented) people were more influenced by subliminally presented schematic faces with angry, neutral, and happy expressions. The emerging research therefore seems to suggest that there is an individual difference in how efficiently the negative emotions caused by threats are dealt with.

In summary, symbolic threats activate a series of automatic processes for the person to cope with the crisis physiologically, cognitively, and affectively, as well as symbolically. The literature has suggested that physiological reactions are the consequence of psychological threat appraisal rather than cause of it; however, as to how cognitive depletion and affective changes relate to psychological and physiological reactions it is still unclear. Is cognitive depletion a consequence of physiological change that follow from threat appraisal, or a consequence of self-regulatory attempt to, for example, suppress negative thoughts or negative emotion? The answer must await future research. Regardless, it seems plausible that cognitive depletion during the experience of threat urges individuals to react in a manner distinct from those who are not threatened. For instance, due to the cognitive limitation, might threatened individuals tend to follow behavioral options that are relatively economical, such as behaviors that are perceptually salient, conforming to a majority or simply have been well practiced? To elaborate on this question, I will now discuss individual differences in threat reaction.

PSYCHOLOGICAL RESOURCES AND
THREAT REACTIONS

There are individual differences in threat reactions. Some people are more robust than others at the face of an impending symbolic threat. Also, once threatened, some are anticipated to respond in greater magnitudes than others, with more intense physiological arousal and negative affect, taking longer to recover from them, and/or showing more depletion of working memory. Moreover, the manner in which symbolic affirmation is shown may also differ across individuals.

Many personality variables are associated with a diversity of threat reactions (Cohen & Edwards, 1989). Literature has suggested that psychological defense against threats may be tighter among those with higher self-esteem (e.g., Crocker & Park, 2004; Pyszczynski et al., 2004), a stronger sense of personal control (e.g., Lachman & Weaver, 1998), trait self-control (Gailliot et al., 2006), optimism (e.g., Scheier & Carver, 1985; Rasmussen et al., 2006), sense-making abilities (e.g., Taylor, 1983), self-complexity (e.g., Linville, 1987), hardiness (e.g., Weibe, 1991), secure-attachment style (e.g., Bowlby, 1982; Mikulincer et al., 2002), intrinsic religiosity (e.g., Jonas & Fischer, 2006), and action orientation (Kuhl, 2000).

In particular, self-esteem has received much attention of researchers. Although downsides of high self-esteem (hereafter HSE) accompanied by fragile self-esteem and narcissism are noted (e.g., Baumeister et al., 1993; Jordan et al., 2003), HSE people, in comparison to their low self-esteem (LSE) counterpart, have been found to show more robust physiological responses, both immediately after the threatening incident and over a long time period (Tomaka et al., 1999; Taylor et al., 2003a, b), lower sensitivity to negative daily events (e.g., Campbell & Lavallee, 1993), and lower rate of depression (Hokanson et al., 1989). Also, HSE people tend to be more self-affirming when threatened with negative personal feedback (e.g., Brockner, 1979; McFarlin & Blascovich, 1981; Taylor & Brown, 1988; Kernis et al., 1989; Beauregard & Dunning, 1998; Dodgson & Wood, 1998; Murray et al., 2002; Sommer & Baumeister, 2002), in situations involving personal and relational uncertainties (McGregor & Marigold, 2003), and when own mortality is made salient (see for a review, Pyszczynski et al., 2004). Evidence then suggests that HSE individuals may have greater psychological resources to avoid and deal with threats.

What might be the reason? According to Terror Management Theory (Greenberg et al., 1997) individuals gain self-esteem from the self-perception of possessing the qualities prescribed by the cultural norms and worldviews. Thus, cultural worldviews are the basis of self-esteem, and both of them together provide the person with the psychological resource to cope with threats. Hart et al. (2005) maintain a similar view about the strength of securely attached individuals. In their view, individuals internalize societal norms through developing a secure attachment with an authority figure early in their life. In contrast, sociometer theory (Leary & Baumeister, 2000) explains that individuals gain self-esteem through belongingness; humans as social animals depend on group living, coop-eration, and social support to survive. As such, self-esteem is an indicator of the person's acceptance and rejection by others, and assists the person to monitor and regulate his/her social adaptation.

Regardless of theories, then, HSE individuals are suggested to be those who accumulate plentiful psychological resources over time through posi-tive interactions with others. Nonetheless, when one is faced with a looming threat, an opportunity to think of own strengths, meanings that seem impor-tant, and individuals and groups who are accommodating to the self can pro-vide an immediate boost to one's psychological resources, and thereby produce heartier responses to symbolic threats (Tomaka et al., 1993, 1999; Tomaka & Blascovich, 1994; Harmon-Jones et al., 1997; Clark et al., 1999; Pruessner et al., 1999; Matheson & Cole, 2004; Seery et al., 2004; Creswell et al., 2005; Schmeichel & Martens, 2005; Jonas & Fischer, 2006). Thus, individuals' psy-chological resources may be best considered as contingent upon both long-term and short-term experiences in life.

Research has also suggested that people with HSE and LSE show distinc-tive styles of symbolic affirmation. For instance, Vohs and Heatherton (2001) and Heatherton and Vohs (2000) found in the United States that LSE people responded to a self threat in an interdependent way, making pleasant impressions on their interaction partners, whereas HSE people reacted in a more autonomous fashion, emphasizing their strengths at the cost of giving a negative impression. This result is puzzling because if the threat had a greater impact on the LSE than HSE people, it is the LSE people rather than their HSE counterpart who ought to validate independence that is culturally normative in the North American context (Markus & Kitayama, 1991). Several other studies have also reported that LSE people engage in *less* ingroup favoritism, fewer attempts to improve their self-image, and instead show spontaneous self-deprecation and withdrawal after various threats (Crocker et al., 1987; Mussweiler et al., 2000; Sommer & Baumeister, 2002). Hence, symbolic affirmation of LSE suggests lesser aggres-siveness and personal agency which might be implied by their limited psycho-logical resources.

If LSE individuals' threat reactions are constrained by their limited psy-chological resource, would threats lead them to cope by engaging in automatic behavior such as non-conscious mimicry which is perhaps more affordable even under limited resources? The previous research has suggested that automatic mimicry serves as "social glue," enhancing interpersonal liking in both directions (e.g., Chartrand & Bargh, 1999; van Baaren et al., 2004). Automatic mimicry is also associated with interdependence. Individuals with more interdependent self and experimental manipulation of interdependence yield greater mimicry in the laboratory setting (van Baaren et al., 2003; Ashton-James et al., 2007).

Preliminary research conducted in Australia found evidence to support this prediction (Kashima et al., 2007). Australian university students were asked to think of their own death (mortality salience), own felt uncertainty (uncertainty salience), or watching TV (control), using the traditional method of mortality manipulation, and uncertainty manipulation that modified this by replacing the word "death" with "uncertainty." After a filler task, a male experimenter who was blind to the experimental condition interviewed subjects ostensibly about their study habit, during which he performed a series of well-rehearsed actions such as touching his eyebrow and guarding his mouth, giving opportunities for subjects to mimic these behaviors. The interviews were videotaped, and the number of target behaviors that each subject mimicked was coded by two independent coders.

The number of behaviors mimicked was predicted from an interaction effect of threat and self-esteem. LSE people mimicked significantly more when threatened (versus not threatened), equally for uncertainty and mortality threats. Hence, LSE took on the opportunity to deal with the threats by engaging in a cognitively undemanding, energy-saving, implicit solution. By contrast, HSE people mimicked significantly less after these threats. Thus, the study demonstrated that the threat impact on mimicry depends on the level of self-esteem. Similar to Vohs and Heatherton's (2001) finding, the HSE people behaviorally differentiated themselves from their interaction partner in the threat conditions. Apparently, HSE people react to threats more actively and autonomously, whereas LSE people respond to threats in less agentic, conforming manners.

This study also found that in the no threat condition mimicry was greater among HSE individuals. Further, in the no threat condition, those who mimicked more rated the experimenter as more likeable, and they were rated by independent judges to be more likeable. Mimicry was therefore like "social glue" and reflected interdependence. In this condition HSE people were more sociable than LSE people, perhaps revealing their better social adjustment. In the threat conditions, by contrast, LSE rather than HSE people mimicked more, and the extent of mimicry was unrelated with both the likeability ratings. In these conditions, therefore, mimicry might have reflected other-directedness or dependence rather than interdependence, and it was in this context that the LSE people engaged in this behavior.

Does mimicry satisfy the thwarted motives? Their data suggest a tentative yes. The control subjects who mimicked more subsequently rated their affiliation needs more highly. In contrast, correlation between mimicry and affiliation needs was non-significantly negative in the threat conditions, suggesting that mimicry might have satisfied affiliation needs to compensate for the needs for symbolic immortality and uncertainty. More research is required to clarify if automatic behaviors such as mimicry act as a part of fluid motive compensation mechanism, and how individuals use this path of coping when they are depleted with psychological resources.

CULTURE AND THREAT REACTIONS

The psychological *mechanism* of fluid compensation is likely to be universal. People are threatened symbolically by a thought of an important meaning being impaired in some way, and recover from such psychological injury by ensuring that the same or an alternative meaning is kept intact. Through this process of symbolic affirmation, the meanings that are important and relevant are reproduced and validated by people thereby increasing their levels of accessibility in people's minds (see Hong et al., 2000, for a discussion on contextual accessibility of cultural meanings).

However, cultural groups often differ in degrees to which they find particular meaning important or contextually accessible, and because of this difference they may show variations in *content* of symbolic affirmation they engage in within a context. For instance, the notion of honor is more important for some cultural groups than others according to Cohen et al. (1996). In cultures where honor is relatively important (versus unimportant), people might more frequently think about a potential of their honor being injured in a social situation, which would pose a symbolic threat. Extant research provides evidence for cultural variations in the content of both symbolic threat and symbolic affirmation.

CULTURAL VARIATION IN SYMBOLIC THREAT

Self-enhancement motive across cultures and especially whether or not East-Asians have this motive is hotly debated in the current literature (e.g., Heine et al., 2007; Sedikides et al., 2007). One of the first cross-cultural comparisons of self-serving reactions to ego-threat has shown that the Japanese were more self-critical than Americans (Kashima & Triandis, 1986). Subsequent studies conducted by Heine and his colleagues replicated this pattern, making a conclusion that Japanese are less prone to a threat to the self, at least in comparison to North Americans. For example, in Heine et al.'s (2001) study, Japanese chose to perform the same task despite negative feedback on their previous performance, whereas North Americans chose to work on a different task after receiving negative feedback than positive feedback. In contrast, an alternative view suggests that it is because of the cultural norm of modesty that East-Asians sometimes show self-effacement or self-criticism, rather than a lack of self-enhancement motive. Proponents of this view have shown that after threatened by negative feedback, Japanese engaged in self-enhancement if it had been made certain that doing so would have no relational implications (Kudo & Numazaki, 2003) or the situation was explicitly competitive in nature (Takata, 2003).

Several studies have shown that European-Americans react more strongly than East-Asians or Asian-Americans when the sense of personal choice is impaired. For example, in Iyengar and Lepper's (1999) study, task performance of European-American children, relative to that of Asian-American children, was affected more by the lack of choice in task they performed and especially, when the task performed had been selected by a trusted authority or by an ingroup member. Similarly, Hoshino-Browne et al. (2005) demonstrated that North American and Asian participants differed in their sensitivity to cognitive dissonance depending on whether it was based on personal choice versus relational choice. Responses to these two types of cognitive dissonance by Canadians, Japanese, and Asian-Canadians suggested that Canadian culture enhanced the dissonance based on personal choice, whereas East Asian culture enhanced the dissonance based on relational choice. Further, a prior affirmation of independent self reduced personal dissonance, whereas a prior affirmation of interdependent self reduced the relational dissonance (as also Heine & Lehman, 1997; Kitayama et al., 2004). Interestingly, both the independent and interdependent affirmations boosted the psychological resources of the bicultural Asian-Canadians.

In turn, a claim has been made by Navarrete and his colleagues (Navarrete et al., 2004) that the degrees to which interdependence with other people is essential for survival influence how much people show conformity to their ingroup norms in situations that heighten the need for social coalition. Using the terror management research paradigm, they found that thinking about social isolation (Navarrete et al., 2004) and the need for building a house (Navarette, 2004, Study 1) led Costa Ricans to defend their ingroup ideology more, whereas thinking about their own mortality did not trigger the same response. In contrast, the opposite pattern of responses was obtained from undergraduate participants from Los Angeles. In support of the view that this cross-cultural difference in pattern was due to the higher need for social bonds in Costa Rica than in the United States, Navarrete (2004, Study 2) also found that Costa Ricans had more interdependent orientation than North Americans, and that thinking of social isolation and own mortality led North Americans to show greater ingroup bias, particularly if they believed that the world is dangerous, or if they endorsed the collectivist values.

CULTURAL VARIATION IN SYMBOLIC AFFIRMATION

A cross-cultural divergence in symbolic affirmation has been shown in several recent studies. Indicating that culture influences symbolic affirmation, Bagozzi et al. (2003) reported that Dutch and Filipino salespeople compensated differently for the sense of shame triggered by the clients' dissatisfaction with their service: Dutch salespeople responded to the threat by affirming personal self, which led to more self-protective actions and less use of adaptive resources, yielding poor outcomes. In contrast, Filipinos responded by affirming social self, which led to greater repairing of relationships, citizenship behaviors, and better outcomes. Heine et al. (2001) on the other hand highlighted that Canadians and Japanese respond to self-threatening information differently. Whereas Canadians responded to the threat by affirming their self-esteem by engaging in an alternative task that made self-enhancement possible, Japanese responded to the threat by engaging in self-improvement on the same task.

Taylor et al. (2007) have recently reported that although Asian-Americans report that they seek social support less often than do European-Americans (Kim et al., 2006; Taylor et al., 2004), they in fact receive more adaptive benefit when thinking about their support groups. Participants in their study were led to anticipate a stressful task involving a public presentation, and while in waiting they thought of either explicit social support, that is, how to seek and use friends' advice and emotional support, or implicit social support, that is, just thinking about their valued ingroup. The verbal and neuroendocrine responses indicated that European-Americans coped better with the explicit than implicit support, perhaps because an explicit discussion of problems was beneficial but simply thinking about the ingroup provided them with further pressure. By contrast, Asian-Americans coped better with the implicit than explicit support; in cultures where interdependence is emphasized, simply thinking of the existence of supportive others with no worry to annoy them may be sufficiently beneficial.

THE ROLE OF SELF-ESTEEM IN FLUID MOTIVE COMPENSATION ACROSS CULTURES

The cross-cultural studies discussed above did not examine the effects of individual difference in psychological resources in threat reactions. Are LSE individuals across cultures more vulnerable to threats and inclined to engage in symbolic affirmation more? Self-esteem is a culture-dependent construct in that it develops on the basis of the individual belief that one lives up to the standards set by the cultural norms (Rosenberg, 1965; Pyszczynski et al., 2004). Therefore, in all societies, those who conform more to their cultural mandate should have higher self-esteem. Yet, cultures also differ in how they encourage self-esteem to be expressed in social situations (Heine et al., 1999). According to Kitayama et al. (1997), independent cultures prescribe self-enhancement whereas interdependent cultures prescribe self-criticism. Then, potentially, HSE people in the interdependent cultures may not develop as much psychological resource as their counterparts in the independent cultures do; hence, culture may moderate the role of self-esteem in threat reaction. This is however a more likely expectation if self-enhancement, rather than the sense of being a valuable cultural member, is the main underpinning of psychological resource. On the other hand, if the sense of being a valuable cultural member is primarily responsible for the development of psychological resource, then HSE people's advantage in psychological resource and in coping with threats should be observed in the interdependent cultures as well.

Brockner and Chen (1996) tested this important question in People's Republic of China and the United States of America by using the ego-threat paradigm often used in the North American research. Participants' trait self-esteem and independent self-construal were assessed first, followed by orthogonal manipulations of personal failure and ingroup failure through bogus feedback. Self-enhancement as a response to the ego-threat was measured via ingroup favoritism and discounting of ability in causal attribution of failure. Contrary to anticipation that Chinese may find group identity threat more threatening than Americans, the ingroup failure manipulation had little impact on both cultural groups. More interestingly, the result of the study indicated that both Chinese and Americans with HSE self-enhanced more after personal failure feedback, if they were independent rather than interdependent in their self-orientation. Indeed Chinese and Americans in this study had equivalent self-orientation. Therefore, the tendency among HSE individuals to self-enhance in response to the threat was equivalent. This study clearly supported that HSE individuals are ready to strike back when a threat is presented to the self and if they have independent self; however, the study findings are silent about how individuals respond to threats in different cultural groups if they have LSE, or if they are interdependent.

More recently, Kashima et al. (2004) approached the question using mortality threats and observing the Japanese and Australians' responses to mortality threats in relations to their self-esteem levels. In addition to the standard personal mortality condition, this study also tested a cultural difference in symbolic threat by devising a collective mortality condition by asking subjects to "imagine that your country was suddenly destroyed by a meteorite, killing all the people" and to respond to two questions concerning "your death and the death of all the people in your country." They predicted that Australians would be threatened more by personal mortality than by collective mortality, whereas Japanese would be threatened by collective mortality more than by personal mortality. Furthermore, they tested a prediction involving a cultural difference in symbolic affirmation such that a mortality threat would lead Australians to affirm the self-view that they would engage in individualist behaviors, whereas it would lead Japanese to reject the individualist self-view.

The predictions about both symbolic threats and symbolic affirmation were supported by the data. Australians responded by affirming their individualist self-view more in the personal mortality condition than both the collective mortality and no mortality conditions. By contrast, the Japanese responded by rejecting individualist self-view more in the collective mortality condition than both the personal mortality and no mortality conditions. Furthermore, it was confirmed that LSE individuals in both Japan and Australia engaged in their respective symbolic affirmation more than the HSE individuals, suggesting that LSE people were similarly more prone to mortality threats in both cultures.

The pattern of the results just described is illustrated in Figure 19.2 in which LSE and HSE values have been estimated at $M - 1\ SD$ and $M + 1\ SD$, respectively. It may be noticed that the grand mean of individualist self-view was higher in Japan than in Australia. This may reflect a reference group effect; in other words, the mean difference is not interpretable. A more important aspect of the result is that the LSE individuals endorsed individualist self-view more, particularly in the personal mortality condition in Australia, and endorsed individualist self-view least, particularly in the collective mortality condition in Japan. In contrast, the HSE individuals in both countries showed little effect by mortality threats.

Further analysis of data also found that HSE was associated with greater endorsement of cultural norm in the control condition in both cultural samples; a stronger rejection of individualist self-view by Japanese and a stronger endorsement of this self-view by Australians. This was consistent with the theory that self-esteem is based on the sense of being a good cultural member. By contrast,

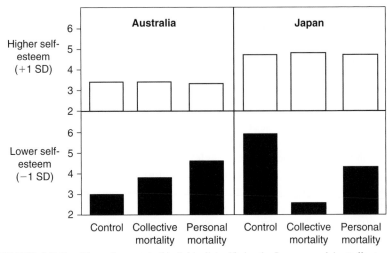

FIGURE 19.2   The endorsement of individualist self-view by Japanese and Australians with high versus low self-esteem in control, collective mortality, and personal mortality conditions.

in the mortality conditions, LSE, rather than HSE, was seen to be associated with the endorsement of the respective cultural norm (see Table 19.1). Clearly, therefore, where the cultural norm is salient and a threat is imposed, LSE people are likely to conform to the norm.

In sum, both Brockner and Chen (1996) and Kashima, E.S. et al. (2004) suggested that personal self-esteem is a potentially important moderator of symbolic threat reactions, although the pattern of moderation differed between these two studies. HSE people responded to ego-threat more autonomously and aggressively by self-enhancing, especially if they endorsed independent self-view; however, the HSE people responded little to mortality threat. By contrast, LSE people did not respond to ego-threat with self-enhancement, but reacted to mortality threat by conforming to the culturally normative self-view.

TABLE 19.1   Correlation Between Self-esteem and Endorsement of Individualist Values in Control, Collective Mortality, and Personal Mortality Conditions

	Japan			Australia		
	n	r	p	n	r	p
Control	36	−0.33	<0.06	22	0.31	<0.2
Collective mortality	21	0.50[*]	<0.03	27	−0.22	<0.3
Personal mortality	35	0.31	<0.07	25	−0.28	<0.2

[*]$P < .05$

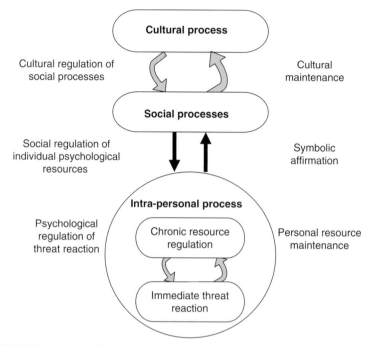

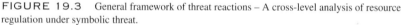

FIGURE 19.3   General framework of threat reactions – A cross-level analysis of resource regulation under symbolic threat.

THE FRAMEWORK OF SYMBOLIC THREAT

In this section of the paper, I will present a general framework of threat reactions. This framework describes symbolic threat, its precursors and consequences as forming three layers: cultural, social, and personal (see Figure 19.3).

I define culture in this paper as a collection of meanings and practices shared by a large group of people. Culture is also a dynamic process: the meanings and practices that constitute a culture are in constant flux. Culture provides members of the group with both the potential causes for symbolic threats and their means for coping with them. This cultural regulation of symbolic threat is mediated by social process, the interactions among group members that make use of symbols. Social process produces two impacts. One is the maintenance of meanings within the culture. Meanings that are used more frequently and effectively in the process of symbolic threat are more likely to be maintained as part of the culture. The other is regulation of individual psychological resource. People threaten others symbolically by using meanings (as well as non-symbolically, sometimes, through physical aggression as many animals do; e.g., Sapolsky, 2004). Within the big circle presented at the bottom of the diagram are intra-personal processes of resource regulation. As discussed earlier in the paper, the chronic level of psychological resources, which correlate with self-esteem as an example, are influenced by the social relationships of the person. The chronic level of resources partly determines the person's suscep-tibility to the potential threat. Repeated experiences of threats also affect the chronic level of psychological resource in turn.

A good example of how culture, social process, and intra-personal process merge in threat reaction might be found in stereotyping. Stereotypes are a part of shared knowledge that plays a key role in threat and coping (e.g., Kunda & Spencer, 2003). When an individual is exposed to a stimulus that reminds him/ her of a relevant outgroup, the latter's stereotypes may be activated. Researchers have found that stereotypes can be automatically activated even under high cog-nitive busyness, particularly when the person has been threatened by negative feedback (Bargh & Chartrand, 1999; Spencer et al., 1998). It has been suggested that a well-practiced link between the motive (e.g., self-enhancement) and the cognition (i.e., stereotyping) is the precursor for this automatic stereotyping. In other words, those stereotypes serve a strong motivational function in the spe-cific socio-cultural context, and this is likely to be one of the reasons why they tend to persist within the culture.

Culturally significant meanings such as stereotypes can be a powerful tool of social influence, and as such, they may be used intentionally by socialization agents, leaders, and persuasive communicators. For instance, when a maestro points out that the apprentice lacks perseverance, a culturally desirable quality, this would deeply threaten the apprentice; repeated exposures to such scolding or reproach may deplete his/her resources chronically. Another apprentice who is commended of his/her creativity would gain psychological resource, and repeated compliments would raise his/her resource level chronically. In turn, individu-als who influence others in such manners may gain (or sometimes lose) their psychological resource. Also, in addition to positive and negative interpersonal feedback, a social relation that allows construction of personal meanings may often contribute significantly to psychological resource provision. People find the exchange of culturally relevant meanings gratification. In contrast, social isola-tion is likely to deplete resources just as negative feedback.

Furthermore, psychological resources may be affected by publicly avail-able meanings such as narratives, dictums, songs, inscriptions, and films. For instance, a narrative shared within a group whose members are subjected to per-vasive prejudice and discrimination may assist them to cope, especially if the narrative fosters meanings such as hope, optimism, hardiness, and resilience. A proposition that a group vitality narrative that highlights the notion of future group advances helps people cope with discrimination was tested recently in two studies (Meegan & Kashima, 2007). Lesbians who subscribed to a narrative, such that Lesbians as a group is gradually becoming a vital group, and therefore, there would be no discrimination against them in future generations, showed less negative affect after a reminder of discriminations against their group. Further, women who were randomly allocated to a condition which presented a similar group vitality narrative about women down-regulated their negative affect more effectively compared to a control group.

DIRECTIONS FOR FUTURE RESEARCH

The proposed framework suggests a link between cultural maintenance and the resource regulatory process of individuals mediated by social processes. Though this is admittedly a broad and crude framework, it can be generative as a guide for future research, especially if it is married with extant frameworks of cultural knowledge pertaining to, for instance, universal values, self models, and social axioms.

The research accumulated in the literature has pointed to independent and interdependent self as a key factor in theorizing threat reactions across cultures, especially when ego-threat and self-affirming reactions to the threat are concerned. Threats with relevance to personal choice, self-expressions, and personal competence are all contingent on the notion of personal agency and independent self-construal. Individuals are the primary agent of problem solving, and therefore, how individuals cope with the threats associated with their sense of personal agency is a key question in this research area. At the same time, however, research that focuses on interdependent self can be advanced more. Hence, questions can be posed as to what symbolic threats interdependent people would find more challenging and how they might try to repair such damages symbolically.

There should be questions that go beyond independence and interdependence. I suggest, as one example, that by adopting Schwartz's Value Circumplex (e.g., Schwartz & Bilsky, 1990) together with the present framework, many specific hypotheses concerning symbolic threats and symbolic affirmation can be generated. For instance, in cultures high on the value of hedonism, would people find an impairment of meanings associated with hedonism (e.g., pleasure, enjoying life) more threatening, and would these people be more likely to respond to any symbolic threat by affirming meanings reflective of the hedonism values? Research may also try to identify an individual difference variable that effectively facilitate coping with a certain type of threat. For example, would religiosity (a part of the benevolence value type which is opposite to hedonism) provide a psychological resource useful for coping with a threat to hedonism? There are a number of values that can be used to generate these hypotheses, and cross-cultural data banks (e.g., Schwartz, 1994) can be used to sample cultures theoretically.

Another model that may be tied fruitfully to the current framework is the tripartite model of the self that posits the self involves three conceptually separate aspects: individual, relational, and collective (Kashima et al., 1995; Brewer & Gardner, 1996; Kashima & Hardie, 2000; Brewer & Chen, 2007). According to this approach, the relative prominence of these three self-aspects varies across cultures, genders, and urban versus rural regions, respectively (Kashima, Y. et al., 2004). The most prominent self-aspect of the person is expected to organize the person's experiences most frequently. For instance, Hardie et al. (2005) have gained a preliminary support for the model such that the strength of a particular self-aspect predicts a tendency to find greater psychological uplift in the life events in the matching domain (e.g., a relational person finds more uplifting experiences in the relational domain) and a tendency to find greater stress in life events in non-matching domains. Such a model can be productively applied to the study of threat reactions further. For instance, the framework may predict that personal self is most important and most frequently provoked and affirmed in individualistic cultures (e.g. Gaertner et al., 1999) but that relational self or collective self are relatively more important in some cultures (e.g., Yuki et al., 2005) and easily impaired but also most frequently affirmed by members of those cultures.

Still another exciting research avenue might be to explore some specific cultural tools which have direct impacts on the individual resource regulatory process. Culture as a collection of symbols and practices provides individuals and groups with various tools to moderate resource regulation, and thereby cultural reproduction. Narratives (Lazarus & Alfert, 1964), axioms (Leung et al., 2002), humors, some specific behaviors such as writing (Pennebaker, 1989) and praying can be powerful moderators of threat reactions. Narratives of heroes, music, and pictures may impact the threat reactions of the individual directly or indirectly through social processes (e.g., a narrative leads someone to criticize his/her child less often and the child is consequently threatened less). These cultural tools, if effective, may be exported to other groups who can benefit from the new cultural tool for enhancing cultural maintenance.

What might be the strength of the cultural approach to threat reaction? Most importantly, it may reduce a potential cultural bias in research focus. We may choose to focus on certain motives rather than others because they seem more important to us, according to our own cultural biases. A truly universal model of threat reactions should aspire to understand the threat reactions of people in diverse cultural communities.

REFERENCES

Allport, G. W. (1943). The ego in contemporary psychology. *Psychological Review, 50*, 451–478.

Arndt, J., Greenberg, J., Pyszczynski, T., & Solomon, S. (1997). Subliminal exposure to death-related stimuli increases defense of the cultural worldview. *Psychological Science, 8*, 379–385.

Arndt, J., Allen, J. J. B., & Greenberg, J. (2001). Traces of terror: Subliminal death primes and facial electromyographic indices of affect. *Motivation and Emotion, 25*, 253–277.

Ashton-James, C., van Baaren, R. B., Chartrand, T. L., Decety, J., & Karremans, J. (2007). Mimicry and me: The impact of mimicry on self-construal. *Social Cognition, 25*, 518–535.

Aspinwall, L. G. (1998). Rethinking the role of positive affect in self-regulation. *Motivation and Emotion, 22*, 1–32.

Bagozzi, R. P., Verbeke, W., & Gavino, J. C., Jr. (2003). Culture moderates the self-regulation of shame and its effects on performance: The case of salespersons in the Netherlands and the Philippines. *Journal of Applied Psychology, 88*, 219–233.

Bandura, A. (1986). *Social foundations of thought and action: A social cognitive theory*. Inglewood Cliffs, NJ: Prentice Hall.

Bargh, J. A., & Chartrand, T. L. (1999). The unbearable automaticity of being. *American Psychologist, 54*, 462–479.

Baumann, N., Kaschel, R., & Kuhl, J. (2005). Striving for unwanted goals: Stress-dependent discrepancies between explicit and implicit achievement motives reduce subjective well-being and increase psychosomatic symptoms. *Journal of Personality and Social Psychology, 89*, 781–799.

Baumeister, R. F. (2005). *The cultural animal: Human nature, meaning, and social life.* Oxford, UK: Oxford University Press.

Baumeister, R. F., & Leary, M. R. (1995). The need to belong: Desire to interpersonal attachments as a fundamental human motivation. *Psychological Bulletin, 116*, 497–529.

Baumeister, R. F., Heatherton, T. F., & Tice, D. M. (1993). When ego threats lead to self-regulation failure: Negative consequences of high self-esteem. *Journal of Personality and Social Psychology, 64*, 141–156.

Baumeister, R. F., DeWall, C. N., Ciarocco, N. J., & Twenge, J. M. (2005). Social exclusion impairs self-regulation. *Journal of Personality and Social Psychology, 88*, 589–604.

Baumeister, R. F., Gailliot, M., DeWall, C. N., & Oaten, M. (2006). Self-regulation and personality: How interventions increase regulatory success, and how depletion moderates the effects of traits on behavior. *Journal of Personality, 74*, 1773–1802.

Beauregard, K. S., & Dunning, D. (1998). Turning up the contrast: Self-enhancement motives prompt egocentric contrast effects in social judgments. *Journal of Personality and Social Psychology, 74*, 606–621.

Blascovich, J., & Tomaka, J. (1996). The biopsychosocial model of arousal regulation. In M. P. Zanna (Ed.), *Advances in experimental social psychology* (Vol. 28, pp. 1–51). New York: Academic Press.

Blascovich, J., Mendes, W. B., Hunter, S. B., Lickel, B., & Kowai-Bell, N. (2001). Perceiver threat in social interactions with stigmatized others. *Journal of Personality and Social Psychology, 80*, 253–267.

Bowlby, J. (1982). *Attachment and loss: Vol I. Attachment (2nd ed.).* New York: Basic Books.

Boyd, R., & Richerson, P. J. (1985). *Culture and the evolutionary process.* Chicago, IL: University of Chicago Press.

Boyd, R., & Richerson, P. J. (1990). Culture and cooperation. In J. J. Mansbridge (Ed.), *Beyond self-interest* (pp. 111–132). Chicago, IL: University of Chicago Press.

Brewer, M. B., & Chen, Y. (2007). Where (who) are collectives in collectivism? Toward conceptual clarification of individualism and collectivism. *Psychological Review, 114*, 133–151.

Brewer, M. B., & Gardner, W. (1996). Who is this "We"? Levels of collective identity and self representations. *Journal of Personality and Social Psychology, 71*, 83–93.

Brockner, J. (1979). Self-esteem, self-consciousness, and task performance: Replications, extensions, and possible explanations. *Journal of Personality and Social Psychology, 37*, 447–461.

Brockner, J., & Chen, Y. (1996). The moderating roles of self-esteem and self-construal in reaction to a threat to the self: Evidence from the People's Republic of China and the United States. *Journal of Personality and Social Psychology, 71*, 603–615.

Campbell, J. D., & Lavallee, L. F. (1993). Who am I? The role of self-concept confusion in understanding the behavior of people with low self-esteem. In R. F. Baumeister (Ed.), *Self-esteem: The puzzle of low self-regard* (pp. 3–20). New York, NY: Plenum Press.

Cannon, W. B. (1914). The emergency function of the adrenal medulla in pain and the major emotions. *American Journal of Physiology, 33*, 356–372.

Carver, C. S. (2001). Affect and the functional bases of behavior: On the dimensional structure of affective experience. *Personality and Social Psychology Review, 5*, 345–356.

Carver, C. S., & Scheier, M. F. (1981). *Attention and self-regulation: A control-theory approach to human behavior.* New York: Springer.

Chartrand, T. L., & Bargh, J. A. (1999). The chameleon effect: The perception-behavior link and social interaction. *Journal of Personality and Social Psychology, 76*, 893–910.

Cheng, C. (2003). Cognitive and motivational processes underlying coping flexibility: A dual-process model. *Journal of Personality and Social Psychology, 84*, 425–438.

Chiu, C. Y., Hong, Y. Y., Mischel, W., & Shoda, Y. (1995). Discriminative facility in social competence: Conditional versus dispositional encoding and monitoring-blunting of information. *Social Cognition, 13*, 49–70.

Clark, R., Anderson, N. B., Clark, V. R., & Williams, D. R. (1999). Racism as a stressor for African Americans: A biopsychosocial model. *American Psychologist, 54*, 805–816.

Cohen, D., Nisbett, R. E., Bowdle, B. F., & Schwarz, N. (1996). Insult, aggression, and the southern culture of honor: An "experimental ethnography". *Journal of Personality and Social Psychology, 70*, 945–960.

Cohen, S., & Edwards, J. R. (1989). Personality characteristics as moderators of the relationship between stress and disorder. In R. W. J. Neufeld (Ed.), *Advances in the investigation of psychological stress* (pp. 235–283). Oxford, England: John Wiley & Sons.

Creswell, J. D., Welch, W. T., Taylor, S. E., Sherman, D. K., Gruenewald, T. L., & Mann, T. (2005). Affirmation of personal values buffers neuroendocrine and psychological stress responses. *Psychological Science, 16*, 846–851.

Crocker, J., & Park, L. E. (2004). The costly pursuit of self-esteem. *Psychological Bulletin, 130*, 392–414.

Crocker, J., Thompson, L. L., McGraw, K. M., & Ingerman, C. (1987). Downward comparison, prejudice, and evaluations of others: Effects of self-esteem and threat. *Journal of Personality and Social Psychology, 52*, 907–916.

Dickerson, S. S., & Kemeny, M. E. (2004). Acute stressors and cortisol responses: A theoretical integration and synthesis of laboratory research. *Psychological Bulletin, 130*, 355–391.

Dickerson, S. S., Gruenewald, T. L., & Kemeny, M. E. (2004). When the social self is threatened: Shame, physiology, and health. *Journal of Personality, 72*, 1191–1216.

Dittes, J. E. (1961). Impulsive closure as reaction to failure-induced threat. *Journal of Abnormal and Social Psychology, 63*, 562–569.

Dodgson, P. G., & Wood, J. V. (1998). Self-esteem and the cognitive accessibility of strengths and weaknesses after failure. *Journal of Personality and Social Psychology, 75*, 178–197.

Easterbrook, J. A. (1959). The effect of emotion on cue utilization and the organization of behaviour. *Psychological Review, 66*, 183–201.

Gaertner, L., Sedikides, C., & Graetz, K. (1999). In search of self-definition: Motivational primacy of the individual self, motivational primacy of the collective self, or contextual primacy? *Journal of Personality and Social Psychology, 76*, 5–18.

Gailliot, M. T., Schmeichel, B. J., & Baumeister, R. F. (2006). Self-regulatory processes defend against the threat of death: Effects of self-control depletion and trait self-control on thoughts and fears of dying. *Journal of Personality and Social Psychology, 91*, 49–62.

Geen, R. G. (1976). Test anxiety, observation, and range of cue utilization. *British Journal of Social and Clinical Psychology, 15*, 253–259.

Greenberg, J., Solomon, S., & Pyszczynski, T. (1997). Terror management theory of self-esteem and cultural worldviews: Empirical assessments and conceptual refinements. In M. P. Zanna (Ed.), *Advances in Experimental Social Psychology* (Vol. 29, pp. 61–139). San Diego, CA: Academic Press.

Hardie, E., Kashima, E. S., & Pridmore, P. (2005). The influence of relational, individual and collective self-aspects on stress, uplifts and health. *Self and Identity, 4*, 1–24.

Harmon-Jones, E., Simon, L., Greenberg, J., Pyszczynski, T., Solomon, S., & McGregor, H. (1997). Terror management theory and self-esteem: Evidence that increased self-esteem reduced mortality salience effects. *Journal of Personality and Social Psychology, 72*, 24–36.

Hart, J., Shaver, P. R., & Goldenberg, J. L. (2005). Attachment, self-esteem, worldviews, and terror management: Evidence for a tripartite security system. *Journal of Personality and Social Psychology, 88*, 999–1013.

Heatherton, T. F., & Vohs, K. D. (2000). Interpersonal evaluations following threats to self: Role of self-esteem. *Journal of Personality and Social Psychology, 78*, 725–736.

Heine, S. J., & Lehman, D. R. (1997). Culture, dissonance, and self-affirmation. *Personality and Social Psychology Bulletin, 23*, 389–400.

Heine, S. J., Lehman, D. R., Markus, H. R., & Kitayama, S. (1999). Is there a universal need for positive self-regard? *Psychological Review, 106*, 766–794.

Heine, S. J., Kitayama, S., & Lehman, D. R. (2001). Cultural differences in self-evaluation: Japanese readily accept negative self-relevant information. *Journal of Cross-Cultural Psychology, 32*, 434–443.

Heine, S. J., Kitayama, S., Lehman, D. R., Takata, T., Ide, E., Leung, C., & Matsumoto, H. (2001). Divergent consequences of success and failure in Japan and North America: An investigation of self-improving motivations and malleable selves. *Journal of Personality and Social Psychology*, *81*, 599–615.

Heine, S. J., Proulx, T., & Vohs, K. D. (2006). The meaning maintenance model: On the coherence of social motivations. *Personality and Social Psychology Review*, *10*, 88–110.

Heine, S. J., Kitayama, S., & Hamamura, T. (2007). Inclusion of additional studies yields different conclusions: Comment on Sedikides, Gaertner, & Vevea (2005). *Journal of Personality and Social Psychology*. *Asian Journal of Social Psychology*, *10*, 49–58.

Higgins, E. T. (1987). Self-discrepancy: A theory relating self and affect. *Psychological Review*, *94*, 319–340.

Hogg, M. A., & Abrams, D. (1993). Towards a single-process uncertainty-reduction model of social motivation in groups. In M. A. Hogg & D. Abrams (Eds.), *Social identity theory: Constructive and critical advances* (pp. 28–47). London: Harvester Wheatsheaf.

Hokanson, J. E., Rubert, M. P., Welker, R. A., Hollander, G. R., & Hedeen, C. (1989). Interpersonal concomitants and antecedents of depression among college students. *Journal of Abnormal Psychology*, *98*, 209–217.

Hong, Y. Y., Morris, M. W., Chiu, C. Y., & Benet-Martínez, V. (2000). Multicultural minds: A dynamic constructivist approach to culture and cognition. *American Psychologist*, *55*, 709–720.

Hornsey, M. J., & Jetten, J. (2004). The individual within the group: Balancing the need to belong with the need to be different. *Personality and Social Psychology Review*, *8*, 248–264.

Hoshino-Browne, E., Zanna, A. S., Spencer, S. J., Zanna, M. P., Kitayama, S., & Lackenbauer, S. (2005). On the cultural guises of cognitive dissonance: The case of Easterners and Westerners. *Journal of Personality and Social Psychology*, *89*, 294–310.

Isen, A. M., & Schmidt, E. (2007). Positive affect facilitates incidental learning and divided attention while not impairing performance on a focal task. Paper presented at the SPSP Conference.

Iyengar, S. S., & Lepper, M. R. (1999). Rethinking the value of choice: A cultural perspective on intrinsic motivation. *Journal of Personality and Social Psychology*, *76*, 349–366.

Jonas, E., & Fischer, P. (2006). Terror management and religion: Evidence that intrinsic religiousness mitigates worldview defense following mortality salience. *Journal of Personality and Social Psychology*, *91*, 553–567.

Jordan, C. H., Spencer, S. J., Zanna, M. P., Hoshino-Browne, E., & Correll, J. (2003). Secure and defensive high self-esteem. *Journal of Personality and Social Psychology*, *85*, 969–978.

Jostmann, N. B., Koole, S. L., van der Wulp, N. Y., & Fockenberg, D. A. (2005). Subliminal affect regulation: The moderating role of action vs. state orientation. *European Psychologist*, *10*, 209–217.

Kashima, E. S., & Hardie, E. A. (2000). The development and validation of the Relational, Individual, and Collective self-aspects (RIC) Scale. *Asian Journal of Social Psychology*, *3*, 19–48.

Kashima, Y., & Triandis, H. C. (1986). The self-serving bias in attributions as a coping strategy: A cross-cultural study. *Journal of Cross-Cultural Psychology*, *17*, 83–97.

Kashima, E. S., Halloran, M., Yuki, M., & Kashima, Y. (2004). The effects of personal and collective mortality salience on individualism: Comparing Australians and Japanese with higher and lower self-esteem. *Journal of Experimental Social Psychology*, *40*, 384–392.

Kashima, E. S., Azzopardi, D., & Kaufmann, L. (2007). Automatic mimicry under mortality and uncertainty threats. Unpublished manuscript.

Kashima, Y., Yamaguchi, S., Kim, U., Choi, S., Gelfand, M. J., & Yuki, M. (1995). Culture, gender, and self: A perspective from individualism-collectivism research. *Journal of Personality and Social Psychology*, *69*, 925–937.

Kashima, Y., Kokubo, T., Kashima, E. S., Boxall, D., Yamaguchi, S., & Macrae, K. (2004). Culture and self: Are there within-culture differences in self between metropolitan areas and regional cities? *Personality and Social Psychology Bulletin*, *30*, 816–823.

Kazen, M., Baumann, N., & Kuhl, J. (2005). Self-regulation after mortality salience: National pride feelings of action-oriented German participants. *European Psychologist, 10,* 218–228.

Kernis, M. H., Brockner, J., & Frankel, B. S. (1989). Self-esteem and reactions to failure: The mediating role of overgeneralization. *Journal of Personality and Social Psychology, 57,* 707–714.

Kim, H. S., Sherman, D. K., Ko, D., & Taylor, S. E. (2006). Pursuit of comfort and pursuit of harmony: Culture, relationships, and social support seeking. *Personality and Social Psychology Bulletin, 32,* 1595–1607.

Kitayama, S., Markus, H. R., Matsumoto, H., & Norasakkunkit, V. (1997). Individual and collective processes in the construction of the self: Self-enhancement in the United States and self-criticism in Japan. *Journal of Personality and Social Psychology, 72,* 1245–1267.

Kitayama, S., Snibbe, A. C., Markus, H. R., & Suzuki, T. (2004). Is there any free choice? Self and dissonance in two cultures. *Psychological Science, 15,* 527–533.

Koole, S. L., & Jostmann, N. B. (2004). Getting a grip on your feelings: Effects of action orientation and external demands on intuitive affect regulation. *Journal of Personality and Social Psychology, 87,* 974–990.

Koole, S. L., Smmets, K., van Knippenberg, A., & Dijksterhuis, A. (1999). The cessation of rumination through self-affirmation. *Journal of Personality and Social Psychology, 77,* 111–125.

Kruglanski, A. W., & Webster, D. M. (1996). Motivated closing of the mind: "Seizing" and "freezing". *Psychological Review, 103,* 263–283.

Kudo, E., & Numazaki, M. (2003). Explicit and direct self-serving bias in Japan: Reexamination of self-serving bias for success and failure. *Journal of Cross-Cultural Psychology, 34,* 511–521.

Kuhl, J. (2000). A functional-design approach to motivation and self-regulation: The dynamics of personality systems interactions. In M. Boekaerts, P. R. Pintrich, & M. Zeidner (Eds.), *Handbook of self-regulation* (pp. 111–169). San Diego, CA: Academic Press.

Kunda, Z. (1990). The case for motivated reasoning. *Psychological Bulletin, 108,* 480–498.

Kunda, Z., & Spencer, S. J. (2003). When do stereotypes come to mind and when do they color judgment? A goal-based theoretical framework for stereotype activation and application. *Psychological Bulletin, 129,* 522–544.

Lachman, M. E., & Weaver, S. L. (1998). The sense of control as a moderator of social class differences in health and well-being. *Journal of Personality and Social Psychology, 74,* 763–773.

Landau, M. J., Johns, M., Greenberg, J., Pyszczynski, T., Martens, A., Goldenberg, J. L., & Solomon, S. (2004). A function of form: Terror management and structuring the social world. *Journal of Personality and Social Psychology, 87,* 190–210.

Lazarus, R. S., & Alfert, E. (1964). Short-circuiting of threat by experimentally altering cognitive appraisal. *Journal of Abnormal & Social Psychology, 69,* 195–205.

Lazarus, R. S., & Folkman, S. (1984). *Stress, appraisal, & coping.* New York: Springer.

Leary, M. R., & Baumeister, R. F. (2000). The nature and function of self-esteem: Sociometer theory. In M. P. Zanna (Ed.), *Advances in Experimental Social Psychology* (Vol. 32, pp. 1–62). New York: Academic Press.

Lerner, J. S., Gonzalez, R. M., Dahl, R. E., Hariri, A. R., & Taylor, S. E. (2005). Facial expressions of emotion reveal neuroendocrine and cardiovascular stress responses. *Biological Psychiatry, 58,* 743–750.

Leung, K., Bond, M. H., de Carrasquel, S. R., Muñoz, C., Hernández, M., Murakami, F., Yamaguchi, S., Bierbrauer, G., & Singelis, T. M. (2002). Social axioms: The search for universal dimensions of general beliefs about how the world functions. *Journal of Cross-Cultural Psychology, 33,* 286–302.

Linville, P. W. (1987). Self-complexity as a cognitive buffer against stress-related illness and depression. *Journal of Personality and Social Psychology, 52,* 663–676.

Markus, H. R., & Kitayama, S. (1991). Culture and the self: Implications for cognition, emotion, and motivation. *Psychological Review, 98,* 224–253.

Maslow, A. H. (1943). Conflict, frustration, and the theory of threat. *Journal of Abnormal & Social Psychology, 38,* 81–86.

Matheson, K., & Cole, B. M. (2004). Coping with a threatened group identity: Psychological and neuroendocrine responses. *Journal of Experimental Social Psychology, 40*, 777–786.

McFarlin, D. B., & Blascovich, J. (1981). Effects of self-esteem and performance feedback on future affective preferences and cognitive expectations. *Journal of Personality and Social Psychology, 40*, 521–531.

McGregor, I., & Marigold, D. C. (2003). Defensive zeal and the uncertain self: What makes you so sure? *Journal of Personality and Social Psychology, 85*, 838–852.

Meegan, C., & Kashima, E. S. (2007). Group vitality narrative and its impact on down-regulation of negative affect caused by perceived pervasive discrimination. Unpublished manuscript.

Mikulincer, M., Gillath, O., & Shaver, P. R. (2002). Activation of the attachment system in adulthood: Threat-related primes increase the accessibility of mental representations of attachment figures. *Journal of Personality and Social Psychology, 83*, 881–895.

Murray, S. L., Rose, P., Bellavia, G. M., Holmes, J. G., & Kusche, A. G. (2002). When rejection stings: How self-esteem constrains relationship-enhancement processes. *Journal of Personality and Social Psychology, 83*, 556–573.

Mussweiler, T., Gabriel, S., & Bodenhausen, G. V. (2000). Shifting social identities as a strategy for deflecting threatening social comparisons. *Journal of Personality and Social Psychology, 79*, 398–409.

Navarrete, C. D. (2004). Death concerns and other adaptive challenges: The effects of coalition-relevant challenges on worldview defense in the US and Costa Rica. *Group Processes and Intergroup Relations, 7*, 411–427.

Navarrete, C. D., & Fessler, D. M. T. (2005). Normative bias and adaptive challenges: A relational approach to coalitional psychology and a critique of Terror Management Theory. *Evolutionary Psychology, 3*, 297–325.

Navarrete, C. D., Kurzban, R., Fessler, D. M. T., & Kirkpatrick, L. A. (2004). Anxiety and intergroup bias: Terror management or coalitional psychology?. *Group Processes and Intergroup Relations, 7*, 370–397.

Pennebaker, J. W. (1989). Confession, inhibition, and disease. In L. Berkowitz (Ed.), *Advances in Experimental Social Psychology* (Vol. 22, pp. 211–244). San Diego, CA: Academic Press.

Powers, S. I., Pietromonaco, P. R., Gunlicks, M., & Sayer, A. (2006). Dating couples' attachment styles and patterns of cortisol reactivity and recovery in response to a relationship conflict. *Journal of Personality and Social Psychology, 90*, 613–628.

Pruessner, J. C., Hellhammer, D. H., & Kirschbaum, C. (1999). Low self-esteem, induced failure and the adrenocortical stress response. *Personality and Individual Differences, 27*, 477–489.

Pyszczynski, T., Greenberg, J., & Solomon, S. (1999). A dual-process model of defense against conscious and unconscious death-related thoughts: An extension of terror management theory. *Psychological Review, 106*, 835–845.

Pyszczynski, T., Greenberg, J., Solomon, S., Arndt, J., & Schimel, J. (2004). Why do people need self-esteem? A theoretical and empirical review. *Psychological Bulletin, 130*, 435–468.

Rasmussen, H. N., Wrosch, C., Scheier, M. F., & Carver, C. S. (2006). Self-regulation processes and health: The importance of optimism and goal adjustment. *Journal of Personality, 74*, 1721–1747.

Reis, H. T., Collins, W. A., & Berscheid, E. (2000). The relationship context of human behavior and development. *Psychological Bulletin, 126*, 844–872.

Rosenberg, M. (1965). *Society and the adolescent self-image.* Princeton, NJ: Princeton University Press.

Sapolsky, R. (2004). Social status and health in humans and other animals. *Annual Review of Anthropology, 33*, 393–418.

Scheier, M. F., & Carver, C. S. (1985). Optimism, coping, and health: Assessment and implications of generalized outcome expectancies. *Health Psychology, 4*, 219–247.

Schmeichel, B. J., & Martens, A. (2005). Self-affirmation and mortality salience: Affirming values reduces worldview defense and death-thought accessibility. *Personality and Social Psychology Bulletin, 31*, 658–667.

Schmeichel, B. J., Vohs, K. D., & Baumeister, R. F. (2003). Intellectual performance and ego depletion: Role of the self in logical reasoning and other information processing. *Journal of Personality and Social Psychology, 85,* 33–46.

Schwartz, S. H. (1994). Beyond individualism/collectivism: New cultural dimensions of values. In U. Kim, H. C. Triandis, C. Kagitcibasi, S.-C. Choi, & G. Yoon (Eds.), *Individualism and collectivism: Theory, method, and application* (pp. 85–121). Thousand Oaks, CA: Sage Publications.

Schwartz, S. H., & Bilsky, W. (1990). Toward a theory of the universal content and structure of values: Extensions and cross-cultural replications. *Journal of Personality and Social Psychology, 58,* 878–891.

Sedikides, C., & Strube, M. J. (1997). Self evaluation: To thine own self be good, to thine own self be sure, to thine own self be true, and to thine own self be better. In M. P. Zanna (Ed.), *Advances in Experimental Social Psychology* (Vol. 29, pp. 209–269). San Diego, CA: Academic Press.

Sedikides, C., Gaertner, L., & Vevea, J. L. (2007). Inclusion of theory-relevant moderators yield the same conclusions as Sedikides, Gaertner, and Vevea (2005): A meta-analytical reply to Heine, Kitayama, and Hamamura (2007). *Asian Journal of Social Psychology, 10,* 59–67.

Seery, M. D., Blascovich, J., Weisbuch, M., & Vick, S. B. (2004). The relationship between self-esteem level, self-esteem stability, and cardiovascular reactions to performance feedback. *Journal of Personality and Social Psychology, 87,* 133–145.

Sherman, D. K., & Cohen, G. L. (2006). The psychology of self-defense: Self-affirmation theory. In M. P. Zanna (Ed.), *Advances in Experimental Social Psychology* (Vol. 38, pp. 183–242). Amsterdam: Elsevier.

Sommer, K. L., & Baumeister, R. F. (2002). Self-evaluation, persistence, and performance following implicit rejection: The role of trait self-esteem. *Personality and Social Psychology Bulletin, 28,* 926–938.

Spencer, S. J., Fein, S., Wolfe, C., Hodgson, H. L., & Dunn, M. A. (1998). Stereotype activation under cognitive load: The moderating role of self-image threat. *Personality and Social Psychology Bulletin, 24,* 1139–1152.

Steele, C. M. (1988). The psychology of self-affirmation: Sustaining the integrity of the self. In M. P. Zanna (Ed.), *Advances in Experimental Social Psychology* (Vol. 21, pp. 262–302). San Diego, CA: Academic Press.

Steele, C. M., Spencer, S. J., & Lynch, M. (1993). Self-image resilience and dissonance: The role of affirmational resources. *Journal of Personality and Social Psychology, 64,* 885–896.

Steele, C. M., Spencer, S. J., & Aronson, J. (2002). Contending with group image: The psychology of stereotype and social identity threat. In L. Berkowitz (Ed.), *Advances in Experimental Social Psychology* (Vol. 34, pp. 379–440). San Diego, CA: Academic Press.

Swann, W. B., Jr. (1987). Identity negotiation: Where two roads meet. *Journal of Personality and Social Psychology, 53,* 1038–1051.

Tajfel, H. (1981). *Human groups and social categories.* Cambridge: Cambridge University Press.

Takata, T. (2003). Self-enhancement and self-criticism in Japanese culture. An experimental analysis. *Journal of Cross-Cultural Psychology, 34,* 542–551.

Taylor, S. E. (1983). Adjustment to threatening events: A theory of cognitive adaptation. *American Psychologist, 38,* 1161–1173.

Taylor, S. E., & Brown, J. D. (1988). Illusion and well-being: A social psychological perspective on mental health. *Psychological Bulletin, 103,* 193–210.

Taylor, S. E., Neter, E., & Wayment, H. A. (1995). Self-evaluation processes. *Personality and Social Psychology Bulletin, 21,* 1278–1287.

Taylor, S. E., Klein, L. C., Lewis, B. P., Gruenewald, T. L., Gurung, R. A. R., & Updegraff, J. A. (2000). Biobehavioral responses to stress in females: Tend-and-befriend, not fight-or-flight. *Psychological Review, 107,* 411–429.

Taylor, S. E., Lerner, J. S., Sherman, D. K., Sage, R. M., & McDowell, N. K. (2003). Portrait of the self-enhancer: Well-adjusted and well-liked or maladjusted and friendless? *Journal of Personality and Social Psychology, 84,* 165–176.

Taylor, S. E., Lerner, J. S., Sherman, D. K., Sage, R. M., & McDowell, N. K. (2003). Are self-enhancing cognitions associated with healthy or unhealthy biological profiles?. *Journal of Personality and Social Psychology, 85*, 605–615.

Taylor, S. E., Sherman, D. K., Kim, H. S., Jareho, J., Takagi, K., & Dunagan, M. S. (2004). Culture and social support: Who seeks it and why? *Journal of Personality and Social Psychology, 87*, 354–362.

Taylor, S. E., Welch, W. T., Kim, H. S., & Sherman, D. K. (2007). Cultural differences in the impact of social support on psychological and biological stress responses. *Psychological Science, 18*, 831–837.

Tesser, A. (1988). Toward a self-evaluation maintenance model of social behavior. In L. Berkowitz (Ed.), *Advances in Experimental Social Psychology* (Vol. 21, pp. 181–227). San Diego, CA: Academic Press.

Tesser, A. (2000). On the confluence of self-esteem maintenance mechanisms. *Personality and Social Psychology Review, 4*, 290–299.

Tomaka, J., & Blascovich, J. (1994). Effects of justice beliefs on cognitive appraisal of and subjective, physiological, and behavioral responses to potential stress. *Journal of Personality and Social Psychology, 67*, 732–740.

Tomaka, J., Blascovich, J., Kelsey, R. M., & Leitten, C. L. (1993). Subjective, physiological, and behavioral effects of threat and challenge appraisal. *Journal of Personality and Social Psychology, 65*, 248–260.

Tomaka, J., Blascovich, J., Kibler, J., & Ernst, J. M. (1997). Cognitive and physiological antecedents of threat and challenge appraisal. *Journal of Personality and Social Psychology, 73*, 63–72.

Tomaka, J., Palacios, R., Schneider, K. T., Colotla, M., Concha, J. B., & Herrald, M. M. (1999). Assertiveness predicts threat and challenge reactions to potential stress among women. *Journal of Personality and Social Psychology, 76*, 1008–1021.

Triandis, H. C. (1979). Values, attitudes, and interpersonal behavior. *Nebraska Symposium on Motivation, 27*, 195–259.

van Baaren, R. B., Maddux, W. W., Chartrand, T. L., de Bouter, C., & van Knippenberg, A. (2003). It takes two to mimic: Behavioral consequences of self-construals. *Journal of Personality and Social Psychology, 84*, 1093–1102.

van Baaren, R. B., Holland, R. W., Kawakami, K., & van Knippenberg, A. (2004). Mimicry and prosocial behavior. *Psychological Science, 15*, 71–74.

van den Bos, K., & Lind, E. A. (2002). Uncertainty management by means of fairness judgments. In M. P. Zanna (Ed.), *Advances in Experimental Social Psychology* (Vol. 34, pp. 1–60). San Diego, CA: Academic Press.

Vohs, K. D., & Heatherton, T. F. (2001). Self-esteem and threats to self: Implications for self-construals and interpersonal perceptions. *Journal of Personality and Social Psychology, 81*, 1103–1118.

Vohs, K. D., Baumeister, R. F., & Ciarocco, N. J. (2005). Self-regulation and self-presentation: Regulatory resource depletion impairs impression management and effortful self-presentation depletes regulatory resources. *Journal of Personality and Social Psychology, 88*, 632–657.

Wachtel, P. L. (1968). Anxiety, attention and coping with threat. *Journal of Abnormal Psychology, 73*, 137–143.

Weibe, D. J. (1991). Hardiness and stress moderation. A test of proposed mechanisms. *Journal of Personality and Social Psychology, 60*, 89–99.

Yang, K., & Yang, P. L. (1973). The effects of anxiety and threat on the learning of balanced and unbalanced social structures. *Journal of Personality and Social Psychology, 26*, 201–207.

Yuki, M., Maddux, W. W., Brewer, M. B., & Takemura, K. (2005). Cross-cultural differences in relationship- and group-based trust. *Personality and Social Psychology Bulletin, 31*, 48–62.

20

VALUES AND SOCIAL AXIOMS

KWOK LEUNG*AND FAN ZHOU†

*City University of Hong Kong, China
†Zhejiang University, Hangzhou, China

There is a long tradition of research on the interplay between cognitive and motivational processes in psychology (e.g., Forgas, 2000). Cognitive and motivational processes are quite distinct, but they often exert mutual influence on each other (e.g., Jost et al., 2003). It is well known that motivational processes may orient people to perceive and interpret social reality in a particular manner (e.g., Goodwin et al., 2001), but that people who possess certain cognitions may react to the same event with different affective reactions (e.g., Schachter & Singer, 1962).

Motivational constructs and cognitions vary along a continuum of specificity. On the one end of the spectrum, some motivational constructs and cognitions are tied to a specific context, such as those learned expectations one has developed about a specific Chinese restaurant one frequents. Moving toward the middle of the spectrum, some motivational constructs and cognitions are about general contexts or categories of objects, such as those about meals or restaurants in general. On the other end of the spectrum, there exist motivational constructs and cognitions that are context- and category-free, such as those about what and how one eats.

The purpose of this chapter is to provide a critical analysis of the relationships between two classes of general motivational and cognitive constructs: values and social axioms. In distinction from previous work on motivational and cognitive processes, research on these two constructs has taken into account the influence of culture. Their cultural generality has been demonstrated by large-scale cross-cultural research, making it possible to develop truly pan-cultural theoretical frameworks. The chapter also explores the interplay between values and social axioms in influencing behavior, and presents a number of directions for future research.

CONCEPTUAL FOUNDATION OF VALUES AND AXIOMS

VALUES AS GENERALIZED GOALS

Values represent priorities in life and serve a motivational function in focusing people's attention and effort on goals deemed as important to the person (e.g., Rokeach, 1972; Schwartz, 1996). As such, values can be regarded as generalized or trans-situational goals because people have an affinity toward the goals indicated by their value profiles.

Schwartz's (1992) framework of values is the most comprehensive attempt to provide a universal structure of values. Previous work on values emerged from a specific cultural context, such as the United States (e.g., Rokeach, 1972), but Schwartz has included values from diverse cultural sources and evaluated the culture-generality of his structure in a large-scale cultural research program. Based on smallest space analysis, Schwartz (1992) examined the spatial relationships among a broad range of values and identified a two-dimensional representation as optimal. Ten value types are proposed, which are organized in the form of a circumplex (see Figure 20.1).

Schwartz's value structure has been confirmed across diverse cultures (Schwartz, 1992; Schwartz & Boehnke, 2004). Many meaningful relationships between his value types and other variables have been reported, such as those with worries (Schwartz et al., 2000) and with voting behavior (Barnea & Schwartz, 1998).

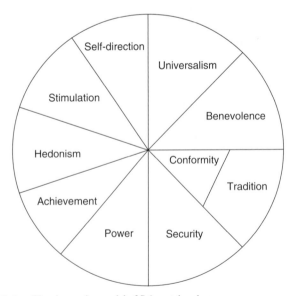

FIGURE 20.1   The circumplex model of Schwartz's values.
Source: Adapted from Schwartz (1992).

SOCIAL AXIOMS AS GENERALIZED BELIEFS

Beliefs as a type of cognition also vary along a continuum of specificity. While some beliefs are tied to a specific context, domain, or object, some beliefs are general and context-free, and thus may be regarded as "generalized expectancies," a concept first proposed by Rotter (1966) in describing locus of control. We have used the term "social axioms" to label this type of general beliefs (Leung et al., 2002). Social axioms are axiomatic because they represent basic premises that people endorse and rely upon, without meticulous evaluation and scrutiny of their validity, to make sense of their life space and to guide their actions and life course. The term "social" is used to refer to the assumption that social axioms are acquired through social experiences, often refer to one's social world and have implications for one's social living. Social axioms are defined by Leung and Bond (2007, p. 198) as follows:

> Social axioms are generalized beliefs about people, social groups, social institutions, the physical environment, or the spiritual world as well as about categories of events and phenomena in the social world. These generalized beliefs are encoded in the form of an assertion about the relationship between two entities or concepts.

Social axioms follow the structure of "A is related to B," and the relationship may be causal or correlational, whereas a value assumes the form of "A is good/desirable/important." It is possible that an evaluative dimension may underlie social axioms, because semantic objects are characterized by an evaluative dimension (Osgood et al., 1957). However, the evaluative connotation of a value is more explicit than the evaluative connotation of a social axiom. For instance, when respondents are asked to report on the value they attach to, say, power, they report the importance or desirability they accord to power. In contrast, when respondents are asked to evaluate the likelihood of a social axiom, such as "powerful people tend to exploit others," their focus is on the perceived link between powerful people and their behaviors. Exploitation of others is obviously undesirable, and a strong belief in this statement may be associated with a negative evaluative reaction to the exploitation of others. Nonetheless, the evaluative connotation of an axiom is implicit, because respondents are not asked to report on the desirability or importance of their belief.

To put together a comprehensive set of social axioms, Leung et al. (2002) began with the psychological literature on beliefs, which is mostly Euro-American in origin. To increase the cultural diversity of the beliefs, Leung et al. also interviewed informants and analyzed cultural sources from Hong Kong and Venezuela. A Social Axioms Survey with 182 items was assembled based on the items collected, and this survey was administered to college students and adults in these two cultures. Exploratory factor analysis suggested a five-factor structure that was quite congruent across the two cultural groups. Leung et al. (2002) then evaluated the universality of the five-dimensional structure in three more cultural groups: United States, Japan, and Germany. Both confirmatory factor analysis and factor analysis based on Procrustes rotation supported the cross-cultural equivalence of the original, five-factor structure.

To provide a more definitive test of the universality of the five-factor structure of social axioms, Leung and Bond (2004) orchestrated a global project with the involvement of over 50 collaborators from 40 national/cultural groups. An important feature of the data analysis they conducted is that a meta-analytic procedure for factor analysis was followed (Becker, 1996). In this procedure, no a priori structure was privileged by becoming the standard template against which the data were assessed. In other words, the five-factor structure previously identified was not used as a template against which the data collected were evaluated. Instead, the correlation matrix of each cultural group was normalized by Fisher transformation. An overall matrix was formed by averaging the matrices over all the cultural groups, and the resulting matrix was then transformed back into a correlation matrix for an exploratory factor analysis. This procedure weights each culture's correlation matrix equally and does not assume any specific dimensional structure in the data.

The exploratory factor analysis of the overall matrix suggested that a five-dimensional structure was optimal, both for the 40 sets of student data as well as the 13 sets of adult data collected. This five-dimensional structure resembles the structure reported by Leung et al. (2002). The final structure adopted for the student samples is based on 39 items, which optimizes cross-cultural equivalence across the 40 cultural groups studied (see Table 20.1 for the five-factor structure and composition).

Factor one is labeled *social cynicism*, because the items suggest a negative view of human nature, a bias against some social groups, a mistrust of social institutions, and a belief that people tend to ignore ethical means in pursuing their goals. The second factor is labeled *social complexity*, because the items suggest a belief complex that there are multiple ways to solve a problem, and that people's behavior may vary across situations. The third factor is labeled *reward for application*, because the items suggest a belief complex that the investment of effort, knowledge, careful planning, and other resources will lead to positive outcomes. The fourth factor was labeled *spirituality* but subsequently renamed *religiosity*, because the items endorse the existence of a supernatural being and a complex of beliefs about the beneficial social functions of religious institutions and practices. The fifth factor is labeled *fate control*, because the items suggest a belief complex claiming that life events are pre-determined by external forces, but that there are ways for people to influence the negative impact of these forces. This five-factor structure was subsequently confirmed by multi-level factor analysis, which is a more stringent analytic technique (Cheung et al., 2006). These five factors are relatively orthogonal, with the size of their relations varying slightly by cultural group, and scores on these five axiom dimensions provide an important profile of a person's general beliefs about the social world. We consider the axiom dimensions to contain "valuable" beliefs (Preston & Epley, 2005), because they can be applied to diverse contexts and are good predictors of social behavior.

In support of the validity of the axiom dimensions, a number of individual-level studies have reported meaningful relationships between them and a wide

TABLE 20.1 The Five Pan-Cultural Axiom Dimensions

Item	1 Social cynicism	2 Social complexity	3 Reward for application	4 Religiosity	5 Fate control
Powerful people tend to exploit others	0.60				
Power and status make people arrogant	0.59				
Kind-hearted people usually suffer losses	0.57				
Kind-hearted people are easily bullied	0.53				
People will stop working hard after they secure a comfortable life	0.45				
Old people are usually stubborn and biased	0.45				
The various social institutions are biased toward the rich	0.44				
It is rare to see a happy ending in real life	0.44				
To care about societal affairs only brings trouble for yourself	0.42				
People deeply in love are usually blind	0.39				
Young people are impulsive and unreliable	0.38				
People may have opposite behaviors on different occasions		0.60			
Human behavior changes with the social context		0.54			
One's behaviors may be contrary to his or her true feelings		0.54			
One has to deal with matters according to the specific circumstances		0.48			
Current losses are not necessarily bad for one's long-term future		0.40			
There is usually only one way to solve a problem		0.39			
Hard working people will achieve more in the end			0.59		
Adversity can be overcome by effort			0.56		
Every problem has a solution			0.50		
Knowledge is necessary for success			0.49		
One who does not know how to plan his or her future will eventually fail			0.45		

(continues)

TABLE 20.1 *(continued)*

Item	1 Social cynicism	2 Social complexity	3 Reward for application	4 Religiosity	5 Fate control
Competition brings about progress			0.42		
Failure is the beginning of success			0.40		
Caution helps avoid mistakes			0.36		
Belief in a religion helps one understand the meaning of life				0.75	
Religious faith contributes to good mental health				0.72	
There is a supreme being controlling the universe				0.62	
Belief in a religion makes people good citizens				0.61	
Religion makes people escape from reality				0.59	
Religious beliefs lead to unscientific thinking				0.54	
Religious people are more likely to maintain moral standards				0.51	
Individual characteristics, such as appearance and birthday, affect one's fate					0.60
There are many ways for people to predict what will happen in the future					0.60
There are certain ways to help us improve our luck and avoid unlucky things					0.52
Most disasters can be predicted					0.51
Fate determines one's successes and failures					0.48
Good luck follows if one survives a disaster					0.48

Source: Adapted from Leung and Bond (2004).

spectrum of variables. In an American study, Singelis et al. (2003) found that social cynicism correlated negatively with interpersonal trust; social complexity correlated positively with cognitive flexibility; reward for application was related to trying harder the next time when unsuccessful; religiosity correlated positively with traditional Christian beliefs, and with seeking advice from a spiritual adviser, praying, and reading the scriptures; fate control correlated positively with an external locus of control, negatively with traditional Christian beliefs, and positively with spiritual beliefs, supernatural beliefs, and belief in precognition.

Bond et al. (2004a) examined the relationships between axioms and behavioral intentions in Hong Kong, and found some meaningful relationships. For instance, social cynicism was negatively related to the use of collaborative and compromising styles of conflict resolution, whereas Social Complexity related positively to the use of compromise and collaboration. In addition, fate control was related positively to distancing, a coping style characterized by being passive and the avoidance of thinking about difficulties.

CROSS-CULTURAL DIFFERENCES IN SOCIAL AXIOMS

Leung and Bond (2004) have reported significant variation in the five axiom dimensions across the forty cultures in their sample. The implications of these cross-cultural differences can be explored because "citizen" scores can be obtained for a cultural group by aggregating the responses of the individuals from this culture. For social cynicism, Dutch, Canadians, and Caucasian Americans reported the lowest scores, and Greeks, Germans, and Georgians reported the highest scores. For social complexity, Peruvians, Romanians, and Pakistanis reported the lowest scores, and Taiwanese, Germans, and Norwegians reported the highest scores. For reward for application, Dutch, Italians, and Czechs reported the lowest scores, and Pakistanis, Indians, and Malaysians reported the highest scores. For religiosity, Spaniards, Norwegians, and Belgians reported the lowest scores, and Indonesians, Malaysians, and Pakistanis reported the highest scores. Finally, for fate control, Norwegians, Spaniards, and Italians reported the lowest scores, and Nigerians, Thais, and Pakistanis reported the highest scores.

These citizen scores can be correlated with a wide range of culture-level variables, and the culture-level correlations obtained generally support the interpretation of the five axiom dimensions described above. For instance, people from cultures high in social cynicism tend to report lower life satisfaction. People from cultures high in social complexity tend to show stronger interest in politics. People from cultures high in reward for application tend to have more working hours per week. People from cultures high in religiosity tend to show higher agreeableness, one of the big-five personality dimensions, and higher church attendance. Finally, people from cultures high in fate control are more likely to die from heart diseases. This relationship between fate control and heart diseases is interesting and suggests that fate control may be related to a passive approach to health problems, such as less diet restriction, resulting in more heart diseases.

Research on the implications of cross-cultural differences in axiom dimensions at the individual level has just begun, but the results tend to support the usefulness of axioms as a useful construct to explain cultural differences in social behaviors. For instance, Fu et al. (2004) found in a cross-cultural study that people from cultures that were higher in social cynicism tended to regard assertive influence tactics as more effective. Socially cynical beliefs are associated with negative views of human nature, which should preclude the use of tactics that require mutual trust and encourage the display of power in securing compliance from others. In summary, the use of axioms to account for cultural differences in cognition, motivation, and behavior is a very promising area of research and should be actively pursued in future studies.

A FUNCTIONALIST APPROACH TO VALUES AND SOCIAL AXIOMS

Many theorists regard attitudinal constructs instrumental to human functioning and survival (e.g., Katz, 1960; Kruglanski, 1989). Along this line of logic, Schwartz (1992, p. 4) has also argued that his value structure is universal because all human groups need to cope with a common set of problems, viz., "... needs of individuals as biological organisms, requisites of coordinated social interaction, and survival and welfare needs of groups." The culture-generality of these three survival issues has given rise of a common scheme of value types to guide people's actions and choices in diverse cultures.

Leung and Bond (2004) have followed a similar logic in accounting for the universality of their axiom structure. In a nutshell, social axioms also help individuals cope with the universal problems of individual and group survival, thus giving rise to their culture-generality. Drawing upon evolutionary psychology, Leung and Bond (2004) have further argued that social axioms guide people to function effectively in two broad domains: social interaction and problem-solving (Keller, 1997). In the social domain, detecting deception is important for protecting one's security and advancing one's self-interest, an ability which has immense survival value (e.g., Humphrey, 1983; Whiten & Byrne, 1997). Social cynicism is related to detection of deception because it is concerned with the potential for exploitation, oppression, discrimination, and other negative elements endemic in social life. It represents a judgment of whether one lives in a benign or malevolent social world, and if this world is widely seen as malevolent (Bond et al., 2004b), one sensibly becomes suspicious of other people and vigilant in protecting one's self-interest.

Leung and Bond (2004) proposed three fundamental issues in the problem-solving domain. First, individuals need to determine whether or not it is useful to actively deal with the problems they encounter in life. Fate control represents a cognitive response to this decision, and people high in fate control see events as generally pre-determined, but they also believe that there are ways to alter these external forces. In other words, people who endorse fate control try to adapt to their perceived fate, but at the same time they are also active in finding ways to improve their fate. Second, people need to know how much personal effort and resource investment they need to exercise in order to solve the problems they encounter in life. Reward for application represents a general cost–benefit analysis of the coping responses to environmental demands. Striving is likely only if effort is seen as instrumental to problem-solving, and the problem domain is influenceable to some degree by individual inputs. Third, people need to believe that there are good solutions for solving life problems, and Social Complexity is central to this assessment. Whether or not people believe in inconsistency in human behavior and the existence of multiple solutions have important implications for their problem-solving styles. People who see the world in a "complex" fashion are likely to adopt a contingency approach to problem-solving and pay more attention to the context of the problems that they encounter.

Finally, humans have a need to seek meaning for their existence (e.g., Williams, 1997), and religious activities provide meaning to human existence, and a group context in which to pursue that meaning. Religiosity represents a cognitive response to the spiritual needs of humans and assesses whether a supreme being exists and whether religious institutions and observances have beneficial effects on people and on society. People high in religiosity are likely to be in favor of religious activities and religious in belief and practice themselves.

Although we argue that value types and axiom dimensions are recognized in a wide range of cultures, we do not imply that there are no cultural differences in values and axioms. Quite the contrary, cultural differences in these two constructs have been shown to relate to cultural differences in a wide range of phenomena (e.g., Schwartz & Sagie, 2000; Leung & Bond, 2004).

RELATIONSHIPS BETWEEN
VALUES AND AXIOMS

While we argue that values and axioms are distinct constructs, they are not without overlap. People may perceive and interpret social reality through a lens of values. Goodwin et al. (2001), for example, illustrated this possibility in their finding that values were related to people's perceptions about the availability of social support in three post-communist nations. Cognitions also have an impact on values by influencing the goals that people pursue. This possibility is illustrated by the well-known relationships between self-efficacy, a general belief about one's ability in task accomplishment, and the importance that people attach to their goals, such as career goals (Kahn & Scott, 1997).

Leung et al. (2007) have examined the relationships between Schwartz's values and social axioms in five cultural groups: Hong Kong, Mainland China, the Netherlands, Estonia, and Israel. As predicted, some social axioms showed weak relationships with some values, and these relationships were quite similar across the five cultural groups: social cynicism was correlated positively with power and conformity, and negatively with self-direction. Reward for application was correlated positively with achievement, power, and conformity, but negatively with hedonism and tradition. Social complexity was correlated positively with self-direction and benevolence, but negatively with tradition and power. Fate control correlated with tradition positively and self-direction negatively. Finally, religiosity correlated positively with tradition, conformity, and benevolence, but negatively with hedonism, stimulation, self-direction, power, and achievement.

How do we explain the relationships between values and axioms? An axiom is defined as people's perception of a relationship between two entities that are not related to themselves. Axioms may be viewed as a representation, a script, or a schema about the social world. The affective content of these beliefs is low, which is consistent with the small correlations they show with values, and they seem best regarded as "cold cognitions" (Schwarz, 1998). We argue that the law of "cognitions-to-be-consistent," such as Festinger's (1957) well-known theory of cognitive dissonance, suggests that people may feel a need to have consistent beliefs and values, thus giving rise to some relationships between certain values and axioms.

One of three mechanisms may account for the relationships between values and beliefs. Axioms may give rise to values, values may give rise to values, or axioms are related to values because of a common cause. We acknowledge that the relationships between axioms and values may be complex, and for a given relationship, all three causal processes may be at work. However, to simplify the discussion, we focus on a single causal process between a given relationship of axiom and value to illustrate the following arguments.

THE INFLUENCE OF AXIOMS ON VALUES

The first mechanism assumes that some axioms influence the formation of some values through a consistency mechanism. Some theorists conceptualize attitudes as the end result of a syllogistic network of beliefs (Wyer, 1974). Consider two entities A and B. The basic rationale is that if one holds a belief that A usually co-emerges with B, and if B is thought to be desirable, then A becomes a goal that people think they should pursue.

More complex models of this type take the probabilities of the connection between A and B into consideration. We borrow this logic to explain the influence of axioms on values. An axiom assumes the structure that A is related to B. Again, take "powerful people tend to exploit others" as an example from social cynicism. "Powerful people" is one entity and "exploit others" is the other entity. Values represent trans-situational goals, and a value such as Power represents a high importance attached to activities that will result in more power for the actor. If people hold social cynicism beliefs, they are likely to endorse the belief that powerful people are exploitative, social institutions are biased against the poor and powerless, and some groups possess negative attributes. Being exploited is obviously undesirable, and for people who hold cynical beliefs, an obvious strategy to avoid exploitation is to be in a position of power. This logic explains why the endorsement of social cynicism is likely to lead to a higher value attached to power, which was what Leung et al. (2007) found. This consistency mechanism may be termed the *goal congruence* mechanism (see Panel A of Figure 20.2).

Panel A: Goal congruence/affiliation mechanisms

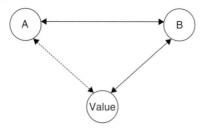

Panel B: Value-directed experience

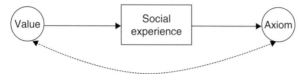

Panel C: Common causes of axioms and values

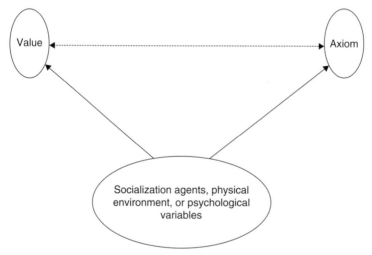

FIGURE 20.2   Mechanisms for explaining the relationships between values and axioms. *Note*: In Panel A, A and B refer to the two elements of an axiom. In all panels, a dotted line represents an observed relationship between an axiom and a value generated by the hypothesized mechanism depicted in the panel.

To illustrate the goal congruence mechanism further, let us consider the positive correlation between social cynicism and Conformity and the negative correlation between social cynicism and self-direction reported by Leung et al. (2007). As argued before, being exploited is undesirable, and if people endorse cynical beliefs, they need to find effective ways to cope with powerful people and social institutions that may be biased against them. One strategy is to comply with the requirements of powerful people and social institutions so as to avoid suffering from their sanctions, giving rise to a higher endorsement of conformity and a lower endorsement of self-direction. These values thus become strategically sensible for persons who believe in a socially malevolent world.

An extension of the above reasoning is that if B is regarded as desirable, values that are closely affiliated with A should also be endorsed. We term this mechanism the *goal affiliation* mechanism (see Panel A of Figure 20.2). Take religiosity as an example. People who endorse religiosity believe in the positive consequences of religion, such as higher moral standards and better mental health. Obviously, these positive consequences are desirable, and an effective strategy to promote these positive consequences is to support religion and religious activities. Religion is a core part of tradition for most cultures, continuing into the present, and this association is able to explain the positive correlation between religiosity and the value of tradition.

Leung et al. (2007) found that religiosity also correlated positively with conformity and benevolence, and negatively with hedonism, stimulation, self-direction, power, and achievement, and the mechanism of goal affiliation can provide one explanation for these correlations. Beit-Hallahmi and Argyle (1997) suggested that all the major religions emphasize compliance with religious teachings as a pathway to spiritual growth (Conformity and negative self-direction) and kind-heartedness (benevolence), and the rejection of pleasure (hedonism), excitement (stimulation), and domination as well as materialism (power and achievement). If people endorse religiosity and accept religion as a positive social force, they are likely to accept the values that are embraced by major religions in the world, which explains its correlations with the values reported above.

THE INFLUENCE OF VALUES ON AXIOMS

A second mechanism potentially responsible for the correlations between axioms and values derives from the assumption that certain values give rise to certain axioms. Specifically, a value guides people to focus on a set of goals and motivates them to engage in activities calculated to achieve these goals, resulting in the emergence of some specific beliefs. For example, people who endorse the value of tradition may focus their activities mainly within the traditional realm and avoid activities that contradict traditional practices and norms. Traditions are typically associated with well-defined norms and practices, and discourage self-generated goals and understandings. Thus, people who immerse themselves in traditional activities are likely to see the social world as well defined and hence unambiguous. Furthermore, tradition often prescribes what is best for a given social situation, which may give rise to the belief that there exists best ways to handle problems and situations. This analysis suggests that compliance with cultural traditions is conducive to the endorsement of low social complexity, a belief complex that emphasizes the existence of a single best solution and that there is a consistency to human behaviors. We term this mechanism the mechanism *of value-directed experience*, because the value of tradition results in the person having social experiences that promote a lower level of belief in social complexity (see Panel B of Figure 20.2).

To further illustrate the mechanism of value-directed experience, consider the correlation between the belief complex of fate control and the value type of tradition reported by Leung et al. (2007). As argued before, the endorsement of tradition is associated with immersion in traditional activities, which are guided by prescriptive norms and practices. Heightened experience with such activities is likely to result in the belief that events are shaped by external fatalistic forces, because people's behaviors are mostly driven by group-supported, traditional norms and practices. In contrast, people who reject the value of tradition are likely to follow their own preferences in conducting their daily life, and the heightened experience with self rather than tradition-guided behavior should result in a lower belief in fatalistic forces.

COMMON CAUSE AND THE OVERLAP BETWEEN VALUES AND AXIOMS

The third mechanism assumes that a common cause, or a third variable, leads to the association of axioms and values (see Panel C of Figure 20.2). Third variables may represent environmental forces, because we know that people's proximal environment can shape their values and axioms. For example, it has been found that participation in pro-social activities leads to the emergence of pro-social values (Pratt et al., 2003). The environment can be broken down into two aspects: social and physical. The influence of the social environment is mainly through socialization agents, such as schools, parents, friends, and media, which nurture particular values and axioms in people, both implicitly and explicitly. Take the widely concerned influence of media violence as an example. Some research has shown that exposure to media violence acts as a powerful social agent that can change youths' aggressive scripts, interpersonal schemas, and aggression-supporting beliefs, and increase their aggressive behavior (see Anderson et al., 2003, for a review). We argue that socialization agents may bring about the co-variation of certain values and axioms. For instance, they may consistently emphasize the importance of power, thus inculcating this value in people. At the same time, we expect that they also instruct people to be vigilant about potential exploitation by other people and social institutions, thus promoting social cynicism, giving rise to a co-variation between power and social cynicism, which was what Leung et al. (2007) found.

For socialization to be a viable explanation for the link between social cynicism and power, however, we need to postulate the existence of a mechanism that drives the socialization of social cynicism on the one hand and the socialization of power on the other. We propose an isomorphic mechanism that links values with axioms at the societal level. Going back to the example of social cynicism and power, we previously argue that from an individual's point of view, the endorsement of social cynicism is likely to give rise to the endorsement of power. This reasoning is likely to be shared by many members of a given society, thus giving rise to an implicit consensus regarding the link between social cynicism and power. Socialization practices are based on consensus within a society, and we argue that the individual logic with regard to social cynicism and Power is encapsulated in the mundane exchanges and actions of socialization agents. In other words, the links between certain values and axioms driven by individual psychological processes are isomorphic with the links that are engendered by the influence of socialization agents throughout a society.

The influence of the physical environment on human behavior is well known. For instance, in Berry's (1976) eco-cultural model, the ecology of a society is viewed as an antecedent of individual behaviors. More recently, van de Vliert and his colleagues (e.g., Van de Vliert et al., 2004; Van de Vliert, 2006) have shown that climate has some intriguing relationships with a variety of human behaviors, including leadership and motives for volunteer work. Following this line of reasoning, we postulate that some ecological features of a cultural group may promote the links of certain values with certain axioms through some social experiences engendered by these ecological features. A good example is poverty, which has both environmental as well as social causes. Although psychological processes may to some extent alter the poverty experience, poverty can be defined by objective standards and exercises material effects on the daily life of human beings. If an individual lives in poverty, he or she is likely to find the values associated with power and wealth appealing. In an impressive research program of values, Abramson and Inglehart (1995) reported that values associated with materialism are indeed more strongly endorsed in poorer societies. Poverty is associated with discomfort and inconvenience, and even hunger, extreme temperatures, and sickness. People suffering from poverty are obviously keen to embrace values associated with achievement and power, which prescribe goals and activities that deliver them out of poverty. In fact, Schwartz and Sagie (2000) found that low socioeconomic development was related to the endorsement of the values of power, conformity, tradition, security, and achievement.

With regard to the relationships between axioms and poverty, Leung and Bond (2004) found that reward for application has a positive correlation with wealth at the level of national culture as measured by GDP per capita. In other words, citizens of a poor society are more likely to endorse reward for application than are citizens of a wealthy society. A likely explanation for this association is that in poor society, people are struggling constantly for a decent living, and their life experiences may give rise to the belief that striving results in more food, shelter, and money. In contrast, life is comfortable for most people in wealthy societies, who see no need to struggle on a daily basis. Furthermore, in these societies, welfare benefits cushion low-income families and taxes tend to be high, both of which may reduce the perceived link between effort and reward. This analysis suggests that poverty is able to engender both values associated with power and achievement and beliefs associated with reward for application.

The links between power and achievement and reward for application are therefore partly explainable by societal wealth.

While the above discussion focuses on variables that are from the environment, it is also possible that third variables may have an intra-individual origin. For instance, a significant relationship was found between the axiom dimension of religiosity and the value of conformity. One may argue that anxiety about social chaos and immorality may lead to the endorsement of the axiom dimension of religiosity as well as the value of conformity. To sum up, many hypotheses can be formulated with regard to the influence of third variables on the relationships between axioms and values, and this area is definitely a fruitful area for future research.

THE ROLES OF VALUES AND SOCIAL AXIOMS IN INFLUENCING BEHAVIOR

DIFFERENTIAL ROLES OF VALUES AND SOCIAL AXIOMS

Context-free constructs bear some relationships with specific behaviors, but the relationships are typically weak (e.g., Fishbein & Ajzen, 1975). Values and axioms often show some meaningful relationships with behaviors, but, as with other context-free constructs, the relationships are not strong (e.g., Bardi & Schwartz, 2003; Bond et al., 2004a). A useful way to conceptualize their influences on behavior is to view beliefs and values as distal antecedents which function to orient people toward certain behavioral tendencies. We argue that values and axioms differ in the ways they influence behaviors, however.

A simple, but useful way to conceptualize the roles of values and social axioms in guiding actions and behaviors is that values answer the "what" question in life, and social axioms the "why" question. Values represent trans-situational goals and guiding principles in terms of defining what people would like to pursue in life (Schwartz, 1992). For instance, those who value power and wealth will focus their attention and energy on activities that bring them influence and money. In contrast, social axioms are analogous of a map that people have about their social world, which helps people navigate their daily life effectively. For instance, if people are high in social cynicism and see the world as malevolent (Bond et al., 2004b), they are less likely to engage in actions that require other people to be co-operative and trustworthy.

The different roles of axioms and values in guiding action can be illustrated by how a conflict is handled. Values provide an account of why people prefer some goals over others in handling a conflict. For instance, Ohbuchi et al. (1999) showed that the collectivistic values of Japanese led them to emphasize relationship goals in handling a conflict in order to maintain a positive relationship with others, whereas the individualistic values of Americans led to an emphasis on justice goals in order to restore justice in conflict resolution.

By contrast, axioms influence the choice of conflict resolution strategies in that the endorsement of an axiom may lead to the use of a particular strategy of conflict resolution. For instance, Bond et al. (2004a) found that people high in social cynicism were less likely to use collaboration and compromise to resolve a conflict. These people tend to see others as generally exploitative, which may discourage their use of collaboration and compromising, both of which require mutual trust for them to be effective.

In summary, values guide the choice of goals of behavior and the choice of means that are value compatible, whereas social axioms guide the choice of means based on perceived effectiveness for goal attainment.

THE INTEGRATIVE EFFECTS OF VALUES AND AXIOMS ON BEHAVIOR

Perhaps the most well-known model that is relevant to the integration of values and axioms is the expectancy model (Vroom, 1964; Fishbein & Ajzen, 1975). The central idea of this model is that an individual is likely to engage in an action if the action has a high likelihood of generating a desirable outcome. The extent to which an outcome is regarded as desirable, i.e., its valence, is related to values. For instance, material gain is likely to be regarded as highly desirable by people who endorse achievement. The perceived likelihood of a given action to generate a specific outcome, i.e., the expectancy, is a belief and may therefore be related to an axiom dimension. For instance, if one believes that there are equally good solutions to a problem, a facet of social complexity, one will stop searching for the best solution if a good solution has been identified.

The expectancy model provides a framework to integrate values and beliefs that are tied to a specific situation or object, because the common situation or object provides the basis for integrating the corresponding values and beliefs (e.g., Fishbein & Ajzen, 1975). However, because values and axioms are context-free, their integration seems more complicated because there is usually no obvious, a priori way to pair them up. For a given goal-directed behavior, values usually play the role of a distal antecedent, because the proximal goal should show some association with a general value. However, the role of axioms is less obvious, because as general beliefs, they may not bear upon the specific behavioral options of a given situation. Axioms are relevant only if they are related to the feasible actions that are capable of achieving a valued goal. For instance, axiom dimensions are related to preferences for conflict resolution procedures, but their relationships with career choices are less obvious (Bond et al., 2004a). In the absence of prior research, however, it is unclear at this point how to systematically identify the behaviors that are under the joint influence of values and axioms.

The nature of the joint influence of values and axioms on behavior is also unclear, and one possibility is that values and axioms may interact to influence behavior. The effect of some axioms on a given behavior may be accentuated if people endorse a certain value. The underlying logic is that the endorsement of a value may accentuate the importance of making the right choice or taking the optimal course of action in a given situation. Axioms are usually distal antecedents of specific behaviors, but the vigilance associated with a certain value in selecting the right choice or the right course of action may activate certain axioms and bring them to the forefront of the decision-making process. For instance, if people value power, they will be careful about how to handle their relationship with decision-makers who can influence the outcomes they achieve. Or, if people value benevolence, they will be careful about how to handle their relationship with recipients of their benevolent acts so as not to offend or alienate them.

Another possibility for the interactive effects of values and axioms is that for behaviors that are closely tied to a certain axiom, the role of values may be suppressed. For instance, persistence after failure is related to reward for application (Singelis et al., 2003), so people low in reward for application may give up after repeated failures, regardless of how much they endorse the value of achievement. Similarly, persons high in fate control may be less persistent in helping others regardless of how much they endorse the value of benevolence. Obviously, these are mere conjectures and need to be evaluated empirically in the future. The exploration of how values and axioms interact to influence behaviors is a fruitful area for future research.

CONCLUSIONS

Schwartz's (1992) circumplex model of values and Leung and Bond's (2004) analysis of social axioms are large-scale attempts to map out a psychological structure that is universal across diverse cultures. Values and axioms are constructs that have been developed to explain general psychological processes, and hence are well suited for explaining a wide range of individual preferences and behaviors. A distinctive feature of these two frameworks is that they have also been developed with the explicit aim of taking into account the cultural diversity around the world. Thus, unlike most motivational and cognitive theories in the literature, which are primarily tied to the Euro-American cultural context (e.g., for reviews, see Sampson, 1981; Nisbett, 2003), these two frameworks are intended to be pan-cultural and hence are well suited for the explanation of differences in preferences and behaviors across diverse cultural boundaries.

In this chapter, we have attempted to explore how values and axioms are related to each other, and how they may jointly influence behaviors. Research on values has a long history, but the social axiom framework is in its infancy and does not allow a rigorous and evidence-based analysis of its relationships with values. Nonetheless, we have speculated on a number of important issues for understanding their interplay, and identified a number of avenues for future research. Hopefully, our analysis will provide the impetus for more research on general values and beliefs, and their role as distal and proximal antecedents of behaviors within and across diverse cultural contexts.

ACKNOWLEDGMENT

We thank the constructive comments of the editors as well as Michael Bond and Shalom Schwartz. This chapter is supported by a grant provided by the Hong Kong Research Grants Council (CityU 1466/05H).

REFERENCES

Abramson, P. R., & Inglehart, R. (1995). *Value change in global perspective*. Ann Arbor, MI: University of Michigan Press.

Anderson, C. A., Berkowitz, L., Donnerstein, E., Huesmann, L. R., Johnson, J. D., Linz, D. et al. (2003). The influence of media violence on youth. *Psychological Science in the Public Interest, 4*, 81–110.

Bardi, A., & Schwartz, S. H. (2003). Values and behaviors: Strength and structure of their relations. *Personality and Social Psychology Bulletin, 29*, 1207–1220.

Barnea, M., & Schwartz, S. H. (1998). Values and voting. *Political Psychology, 19*, 17–40.

Becker, G. (1996). The meta-analysis of factor analyses: An illustration based on the cumulation of correlation matrices. *Psychological Methods, 1*, 341–353.

Beit-Hallahmi, B., & Argyle, M. (1997). *The psychology of religious behaviors, beliefs and experience*. UK: Routledge.

Berry, J. W. (1976). *Human ecology and cognitive style: Comparative studies in cultural and psychological adaptation*. New York: Russell Sage.

Bond, M. H., Leung, K., Au, A., Tong, K. K., & Chemonges-Nielson, Z. (2004a). Combining social axioms with values in predicting social behaviors. *European Journal of Personality, 18*, 177–191.

Bond, M. H., Leung, K., Au, A., Tong, K. K., de Carrasquel, S. R., Murakami, F. et al. (2004b). Culture-level dimensions of social axioms and their correlates across 41 cultures. *Journal of Cross-Cultural Psychology, 35*, 548–570.

Cheung, M. W. L., Leung, K., & Au, K. (2006). Evaluating multilevel models in cross-cultural research: An illustration with social axioms. *Journal of Cross-Cultural Psychology, 37*, 522–541.

Festinger, L. (1957). *A theory of cognitive dissonance*. Evanston, IL: Row-Peterson.

Fishbein, M., & Ajzen, I. (1975). *Belief, attitude, intention, and behavior: An introduction to theory and research*. Reading, MA: Addison-Wesley.

Forgas, J. P. (2000). *Feeling and thinking: The role of affect in social cognition*. Cambridge, England: Cambridge University Press.

Fu, P. P., Kennedy, J., Yukl, G., Bond, M. H., Peng, T. K., Srinivas, E. S. et al. (2004). Exploring the effect of cultural values on the relationship between social beliefs and managerial influence strategies in twelve cultures: A meso approach using HLM. *Journal of International Business Studies, 35*, 284–305.

Goodwin, R., Nizharadze, G., Luu, L. N., Kosa, E., & Emelyanova, T. (2001). Social support in a changing Europe: An analysis of three post-communist nations. *European Journal of Social Psychology, 31*, 379–393.

Humphrey, N. K. (1983). The adaptiveness of mentalism. *Behavioral and Brain Science, 6*, 343–390.

Jost, J. T., Glaser, J., Kruglanski, A. W., & Sulloway, F. J. (2003). Political conservatism as motivated social cognition. *Psychological Bulletin, 129*, 339–375.

Kahn, J. J., & Scott, N. A. (1997). Predictors of research productivity and science-related career goals among counseling psychology doctoral students. *The Counseling Psychologist, 25*, 38–67.

Katz, D. (1960). The functional approach to the study of attitudes. *Public Opinion Quarterly, 24*, 163–204.

Keller, H. (1997). Evolutionary approaches. In J. W. Berry, Y. H. Poortinga, & J. Pandey (Eds.), *Handbook of cross-cultural psychology*, (Vol. 1) pp. 215–255. Boston, MA: Allyn and Bacon.

Kruglanski, A. W. (1989). *Lay epistemics and human knowledge: Cognitive and motivational bases.* New York: Plenum.

Leung, K., & Bond, M. H. (2004). Social axioms: A model of social beliefs in multi-cultural perspective. In M. P. Zanna (Ed.), *Advances in Experimental Social Psychology,* (Vol. 36) pp. 119–197. San Diego, CA: Academic Press.

Leung, K., & Bond, M. H. (2007). Psycho-logic and eco-logic: Insights from social axiom dimensions. In F. van de Vijver, D. van Hemert, & Y. P. Poortinga (Eds.), *Individuals and cultures in multilevel analysis* (pp. 197–219). Mahwah, NJ: Lawrence Erlbaum Associates.

Leung, K., Bond, M. H., Reimel de Carrasquel, S., Muñoz, C., Hernández, M., Murakami, F., Yamaguchi, S., Bierbrauer, G., & Singelis, T. M. (2002). Social axioms: The search for universal dimensions of general beliefs about how the world functions. *Journal of Cross Cultural Psychology, 33,* 286–302.

Leung, K., Au, A., Huang, X., Kurman, J., Niit, T., & Niit, K. K. (2007). Social axioms and values: A cross-cultural examination. *European Journal of Personality, 21,* 91–111.

Nisbett, R. E. (2003). *The geography of thought: How Asians and westerners think differently, and why.* New York: Free Press.

Ohbuchi, K., Fukushima, O., & Tedeschi, J. T. (1999). Cultural values in conflict management: Goal orientation, goal attainment, and tactical decision. *Journal of Cross-Cultural Psychology, 30,* 51–71.

Osgood, C. E., Suci, G. J., & Tannenbaum, P. H. (1957). *The measurement of meaning.* Urbana, IL: University of Illinois Press.

Pratt, M. W., Hunsberger, B., Pancer, S. M., & Alisat, S. (2003). A longitudinal analysis of personal values socialization: Correlates of a moral self-ideal in late adolescence. *Social Development, 12,* 563–585.

Preston, J., & Epley, N. (2005). Explanations versus applications: The explanatory power of valuable beliefs. *Psychological Science, 18,* 826–832.

Rokeach, M. (1972). *Beliefs, attitudes, and values.* San Francisco, CA: Jossey-Bass.

Rotter, J. B. (1966). Generalized expectancies for internal versus external control of reinforcement. *Psychological Monographs, 80,* 1–28.

Sampson, E. E. (1981). Cognitive psychology as ideology. *American Psychologist, 36,* 730–743.

Schachter, S., & Singer, J. (1962). Cognitive, social and physiological determinants of emotional state. *Psychological Review, 69,* 379–399.

Schwarz, N. (1998). Warmer and more social: Recent developments in cognitive social psychology. *Annual Review of Sociology, 24,* 239–264.

Schwartz, S. H. (1992). Universals in the content and structure of values: Theory and empirical tests in 20 countries. In M. Zanna (Ed.), *Advances in experimental social psychology* (Vol. 25) pp. 1–65. New York: Academic Press.

Schwartz, S. H. (1996). Value priorities and behavior: Applying a theory of integrated value systems. In C. Seligman, J. M. Olson, & M. P. Zanna (Eds.), *The psychology of values: The Ontario Symposium,* (Vol. 8) pp. 1–24. Hillsdale, NJ: Erlbaum.

Schwartz, S. H., & Boehnke, K. (2004). Evaluating the structure of human values with confirmatory factor analysis. *Journal of Research in Personality, 58,* 88–107.

Schwartz, S. H., & Sagie, G. (2000). Value consensus and importance: A cross-national study. *Journal of Cross-Cultural Psychology, 31,* 465–497.

Schwartz, S. H., Sagiv, L., & Boehnke, K. (2000). Worries and values. *Journal of Personality, 68,* 309–346.

Singelis, T. M., Hubbard, C., Her, P., & An, S. (2003). Convergent validation of the social axioms survey. *Personality and Individual Differences, 24,* 269–282.

Van de Vliert, E. (2006). Autocratic leadership around the globe: Do climate and wealth drive leadership culture? *Journal of Cross-Cultural Psychology, 37,* 42–59.

Van de Vliert, E., Huang, X., & Levine, R. V. (2004). National wealth and thermal climate as predictors of motives for volunteer work. *Journal of Cross-Cultural Psychology, 35,* 62–73.

Vroom, V. H. (1964). *Work and motivation*. New York: Wiley.

Whiten, A., & Byrne, R. W. (Eds.) (1997). *Machiavellian intelligence II: Extensions and evaluations*. Cambridge, England: Cambridge University Press.

Williams, K. D. (1997). Social ostracism. In R. M. Kowalski (Ed.), *Aversive interpersonal behaviors* (pp. 133–170). New York: Plenum Press.

Wyer, R. S., Jr. (1974). *Cognitive organization and change: An information-processing approach*. Hillsdale, NJ: Lawrence Erlbaum Associates.

21

COGNITIVE, RELATIONAL AND SOCIAL BASIS OF ACADEMIC ACHIEVEMENT IN CONFUCIAN CULTURES: PSYCHOLOGICAL, INDIGENOUS, AND CULTURAL PERSPECTIVES

UICHOL KIM* AND YOUNG-SHIN PARK[†]

*College of Business Administration, Inha University, Korea
[†]College of Education, Inha University, Korea

INTRODUCTION

In psychology, biological theories are popular explanations of human cognition, emotion and behavior. In establishing psychology as a discipline, behaviorism became the dominant paradigm emphasizing biology as the basis of human behavior (Koch & Leary, 1985). In psychiatry, Freudian theory and the medical diagnosis and treatment of the mentally ill are still pervasive (Kleinman, 2005). On the third camp, humanists criticize behaviorists and psychiatrists for the negative portrayal of human beings and for not examining human potential and creativity. However, even the leading advocate of humanism, Abraham Maslow,

This chapter was published with the support of INHA UNIVERSITY Research Grant.

491

viewed biological needs as being basic and psychological needs (e.g., emotional, relational and social needs) as secondary (Maslow, 1943).

Bandura (1999) criticizes general psychology for portraying human beings as passive recipients of stimulation and the brain as a simple store of information. Shweder (1991, p. 80) points out that "epistemologically speaking, knowledge-seeking in general psychology is the attempt to get a look at the central processing mechanism untainted by content and context." Harré (1999) notes that traditional psychological theories view knowledge as being hierarchically organized and accessed, combined, and integrated without individuals' awareness. Bandura (1999) points out that the agentic and creative aspects of human cognition, motivation and behavior have been largely ignored in general psychology.

The emphasis on biology is an extension of the evolutionary theories that dominate the field. Although animal behavior can be explained in terms of physiology and biological evolution, can the same be said about human cognition, motivation and behavior? If biology is the basis of human behavior, then what role do creativity and culture play in explaining human thought, emotions and behavior? In order to answer these questions, we need to return to prehistoric times and examine how we have become modern human beings (i.e., *Homo sapiens sapiens*, "wise wise human"). Mithen (2007, p. 1977) points out that "there was a complex network of evolving relationships between anatomy, brain size, foraging behavior, sociality, vocalization, technology and environment" and "the most reasonable interpretation of the evidence is that there was feedback between each of these developments within a continuous nexus of evolutionary change."

While the main motivation force in the early human history focused on survival and adaptation, humans were able to gradually develop the necessary cognitive capabilities to understand, predict and manage the environment through creativity and innovations. Although our body provides the physiological basis of the self, our cognitive and affective capabilities have provided symbolic approximations of the world. These symbolic approximations become more sophisticated through repeated cycles of observation, testing, verification and modification. The shared symbolic understanding and management of the world represents culture. Cultural knowledge is recorded outside of our body and is transmitted through enculturation, socialization and education. In modern life, education plays a key role in teaching the accumulated knowledge that helps our children to understand, predict and manage the world.

CREATIVITY ADAPTATION, AND MASTERY

At the dawn of time, the main motivation force in life was survival. As a physically weaker species, humans were at a constant mercy of predators and harsh climate. A separate genus *Homo* emerged around 2.5 million years ago, which originally diverged from apes about five millions years ago (Collard & Wood, 2007). Humans and other species within the *Homo genus* possess characteristic features such as walking upright, possessing a relatively large brain size and engaging complex social behavior (Berger & Hilton-Barber, 2000). Mithen (2007, p. 1966) notes that "the paradox we face is that *Homo sapiens* are almost is genetically almost identical to the chimpanzee, our closest living relative with whom we shared that 6-million year-old ancestor, but cognitively and behaviorally radically different." The critical feature that distinguishes *Homo sapiens sapiens* from apes appears to be creativity: The cognitive capability of reasoning, abstract thinking, generative forethoughts, planning, implementation of thoughts into action and the development of syntactic language (Berger & Hilton-Barber, 2000; Wells, 2002; Mithen, 2007).

Early human beings struggled to adapt and survive in the harsh environment. Through a series of cognitive, social and cultural transformations, they began to exert greater control over their environment. Early humans were originally the hunted and not the hunters; they survived by foraging roots, plants, fruits, and by scavenging (Berger & Hilton-Barber, 2000). The first major transformation came with the production and use of stone tools around 2.6 million years ago (Toth & Schick, 2007). Although other animals use tools (e.g., sea otters, crows, finches and chimpanzees), the manufacturing process of shaping and flaking of stones has not been found in non-human species (Toth & Schick, 2007). For example, when a pygmy chimpanzee named Kanzi, his sister and offspring were trained for over 15 years in tool-making and usage, they experienced distinct limitations due to biomechanical differences (i.e., they lack opposable thumbs) and limited cognitive capability (Toth & Schick, 2007). Stone tools allowed humans to move from being the hunted to hunters. Making, refining and teaching the use of tools is a cultural achievement since "stone technology is based on learned behavior and is not directly transmitted biologically" (Conrad, 2007, p. 2005).

The second major cognitive transformation came about 1.1 million years ago, when *Homo erectus* first learned the controlled use of fire (Berger & Hilton-Barber, 2000; Gore, 2000). Like all animals, it is natural to fear the destructive forces of fire. Humans, however, learned to control their fears and the destructive forces of the fire for protection and warmth. As long as the flame was maintained, no animal, however fierce or strong, would dare to attack them.

Humans learned to cook food over fire, which significantly changed their diet, physiology and lifestyle. Tenderizing food over fire allowed humans to consume more calories, which subsequently transformed their physiology (Berger & Hilton-Barber, 2000). With fire tenderizing food, humans no longer needed strong facial muscles and large teeth to chew. This allowed the gradual increase in the size of the skull to accommodate a larger brain. Cooking reduced the amount of time needed to chew and digest food, while significantly increasing the total calorie intake.

Aiello and Wheeler (1995) point out that the human brain has a high metabolic cost since brain tissues require significantly more calories than muscle tissues. With the enhanced quality of diet through cooking, humans could accommodate a larger brain and a small gut (Aiello & Wheeler, 1995). With a larger brain, cognitive capabilities became more sophisticated, which in turn allowed humans to develop the necessary cognitive skills in collectively planning and executing hunts for large animals (Berger & Hilton-Barber, 2000). With the use of tools, fire and social cooperation, humans were able to hunt for large animals and obtain more food. This in turn supported a large brain and provided leisure time for them to develop additional cognitive and social skills.

Early humans displayed compassion by taking care of the sick and injured (Berger & Hilton-Barber, 2000; Gore, 2000). In a harsh environment with limited food supply and in constant danger of being attacked by predators, it would be advantageous to abandon the weak and sick. However, fossil records indicate that humans cared for the weak and the sick (Gore, 2000). Conrad (2007, p. 2015) notes that the "deliberate burial of kin is linked to personal and emotional ties between the living and the dead." In addition, items recovered from gravesites give information about the status of the individual and the tools that they may have needed in the afterlife (Conrad, 2007).

The third major cognitive transformation is the development of language. Mithen (2007, p. 1974) points out that the brain size began to increase dramatically around 60,000 years ago, which is likely to be related to the evolution of language. He suggests that living in a larger social group may have "imposed selective pressures for an enlargement of the brain and enhanced communication." Language allows coordination of group activities and development of symbolic knowledge that is critical to the further development of creativity. The cognitive impact that "language has on an individual is magnified a multitude of times by the manner in which language connects people's minds into a single network" and "ideas are then able to 'migrate' between minds" (Mithen, 2007, p. 1991). The sharing of these ideas through language can "allow the communal construction of extremely delicate and difficult intellectual trajectories and progressions" (Clark, 1996, p. 206).

The fourth major cognitive transformation is the anchoring of symbolic ideas in the material world through the development of jewelry, art and music. Art and jewelry do not have practical functional values, except to provide the symbolic connectedness of the individual to the group (Conrad, 2007). The earliest art forms excavated are: (1) a lion-man figurine (i.e., possessing the head of a lion and the body of a man) from Hohlenstein-Stadel, Germany, dating back to 33,000 years ago; (2) the Grotte Chauvet paintings of animals from France, dating back to 32,000 years ago; and (3) the Aurignacian flute made from mammoth ivory, dating back to 33,000 years ago (Conrad, 2007). Ideas and utterances are not durable since they can remain only in the mind of the speaker or listener. Transforming ideas into art forms make them durable and can connect individuals across time and space (Mithen, 2007).

Although reality is constrained by physical necessities, ideas can be fluid and innovative. Although an actual lion-man does not exist in nature, a figurine can be created through constructive imagination. These artifacts help to articulate what is possible and to share these ideas, beliefs and values beyond the physical realm (Mithen, 2007). Art and music can serve as a "cognitive anchor and extend the capacities of the mind" and allow "information and ideas to be recalled and communicated across time and space far in excess of what a human body and brain are able to do alone" (Mithen, 2007, p. 1993). They allow the record, transmission and refinement of ideas beyond any individual and the human body. If the human physiology is the hardware, ideas that are communicated, shared and transmitted are the software of the mind and it is the basis of culture (Hofstede, 1991). These ideas were subsequently refined and extended into religious thoughts, philosophy and science (Kim et al., 2003).

The fifth major transformation is the domestication of animals and plants. Domestication, agriculture and the making of pottery developed around 10,000 years ago (Mithen, 2007). Animals, like cows, goats, pigs and chickens, existed in the wild and humans have traditionally hunted, killed and consumed them. They have, however, learned to control their natural tendencies and domesticate them as a way of producing and storing food. Also, humans have learned to control the natural instincts of predators (e.g., wolves and cats) so that they serve as protectors, workers or companions. They have learned to cultivate natural resources such as wheat, rice and potato, and harvest crops from the land. With increased agricultural efficiency, irrigation and storage, enough food could be produced to support a large number of people and a sedentary lifestyle. Social, religious, legal and political institutions were created to manage a large number of people who lived in close proximity (Kim et al., 2002).

Using fire, formless clay was transformed into pottery, which could be used to cook food and to store water. It was transformed into bricks, which allowed humans to build houses and become mobile. How could humans transform formless clay into a cup, house or an art form that did not exist in nature? They made a cup from formless clay since they had an idea of a container and capabilities to transform an idea into a cup. They were able to make a cup because they developed reflective and generative cognitive capabilities (Bandura, 1997). Berger & Hilton-Barber (2000, p. 18) point out that humans "are able, if we choose so, to alter our actions in any situation based upon the accumulated knowledge and wisdom of those hundreds of thousands of generation that have preceded us," and "our brain and our ability to communicate our thoughts through language allow us to analyze situations and pass on information at a level that no other animal can, not even our most closely related biological relatives, the chimpanzee."

A renowned geneticist, Spencer Wells, traced the genetic makeup of *Homo sapiens sapiens* and concluded that humans have emerged as a separate species around 60,000 years ago from a single tribe in Kalahari, Africa (Wells, 2002). The critical feature that separates humans from other species is the capability of creative forethought, planning, conceptualization and implementation of ideas into reality (Wells, 2002). Syntactic language became the medium through which ideas were communicated, refined and recorded. Creativity is a hallmark of humanity that separates human beings from other animals (Wells, 2002).

With each succeeding generation, new knowledge became accumulated and was passed on orally, and later in written forms around 7000 years ago. Industrialization, commerce, science and technology transformed subsistence economies into urban centers and modern nations. Currently, information technology, democracy and the rule of law protect the right of individuals in society, and people enjoy freedom and quality of life that is unparalleled in human history (Kim et al., 2003).

CULTURAL TRANSFORMATIONS

The motivation to understand, predict and manage our environment went beyond the need for survival (Bandura, 1997). Understanding our environment and ourselves became a central motive in our adaptation and mastery. Religion, philosophy and science emerged to answer the basic question of our existence, which are cultural creations constructed to understand and manage the physical and human world (Kim et al., 2002, 2003). The knowledge they generated are passed on to our children through socialization and formal education.

Myths and superstitions emerged as our attempt to explain the physical, biological and human world by resorting to supernatural forces. They were extensions of the mind and were symbolically expressed through ornaments, art, music and oral narratives. They did not provide any functional value, except for providing self-expressiveness, emotional security and communal identity (Mithen, 2007). With time, myths and superstitions gave away to major religions (e.g., Buddhism, Christianity, Hinduism, Islam and Judaism), which provided a comprehensive, systematic and integrated belief system of the truth, the whole truth and nothing but the truth. Once accepted, it became the only, absolute, and universal truth. Based on these beliefs, explicit guidelines were established, outlining how humans should live. Religion is an example of how symbolic ideas are systematized and transformed into social institutions that regulate the lives of people (Kim et al., 2003).

Major challenges to religion came with the emergence of philosophy. Questions that Socrates raised to his students (e.g., *know thyself; what is the essence of beauty?*) were revolutionary since many Greeks believed that their lives were controlled by whims of gods and that they could appease them through religious rituals and offerings. Socrates wanted his students to be freed from these superstitions and to use critical reasoning to discover universal knowledge. This type of free-thinking threatened the religious establishment, and he was sentenced to death in 399 BC. His ideas, however, did not die. They were recorded, extended and refined by succeeding generations, such as Plato, Aristotle, Avicenna and Déscartes. Socrates' ideas paved the way for the development of science, in which reflective thinking, reasoning and observation became formalized and systematized through verification and falsification.

In mathematics, Pythagoras discovered that all right-angled triangles followed the universal law of $a^2 + b^2 = c^2$. Although human beings were imperfect, we could understand the universal truth through the use of reason. When Archimedes discovered the Law of Displacement, he ran outside shouting, *"Eureka!"* At this time, common sense told us that all matters were unique. Archimedes discovered a universal property called mass, which could be quantified and standardized. In the field of medicine, Hippocrates rejected superstitious temple medicine and developed a rational and naturalistic medicine.

Philosophy, religion, arts and science provide a way of constructing, anchoring and communicating our ideas, beliefs, knowledge and culture and provide a coherent integration. Culture allows us to define who we are and what is meaningful, as well as communicating with others and managing our environment. Culture represents *the collective utilization of natural and human resources to achieve desired outcomes* (Kim, 2001). To understand culture, we need to understand the goals and aspirations of people, the process by which they strive to achieve these goals and the human and natural resources that are used in attaining these goals (Kim, 2000, 2001).

In modern societies, culture is as basic to understanding human thought, emotion and behavior as our physiology. Without culture, humans would not be able to think, feel or behave the way we do. Just as we use our eyes to see the world, it is *through* culture that we think, feel and behave (Shweder, 1991). Because we think *through* culture, it is difficult to recognize our own culture. For a person born and raised in a particular culture, that culture feels supremely natural.

Cultures differ in ways people understand, manage and contribute to the world (Kim et al., 2006). The basic difference across cultures is a difference in emphasis rather than quality. For example, in the West, there is an emphasis on individuality and rationality. When Socrates asked his students to *know thyself,* Déscartes concluded, *I think, therefore I am.* In East Asia, Confucianism emphasizes human relationships and emotions that bind individuals together. In Confucianism, people define themselves through relationships and emotions: *I feel, therefore I am.* Relationships and emotions are central to understanding the self. Our parents and ancestors represent our past since they provided us with the basis of who we are (i.e., our body) and have raised us in a family environment that they created for us. Our children represent our future. In schools, Confucianism taught universal ethics and laws which are essential for developing a broad understanding of humanity, compassion and justice (Kim et al., 2006).

Similarly, Buddhism emphasizes universal justice, compassion and humanity. It is through understanding the relatedness of individuals, people and nature that we can develop a universal sense of compassion, justice and understanding. It is not through satisfying our needs, as Maslow's theory states, but regulating our needs through discipline and detachment that humans are able to self-actualize. Buddhism rejects the narrow Confucian emphasis on the family and interpersonal emotions, and emphasizes universal compassion and justice. Buddhism provides an alternative view of how creativity is achieved by rejecting individualism, hedonism and rationality and by affirming the transcendental relatedness of the self to others, nature and the universe. While Confucianism focuses on the

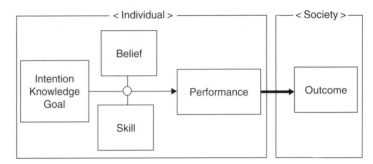

FIGURE 21.1   Facets of self-efficacy.

family and society, Buddhism focuses on the inner lives of individual and universal connectedness.

HUMAN BEHAVIOR

Human beings are agents of our action motivated to control events that influence our lives (Bandura, 1997). We interpret human behavior in terms of cognition, emotions and agency (i.e., intention, motive and responsibility). People develop a *theory of mind* to explain the behavior of themselves and others (Premack & Woodruff, 1978; Mithen, 2007). It is defined as the ability to attribute desires, intentions and beliefs to oneself and others, and to explain their behavior in terms of these inner states (Premack & Woodruff, 1978; Mithen, 2007).

Bandura (1997, p. 3) identifies self-efficacy as an important mediating factor between environment and behavior. He defines self-efficacy as "beliefs in one's capabilities to organize and execute the courses of action required to produce given attainments." Self-efficacy can be divided into four components: (1) intention, knowledge and goal; (2) belief; (3) skills and (4) performance (see Figure 21.1). For example, the goal of doing well on a math test can vary from one student to another. Individuals also vary in their belief in their skills to do well on a test. This belief will be confirmed or disconfirmed through their performance on an actual test. The actual score on the test can lead to outcomes (e.g., whether they will receive a scholarship or enter a desired university). An outcome is probabilistic since performance may not always result in the same outcome for any given performance (e.g., it may depend on the ability of their competitors, task and the evaluation criteria). Behavior and outcome have multiple determinants, and culture plays an important role in influencing the behaviors that will be rewarded or punished (Yamaguchi, 1994; Bandura, 1999; Kim & Park, 2006).

EDUCATION AND ACADEMIC ACHIEVEMENT

Formal education has become an important aspect of modern life. Historically, children had to learn practical skills, such as hunting, farming or trade skills.

In modern societies, children must spend a minimum of 9 years in compulsory education, and most spent an average of 12–16 years obtaining a formal education.

The benefits of education for an individual and nations have been systematically documented (OECD, 2003). At the individual level, financial returns of education are significant: a Korean employee with a university degree earns 155% more than a person with a high school degree and 283% more than a person with an elementary education (Korea National Statistical Office, 2008). In the United States, university graduates earn on average 86% more than non-graduates (Time Magazine, 2004). At the national level, education is one of the most important factors contributing to economic development (OECD, 2003).

Governments have sponsored large-scale international studies to analyze factors that influence the academic achievement of middle and high school students (e.g., TIMSS[1] and PISA[2]). In these studies, East Asian students are top achievers in mathematics, sciences, reading and problem-solving. In math, students from Singapore are the top performers, followed by students from South Korea (abbreviated as Korea), Taiwan, Hong Kong and Japan (TIMSS, 1999). In the sciences, Taiwanese students are the top performers, followed by Singapore, Hungary, Korea and Japan. In the 31-nation OECD study of ninth-grade students (PISA, 2000), Japanese students are top achievers in math, Korean students are the top achievers in the sciences, and they are near the top in reading (ranked 8th and 6th, respectively). In problem-solving, Korean students are ranked first and Japanese students third (PISA, 2003). This pattern of results has been found in subsequent studies (PISA, 2003, 2006).

Although the US government spends more money per student, has smaller classes and provides larger research funds to develop teaching material and curricula, US students perform far below their East Asian counterparts. They are ranked 19th in math 18th in the sciences (TIMSS, 1999). In PISA (2000), they are ranked 15th in reading, 19th in math and 14th in scientific literacy. In problem-solving, US students are ranked 24th among OECD countries (PISA, 2003). Similar patterns of results were found in subsequent studies (PISA, 2003, 2006).

These results baffle many educators since they contradict existing psychological, educational and sociological theories that emphasize individualistic values (e.g., intrinsic motivation, primary control, self-esteem, individual creativity, small class size, active learning and individualized instruction). These aspects have been incorporated into the curricula, teaching methods and educational system in economically developed countries in the West (e.g., Denmark, Germany

---

[1] A 39-nation study of Grade 8 students sponsored by National Center for Education Statistics, US Government, www.nces.ed.gov/timss.

[2] A 31-nation study of 15 year old students sponsored by the Organisation for Economic Cooperation and Development. It increased to 40 nations in 2003 and 57 in 2006, www.pisa.oecd.org.

and the United States). However, students from these countries perform at much lower levels than students from East Asia.

Consistent with cultural values, survey results from these studies indicate that US students maintain strong individualistic values (i.e., they maintain high self-esteem and intrinsic motivation). Nearly half of US students *strongly agreed* that their motivation for studying math is "to get the desired job," affirming their individualistic value. However, only one-tenth of Korean and Japanese students gave the same response (TIMSS, 1999). The vast majority of Korean students report relational and social motivation: 85% agreed that their motivation is to "enter a desired university" and 62% agreed that it is "to please their parents" (TIMSS, 1999).

Although US students perform lower then their East Asian counterparts, they have the highest score in the self-concept for sciences and fourth highest in the self-concept for mathematics (TIMSS, 1999). In contrast, East Asian students had relatively lower scores: Korean students are ranked 32nd for self-concept for math and 21st for the sciences, 34th and 16th for Japanese students and 30th and 18th for Taiwanese students. Similar patterns of results were found in PISA (2003, 2006) studies, in which Japanese and Korean students had high performances, but lower self-concepts relative to US students.

These patterns of results question the validity of Western theories that focus on individualistic values. Also, it raises the following question: What are the factors that explain the high level of achievement among East Asian students?

CULTURE AND EDUCATION IN EAST ASIA

China, Japan and Korea share the Confucian heritage in which education and self-regulation are viewed as an important goal and as the means to achieving success (Kim & Park, 2003). In contrast to the Western emphasis on the individuated self, Confucianism focuses on emotions that bind individuals and family members together (Kim, 2001). The Chinese, Japanese and Korean word for human being is *ingan* "人間", which can be translated literally as "human between." It is not what happens within an individual, but between individuals that makes us human (Kim, 2001). Mencius stated that "If you see a child drowning and you don't feel compassion, then you are not a human being." It is compassion that helps us to relate to the child and to take the necessary actions to save the child. The love, sacrifice and devotion of parents for their children are viewed as being necessary and essential for a child to become human. Human essence is relational and can be defined in terms of universal emotions that bind people together.

Confucius articulated the need to cultivate oneself to achieve harmony with others and the environment. Self-cultivation involves examining oneself from within and learning from others: "When you meet someone better than yourself, turn your thoughts to becoming his equal. When you meet someone who is not as good as you are, look within and examine your own self" (Confucius, 1979). Self-cultivation involves constant self-examination: "Every day I examine myself on three counts. In what I have undertaken on another's behalf, have I failed to do my best? In my dealings with my friends, have I failed to be trustworthy in what I say? Have I passed on to others anything that I have not tried out myself?" (Confucius, 1979). In Confucianism, self-cultivation and learning is a lifelong process and the basis of all activities.

In Confucian societies, individuals of merit were selected through national examinations to serve the public. In China and Korea, Confucian academies were established around 1000 years ago. Successful candidates in the national examination were given official positions as a government, military or local official. In return for their service, they were given a track of land for three generations. Success on the national examination was an indication of their knowledge, wisdom and moral integrity, and it provided a chance for upward social mobility. Since educational success also benefited family members for three generations, it became the most effective way of fulfilling one's filial piety. In traditional Confucian societies, passing the national examination was the most effective way to move up in social status and wealth.

Although the formal aspects of Confucianism have declined with modernization, the emphasis on educational achievement remains strong (Tsuneyoshi, 2001; Park & Kim, 2004b; Hwang, 2007). The content and mode of instruction of education in modern East Asia has changed from the traditional emphasis on Confucian Classics and literature, to science, technology and global knowledge.

The second major transformation is the change of emphasis from the past to the future. Confucian philosophy has traditionally emphasized the past, the status quo and the role of ancestors and the elderly. In modern society, the relational shift has changed from the past and ancestors to the future, change and children.

THE ROLE OF PARENTS AND FAMILY

East Asian parents are instrumental in motivating their children to achieve educational success. Mothers in modern Confucian cultures view unselfish devotion to their children as a critical feature of their personhood and motherhood. Researchers have found that East Asian mothers' personal identities are often defined by their role as a mother, and they become emotionally tied to their children and see their children as extensions of themselves and their future (Azuma, 1986; Ho, 1986; Park & Kim, 2004a). Children's accomplishments and failures become their own, and children vicariously fulfill their own dreams and goals. Attaining this vicarious gratification is one of the most important aspects of motherhood, and it is one of the most valued aspects of raising children (Azuma, 1986; Ho, 1986; Park & Kim, 2004a; Kim et al., 2005).

When a child is born, East Asian mothers remain close to their child to make the child feel secure, make the boundary between herself and the child minimal, and meet all the needs of the child, even if it means a tremendous sacrifice and devotion on her own part (Azuma, 1986; Ho, 1986; Park & Kim, 2004a). Children's strong dependency needs, both emotional and physical, are satisfied by their mothers' indulgent devotion. As children mature, they sense that it is through their mother that they can obtain gratification, security and love. Children become motivated to maintain the close relationship and they do so by taking a more active role incorporating their mothers' values and behaving according to their mother's wishes. The feeling of relatedness helps children to assimilate their mothers' values and beliefs as their own, and they learn to develop proxy control. By maintaining a close relationship and by pleasing their mother, their mothers satisfy their needs and provide a positive environment.

SCHOOL ENVIRONMENT AND EDUCATION

The phenomenal educational attainment in East Asian societies has been systematically documented (Stevenson et al., 1986; Stevenson & Lee, 1990). In addition to the supportive environment that parents provide, self-regulation, proxy control and compatibility of values in the family and school environment are important aspects of educational success in Confucian cultures.

Self-regulation

An important factor in academic achievement of East Asian students is the belief in self-regulation and discipline. Effort is believed to lead to success, especially in education (Stevenson & Lee, 1990; Yu & Yang, 1994; Kim & Park, 2003; Hwang, in press). Lebra (1976) has found that over 70% of Japanese respondents attribute success to diligence, effort and endurance and only 1% to ability. Researchers similarly found that East Asian adolescents and adults attribute educational success to effort (Stevenson et al., 1986; Yu & Yang, 1994; Park & Kim, 1998; Hwang, in press).

Consistent with Confucian philosophy, individual striving is viewed as a necessary component of the self-cultivation process. Excellence in performance provides evidence that children have developed a moral character through perseverance and persistence. It is a visible demonstration that they have deeper abilities to be a virtuous person. Holloway et al. (1986, p. 272) point out that "the emphasis on individual effort includes a sense of responsibility to the group to which one belongs." In Confucian societies, individuals are pressured to contribute to the group through persistent effort.

Proxy Control

As children mature, they are expected to extend their close mother–child identification to their teachers. A mother's job is to use her close relationship with her children to prepare her children for school life and to control the environment for them. She becomes a mediator between the home environment and the school environment, and she serves as a proxy for her children providing a positive environment for achievement and by negotiating with the teachers on their behalf (Azuma, 1986; Ho, 1986; Park & Kim, 2004a).

In Confucian cultures, the relationship between teachers and their students is seen as an extension of the mother–child relationship. A typical climate of East Asian schools affirms the strong relational bond between teachers and students; teachers pressure the student to strive for personal excellence and encourage students to cooperate in a group (Azuma, 1986; Ho, 1986; Park & Kim, 2004b). Children are motivated to please the teacher and their attention is focused on the teacher. Even in a class size that is as large as 40 or 50, East Asian students are attentive and devoted to doing their schoolwork and homework (Azuma, 1986; Park & Kim, 2004; Stevenson et al., 1986). Through proxy control, children are able to grow up in a positive family and school environment that supports their educational endeavors. By maintaining a close relationship, they are able to receive social support from parents, teachers and friends, which are important for their academic achievement and subjective well-being.

Compatibility of Values

In East Asia, there is a greater congruence between the values emphasized in the home environment and those learned in the school environment than there is in the United States (White & LeVine, 1986). In the United States, individualistic values are often in conflict with the relatively rigid classroom structure, standardized curricula and the hierarchical teacher–student relationship (White & LeVine, 1986). In addition, US students, parents, teachers and administrators often hold different views about the importance of education in relation to personal happiness (Farkas et al., 1990). The diversity of viewpoints are considered the strength of individualistic societies (White & LeVine, 1986; Hsia, 1988).

There is greater congruence in the goals of education and the method of achieving this goal among East Asians (Azuma, 1986; Yu & Yang, 1994; Park & Kim, 2004) and Asian Americans when compared to European Americans (Hsia, 1988; Farkas et al., 1990). This compatibility of values promote collective efficacy, which in turn promotes educational achievement (Bandura, 1997).

EMPIRICAL ANALYSIS

A research program has been conducted in Korea to explore the cognitive, motivational and relational factors influencing the academic achievement of children and adolescents. In the first phase, adolescents, parents, teachers and administrators participated in focus group interviews to assess adolescent development trajectories and achievement (Ahn et al., 1997). Second, ecological analyses of adolescents' homes, schools and neighborhoods were conducted. Third, based on the above analyses, an open-ended questionnaire was developed to explore Korean students' and adults' perceptions of success and failure (Kim & Park, 2003; Park & Kim, 2004). Fourth, structured questionnaires were developed to examine factors that contribute to academic achievement. The concept of agency is measured through self-efficacy scales developed by Bandura (1995) and relational efficacy and efficacy for promoting social harmony have been developed to capture important aspects of Korean culture (Kim & Park, 1999). Scales to measure achievement motivation (Yu & Yang, 1994), academic aspiration, parental achievement pressure, social support and parent–child relationship (Kim & Park, 1999) and life-satisfaction (Taft, 1986) have been included. The structured questionnaires were administered to cross-sectional and longitudinal samples of elementary school, middle school, high school and university students.

QUALITATIVE ANALYSIS

Using the indigenous psychological approach (Kim, 2000, 2001), an open-ended questionnaire was administered to a sample of Korean students and adults in 1997 and a follow-up study was conducted in 2000 (Kim & Park, 2003). The goal was to examine respondents' perceptions and evaluations of their success and failure experiences and the psychological, relational and social factors that contributed to the outcome.

Since the pattern of results obtained in 1997 and 2000 are similar, the results of the study conducted in the year 2000 will be provided. In 2000, the questionnaire was administered to a sample of students (116 elementary, 88 middle and 72 high school) and their parents (236 fathers and 271 mothers). Participants were asked to list three important successes in their lives and to select one achievement that they are most proud of. The participants were asked to list the person who was most helpful and the type of support they received. They were asked to list the most important factor that contributed to their success. A similar set of questions were asked about their failure experiences.

Figure 21.2 provides the results of their proudest achievement. The most frequent response for students was academic achievement, followed by friendship and self-development. The most frequent response for both fathers and mothers of these students was harmonious family life, followed by occupational achievement, financial independence and self-development.

As for the person who provided the necessary support to succeed, students listed parents most frequently (41%), followed by teachers (18%), friends (14%) and "myself" (10%). For parents, the spouse was listed most frequently (32%), followed by parents (20%) and "myself" (11%). As for the type of social support received, 37% of the students listed emotional support, followed by information support (26%) and financial support (18%). For their parents, they listed emotional support (40%), followed by financial support (18%), positive environment (15%) and informational support (11%).

Figure 21.3 lists the most important factor that contributed to success. For students, self-regulation (i.e., effort, hard work and persistence) was mentioned most frequently, followed by family environment, social support and personality. For fathers, self-regulation was mentioned most frequently, followed by family environment, personality and social support. For mothers, family environment

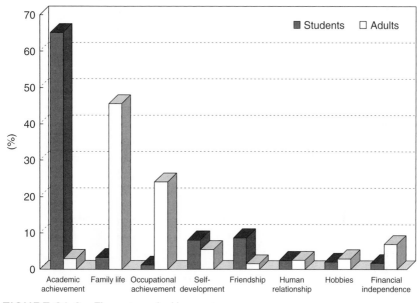

FIGURE 21.2   The most proud achievement.

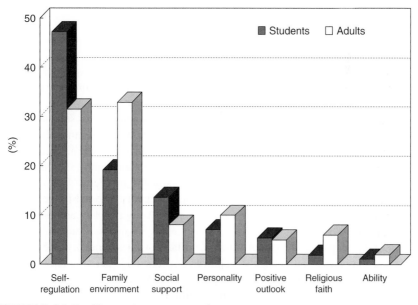

FIGURE 21.3   The most important reason for success.

was mentioned most frequently, followed by self-regulation, social support and personality. Both students and their parents report that positive personality is needed to maintain good human relationships. The importance of ability is listed by only 1% of students and 2% of parents.

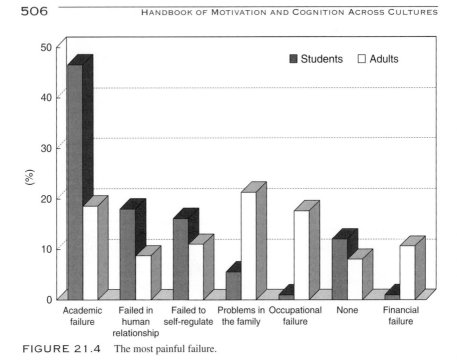

FIGURE 21.4   The most painful failure.

When students are asked to list their most painful failure experiences, academic failure is listed most frequently by students, followed by failure in human relationships and self-regulation (see Figure 21.4). For parents, problems in the family are listed most frequently, followed by academic failure, occupational failure and failure to self-regulate.

As for the person who influenced their failure, the majority of students (66%) and their parents (57%) blamed themselves, followed by friends (students = 18%, adults = 16%), family members (students = 3%, adults = 12%) and their parents (students = 8%, adults = 9%). As for the reason for their failure, students attributed a lack of self-regulation, followed by personality problems, lack of ability and problems in relationships (see Figure 21.5). Parents reported failure to self-regulate, followed by negative environment, personality problem and bad family environment.

Overall, the pattern of results affirms Confucian values. Korean students place a prime importance on academic achievement. For their parents, family life is the most important, followed by occupational success. Both students and adults view academic failure as one of the most painful experiences.

In order to succeed in Korea, whether it is academic, relational or occupational, people believe that self-regulation is the most effective strategy. In addition, social support received from parents and family members is reported to be very important. The type of support they value the most is emotional support. In contrast to the importance placed on self-regulation and social support, ability

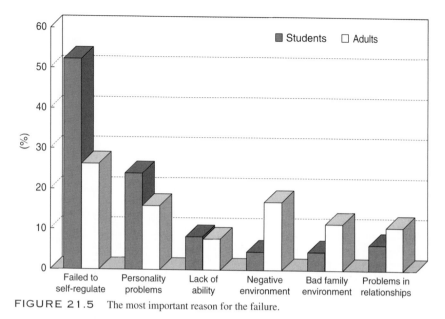

FIGURE 21.5   The most important reason for the failure.

was listed by less than 2% of the sample. Both students and adults emphasized good personality as a way of maintaining harmonious relationships.

As for failure experiences, respondents are most likely to blame themselves for the failure. Respondents are most likely to report a lack self-regulation as a key factor for their failure. Unlike achievement, where respondents report family and social support as important factors for their success, they are more likely to report their personality and lack of ability as important factors for their failure.

These results challenge existing psychological theories that claim the belief in ability and self-serving bias are universal. Similar patterns of results have been reported by researchers in East Asia (Bond et al., 1982; Hwang, in press; Muramoto et al., 2008). These results point to the importance of understanding cultural values and beliefs in explaining academic achievement. However, due to the qualitative nature of the data, it is not possible to infer causality. Based on these qualitative results, a series of empirical studies have been conducted to explore the factors that can explain the academic achievement of Korean adolescents.

CROSS-SECTIONAL ANALYSIS

A series of cross-sectional studies was conducted in 1997 through 2007 to examine factors that influence the academic achievement of Korean adolescents (Ahn et al., 1997; Park & Kim, 2004a, b; Kim & Park, 2006). In 1998, a stratified national sample of 5504 eighth-grade students completed the structured question-naire described above (Kim & Park, 1999). The results indicate that academic

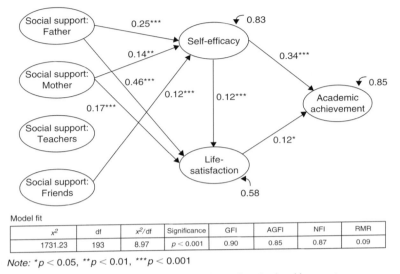

Model fit

x^2	df	x^2/df	Significance	GFI	AGFI	NFI	RMR
1731.23	193	8.97	$p < 0.001$	0.90	0.85	0.87	0.09

Note: $*p < 0.05$, $**p < 0.01$, $***p < 0.001$

FIGURE 21.6   Factor influencing life-satisfaction and academic achievement.
Source: Adapted from Park et al. (2000).

achievement is positively correlated to subscales of self-efficacy ($r = 0.13$–0.53), achievement motivation ($r = 0.31$), academic aspiration ($r = 0.55$), parental social support ($r = 0.22$), parental achievement pressure ($r = 0.22$) and family's socio-economic status ($r = 0.30$).

Based on the 1998 study, a total of 961 elementary school, 898 middle school and 1236 high school students completed the structured questionnaire (Park et al., 2000). For high school students, self-efficacy has direct positive influence on life-satisfaction and academic achievement (see Figure 21.6). Life-satisfaction has a moderate positive influence on academic achievement. Support received from parents and friends has a direct positive influence on adolescents' self-efficacy. Social support from parents has a direct positive influence on life-satisfaction. The influence of teachers is non-significant. A similar pattern of results has been found for elementary school, middle school and university students, with the exception of teachers' social support positively influencing life-satisfaction among elementary and middle school students (Park et al., 2000; Park & Kim, 2004b).

The results indicate the important mediating role self-efficacy plays in influencing academic achievement and life-satisfaction. Second, social support plays an important role in elevating both academic achievement and life-satisfaction directly and indirectly. The important contributions made by parents and social support have been documented in Europe and North America (Bandura, 1997; Caprara et al., 2006). Third, the influence of teachers decreases with the increasing age of students, while the influence of parents, especially fathers, increases with

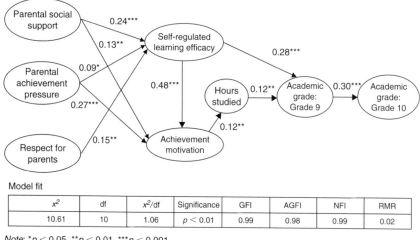

Model fit

x^2	df	x^2/df	Significance	GFI	AGFI	NFI	RMR
10.61	10	1.06	$p < 0.01$	0.99	0.98	0.99	0.02

Note: $*p < 0.05$, $**p < 0.01$, $***p < 0.001$

FIGURE 21.7 Longitudinal analysis of academic achievement.
Source: Adapted from Park et al. (2004).

age. Fourth, social support from friends has a moderate influence on self-efficacy for all age groups.

LONGITUDINAL STUDY

A series of longitudinal studies were conducted to examine influences that parents have on their children and the mediating role of self-efficacy and achievement motivation on academic achievement (Park et al., 2004a). A total of 830 ninth-grade students participated in the study, and 656 students participated in the study when they became tenth-graders. The questionnaire used in the cross-sectional study was used in the longitudinal study. In addition, respect for parents and a sense of indebtedness to parents, which were developed using indigenous psychological methods, was included (Park & Kim, 2004a). This result is from an 8-year longitudinal project.

As depicted in Figure 21.7, efficacy for self-regulated learning and studying time has direct positive effects on academic achievement (see Figure 21.7). While achievement motivation has a positive influence on studying time, parental support, parental achievement, pressure and respect for parents have a direct positive effect on efficacy for self-regulated learning. Parental social support and achievement pressure have direct positive effects on adolescents' achievement motivation. When a sense of indebtedness was included in the place of respect for parents, a similar pattern of results were found. However, a sense of indebtedness to parents has a direct positive effect on adolescents' achievement motivation, which in turn has a direct positive effect on academic achievement (Park et al., 2004a).

DISCUSSION

Consistent with Confucian values, Korean students and adults view education as an important life goal, and persistent effort and discipline as the means to the goal. The social support received from parents and family members are viewed as essential ingredients. Emotional support in the form of encouragement, praise and understanding are valued. Koreans believe that ability can be acquired and personality can be polished through persistent effort. These results question the validity of Western theories that focus narrowly on individualistic values.

First, most developmental theories do not examine the influence of parents on child and adolescent development. Freudian, Piagetian, behavioral and humanistic theories do not systematically examine the role of parents. Although attachment theory examines the role of parents, it supports individualistic values by asserting that separation and individuation are necessary for healthy human development (Rothbaum et al., 2000). In Korea, parental support and influence are strong during childhood and adolescence, and continue to persist even in adulthood (Park & Kim, 2004a, b). The importance of the parental role in adolescent development has also been confirmed in studies conducted in Europe and the United States (Bandura, 1997; Pajares & Urban, 2006). Social support is an important factor in elevating the self-efficacy of adolescents, which increases their academic achievement and life-satisfaction.

Second, the concept, such as a sense of indebtedness to parents, has a very different connotation in Korea (Park & Kim, 2004a). In many Western psychological theories, guilt is presumed to be based on irrational beliefs, neurotic fears or forbidden wishes. The extensive experience of guilt is believed to cause developmental problems in adolescence and adulthood. In Korea, it is considered appropriate that children feel guilty and indebted toward their parents for the devotion, sacrifice and love they have received from them (Park & Kim, 2004a). Children feel indebted to their parents since they cannot return the love and care that they have received. Guilt in Korea has a positive aspect and is viewed as an important interpersonal emotion that promotes filial piety, achievement motivation and relational closeness.

Third, East Asian students are high achievers since they live in a culture in which education is valued and self, proxy and collective efficacy for academic achievement is high (Stevenson et al., 1986; Yu & Yang, 1994; Tsuneyoshi, 2001; Kim & Park, 2005). Children are taught to discipline themselves and to focus on academic achievement. Many high school students study up to 14–16 hours a day. Parents play a key role in providing emotional, informational and financial support and creating a positive environment to ensure that their children succeed in school. They set high goals for their children and pressure them to excel in school. The high standard is responsible for the awareness that they are not the best and propels them to work harder.

Fourth, parents provide a positive environment so that their children can focus their attention on academic work. Their peers also view educational success as the most important life goal. Schools and teachers complete the picture by teaching adolescents the necessary academic skills to reach this goal. It is the concerted effort of students, parents, teachers and administrators that promote high self, relational and collective efficacy for academic achievement in Korea (Kim & Park, 2005).

Fifth, family and close ingroup members are highly influential, while professional relationships play a secondary role. The support received from teachers is important when children are young, but their influence decreases as they become older.

Sixth, self-serving bias has not been found in Korea. Korean students and adults attribute their success to persistent effort and social support, and failure to a lack of effort and ability. Very few Korean respondents emphasize innate ability as being responsible for their success. Instead, they report that a lack of persistent effort resulted in their lack of ability and personality problems, which are responsible for their failures. They understand the importance of taking responsibility for their actions and the importance of working hard and receiving social support in order to succeed.

These results point to the limitation in traditional psychological theories that focus on individualistic values. Results from the series of empirical studies conducted in Korea affirm the important mediating role of self-efficacy in influencing academic achievement and life-satisfaction. The ingredients necessary for academic success is not limited to Korea or Confucian cultures. Similar patterns of results have been found in other East Asian countries (Stevenson et al., 1986; Stevenson & Lee, 1990; Yu & Yang, 1994; Tsuneyoshi, 2001), Europe and the United States (Bandura, 1997; Pajares & Urban, 2006). Within the United States, Asian American students are high achievers since they possess the characteristics described in the above section (Hsia, 1988; Farkas et al., 1990). Similarly, socialization practices of discipline and emphasis on education in Finland are closely parallel to those values found in East Asia, which may be responsible for the high level of educational achievement of Finnish students (Helgesen & Kim, 2002).

In high schools, Korean students are high achievers, but it comes at a cost. In 1996, when Korean students were asked to describe the most stressful aspect of their lives, 28% reported "pressure to achieve academically" (Park & Kim, 2004b). During the economic crisis in 1999, the number increased to 44%. Even with the pressure and stress, when students succeed academically, they are given social, relational and economic rewards and feel that it is worth the investment (Park & Kim, 2004b).

However, the Korean society is not prepared to deal with those students who cannot adjust to the rigid school system and cope with the pressure to achieve, and fail to do well academically (Park & Kim, 2004b). The rates of students who refuse to attend school, delinquency and school violence have been increasing in recent years (Park & Kim, 2004b). Nearly half of teachers and students feel that teachers and administrator have lost their leadership and authority to teach and regulate students, and around half of the elementary, middle and high school students report experiencing school violence (Park et al., 2004b). This pattern of results has also been found in Japan (Tsuneyoshi & Akita, in press).

In contrast to Korean high schools, there is a lack of concerted efforts among students, parents, professors and administrators to promote high academic achievement at the university level (Kim, 2006). Once students enter a university, the pressure and efforts to achieve academically are not maintained (Kim, 2006). Compared to their high school years, students spend less time on their academic work and more time socializing, pursuing individual interests and enjoying life. This is the case since the entrance into a university is highly competitive, but graduation from a university is relatively easy. Parents do not invest as much time or money in their children's education nor do they pressure them to study. With the lackluster performance at the university level, the Korean government is pressuring universities to adopt global standards in fostering competition, research and excellence.

Students, teachers and parents in East Asia have high efficacy in promoting academic achievement, but low efficacy in dealing with delinquency, truancy and school violence, and they are unable to stem the rising tide (Park & Kim, 2004b; Tsuneyoshi & Akita, in press). East Asian societies have been able to foster the development of self, proxy and collective control in promoting high academic achievement in high schools, but not at the university level. East Asian societies have yet to develop the necessary control in stemming the rising rates in drop-outs, delinquency and school violence. These are the two important education challenges that East Asian societies face. It will be up to the next generation to find creative and innovative solutions to these challenges.

REFERENCES

Ahn, K. D., Hwang, J. K., Kim, U., & Park, Y. S. (1997). *Adolescent culture of Korea: Psycho-social structure and dynamics.* Seoul: Academy of Korean Studies.

Aiello, L. C., & Wheeler, P. (1995). The expensive-tissue hypothesis. *Current Anthropology, 36,* 199–200.

Azuma, H. (1986). Why study child development in Japan?. In H. Stevenson, H. Azuma, & K. Hakuta (Eds.), *Child development and education in Japan* (pp. 3–12). New York: W.H. Freeman.

Bandura, A. (1995). Manual for the construction of self-efficacy scales. Unpublished manuscript, Department of Psychology, Stanford University, USA.

Bandura, A. (1997). *Self-efficacy: The exercise of control.* New York: Freeman.

Bandura, A. (1999). Social cognitive theory: An agentic perspective. *Asian Journal of Social Psychology, 2,* 21–42.

Berger, L. R., & Hilton-Barber, B. (2000). *Footsteps of eve: The mystery of human origins.* Washington, DC: National Geographic Books.

Bond, M. H., Leung, K., & Wan, K. C. (1982). The social impact of self-effacing attributions: The Chinese case. *Journal of Social Psychology, 118,* 157–166.

Caprara, G. V., Scabini, E., & Regalia, C. (2006). The impact of perceived family efficacy beliefs on adolescent development. In F. Pajares & T. Urdan (Eds.), *Self-efficacy beliefs of adolescents* (pp. 97–116). Greenwich, CT: Information Age Publishing.

Clark, A. (1996). *Being there: Putting brain, body and world together again.* Cambridge, MA: MIT press.

Collard, M., & Wood, B. (2007). Defining the genus homo. In W. Henke & I. Tattesall (Eds.), *Handbook of Paleoanthropology, Vol. 3* (pp. 1575–1610). New York: Springer.

Confucius (1979). *The Analects*. Translated by D. C. Lau. New York: Penguin Books.

Conrad, N. (2007). Cultural evolution in Africa and Eurasia during the middle and late Pleistocene. In W. Henke & I. Tattesall (Eds.), *Handbook of Paleoanthropology, Vol. 3* (pp. 2001–2038). New York: Springer.

Farkas, G., Grobe, R. P., Sheehan, D., & Shuan, Y. (1990). Cultural resources and school success: Gender, ethnicity and poverty groups within an urban school district. *American Sociological Review*, *55*, 127–142.

Gore, R. (2000). The dawn of humans: People like us. *National Geographic*, July, 90–117.

Harré, R. (1999). The rediscovery of the human mind: The discursive approach. *Asian Journal of Social Psychology*, *2*, 43–62.

Helgesen, G., & Kim, U. (2002). *Good government: Nordic and East Asian perspectives*. Copenhagen: Danish Institute of International Affairs.

Ho, D. Y. F. (1986). Chinese patterns of socialization: A critical review. In M. H. Bond (Ed.), *The psychology of the Chinese people* (pp. 1–37). Oxford: Oxford University Press.

Hofstede, G. (1991). *Cultures and organizations: Software of the mind*. New York: McGraw Hill Book.

Holloway, S., Kasgiwagi, K., & Azuma, H. (1986). Causal attributions by Japanese and American mothers and children about performance in mathematics. *International Journal of Psychology*, *21*, 269–286.

Hsia, J. (1988). *Asian Americans in higher education and work*. Hillsdale, NJ: Lawrence Erlbaum Associates.

Hwang, K. K. (in press). Life goals, achievement motivation and value of effort in Confucian society. To appear in U. Kim & Y. S. Park (Eds.), *Asia's educational miracle: Psychological, social and cultural perspectives*. New York: Springer.

Kim, U. (2000). Indigenous, cultural, and cross-cultural psychology: Theoretical, philosophical, and epistemological analysis. *Asian Journal of Social Psychology*, *3*, 265–287.

Kim, U. (2001). Culture, science and indigenous psychologies: An integrated analysis. In D. Matsumoto (Ed.), *Handbook of culture and psychology* (pp. 51–76). Oxford: Oxford University Press.

Kim, U. (2006). Korea's universities: The flip side of educational miracle. *Korea Herald*, December 5.

Kim, U., Aasen, H. S., & Ebadi, S. (2003). *Democracy, human rights, and Islam in modern Iran: Psychological, social and cultural perspectives*. Bergen: Fagbokforlaget.

Kim, U., Helgesen, G., & Ahn, B. M. (2002). Democracy, trust, and political efficacy: Comparative analysis of Danish and Korean political culture. *Applied Psychology: An International Review*, *51*(2), 317–352.

Kim, U., & Park, Y. S. (1999). Psychological and behavioral pattern of Korean adolescents: With specific focus on the influence of friends, family, and school. *Korean Journal of Educational Psychology*, *13*, 99–142.

Kim, U., & Park, Y. S. (2003). An indigenous analysis of success attribution: Comparison of Korean students and adults. In K. S. Yang, K. K. Hwang, P. Pedersen, & I. Daibo (Eds.), *Progress in Asian social psychology: Conceptual and empirical contributions* (pp. 171–195). New York: Preager.

Kim, U., & Park, Y. S. (2005). Integrated analysis of indigenous psychologies: Comments and extensions of ideas presented by Shams, Jackson, Hwang and Kashima. *Asian Journal of Social Psychology*, *8*, 75–95.

Kim, U., & Park, Y. S. (2006). The scientific foundation of indigenous and cultural psychology: The transactional approach. In U. Kim, K. S. Yang, & K. K. Hwang (Eds.), *Indigenous and cultural psychology: Understanding people in context* (pp. 3–25). New York: Springer.

Kim, U., Park, Y. S., Kwon, Y. E., & Koo, J. S. (2005). Values of children, parent–child relationship, and social change in Korea: Indigenous, psychological, and cultural analysis. *Applied Psychology: International Review*, *54*, 313–316.

Kim, U., Yang, K. S., & Hwang, K. K. (2006). *Indigenous and cultural psychology: Understanding people in context*. New York: Springer.

Kleinman, A. (2005). *Rethinking psychiatry: From cultural category to personal experience*. New York: The Free Press.

Koch, S., & Leary, D. E. (1985). *A century of psychology as science*. New York: McGraw Hill.

Korean Statistic Office (2005). *Annual statistics*. Seoul: Government of Korea.

Lebra, T. S. (1976). *Japanese patterns of behavior*. Honolulu: East-West Center.

Maslow, A. (1943). A theory of human motivation. *Psychological Review, 50*, 370–396.

Mithen, S. (2007). The network of brain, body, language, and culture. In W. Henke & I. Tattesall (Eds.), *Handbook of Paleoanthropology, Vol. 3* (pp. 1965–2000). New York: Springer.

Muramoto, Y., Yamaguchi, S., & Kim, U. (2008). Self-serving and group-serving bias: Comparative analysis of Japanese, Korean, and US results. Submitted for publication to *Asian Journal of Social Psychology*.

OECD (2003). *Financing education: Investments and returns analysis of the World Education Indicators* (2002 Edition). Paris: OECD Publishing.

Pajares, F., & Urban, T. (2006). *Self-efficacy beliefs of adolescents*. Greenwich, CT: Information Age Publishing.

Park, Y. S., & Kim, U. (1998). Locus of control, attributional style, and academic achievement: Comparative analysis of Korean, Korean-Chinese, and Chinese students. *Asian Journal of Social Psychology, 1*, 191–208.

Park, Y. S., & Kim, U. (2004a). *Parent–child relationship in Korea: Indigenous psychological analysis of self-concept and family role*. Seoul: Kyoyook Kwahaksa.

Park, Y. S., & Kim, U. (2004b). *Adolescent culture and parent–child relationship in Korea: Indigenous psychological analysis*. Seoul: Kyoyook Kwahaksa.

Park, Y. S., Kim, U., Chung, K. S., Lee, S. M., Kwon, H. H., & Yang, K. M. (2000). Causes and consequences of life-satisfaction among primary, junior high, senior high school students. *Korean Journal of Health Psychology, 5*, 94–118.

Park, Y. S., Kim, U., & Chung, K. (2004a). Longitudinal analysis of the influence of parent–child relationship on adolescents' academic achievement: With specific focus on the mediating role of self-efficacy and achievement motivation. *Korean Journal of Psychological and Social Issues, 10*, 37–59.

Park, Y. S., Kim, U., & Tak, S. Y. (2004b). Indigenous psychological analysis of delinquency among Korean adolescents: Comparison of adolescents under probation and high school students. *Korean Journal of Psychological and Social Issues, Special Issue, 10*(1), 107–145.

PISA (2000). *Measuring student knowledge and skills: The PISA 2000 Assessment of reading, mathematical and scientific literacy*. Paris: OECD Publishing.

PISA (2003). *Learning for tomorrow's world: First results from PISA 2003*. Paris: OECD Publishing.

PISA (2006). *Education at a glance: OECD indicators 2006*. Paris: OECD Publishing.

Premack, D. G., & Woodruff, G. (1978). Does the chimpanzee have a theory of mind?. *Behavioral and Brain Sciences, 1*, 515–526.

Rothbaum, F., Weisz, J., Pott, M., Miyake, K., & Morelli, G. (2000). Attachment and culture: Security in the United States and Japan. *American Psychologist, 55*, 1093–1104.

Shweder, R. A. (1991). *Thinking through cultures – Expeditions in cultural psychology*. Cambridge: Harvard University Press.

Stevenson, H., & Lee, S. Y. (1990). Context of achievement: A study of American, Chinese, and Japanese children. *Monographs of the Society for Research in Child Development, 55*, 1–95.

(1986). . New York: W. H. Freeman.

Taft, R. (1986). The psychological study of the adjustment and adaptation of immigrants to Australia. In N. T. Feather (Ed.), *Survey of Australian Psychology: Trend for Research*. Sydney: George Allen and Unwin.

Time Magazine (2004). Learn to earn. September 27, p. 22.

TIMSS (1999). *Highlights from the Third International Mathematics and Science Study – Repeat (TIMSS–R)*. Washington, DC: National Center for Educational Statistics.

Toth, N., & Schick, K. (2007). Overview of paleolithic archeology. In W. Henke & I. Tattesall (Eds.), *Handbook of paleoanthropology, Vol. 3* (pp. 1943–1964). New York: Springer.

Tsuneyoshi, R. K. (2001). *The Japanese model of schooling*. New York: Routledge Falmer.

Tsuneyoshi, R. K., & Akita, K. (in press). The Japanese solution to the East Asian syndrome: The establishment of the integrated studies period and its implications. To appear in U. Kim & Y. S. Park (Eds.), *Asia's educational miracle: Psychological, social and cultural perspectives.* New York: Springer.

Wells, S. (2002). *The journey of man: A genetic odyssey*. Princeton, NJ: Princeton University Press.

White, M. I., & LeVine, R. A. (1986). What is an *li ko* (Good child)?. In H. Stevenson, H. Azuma, & K. Hakuta (Eds.), *Child development and education in Japan* (pp. 55–62). New York: W. H. Freeman.

Yamaguchi, S. (1994). Collectivism among the Japanese: A perspective from the self. In U. Kim, H. C. Triandis, C. Kagitcibasi, S. C. Choi, & G. Yoon (Eds.), *Individualism and collectivism: Theory, method, and applications* (pp. 175–188). Thousand Oaks, CA: Sage.

Yu, A. B., & Yang, K. S. (1994). The nature of achievement motivation in collectivistic societies. In U. Kim, H. C. Triandis, C. Kagitcibasi, S. C. Choi, & G. Yoon (Eds.), *Individualism and collectivism: Theory, method, and applications* (pp. 239–250). Thousand Oaks, CA: Sage Publication.

22

DIALECTICAL EMOTIONS: HOW CULTURAL EPISTEMOLOGIES INFLUENCE THE EXPERIENCE AND REGULATION OF EMOTIONAL COMPLEXITY

JENNIFER L. GOETZ[*], JULIE SPENCER-RODGERS[†] AND KAIPING PENG[*]

*University of California, Berkeley, CA, USA
†University of Victoria, British Columbia, Canada

Our goal in this chapter is to discuss how culture influences the experience and regulation of emotional complexity, or the co-occurrence of positive and negative emotions. A growing corpus of research indicates that Western and Eastern folk epistemologies and systems of thought differ in important ways. Whereas Western folk epistemologies stress analytical thinking, constancy, and non-contradiction, Eastern folk epistemologies emphasize holism, change, and contradiction (Peng & Nisbett, 1999; Nisbett et al., 2001). These beliefs about the world and the nature of knowledge influence attention processes (Masuda & Nisbett, 2001), causal attribution (Choi et al., 1999), the resolution of social contradictions

(Peng & Nisbett, 1999), and contradictory self-views (Spencer-Rodgers et al., 2004; Chen et al., 2006). We argue these cultural differences also have important consequences for the experience of positive and negative emotions.

We begin by discussing traditional Western approaches to emotional experience, focusing in particular on the association between positive and negative emotions. Next, we discuss the ways in which dialecticism is likely to influence experiences of emotional complexity. Finally, we review evidence for cultural differences in emotional complexity and discuss its implications for psychological well-being, as well as other areas of future research.

IS EMOTIONAL COMPLEXITY POSSIBLE?

Western folk epistemologies and modes of thinking are largely rooted in Greek and Aristotelian logic (Lewin, 1935). They can be characterized as "linear" or "synthesis-oriented" because they tend to emphasize coherence, stability, and the resolution of contradiction through integration and synthesis (Lewin, 1951; Festinger, 1957; Heider, 1958; Peng & Nisbett, 1999). This perspective can be represented by three principles (Lewin, 1935; Peng & Nisbett, 1999; Spencer-Rodgers et al., 2004). The first is the law of identity or the notion that if A is true now, then it is always true (A equals A). The second is the law of non-contradiction or the idea that no statement can be both true and false (A cannot equal not-A). Finally, the third is the law of the excluded middle or the belief that any statement of fact must be either true or false.

From a linear perspective, contradiction is largely untolerated and inconsistencies lead to psychic tension that should be reconciled through synthesis (Peng & Nisbett, 1999). For example, cognitive dissonance theory (Festinger, 1957) rests on the assumption that incongruities between one's actions and one's attitudes represent a conflict to be resolved. We contend that these conceptions about contradiction lead Westerners to be less likely to experience positive and negative emotions simultaneously and less likely to acknowledge and tolerate emotional complexity when it arises.

Western scientific conceptions of affect and emotion have been traditionally consistent with Aristotelian logic and the notion that negative and positive emotions are discrete, oppositional phenomena that cannot co-occur. Discrete emotion researchers assume that emotions evolved as adaptations to specific problems (e.g., Darwin, 1872/1998; Lazarus, 1991; Ekman, 1992). When confronted with novel stimuli in the environment, one fundamental decision to be made concerns whether it is threatening or advantageous to the self (see Lazarus, 1991). Threatening stimuli evoke emotions like fear to help individuals quickly escape dangerous situations. In contrast, advantageous stimuli evoke emotions like happiness and love to help individuals establish and maintain close contact with those who are beneficial to survival. Likewise, dimensional approaches to emotion and affect argue that valence is an underlying aspect of all reactions to the environment (e.g., Russell, 1980). From this perspective, pleasantness and unpleasantness are opposite ends of a single dimension that cannot be experienced together (e.g., Russell, 1980; Russell & Carroll, 1999).

In contrast to these traditions, recent theorizing suggests that positive and negative emotions may be experienced simultaneously (Cacioppo & Berntson, 1994; Cacioppo et al., 1999; Schimmack, 2005). Although outward behavior often appears bipolar (e.g., representing approach or avoidance), the biological systems that underlie positive and negative emotions are largely uncoupled and independent (Cacioppo et al., 1999). Recent studies have succeeded in eliciting the co-occurrence of positive and negative emotions in Western populations (Larsen et al., 2001, 2004; Williams & Aaker, 2002; Schimmack, 2005). For example, the film *Life is Beautiful*, in which a Jewish man's efforts to protect his son in a World War II concentration camp are often humorous, elicited both happiness and sadness in college students (Larsen et al., 2001). Emotional complexity has also been induced with advertisements that emphasize both positive and negative aspects of a situation, such as the death of a grandmother who lived long enough to meet her granddaughter (Williams & Aaker, 2002). In our own lab, when asked to describe events in which they felt complex emotions, participants described important life events like graduation, beginning or ending a romantic relationship, and the death of loved ones (Goetz et al., 2007). Finally, research on counterfactuals suggests that even minor, relatively insignificant events can elicit co-occurrence of positive and negative emotions. For example, a win of $3 elicited both happiness and disappointment in participants who knew they could have won $9 (Larsen et al., 2004). Despite these exceptions, most research finds that Americans report feeling either positive or negative in their daily lives, not both (Diener & Iran-Nejad, 1986; Larsen et al., 2001). Thus although experiences of complex emotions may be possible, they are rare.

Even Western theorists who hold that emotional complexity is possible retain the assumption that co-occurrence of positive and negative emotions has antagonistic consequences (e.g., Cacioppo et al., 1999; Larsen et al., 2001). Positive emotions promote approach and appetitive behavior, whereas negative emotions promote avoidant behavior. From this perspective, emotional complexity should be unpleasant, unstable, and relatively short-lived. This is in contrast to a dialectical view, in which emotional complexity should be considered natural and accepted.

THEORETICAL PREDICTIONS: DIALECTICISM APPLIED TO EMOTION

East Asian folk epistemologies, which are largely based on Confucianism, Taoism, and Buddhism, can be described as "dialectical" because they emphasize the principles of change, holism, and contradiction (Peng & Nisbett, 1999). The principle of change asserts that all phenomena exist in a state of flux and are constantly evolving. The principle of holism posits that all things are fundamentally interconnected and mutually dependent. Finally, the principle of contradiction holds that all phenomena are composed of contradictory elements that exist in a harmonious state of balance. Partly because change is constant, contradiction is constant. These principles stand in stark contrast to the linear epistemologies of the West.

We argue there are two major ways in which dialecticism influences emotional complexity in East Asian cultures. First, dialecticism makes the co-occurrence of positive and negative emotions more likely. Second, dialecticism makes the experience of emotional complexity more natural and comfortable.

DIALECTICISM AND THE ELICITATION OF EMOTIONAL COMPLEXITY

Why might dialecticism lead to more complex, contradictory emotions? Evidence for this assertion comes from research showing that dialecticism, and more specifically the principle of holism, is related to more complex perceptions of the self, others, and physical events. Holistic thinking encourages individuals to adopt multiple perspectives, and perspective-taking, in turn, may be linked to greater emotional complexity. Individuals who adopt multiple perspectives, therefore, are likely to experience a larger number of distinct emotions in any given situation than individuals who are linear and one-dimensional in their approach. They are also more likely to experience contradictory emotions as they examine phenomena from multiple angles. Similarly, the dialectical principle of change encourages individuals to adopt a broader temporal perspective and to expect positive and negative emotions to recur cyclically.

Consistent with the principle of holism, dialecticism is related to more contradictory and contextualized self-views (Spencer-Rodgers et al., 2004; Chen et al., 2006), more contextualized perception of others' behavior (Morris & Peng, 1994), and even more contextualized perceptions of physical scenes and events (Ji et al., 2000; Masuda & Nisbett, 2001). Given the close relationship between self-views, social cognition, and emotion (Smith & Ellsworth, 1985; Lazarus, 1991; Mesquita & Frijda, 1992), dialecticism is also likely to influence the number of emotions one experiences in a particular situation. By eliciting more emotions within any given moment (what we call "multiple emotion" experiences), dialecticism increases the likelihood that positive and negative emotions will co-occur.

In the domain of self-perception, cross-cultural scholars have found that East Asians conceptualize themselves differently depending on the context (Kanagawa et al., 2001; Suh, 2002). They also exhibit less internal consistency in their self-conceptions at any given moment in time (Choi & Choi, 2002; Spencer-Rodgers et al., 2004). For example, Choi and Choi (2002) examined the dialectical tendency to accept seeming contradiction, and more specifically, to endorse contradictory statements about the self (e.g., How extraverted are you? versus How introverted are you?). They found that Koreans held less consistent beliefs regarding their personality characteristics and values than did Americans. Research in our lab shows that dialecticism, as assessed with the Dialectical Self Scale (DSS; Spencer-Rodgers et al., 2007b), is associated with more contextualized (Chen et al., 2006) and contradictory (Spencer-Rodgers et al., 2004) self-conceptions. In a priming study, Chinese and American participants were asked to think about events that had positive and negative consequences for the self (e.g., moving away from home for the first time). These ambivalent experiences elicited greater emotional complexity among East Asians than Americans (Spencer-Rodgers et al., 2007a). Because dialectical individuals adopt multiple perspectives with respect to the self, they are also more likely to experience a broad range of emotions.

In the domain of social perception, studies show that East Asian, dialectical individuals take more possible causes of an event into account than do non-dialectical individuals (Choi et al., 1999). Whereas Americans focus on internal state and trait explanations of behavior, East Asians take both internal and external attributes into account (Morris & Peng, 1994; Lee et al., 1996; Hallahan et al., 1997). Research on the actor–observer bias also shows that East Asians are less likely to deemphasize the influence of the situation when judging others' behaviors versus their own (Choi & Nisbett, 1998). For instance, Koreans took more information into account when explaining both deviant and prosocial behaviors than Americans (Choi et al., 2003). Because dialectical individuals consider more possible explanations of an event as plausible, they are more likely to experience a broad range of emotions.

Some researchers have proposed that perspective-taking and empathic emotion may be important precursors to emotional complexity (Beach et al., 1998; Larsen et al., 2001). Given the dialectical focus on context and situation, East Asians spontaneously take the perspectives of others more than do Westerners. In recalled experiences in which they were the central figure, East Asians were more likely to take a third-person perspective than Whites (Cohen & Gunz, 2002). Even when they were not involved in the social event in question, another study found that White Americans focused more on the main characters and Chinese focused more on peripheral others (Chua et al., 2005). Dialectical individuals, who are more likely to think spontaneously about situations from other people's perspectives, are more likely to feel multiple emotions than non-dialectical individuals.

The pathways discussed thus far suggest that dialectical epistemologies are likely to lead to multiple emotions, or many emotions in response to any given event or moment. Why should a greater *number* of emotions in turn lead to greater emotional *complexity*, or the co-occurrence of positive and negative emotions? First, the experience of more emotions at once creates more opportunities for positive and negative emotions to co-occur. In the next section, we discuss how East Asians are more likely to accept and acknowledge experiences of emotional complexity when they occur. Second, because East Asians may encounter more situations that elicit emotional complexity, they may be more attuned to emotional complexity in others. Members of interdependent cultures must adapt to the needs of important ingroup members and the requirements of the situation, even if these contradict their own needs and goals. Thus East Asians may experience greater conflict between their personal goals and social norms. Perspective-taking and empathy for close others are also likely to bring to mind more conflicting goals than would otherwise arise (Beach & Tesser, 1993). Therefore, contradictory emotion arising from perspective-taking and empathy may be more common for East Asians than for Westerners.

Finally, the dialectical focus on change encourages individuals to consider events within a larger temporal context and a continual process of transformation (Ji et al., 2001). Because all phenomena are thought to change into their opposites in a never-ending process of reversal (e.g., good becomes bad, bad becomes good), positive and negative emotions are expected to alternate in a cyclical pattern. Research on the perception of change in East Asian cultures indicates that the existence of an extreme state at present suggests that the opposite state is imminent. For example, Chinese participants were more likely to predict that various phenomena would undergo a change from an initial state than were Americans (Ji et al., 2001). If all phenomena exist in a state of flux and are constantly changing, it stands to reason that both positive and negative elements will eventually occur. This also suggests that East Asians are more likely to experience opposite-valence emotions in response to an event, as no event is thought to be all-good or all-bad.

DIALECTICISM AND TOLERANCE FOR COMPLEX EMOTIONS

Dialecticism is also likely to influence emotional complexity through beliefs about contradiction. Although "dialecticism" has a long history in both Eastern and Western philosophy and religion, as is reflected in the writings of Plato, St. Augustine, Hegel, Goethe, and Marx (Peng et al., 2006), Eastern and Western dialectics are fundamentally different (Peng & Nisbett, 1999). The main distinction lies in the relative emphasis these philosophical traditions place on tolerance for contradiction (Eastern) versus the need for synthesis (Western). In East Asia, all phenomena are thought to change into their opposites in an eternal cycle of reversal (e.g., sickness turns into health, health turns into sickness, etc.), and all forces are seen as possessing the seeds of their opposite. Consequently, no phenomenon is ever completely devoid of its antithesis (e.g., all joy contains some sorrow, and all sorrow contains some joy). The East Asian view of contradiction is best illustrated by the Yin/yang (*Tai-ji*) symbol. Yin and yang represent mutually dependent opposites that are balanced, complementary, and harmonious. From this perspective, an emotion, such as joy is less the "opposite" of sorrow, than it is its natural complement. Because the seeds of happiness exist within misery (and vice versa), both emotions are seen as co-existing within all individuals, at all times. In contrast, the Western view of contradiction is more divisive (e.g., happy or sad, good or bad, right or wrong) and contradictory phenomena are conceptualized as largely separate and dichotomous.

Due to dialectical tolerance for contradiction, opposite-valence emotions are likely to be viewed as more closely related in East Asian than Western, linear cultures. Positive and negative emotions are not mutually exclusive in Eastern representations, nor are they necessarily antagonistic. The principles of change and contradiction suggest that it is natural and expected that positive and negative emotions occur together. Moreover, fundamental differences in the conception of opposite-valence emotions make the experience of emotional complexity less problematic for East Asians. Whereas Westerners view emotional complexity as an indicator that their inner life is conflicted and must be resolved, East Asians are likely to view it as a natural and perhaps even comfortable state. Therefore, once emotional complexity is elicited, dialectical individuals are more likely to acknowledge and accept it and they should be less likely to feel uncomfortable and make efforts to regulate it than Westerners.

LEVELS OF ANALYSIS IN EMOTIONAL COMPLEXITY

The existence of emotional complexity and its cultural specificity can be analyzed at many levels. We divide these levels broadly into: (1) retrospective, global memories; (2) actual, global experience; and (3) actual, momentary experience.

Retrospective reports of global emotional experience are the most abundant, and hence most commonly examined with regard to the question of emotional complexity. For example, participants are often asked "How do you feel in general?" or "On average, how often do you feel the following emotions?" (e.g., Bagozzi et al., 1999; Kitayama et al., 2000). Sometimes the timeframe of this question is more specific, such as "How often have you felt the following emotions in the past month?" (e.g., Schimmack et al., 2002). Reports of recalled affect have been shown to reflect more about emotion beliefs than actual experience. In a series of studies with American participants, researchers compared actual aggregates of momentary reports from a single experience sampling study with multiple retrospective aggregates (Diener & Emmons, 1985). Results revealed that the larger the time period over which participants were asked to aggregate, the more their reports diverged from calculated aggregates based on momentary reports. In one study, participants filled out momentary, daily retrospective, and 3-week retrospective reports. While momentary reports had the highest inverse correlation of positive and negative affect ($r = -0.57$), daily reports had a weaker correlation ($r = -0.31$), and 3-week reports had the weakest association ($r = -0.10$). Thus global or retrospective reports may tell us more about differences in lay beliefs about emotion than the actual structure of emotion. For example, while members of dialectical cultures may encode both positive and negative emotions, members of linear cultures may be biased toward retaining only memories of positive emotions. It is also possible that members of Western cultures aggregate frequency estimates on the basis of valence, whereas East Asian cultures use different heuristics, such as arousal (Tsai et al., 2006) or engagement (Kitayama et al., 2006).

The actual, momentary experience of positive and negative emotions can be considered the gold-standard indicator of emotional complexity. Since momentary reports are closest to actual experience, they are least likely to be influenced by lay beliefs or recall bias (Diener & Emmons, 1984). However, single-moment reports pose the problem of confounding response style with actual emotional experience (Schimmack, 2001). By sampling multiple time points, response style can be controlled for and the data can answer questions about state and trait experiences (Zelenski & Larsen, 2000). For example, using within-person correlations, one can ask, "What was the average relationship between positive and negative emotions at the level of *momentary* experience?" Using between-person correlations, one can ask, "What was the average relationship between positive and negative emotions at the level of *overall* experience?" Both questions are relevant to an examination of cultural differences in emotional complexity.

DIALECTICISM AND EXPERIENCES OF EMOTIONAL COMPLEXITY

One of the first papers to report cultural differences in emotional complexity asked participants to report how much positive and negative affect they tended to feel in general (Bagozzi et al., 1999). Specifically, they rated the frequency and intensity of 72 positive and negative emotions. Whereas American participants' reports showed a negative correlation between positive and negative affect, Chinese participants showed no such pattern. For Chinese women, positive and negative affect were positively correlated. For Chinese men, they were uncorrelated. The researchers also asked participants to report how they were feeling "right now." Consistent with reports of overall frequency, momentary reports revealed positive correlations between positive and negative emotions for Chinese participants. Americans, on the other hand, exhibited negative correlations. A replication of the study also found positive correlations for momentary experience among Koreans (Bagozzi et al., 1999).

These findings were some of the first to suggest that the structure of affective experience could vary across cultures. Subsequently, similar findings were reported using a list of 31 terms derived from Japanese emotions (Kitayama et al., 2000). The authors found a positive correlation between the frequency of positive and negative emotions among Japanese participants, but found a negative correlation among American participants. Together, these studies suggest that East Asians have more experiences of emotional complexity than do Westerners. Some researchers theorized that these differences were related to East Asian dialecticism (Bagozzi et al., 1999), but others argued they were the result of cultural differences in collectivism/interdependence (Kitayama et al., 2000).

A larger study sought to test possible explanatory factors for cultural differences in the structure of affect (Schimmack et al., 2002). The researchers compared two cultural dimensions: dialecticism and collectivism. College students in 38 nations were asked how frequently they had experienced four positive (affection, pride, contentment, and joy) and four negative (guilt, fear, anger, and sadness) emotions during the past month. Consistent with predictions, dialectical cultures (e.g., Hong Kong, Japan, China) exhibited less negative correlations between pleasant and unpleasant emotions, whereas non-dialectical cultures (e.g., United States, Puerto Rico, Egypt) revealed strong negative correlations. In addition, dialecticism was a better predictor of these cultural differences in complexity than was collectivism. Many collectivistic (but non-dialectical) cultures in Africa and Latin America revealed negative correlations between the frequency of pleasant and unpleasant emotions. Hence dialecticism, not collectivism, appears to be related to the greater co-occurrence of positive and negative emotions.

In our own work, we found evidence to connect a direct measure of dialecticism to increased emotional complexity (Goetz et al., 2007). Participants from China and the United States were randomly assigned to describe an event in which they either felt mixed or single emotions. In addition, we administered a survey-based measure of dialecticism, the DSS (Spencer-Rodgers et al., 2007b). Mainland Chinese were more likely than Americans to endorse such statements on the DSS as "When I hear two sides of an argument, I often agree with both" (principle of contradiction) and "I sometimes find that I am a different person by the evening than I was in the morning" (principle of change). Although both Chinese and American participants were able to describe simple and mixed emotional experiences, consistent with dialecticism, Chinese participants reported feeling mixed emotional experiences more often than did American participants. This was true even when the mixed emotions were of opposite valence (e.g., "happiness" and "sadness"). Analysis of the dialecticism measure revealed that those high in dialecticism reported more frequent mixed emotions and those low in dialecticism reported less frequent mixed emotions. Finally, dialecticism fully mediated the relationship between culture and the reported frequency of mixed emotional experiences (Goetz et al., 2007). In a separate study, priming of dialectical concepts was related to experience of emotional complexity. Chinese and American participants were asked to think about ambivalent experiences that had both positive and negative consequences for the self (e.g., graduation). Participants in the dialectical condition experienced significantly greater emotional complexity than did those in the control condition, and the dialecticism measure mediated cultural differences in emotional complexity (Spencer-Rodgers et al., 2007a).

The above mentioned studies provide cumulative evidence for the influence of cultural epistemologies on the experience of positive and negative affect. Across multiple studies, the traditional inverse relationship between the frequency of positive and negative affect has been found in American samples, but not in East Asian samples. In some cases, East Asians have reported positive associations.

However, it is unclear if these cultural differences happen at the level of momentary experience or if they result from differences in recall or overall trait level experience.

Two studies have assessed momentary affect over multiple time points in an attempt to disentangle these effects (Scollon et al., 2005; Perunovic et al., 2007). The first study utilized an experience sampling methodology and had American and Japanese students report their momentary affect at multiple time points over one week (Scollon et al., 2005). Overall experience of positive and negative affect were unrelated for European American students, but were positively associated for Asian American and Japanese students. Consistent with previous research, Asians who tended to feel more positive emotions also tended to feel more negative emotions. This was especially true for the experience of pride, which was positively correlated with the experience of negative emotions in the Asian samples. Contrary to previous findings, however, there were no significant differences in emotional complexity at the state level. All cultures had strong within-person, negative associations between positive and negative affect, indicating that positive and negative affect did not co-occur. When they compared the cultural groups, the researchers did find a non-significant trend for a weaker negative association among the Asian groups (Scollon et al., 2005). These findings suggest that cultural differences in emotional complexity occur at the level of overall experience, but not the momentary level (see also Yik, 2007).

In contrast, another study found evidence for cultural differences in emotional complexity at both the state and trait levels (Perunovic et al., 2007). Rather than examine emotional complexity between individuals of different cultures, this study used a daily diary design to examine within-person variation in East Asian Canadian biculturals. Consistent with linear epistemologies, when participants identified with Western culture or recently spoke a non-Asian language, positive and negative affect were inversely associated at the state level. Consistent with dialectical epistemologies, when participants identified with Asian culture or recently spoke an Asian language, positive and negative affect were unrelated to each other. In addition, East Asian Canadians had a non-significant positive association at the trait level, whereas European Canadians had a marginal negative association (Perunovic et al., 2007). Thus, even within an individual, cultural epistemologies may influence emotional experience at least among biculturals.

AREAS OF FUTURE RESEARCH: UNDERLYING CAUSES
OF EMOTIONAL COMPLEXITY

Do folk epistemologies relate to the experience of emotional complexity? The research clearly shows that individuals from different cultures differ in their overall reports of emotional experience. Consistent with linear epistemologies and a conception of positive and negative as antagonistic opposites, Westerners report an inverse relationship between experiences of positive and negative emotion at both the trait and state levels (Bagozzi et al., 1999; Kitayama et al., 2000;

Schimmack et al., 2002; Spencer-Rodgers et al., 2004; Perunovic et al., 2007). In contrast, East Asians report either no relationship or a positive relationship between negative and positive emotion. In addition, dialecticism is positively related to the frequency with which individuals feel mixed emotions (Goetz et al., 2007). These patterns are consistent with a dialectical epistemology in which positive and negative emotions are conceptualized more as complements than as opposites.

Do these self-reports reflect actual experience, beliefs about emotional experience, or biases in encoding and recalling emotional experience? The studies reviewed here support the argument that, at the trait level, these cultural differences are not simply the result of recall bias or beliefs about emotion. Members of dialectical cultures who experienced more positive affect also experienced more negative affect (Scollon et al., 2005). However, analysis of data from multiple timepoints suggests that these cultural differences may or may not occur at the state level (Scollon et al., 2005; Perunovic et al., 2007). Clearly, more research is needed for replication and clarification of these findings.

The role of folk epistemologies in emotional complexity has received some empirical support (Schimmack et al., 2002; Goetz et al., 2007). When explicitly compared to collectivistic cultures, dialectical cultures were less likely to show an inverse relationship between positive and negative emotions (Schimmack et al., 2002). In addition, a cultural difference in frequency of mixed emotions was mediated by a measure of dialecticism (Goetz et al., 2007). However, the mechanisms by which folk epistemologies influence emotional complexity have yet to be tested. Are cultural differences in emotional complexity simply the result of differences in the actual events that occur in different cultures? One criticism of studies of emotion structure is that they often involve emotion reports in unspecified and ambiguous settings (Schimmack, 2001). In addition to missing theoretically interesting experiences, this makes it unclear what caused the emotions that participants report. Studies in Western samples suggest that special events are needed to elicit complex emotion (Larsen et al., 2001, 2004). Perhaps members of East Asian cultures experience more complexity because they are presented with more complex situations than are members of Western cultures.

Our work on this topic suggests that the meaning of an event, rather than the event itself, is important in eliciting emotional complexity (Goetz et al., 2007). After collecting descriptions of mixed (multiple emotion) and simple (single emotion) emotional events, we coded for whether the situations were social or not, for the number of people involved in the event, and for the general context of the event (e.g., academics, family, friends, and romantic relationships). There were few differences across culture in the types of events that elicited mixed versus simple emotions. However, the meanings of events appeared to differ dramatically. Chinese participants reported that events had more conflicted goal implications than did Americans. Chinese were more likely than Americans to report that an event both helped and hurt their goals. In addition, Chinese participants mentioned more possible causes of events than did American participants.

Finally, Chinese engaged in more efforts to think about the situation in a way that changed the way they felt about it than did Americans. These findings suggest that the interpretation of life events is especially germane to cultural differences in emotional complexity.

Another study in our lab tested cultural variation of emotions in a more controlled situation (Shiota et al., 2007a). Asian and European American romantic couples were invited to the laboratory and asked to engage in a series of semi-structured tasks that could elicit both positive and negative emotions. The couples teased each other, discussed a current concern in their relationship, talked about their first date, and then rated the emotions they were feeling after each discussion. Given the positive and negative aspects of these events, the discussions could readily bring about both positive and negative emotions.

For each discussion, the researchers analyzed the relationship between situationally appropriate opposing positive and negative emotions (e.g., love and contempt). Results revealed that Asian Americans experienced a greater mix of positive and negative emotions than did European Americans. After discussing a current concern, Asian Americans' reports of love, sympathy, and contempt were positively correlated, whereas European Americans' reports were negatively correlated. Likewise, after discussing their first date, Asian Americans' reports of love and contempt were positively correlated, whereas European Americans' reports were negatively correlated (Shiota et al., 2007a). Although the situations were not identical, these semi-controlled interactions suggest that the experience of mixed emotions resulted from how the participants thought about each situation, not necessarily the characteristics of the situation itself.

Based on cognitive appraisal theories of emotion (e.g., Mesquita & Frijda, 1992), we argue that epistemologies influence emotional experience through the psychological meanings and interpretation of events. In accordance with the principle of holism, dialectical individuals are more likely to take multiple perspectives into account, and are less likely to discount one perspective at the expense of another (Peng & Nisbett, 1999). Research on the self has shown that dialecticism is related to more complex, contradictory, and contextualized views of the self (Chen et al., 2006; Spencer-Rodgers et al., 2004, 2007a,b), which may in turn lead to emotionally complex reactions to self-relevant events. In addition, it is likely that the contextual attribution styles documented in East Asian individuals will likewise lead to emotional complexity.

Other theories have been put forth to explain the relationship between culture and emotional complexity. Members of collectivistic cultures may have more conflicted goal structures (Scollon et al., 2005), which may cause individuals to feel both more positive and negative emotions. In addition, collectivistic emphasis on harmony and the middle way may cause East Asians to avoid intense arousal (e.g., Tsai & Levenson, 1997; Gross & John, 1998). In avoiding extremes, however, it is unclear if this emphasis leads to neutrality and lack of emotion, or if it could create emotional balance in the form of contradictory emotions. Finally, cultural norms about the value and function of emotions such as pride and shame may create emotional complexity (e.g., Goetz & Keltner, 2007). In collectivistic cultures, the experience and expression of pride can elicit negative responses in others and negative emotions in the self. In contrast, an emotion like shame can elicit forgiveness and positive reconciliation behaviors. In one study of cultural values and beliefs, researchers (Eid & Diener, 2001) examined norms for experiencing eight emotions, including pride and guilt, across four cultures (United States, Australia, Taiwan, and China). While pride was considered both acceptable and desirable in the United States and Australia, norms in China and Taiwan were indifferent and even negative toward pride. Guilt was very undesirable in all countries except for China.

In summary, East Asians may be more likely than Westerners, at least at the aggregate level, to experience positive and negative emotions at the same time. In addition, East Asian individuals who experience positive emotions often are also likely to experience negative emotions more often. In contrast, Westerners who experience positive emotions often are less likely to experience negative emotions. These cultural differences appear to be related to dialectical epistemologies and beliefs about the nature of contradiction and change. How do individuals react to experiences of emotional complexity? Is emotional complexity uncomfortable and distressing? Or is emotional complexity perceived as a natural part of life? In the next section, we discuss the downstream effects of cultural epistemologies on emotional complexity.

REGULATION OF EMOTIONAL COMPLEXITY AND IMPLICATIONS FOR WELL-BEING

In addition to influencing actual experience of emotional complexity, cultural epistemologies are likely to influence the beliefs people have about the relationship between positive and negative emotions. According to the dialectical principle of contradiction, opposites are not so much opposites as complementary parts of a whole. From this perspective, without sadness happiness does not exist. Without anger, one cannot know love and compassion. Tolerance for contradiction is likely to influence the interpretations people place on their emotional complexity.

In contrast, a linear perspective sees co-activation of positive and negative emotions as incongruous and unnatural. Such a state may indicate confusion, indecision, and generally a need for more emotional processing and regulation (Festinger, 1957). Researchers have suggested that complex emotions should be unstable and short-lived because they cannot clearly drive behavior (Cacioppo et al., 1999). In contrast, the dialectical perspective on emotional complexity is generally one of acceptance (Bagozzi et al., 1999). Positive and negative emotions are expected to occur together and emotional complexity is considered a natural outcome of the existence of contradiction in the world. As such, emotional complexity is viewed as more comfortable, more acceptable, and in less need of regulation. Given the dialectical aversion to extremes, emotional complexity may even be considered more desirable than emotional polarity (e.g., Tsai & Levenson, 1997).

Research shows that individuals with dialectical epistemologies are more likely to accept contradiction in their emotional experiences (Williams & Aaker, 2002; English et al., 2007). In one study, European and Asian American students were presented with advertisements pretested to evoke equal mean levels of happiness and sadness in both cultures (Williams & Aaker, 2002). Participants rated their attitude (bad–good) toward the advertisement and indicated how much they were feeling discomfort and other specific emotions (e.g., happy, sad). European and Asian Americans reported feeling similar levels of mixed emotion. However, European Americans reported feeling more discomfort than did Asian Americans in the mixed emotion condition. They also had more negative attitudes toward the advertisement overall (Williams & Aaker, 2002).

In our work (English et al., 2007), American and Chinese participants were asked to describe a series of complex and simple emotional experiences. Americans' descriptions of complex emotional experiences varied dramatically from their descriptions and responses to simple emotional experiences. Americans reported that, in comparison to simple emotions, they were less comfortable with complex emotions. In contrast, Chinese were no less comfortable with complex than simple emotions. Participants then rated the degree to which they expressed and sought to control their emotions. Participants' descriptions of their emotional experiences were also coded for mention of effort to suppress emotional expression. Although there were no cultural differences in self-reported emotional expression, there was a culture by type of emotion interaction for suppression. American participants mentioned more efforts to suppress complex than simple emotions, whereas Chinese participants mentioned more efforts to suppress simple than complex emotions (English et al., 2007). This finding suggests that expression of complex emotion may be more acceptable to Chinese participants.

Recent research also suggests that dialectical individuals are more likely to perceive contradictory emotions in other's facial expressions (Shiota et al., 2007b). The authors showed photographs of prototypical expressions of amusement, anger, sadness, embarrassment, and fear to Japanese and American participants. Participants were asked to rate the intensity of emotions the individuals in the photographs were experiencing. In order to test for perception of contradictory emotions, a discrepancy score was calculated between the intensity of the target emotions (e.g., happiness) and the intensity of opposing, contradictory emotions (e.g., anger). Overall, Japanese participants tended to have smaller discrepancies between target and contradictory emotions than did American participants (Shiota et al., 2007b), suggesting that Japanese participants perceived more emotional complexity in the photographs than did Americans.

Interestingly, the use of validated prototypical emotion displays with "target" emotions allowed the authors to ask very specific questions about the nature of emotional complexity. In this context, they were able to test two mechanisms that could lead to emotional complexity. One possible route to emotional complexity could be moderation or blunting of the "target" or primary emotion in the photograph. Another possible route could be facilitated experience of "opposites" of the target emotion. Either of these routes would result in more emotional complexity with the metrics discussed so far (e.g., a smaller negative correlation or a smaller discrepancy between positive and negative emotions). The results suggest that when looking at negative emotion targets, emotional complexity among Japanese participants was driven by moderation. For embarrassment and happiness, however, it was driven both by moderation of the target emotion and by enhancement of the opposite emotions (Shiota et al., 2007b). Hence both mechanisms appear to be important to emotional complexity among Japanese.

In sum, a growing body of research suggests East Asians are more comfortable with emotional complexity than are Westerners. More research is needed to explain the underlying mechanisms and to address the possible link between dialectical epistemologies and the experience and regulation of emotional complexity. In addition to questions about the immediate implications of emotional complexity, it is unclear what relation emotional complexity has with overall psychological well-being. Is emotional complexity a bad thing? Does it cause individuals to have lower overall well-being? We address these questions in the following section.

IMPLICATIONS FOR PSYCHOLOGICAL WELL-BEING

To our knowledge, no research has specifically addressed whether cultural variation in emotional complexity has implications for psychological well-being. However, a significant body of research has examined cultural variations in well-being, including the role of contradictory self-views and dialecticism. We draw on this research here to make predictions for the implications of emotional complexity on overall well-being.

Dialectical epistemologies have important implications for cultural differences in self-evaluations and psychological well-being. In particular, the tendency to tolerate contradictory feelings toward the self and one's life in general can give rise to cultural variation in self-reported psychological well-being. The cross-cultural literature documents a fairly robust and pervasive tendency for East Asians to report lower levels of self-esteem and life satisfaction, and more negative affect, anxiety, and depression than do Westerners (Diener & Diener, 1995; Heine et al., 1999; Kitayama et al., 2000). A large number of potential explanations for these findings have been examined by cross-cultural scholars. Our research shows that dialectical epistemologies account, in part, for the observed cross-cultural differences in self-reported well-being (Spencer-Rodgers et al., 2004). In the following section, we review evidence on this topic and examine whether these findings reflect true underlying differences in well-being. Rather than being indicative of psychological maladjustment, we believe that these cultural differences are due to dialectical epistemologies which encourage East

Asians to endorse contradictory statements (e.g., "I am satisfied with my life" versus "I am dissatisfied with my life"). Indeed, the co-occurrence of positive and negative self-attitudes and emotions may actually be less problematic for members of dialectical cultures.

SELF-REPORTED DIFFERENCES IN WELL-BEING

How does dialecticism give rise to cultural variation in self-reported well-being? As outlined earlier in this chapter, a principal consequence of naïve dialecticism is that East Asians more comfortably acknowledge and accept psychological or "natural contradiction," in Piagetian terms (Piaget, 1980). Psychological contradiction is said to exist when two or more opposing phenomena (e.g., self-love and self-hatred) do not easily co-exist within the psyche, even though they are not logically incompatible. In Western cultures, discrepancies in one's emotions, cognitions, or behaviors are thought to give rise to a state of tension (Lewin, 1951), disequilibrium (Heider, 1958), or dissonance (Festinger, 1957), which activates a need for consonance (Festinger, 1957). When presented with conflicting information about an attitude object, including the self or one's life, Americans tend to examine both sides of the contradiction, and then search for synthesis and the resolution of incongruity (Peng & Nisbett, 1999; Spencer-Rodgers et al., 2004). Because Americans are motivated to emphasize and elaborate positive aspects of themselves (Heine & Hamamura, 2007) and to provide internally consistent responses to psychological measures, their global scores on various psychological instruments tend to be higher than those of East Asians.

As a result of dialectical epistemologies, East Asians are less motivated to exhibit internal consistency in their emotions, cognitions, and behaviors (Peng & Nisbett, 1999; Choi & Choi, 2002; Spencer-Rodgers et al., 2004). The cognitive tendency to accept psychological contradiction leads members of dialectical cultures to emphasize and elaborate negative aspects of themselves and to endorse indicators of psychological ill health (Spencer-Rodgers et al., 2004). Although East Asians and Americans tend not to differ in their rating of positively keyed items, such as "How satisfied are you with your life?" they often differ significantly in their tendency to endorse negatively keyed items, such as "How dissatisfied are you with your life?" Because members of dialectical cultures are inclined to see both perspectives (good and bad), they are more likely to acknowledge negative aspects of themselves and their lives. Moreover, in collectivist/interdependent countries, the cultural norm is to characterize the self in a self-effacing manner, whereas in individualist/independent societies, the cultural mandate is to present oneself in a self-enhancing light (Heine & Hamamura, 2007). East Asians generally describe themselves in less positive terms (Bond, 1986; Heine et al., 1999) and exhibit greater self-discrepancies, e.g., between the actual and ideal self (Heine & Lehman, 1999) and the public and private self (Triandis, 1995). In contrast to the Western, unitary self, members of dialectical cultures possess multiple selves that may stand in opposition to one another.

TRUE UNDERLYING DIFFERENCES IN WELL-BEING

Do these cultural differences in self-reported well-being reflect true underlying differences in maladjustment or dialectical epistemologies? Recently, Hamamura et al. (2007) examined whether the East Asian tendency to endorse negatively keyed items and contradictory statements was due to their dialectical epistemologies. They asked European-heritage and East-Asian heritage participants to rate themselves on 60 adjectives. They found that ambivalent or contradictory responding on the personality measure was correlated with participants' responses on the DSS. The tendency to endorse opposing or contradictory statements was correlated with participants' responses on the DSS (Spencer-Rodgers et al., 2007b), and cultural differences in contradictory responding were mediated by dialecticism. Contradictory responding is more than simply a "response style" however; it reflects a fundamental epistemology and way of understanding reality.

These findings have important implications for the manner in which psychologists measure psychological and emotional well-being across cultures. Much like research on emotional complexity, research conducted in our lab suggests that psychological constructs such as "self-esteem" and "well-being" may actually be two-dimensional constructs among members of dialectical cultures (Spencer-Rodgers et al., 2004). That is, positive self-esteem (well-being, etc.) may be conceptually and empirically distinct from negative self-esteem (well-being, etc.). If so, Western measures of psychological well-being may not be appropriate for use with East Asian cultures. A number of scholars have pointed to the dangers of using linear-individualist measures when assessing the self-esteem and psychological well-being of dialectical cultures (Kitayama & Markus, 1999; Suh, 2002; Cross et al., 2003; Spencer-Rodgers et al., 2004), noting that these instruments may lead to inaccurate or invalid cross-cultural comparisons.

In addition to having distinct meanings in various cultures, East Asians and Americans are motivated to emphasize different affective experiences and aspects of well-being. Whereas Americans seek to maximize positive emotions and feelings of self-worth, members of dialectical cultures are motivated to maintain a balance between positive and negative emotions. East Asians value less intense positive affect, such as calm (Tsai et al., 2006), and favor interpersonally engaging emotions, such as guilt, shame, and respect (Kitayama et al., 2006), which are important to the maintenance of group harmony in collectivist societies. In accordance with the dialectical tendency to tolerate contradiction, East Asians also possess more realistic and balanced self-appraisals and well-being judgments (Kitayama & Markus, 1999). Whereas self-esteem scores are highly skewed in American samples (e.g., among European Americans, Latinos, and African Americans), estimates of self-worth more closely approximate a normal distribution among East Asians (Diener & Diener, 1995).

Although dialecticism is associated with lower *self-reported* psychological well-being, this finding may be largely due to dialectical epistemologies (Hamamura et al., 2007). In actuality, the co-occurrence of positive and negative emotions may be less troubling and detrimental to an overall sense of well-being among East Asians. Based on the cross-cultural literature on the self, it would be reasonable to hypothesize that emotional complexity is less problematic for East Asians. In Western cultures, the possession of a consistent self-concept is typically associated with psychological well-being (Baumgardner, 1990; Campbell, 1990; Suh, 2002). East Asians place less emphasis on the consistency of the self. Because they are more dialectical, and perhaps because they are more interpersonally flexible (by adapting to the needs of ingroup members and the requirements of the situation), the link between cross-situational consistency and psychological well-being is attenuated among East Asians. Suh (2002) found that identity consistency is less strongly related to psychological well-being among Koreans than Americans. Similarly, Cross and colleagues (Cross et al., 2003) have shown that self-concept consistency is less central to psychological well-being for individuals who are highly relational-interdependent in their self-construals.

Very little research has examined the direct association between emotional complexity and psychological well-being across cultures. In our lab, we have found that emotional complexity is related to lower life satisfaction among East Asians and Americans. Notably, however, this association was weaker for Chinese participants ($r \approx -0.30$) than for European American participants ($r \approx -0.60$) (Spencer-Rodgers et al., 2007a). As outlined earlier, Chinese participants are more comfortable with complex emotions and are less likely to suppress these emotions, relative to Americans (Goetz et al., 2007). Finally, although East Asians exhibit greater ambivalence toward a variety of attitude objects (Spencer-Rodgers et al., 2004; Wonkyong et al., 2006), attitudinal ambivalence is less highly correlated with emotional complexity among East Asians. Wonkyong et al. (2006) primed people's conflicted evaluations about a variety of social issues (e.g., abortion, capital punishment, etc.) through a repeated expression paradigm and then examined the extent to which they felt "torn" or mixed emotions about the issues. There was a strong association between attitudinal ambivalence and emotional complexity among European Canadians, but a significantly weaker correlation among Asian Canadians. Although preliminary, these results suggest that attitudinal ambivalence and emotional complexity are less troubling for members of dialectical than non-dialectical cultures. We see this as an area of research that is ripe for further investigation.

CONCLUSIONS AND FUTURE RESEARCH

Emotional complexity is something we have all felt at some time or another. Whether it was the intense ambivalence felt at college graduation or the blend of happiness and jealousy when a friend outperformed us, life events present many opportunities for complex emotions. Research in this chapter suggests that beliefs about the nature of contradiction, interconnections, and change in the world relate to the subjective experience of complex emotions. Individuals from dialectical cultures that tolerate contradiction report feeling emotional complexity more frequently, are more comfortable with emotional complexity, and may be less likely to regulate it. These findings raise questions about emotional co-occurrence, as well as the role of culture in emotional experience.

Although recent theorizing about emotion has shifted toward acceptance of the possibility of emotional co-occurrence, there remains an underlying belief that positive and negative emotional mixes are inherently unstable states that represent indecision or a state to be resolved (Cacioppo et al., 1999). This is consistent with lay and scientific theories of emotion that assume a large role for emotion in determining behavior (e.g., Frijda et al., 1989; Ekman, 1992). Perhaps in Western cultures that value autonomy and choice, this relationship has been overemphasized. There are other determinants of behavior, such as societal expectations and social roles, and these may have a stronger influence than Western scholars have been willing to concede in emotion research. East Asian cultures are highly interdependent and have "tight" social norms that define clear, agreed upon standards for social behavior (Triandis, 1995). Therefore, in contrast to individualistic cultures, definite, simple emotions may not be needed to motivate social behavior. Indeed, polarized and strong emotional experiences may be considered threatening and undesirable (e.g., Tsai et al., 2006).

If the emotion-behavior link is more tenuous when social prescriptions are strong, one can theorize about other cultures in which emotional complexity is more stable and less problematic. There are many situations in which individuals have little control over their behavior or the environment in which they live. Consequently, people may have to tolerate greater emotional complexity if they live in cultural milieus in which they can exert less control over their environment. For example, Snibbe and Markus (2005) have found that working-class Americans with less education emphasize changing oneself to fit the environment, whereas those with more education emphasize changing one's environment to fit oneself. Perhaps emotional complexity is more acceptable for working-class Americans than it is for middle class Americans. In sum, emotional complexity may be more acceptable in general when emotions do not drive behavior and emotional complexity may promote adaptive functioning like behavioral flexibility. Emotional complexity may serve to prime many possible behaviors. This priming may allow for more flexible behavior and responses to situations. In addition, in situations in which one's inner state must be subjugated to norms or situational demands, emotional complexity may serve as a helpful way to tolerate negative and unchangeable aspects of life (Larsen et al., 2003).

Although we argue that emotional complexity is more likely and more acceptable in East Asian cultures, it is unclear whether emotional complexity among East Asians can be considered comfortable. We have argued, and the data support, that East Asians are less uncomfortable with emotional complexity than are Americans. However, it remains to be seen whether emotional complexity represents a desirable state. Our own data suggest that complex emotional experiences are more uncomfortable for Americans than are simple emotional experiences, but Chinese participants showed no differences. In their study of Asian and Caucasian Americans, Williams and Aaker (2002) found a similar pattern. However, do East Asians find emotional complexity to be an overall comfortable state? This is a question only more careful data collection and analysis can answer.

The research reported here suggests many new areas of research at the intersection of culture and emotional complexity. We have proposed that dialectical epistemologies and conceptions about contradiction are central to the experience and regulation of emotional complexity. However, only two studies have found direct evidence for a mechanistic link between dialecticism and emotional complexity. Future studies can increase understanding of the role of culture in emotional complexity with greater focus on possible pathways of influence. Under what conditions – cultural or situational – is emotional complexity likely to arise? In addition, future studies can provide insight by expanding research beyond subjective experience. By examining cognitive appraisals, expressive and regulatory behavior, as well as social consequences, one can gain insight into the broader emotion process. Finally, the implications for emotional complexity on well-being are largely unexplored.

REFERENCES

Bagozzi, R. P., Wong, N., & Yi, Y. (1999). The role of culture and gender in the relationship between positive and negative affect. *Cognition and Emotion, 13*, 641–672.

Baumgardner, A. H. (1990). To know oneself is to like oneself: Self-certainty and self-affect. *Journal of Personality and Social Psychology, 58*, 1062–1072.

Beach, S. R. H., & Tesser, A. (1993). Decision making power and marital satisfaction: A self-evaluation maintenance perspective. *Journal of Social and Clinical Psychology, 12*, 471–494.

Beach, S. R. H., Tesser, A., Fincham, F. D., Jones, D. J., Johnson, D., & Whitaker, D. J. (1998). Pleasure and pain in doing well, together: An investigation of performance-related affect in close relationships. *Journal of Personality and Social Psychology, 74*, 923–938.

Bond M. H. (Ed.) (1986). *The Psychology of the Chinese people*. Hong Kong: Oxford University Press.

Cacioppo, J. T., & Berntson, G. G. (1994). Relationship between attitudes and evaluative space: A critical review, with emphasis on the separability of positive and negative substrates. *Psychological Bulletin, 115*, 401–423.

Cacioppo, J. T., Gardner, W. L., & Berntson, G. G. (1999). The affect system has parallel and integrative processing components: Form follows function. *Journal of Personality and Social Psychology, 76*, 839–855.

Campbell, J. (1990). Self-esteem and clarity of the self-concept. *Journal of Personality and Social Psychology, 59*, 538–549.

Chen, S., English, T., & Peng, K. (2006). Self-verification and contextualized self-views. *Personality and Social Psychology Bulletin, 32*, 930–942.

Choi, I., & Choi, Y. (2002). Culture and self-concept flexibility. *Personality and Social Psychology Bulletin, 28*(11), 1508–1517.

Choi, I., & Nisbett, R. E. (1998). Situational salience and cultural differences in the correspondence bias and actor–observer bias. *Personality and Social Psychology Bulletin, 24*, 949–960.

Choi, I., Nisbett, R. E., & Norenzayan, A. (1999). Causal attribution across cultures: Variation and universality. *Psychological Bulletin, 125*, 47–63.

Choi, I., Dalal, R., Kim-Prieto, C., & Park, H. (2003). Culture and judgment of causal relevance. *Journal of Personality and Social Psychology, 84*, 46–59.

Chua, H. F., Leu, J., & Nisbett, R. E. (2005). Culture and diverging views of social events. *Personality and Social Psychology Bulletin, 31*, 925–934.

Cohen, D., & Gunz, A. (2002). As seen by the other…: Perspectives on the self in the memories and emotional perceptions of Easterners and Westerners. *Psychological Science, 13*, 55–59.

Cross, S. E., Gore, J. S., & Morris, M. (2003). The relational self-construal, self-consistency, and well-being. *Journal of Personality and Social Psychology, 85*, 933–944.

Darwin, C. (1872/1998). *The expression of the emotions in man and animals.* New York: Oxford University Press.

Diener, E., & Diener, M. (1995). Cross-cultural correlates of life satisfaction and self-esteem. *Journal of Personality and Social Psychology, 68*, 653–663.

Diener, E., & Emmons, R. A. (1984). The independence of positive and negative affect. *Journal of Personality & Social Psychology, 47*, 1105–1117.

Diener, E., & Emmons, R. A. (1985). The independence of positive and negative affect. *Journal of Personality and Social Psychology, 47*, 1105–1117.

Diener, E., & Iran-Nejad, A. (1986). The relationship in experience between various types of affect. *Journal of Personality and Social Psychology, 50*, 1031–1038.

Eid, M., & Diener, E. (2001). Norms for experiencing emotions in difference cultures: Inter- and Intranational differences. *Journal of Personality & Social Psychology, 81*, 869–885.

Ekman, P. (1992). An argument for basic emotions. *Cognition and Emotion, 6*, 169–200.

English, T., Goetz, J. L., Peng, K., & Wang, L. (2007). Cultural variation in responses to emotional complexity. Manuscript in preparation.

Festinger, L. (1957). *A theory of cognitive dissonance.* Stanford: Stanford University Press.

Frijda, N. H., Kuipers, P., & ter Schure, P. (1989). Relations among emotion, appraisal, and emotional action readiness. *Journal of Personality and Social Psychology, 57*, 212–228.

Goetz, J. L., & Keltner, D. (2007). Shifting meanings of self-conscious emotions across cultures: A social functional approach. In J. L. Tracy, R. W. Robins, & J. P. Tangney (Eds.), *The self-conscious emotions: Theory and research* (pp. 153–173). New York: Guilford.

Goetz, J. L., English, T., Peng, K., & Wang, L. (2007). Dialectical emotions: Culture and the experience of emotional complexity. Manuscript in preparation.

Gross, J. J., & John, O. P. (1998). Mapping the domain of expressivity: Multimethod evidence for a hierarchical model. *Journal of Personality and Social Psychology, 74*, 170–191.

Hallahan, M., Lee, F., & Herzog, T. (1997). It's not just whether you win or lose; it's also where you play the game. *Journal of Cross-Cultural Psychology, 28*, 768–778.

Hamamura, T., Heine, S. J., & Paulhus, D. L. (2007). Cultural differences in response styles: The role of dialectical thinking. Unpublished manuscript. University of British Columbia" should be updated to read "Hamamura, T., Heine, S., & Paulhus, D. (2008). Cultural differences in response styles: The role of dialectical thinking. *Personality and Individual Differences, 44*, 932-942.

Heider, F. (1958). *The psychology of interpersonal relations.* New York: Wiley.

Heine, S. J., & Hamamura, T. (2007). In search of East Asian self-enhancement. *Personality and Social Psychology Review, 11*, 4–27.

Heine, S. J., & Lehman, D. R. (1999). Culture, self-discrepancies, and self-satisfaction. *Personality and Social Psychology Bulletin, 25*, 915–925.

Heine, S. J., Lehman, D. R., Markus, H. R., & Kitayama, S. (1999). Is there a universal need for positive self-regard? *Psychological Review, 106*, 766–794.

Ji, L.-J., Peng, K., & Nisbett, R. E. (2000). Culture, control, and perception of relationships in the environment. *Journal of Personality and Social Psychology, 78*, 943–955.

Ji, L.-J., Nisbett, R. E., & Su, Y. (2001). Culture, change, and prediction. *Psychological Science, 12*, 450–456.

Kanagawa, C., Cross, S., & Markus, H. (2001). "Who am I?" The cultural psychology of the conceptual self. *Personality and Social Psychology Bulletin, 27*, 90–103.

Kitayama, S., & Markus, H. R. (1999). Yin and yang of the Japanese self: The cultural psychology of personality coherence. In D. Cervone & Y. Shoda (Eds.), *The coherence of personality: Social cognitive bases of personality consistency, variability, and organization* (pp. 242–302). NY: Guilford.

Kitayama, S., Markus, H. R., & Kurokawa, M. (2000). Culture, emotion, and well-being: Good feelings in Japan and the United States. *Cognition and Emotion, 14*, 93–124.

Kitayama, S., Mesquita, B., & Kurokawa, M. (2006). Cultural affordances and emotional experience: Socially engaging and disengaging emotions in Japan and the United States. *Journal of Personality and Social Psychology, 91*, 890–903.

Larsen, J. T., McGraw, A. P., & Cacioppo, J. T. (2001). Can people feel happy and sad at the same time? *Journal of Personality and Social Psychology, 81*, 684–696.

Larsen, J. T., Hemenover, S. H., Norris, C. J., & Cacioppo, J. T. (2003). Turning adversity to advantage: On the virtues of the coactivation of positive and negative emotions. In L. Aspinwall & U. M. Staudinger (Eds.), *A psychology of human strengths* (pp. 211–225). Washington, DC: American Psychological Association.

Larsen, J. T., McGraw, A. P., Mellers, B. A., & Cacioppo, J. T. (2004). The agony of victory and thrill of defeat. *Psychological Science, 15*, 325–330.

Lazarus, R. (1991). *Emotion and adaptation.* New York: Oxford University Press.

Lee, F., Hallahan, M., & Herzog, T. (1996). Explaining real life events: How culture and domain shape attributions. *Personality and Social Psychology Bulletin, 22*, 732–741.

Lewin, K. (1935). *Dynamic theory of personality.* New York: McGraw-Hill.

Lewin, K. (1951). *Field theory in social science.* New York: Harper.

Masuda, T., & Nisbett, R. E. (2001). Attending holistically versus analytically: Comparing the context sensitivity of Japanese and Americans. *Journal of Personality and Social Psychology, 81*, 922–934.

Mesquita, B., & Frijda, N. H. (1992). Cultural variations in emotions: A review. *Psychological Bulletin, 112*, 179–204.

Morris, M. W., & Peng, K. (1994). Culture and cause: American and Chinese attributions for social and physical events. *Journal of Personality and Social Psychology, 67*, 949–971.

Nisbett, R. E., Peng, K., Choi, I., & Norenzayan, A. (2001). Culture and systems of thought: Holistic versus analytic cognition. *Psychological Review, 108*, 291–310.

Peng, K., & Nisbett, R. E. (1999). Culture, dialectics, and reasoning about contradiction. *American Psychologist, 54*, 741–754.

Peng, K., Spencer-Rodgers, J., & Zhong, N. (2006). Naive dialecticism and the Tao of Chinese thought. In U. Kim, K.-S. Yang, & K.-K. Hwang (Eds.), *Indigenous and cultural psychology: Understanding people in context* (pp. 247–262). New York: Springer.

Perunovic, W. Q. E., Heller, D., & Rafaeli, E. (2007). Within-person changes in the structure of emotion: The role of cultural identification and language. *Psychological Science, 18*, 607–613.

Piaget, J. (1980). *Experiments in contradiction.* University of Chicago Press.

Russell, J. A. (1980). A circumplex model of affect. *Journal of Personality and Social Psychology, 39*, 1161–1178.

Russell, J. A., & Carroll, J. M. (1999). On the bipolarity of positive and negative affect. *Psychological Bulletin, 125*, 3–30.

Schimmack, U. (2001). Pleasure, displeasure, and mixed feelings: Are semantic opposites mutually exclusive? *Cognition & Emotion, 15*, 81–97.

Schimmack, U. (2005). Response latencies of pleasure and displeasure ratings: Further evidence for mixed feelings. *Cognition and Emotion, 19*, 671–691.

Schimmack, U., Oishi, S., & Diener, E. (2002). Cultural influences on the relation between pleasant emotions and unpleasant emotions: Asian dialectic philosophies or individualism-collectivism? *Cognition and Emotion, 16*, 705–719.

Scollon, C. N., Diener, E., Oishi, S., & Biswas-Diener, R. (2005). An experience sampling and cross-cultural investigation of the relation between pleasant and unpleasant affect. *Cognition and Emotion, 19*, 27–52.

Shiota, M. N., Campos, B., Gonzaga, G. C., Keltner, D., & Peng, K. (2007a). Dialectical epistemology and cultural differences in emotional complexity during interaction with a romantic partner. Manuscript under review.

Shiota, M. N., Mori, S. C., Keltner, D., & Peng, K. (2007b). Dialecticism and emotion: Cultural differences in complexity when interpreting emotional faces. Manuscript under review.

Smith, C. A., & Ellsworth, P. C. (1985). Patterns of cognitive appraisal in emotion. *Journal of Personality & Social Psychology, 48*, 813–838.

Snibbe, A. C., & Markus, H. R. (2005). You can't always get what you want: Educational attainment, agency, and choice. *Journal of Personality and Social Psychology, 88*, 703–720.

Spencer-Rodgers, J., Peng, K., Wang, L., & Hou, Y. (2004). Dialectical self-esteem and East–West differences in psychological well-being. *Personality and Social Psychology Bulletin, 30*, 1416–1432.

Spencer-Rodgers, J., & Peng, K. (2004). The dialectical self: Contradiction, change, and holism in the East Asian self-concept. In R. M. Sorrentino, D. Cohen, J. M. Olsen, & M. P. Zanna (Eds.), Culture and social behavior: The Ontario symposium (Vol. 10, pp. 227-249). Mahwah, NJ: Erlbaum.

Spencer-Rodgers, J., Peng, K., & Wang, L. (2007a). Unpublished data. University of California, Berkeley.

Spencer-Rodgers, J., Srivastava, S., English, T., Boucher, H. C., Paletz, S., Wang, L., & Peng, K. (2007b). The dialectical self scale. Unpublished manuscript. University of California, Berkeley.

Suh, E. M. (2002). Culture, identity consistency, and subjective well-being. *Journal of Personality and Social Psychology, 83*, 1378–1391.

Triandis, H. C. (1995). *Individualism and collectivism*. Boulder: Westview.

Tsai, J. L., & Levenson, R. W. (1997). Cultural influences of emotional responding: Chinese American and European American dating couples during interpersonal conflict. *Journal of Cross-Cultural Psychology, 2*, 600–625.

Tsai, J. L., Knutson, B., & Fung, H. H. (2006). Cultural variation in affect valuation. *Journal of Personality and Social Psychology, 90*, 288–307.

Williams, P., & Aaker, J. L. (2002). Can mixed emotions peacefully coexist? *Journal of Consumer Research, 28*, 636–649.

Wonkyong, B. L., Newby-Clark, I., & Zanna, M. P. (January 2006). Cross-cultural differences in the relation between potential and felt ambivalence. Poster session presented at the annual meeting of the Society for Personality and Social Psychology, Palm Springs, CA.

Yik, M. (2007). Culture, gender, and the bipolarity of momentary affect. *Cognition and Emotion, 21*, 664-680.

Zelenski, J. M., & Larsen, R. J. (2000). The distribution of basic emotions in everyday life: A state and trait perspective from experience sampling data. *Journal of Research in Personality, 34*, 178–197.

23

CULTURE, EMOTION, AND MOTIVATION

DAVID MATSUMOTO AND JESSIE WILSON

San Francisco State University, San Francisco, CA, USA

Any discussion of motivation and behavior is incomplete without incorporating the role and functions of emotion as a source of motivation for behavior. In this chapter, we describe a theory of how emotions serve as one important source of motivation by priming individuals to behave in certain ways. We also discuss how culture – as a meaning and information system – influences emotion–behavior linkages. We argue that the function of culture is to prevent social chaos, maintain social order, and ensure group efficiency, given the ecological environment and the resources available in it to survive. It does this by identifying social roles, normative behaviors, expectations, value and belief systems related to interpersonal relationships and the environment, and with regard to emotion itself. It also creates a belief system involving worldviews and self-construals to help to reinforce, maintain, and achieve this purpose. Our thesis, therefore, is that, when emotions are elicited, culture calibrates the primed individual to the behavioral repertoires available and necessary in that culture as identified by the social roles, norms, and expectations in order to serve as motivators for desired behaviors. We view behaviors as occurring in specific situational contexts as role performances, and individuals as actors playing roles defined by culture.

We begin with a discussion of our understanding of culture, and then emotion. We then discuss how culture influences behavior by calibrating the individual behavioral responses when emotions are elicited to culturally appropriate behavioral repertoires. We discuss the possibility of both biologically driven universal behavioral responses, as well as culture-specific responding. Throughout we integrate and synthesize the available literature, and highlight gaps in the literature that can serve as guidelines for future research.

WHAT IS CULTURE?

A DEFINITION OF CULTURE

To understand our perspective on the role of emotion and culture in motivating behavior, it is important to situate our perspective within a larger framework of how we understand the interrelationship between basic human nature, culture, and personality in shaping behavior. To do that we must provide our definition of culture, which we do here, and emotion, which we do in the next section.

In order to survive, humans must satisfy basic physical needs of eating, drinking, breathing, sleeping, eliminating, reproducing, seeking shelter, and otherwise staying healthy. Each of these needs is ultimately related to reproductive success and survival, which are the ultimate goals of an evolutionary life. In order to meet these needs a variety of social problems must be solved, including negotiating complex status hierarchies, forming successful work and social groups, attracting mates, fighting off potential rivals for food and sexual partners, giving birth and raising children, and battling nature (Buss, 1988, 2001). These problems still exist in our everyday lives today. To aid in resolving these problems, various social motives have evolved. Sheldon (2004) proposed that these social motives can be organized around three major themes: autonomy, competence, and relatedness. Similarly, Hogan (1982) posited the importance of the needs to get along and get ahead.

Different environments introduce different problems that humans must deal with in order to survive, and thus human groups need to create different solutions to these different problems. Fortunately, they need not create entirely new solutions in each generation. Because humans are social animals, they survive by taking advantage of the power of the group. Groups create solutions to the problems posed by their environments in order to address biological needs and social motives; these solutions involve adaptations to the specific environments in which groups exist. They are called *environmental adaptations* (Bowlby, 1969), and form the basis of culture. In our view, therefore, culture is the complex set of ways that emerges when a group uses the basic tools inherent in its members to address the problems presented by their ecological context in order to meet biological needs and social motives. Culture is a set of solutions developed over time to solve the problem of how to survive.

All animals engage in environmental adaptation; and because many animals are social, many have culture, or at least a rudimentary form of it (Matsuzawa, 2001; Boesch, 2003; McGrew, 2004; Whiten et al., 2005). Human cultures, however, are different from animal cultures in several respects. These differences are rooted in uniquely human cognitive abilities including language (Premack, 2004), the ability to believe that other people are intentional agents, self–other knowledge (Tomasello, 1999), and the ability to continually build upon improvements and discoveries (ratcheting) (Tomasello et al., 1993). Although rudimentary variants of these abilities may exist in animals, these abilities make human social life much more complex than that of animals.

This complexity exists for several reasons. First, humans are members of multiple groups, each having its own purpose, hierarchy, and networking system. Humans are unique in that they live in large communities with both kin and non-kin. And humans have the capacity for a great diversity of thought and action.

For all these reasons, the great complexity of human social life can easily lead to social chaos. Human cultures, therefore, evolved to help deal with this complexity, prevent social chaos, maintain social order, and ensure efficient group functioning, by giving meaning to this social complexity. Human cultures allow humans to make greater differentiations in their social lives, and institutionalize much of it. Thus, we define human culture as *a unique meaning and information system, shared by a group and transmitted across generations, that allows the group to meet basic needs of survival, by coordinating social behavior to achieve a viable existence, to transmit successful social behaviors, to pursue happiness and well-being, and to derive meaning from life* (Matsumoto, 2007; Matsumoto & Juang, 2007).

CULTURE AND SITUATIONAL CONTEXT

One of the most important ways in which cultures maintain social order is by proscribing preferred modes of behaviors in specific situational contexts through social roles, normative behaviors, and expectations associated with those situational contexts. Cultures do so by first ascribing meaning to the various situational contexts in which individuals exist. There are many components of situational contexts, including time, place, interactants, the content of activities or conversations, the reasons why the interactions are occurring in the first place, and the possibility of any future interactions between the same interactants. All of these factors combine to produce the unique situational contexts in which human lives are woven. Human cultures aid humans in navigating this complex mesh of situations by ascribing meanings to them.

These meanings create *expectations* for the actors in context in terms of normative behaviors, which are the behaviors that each culture expects its members to engage in given the specific situational context in which they live in order to achieve the goal of surviving in a culturally appropriate fashion. The expectations concerning normative behaviors are summarized for each individual member of a culture in a social role (Matsumoto, 2007). These serve as guidelines that help to maintain social order so that the group can adapt to the environment and survive. Social roles define the range of acceptable behaviors of an individual in a context, identifying both culturally appropriate and inappropriate behaviors.

Social roles are like scripts in a play (Goffman, 1959), because they delineate the types of behaviors that are expected in the specific situational context based on the specific meanings ascribed to that context. Because cultures define the meaning of the situational context, the scripts associated with the contexts are culturally dependent, and can produce both cultural similarities and differences. Cultural similarities in the meaning ascribed to specific situational contexts would be related to similarities in social roles and normative behaviors, while cultural differences in situational meaning would be associated with cultural differences in role expectations and normative behavior expectations. While situational context provides the general scripts of behavior, cultures adjust those scripts according to their context-specific frameworks and expectations.

Thus, as inherently social animals, humans live in a complex mix of situational contexts. Behaviors occur in these contexts, and as such are influenced by culture (via social roles, norms, and expectations). During the process of enculturation humans learn, implicitly and explicitly, of the various roles they play because of the meanings inherent in various social situations, and of appropriate and inappropriate behaviors. In this view, cultural knowledge consists of interrelated sets of social roles, normative behaviors, and expectations of many different situational contexts. This view of culture is consonant with a growing awareness within cultural psychology of culture as situated cognition (Matsumoto et al., 1997; Hong et al., 2000; Oyserman & Lee, 2007). (Behaviors are also heavily influenced by personality and individual differences, a topic that will not be discussed in this chapter.) For this reason, we view behaviors as role performances, and individuals engaging in behaviors as actors (Figure 23.1).

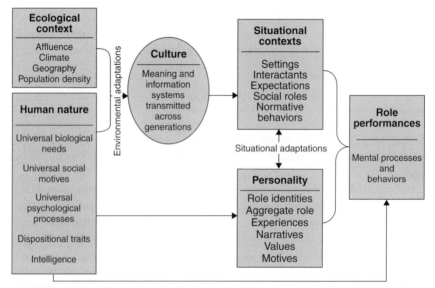

FIGURE 23.1   The relative contributions of basic human nature, culture, and personality to mental processes and behaviors (Matsumoto, in press).

WHAT IS EMOTION?

A DEFINITION OF EMOTION

Humans experience a wide range of affective phenomena. Being tired, bored, sleepy, excited, and hungry are states associated with affect, as are anger, fear, sadness, love, shame, pride, embarrassment, and jealousy. Although the terms affect, feeling, and emotion are often used interchangeably, we believe that emotions are a special type of affective phenomenon. We define emotion as *transient, bio-psycho-social reactions designed to aid individuals in adapting to and coping with events that have immediate implications for their well-being.* They are biological because they involve the brain, the muscles, the autonomic system, and other aspects of human physiology. They are psychological because they involve specific mental processes required for elicitation and regulation of response. And they are social because they often are elicited by social factors, and often have social meaning when elicited and displayed. Emotions are one of the universal psychological processes that are an inherent part of basic human nature.

Consistent with other writers who have suggested the existence of a genetically coded, inheritable, biologically based processing system that activates emotional states (Tomkins, 1962; Lazarus, 1991; Ekman, 1992; Levenson, 1999; Cosmides & Tooby, 2000), Levenson (1999) called the base processing system that elicited emotions the "core emotion system." He suggested that the core system was designed in evolution to deal with species-constant problems related to survival in a time-tested, predictable, and automatic fashion. These problems could occur in interactions with nature or with other humans. The core emotion system is hard-wired, fairly impermeable to modification by experience, and relatively unchanged throughout the lifespan.

Our understanding of the core emotion system extends Levenson's (1999) conceptualization by elaborating two components (Figure 23.2, bottom). The first is a scanner that constantly monitors the environment for emotionally relevant stimuli. Cognitive processes such as attention and perception are involved in this scanning process. Perception involves the creation of schemas or mental representations of the perceived stimulus; then, perceived stimuli are evaluated in an appraisal process. The evaluation uses a combination of emotion-eliciting themes related to their implications for the immediate welfare of the individual and/or kin (Lazarus (1991) called them core relational themes), and cognitive schemas describing the characteristics of the eliciting event. The themes and schemas are stored in what we call the *emotion schema database*. The appraised themes and schemas are compared against the themes and schemas encoded in the emotion schema database, and if they match, a group of responses are initiated, including expressive behavior, physiology, cognitions, subjective experience, and motor behaviors. The group of responses are coordinated, integrated, and organized, and constitute what is known as an "emotion." Emotional responses, in turn, affect

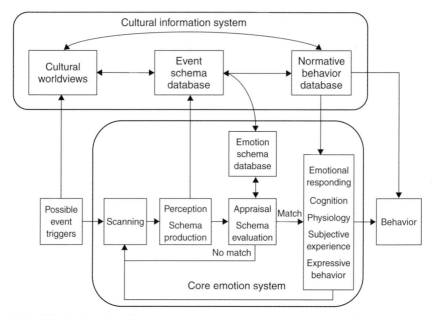

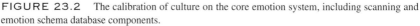

FIGURE 23.2   The calibration of culture on the core emotion system, including scanning and emotion schema database components.

the scanning component of the core system. In our view, the term "emotion" is a metaphor or summary description that refers to a particular group of coordinated response systems.

**THE INTRAPERSONAL FUNCTIONS OF
EMOTION: PRIMING BEHAVIOR**

Modern-day ideas concerning the intrapersonal functions of emotion have their roots in Darwin (1872/1998), who proposed an evolutionary, adaptive function for emotion. Darwin suggested that facial, verbal, and non-verbal expressions of emotion are part of an innate physiological response system signaling behavioral intentions and roles in social interactions. Darwin further suggested that progenitors who could utilize this response system effectively could better fulfill biological needs such as eating, procreation, acquiring shelter, or saving one's young from an attack. Core survival needs such as these, often referred to as fundamental life tasks (Lazarus, 1991; Johnson-Laird & Oatley, 1992; Ekman, 1999), elicit prototypical or biologically based behaviors (action preparedness) that are executed quickly and effectively in order for an individual's survival. Emotions and the emotion response system, Darwin surmised, are responsible for these prototypical behaviors that help meet the fundamental life tasks of survival.

Tomkins (1962, 1963) expanded upon the evolutionary theory. Contrary to the then ubiquitous conjecture that psychoanalytic drives was at the heart of human motivation, Tomkins posited that eight primary, innate emotions – interest, joy, surprise, distress, fear, shame, contempt, and anger – were biologically inherent in all humans, and that acted as a primary motive in an individual's behavioral response to the environment. To understand motivation one must understand emotion, Tomkins argued, as emotion *is* motivation.

Over the years other writers have commented on the intrapersonal function of emotion to prepare individuals to respond behaviorally to eliciting events (Frijda et al., 1989; Levenson, 1999). Frijda et al. (1989), e.g., call this function of emotion action-readiness. Collectively they all suggest that emotions prepare individuals to respond to eliciting stimuli by coordinating a system of responses; anger prepares the body to fight, and fear prepares it for flight.

A number of studies have provided evidence for linkages between emotion and behavior. In studying facial expressions of emotion in children, for instance, Ekman et al. (1972b) found that boys who smiled more while watching a violent movie or sports scene were afterward more likely to engage in hurtful behavior toward another child. Similarly, Matsumoto et al. (1986) studied facial expressions of emotion produced by preschool children as they played a modified version of the prisoner's dilemma game, and showed that children who expressed Duchenne smiles after their partner cooperated with them were in turn more likely to demonstrate cooperative behaviors. Duchenne smiles are smiles that have been identified as signs of true enjoyment (Ekman et al., 1990; Frank & Ekman, 1993; Frank et al., 1993), and involve innervation of orbicularis oculi, the muscle surrounding the eyes, and zygomatic major, which pulls the lip corners up. Children who expressed non-Duchenne smiles after having experienced uncooperative behavior from their partner were more likely to withdraw their own allegiance and led to further defections. Keltner et al. (1995) demonstrated relationships between aggressive and delinquent social behavior of adolescent boys as reported by their teachers with the boys' facial displays of anger; interestingly, an absence of aggressive behaviors was negatively correlated with facial expressions of fear.

A recent study from our laboratory also highlighted the universal linkage between emotion and behavior. In this study (Matsumoto & Yamagishi, in preparation), Japanese university undergraduates participated in the Ultimatum game while their facial behaviors were videotaped. In the first condition, participants were given an unfair offer from a partner, and had to decide to either accept or reject it. If they accepted it, they would both receive what was offered; if the participants rejected the offer, neither would get anything. Because these initial offers were all unfair, expressions of anger were displayed most frequently by all participants. Yet, only expressions of contempt or sadness predicted whether or not the participants would accept or reject the offers; greater displays of either of these emotions were associated with rejection.

In a subsequent condition in the same experiment, the participants then made their own offers back to their partners. These offers were either fair or unfair. Interestingly, participants who showed more positive emotions (enjoyment, interest, or Duchenne smiling) in the *first* condition were more likely to give fair offers themselves later. This is an interesting finding because recall that all participants received an unfair offer in that first condition. This suggests that participants who displayed more positive emotions were either more forgiving of their partners, and thus made more conciliatory, fair, offers subsequently. Or, positive emotions may lead to greater variability in behavior (Hertel & Fiedler, 1994), which may have led to greater frequencies of fair offers.

Although these studies suggest direct linkages between emotion and behavior, as we mention above we believe that emotion primes the individual to engage in behavior, by activating and coordinating cognitive, bodily, and motivational states. Thus our position of the linkage between emotion and behavior is consistent with a recent review of the topic by Baumeister et al. (2007), who argued for indirect rather than direct linkages between emotion and behavior. (We do *not* agree, however, with these authors' claims that contemporary theories of emotion posit one-to-one, direct links with behavior.) We also agree with these authors' suggestions of the learning function of emotion, i.e., the notion that emotions help individuals learn associations between event triggers and behavioral consequences so as to be better equipped to react in similar situations in the future.

THE INTERPERSONAL FUNCTIONS OF EMOTION:
EVOKING RESPONSES IN OTHERS

Emotions not only prime an individual to engage in behavior; their expressions also coordinate social interactions through their informative, evocative, and incentive functions (Keltner & Kring, 1998). They provide information to perceivers about the individual's emotional state (Scherer, 1986; Ekman, 1993), behavioral intentions (Fridlund, 1994), relational status vis-à-vis the target of the expression (Keltner, 1995; Tiedens et al., 2000), and objects and events in the social environment (Mineka & Cook, 1993). This view of facial expression emerged in developmental studies of emotional exchanges between parents and children (Klinnert et al., 1983, 1986; Hertenstein & Campos, 2004), as well as ethological studies of social behaviors like flirting, reconciliation, aggression, and play, and is consistent with claims regarding the co-evolution of signal and perceiver response to displays (Eibl-Eibesfeldt, 1989). Thus, an individual's emotional expression serves as a "social affordance" which evokes "prepared" responses in others (Esteves et al., 1994). Anger, e.g., might have evolved to elicit fear-related responses and the inhibition of inappropriate action (Dimberg & Ohman, 1996); note that Japanese often label another person's angry expression as "scary" (Matsumoto, 2006). Distress calls might have evolved to elicit sympathetic responses in observers (Eisenberg *et al.*, 1989). Through these processes, emotional communication helps individuals in relationships – parent and child, mates, boss and subordinates – respond to the demands and opportunities of their social environment. They are basic elements of social interaction, from flirtatious exchanges to greeting rituals.

Facial expressions of emotion facilitate specific behaviors in perceivers. Because facial expressions of emotion are universal social signals, they contain meaning not only about the expressor's intent and subsequent behavior, but also about what the perceiver is likely to do. Marsh et al. (2005) showed observers fearful and angry faces, and asked them to either push or pull a lever when they saw them. These motor responses were associated with approach and avoidance behaviors; anger facilitated avoidance-related behaviors, while fear facilitated approach-related behaviors. Winkielman et al. (2005) conducted two studies that demonstrated that subliminal presentation of smiles produced increases in how much beverage people poured and consumed, and how much they were willing to pay for it; presentation of angry faces decreased these behaviors. Also, emotional displays evoke specific, complementary emotional responses from observers – for example, anger has been found to evoke fear (Esteves et al., 1994; Dimberg & Ohman, 1996), whereas distress evokes sympathy and aid (Eisenberg et al., 1989).

Facial expressions of emotion regulate social interaction. In the developmental literature, this concept has been investigated under the rubric of social referencing (Klinnert et al., 1983), i.e., the process whereby infants seek out emotional information from others to disambiguate a situation, and then use that information to act. To date, the strongest demonstration of social referencing comes from work on the visual cliff. In the first study to investigate social referencing in the visual cliff, Campos and his colleagues (Sorce et al., 1985) placed mothers on the far end of the cliff from the infant. Mothers first smiled to the infants and placed a toy on top the safety glass to attract them; infants invariably began crawling to their mothers. When the infants were in the center of the table, however, the mother then posed an expression of either fear, sadness, anger, interest, or joy, corresponding to the expressions published by Ekman & Friesen (1975) and Izard (1971). The results showed clearly different results for the different faces. No infant crossed the table when the mother showed fear; only 1 (of 17) did when the mother posed anger. Only 33% crossed when the mother posed sadness, and approximately 75% of the infants crossed when the mother posed joy or interest.

Other studies provide similar support for facial expressions as regulators of social interaction. In one (Bradshaw, 1986), cited in Campos et al. (2003), experimenters posed facial expressions of neutral, anger, or fear toward babies as they moved toward a target object. The dependent variable was the amount of inhibition the babies showed in touching the object. The results for 10- and 15-month olds were the same: anger produced the greatest inhibition, followed by disgust, with neutral the least. This study was replicated (Hertenstein & Campos, 2004), using joy and disgust expressions, altering the method so that the infants were not allowed to touch the toy until 1 hour after exposure to the expression. At 14-months of age, significantly more infants touched the toy in the joy condition (compared with a distractor object), but fewer touched the toy in the disgust condition.

Not surprisingly, the social value of facial expressions of emotion has been shown in other primate species as well. Miller and his colleagues (Miller et al., 1959, 1963, 1966, 1967) demonstrated that monkeys shown a facial expression of distress by a conspecific will perform a conditioned task more readily than a monkey shown a neutral expression. Presumably, the perception of another's distress is sufficiently motivating to an individual to engage in specific types of behaviors, because distress is a call for help and motivational in this manner. Miller's paradigm, in fact, was the basis for an early measure in the human emotional intelligence domain developed by Buck (1976). Itakura (1993) reported a different contingency learning study with a female chimp who showed negative emotional behaviors when she made an error. Collectively, the studies reviewed in this section demonstrate that emotions have important interpersonal functions, regulating the behavior of others.

CULTURAL INFLUENCES ON EMOTION – BEHAVIOR LINKS

THE CULTURAL CALIBRATION OF EMOTIONAL RESPONDING AND SUBSEQUENT BEHAVIORS

Figure 23.2 illustrates how cultures can calibrate two aspects of the core emotion system. The first involves the calibration of the system to culturally available events to ensure that emotions are elicited appropriately to the many events available in human cultural life. We posit that this occurs through the continual encoding of cultural event schemas that require an emotional response to the emotion schema database (i.e., intervention at the front end of the system). The second involves the calibration of the response system to cultural norms, social roles, and expectations for behaviors (i.e., intervention at the back end of the system). This chapter is concerned only with the outputs of this process, i.e., on the cultural calibration occurring at the back end of the system, depicted on the far right, in which emotions lead to behaviors. For a detailed discussion of the entire model, see Matsumoto et al. (2007b).

Although emotions prime behaviors, not everyone who is angry actually does fight, nor does everyone who is afraid actually flee. In these cases, anger and fear *prepare* the individual to do so by *priming* a set of behaviors associated with each emotion. These behaviors may be verbal or motor. The preparatory functions of emotion are served by initiating the response system described above, and especially by recruiting physiological reactions and turning on basic cognitive processes that prepare an individual to respond in specific, adaptive ways. Emotions help individuals deal with eliciting events by limiting the possible behavioral responses that the individual can engage in. That is, of all the infinitely possible actions we *could* do, emotions are adaptive because they restrict the range of behavioral choices for us to that which is most conducive to responding to the eliciting event. When angry, therefore, behaviors related to verbal or physical aggression are primed; when afraid, behaviors related to protection or escape are primed. These linkages between emotion and the activated behavioral repertoires that are primed are universal.

Engaging in such behaviors, however, depend on a host of other factors. One likely factor is the intensity of the emotional response. Emotion-directed expressions and behaviors will be more likely to occur when the intensity of the emotion is high. Becoming enraged (high intensity anger) will be more likely to produce aggressive behaviors such as hitting, kicking, biting, screaming, or yelling compared to when one is just aggravated (low intensity anger). Being terrified (high intensity fear) will be more likely to produce freezing or escape than will being apprehensive (low intensity fear). Thus the linkage between emotion and probability of behavioral occurrence is likely universal, but moderated by the intensity of the emotional response.

That having been said, of course there are enormous individual differences in the types and intensities of emotions people have, even in the same contexts. These differences among emotional reactions prime behaviors differently, and may in fact be maladaptive. Too much emotion, e.g., can lead to behavioral consequences that do not take into account the appropriate responses dictated by social norms. Becoming infuriated at a "little" event, for instance, can lead to yelling, screaming, and even physical aggression in some, causing them to later regret their emotion-driven behaviors. The opposite can also be true; too *little* emotion may lead to non-responses, which may be maladaptive if some emotion and behavior were more appropriate. Maladaptive response may also be a consequence of the wrong emotions elicited. But we view these cases as the exception rather than the norm. The norm provides guidelines for groups of individuals, and while individuals may be at either end of the spectrum of appropriate or inappropriate behaviors, the cultural calibration of emotion ensures that the majority of individuals engage in appropriate emotional responding, leading to social role and norm-driven appropriate behavioral reactions.

Another important factor that moderates the emotion–behavior linkage is culture. (We do not deal here with the influence of personality and individual difference variables on behavior, which are equally important.) As mentioned earlier, one of the functions of culture is to provide guidelines for preferred behaviors in order to prevent social chaos, maintain social order, and ensure group efficiency. Cultures do so by ascribing meaning to specific situational contexts, which in turn provide a means of proscribing a set of normative behaviors in the form of social roles in those situational contexts. Norms via social roles also create expectations for preferred modes of behavior. Thus of all the *possible* behavioral responses available to an individual when an emotion is elicited, culture limits the set of likely responses by providing individuals with a menu of choices of behaviors that are appropriate to that culture, given the social roles, norms, expectations, and situational meaning. (We posit that this information is the contents of the normative behavior database in Figure 23.2.) That is, culture defines the available behavioral repertoires provided to individuals when emotions are aroused. This repertoire is defined by what the culture has determined in its history to be most adaptive in maintaining social order, thereby ensuring survival and genetic transmission. In this fashion, one of the most important goals of enculturation for all individuals in all cultures is the *calibration* of individual core emotion systems with the appropriate behavioral repertoires in those cultures for each specific emotion and situation.

Adamopoulous and Lonner (2001) discussed two ways in which culture influenced behavior, the first by restricting normally available behaviors, the second by enabling new behaviors. We agree that culture does both in moderating the emotion–behavior linkage. By defining social roles, norms, and expectations and limiting the available behavioral repertoire, culture restricts the possible list of normally approved behaviors that are appropriate for any given emotional reaction in any given situational context. At the same time, cultures can enable new behaviors that are incongruent with the universal emotion–behavior linkage, depending on the specific emotion and situational context. Culture, therefore, provides the behavioral maps available and appropriate to individuals in specific contexts. Individuals engage in these behavioral maps as part of role performances in their respective cultures.

EVIDENCE

Biologically Based Universality in Expressive Behaviors

Darwin (1872/1998) suggested that expressive behaviors are the residual actions of more complete behavioral responses. Facial (and vocal) expressions are part of emotion-related actions, and occur in combination with other bodily responses – postural, gestural, skeletal muscle movements, and physiological responses. Thus, we express anger by furrowing the brow and tightening the lips with teeth displayed because these actions are part of an attack response; we express disgust with an open mouth, nose wrinkle, and tongue protrusion as part of a vomiting response. Facial expressions, then, are elements of a coordinated response involving multiple response systems.

The first study to demonstrate universality in expressive behavior was Ekman's (1972) classic study of Americans and Japanese participants who viewed neutral and stressful films and, unbeknownst to them, whose facial behaviors were recorded throughout the entire experiment. Ekman coded the last 3 minutes of facial behavior during the neutral films, and the entire 3 minutes of the last stress film clip using a modified version of facial affect scoring technique (FAST), a precursor to the facial action coding system (FACS; Ekman & Friesen, 1978). FAST identified facial configurations of six emotions – anger, disgust, fear, happiness, sadness, and surprise. But, the facial coding procedure was modified to include *all* lower face actions, rendering the coding equivalent to FACS. (The upper and middle face FAST codes already comprehensively assessed the FACS codes in these areas.) The generated codes corresponded to the facial expressions portrayed in the stimuli used in their judgment studies (Ekman et al.,

1969, 1972a; Ekman, 1972), and subsequently in the descriptions of the universal emotions in *Unmasking the Face* (Ekman & Friesen, 1975), in their stimulus set *Pictures of Facial Affect* (Ekman & Friesen, 1976), in Matsumoto and Ekman's (1988) *Japanese and Caucasian Facial Expressions of Emotion* set, and to the facial configurations identified as emotion signals in Ekman and Friesen's EMFACS (Emotion FACS; (Matsumoto et al., 1991; Levenson, 2005) coding system. Two sets of analyses were performed on the facial codes, one involving separate facial areas, and the other involving the whole face. The rank order correlations on the facial behavior codes from the separate areas between the American and Japanese participants ranged from 0.72 for the eyes-lids area to 0.92 on the brows–forehead area. When the codes were combined into emotion-related configurations the correlations ranged from 0.86 in the brows–forehead region to 0.96 in the lower face. Disgust, sadness, anger, and surprise were the most frequently displayed emotions; but fear and happiness were also evident. When facial codes were combined for whole face emotions, according to the theoretical rationales of Darwin and Tomkins (1962, 1963), and the empirical findings from judgment studies (below), the correlation between the Americans and the Japanese on the frequencies of whole face emotions expressed spontaneously was 0.88.

Since then there have been at least 74 other studies that have actually measured facial behaviors that occurred in reaction to emotionally evocative situations, and reported that the facial configurations originally posited by Darwin (1872/1998) and verified (and somewhat modified) by Ekman (Ekman & Friesen, 1975; Ekman, 2003) actually occur (Matsumoto et al., 2006a). These studies have involved a variety of emotion elicitation methodologies, and participants from many different countries and cultures, demonstrating the universality of facial expressions of emotion.

Several bodies of evidence strongly suggest the biological basis of this universality in expressive behaviors. The facial expressions considered to be universal among humans have been observed in non-human primates as well (de Waal, 2003). Chimpanzees have a fully functional facial mimetic musculature that, while not as differentiated as that of humans, includes the same mimetic muscles that are used in emotional expressions (Bard, 2003; Burrows et al., 2006). The additional facial muscles for humans may be related to speech, speech illustration, conversation regulation, and the ability to eat while talking (Ekman & Friesen, 1969). Moreover, the chimpanzee facial musculature produces many of the same appearance changes in the face as does the human musculature, according to a comparison of the human and chimpanzee versions of the FACS (Vick et al., submitted).

Another source of evidence for the biological basis of emotion–expression linkages comes from studies of congenitally blind individuals. Early case and anecdotal studies (Dumas, 1932; Goodenough, 1932; Thompson, 1941; Fulcher, 1942; Freedman, 1964; Eibl-Eibesfeldt, 1973) reported many similarities between blind and sighted individuals in their spontaneous (but not voluntary) facial expressions of emotion. The findings from these studies have been bolstered more recently by studies that have actually measured the spontaneous facial behaviors of blind individuals when emotions were aroused, showing similarities with the facial behaviors of sighted individuals in children (Cole et al., 1989) and adults of many different cultures (Galati et al., 2001, 2003). In one of our recent studies in this area (Matsumoto & Willingham, 2007), we measured the spontaneous facial expressions of emotion of congenitally and non-congenitally blind athletes at the 2004 Paralympic Games, and compared those expressions to those of sighted athletes at the 2004 Olympic Games. The correlation between the individual facial muscle actions of congenitally blind and sighted athletes was 0.88; for non-congenitally blind and sighted athletes it was 0.96. Facial behaviors of blind individuals are also more concordant with kin compared to strangers (Peleg et al., 2006), and between monozygotic twins raised apart compared to dizygotic twins raised together (Kendler et al., 2007). These findings provide strong evidence for the biological bases of emotion–expression linkages.

Cultural Influences on Expressive Behaviors

Culture influences expressive behaviors by calibrating the biologically based emotion–expression linkage with culturally appropriate modes of expression via social norms known as display rules. Cultural display rules are rules learned early in life that dictate the management and possible modification of an emotional response depending on social circumstances (Ekman & Friesen, 1969). Depending on the situational context, display rules may act to amplify, deamplify, neutralize, qualify, or conceal an emotional response (Ekman & Friesen, 1969), creating a complex and elaborate range of expressive behavior when emotions are aroused. They are part of the normative behaviors cultures use to produce social roles appropriate for specific situational contexts. In order for individuals to engage in normative behaviors, they need to regulate their emotions (Tomkins, 1962, 1963; Buck, 1985; Frijda et al., 1989). The social role of "being a good daughter-in-law," e.g., may require a woman in certain contexts to endure snide comments or to be dealt with as a second class citizen. In order to enact this social role correctly, women need to regulate their emotions and thus their behaviors in those situations. Display rules aid this process because they provide a way of behaving that is consonant with the normative, expected behaviors within a certain social role, even if those behaviors are inconsistent with a basic emotion. Display rules serve a vitally important function in culture by helping to regulate emotional behaviors related to social roles and their scripts, enabling individuals to enact their social roles, which aids within-group social coordination and ultimately group and individual survival.

The first study to document the existence of display rules was Ekman's (1972) study of Americans and Japanese mentioned above. While the participants displayed the same facial expressions of emotion in the first condition when they viewed the stressful films alone, in a second condition they watched the films again in the presence of a higher-status experimenter. In this condition, the

Americans continued to generally show their signs of disgust and displeasure; the Japanese, however, tended to smile. This finding is notable because these were the same participants who in the first condition displayed the same facial expressions.

There have only been a handful of subsequent studies that elicited emotions in participants of different cultures in at least two different situational contexts, videorecorded their actual expressive behavior, and measured them in precise, moment-to-moment fashion (Matsumoto & Kupperbusch, 2001; Matsumoto & Willingham, 2006). These studies have demonstrated that, when social roles allow for expressions to occur spontaneously, people around the world express emotions in the same ways facially. In different situational contexts, however, individuals modify their expressive behavior in order to be socially appropriate, thereby fulfilling cultural requirements of maintaining social order.

Display rules are cultural because social roles are based on culturally prescribed meanings of the situational context. There may be both universal and culture-specific aspects of these meanings. For example, all individuals have a mother and father. Because mothers and fathers play some of the same roles across cultures with regard to childbirth, childrearing, and family dynamics (Georgas et al., 2006), there may be some meanings of self-father and self-mother relationships that are universal. Likewise, recent work has demonstrated that people all around the world have a universal display rule to express more positive emotions when with family and close friends, but to suppress their negative emotions with strangers (Matsumoto et al., 2006b). These display rules correspond exactly to what has been found in studies of actual spontaneous expressive behavior (Ekman, 1972; Fridlund, 1991; Wagner & Smith, 1991; Buck et al., 1992; Fridlund et al., 1992; Matsumoto & Kupperbusch, 2001). These universal display rules can be produced by cross-cultural similarities in the meaning of social contexts and social roles (Matsumoto, in press). Close friends, for instance, probably have similar psychological meaning across cultures, and are associated with similar social roles (e.g., "to be a good friend").

Cultural differences in expression may also occur because of cultural differences in the specific meanings attributed to social roles associated with specific situational contexts. For example, there may be considerable cultural differences in the meaning of self-mother and self-father relationships, which in turn are associated with culturally different implications for these interactions. In some cultures the father may be seen as an exalted authority figure, pitting the mother and children together against him as a team. Other cultures may view the mother and father, and sometimes the children, as equal partners in the family relationship. "Being a good research participant" may mean "to be yourself, and to act as if you were alone" in some cultures, or to "maintain a good impression regardless of how you truly feel" in others. It is likely that something similar occurred in Ekman's (1972) study, in which Americans continued to display their feelings of disgust when with the experimenter, while Japanese tended to smile in order to mask their feelings.

Because people of all cultures must deal with the same problems of social coordination, there is likely to be some aspects of social roles, and thus cultural display rules, that are universal. Thus, e.g., all people of all cultures we have surveyed in our 32-country study of display rules endorse greater expression when with ingroup members – family and close friends – than with outgroups – casual acquaintances, strangers, etc. (Matsumoto et al., in press). At the same time, because all cultures exist in different ecologies, they have the potential to create different solutions to the same problems of living. Thus in the same study members of individualistic cultures tend to endorse greater expression of negative emotions to ingroups and positive emotions to outgroups, while members of collectivistic cultures endorse greater expression of positive emotions toward ingroups and negative emotions toward outgroups.

These kinds of cultural differences may produce different social roles because of the different meanings they ascribe to situational contexts, and thus produce different cultural display rules. Expressions have signal value and social function, and thus how, when, and why they are displayed are essential elements of normative behaviors (display rules) related to social roles in situational contexts. Display rules can act to augment expressions, neutralize them, conceal them, or qualify them (Ekman & Friesen, 1969), and thus allow for a rich and textured expressive repertoire in all cultures. In all cases, cultures modulate the emotion–expression linkage by calibrating the expressive response to the culturally appropriate social norms associated with that situational context in which the emotion arose.

Motor Behaviors

To our knowledge, the only study that has examined cross-cultural differences in motor behaviors that result as a function of emotion elicitation is Scherer and Walbott's large-scale study involving approximately 3000 respondents from 37 countries who provided self-report data concerning their behaviors when they experienced each of seven emotions. They obtained data concerning approach versus withdrawal behaviors, and reported statistically significant cross-country differences on it (Scherer & Wallbott, 1994). Because the effect size (η) associated with this effect (0.20) was relatively smaller than the effect size associated with differences among emotions (0.87), Scherer and Wallbott (1994) interpreted this finding as evidence for universality in motor responses when emotions are elicited. The significant and not insubstantial effect size for country differences, however, suggests that there is room for culture-specific patterning of motor behaviors when different emotions are aroused, as suggested above by our model. This area is clearly ripe for future cross-cultural research that examines motor behavioral consequences of emotion elicitation.

Verbal Behaviors

Scherer and Wallbott's (1994) study also reported statistically significant country differences on verbal utterances, defined as a range from silence, short utterances, one or two sentences, and lengthy utterances. As with motor behaviors, the effect size associated with the country differences (0.36) was considerably smaller than that associated with emotion differences (0.80). Matsumoto et al. (2007a) conducted a reanalysis of these data using multilevel random coefficient modeling (MRCM), and demonstrated that the verbal utterances for four of the seven emotions studied were significantly negatively correlated with the cultural dimension known as long term orientation (Hofstede, 2001). This dimension refers to the degree to which cultures encourage delayed gratification of material, social, and emotional needs among its members. The findings indicated, therefore, that cultures with a relatively greater long term perspective on gratification of needs tended to have relatively smaller means on verbal utterances when emotions were aroused.

Still, the studies described immediately above are the only studies to our knowledge that examine verbal behaviors that occur as a result of emotion elicitation across cultures. Clearly, this area is also ripe for future cross-cultural research that examines the verbal behaviors associated with emotional arousal across cultures.

THE CULTURAL CALIBRATION OF THE PERCEIVER'S BEHAVIORS

As described earlier, emotions and expressions also have interpersonal functions, evoking and providing incentives for emotional and behavioral responses in others. We propose that culture not only calibrates the emoter's behaviors but also calibrates the emotions and behaviors of the perceiver as well. For example, one way of talking about or describing faces in Japanese culture, is to label them as *kowai kao* (literally, fearful faces). This is done, however, to describe faces that express anger, not fear, and is typically used in situations in which the person expressing the anger is angry, or simulates anger. That Japanese observers label these angry expressions as fearful says more about cultural norms and beliefs about the appropriate responses to anger, as being fearful, than about angry faces as being interpreted as expressing fear. That is, angry faces are perceived accurately as anger, but may lead to fearful circumstances for the perceiver, which is a cultural spin on the perceived emotion. Cultures likely create different, culture-specific meanings for different expressed emotions, resulting in culture-specific social roles, norms, and expectations for the perceiver's behavior as well. We know of no data to test these claims, however; clearly, future research needs to turn its attention to how the emotions of one person affect the emotions and behaviors of others, and how culture moderates this linkage.

CONCLUSION

In this chapter we have described a theory of how emotions serve as one important source of motivation by priming individuals to behave in certain ways.

We also argued that the functions of culture – as a meaning and information system – are to prevent social chaos, maintain social order, and ensure group efficiency, given the ecological environment and the resources available in it to survive. Culture proscribes social roles, normative behaviors, and expectations; value and belief systems related to interpersonal relationships, the environment, and with regard to emotion itself; and belief systems involving worldviews and self-construals. We believe that when emotions are elicited, culture calibrates the primed individual to the behavioral repertoires available and necessary in that culture as identified by the social roles, norms, and expectations in order to serve as motivators for desired behaviors. Behaviors occurring in specific situational contexts are role performances, and individuals are actors playing roles defined by culture. We also believe that culture calibrates the behaviors of the perceivers of emotion, thereby ensuring the regulation of social interaction.

There are many aspects of culture–emotion–behavior linkages that we did not discuss in this chapter, and these deserve mention and future examination as well. For instance, we did not discuss how cultures calibrate the core emotion system to the available events in the culture in order to elicit emotions in the first place (the front end of the model in Figure 23.2). Instead, our discussion was focused on the behavioral consequences once emotions were elicited. Yet, cultures play a major role in calibrating the core emotion elicitation system to the available events in the culture so that individuals can have appropriate emotional reactions in the first place, thereby priming a set of appropriate behavioral responses as determined by social roles, norms, and expectations.

The literature reviewed above make it clear that there is considerable evidence for the utility of the model with regard to expressive behaviors. This is probably because researchers interested in emotion and behavior tend to focus on the behaviors most closely related to emotion, and these are the behaviors associated with the expression of the elicited emotion. Still, if emotions prime individuals to act in certain ways, then studies of emotion–behavior links clearly need to go beyond the immediate expressive reactions that occur when emotions are aroused, and examine the subsequent instrumental, goal-directed motor and verbal behaviors that occur after emotions have been elicited. Our review described above indicated that there is a glaring paucity of cross-cultural studies that have examined actual behaviors – motor or verbal – in specific situations after emotions have been aroused, on the part of both expressors and perceivers. In fact, we believe that there is a dearth of research on actual motor or verbal behaviors across cultures even without the incorporation of emotion. Behavioral research is difficult, time-consuming, and labor-intensive. Yet, clearly research attention needs to be turned to the examination of actual behaviors – not just self-reports – to complement the existing literature that is overwhelming focused on paper-and-pencil measures. We hope that this chapter can serve as a call for more of such research across cultures in the future.

REFERENCES

Adamopoulous, J., & Lonner, W. J. (2001). Culture and psychology at a crossroad: Historical perspective and theoretical analysis. In D. Matsumoto (Ed.), *The handbook of culture and psychology* (pp. 11–34). New York: Oxford University Press.

Bard, K. A. (2003). Development of emotional expressions in chimpanzees (Pan troglodytes). *Annals of the New York Academy of Sciences, 1000*, 88–90.

Baumeister, R. F., Vohs, K. D., DeWall, N., & Zhang, L. (2007). How emotion shapes behavior: Feedback, anticipation, and reflection, rather than direct causation. *Personality and Social Psychology Review, 11*(2), 167–203.

Boesch, C. (2003). Is culture a golden barrier between human and chimpanzee? *Evolutionary Anthropology, 12*, 82–91.

Bowlby, J. (1969). *Attachment*. New York: Basic Books.

Bradshaw, D. (1986). Immediate and prolonged effectiveness of negative emotion expressions in inhibiting infants' actions. Unpublished Doctoral Dissertation, University of California, Berkeley, CA.

Buck, R. W. (1976). A test of nonverbal receiving ability: Preliminary studies. *Human Communication Research, 2*(2), 162–171.

Buck, R. W. (1985). Prime theory: An integrated view of motivation and emotion. *Psychological Review, 92*(3), 389–413.

Buck, R. W., Losow, J. I., Murphy, M. M., & Costanzo, P. (1992). Social facilitation and inhibition of emotional expression and communication. *Journal of Personality and Social Psychology, 63*(6), 962–968.

Burrows, A. M., Waller, B. M., Parr, L. A., & Bonar, C. J. (2006). Muscles of facial expression in the chimpanzee (Pan troglodytes): Descriptive, comparative, and phylogenetic contexts. *Journal of Anatomy, 208*, 153–167.

Buss, D. M. (1988). The evolution of human intrasexual competition: Tactics of mate attraction. *Journal of Personality and Social Psychology, 54*(4), 616–628.

Buss, D. M. (2001). Human nature and culture: An evolutionary psychological perspective. *Journal of Personality, 69*(6), 955–978.

Campos, J., Thein, S., & Owen, D. (2003). A Darwinian legacy to understanding human infancy: Emotional expressions as behavior regulators. In P. Ekman, J. Campos, R. J. Davidson, & F. B. M. De Waal (Eds.), *Emotions inside out: 130 years after Darwin's The expression of the emotions in man and animals* (Vol. 1000, pp. 110–134). New York: New York Academy of Sciences.

Cole, P. M., Jenkins, P. A., & Shott, C. T. (1989). Spontaneous expressive control in blind and sighted children. *Child Development, 60*(3), 683–688.

Cosmides, L., & Tooby, J. (2000). Evolutionary psychology and the emotions. In M. Lewis & J. M. Haviland-Jones (Eds.), *Handbook of emotions* (2nd ed, pp. 91–115). New York: Guilford Press.

Darwin, C. (1872/1998). *The expression of emotion in man and animals*. New York: Oxford University Press.

de Waal, F. B. M. (2003). Darwin's legacy and the study of primate visual communication. In P. Ekman, J. Campos, R. J. Davidson, & F. B. M. De Waal (Eds.), *Emotions inside out: 130 years after Darwin's The Expression of Emotion in Man and Animals* (pp. 7–31). New York: New York Academy of Sciences.

Dimberg, U., & Ohman, A. (1996). Behold the wrath: Psychophysiological responses to facial stimuli. *Motivation and Emotion, 20*(2), 149–182.

Dumas, F. (1932). La mimique des aveugles [Facial expression of the blind]. *Bulletin de l'Academie de Medecine, 107*, 607–610.

Eibl-Eibesfeldt, I. (1973). The expressive behavior of the deaf-and-blind born. In M. von Cranach & I. Vine (Eds.), *Social communication and movement* (pp. 163–194). London: Academic Press.

Eibl-Eibesfeldt, I. (1989). *Human ethology.* New York: Aldine de Gruyter Press.

Eisenberg, N., Fabes, R. A., Miller, P. A., Fultz, J., Shell, R., Mathy, R. M. et al. (1989). Relation of sympathy and distress to prosocial behavior: A multimethod study. *Journal of Personality and Social Psychology, 57,* 55–66.

Ekman, P. (1972). Universal and cultural differences in facial expression of emotion. In J. R. Cole (Ed.), *Nebraska Symposium on Motivation, 1971* (Vol. 19, pp. 207–283). Lincoln, NE: Nebraska University Press.

Ekman, P. (1992). An argument for basic emotions. *Cognition and Emotion, 6*(3–4), 169–200.

Ekman, P. (1993). Facial expression and emotion. *American Psychologist, 48*(4), 384–392.

Ekman, P. (1999). Basic emotions. In T. Dalgleish & T. Power (Eds.), *The handbook of cognition and emotion* (pp. 45–60). Sussex: John Wiley and Sons, Ltd.

Ekman, P. (2003). *Emotions revealed.* New York: Times Books.

Ekman, P., & Friesen, W. V. (1969). The repertoire of nonverbal behavior: Categories, origins, usage, and coding. *Semiotica, 1,* 49–98.

Ekman, P., & Friesen, W. V. (1975). *Unmasking the face; a guide to recognizing emotions from facial clues.* Englewood Cliffs, NJ: Prentice-Hall.

Ekman, P., & Friesen, W. V. (1976). *Pictures of facial affect.* Palo Alto, CA: Consulting Psychologists Press.

Ekman, P., & Friesen, W. V. (1978). *Facial action coding system: Investigator's guide.* Palo Alto, CA: Consulting Psychologists Press.

Ekman, P., Sorenson, E. R., & Friesen, W. V. (1969). Pancultural elements in facial displays of emotion. *Science, 164*(3875), 86–88.

Ekman, P., Friesen, W. V., & Ellsworth, P. (1972a). *Emotion in the human face: Guide-lines for research and an integration of findings.* New York: Pergamon Press.

Ekman, P., Liebert, R. M., Friesen, W. V., Harrison, R., Zlatchin, C., Malmstrom, E. J. et al. (1972b). Facial expressions of emotion while watching televised violence as predictors of subsequent aggression. In G. A. Comstock, E. A. Rubinstein, & J. P. Murray (Eds.), *TELEVISION AND SOCIAL BEHAVIOR: A technical report to the Surgeon General's Scientific Advisory Committee on Television and Social Behavior* (Vol. I: TELEVISION'S EFFECTS: FURTHER EXPLORATIONS, pp. 22–58). Washington, DC: US Government Printing Office.

Ekman, P., Davidson, R. J., & Friesen, W. V. (1990). The Duchenne smile: Emotional expression and brain physiology: II. *Journal of Personality & Social Psychology, 58*(2), 342–353.

Esteves, F., Dimberg, U., & Ohman, A. (1994). Automatically elicited fear: Conditioned skin conductance responses to masked facial expressions. *Cognition and Emotion, 8*(5), 393–413.

Frank, M. G., & Ekman, P. (1993). Not all smiles are created equal: The differences between enjoyment and nonenjoyment smiles. Special Issue: Current issues in psychological humor research. *Humor: International Journal of Humor Research, 6*(1), 9–26.

Frank, M. G., Ekman, P., & Friesen, W. V. (1993). Behavioral markers and recognizability of the smile of enjoyment. *Journal of Personality and Social Psychology, 64*(1), 83–93.

Freedman, D. G. (1964). Smiling in blind infants and the issue of innate versus acquired. *Journal of Child Psychology and Psychiatry, 5,* 171–184.

Fridlund, A. (1991). Sociality of solitary smiling: Potentiation by an implicit audience. *Journal of Personality and Social Psychology, 60*(2), 229–240.

Fridlund, A. (1994). *Human facial expression: An evolutionary view.* San Diego, CA: Academic Press.

Fridlund, A., Kenworthy, K. G., & Jaffey, A. K. (1992). Audience effects in affective imagery: Replication and extension to dysphoric imagery. *Journal of Nonverbal Behavior, 16*(3), 191–212.

Frijda, N. H., Kuipers, P., & ter Schure, E. (1989). Relations among emotion, appraisal, and emotional action readiness. *Journal of Personality and Social Psychology, 57*(2), 212–228.

Fulcher, J. S. (1942). "Voluntary" facial expression in blind and seeing children. *Archives of Psychology, 272,* 5–49.

Galati, D., Miceli, R., & Sini, B. (2001). Judging and coding facial expression of emotions in congenitally blind children. *International Journal of Behavioral Development, 25*(3), 268–278.

Galati, D., Sini, B., Schmidt, S., & Tinti, C. (2003). Spontaneous facial expressions in congenitally blind and sighted children aged 8–11. *Journal of Visual Impairment and Blindness, July,* 418–428.

Georgas, J., Berry, J. W., Van de Vijver, F. J. R., Kagitcibasi, C., & Poortinga, Y. H. (2006). *Families across cultures: A 30-notion psychological study.* Cambridge: Cambridge University Press.

Goodenough, F. L. (1932). Expression of emotions in a blind-deaf child. *Journal of Abnormal and Social Psychology, 27,* 328–333.

Goffman, E. (1959). *The presentation of self in everyday life.* Garden City, NY: Doubleday.

Hertel, G., & Fiedler, K. (1994). Affective and cognitive influences in a social dilemma game. *European Journal of Social Psychology, 24,* 131–145.

Hertenstein, M. J., & Campos, J. J. (2004). The retention effects of an adult's emotional displays on infant behavior. *Child Development, 75*(2), 595–613.

Hofstede, G. H. (2001). *Culture's consequences: Comparing values, behaviors, institutions and organizations across nations* (2nd ed.). Thousand Oaks, CA: Sage Publications.

Hogan, R. (1982). A socioanalytic theory of personality. In M. Page (Ed.), *Nebraska Symposium on Motivation* (Vol. 30, pp. 55–89). Lincoln, NE: University of Nebraska Press.

Hong, Y. Y., Morris, M., Chiu, C.-Y., & Benet-Martinez, V. (2000). Multicultural minds: A dynamic constructivist approach to culture and cognition. *American Psychologist, 55,* 709–720.

Itakura, S. (1993). Emotional behavior during the learning of a contingency task in a chimpanzee. *Perceptual and Motor Skills, 76*(2), 563–566.

Izard, C. E. (1971). *The face of emotion.* East Norwalk, CT: Appleton-Century-Crofts.

Johnson-Laird, P. N., & Oatley, K. (1992). Basic emotions, rationality, and folk theory. *Cognition and Emotion, 6*(3–4), 201–223.

Keltner, D. (1995). The signs of appeasement: Evidence for the distinct displays of embarrassment, amusement, and shame. *Journal of Personality and Social Psychology, 68,* 441–454.

Keltner, D., & Kring, A. M. (1998). Emotion, social function, and psychopathology. *Review of General Psychology, 2*(3), 320–342.

Keltner, D., Moffitt, T., & Stouthamer-Loeber, M. (1995). Facial expressions of emotion and psychopathology in adolescent boys. *Journal of Abnormal Psychology, 104,* 644–652.

Kendler, K.S., Halberstadt, L.J., Butera, F., Myers, J., Bouchard, T., & Ekman, P. (2007). The similarity of facial expressions in response to emotion-inducing films in reared-apart twins. *Psychological Medicine,* Oct 1 [Epub ahead of print].

Klinnert, M. D., Campos, J. J., & Sorce, J. F. (1983). Emotions as behavior regulators: Social referencing in infancy. In R. Plutchik & H. Kellerman (Eds.), *Emotion: Theory, research, and experience* (pp. 57–86). New York: Academic Press.

Klinnert, M. D., Emde, R. N., Butterfield, P., & Campos, J. (1986). Social referencing: The infant's use of emotional signals from a friendly adult with a mother present. *Developmental Psychology, 22*(4), 427–432.

Lazarus, R. (1991). *Emotion and adaptation.* New York: Oxford University Press.

Levenson, R. W. (1999). The intrapersonal functions of emotion. *Cognition and Emotion, 13*(5), 481–504.

Levenson, R.W. (2005). FACS/EMFACS emotion predictions, Computer program available from Robert W. Levenson, University of California, Berkeley, CA.

Marsh, A. A., Ambady, N., & Kleck, R. E. (2005). The effects of fear and anger facial expressions on approach- and avoidance-related behaviors. *Emotion, 5*(1), 119–124.

Matsumoto, D. (2006). Culture and cultural worldviews: Do verbal descriptions of culture reflect anything other than verbal descriptions of culture?. *Culture and Psychology, 12*(1), 33–62.

Matsumoto, D. (2007). Culture, context, and behavior. *Journal of Personality, 75*(6), 1285–1319.

Matsumoto, D. (in press). Culture, context, and behavior. *Journal of Personality.*

Matsumoto, D., & Ekman, P. (1988). Japanese and Caucasian facial expressions of emotion and neutral faces (JACFEE and JACNeuF). Available from www.paulekman.com.

Matsumoto, D., & Juang, L. (2007). *Culture and psychology* (4th ed.). Belmont, CA: Wadsworth.

Matsumoto, D., & Kupperbusch, C. (2001). Idiocentric and allocentric differences in emotional expression and experience. *Asian Journal of Social Psychology, 4,* 113–131.

Matsumoto, D., & Willingham, B. (2006). The thrill of victory and the agony of defeat: Spontaneous expressions of medal winners at the 2004 Athens Olympic Games. *Journal of Personality and Social Psychology, 91*(3), 568–581.

Matsumoto, D., & Willingham, B. (2007). Spontaneous facial expressions of emotion of congenitally and non-congenitally blind individuals. Manuscript currently submitted for publication.

Matsumoto, D., & Yamagishi, T. (in preparation). Facial expressions of emotion predict actions in the Ultimatum Game.

Matsumoto, D., Haan, N., Gary, Y., Theodorou, P., & Cooke-Carney, C. (1986). Preschoolers' moral actions and emotions in prisoner's dilemma. *Developmental Psychology, 22*(5), 663–670.

Matsumoto, D., Ekman, P., & Fridlund, A. (1991). Analyzing nonverbal behavior. In P. W. Dowrick (Ed.), *Practical guide to using video in the behavioral sciences* (pp. 153–165). New York: John Wiley & Sons.

Matsumoto, D., Weissman, M., Preston, K., Brown, B., & Kupperbusch, C. (1997). Context-specific measurement of individualism–collectivism on the individual level: The IC Interpersonal Assessment Inventory (ICIAI). *Journal of Cross-Cultural Psychology, 28,* 743–767.

Matsumoto, D., Keltner, D., O'Sullivan, M., & Frank, M. G. (2006a). What's in a face? Facial expressions as signals of discrete emotions. Manuscript currently submitted for publication.

Matsumoto, D., Yoo, S. H., Alexandre, J., Altarriba, J., Anguas-Wong, A. M., Arriola, M. et al. (2006b). Universal effects of contexts on display rules for emotional behaviors. Manuscript currently submitted for publication.

Matsumoto, D., Nezlek, J., & Koopmann, B. (2007a). Evidence for universality in phenomenological emotion response system coherence. *Emotion, 7*(1), 57–67.

Matsumoto, D., O'Sullivan, M., & Keltner, D. (2007b). Culture and emotion: The preservation of social order through the cultural calibration of emotion. Manuscript currently submitted for publication.

Matsumoto, D., Yoo, S. H., Fontaine, J. R. J., Anguas-Wong, A. M., Arriola, M., Ataca, B. et al. (2008). Mapping expressive differences around the world: The relationship between emotional display rules and Individualism v. Collectivism. *Journal of Cross-Cultural Psychology, 39*(1), 55–74.

Matsuzawa, T. (2001). *Primate origins of human cognition and behavior.* New York: Springer-Verlag Publishing.

McGrew, W. C. (2004). *The cultured chimpanzee: Reflections on cultural primatology.* New York: Cambridge University Press.

Miller, R. E., Murphy, J. V., & Mirsky, I. A. (1959). Relevance of facial expression and posture as cues in communication of affect between monkeys. *Archives of General Psychiatry, 1,* 480–488.

Miller, R. E., Banks, J. H. Jr., & Ogawa, N. (1963). Role of facial expression in 'cooperative-avoidance conditioning' in monkeys. *Journal of Abnormal and Social Psychology, 67*(1), 24–30.

Miller, R. E., Banks, J. H. Jr., & Kuwahara, H. (1966). The communication of affects in monkeys: Cooperative reward conditioning. *Journal of Genetic Psychology, 108*(1), 121–134.

Miller, R. E., Caul, W. F., & Mirsky, I. A. (1967). Communication of affects between feral and socially isolated monkeys. *Journal of Personality and Social Psychology, 7*(3), 231–239.

Mineka, S., & Cook, M. (1993). Mechanisms involved in the observational conditioning of fear. *Journal of Experimental Psychology: General, 122*(1), 23–38.

Oyserman, D., & Lee, S. W.-S. (2007). Priming 'culture': Culture as situated cognition. In S. Kitayama, & D. Cohen (Eds.), *Handbook of cultural psychology.* New York: Guilford Press.

Peleg, G., Katzir, G., Peleg, O., Kamara, M., Brodsky, L., Hel-Or, H. et al. (2006). Heriditary family signature of facial expression. *Proceedings from the National Academy of Sciences, 103*(43), 15921–15926.

Premack, D. (2004). Is language the key to human intelligence?. *Science, 303,* 318–320.

Scherer, K. R. (1986). Vocal affect expression: Review and a model for future research. *Psychological Bulletin, 99,* 143–165.

Scherer, K. R., & Wallbott, H. (1994). Evidence for universality and cultural variation of differential emotion response-patterning. *Journal of Personality and Social Psychology, 66*(2), 310–328.

Sheldon, K. M. (2004). *The psychology of optimal being: An integrated, multi-level perspective.* Mahwah, NJ: Erlbaum.

Sorce, J. F., Emde, J. J., Campos, J. J., & Klinnert, M. D. (1985). Maternal emotional signaling: Its effect on the visual cliff behavior of 1-year-olds. *Developmental Psychology, 21,* 195–200.

Thompson, J. (1941). Development of facial expression of emotion in blind and seeing children. *Archives of Psychology, 37,* 1–47.

Tiedens, L. Z., Ellsworth, P. C., & Mesquita, B. (2000). Stereotypies about sentiments and status: Emotional expectations for high- and low-status group members. *Personality and Social Psychology Bulletin, 26*(5), 560–574.

Tomasello, M. (1999). *The cultural origins of human cognition.* Cambridge, MA: Harvard University Press.

Tomasello, M., Kruger, A. C., & Ratner, H. H. (1993). Cultural learning. *Behavioural and Brain Sciences, 16,* 495–552.

Tomkins, S. S. (1962). *Affect, imagery, and consciousness* (Vol. 1: The positive affects). New York: Springer.

Tomkins, S. S. (1963). *Affect, imagery, and consciousness* (Vol. 2: The negative affects). New York: Springer.

Vick, S.-J., Waller, B. M., Parr, L. A., Pasqualini, M. S., & Bard, K. A. (2007). A cross-species comparison of facial morphology and movement in humans and chimpanzees using the Facial Action Coding System (FACS). *Journal of Nonverbal Behavior, 31*(1), 1–20 .

Wagner, H. L., & Smith, J. (1991). Facial expression in the presence of friends and strangers. *Journal of Nonverbal Behavior, 15,* 201–214.

Whiten, A., Horner, V., & De Waal, F. B. M. (2005). Conformity to cultural norms of tool use in chimpanzees. *Nature, 437*(7059), 737–740.

Winkielman, P., Berridge, K. C., & Wilbarger, J. L. (2005). Unconscious affective reactions to masked happy versus angry faces influence consumption behavior and judgments of value. *Personality and Social Psychology Bulletin, 31*(1), 121–135.

MEASUREMENT

24

MEASURING COGNITION AND MOTIVATION ACROSS CULTURAL GROUPS

RONALD FISCHER AND VIVIAN MIU-CHI LUN

Centre for Applied Cross-Cultural Research, Victoria University of Wellington, Wellington, New Zealand

Globalization has led to fundamental changes in the work and life of most people around the world. We work with individuals from other cultural backgrounds, children learn in culturally diverse classrooms, and health care professionals deal with clientele of other cultural background. In all these contexts, the assessment of cognitive and motivational factors is paramount. In work settings, individuals are selected and promoted based on their cognitive capacities and motivations; pupils are selected into classes or universities based on their academic record and mental abilities and the assessment of motivational factors and mental capabilities of clients is important for making appropriate diagnoses in the mental health domain. Therefore, we need to address to what extent existing tests are adequate and can be used with culturally diverse populations. The aim of the current chapter is therefore to (a) outline criteria and principles for assessing equivalence and bias (or cultural fairness) of psychological tests, (b) provide a brief review of methods that could be used for examining the applicability of tests, (c) provide a selected review of specific tests and domains and their cross-cultural applicability, and (d) present some avenues for further research. Our review will specifically focus on tests of mental ability as used in educational and work settings and assessment of motivation in work settings using measures of commitment to the organization. In doing so, we will focus on the application of these techniques in cross-cultural research within the last decade.

CHALLENGES IN TESTING ACROSS
CULTURAL BOUNDARIES

The issue of bias and lack of equivalence in cross-cultural psychological test-ing has been addressed extensively in the psychometric literature. It is widely accepted by scholars that there is a hierarchy of equivalence and potential biases (e.g., Messick, 1991; van de Vijver & Leung, 1997; Vandenberg & Lance, 2000; Lubke et al., 2003; Fontaine, 2005). In the cross-cultural assessment framework, four levels of equivalence and associated biases are generally distinguished (Fontaine, 2005) to address three fundamental questions: (1) do the same theo-retical constructs account for test behavior, (2) can we use the same observed variables to measure the theoretical construct, and (3) can we compare the scores on the assumed latent variable across cultural groups?

THE FOUR LEVELS OF EQUIVALENCE AND
ASSOCIATED BIASES

Functional Equivalence

The most basic and fundamental level is construct or functional equivalence. Whether a specific construct such as intelligence exists in other cultures needs to be addressed prior to operationalizing and measuring the constructs and this question can only be addressed by extensive theoretical analysis as well as combining series of qualitative and quantitative studies in each cultural group individually (Johnson, 2006). The main question is whether the same construct can account for behavioral differences in each group. Greenfield (1997) offered good examples of how intelligent behaviors were differently understood in vari-ous cultures. For instance, being slow and conforming are viewed as intelligent in Africa (Wober 1974; cited in Greenfield, 1997), which is different from the Western culture where intelligence is often discussed in relation to high mental processing speed. In this case, intelligent behavior is understood very differently in African and Western cultures.

If there is substantial difference across cultural groups in terms of the mean-ing of the construct of interest, the construct cannot be compared across cultural groups. It is nevertheless still possible to construct an instrument within each group that measures the construct reliably and validly and captures all relevant aspects of the construct in each group. Since the construct cannot be compared across groups, the only comparison that can be made across groups is an exami-nation of whether the construct of interest relates in a similar manner to other related and unrelated variables. This so-called nomological net of convergent and discriminant relationships can be used to answer the question whether the construct is functionally equivalent across cultural groups.

The bias associated with a lack of functional equivalence is called the cultural specificity of the theoretical variable. In this case, the construct of interest exists only in this one specific cultural context. Fontaine (2005) uses the example of "reading disabilities" which only makes sense in literate societies. It is often difficult to ascertain whether seemingly different constructs are in fact different cultural interpretations or constructions of similar underlying mechanisms (in the case of mental ability, these are often seen as biologically influenced). Taking mental ability as a phenomenon rooted in processing efficiency which refers to the speed of processing and controlled attention (Jensen, 1998), then the underlying function is the same regardless of culture and only the expression of this mental capacity might be culturally influenced.

Structural Equivalence

The second level of equivalence refers to structural equivalence, namely whether the same observed variables or items can be used to assess the same underlying theoretical variable across cultural groups. Van de Vijver and Leung (1997) discussed structural equivalence under construct (functional) equivalence, but it is preferred to separate the measurement aspect from the theoretical discussion of functional equivalence of the theoretical construct (Fontaine, 2005). Functional equivalence is a prerequisite for structural equivalence. If a researcher decides that a construct is absent in one culture or the construct of interest has a different function, then comparisons are implausible. In this case, emic research might focus on function and meaning of constructs (or the meaning of lacking constructs) within particular cultural contexts. If functional equivalence is assumed, researchers can proceed and test for structural equivalence.

At this level of equivalence, the questions of the representativeness and relevance of observed variables are important (van de Vijver & Leung, 1997; Fontaine, 2005). During the testing session, individuals respond to a small set of stimuli that are supposed to reflect the particular theoretical variable of interest. The resulting score is then generalized beyond the performance in the particular testing situation and is assumed to reflect some stable characteristic of the testee. Therefore, it is important to consider whether this small subset of items is relevant and representative for the measurement of the larger construct across cultures. Irrelevant items would measure some other theoretical construct and this would introduce systematic error in the measurement. For example, if an instrument measuring intrinsic motivation uses complex language and unfamiliar words, this item would also reflect verbal abilities. Representativeness refers to the extent to which items capture the whole range of the theoretical domain. For example, intelligence might be defined as much broacher in some contexts than others. If the narrower definition is used and a test is applied in a population where intelligence is seen as a broader construct, then the test does not cover the whole range of the domain, which is a bias called Domain Under-representation.

Structural equivalence also demands that items have non-trivial weight parameters across cultural groups. This means that the items have to have the same internal structure across groups and the same items are supposed to load on the same factor in each cultural group. This is the most basic question that can be answered using structure-oriented tests (Confirmatory Factory Analysis [CFA],

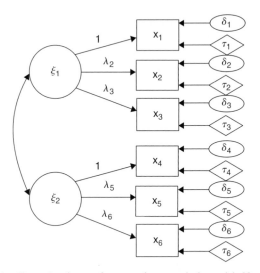

FIGURE 24.1　Example of a confirmatory factor analysis model. Note: The relationship between observed items and latent factors in CFA can be graphically represented in diagrams. Latent and unobserved variables are represented by circles, ovals or parallelograms, whereas manifest variables are usually represented by squares or boxes. The relationship between the variables is indicated by lines. Lines with one arrow pointing to a specific variable represent a hypothesized direct relationship where the variable with the arrow pointing to is the DV. Variables linked by lines with arrows at both ends indicates that the variables simply covary with no implied direction of the effect. The individual parameter are denoted by Greek letters. The latent variables in a CFA are represented by ξ (ksi); the observed variables are labeled x, the loadings of the observed variables on the latent variables are represented by λ (lambda), and the errors of measurement or unique factors or residuals are called δ (delta). The intercepts of the observed items are indicated with τ (tau). The loading of one item per latent factor has been constrained to one. This is the most common option for allowing identification (see Bollen, 1989; Byrne, 1998).

Exploratory Factor Analysis [EFA], Multidimensional Scaling [MDS]) with standard programs such as SPSS, LISREL, AMOS, or EQS. Among these techniques, EFA and MDS do not assume that the researcher has a specific structure in mind and therefore, these techniques are exploratory, whereas CFA requires that the researcher has a specific structure that is imposed on the data which are used to test the fit of that specific structure to real life observations (see Figure 24.1 for a schematic model of a confirmatory factor model).

Van de Vijver and Leung (1997) provided some examples that can be used to compare reliabilities and internal consistencies across cultural groups. Fischer and Fontaine (in press) discussed the procedures for running EFA and MDS with SPSS since demonstration of structural equivalence requires some additional steps. Specifically, both techniques may show results that appear different across cultural groups that may be due to sample fluctuations. Therefore, it is advantageous to use target-rotation before comparing the structure in different groups. This can be done with procrustean rotation which is discussed in Fischer and Fontaine (in press). CFA requires researchers to specify the expected factor structure, therefore, assessing structural equivalence (or form invariance in CFA terms, Cheung & Rensvold, 2000) is straightforward (e.g., Bollen, 1989; Byrne, 1998). However, if a test shows structural equivalence, it is still not possible to compare scores either directly or indirectly (for example in the form of score patterns or profiles) across cultural groups. This is an important issue, since merely showing a similarity of factor structures does not mean the observed test scores are comparable across cultures.

Turning to biases next, we already referred to one potential source of bias, namely domain underrepresentation. If the construct exists in all culture of interest, the researcher has to make sure that the appropriate stimulus material is selected in each cultural context to elicit the behavioral responses indicative of the underlying construct. The issue of item relevance is closely linked to domain underrepresentation since items representative of the intended construct have to be relevant in the specific cultural context. For example, verbal intelligence tests that capture domain specific knowledge specific to one particular cultural context (historical events, place names, etc.) may be better seen as an indicator of academic performance rather than as indicator of general mental ability.

If the set of items that elicits the appropriate behavioral response indicative of the latent construct (e.g., intelligence or motivation) is very different across cultural groups, it could be questioned whether the underlying construct is in fact comparable. In this case, domain under-representation and cultural specificity of the underlying construct might be closely related and sometimes these two sources are discussed together as a form of construct bias (e.g., van de Vijver & Leung, 1997).

Metric Equivalence

The next higher level of equivalence is metric equivalence (Fontaine, 2005) or measurement unit equivalence (van de Vijver & Leung, 1997). This answers the question whether it is possible to compare patterns of scores across cultural or ethnic groups. The important issue is whether the measurement units are identical across groups and identical weight parameters (e.g., factor loadings) are found in each cultural group. To show metric equivalence we have to demonstrate that the loadings of the items on the underlying factors or the location of items in a specific space is identical across cultural groups. A change in the latent variable is expected to lead to the same change in the observed variable in all cultural groups, implying that the measurement units are the same, and the same metric scale is being used. However, the origins of the scale might still differ, which makes it inappropriate to compare the observed test scores directly across all cultural groups. This is analogous to comparing temperature using a Kelvin scale and a Celsius scale. The temperature measured with these two scales cannot be compared directly but it is possible to compare relative temperature differences between night and day.

Applying a similar logic to psychological constructs, it is possible to compare relative differences across cultural groups, but the absolute score levels cannot be compared. For example, if metric equivalence of a scale is achieved in two cultural groups, it is possible to draw conclusions like that verbal intelligence scores are one standard deviation above abstract reasoning levels in one group, whereas the scores for verbal intelligence in a second group are only half a standard deviation above the abstract reasoning scores. However, it will not be appropriate to compare directly the observed scores and interpret the differences as real differences of underlying intelligence between the two groups.

Various biases can threaten metric equivalence, including method and item biases. Method bias refers to biases that affect all (or at least a substantial part) of an instrument, whereas item bias refers to factors that influence only individual items in the instrument. Method bias is often divided into administration, instrument, and sample bias. In fact, these biases would also threaten both structural equivalence and full score equivalence, so we will discuss these in more details below after the introduction of the last form of equivalence. Here, we would only introduce one specific type of item bias which is called non-uniform item bias. Metric equivalence is concerned with the equivalence of factor loadings across cultural groups. In other words, the weight parameter has to be identical across cultural groups. If this is not the case, the extent of bias for any respondent in a group depends on his or her relative position on the latent variable. This can be visually illustrated using the regression analogy. In CFA (see Figure 24.1 for a graphical display of the CFA model and an explanation of terms), the loadings of items on latent factors are similar to regression lines. The latent factor is "causing" changes in the observed variable. Therefore, a different regression line (item loadings or parameter λ in technical terms) in two different groups would indicate non-uniform bias. For one group, an increase in the latent factor is associated with more changes in the observed variable, compared to the other group (see Figure 24.2).

Metric equivalence can be tested with a variety of tests. CFA as implemented in programs such as LISREL, AMOS, or EQS can be used to constrain the factor loadings to be identical across cultural groups (see Bollen, 1989; Byrne, 1998; Cheung & Rensvold, 2000; Vandenberg & Lance, 2000). Two-factorial analysis of variance can also be used to test for metric equivalence (see van de Vijver & Leung, 1997). An interaction between culture and item would indicate a lack of metric equivalence and the presence of non-uniform bias. Using two-parameter logistic models, unequal item difficulty parameters would indicate uniform bias. If the tests are in the form of correct–incorrect answers, the Mantel-Haenszel statistic can be used (see van de Vijver & Leung, 1997).

Full Score Equivalence

The highest level of equivalence is full score equivalence (Fontaine, 2005) or scalar equivalence (van de Vijver & Leung, 1997). If this level is satisfied, we can directly compare the scores at face value across cultural groups and interpret

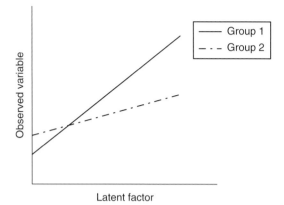

FIGURE 24.2 Figure showing an item with non-uniform item bias. The regression lines represent the factor loading of the observed variable on the latent factor. Note that the regression lines are different and therefore, the item is a better predictor of the latent factor in group 1 than group 2.

any differences in terms of latent constructs. In this case, individuals with the same score are expected to have the same underlying latent score, independent of cultural context, and differences in observed scores indicated "true" differences in latent underlying scores. Statistically, the question that needs to be addressed is whether the intercepts linking the observed and latent variable are identical across cultural groups. Only in the absence of intercept differences can any observed differences between individuals from different ethnic or cultural groups be interpreted in terms of the underlying theoretical construct. Researchers such as Hartman et al. (2007), Lynn and Vanhanen (2002), or Ruston et al. (2002, 2003) claiming that observed intelligence test score differences are related to an underlying and true difference in latent intelligence assume full score equivalence of the instruments. However, contrary to what would be expected, these researchers often fail to present evidence of full score or scalar equivalence, which may weaken their claims.

Item biases that are associated with a lack of full score equivalence are uniform item biases. In this case, the item loads in the same way on the latent underlying construct but one group scores systematically higher or lower than the other(s). For example, the loadings (regression slopes) of the individual indicators on the latent factors can be identical but there might still be systematic differences between the groups that do not reflect latent mean differences. The same techniques as for establishing metric equivalence can be used. CFA can be used to test the equality of item intercepts in multi-group analyses (see Cheung & Rensvold, 2000; Fischer & Fontaine, in press). Two-factorial analysis of variance can detect uniform bias which is indicated by main effects of culture (see van de Vijver & Leung, 1997). Dichotomous items can be analyzed using the Mantel-Haenszel statistic (see van de Vijver & Leung, 1997). For two-parameter logistic models, unequal item discrimination parameters would indicate uniform bias (see Figure 24.3).

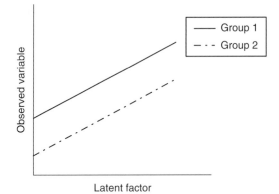

Latent factor

FIGURE 24.3   Figure showing an item with uniform item bias. The regression lines represent the factor loading of the observed variable on the latent factor in two groups. Note that the intercept is different and indicates that the item is consistently easier in one group than in the other.

As we previously suggested, method bias could pose threats to structural equivalence, metric equivalence, and full score equivalence (Fontaine, 2005). It refers to any biasing effect caused by the methods employed and the context of measurement, including instrument bias, administration bias, and sample bias. Instrument bias could be caused by the specific item content, and the participants' response format or response styles. There is some evidence that individuals from different cultural contexts use Likert-type response scales differently (see Smith, 2004; Fischer et al., in press; Smith & Fischer, in press). This is an issue that affects the whole instrument and not just individual items (which would be an issue of item bias). Social desirability, extremity scoring, and acquiescence are some response styles that introduce biases or noise in the cross-cultural assessment, and these biases can be addressed by multiple-group CFA discussed above (comparing models with constrained intercepts and loadings across cultural groups; see Cheung & Rensvold, 2000). Lack of familiarity with the test stimulus or the response format may cause unnecessary difficulty to the testee. For example, it was found that for performance items, telling the children what to do instead of asking them to say something would be better in hierarchically organized cultures where children are used to respond to verbal comments with non-verbal actions (Greenfield, 1997). Making use of information derived from qualitative research would prevent introducing test unfamiliarity to the participants.

Administration bias refers to biases caused by the ways in which the test is administered. According to Fontaine (2005) and van de Vijver and Leung (1997), potential administration bias include (1) differences in physical conditions (such as temperature or room size) and social environment (e.g., group testing versus individual testing); (2) different instructions for the respondents because of ambiguous guidelines or differential expertize of the test administrators; and

(3) communication barriers between the test administrator and the testee due to language differences, the use of an interpreter, or different interpretation of the instructions. Standardizing the instructions used for test administration according to the characteristics of the cultures of interest would alleviate the impact of these biases. One important trade-off is the applicability of procedures to the local context versus standardization across context. For example, in collectivistic settings, researchers might be required to establish more rapport with participants (Pe-Pua, 1990) which might lead to additional information being conveyed to participants. However, not engaging in this relationship would not result in meaningful data since participants do not trust the researcher.

Sample bias is due to the incomparability of the cultural samples on characteristics other than the target variable. For instance, in the assessment of intelligence, if the groups differed significantly in their social economic status (SES) or educational levels, any differences observed on the intelligence test scores could be alternatively explained by these differences in SES or education levels, instead of being interpretable in terms of cultural differences in cognitive ability. Therefore, consideration should go into the selection of equivalent samples prior to commencing research and assessment of any possible confounding variables should be attempted during the data collection stage. Statistical technique such as ANCOVA, MANCOVA, and hierarchical multiple regressions can then be used to control for possible influences of known (and measured) covariates.

PROBLEMS ASSOCIATED WITH NOT ADDRESSING EQUIVALENCE AND BIAS

So far, we have only reviewed the procedures for establishing equivalence and indicated that it is inappropriate to interpret any observed difference if equivalence is not established. We also repeatedly stressed that the failure of not demonstrating full score equivalence precludes any direct comparison of scores across groups. Once metric equivalence is demonstrated, patterns can be compared indirectly. Profile interpretations (e.g., subtest differences of mental ability tests relative to each other) are admissible. Researchers may also interpret the means of instruments, as long as they are aware that they can not make any claims about underlying latent traits or constructs. For example, it may be possible to say that one group scores lower than another one on a particular IQ test. However, this will not allow any interpretation in terms of mental abilities. Any interpretation has to stay at the measured score level (e.g., one group is doing worse in solving abstract figure completion tasks).

For practical work this may be sufficient. Nevertheless, even this is riddled with problems if there are differences in means or loadings across groups that are not examined. Aguinis and Smith (2007) demonstrated that comparing scores from two different populations that show different validities (e.g., relationship between mental ability and job performance) as if they were coming from the same population will result in potentially serious selection errors. These so-called bias-based selection-errors arise from assuming that tests are unbiased if in fact they are biased. The authors empirically demonstrated that these errors potentially lead to unwanted discrimination against minority groups, overselection of minority or majority group members, hiring of unsuitable candidates or rejecting of highly qualified candidates (all depending on the specific means and variances of the two groups). Most importantly from a practical perspective, this might lead to situations where decision makers are faced with the unpleasant realization that their newly hired employees or the selected students do not perform as well as would have been predicted. The authors also provided a computer program that can be used to assess the likelihood of these scenarios prior to the selection of candidates.

Therefore, neglect of bias and failure of equivalence can have significant practical and societal implications. Conclusions drawn from studies that do not meet specific levels of equivalence are invalid and open to alternative interpretations. The continuing debate on mental differences and differential performance on tests between ethnic groups in the United States also contributes to anxiety or lowered self-esteem among minority groups that are often disadvantaged by these tests (e.g., Crosby et al., 2006). Next, we are reviewing some selected tests and instruments in the areas of cognition and motivation. Table 24.1 summarizes the four levels of equivalence and biases, and gives some possible alternative explanations if a test fails a particular level of equivalence. Van de Vijver and Leung (1997) provide more specific examples of biases.

TABLE 24.1   Summary of the Four Levels of Equivalence, Biases, and Examples of Alternative Explanations if the Equivalence Is not Achieved

Level of Equivalence	Biases	Examples of Alternative Explanations
Functional equivalence	Cultural specificity	*Cognitive research:* • Intelligence is constructed differently in different contexts (e.g., definition of intelligence in terms of mental operation speed might be contrary to intelligence conceptualized in more social terms). *Motivation research:* • Organizational commitment is conceptually broader in some cultures (e.g., commitment might include elements of organizational citizenship behaviors compared to Western cultures where the two concepts are distinctive from one another).

(continues)

TABLE 24.1   *(continued)*

Level of Equivalence	Biases	Examples of Alternative Explanations
Structural equivalence	Domain under-representation/ Representativeness Method bias • Instrument bias • Administration bias • Sample bias	*Cognitive research:* • Culture-specific knowledge being assessed in subtests (e.g., geographical or historical knowledge) • Social components of intelligence not being assessed in intelligence tests. • Lack of familiarity with individualized testing or testing more generally (e.g., speed testing). • Comparison of samples differing along a number of dimensions (culture, education, SES, reading abilities, and so on). *Motivation research:* • Western instruments of commitment missing social aspects of commitment that are important in another cultural group. • Familiarity with rating scales.
Metric equivalence	Non-uniform item bias	*Cognitive research:* • Individual items or subtests assessing culture-specific knowledge or abilities have higher loadings on their latent factor in the culture these items came from compared to another culture, where the items or subtests are inappropriate. *Motivation research:* • Translation problems of individual items leading to differential factor loadings. • Negatively phrased items loading on separate factors in some cultures in which disagreement is not voiced directly. • Items measuring social pressures and costs associated with leaving might not be indicators of commitment in individualistic settings.
Full score equivalence	Uniform item bias	*Cognitive research:* • Item familiarity (e.g., the translation of the English question: "Where is a bird with webbed feet most likely to live?" into Swedish gives clues for the correct answer since the translation of "webbed feet" is "swimming feet") systematically increase the rate of correct responses of an item in a particular culture. *Motivation research:* • Complex wording of items or poor translation increasing the mean of individual items independent of the overall commitment score. • Negatively phrased items might be interpreted differently and item means might be elevated or depressed.

REVIEW OF COGNITIVE ASSESSMENT RESEARCH: INTELLIGENCE TESTING

Different tools were developed to assess the cognitive abilities of individuals; among those more commonly used are standardized intelligence tests, scholastic aptitude tests, and achievement tests. Our current focus will be primarily on intelligence testing. Studies concerning the development and application of culture free or culture fair intelligence test became the focus of much research endeavors since the researchers in the field recognized the need to test culturally diverse groups (Knapp, 1960). Dating back to the 1920s and 1930s, there had already been attempts to apply intelligence tests originated in Western cultures in samples from other cultures (e.g., Menzel, 1935). Since then, more intelligence testing comparing different cultural or ethnic groups has been conducted in culturally diversified countries such as the United States (Knapp, 1960) or New Zealand (Walters, 1958). During those days, researchers were aware of the possible influence of cultures on intelligence testing among samples of different backgrounds, yet, not much was (or could be) done to address the issue which resulted in complicated interpretation of the results. For a brief historical overview of cross-cultural testing on cognitive ability, the interested reader may also refer to the meta-analytic study on ethnic differences in cognitive ability in the United States by Roth et al. (2001).

A major issue in the cross-cultural study of intelligence concerns the definitions of intelligence across different cultures. As suggested in our previous discussion of functional equivalence, it is often the case that people from non-Western cultures define intelligence and intelligent behaviors very differently than those from the Western cultures (e.g., Berry & Bennett, 1992). It is therefore important to understand more thoroughly the meaning or definition of intelligence in each culture of interest prior to administering any intelligence tests for cross-cultural comparison.

In addition to the definition of intelligence, another factor worth considering in cross-cultural intelligence testing is the meaning of testing across different cultures. In the development of an ability test measuring verbal problem-solving skills among rural Zulu-speaking children, Solarsh and Alant (2006) noted that "testing is in itself a particularly Western middle class phenomenon, as the manner, content and criteria for evaluation are firmly embedded within Western middle class culture and standard" (p. 110). In order to address the potential method biases relating to the testing situations in the assessment of rural Zulu-speaking children in South Africa, Solarsh and Alant (2006) conducted a series of qualitative studies to refine aspects such as the cultural sensitivity of test content, adaptation of test stimuli (such as pictures or format of questions), method of presentation, and test administration/scoring. This indigenous intelligence test for the Zulu-speaking children offers an avenue for establishing a nomological net of convergent or discriminant variables (e.g., correlating the children's test scores with their academic performance in school) which would then enable the investigation of functional equivalence of the construct "intelligence" between Zulu and other cultures.

Besides developing indigenous measure of intelligence, another common strategy in cross-cultural intelligence testing is to adapt one version of test for use in another culture. In a cross-cultural research of intelligence testing among school children in India and in the Netherlands, a Dutch test, the Revised Amsterdamse Kinder Intelligentie Test (RAKIT) was adapted to the Indian context (Bleichrodt et al., 1999). During the pilot study of the adapted test, several items in the original RAKIT were identified as describing typical Dutch objects, products, and situations which were not appropriate for testing the Indian children. As a result, those items related to verbal intelligence were omitted in the Indian version. In this case, the assessment of verbal intelligence among the Indian children by means of the Indian version of RAKIT became more susceptible to domain under-representation bias. Bleichrodt et al. (1999) also tested the factor structure of both test batteries by means of principal component analysis with Procrustean rotation on the subtests. The degree of invariance of the three resulting factors was assessed using Tucker's phi coefficients (see van de Vijver & Leung, 1997; Fischer & Fontaine, in press). Appropriate values for showing structural invariance are debated. The Tucker's phi coefficients in their study were 0.87, 0.90, and 0.89 which the authors interpreted as showing comparable factor structures at the subtest level in India and the Netherlands. Other authors (Van de Vijver & Poortinga, 2002) have suggested that higher coefficients (larger than 0.90) would indicate factor structure similarity. Another problem is that the study was conducted at the subtest level and therefore, the results can be only seen as indicating some more stringent form of functional equivalence of the instrument in both cultures (investigating the nomological net of the subtests). Hence, the functional equivalence of the two tests was supported by the fact that the subtests loaded on similar factors in the two cultures. The statistical procedures taken by Bleichrodt et al. (1999) was similar to what is used to test for the structural equivalence of the scales; however, without offering information about the item biases in each subtests and given that the authors only conducted the analyses at the subtests level, it would be inappropriate to claim that the two instruments showed structural equivalence.

Intelligence tests are generally applied in different cultural groups to say something about the underlying intelligence of these groups. Significant differences across different ethnic or cultural groups have been repeatedly reported (e.g., Rushton, 2001, 2002; Lynn & Vanhanen, 2002; Rushton et al., 2004; Hartman et al., 2007). The findings in these studies are often discussed in relation to the "Jensen effect," a term formulated by Rushton (1998) to state that the performance differences between ethnic groups on intelligence tests are positively correlated to the tests' g loadings. A test loading higher on g should show greater ethnic group differences. According to Jensen & Weng (1994), g is the general factor shared among all mental ability tests. Although there are many different conceptualizations and measurements of mental ability or intelligence (e.g., Sternberg, 1985, 1996; Carroll, 1993; Jensen, 1998), major theories of cognitive ability share some common features, including the suggestion of a common factor g underlying human cognitive abilities (such as mathematical or verbal abilities) (Roth et al., 2001).

According to this view of intelligence in relation to the g factor, the formulation of the "Jensen effect" implies that any observed ethnic difference on intelligence test scores reflects an actual ethnic difference on mental capacity. These differences are then taken at face value and used to make claims about the relationship between a group's mental ability and its socioeconomic advancement (e.g., Lynn & Vanhanen, 2002). However, these tests have rarely been investigated in terms of measurement equivalence. We should be cautious about claiming differences in underlying abilities because of the potential biases involved in the administration processes and the test properties itself (Helms-Lorenz et al., 2003; Cronshaw et al., 2006). In equivalence of tests across groups and presence of biases are likely alternative explanations of observed differences and should be taken seriously.

For example, Rushton and his colleagues devoted much research efforts in the study of Black–White difference on intelligence, which often showed support to the "Jensen effects." In one of those studies, Rushton et al. (2004) claimed that Raven's Advanced Progressive Matrices (APM; Raven et al., 1998) was unbiased. They conducted a multi-group CFA in which they forced 14 items of the APM (out of 36 items in total) to load on a single latent factor g among their sample of African, East Indian, and White engineering students. They found acceptable model fit when constraining factor loadings for all groups to be equal and therefore they concluded that "the factor structure of cognitive ability in this study is equivalent for Africans and non-Africans" (Rushton et al., 2004, p. 225). However, as discussed above, this only shows metric equivalence and does not allow an unambiguous interpretation of mean differences. Therefore, their observation that White students outperformed the East Indians who in turn outperformed African students on the APM cannot be directly interpreted in terms of underlying mental ability. Observed differences could have been caused by a number of alternative factors, including different item familiarity, familiarity with testing procedures, differences in the physical setting of the test administration, socioeconomic, and/or educational differences across the samples or tester effects (e.g., a person from a different ethnic group administering the tests). The interpretation of the observed mean differences in terms of ethnic differences in intelligence as an underlying latent variable is not warranted by their study. However, these authors have to be lauded for conducting tests at the item level.

In another study conducted by te Nijenhuis et al. (2004), the RAKIT test mentioned above was administered to compare the cognitive ability between immigrant and Dutch school children. The researchers performed item level analyses using Mantel-Haenszel analyses. They found that some items were biased against the immigrant group, and upon further inspection of those biased items, they suggested that some words may be difficult for immigrant children to understand. Even so, they proposed that the influence of these item biases would be small if one works at the sum score level. te Nijenhuis et al. (2004) also subjected the test to multi-group CFA to test the factorial invariance of a model with a hierarchical factor g and the subtests being the lower order factors. They found that the model fit did not decrease after constraining the factor loadings to be the same across all cultures. te Nijenhuis et al. (2004) conducted the analyses at the subtest level instead of at the item level. Therefore, like Bleichrodt et al. (1999), the results could only be regarded as indicating functional equivalence instead of any other higher level of equivalence.

As far as we know, there had not been much attempt in addressing full score equivalence of intelligence tests across cultures. Lubke et al. (2003) outlined all the equations involved in testing full score equivalence and described all the necessary steps. Unfortunately, they also conducted their re-analysis of a published data set at the subtest level.

As our review has shown, the functional equivalence of intelligence tests across cultures has been addressed most frequently. However, more work has to be done to appropriately demonstrate structural equivalence and metric equivalence. Most tests of equivalence were conducted at the subtest level. This is appropriate if item biases have been first investigated. This could be done using item response theory (IRT, see van de Vijver & Leung, 1997 for reviews in the cross-cultural literature) or any other of the tests listed above. Once this has been shown, further tests at the subtest level are appropriate. Given the prevalence of research on the ethnic or cultural group difference on intelligence test, the need to investigate the full score equivalence of the instruments being used is acute. Without demonstrating this, the validity of claims about observed group difference on intelligence testing can be challenged, the applications of such tests in clinical, work and educational settings could be labeled as unethical and no real progress in our understanding of cross-cultural differences in cognitive abilities can be achieved.

REVIEW OF MOTIVATION RESEARCH IN THE ORGANIZATIONAL LITERATURE: ORGANIZATIONAL COMMITMENT

Work motivation is of great concern for organizational scholars and practitioners. Maintaining a highly motivated work force is seen as essential for organizational survival. Various theories have been proposed to increase and maintain motivation of employees (for reviews see for example Kanfer, 1990; Wood, 2000). One of the key variables in motivating frameworks is the commitment of employees to their organization (Smith et al., 2001). Highly motivated individuals are thought to be strongly identified with the organization, its values and goals. Commitment has been defined in a number of ways and current research distinguishes at least three main forms of commitment (Meyer & Allen, 1991; Meyer et al., 2002; Cohen, 2003; Meyer et al., 2004). These are affective, continuance, and normative commitment. Affective commitment, as an emotional attachment to organizations is characterized by a genuine want or desire to belong to the organization. Employees who are affectively committed strongly identify with the values, norms, and goals of the organization (following earlier work by Porter et al., 1974). Second, continuance commitment is identified as the alleged costs associated from leaving or altering one's involvement with a current organization. Therefore, continuance commitment is seen as an individual's perceived need to remain with an organization (see Becker, 1960). Finally, normative commitment is viewed as a sense of obligation or a feeling that one ought to remain with the organization (Meyer & Allen, 1991). It captures normative pressures and perceived obligations by important others. Research has shown that these components of organizational commitment are empirically distinct in their both antecedents and consequences (Meyer et al., 2002). These forms, but especially affective commitment, are routinely used in employee opinion and motivation surveys. Results are used to design or evaluate training or intervention programs, to judge the effectiveness of organizations (e.g., benchmarking) or leaders (leadership evaluation surveys) and to provide feedback about the motivation level of employees to management. However, this widespread use in both national and international organizations is paralleled by research demonstrating differences in form and level in different cultural groups.

Since Cole's (1979) initial comparison of behavioral commitment levels in Japan and the United States, researchers have focused on differences and similarities in commitment across cultural groups. Early research was driven by the observation that decreasing morale among North American workers coincided with a cycle of economic decline, while the healthy growth of the Japanese economy coincided with Japanese workers that demonstrated high levels of behavioral commitment (low turnover). This observation led to the belief that fostering high levels of commitment could help with economic growth in the United States. However, researchers investigating cultural differences were quick to notice that this apparent behavioral commitment did not coincide with employee self-report of their identification with their company and the goals and values of their company (e.g., Lincoln & Kalleberg, 1990). Such findings have generated a substantial amount of research, and presence or absence of differences in commitment have been explained using cultural (e.g., Randall, 1993; Cohen, 2003; Fischer & Mansell, 2007), economic (Fischer & Mansell, 2007), structural (e.g., Lincoln & Kalleberg, 1990; for a review see Besser, 1993), organizational and methodological artifact variables (e.g., Lincoln & Kalleberg, 1990; Smith et al., 2001). Wasti and Öender (in press) recently reviewed this literature and suggested a complex interplay of economic, structural, organizational, and cultural factors. However, the question regarding the equivalence or bias of commitment has rarely been asked and assessed. In the following, we will review the present evidence regarding this issue.

Starting with functional equivalence, the definitions derived in the Western literature have been relatively precise and focused. However, the extent to which such definitions capture the understanding of commitment in different cultural contexts is yet unclear (Fischer & Mansell, 2007; Wasti & Öender, in press). For example, Fischer and Mansell (2007) in their meta-analysis of commitment across cultures found that the three components showed considerable overlap in lower income contexts and therefore, these commitment components might not be functionally equivalent across economic contexts. Considering nomological networks of relationships, a meta-analysis by Meyer et al. (2002) showed considerable differences in antecedents, correlates and consequences of all three components of commitment between studies conducted in North America (United States, Canada) versus outside North America.

Alnajjar (1996) developed a measure of organizational commitment that used quite different components compared to the standard three-componential model of commitment. In his research in the United Arab Emirates, commitment was conceptualized as involving disciplinary requirements (e.g., punctuality, performance to the required work standards, and physical appearance), concerns about the organization (concerns of organizational climate, the social status, and loyalty of workers to the organization) and updating (enhancing one's abilities through study and creativity related to one's job). It is interesting to note that this conceptualization is closer to other Western constructs such as organizational citizenship behavior (Organ, 1990; Organ & Paine, 1999) than organizational commitment as discussed in the Western literature.

Wasti (2002) conducted a study in a Turkish context arguing that continuance commitment has been too narrowly defined for this particular cultural context. In more collectivistic and relational societies such as Turkey, loyalty and trust are quintessential and lead to a preference for paternalistic management practices. Employers are likely to give jobs to family members or friends, which will put them in a position of dependency and obligation. This obligation then leads to attempts to "maintain the face" and credibility of the employee and return the favor. These normative pressures to stay then become an additional social part of continuance commitment. Therefore, in Turkey continuance commitment calculations involve both financial and rational considerations (investments, benefits) as well as social costs (loss of face, credibility). An instrument was then developed based on in-depth interviews including both aspects and the factor structure was found to hold well (Wasti, 2002).

Consequently, these studies suggest that the functional equivalence is not clearly established for the construct. Although the three components as defined in the West have been applied repeatedly in studies around the world, the nomological net seems to be different in studies outside North America, the correlation between the components changes depending on the economic context and emic or culturally sensitive conceptualizations of commitment have suggested that the concept might have different content across cultural contexts. Therefore, the construct might show cultural specificity.

Bearing these limitations in mind, the subsequent discussion of equivalence has to be treated cautiously. Given the widespread use of Western scales in internationally operating organizations, it might be argued that local conceptualizations of commitment are less relevant since employees have to operate within a Western-dominated and structured environment. Local employees have to respond to managerial directives and techniques and their evaluation is conducted using Western concepts. Hence, the use of Western instruments for adequate motivation might be appropriate. With this argument in mind, the next levels of equivalence can be examined.

As discussed previously, the issues of representativeness and relevance need to be addressed at this stage. Work by Wasti (2002) demonstrated that some items can be added to commitment scales in order to increase relevance and representativeness. Individual researchers have also occasionally dropped items. The reasons might have been to avoid reversed scored items that are harder to understand (Pearson & Chong, 1997; see van de Vijver & Leung, 1997); because inclusion of specific individual items yielded low alphas in the particular sample (Khatrie et al., 2001) or because items did not load on the expected factor (Kalliath & O'Driscoll, 1998). Occasionally, items were added to capture local meanings and understandings (Roe et al., 2000). Structural equivalence also requires that the weight parameters (e.g., factor loadings) are non-trivial in all cultural groups, indicating that the international consistency is similar. However, comparisons of internal consistency (e.g., Cronbach's alpha) were virtually absent in any comparative study included in Fischer and Mansell's (2007) meta-analysis. Use of exploratory or confirmatory factor analysis was relatively common in single country studies, but the comparability of factor structures was rarely investigated. One of the few examples is the study by Riordan and Vandenberg (1994). They compared commitment scores in US and Korean samples and demonstrated that all items loaded on a single factors in both samples. Vandenberghe et al. (2001) compared commitment levels to various entities (including the organization, the work group and Europe) in samples from 15 European Union nations. They compared French and English language versions as well as subgroups of samples (grouped by cultural similarity using Hofstede's indicators). Overall, they found supporting evidence for structural equivalence across these samples. Palich et al. (1995) in their study of employees from various 15 subsidiaries of one large US multinational split the sample in two groups based on the cultural differences observed by Hofstede (1980). They also found structural equivalence. However, it needs to be noted that these two studies combined various national groups in their analyses, which might have introduced bias. However, given that the analyses were repeated using different sets of national samples, the likelihood is relatively small. Kirkman and Shapiro (2001) conducted EFA's in each of their four national samples individually. Only studies by Walumbwa and Lawler (2003) and Lee and Bruvold (2003) conducted multi-group CFA's using all samples.

Focusing on metric equivalence next, it needs to be shown whether the factor loadings are identical across cultural groups. Some of the studies mentioned above also continued to constrain the factor loadings to be equivalent across samples (using multi-group CFA). If these constraints do not lead to significant model deterioration, score patterns can be compared across samples and metric equivalence can be assumed. Vandenberghe et al. (2001), Palich et al. (1995), Walumbwa and Lawler (2003), and Lee and Bruvold (2003) claimed metric equivalence since model fit did not get considerably worse. Vandenberghe et al.

(2001) nevertheless noted that the English and French versions of the commitment scale to one's occupation did not work so well. Riordan and Vandenberg (1994) in contrast reported that three items showed discrepancies between the two samples. They relaxed the constraints for these items (called partial measurement invariance) and proceeded with testing mean differences. However, as discussed before, this is not yet appropriate since only metric equivalence was achieved.

The highest level is full score equivalence. To the best of our knowledge, only two studies tested this level appropriately. Walumbwa and Lawler (2003) constrained the intercepts to be equal across Indian, Chinese, and Kenyan employees. They reported no significant deterioration of model fit and concluded that their data met the requirement of full score equivalence. In contrast, Lee and Bruvold (2003) did not find full score equivalence, but by freeing up at least two items on their multi-item measures they were able to show partial full score equivalence. The other three studies reviewed above evaluated error variances across cultural groups and found that these were generally equal across cultural groups. This provides interesting and important information about item bias, but it does not address the issue of full score equivalence. We will return to the issue of error variances in the final section of this chapter. Consequently, the direct comparison of the means across cultural groups in these three studies is open to alternative interpretations.

In summary, the extensive literature on organizational commitment indicates that functional equivalence of the construct across cultures can be challenged due to different nomological network strengths. Nevertheless, the application of Western instruments has been shown to satisfy structural and metric equivalence in samples with employees in Westernized and multinational organizations. Full score equivalence has been investigated less frequently and the continuing question about cultural differences in commitment can not be addressed before this important aspect has been dealt with in a larger number of studies.

FUTURE DIRECTIONS

In the cognitive testing domain, the debate has become locked about the appropriate testing of differences in mental ability. One central issue that has been argued here and elsewhere (e.g., Lubke et al., 2003; Borsboom, 2006) is that testing of item parameters is necessary to get past this intellectual stalemate. Currently, the debate is focused on equivalence at the subtest level (e.g., using subtests and their loading on the g factor). However, such tests can be best conceptualized as indicators of functional equivalence because they test whether particular tests (subtests) show the same intercorrelation. This is a functional equivalence question, but does not address the real issue of full score equivalence needed. Our review has also shown that this level is hardly ever investigated. Much research needs to be done in this respect. Current interpretations of emerging differences can be challenged on this ground.

A second issue is constraining error terms in equivalence research and praxis. The traditional equivalence framework has not focused on error terms. However, from a practical perspective errors associated with individual items become important. If there is substantially more error associated with a test in one group, it implies that it is less accurate in predicting the intended construct. Hence, any scores might systematically over- or underestimate the true abilities or motivations of individuals from specific groups. In the selection literature, this becomes an important consideration and error variances of individual items should be constrained to be equal across groups. In the organizational commitment literature, this procedure seems to be more routinely employed, partly because it can be easily implemented with standard programs such as LISREL, AMOS, or EQS. Vandenberg and Lance (2000) suggest that constraining error variances and latent variable variance simultaneously would provide an indicator of equivalence of reliability. This is a desirable diagnostic and should be reported in the testing literature. The mental ability literature should address this question, particularly considering the widespread use of mental testing in Western societies and the significant implications associated with it. More effort is needed in using the procedure to ensure that any claims about any ethnic or cultural differences on cognitive ability are sound.

The current chapter also highlights the clear need for more indigenous or emic research. In fact, the equivalence framework should encourage researchers to fully explore the functions of constructs and concepts in their local cultures. This is an exiting and important area for further research. Too much comparative research is conducted using Western scales resulting in imposed etic research (Berry, 1989). Similarly, equivalence research could be embraced more wholeheartedly by researchers in indigenous research or relativists who argue that psychological constructs are culturally constructed since these tools and procedures reviewed in this chapter provide a means to show the cultural bias of instruments and constructs. Using methods and results that are understandable to a quantitatively oriented audience, a convincing point could be made regarding the culture specificity of psychological constructs. This can then be used for justifying in-depth emic and qualitative research to explore the meanings and functions in specific cultural contexts. Therefore, the equivalence framework can be used to bridge the gap between universalists and relativists in cultural and cross-cultural psychology.

REFERENCES

Aguinis, H., & Smith, M. A. (2007). Understanding the impact of test validity and bias on selection errors and adverse impact in human resource selection. *Personnel Psychology*, *60*, 165–199.

Alnajjar, A. A. (1996). Relationship between job satisfaction and organizational commitment among employees in the United Arab Emirates. *Psychological Reports*, *76*, 315–321.

Becker, H. S. (1960). Notes on the concept of commitment. *American Journal of Sociology*, *66*, 32–42.

Berry, J. W. (1989). Imposed etics-emics-derived etics: The operationalization of a compelling idea. *International Journal of Psychology*, *24*, 721–735.

Berry, J. W., & Bennett, J. A. (1992). Cree conceptions of cognitive competence. *International Journal of Psychology*, *27*(1), 73–88.

Besser, T. L. (1993). The commitment of Japanese workers and U.S. workers: A reassessment of the literature. *American Sociological Review*, *58*, 873–881.

Bleichrodt, N., Hoksbergen, R. A. C., & Khire, U. (1999). Cross-cultural testing of intelligence. *Cross-Cultural Research*, *33*(1), 3–25.

Bollen, K. A. (1989). *Structural equations with latent variables*. New York: Wiley.

Borsboom, D. (2006). The attack of the psychometricians. *Psychometrika*, *71*(3), 425–440.

Byrne, B. M. (1998). *Structural equation modelling with LISREL, PRELIS, and SIMPLIS: Basic concepts, applications, and programming*. Mahwah, NJ: Lawrence Erlbaum Associates.

Carroll, J. B. (1993). *Human cognitive abilities: A survey of factor-analytic studies*. New York: Cambridge University Press.

Cheung, G. W., & Rensvold, R. B. (2000). Assessing extreme and acquiescence response sets in cross-cultural research using structural equation modeling. *Journal of Cross-Cultural Psychology*, *31*(2), 187–212.

Cohen, A. (2003). *Multiple commitments in the workplace: An integrative approach*. Mahwah, NJ: Lawrence Erlbaum.

Cole, E. R. (1979). *Work, mobility and participation: A comparative study of American and Japanese industry*. Los Angeles, CA: University of California Press.

Cronshaw, S. F., Hamilton, L. K., Onyura, B. R., & Winston, A. S. (2006). Case for non-biased intelligence testing against Black Africans has not been made: A comment on Rushton, Skuy, and Bons (2004). *International Journal of Selection and Assessment*, *14*(3), 278–287.

Crosby, F. J., Iyer, A., & Sincharoen, S. (2006). Understanding affirmative action. *Annual Review of Psychology*, *57*, 585–611.

Fischer, R., & Fontaine, J. R. (in press). Individual-level structural equivalence. In D. Matsumoto & F. van de Vijver (Eds.), *Handbook of cross-cultural research methods*. Oxford University Press.

Fischer, R., & Mansell, A. (2007). *Commitment across cultures: A meta-analytical approach*. Unpublished manuscript, Victoria University Wellington, New Zealand.

Fischer, R., Fontaine, J., van de Vijver, F., & van Hemert, D. (in press). What is style and what is bias in cross-cultural comparisons? An examination of response styles in cross-cultural research. In *Proceedings of the 18th International Congress of International Association for Cross-Cultural Psychology*, Spetses, Greece.

Fontaine, J. R. J. (2005). Equivalence. In K. Kempf-Leonard (Ed.), *Encyclopedia of social measurement* (Vol. 1, pp. 803–813). San Diego, CA: Academic Press.

Greenfield, P. M. (1997). You can't take it with you: Why ability assessments don't cross cultures? *American Psychologist*, *52*(10), 1115–1124.

Hartman, P., Kruuse, N. H. S., & Nyborg, H. (2007). Testing the cross-racial generality of Spearman's hypothesis in two samples. *Intelligence*, *35*, 47–57.

Helms-Lorenz, M., Van de Vijver, F. J. R., & Poortinga, Y. H. (2003). Cross-cultural differences in cognitive performance and Spearman's hypothesis: g or c? *Intelligence*, *31*, 9–29.

Hofstede, G. (1980). *Culture's consequences: International differences in work-related values*. Beverly Hills: Sage.

Jensen, A. R. (1998). *The g factor: The science of mental ability*. New York: Praeger.

Jensen, A. R., & Weng, L.-J. (1994). What is a good g? *Intelligence*, *18*, 231–258.

Johnson, T. P. (2006). Methods and frameworks for crosscultural measurement. *Medical Care*, *44*(11 Suppl 3), 17–20.

Kalliath, T., O'Driscoll, M. P. et al. (1998). The relationship between burnout and organizational commitment in two samples of health professionals. *Work & Stress*, *12*(2), 179–185.

Kanfer, R. (1990). Motivation theory and industrial and organizational psychology. In M. D. Dunnette & L. M. Hough (Eds.), *Handbook of industrial and organizational psychology*, 2nd ed (Vol. 1, pp. 75–170). Palo Alto, CA: Consulting Psychologists Press.

Khatri, N., Tze Fern, C. et al. (2001). Explaining employee turnover in an Asian context. *Human Resource Management Journal, 11*(1), 54–74.

Kirkman, B. L., & Shapiro, D. L. (2001). The impact of cultural values on job satisfaction and organizational commitment in self-managing work teams: The mediating role of employee resistance. *Academy of Management Journal, 44*(3), 557–569.

Knapp, R. R. (1960). The effects of time limits on the intelligence test performance of Mexican and American subjects. *Journal of Educational Psychology, 51*(1), 14–20.

Lee, C. H., & Bruvold, N. T. (2003). Creating value for employees: Investment in employee development. *The International Journal of Human Resource Management, 14*, 981–1000.

Lincoln, J. R., & Kalleberg, A. L. (1990). *Culture, control and commitment: A study of work organization and work attitudes in the United States and Japan.* New York: Cambridge University Press.

Lubke, G. H., Dolan, C. V., Kelderman, H., & Mellenbergh, G. J. (2003). On the relationship between sources of within- and between-group differences and measurement invariance in the common factor model. *Intelligence, 31*, 543–566.

Lynn, R., & Vanhanen, T. (2002). *IQ and the wealth of nations.* Westport, CT: Praeger.

Menzel, E. W. (1935). The goodenough intelligence test in India. *Journal of Applied Psychology, 19*(5), 615–624.

Messick, S. (1991). Psychology and methodology of response styles. In R. E. Snow & D. E. Wiley (Eds.), *Improving inquiry in social science* (pp. 161–200). Hilllsdale, NJ: Erlbaum.

Meyer, J. P., & Allen, N. J. (1991). A three-component conceptualization of organizational commitment. *Human Resources Management Review, 1*, 61–89.

Meyer, J. P., Stanley, D. J., Herscovitch, L., & Topolytsky, L. (2002). Affective, continuance, normative commitment to the organization: A meta-analysis of antecedents, correlates and consequences. *Journal of Vocational Behavior, 61*, 20–52.

Meyer, J. P., Becker, T. E., & Vandenberghe, C. (2004). Employee commitment and motivation: A conceptual analysis and integrative model. *Journal of Applied Psychology, 89*, 991–1007.

Organ, D. W. (1990). The motivational basis of organizational citizenship behavior. In B. Staw & L. L. Cummings (Eds.), *Research in organisational behaviour* (Vol. 12, pp. 43–72). Greenwich, CT: JAI Press.

Organ, D. W., & Paine, J. B. (1999). A new kind of performance for industrial and organizational psychology: Recent contributions to the study of organizational citizenship behavior. In C. L. Cooper & I. T. Robertson (Eds.), *International review of industrial and organizational psychology* (Vol. 14, pp. 337–368). Chichester: Wiley.

Palich, L. E., Hom, P. W., & Griffeth, R. W. (1995). Managing in the international context: Testing cultural generality of sources of commitment to multinational enterprises. *Journal of Management, 21*, 671–690.

Pe-Pua, R. (1990). Pagtatanung-tanong: A method for cross-cultural research. In V. G. Enriquez (Ed.), *Indigenous psychology: A book of readings* (pp. 231–249). Quezon City: Akademya Ng Sikoholhiyang Pilipino.

Pearson, C. A., & Chong, J. (1997). Contributions of job content and social information on organizational commitment and job satisfaction: An exploration in a Malaysian nursing context. *Journal of Occupational and Organizational Psychology, 70*, 357–374.

Porter, L. W., Steers, R. M., Mowday, R. T., & Boulian, P. V. (1974). Organizational commitment, job satisfaction, and turnover among psychiatric technicians. *Journal of Applied Psychology, 59*, 603–609.

Randall, D. (1993). Cross-cultural Research on organizational commitment: A review and application of Hofstede's value survey module. *Journal of Business Research, 26*, 91–110.

Raven, J., Raven, J. C., & Court, J. H. (1998). *Manual for Raven's advanced progressive matrices (1998 Edn.).* Oxford, England: Oxford Psychologists Press.

Riordan, C. M., & Vandenberg, R. J. (1994). A central question in cross-cultural research: Do employees of different cultures interpret work-related measures in an equivalent manner?. *Journal of Management, 20*, 643–671.

Roe, R. A., Zinovieva, I. L., Dienes, E., & Ten Horn, L. A. (2000). A comparison of work motivation in Bulgaria, Hungary, and the Netherlands: Test of a model. *Applied Psychology: An International Review, 49*(4), 658–687.

Roth, P. L., Bevier, C. A., Bobko, P., Switzer, F. S., & Tyler, P. (2001). Ethnic group differences in cognitive ability in employment and educational settings: A meta-analysis. *Personnel Psychology, 54*(2), 297–330.

Rushton, J. P. (1998). The "Jensen Effect" and the "Spearman-Jensen Hypothesis" of Black-White IQ differences. *Intelligence, 26*(3), 217–225.

Rushton, J. P. (2001). Black-White differences on the g factor in South Africa: A "Jensen Effect" on the Wechsler Intelligence Scale for Children-Revised. *Personality and Individual Differences, 31*, 1227–1232.

Rushton, J. P. (2002). Jensen Effects and African/Colored/Indian/White differences on Raven's Standard Progressive Matrices in South Africa. *Personality and Individual Differences, 33*, 65–70.

Rushton, J. P., Skuy, M., & Fridjhon, P. (2002). Jensen Effects among African, Indian, and White engineering students in South Africa on Raven's Standard Progressive Matrices. *Intelligence, 30*, 409–423.

Rushton, J. P., Skuy, M., & Fridjhon, P. (2003). Performance on Raven's Advanced Progressive Matrices by African, Indian, and White engineering students in South Africa. *Intelligence, 31*, 123–137.

Rushton, J. P., Skuy, M., & Bons, T. A. (2004). Construct validity of Raven's advanced progressive matrices for African and non-African engineering students in South Africa. *International Journal of Selection and Assessment, 12*(3), 220–229.

Smith, P. B. (2004). Acquiescent response bias as an aspect of cultural communication style. *Journal of Cross-Cultural Psychology, 35*, 50–61.

Smith, P. B., & Fischer, R. (2008). Acquiescence, extreme response bias and levels of cross-cultural analysis. In F. J. R. van de Vijver, D. A. van Hemert, & Y. Poortinga (Eds.), *Individuals and cultures in multi-level analysis*, pp. 283–311. Mahwah, NJ: Lawrence Erlbaum Associates.

Smith, P. B., Fischer, R., & Sale, N. (2001). Cross-cultural industrial and organizational psychology. In C. L. Cooper & I. T. Robertson (Eds.), *International review of industrial and organizational psychology* (Vol. 16, pp. 147–194). Chicester, England: John Wiley & Sons Ltd.

Solarsh, B., & Alant, E. (2006). The challenge of cross-cultural assessment – The test of ability to explain for Zulu-speaking children. *Journal of Communication Disorders, 39*, 109–138.

Sternberg, R. J. (1985). *Beyond IQ: A triarchic theory of human intelligence*. New York: Cambridge University Press.

Sternberg, R. J. (1996). *Successful intelligence*. New York: Simon & Schuster. (Paperback edition: New York: Dutton, 1997).

te Nijenhuis, J., Tolboom, E., Resing, W., & Bleichrodt, N. (2004). Does cultural background influence the intellectual performance of children from immigrant groups? *European Journal of Psychological Assessment, 20*(1), 10–26.

van de Vijver, F., & Leung, K. (1997). *Methods and data analysis for cross-cultural research*. Thousand Oaks, CA: Sage.

Van de Vijver, F. J. R., & Poortinga, Y. H. (2002). Structural equivalence in multilevel research. *Journal of Cross-Cultural Psychology, 33*, 141–156.

Vandenberg, R. J., & Lance, C. E. (2000). A review and synthesis of the measurement invariance literature: Suggestions, practices, and recommendations for organizational research. *Organizational Research Methods, 3*(1), 4–70.

Vandenberghe, C., Stinglhamber, F., Bentein, K., & Delhaise, T. (2001). An examination of the cross-cultural validity of a multidimensional model of commitment in Europe. *Journal of Cross-Cultural Psychology, 32*, 322–347.

Walters, R. H. (1958). The intelligence test performance of Maori children: A cross cultural study. *The Journal of Abnormal and Social Psychology, 57*(1), 107–114.

Walumbwa, F. O., & Lawler, J. J. (2003). Building effective organizations: Transformational leadership, collectivist orientation, work-related attitudes and withdrawal behaviors in three emerging economies. *International Journal of Human Resource Management, 14*, 1083–1101.

Wasti, S. A. (2002). Affective and continuance commitment to the organization: Test of an integrated model in the Turkish context. *International Journal of Intercultural Relations, 26*, 525–550.

Wasti, S. A. & Önder, Ç. (in press). *Commitment across cultures: Progress, pitfalls and propositions.* In H. J. Klein, T. E. Becker & J. C. Meyer (Eds.), Commitment in organizations: Accumulated wisdom and new directions. SIOP Frontier Series.

Wood, R. (2000). Work motivation: Theory, research and practice introduction to the special issue. *Applied Psychology: An International Review, 49*, 318.

INDEX